Lecture Notes in Artificial Intelligence   3025

Edited by J. G. Carbonell and J. Siekmann

Subseries of Lecture Notes in Computer Science

Springer
Berlin
Heidelberg
New York
Hong Kong
London
Milan
Paris
Tokyo

George A. Vouros
Themistoklis Panayiotopoulos (Eds.)

Methods
and Applications
of Artificial Intelligence

Third Hellenic Conference on AI, SETN 2004
Samos, Greece, May 5-8, 2004
Proceedings

 Springer

Series Editors

Jaime G. Carbonell, Carnegie Mellon University, Pittsburgh, PA, USA
Jörg Siekmann, University of Saarland, Saarbrücken, Germany

Volume Editors

George A. Vouros
Department of Information and Communication Systems
Engineering School of Sciences
University of the Aegean 83200, Samos, Greece
E-mail: georgev@aegean.gr

Themistoklis Panayiotopoulos
Knowledge Engineering Lab, Department of Informatics, University of Piraeus
Piraeus, 185 34, Greece
E-mail: themisp@unipi.gr

Library of Congress Control Number: Applied for

CR Subject Classification (1998): I.2, H.3, H.4, H.2.8, F.2.2, I.4

ISSN 0302-9743
ISBN 3-540-21937-4 Springer-Verlag Berlin Heidelberg New York

Springer-Verlag is a part of Springer Science+Business Media

springeronline.com

© Springer-Verlag Berlin Heidelberg 2004
Printed in Germany

Typesetting: Camera-ready by author, data conversion by Olgun Computergrafik
Printed on acid-free paper   SPIN: 10999387   06/3142   5 4 3 2 1 0

Preface

Artificial intelligence has attracted a renewed interest from distinguished scientists and has again raised new, more realistic this time, expectations for future advances regarding the development of theories, models and techniques and the use of them in applications pervading many areas of our daily life. The borders of human-level intelligence are still very far away and possibly unknown. Nevertheless, recent scientific work inspires us to work even harder in our exploration of the unknown lands of intelligence.

This volume contains papers selected for presentation at the 3rd Hellenic Conference on Artificial Intelligence (SETN 2004), the official meeting of the Hellenic Society for Artificial Intelligence (EETN). The first meeting was held in the University of Piraeus, 1996 and the second in the Aristotle University of Thessaloniki (AUTH), 2002.

SETN conferences play an important role in the dissemination of the innovative and high-quality scientific results in artificial intelligence which are being produced mainly by Greek scientists in institutes all over the world. However, the most important effect of SETN conferences is that they provide the context in which people meet and get to know each other, as well as a very good opportunity for students to get closer to the results of innovative artificial intelligence research.

SETN 2004 was organized by the Hellenic Society for Artificial Intelligence and the Artificial Intelligence Laboratory of the Department of Information and Communication Systems Engineering, the University of the Aegean. The conference took place on the island of Samos during 5–8 May 2004. We wish to express our thanks to the sponsors of the conference, the University of the Aegean and the School of Sciences, for their generous support.

The aims of the conference were:

- To present the high-quality results in artificial intelligence research which are being produced mainly by Greek scientists in institutes all over the world.
- To bring together Greek researchers who work actively in the field of artificial intelligence and push forward collaborations.
- To put senior and postgraduate students in touch with the issues and problems currently addressed by artificial intelligence.
- To make industry aware of new developments in artificial intelligence so as to push forward the development of innovative products.

Artificial intelligence is a dynamic field whose theories, methods and techniques constantly find their way into new innovative applications, bringing new perspectives and challenges for research. The growth in the information overload which makes necessary its effective management, the complexity of human activities in relation to the constant change of the environment in which these activities take place, the constantly changing technological environment, as well as the constant need for learning point to the development of systems that are more oriented to the way humans reason and act in social settings. Recent advances in artificial intelligence may give us answers to these new questions in intelligence.

The 41 contributed papers were selected from 110 full papers by the program committee, with the invaluable help of additional reviewers; 13% of the submitted papers were co-authored by members of non-Greek institutions. We must emphasize the high quality of the majority of the submissions. Many thanks to all who submitted papers for review and for publication in the proceedings.

This proceedings volume also includes the two prestigious papers presented at SETN 2004 by two distinguished keynote speakers:

- *"Dynamic Discovery, Invocation and Composition of Semantic Web Services"* by Prof. Katia Sycara (School of Computer Science, Carnegie Mellon University); and
- *"Constraint Satisfaction, Complexity, and Logic"* by Prof. Phokion Kolaitis (Computer Science Department, University of California, Santa Cruz).

Three invited sessions were affiliated with the conference:

- *AI in Power System Operation and Fault Diagnosis*, Assoc. Prof. Nikos Hatziargyriou (Chair);
- *Intelligent Techniques in Image Processing*, Dr. Ilias Maglogiannis (Chair);
- *Intelligent Virtual Environments*, Assoc. Prof. Themis Panagiotopoulos (Chair).

Members of the SETN 2004 program committee did an enormous amount of work and deserve the special gratitude of all participants. Our sincere thanks to the Conference Advisory Board for its help and support.

Special thanks go to Alfred Hofmann and Tatjana Golea of Springer-Verlag for their continuous help and support.

May 2004

George Vouros
Themis Panayiotopoulos

Organization

SETN 2004 is organized by the department of Information and Communication Systems Engineering, Univeristy of the Aegean and EETN (Hellenic Association of Artificial Intelligence).

Conference Chair

George Vouros (University of the Aegean)

Conference Co-chair

Themis Panagiotopoulos (University of Piraeus)

Organizing Committee

George Anastasakis (University of Piraeus)
Manto Katsiani (University of the Aegean)
Vangelis Kourakos-Mavromichalis (University of the Aegean)
Ioannis Partsakoulakis (University of the Aegean)
Kyriakos Sgarbas (University of Patras)
Alexandros Valarakos (University of the Aegean)

Advisory Board

Nikolaos Avouris (University of Patras)
Ioannis Vlahavas (Aristotle University of Thessalonica)
George Paliouras (National Centre for Scientific Research "DEMOKRITOS")
Costas Spyropoulos (National Centre for Scientific Research "DEMOKRITOS")
Ioannis Hatzyligeroudis (Computer Technology Institute (CTI) and University of Patras)

Program Committee

Ioannis Androustopoulos (Athens University of Economics and Business)
Grigoris Antoniou (University of Crete)
Dimitris Christodoulakis (Computer Technology Institute (CTI))
Ioannis Darzentas (University of the Aegean)
Christos Douligeris (University of Piraeus)
Giorgos Dounias (University of the Aegean)

Theodoros Evgeniou (INSEAD, Technology Dept., France)
Nikos Fakotakis (University of Patras)
Eleni Galiotou (University of Athens)
Manolis Gergatsoulis (Ionian University)
Dimitris Kalles (Hellenic Open University and AHEAD Relationship Mediators Company)
Giorgos Karagiannis (Technical University of Athens)
Vangelis Karkaletsis (National Centre for Scientific Research "DEMOKRITOS")
Sokratis Katsikas (University of the Aegean)
Elpida Keravnou (University of Cyprus)
Giorgos Kokkinakis (University of Patras)
Manolis Koubarakis (Technical University of Crete)
Spyridon Lykothanasis (University of Patras)
Giorgos Magoulas (University of Brunel, England)
Filia Makedon (University of the Aegean and Dartmouth College)
Basilis Moustakis (Foundation for Research and Technology-Hellas (FORTH))
Christos Papatheodorou (Ionian University)
Giorgos Papakonstantinou (Technical University of Athens)
Stavros Perantonis (National Centre for Scientific Research "DEMOKRITOS")
Ioannis Pittas (University of Thessaloniki)
Stelios Piperidis (Institute for Language and Speech Processing)
Dimitris Plexousakis (University of Crete)
Giorgos Potamias (Foundation for Research and Technology-Hellas (FORTH))
Ioannis Refanidis (University of Macedonia)
Timos Sellis (Technical University of Athens)
Panagiotis Stamatopoulos (University of Athens)
Kostas Stergiou (University of the Aegean)
George Tsichrintzis (Univeristy of Piraeus)
Petros Tzelepithis (Kingston University)
Maria Virvou (University of Piraeus)
Vasilis Voutsinas (University of Piraeus)

Additional Referees

Adam Adamopoulos
Stergos Afantenos
Nikos Ambazis
Nikos Bassiliades
Grigorios Beligiannis
Christos Berberidis
George Boukeas
Evagelos Dermatas
Gang Feng
Vassilis Gatos

Efstratios Georgopoulos
Ioannis Giannikos
Theodoros Gnardellis
Eleni Golemi
Chris Hutchison
Keterina Kabassi
Ioannis Kakadiaris
Sarantos Kapidakis
Fotis Kokkoras
George Kormentzas

D. Kosmopoulos
Eirini Kotsia
Martha Koutri
Konstantinos Koutsojiannis
Michalis Krinidis
Michalis Lagoudakis
Aristomenis Lambropoulos
Maria Moundridou
Ruediger Oehlmann
Charles Owen
George Petasis
Christos Pierrakeas
Dimitris Pierrakos
Vasileios Plagiannakos
Ioannis Pratikakis
Dimitris Prentzas
Panagiotis Rontogiannis
Elias Sakellariou
Nikos Samaras

George Sigletos
Spyros Skiadopoulos
Dionysios Sotiropoulos
Ioanna-Ourania Stathopoulou
Ioannis Stavrakas
George Stefanidis
Manolis Terrovitis
Athanasios Tsakonas
Ioannis Tsamardinos
Nikolaos Tselios
Victoria Tsiriga
Loukas Tsironis
Nikos Vassilas
Nikolaos Vayatis
Ioannis Vetsikas
Kyriakos Zervoudakis
Vossinakis Spyros
Avradinis Nikos

Table of Contents

Invited Talks

Information Management

Machine Learning

Data Mining and Diagnosis

Knowledge Representation and Search

Natural Language Processing

Invited Session:
AI in Power System Operation and Fault Diagnosis

Invited Session:
Intelligent Techniques in Image Processing

Invited Session: Intelligent Virtual Environments

Constraint Satisfaction, Complexity, and Logic

Phokion G. Kolaitis

Computer Science Department
University of California, Santa Cruz
Santa Cruz, CA 95064, USA
kolaitis@cs.ucsc.edu

Synopsis

Constraint satisfaction problems arise naturally in several different areas of artificial intelligence and computer science. Indeed, constraint satisfaction problems encompass Boolean satisfiability, graph colorability, relational join evaluation, as well as numerous other problems in temporal reasoning, machine vision, belief maintenance, scheduling, and optimization. In their full generality, constraint satisfaction problems are NP-complete and, thus, presumed to be algorithmically intractable. For this reason, significant research efforts have been devoted to the pursuit of "islands of tractability" of constraint satisfaction, that is, special cases of constraint satisfaction problems for which polynomial-time algorithms exist.

The aim of this talk is to present an overview of recent advances in the investigation of the computational complexity of constraint satisfaction with emphasis on the connections between "islands of tractability" of constraint satisfaction, database theory, definability in finite-variable logics, and structures of bounded treewidth.

References

1. A. Bulatov. A dichotomy theorem for constraints on a three-element set. In *Proc. 43rd IEEE Symposium on Foundations of Computer Science*, pages 649–658, 2002.
2. A. Bulatov. Tractable conservative constraint satisfaction problems. In *Proc. 18th IEEE Symposium on Logic in Computer Science*, 2003.
3. V. Dalmau, Ph. G. Kolaitis, and M. Y. Vardi. Constraint satisfaction, bounded treewidth, and finite-variable logics. In *Proc. of Eighth International Conference on Principles and Practice of Constraint Programming*, pages 310–326, 2002.
4. R. Dechter. Constraint networks. In S.C. Shapiro, editor, *Encyclopedia of Artificial Intelligence*, pages 276–185. Wiley, New York, 1992.
5. R. Dechter. Bucket elimination: a unifying framework for reasoning. *Artificial Intelligence*, 113(1–2):41–85, 1999.
6. R. Dechter. *Constraint Processing*. Morgan Kaufmann, 2003.
7. R. Dechter and J. Pearl. Tree clustering for constraint networks. *Artificial Intelligence*, pages 353–366, 1989.
8. R.G. Downey and M.R. Fellows. *Parametrized Complexity*. Springer-Verlag, 1999.

G.A. Vouros and T. Panayiotopoulos (Eds.): SETN 2004, LNAI 3025, pp. 1–2, 2004.

9. T. Feder and M. Y. Vardi. The computational structure of monotone monadic SNP and constraint satisfaction: a study through Datalog and group theory. *SIAM J. on Computing*, 28:57–104, 1998. Preliminary version in *Proc. 25th ACM Symp. on Theory of Computing*, May 1993, pp. 612–622.
10. M. R. Garey and D. S. Johnson. *Computers and Intractability - A Guide to the Theory of NP-Completeness*. W. H. Freeman and Co., 1979.
11. G. Gottlob, N. Leone, and F. Scarcello. A comparison of structural CSP decomposition methods. *Artificial Intelligence*, 124(2):243–282, 2000.
12. G. Gottlob, N. Leone, and F. Scarcello. Hypertree decompositions: A survey. In *Mathematical Foundations of Computer Science - MFCS 2001*, volume 2136 of *LNCS*, pages 37–57. Springer, 2001.
13. M. Grohe. The complexity of homomorphism and constraint satisfaction problems seen from the other side. In *Proc. 44th Symposium on Foundations of Computer Science (FOCS 2003)*, pages 552–561, 2003.
14. P. Jeavons. On the algebraic structure of combinatorial problems. *Theoretical Computer Science*, 200(1–2):185–204, 1998.
15. P. Jeavons, D. Cohen, and M.C. Cooper. Constraints, consistency and closure. *Artificial Intelligence*, 101(1-2):251–65, May 1998.
16. P. Jeavons, D. Cohen, and M. Gyssens. Closure properties of constraints. *Journal of the ACM*, 44(4):527–48, 1997.
17. Ph. G. Kolaitis and M. Y. Vardi. On the expressive power of Datalog: tools and a case study. *Journal of Computer and System Sciences*, 51(1):110–134, August 1995. Special Issue: Selections from Ninth Annual ACM SIGACT-SIGMOD-SIGART Symposium on Principles of Database Systems (PODS), Nashville, TN, USA, 2-4 April 1990.
18. Ph. G. Kolaitis and M. Y. Vardi. Conjunctive-query containment and constraint satisfaction. *Journal of Computer and System Sciences*, pages 302–332, 2000. Earlier version in: *Proc. 17th ACM Symp. on Principles of Database Systems (PODS '98)*.
19. Ph. G. Kolaitis and M. Y. Vardi. A game-theoretic approach to constraint satisfaction. In *Proc. of the 17th National Conference on Artificial Intelligence (AAAI 2000)*, pages 175–181, 2000.
20. Ph. G. Kolaitis. Constraint satisfaction, databases, and logic. In *Proc. of the Eighteenth International Joint Conference on Artificial Intelligence (IJCAI 2003)*, pages 1587–1595, 2003.
21. U. Montanari. Networks of constraints: fundamental properties and application to picture processing. *Information Science*, 7:95–132, 1974.
22. J. Pearson and P. Jeavons. A survey of tractable constraint satisfaction problems. Technical Report CSD-TR-97-15, Royal Holloway University of London, 1997.
23. T.J. Schaefer. The complexity of satisfiability problems. In *Proc. 10th ACM Symp. on Theory of Computing*, pages 216–226, 1978.

Dynamic Discovery, Invocation and Composition
of Semantic Web Services

Katia Sycara

The Robotics Institute
Carnegie Mellon University
Pittsburgh, PA 15213-3890, USA
katia@cs.cmu.edu

1 Introduction

While the Web has emerged as a World Wide repository of digitized information, by
and large, this information is not available for automated inference. Two recent efforts, the *Semantic Web* [1] and *Web Services*[1] hold great promise of making the Web
a machine understandable infrastructure where software agents can perform distributed transactions. The Semantic Web transforms the Web into a repository of computer readable data, while Web services provide the tools for the automatic use of that
data. To date there are very few points of contact between Web services and the Semantic Web: research on the Semantic Web focuses mostly on markup languages to
allow annotation of Web pages and the inferential power needed to derive consequences, utilizing the Web as a formal knowledge base. Web services concentrate on
proposals for interoperability standards and protocols to perform B2B transactions.

We propose the vision of Web services as *autonomous goal-directed agents* which
select other agents to interact with, and flexibly negotiate their interaction model,
acting at times in client server mode, or at other times in peer to peer mode. The resulting Web services, that we call *Autonomous Semantic Web services*, utilize ontologies and semantically annotated Web pages to automate the fulfillment of tasks and
transactions with other Web agents. In particular, Autonomous Semantic Web services use the Semantic Web to support capability based discovery and interoperation
at run time.

A first step towards this vision is the development of formal languages and inference mechanisms for representing and reasoning with core concepts of Web services.
DAML-S (the Darpa Agent Markup Language for Services) [4] is the first attempt to
define such a language. With OWL (Ontology Web Language) on track to become a
W3C recommendation, DAML-S has evolved into OWL-S [9].

In the rest of the paper, we will describe OWL-S and its relations with the Semantic Web and Web services. In addition, we will provide concrete examples of computational models of how OWL-S can be viewed as the first step in bridging the gap
between the Semantic Web and current proposed industry standards for Web services.

---

[1] For introductory papers on Web services see www.webservices.org

G.A. Vouros and T. Panayiotopoulos (Eds.): SETN 2004, LNAI 3025, pp. 3–12 , 2004.
© Springer-Verlag Berlin Heidelberg 2004

2 The Semantic Web

The aim of the Semantic Web is to provide languages to express the content of Web pages and make it accessible to agents and computer programs. More precisely, the Semantic Web is based on a set of languages such as RDF, DAML+OIL and more recently OWL that can be used to markup the content of Web pages. These languages have a well-defined semantics and a proof theory that allows agents to draw inferences over the statements of the language. As an example, an agent may use the semantic markup of the NOAA page reporting the weather conditions in Pittsburgh, and learn that the current condition is Heavy Snow; furthermore, the agent may infer from the semantic markup of the Pittsburgh school board page that in days of heavy snow all the schools are closed; combining the two pieces of information, the agent would infer that indeed today Pittsburgh schools are closed.

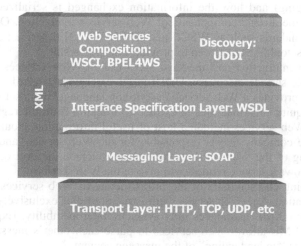

Fig. 1. The Web Services Infrastructure

The second element of the Semantic Web is a set of ontologies, which provide a conceptual model to interpret the information For example, an ontology of weather may contain concepts such as temperature, snow, cloudy, sunny and so on. It may also contain information on the relation between the different terms; for instance, it may say that cloudy and sunny are two types of weather conditions.

The Semantic Web provides the basic mechanisms and knowledge that support the extraction of information from Web pages and a shared vocabulary that Web services can use to interact. Ultimately, the Semantic Web provides the basic knowledge that can be used by Web services in their transactions. But Web services need more than knowledge, they also need an infrastructure that provides reliable communication between Web services, registries to locate Web services to interact with, guarantees of security and privacy during the transaction, reputation services and so on. The specification of such a Web services infrastructure is outside the scope of what is currently thought of as the Semantic Web.

3 Web Services Infrastructure

The recent plethora of proposed interoperability standards for business transactions on the Web has resulted in significant interest in automating program interactions for B2B e-commerce. The development of a Web services infrastructure is one of the current frontiers of Web development, since it attempts to create a Web whose nodes are not pages that always report the same information, but programs that transact on demand.

The Web services infrastructure provides the basic proposed standards that allow Web services to interact. The diagram in Fig.1 shows how some of the most popular proposed standards could fit together. The unifying factor of all these standards is XML as shown by the column on the left that cuts across all layers. The two most popular proposed standards are SOAP [8] and WSDL [2]. SOAP defines a format for message passing between Web services. WSDL describes the interface of a Web service, i.e. how it can be contacted (e.g. through Remote Procedure Call or Asynchronous Messaging) and how the information exchanged is serialized. SOAP and WSDL describe the atomic components of Web services interaction. Other more recent proposed standards such as WSCI[2] and BPEL4WS [3] describe how more than one Web services could be composed to provide a desired result.

In addition to interaction and message specification, Web services registries are useful to facilitate service discovery. UDDI is the emerging standard for a Web services registry. It provides a Web service description language and a set of publishing, browsing and inquiry functionalities to extract information from the registry. UDDI's descriptions of Web services include a host of useful information about the Web service, such as the company that is responsible for the Web service, and most importantly the binding of the Web service (the bindings include the port of the transport protocol) that allows a service requester to invoke the Web service.

One overarching characteristic of the infrastructure of Web services is its lack of semantic information. The Web services infrastructure relies exclusively on XML for interoperation, but XML guarantees only syntactic interoperability. Expressing message content in XML allows Web services to parse each other's messages but does not allow semantic "understanding" of the message content.

Current industry proposals for Web services infrastructure explicitly require Web services' programmers to reach an agreement on the way their Web services interact, and on the format of the messages that they exchange. Furthermore, the programmers should explicitly hard code the interaction between their Web services and how they should interpret the messages that they exchange. Finally, programmers are also responsible for modifying their Web services when something changes in the interaction patterns, or simply something breaks. Ultimately, the growing Web services infrastructure facilitates the emergence of agreements between programmers, and the coding of those agreements, but the result is an infrastructure that is inherently brittle, unable to easily reconfigure to accommodate new Web services, or to react to failures, and inevitably expensive to maintain.

---

[2] For more information on WSCI: Web Service Choreography Interface (WSCI) 1.0 Specification: http://wwws.sun.com/software/xml/developers/wsci/

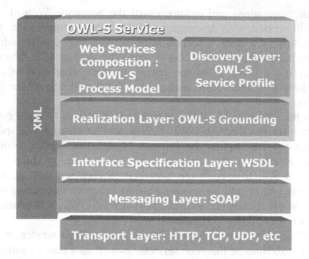

Fig. 2. The OWL-S infrastructure

One way to overcome the brittleness of the Web services infrastructure is to increase the *autonomy* of Web services. Any increase in autonomy allows Web services to reconfigure their interaction patterns to react to changes while minimizing the direct intervention of programmers.

Crucially, what prevents web services from acting autonomously is the lack of explicit semantics, which prevents Web services from understanding what each other's messages mean, and what tasks each Web service performs. In addition, current Web service proposals do not enable the semantic representation of business relations, contract or business rules in a machine understandable way. Enriching the Web services infrastructure with semantics will allow Web services to (a) explicitly express and reason about business relations and rules, (b) represent and reason about the task that a Web service performs (e.g. book selling, or credit card verification) so as to enable automated Web service discovery based on the explicit advertisement and description of service functionality, (c) represent and reason about message ordering, (d) understand the meaning of exchanged messages, (e) represent and reason about preconditions that are required to use the service and effects of having invoked the service, and (f) allow composition of Web services to achieve a more complex service.

4 OWL-S

OWL-S [9] is both a language and an ontology for describing Web services that attempts to close the gap between the Semantic Web and Web services. As ontology, OWL-S is based on OWL to define the concept of Web service within the Semantic Web; as a language, OWL-S supports the description of actual Web services that can be discovered and then invoked using standards such as WSDL and SOAP. OWL-S uses the semantic annotations and ontologies of the Semantic Web to relate the description of a Web service, with descriptions of its domain of operation. For example, a OWL-S description of a stock reporting Web service may specify what data it reports, its delay on the market, and the cost of using the Web service. The clients of the Web service may use a OWL inference engine to infer what kind of data the Web service reports, how to contact it, to make sure that it will deliver the goods after a payment and so on.

Fig. 2 shows the structure of OWL- S and how it relates to other components of the Web services infrastructure. An OWL-S Web service requires the specification of four modules: the Service Profile, the Process Model, the Service Grounding and a OWL-S Service description that connects the other three modules. Furthermore, OWL-S relies on WSDL to specify the interface of Web services, on SOAP[3] to describe the messaging layer and on some transport protocol to connect two Web services. Therefore, at the messaging and transport levels, OWL-S is consistent with the rest of the Web services proposed standards.

The *Service Profile* provides a high level view of a Web service; it specifies the provenance, the capabilities of the Web service, as well as a host of additional properties that may help to discover the Web service. The Service Profile is the OWL-S analog to the Web service representation provided by UDDI in the Web service infrastructure. There are similarities as well as sharp differences between the Service Profile and UDDI service descriptions. Some information, e.g. provenance of a Web service is present in both descriptions. However, the OWL-S Service Profile supports the representation of capabilities, i.e. the task that the service performs, whereas this is not supported by UDDI. UDDI, on the other hand, provides a description of the ports of the Web service. In OWL-S information about ports is relegated to the Grounding and the WSDL description of the Web service.

The *Process Model* provides a description of what a Web service does, specifically it specifies the tasks performed by a Web service, the control flow, the order in which these tasks are performed, and the consequences of each task described as input, outputs, preconditions and effects. A client can derive from the Process Model the needed *choreography*, i.e. its pattern of message exchanges with the Web service by figuring out what inputs the Web services expects, when it expects them, and what outputs it reports and when. The Process Model plays a role similar to the emerging standards such as BPEL4WS and WSCI, but it also maintains a stronger focus on the semantic description of a service choreography and the effects of the execution of the different components of the Web service. Finally, the *Service Grounding* binds the description of abstract information exchange between the Web service and its partners, defined in terms of inputs and outputs in the Process Model, into explicit messages specified in the WSDL description of the Web service and the SOAP message and transport layers.

OWL-S reliance on OWL, as well as WSDL and SOAP shows how the proposed industry Web services standards can be enriched with information from the Semantic Web. OWL-S adds a formal representation of content to Web services specifications and reasoning about interaction and capabilities. OWL-S enabled Web services can use the Semantic Web to discover and select Web services they would like to interact

---

[3] As in the general case of Web services, SOAP is not required. OWL-S Web services can communicate using HTTP Get/Put or other messaging specifications.

with, and to specify the content of their messages during interaction. In addition, they use UDDI, WSDL and SOAP to facilitate the interaction with other Web services.

5 Autonomous Semantic Web Services

In this section, we discuss a computational framework for OWL-S that encompasses utilization of the Service Profile for semantic service discovery, the Process Model for semantically motivated service choreography and the Grounding for message exchange. In addition, we will discuss briefly the Semantic Web Services tools that we have implemented and their complementarities with current web services systems. Specifically we will describe the OWL-S/UDDI Matchmaker, and the architecture of a OWL-S empowered Web service. Finally, we will conclude with the discussion of a test application.

5.1 Autonomous Semantic Service Discovery

At discovery time, a Web service may generate a request that contains the profile of the ideal Web service it would like to interact with. Discovery is then realized by the derivation of whether the request matches the profile of any Web service available at that time.

While OWL-S Profiles and UDDI descriptions of Web services contain different information, they attempt to achieve the same goal: facilitate discovery of Web services. Therefore the combination of OWL-S and UDDI may result in a rich representation of Web services [6]. The differences between OWL-S and UDDI can be reconciled by using UDDI's TModels to encode OWL-S capability descriptions. Once capabilities are encoded, a matching engine that performs inferences based on OWL logics can be used to match for capabilities in UDDI [5]. The result of this combination is the OWL-S / UDDI Matchmaker for Web services.

The Matchmaker receives advertisements of Web services, information inquiries and requests for capabilities through the *Communication module*. Advertisements and information inquiries are then sent to UDDI through the *OWL-S/UDDI Translator*. Requests for capabilities are directed to the *OWL-S Matching Engine*. The OWL-S Matching Engine selects the Web services whose advertised capabilities match the capability requested. The computation of the match is complicated by the fact that the provider and the requester have different views on the functionality of a Web service, and could use different ontologies to express those views. Therefore the selection cannot be based on string or on keywords matching, rather it has to be performed on the basis of the semantic meaning of the advertisements and the request. For example consider a service provider that advertises that it sells food for pets, and a requester looking for a seller of dog food. Relying on keyword matching alone, a UDDI style registry will not be able to match the request to the existing pet food store advertisement, since keyword matching is not powerful enough to identify the relation between pet food and dog food.

However, since the OWL-S profile allows *concepts* rather than keywords to be expressed, and ontologies on the semantic web make relations between concepts explicit, it would be able to perform a semantic match and recognize the relation between the request and the advertisement. For example, an ontology that describes pets may list a relation like "a dog is a pet". This enables the matching algorithm of the OWL-S/UDDI matchmaker, using a OWL reasoner, to also recognize that "dog food" is a type of "pet food" and therefore the pet food store would match the request.

The OWL-S matching algorithm accommodates for the differences between the advertisement and the request by producing *flexible* matches, i.e. matches that recognize the degree of similarity between advertisements and requests, on the basis of the ontologies available to the Web services and the matching engine. Basically, the matching engine attempts to verify whether the outputs in the request are a subset of the outputs generated by the advertisement, and whether the inputs of the advertisement subsume those of the request. When these conditions are satisfied, the advertised service generates the outputs that the requester expects and the requester is able to provide all the inputs that the Web service expects. The degree of satisfaction of these two rules determines the degree of match between the provider and the requester. For more details on the matching algorithm, see [5].

5.2 Autonomous Semantic Web Service Interactions

Semantic Web services also use the OWL-S Process Model and Grounding to manage their interaction with other Web services. The diagram in Fig. 3 shows our design and implementation of the architecture of a OWL-S based Web service. The core of the architecture is represented by three components in the center column: the *Web service Invocation*, the *OWL-S Virtual Machine (VM)* and the *DAML Parser*. The Web service Invocation module is responsible for contacting other Web services and receiving messages from other Web services. The transaction with other Web services may be based on SOAP messaging, or on straight HTTP or any other mode of communication as described by the WSDL specification of the Web service provider. Upon receiving a message, the Web service invocation extracts the payload, or in other words the content of the message and either sends it to the OWL Parser or passes it directly to the OWL-S VM [11][4].

The OWL parser is responsible for reading fragments of OWL ontologies and transforming them into predicates that can be used by the OWL inference engine. The OWL parser is also responsible for downloading OWL ontologies available on the Web, as well as OWL-S descriptions of other Web services to interact with.

The OWL-S VM is the center of our implementation: it uses the ontologies gathered from the Web and the OWL-S specifications of the Web services to make sense of the messages it received, and to decide what kind of information to send next. To make these decisions the OWL-S VM uses a set of rules that implement the semantics of the OWL-S Process Model and Grounding. The OWL-S VM is also responsible for the generation of the response messages; to accomplish the latter task, the OWL-S VM uses the Grounding to transform the abstract information exchanges described by the Process Model into concrete message contents that are passed to the Web service Invocation Module to be transformed into actual messages and sent off to their receivers.

---

[4] Since the publication of citation [11], we have converted the DAML-S Virtual Machine to OWL-S.

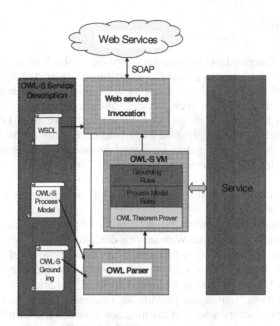

Fig. 3. Description of OWL-S Web Service architecture

The other two columns of the diagram in Fig. 3 are also very important. The column on the left shows the information that is downloaded from the Web and how it is used by OWL-S Web services. Specifically the WSDL is used for Web service invocation, while ontologies and OWL-S specifications of other Web services are first parsed and then used by the OWL-S VM to make decisions on how to proceed. The column on the right shows the service which is displayed essentially as a black box. The service represents the main body of the Web service; it is the module that realizes what the Web service does. For example, the service module of a financial consulting Web service would contain software that performs financial calculations such as suggesting stocks to buy. The service module interacts with the other OWL-S modules to manage the interaction with other Web services, as for instance stock quote Web services, or Web services that report financial news. Through the OWL-S VM, the service retrieves the information received from other Web services or sends additional requests.

OWL-S does not make any explicit assumption on the Service module itself since its goal is to facilitate autonomous interaction between Web services. Nevertheless, the service module is responsible for many of the decisions that have to be made while using OWL-S. The service is responsible for the interpretation of the content of the messages exchanged and for its integration with the general problem solving of the Web service. The service is also responsible for Web services *composition* during the solution of a problem [10]. Specifically, the service module is responsible for the decision of what goals to subcontract to other Web services, or what capability descriptions of potential providers to submit to an OWL-S/UDDI Matchmaker; furthermore, it is responsible for the selection of the most appropriate provider among the providers located by the Matchmaker.

6 Conclusion

In this paper we described the importance of the Semantic Web in the development of the Web services infrastructure and the contribution provided by OWL-S; furthermore, we showed that OWL-S is not just an academic exercise, but it can be used to control the interaction between Web services that use the Semantic Web, thus leading the way towards Semantic Web services. Specifically, we used OWL-S to describe capabilities of Web services so that they can find each other on the basis of the information that they provide, rather than incidental properties such as their name, port, or a free text description. Furthermore, we showed how OWL-S can also be used to control the *autonomous* interaction between Web services without any need of pre-programming hard coding neither the sequence of messages to exchange nor the information to be transmitted.

The work presented here shows the importance of the Semantic Web and the need for widespread ontologies. In the Web service discovery phase, ontologies support the basic information on the changes that result by the execution of Web services; the representation of those changes needs to refer to objects or concepts in the world for which all the parties in the transaction need to have a shared knowledge and understanding. Furthermore, ontologies provide an inference framework that allows Web services to resolve discrepancies and mismatches between the knowledge that they are using. This is particularly relevant in the OWL-S/UDDI matching engine that has to abstract from the superficial differences between the advertisement and the request to recognize whether they describe the same capabilities.

In addition, ontologies play an essential role during Web services interaction, because they provide a shared dictionary of concepts so that Web services can understand each other's messages. Ultimately, ontologies provide the basis for the use of the knowledge exchanged by Web services by supporting inferences when new knowledge is added.

Acknowledgements

This is joint work with Massimo Paolucci and Naveen Srinivasan. The research has been supported by the Defense Advanced Research Projects Agency as part of the DARPA Agent Markup Language (DAML) program under Air Force Research Laboratory contract F30601-00-2-0592 to Carnegie Mellon University.

References

1. T. Berners-Lee, J. Hendler, and O. Lassila.: The semantic web. Scientific American, 284(5):34--43, 2001
2. E. Christensen, F. Curbera, G. Meredith, and S.Weerawarana.: Web Services Description Language (WSDL) 1.1 http://www.w3.org/TR/2001/NOTE-wsdl-20010315 2001.
3. F. Curbera, Y. Goland, J. Klein, F. Leymann, D. Roller, S. Thatte, and S. Weerawarana: Business Process Execution Language for Web Services, Version 1.0

4. The DAML-S Coalition: DAML-S: Web service description for the semantic web In Proceedings of the .First International Web Conference, Sardinia, 2002.
5. M. Paolucci, T. Kawamura, T. R. Payne, and K. Sycara.: Semantic matching of web services capabilities. In Proceedings of the First International Semantic Web Conference, Sardinia, 2002
6. M. Paolucci, T. Kawamura, T. R. Payne, and K. Sycara.: Importing the Semantic Web in UDDI. In Proceedings of E-Services and the Semantic Web 2002.
7. T. R. Payne, R. Singh, and K. Sycara.:Calendar agents on the semantic web.:IEEE Intelligent Systems, 17(3) 84-86, 2002
8. W3C Soap Version 1.2, Recommendation, 24 June 2003.
9. www.daml.org/services/owl-s/1.0/
10. M. Paolucci, N. Srinivasan, K. Sycara, and T. Nishimura, "Toward a Semantic Choreography of Web Services: From WSDL to DAML-S" In *Proceedings of the First International Conference on Web Services (ICWS'03),* Las Vegas, Nevada, USA, June 2003, pp 22-26.
11. M. Paolucci, A. Ankolekar, N. Srinivasan and K. Sycara, "The DAML-S Virtual Machine," In *Proceedings of the Second International Semantic Web Conference (ISWC),* 2003, Sandial Island, Fl, USA, October 2003, pp 290-305.

Data Brokers:
Building Collections through Automated Negotiation

Fillia Makedon[1], Song Ye[1], Sheng Zhang[1], James Ford[1],
Li Shen[1], and Sarantos Kapidakis[2]

[1] The Dartmouth Experimental Visualization Laboratory (DEVLAB)
Department of Computer Science
{makedon,yesong,clap,jford,li}@cs.dartmouth.edu
[2] Department of Archive and Library Sciences
Ionian University, Greece
sarantos@ionio.gr

Abstract. Collecting digital materials is time-consuming and can gain from automation. Since each source – and even each acquisition – may involve a separate negotiation of terms, a collector may prefer to use a broker to represent his interests with owners. This paper describes the Data Broker Framework (DBF), which is designed to automate the process of digital object acquisition. For each acquisition, a negotiation agent is assigned to negotiate on the collector's behalf, choosing from strategies in a *strategy pool* to automatically handle most bargaining cases and decide what to accept and what counteroffers to propose. We introduce NOODLE (Negotiation OntOlogy Description LanguagE) to formally specify terms in the negotiation domain.

1 Introduction

Digital materials collection has traditionally been a complex and time consuming multi-step process. A collector may have multiple requirements that may change over time, from initially identifying needs to signing on to services, to obtaining approvals for purchases. Collecting objects from different providers can be tedious for collectors because each provider may have his own formats, policies, asset value system, and pricing, and a separate negotiation may be necessary or desirable with each party in order to fully satisfy the collector's requirements. Automating object collection has the potential not only to make the process more efficient, but also to address an important challenge that arises as modern collections are developed – namely, the desire to unify the physical and digital. Automating negotiation is central to the automation of object collection.

Generally, negotiation can be understood as the process toward a final agreement on one or more matters of common interest to different parties. It has been widely accepted that there are two major obstacles in automating negotiation: knowledge representation and strategic reasoning [1, 2], or incorporating necessary negotiation knowledge and intelligence into a computer system that will carry out a negotiation. We introduce NOODLE (Negotiation OntOlogy Description LanguagE) to address the knowledge representation issue in negotiation and a *strategy pool* to support a

G.A. Vouros and T. Panayiotopoulos (Eds.): SETN 2004, LNAI 3025, pp. 13–22, 2004.

flexible mechanism for choosing and applying negotiation strategies. This work is built on top of an general-purpose negotiation system: *SCENS* [3] (Secure/Semantic Content Exchange System). In SCENS, we have been working on building a three mode Web Services-based negotiation system that enables automated negotiation on scientific data sharing. NOODLE, which is based on current Semantic Web [4] techniques, is designed to address knowledge representation issue in SCENS by creating a standard language for representing and reasoning about negotiation concepts. NOODLE provides SCENS with a common means to represent different aspects of negotiation.

Here, we incorporate SCENS and the strategy pool into a unifying *Data Broker Framework* (DBF) in order to automate the process of collecting widely varying objects. DBF is a distributed framework designed to match needs with available resources. It can be applied to all types of object owners (*e.g.*, libraries, labs, museums, government centers) and object requesters (*e.g.*, conventional libraries, digital libraries, metadata-based digital libraries [5]).

The remainder of this paper is organized as follows. Section 2 reviews the related work in automated negotiation. Section 3 presents the details of the DBF. Section 4 introduces NOODLE and the strategy pool technique. Finally, Section 5 offers some concluding remarks and notes on future work.

2   Related Work

Of the two main problems in automated negotiation, knowledge representation is more fundamental than negotiation strategy – after all, all negotiation strategies are based on a correct understanding of the concepts and terms used in a negotiation. There have been several previous efforts to find commonalities across different negotiation protocols [6, 7], and with the development of the Semantic Web, it appears possible to solve or partially solve the problem of knowledge representation using ontologies, which are formal models that describe objects, concepts, and the relations between them [8, 9]. Tamma, *et al.* [8] have theoretically analyzed an ontology for automated negotiation, and Grosof and Poon [9] proposed a rule-based approach to representing business contracts that enables software agents to conduct contract-related activities, including negotiation. However, most existing negotiation ontology work has focused on negotiation activities in e-commerce, and as a result existing techniques cannot be efficiently used for general data sharing negotiation, where many different negotiation conditions might be considered rather than a simple optimization on *e.g.* price.

Negotiation, while a very human process, often paradoxically produces the most useful results if automated, with all terms, sequence of requests, and outcomes recorded and supported by a computer system. Agent technologies are widely used in negotiation systems to replace the activities of human beings and thus automate the negotiation process. Distributed Artificial Intelligence (DAI) and Multi-Agent Systems (MAS) [10] laid important groundwork for agent technology research. Other AI techniques are also frequently used in negotiation systems to help people or agents exhibit rational behavior and obtain the best outcomes. Among these existing approaches, a traditional one is to use game theory to analyze the negotiation process to provide a theoretically sound mathematical solution and winning strategy. However,

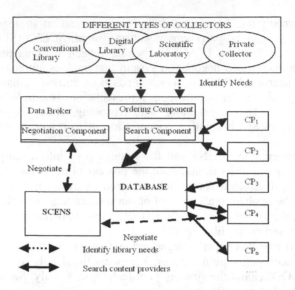

Fig. 1. The Data Broker Framework. The Ordering Component identifies needs of the collector (*dotted arrows*) and feeds these as queries into the Search Component, which retrieves a list of potential content providers (*solid arrows*). The Negotiation Component uses SCENS to negotiate with the content providers for the best offer based on the needs and the optimal strategies for each provider (*dashed arrows*).

this analysis is based on the assumption that the system can get full information about the participants; in the general case, where information and rules are hidden, machine learning technologies are widely used. For example, negotiation can be modeled as a sequential decision-making task using Bayesian updating [11], fuzzy logic [12], defeasible logic [13], or genetics-based machine learning [14]. The latter provides a methodology for constructive models of behavioral processes, in which negotiation rules might be derived and learned from existing rules by means of genetic operations (reproduction, crossover, and activation).

3   The Data Broker Framework

DBF is a distributed framework (as shown in Figure 1): libraries are assumed to use local data brokers that know about local library policies, assets, and similar information. A typical data broker includes the following three major components, which are tightly related to object acquisition: the Ordering Component (OC), the Searching Component (SC), and the Negotiation Component (NC).

3.1   The Ordering Component (OC)

In a conventional library context, the Acquisition Department will order needed content periodically after receiving requests from library users. The *Ordering Component* (OC) similarly identifies a collector's needs by executing several phases automatically (with possible human intervention): (a) the entry of requests by users, and a matching with what is already there, (b) the search for potential providers through a metadata library or database, and (c) the automation of a variety of collection procedures. Essentially, DBF extends the library paradigm by making the acquisition process proactive as well as reactive.

Publishers periodically send out a list of recent publications to libraries, and libraries choose to order some items in the list. Based on its needs, usage history, and the publication lists it receives, a library must decide on acquisition priorities [15, 16]. For example, a book lost or damaged by a user may have to be reordered. If numerous users wish to borrow a specific item from the library but only one copy exists, the library may want to order additional copies.

The above scenarios can be characterized as "reactive" because they react to a need after the need has been expressed. A "proactive" process instead anticipates needs: for example, if the first and second editions of a book exist in the library, the library may wish to order a new third edition. Our system supports both reactive and proactive acquisition processes. OC has an interactive object collection interface for librarians and other collectors to enter object needs. The OC component can request human approval before proceeding into negotiation.

3.2 The Searching Component (SC)

Finding all potential object providers is usually not easy for a collector, especially when some special objects are desired, *e.g.*, images of a film star to be added to a cinematographic collection. For this purpose, our system contains a *Searching Component* (SC), which may contain a database or a digital library such as a metadata-based digital library to facilitate the searching process. This database might contain information about object providers, with listings of available objects and preset trading conditions. SC basically acts as a broker between the object requester and object provider, thus making highly heterogeneous objects interoperable and amenable to an efficient search.

Once a data broker knows what to order, it will need to find appropriate object providers and communicate with them. Here we assume that every object provider has a data broker-like interface. For some specific objects, such as journals, there will be only one or two well-known object providers. However, if a library wants to buy a new book, it may be potentially available everywhere – directly through different book resellers, online bookstores, or publishers, or even from individuals.

3.3 The Negotiation Component (NC)

Different object providers may provide different offers for the same object. Due to budget limits, conventional collectors, such as libraries, hope to find agreeable offers for all needed objects. Negotiation is currently seldom used by libraries in the acquisition process because of its high overhead and uncertain results. Automated negotiation, because of potential for dramatically low cost, can be used for most negotiations, thus making the acquisition process more scalable.

In Figure 1, the broker is conducting negotiation with CP_4 through a negotiation agent. Rather than conducting negotiations directly, the *Negotiation Component* (NC) creates a set of negotiation agents that conduct negotiations autonomously with other

agents [17, 18]. When the broker finds potential providers, NC will generate a negotiation agent for each upcoming negotiation activity. The negotiation agent will communicate with SCENS to obtain the negotiation protocol, which includes the knowledge of how to understand negotiation proposals, conditions, agreements, *etc.* Then it
will be assigned a negotiation strategy and will use this strategy to conduct negotiation with other agents through SCENS. The details of representation of negotiations
and strategies are discussed in Section 4.

3.4 A Sample Scenario

Assume a Data Broker is responsible for representing a client (a library to be popu-
lated) with relevant content providers. It is to acquire objects for the client under a
given set of requirements covering purchase price, duration of use, restrictions (or
lack thereof) on usage, *etc.* The following summarizes its object acquisition process:

1. It identifies the object needs.
2. It identifies all possible object providers, some available locally and some after
   consulting centralized servers, such as a MetaDL server.
3. A negotiation strategy is chosen (but may change or be revised later as negotiation
   proceeds and the system "learns" from past or different types of negotiations).
4. While searching for all sources, it can enter negotiation mode with one of the object providers it has found in order to determine whom to negotiate with later
   (stepwise negotiation).
5. It can conduct multiple such negotiations simultaneously (Figure 1).
6. The negotiation strategy may change, but will always aim to optimize the criteria
   of the object requestor.
7. This can be a cyclical process (since negotiation with an earlier party might resume
   under different conditions) and, in the process, the ranking of object providers can
   change.
8. The process ends or is suspended at the decision of either party, *e.g.* because he is
   not prepared to commit or because a certain time has elapsed. The process can resume at a later time, when conditions may have changed (*e.g.*, changes in price or
   budget). In this case, the data broker should alert the parties of these changes.

4 Structure of the Negotiation Component (NC)

As mentioned above, the Negotiation Component is the most important part of DBF.
The key functionalities of NC are correctly understanding the negotiation ontologies
and choosing appropriate negotiation strategy. NOODLE, described below, is used to
ensure that all negotiation agents have a uniform knowledge of negotiations, including how to conduct them. Negotiation agents are assigned appropriate negotiation
strategies from a *strategy pool* based on the current negotiation task. Appropriate
strategies are generated based on the past history of negotiations.

4.1 NOODLE

NOODLE (Negotiation OntOlogy Description LanguagE) is an important part of
SCENS. With NOODLE, the negotiation protocols, proposals, conditions, and final

agreement will be described in a negotiation agent-understandable manner, which will allow automated negotiation to be supported by SCENS layers 2 and 3. NOODLE is based on DAML+OIL [19], a standard ontology description language. The goal of NOODLE is to help formalize negotiation activities by predefining some commonly used negotiation concepts and terms. Although these concepts and terms could be defined directly on top of the DAML and OIL ontology description languages, NOODLE is focused on providing a standard specifically for negotiation ontologies. The implementation of NOODLE will be available at http://scens.cs.dartmouth.edu, which is still under construction.

Our current definition of NOODLE has three parts: `negotiation.daml`, `proposal.daml`, and `agreement.daml`. In each of these three files, different aspects of negotiation are defined. `Negotiation.daml` defines the skeleton of a negotiation activity, including the number of negotiation parties and the actions that can potentially be used by the requester and owner, such as *Initiate, Reject, Accept, ... etc*. Some actions are used together, with the association defined in `proposal.daml` and/or `agreement.daml`. For example, an *Accept* action will always be followed by an agreement; a *Propose* action likewise is followed by a proposal/offer. Figure 2 shows a part of `negotiation.daml` with the comments removed. `Proposal.daml` defines the format of the messages that are exchanged in any negotiation activity. Basically there are two types of messages, "proposal/offer" and "critique". A proposal/offer is composed of several conditions, and a critique contains comments on one or more conditions. Currently, NOODLE defines several commonly used negotiation conditions in data sharing, such as usage period, payment, user groups, *etc*. Additional conditions can be added easily. After negotiation parties reach final agreement, they need to have something like contracts to sign. `Agreement.daml` defines the format of the final agreement with semantic meanings. Each negotiation party is allowed to review the final agreement before it is signed by a digital signature; after this, it cannot be refuted by any one of negotiation parties unless all parties agree to revoke the agreement.

```
<daml:Class rdf:ID="Negotiation">
  <rdfs:label>Negotiation</rdfs:label>
</daml:Class>

<daml:ObjectProperty rdf:ID="initiate">
  <daml:inverseOf rdf:resource="Negotiation.daml#initiateBy" />
</daml:ObjectProperty>

<daml:ObjectProperty rdf:ID="initiateBy">
  <daml:inverseOf rdf:resource="Negotiation.daml#initiate" />
</daml:ObjectProperty>
```

Fig. 2. A `Negotiation.daml` fragment, showing the class **Negotiation** and two important properties, **initiate** and **initiateBy**. A negotiation can be *initiated by* exactly one negotiation party, which is the party that *initiates* it, and so the two properties are semantically related. Both are needed in order to ensure that reasoning about the negotiation can be conducted automatically. In addition to the above fragment, the full code includes a "cardinality restriction", which ensures that there is a one-to-one relationship as described above.

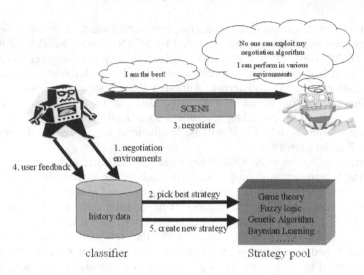

Fig. 3. Strategy Pool: (1) The agent input the negotiation environment parameters into the classifier. (2) The classifier selects a best strategy from the strategy pool. (3) The agent uses this strategy to negotiate with other agents through SCENS. (4) The agent returns the user feedback to the classifier. (5) The classifier generates new rules and creates the new strategy.

4.2 Strategy Pool

There are three important standards for a good negotiation agent. First, it should prevent the other agents easily find its negotiation rules and negotiation strategies. Intuitively, if a collector agent's reservation price for a certain object (generally the highest price the buyer can afford) is determined by a supplier agent after some interaction, the supplier agent can use this information to gain an unfair advantage in later negotiations with this collector. Second, a good agent needs to be flexible, which means it must work well in a variety of negotiation environments. Different environments include different user preferences (*e.g.* user may desire aggressive, neutral, or conservative bidding or bargaining), different user requirements (*e.g.* priority for price *vs.* delivery time), and different profiles of the agents to be negotiated with (agents' reputations). Finally, a negotiation agent needs to be more economical (or no worse) than a human being, taking into account any cost or savings from replacing human negotiators with agents and any required human interventions.

To allow an agent to achieve these three standards, we propose using a *Strategy Pool*. Figure 3 shows that for each negotiation process, the DBF system deploys a new negotiation agent on its behalf. That agent enters the current negotiation environment features into a classifier, which then selects a negotiation strategy or a combination of several strategies from the strategy pool according to past experiences and feedback. The agent then uses this negotiation strategy to negotiate through SCENS. After the negotiation process ends, the agent and its user can provide a negotiation history and feedback on the result to the classifier. Over time, based on the feedback from past negotiation processes, the system can thus make use of machine learning to find the best strategy for each different negotiation environment. Moreover, the classifier may create new negotiation strategies by discovering new negotiation rules or

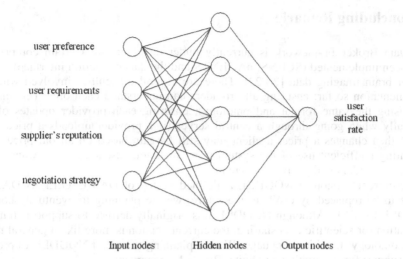

user preference

user requirements

supplier's reputation

negotiation strategy

user satisfaction rate

Input nodes   Hidden nodes   Output nodes

Fig. 4. Using a neural network to choose an appropriate strategy for a given negotiation. The inputs to the neural network are user preferences and requirements (negotiation conditions), the reputation of the current supplier, and current strategies (*left nodes*). The output node (*right*) encodes the expected average user satisfaction rate, which the network attempts to optimize by changing the value of the negotiation strategy input.

combining groups of existing strategies. Each such new strategy can then be added to the strategy pool for later use.

By using the strategy pool framework, we argue that the negotiation agent in the DBF system is made more flexible. This is because the negotiation strategy picked for the agent for a particular negotiation process is generally one that performed well on similar negotiation cases in the past (if such cases are known). Another advantage is that the strategy in each negotiation process is potentially different and is always subject to revision, which should make it more difficult for other agents to deduce or induce the strategy the agent uses; this may reduce any potential vulnerability arising from the discovery of "secret" information (such as reserve prices).

The learning in a DBF system can take one of two forms. In the first, the classifier can use a supervised learning process such as neural network (see Figure 4) to help it benefit from its experiences. To do that, after each negotiation process, the user performs some evaluation – say, assigns a ranking score to show his satisfaction rate on the negotiation result. Thus, a more favorable strategy will be chosen the next time based on the set of environments. In the second learning formulation, the classifier can use the data mining techniques to find the interesting association rules like "in those negotiation process getting the top 10% user satisfaction, 80% of buyer agents bid with a 5% concession from their previous bid when the supplier agents have the same percent concession". Such a rule may be helpful, but not be in the current strategies. Therefore, we can incorporate this rule into those strategies where appropriate to form new strategies, which will then be loaded into the strategy pool.

5 Concluding Remarks

The Data Broker Framework is currently under development. Certain components have been implemented (SCENS, nAGENTS and the data collection interface) for the area of brain imaging data [20-22]. There are several difficulties involved with the implementation so far: ensuring all providers can understand each other (*i.e.* encode their using the same format and ontology); ensuring each provider updates offers, especially when going through a central server (if a provider uploads a pricelist to server, then changes a price, a client may still bargain based on an old price); and preventing inefficient use of the system (*e.g.,* malicious users who just want to see how low providers will go, but not actually buy anything).

The current version of NOODLE is defined on top of DAML+OIL. As DAML+OIL is to be replaced by OWL in the future, we are planning to eventually convert NOODLE to OWL. Although NOODLE was originally defined to support automated negotiation for scientific data sharing, the current version is more like a general negotiation ontology definition language. We are planning to extend NOODLE to provide better support for negotiation on Digital Rights Management.

References

1. Beam, C. and A. Segev., Automated Negotiations: A Survey of the State of the Art. 1997.
2. Kraus, S., Negotiation in multiagent environments. 2001, Cambridge, MA: The MIT Press.
3. Ye, S., et al. SCENS: A system for the mediated sharing of sensitive data. In Third ACM+IEEE Joint Conference on Digital Libraries (JCDL03). 2003. Houston, TX.
4. SemanticWeb, http://www.thesemanticweb.org.
5. Makedon, F., et al. MetaDL: A digital library of metadata for sensitive or complex research data. In ECDL02. 2002. Rome, Italy.
6. Bartolini, C. and C.P.N. Jennings. A generic software framework for automated negotiation. In First International Conference on Autonomous Agent and Multi-Agent Systems. 2002.
7. Lomuscio, A., M. Wooldridge, and N. Jennings, A Classification Scheme for Negotiation in Electronic Commerce. Agent Mediated Electronic Commerce: A European Perspective, ed. D. F. and C. Sierra. 2000, Berlin: Springer-Verlag.
8. Tamma, V., M. Wooldridge, and I. Dickinson. An ontology for automated negotiation. In The AAMAS 2002 workshop on Ontologies in Agent Systems (OAS2002). 2002. Bologna, Italy.
9. Grosof, B. and T. Poon. SweetDeal: Representing Agent Contracts with Exceptions using XML Rules, Ontologies, and Process Descriptions. In WWW 2003. 2003. Budapest, Hungary: ACM Press.
10. Gilad, Z. and J.S. Rosenschein, Mechanisms for Automated Negotiation in State Oriented Domains. Journal of Artificial Intelligence Research, 1996. **5**.
11. Zeng, D. and K. Sycara, Bayesian learning in negotiation. International Journal of Human-Computer Studies, 1998. **48**: 125–141.
12. Kowalczyk, R. and V. Bui. On fuzzy e-negotiation agents: Autonomous negotiation with incomplete and imprecise information. In DEXA Workshop 2000. 2000.
13. Governatori, G., A.H.M. ter Hofstede, and P. Oaks. Defeasible logic for automated negotiation. In Fifth CollECTeR Conference on Electronic Commerce. 2000. Deakin University, Burwood, Victoria, Australia.

14. Matwin, S., T. Szapiro, and K. Haigh, Genetic algorithms approach to a negotiation support system. IEEE Transactions on Systems, Man, and Cybernetics, 1991. **21**.
15. Capron, L., The Long-term performance of horizontal acquisitions. Strategic Management Journal, 1999. **20**: 987-1018.
16. Hayward, M.L.A., When do firms learn from their acquisitions experience? Evidence from 1990-1995. Strategic Management Journal, 2002(23): 21-39.
17. Kraus, S., Negotiation and cooperation in multi-agent environments. Artificial Intelligence, 1997. **94**(1-2): 79-98.
18. Arizona Health Sciences Library, Collection Development Policy for Electronic Resources.
19. DAML+OIL, http://www.daml.org/2001/03/daml+oil.
20. Wang, Y., et al. A system framework for the integration and analysis of multi-modal spatio-temporal data streams: A case study in MS lesion analysis. In EMBS IEEE 29th Annual Northeast Bioengineering Conference. 2003. Capri, Italy.
21. Makedon, F., et al. Multi-functional data collection interfaces for biomedical research collaboration. In Human Computer Interaction (HCI). 2003. Crete.
22. Steinberg, T., et al. A spatio-temporal multi-modal data management and analysis environment: A case study in MS lesions. In 15th International Conference on Scientific and Statistic Database Management (SSDBM). 2003. Cambridge, MA.

P2P-DIET: Ad-hoc and Continuous Queries in Peer-to-Peer Networks Using Mobile Agents*

Stratos Idreos and Manolis Koubarakis

Intelligent Systems Laboratory
Dept. of Electronic and Computer Engineering
Technical University of Crete
GR73100 Chania, Crete, Greece
{sidraios,manolis}@intelligence.tuc.gr

Abstract. This paper presents P2P-DIET, a resource sharing system that unifies ad-hoc and continuous query processing in super-peer networks using mobile agents. P2P-DIET offers a simple data model for the description of network resources based on attributes with values of type text. It also utilizes very efficient query processing algorithms based on indexing of resource metadata and queries. The capability of location-independent addressing is supported, which enables P2P-DIET clients to connect from anywhere in the network and use dynamic IP addresses. The features of stored notifications and rendezvous guarantee that all important information is delivered to interested clients even if they have been disconnected for some time. P2P-DIET has been developed on top of the Open Source mobile agent system DIET Agents and is currently been demonstrated as a file sharing application.

1 Introduction

In peer-to-peer (P2P) systems a very large number of autonomous computing nodes (the *peers*) pool together their resources and rely on each other for *data* and *services*. P2P systems are application level *virtual* or *overlay networks* that have emerged as a natural way to share data and resources. Popular P2P *data sharing* systems such as Napster, Gnutella, Freenet, KaZaA, Morpheus and others have made this model of interaction popular.

The main application scenario considered in recent P2P data sharing systems is that of *ad-hoc querying*: a user poses a query (e.g., "I want music by Moby") and the system returns a list of pointers to matching files owned by various peers in the network. Then, the user can go ahead and download files of interest. The complementary scenario of *selective information dissemination (SDI)* or *selective information push* [8] has so far been considered by few P2P systems [1,10]. In an SDI scenario, a user posts a *continuous query* to the system to receive notifications whenever certain *resources* of interest appear in the system

---

* This work was carried out as part of the DIET project (IST-1999-10088), within the UIE initiative of the IST Programme of the European Commission.

G.A. Vouros and T. Panayiotopoulos (Eds.): SETN 2004, LNAI 3025, pp. 23–32, 2004.

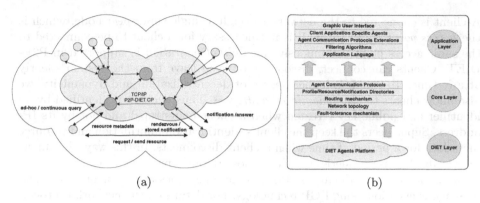

(a)   (b)

Fig. 1. The architecture and the layered view of P2P-DIET

(e.g., when a song of Moby becomes available). SDI can be as useful as ad-hoc querying in many target applications of P2P networks ranging from file sharing, to more advanced applications such as alert systems for digital libraries, e-commerce networks etc.

At the Intelligent Systems Laboratory of the Technical University of Crete, we have recently concentrated on the problem of SDI in P2P networks in the context of project DIET[1]. Our work, summarized in [9], has culminated in the implementation of P2P-DIET, a service that unifies ad-hoc and continuous query processing in P2P networks with super-peers. Conceptually, P2P-DIET is a direct descendant of DIAS, a distributed information alert system for digital libraries, that was presented in [10] but was never implemented. P2P-DIET combines ad-hoc querying as found in other super-peer networks [2] and SDI as proposed in DIAS. P2P-DIET goes beyond DIAS in offering many new features discussed above: client migration, dynamic IP addresses, stored notifications and rendezvous, simple fault-tolerance mechanisms, message authentication and encryption. P2P-DIET has been implemented on top of the open source DIET Agents Platform[2] [3] and it is currently available at http://www.intelligence.tuc.gr/p2pdiet. This paper concentrates on the architecture, functionality and agents of P2P-DIET.

A high-level view of the P2P-DIET architecture is shown in Figure 1 (a). There are two kinds of nodes: *super-peers* and *clients*. All super-peers are equal and have the same responsibilities, thus the super-peer subnetwork is a *pure* P2P network (it can be an arbitrary undirected graph). Each super-peer serves a fraction of the clients and keeps *indices* on the resources of those clients.

Clients can run on user computers. Resources (e.g., files in a file-sharing application) are kept at client nodes, although it is possible in special cases to store resources at super-peer nodes. Clients are equal to each other only in terms of download. Clients download resources directly from the resource owner client.

---

[1] http://www.dfki.de/diet

[2] http://diet-agents.sourceforge.net/

A client is connected to the network through a single super-peer node, which is the *access point* of the client. It is not necessary for a client to be connected to the same access point continuously since *client migration* is supported in P2P-DIET. Clients can connect, disconnect or even leave from the system silently at any time. To enable a higher degree of decentralization and dynamicity, we also allow clients to use *dynamic IP addresses*. Thus, a client is identified by an identifier and public key (created when a client bootstraps) and not by its IP-address. Super-peers the keep the client's identification information and resource metadata for a period of time when a client disconnects. In this way, the super-peer is able to answer queries matching those resource metadata even if the owner client is not on-line. Finally, P2P-DIET provides message authentication and message encryption using PGP technology. For details on the network protocols and implementation see [6].

The rest of the paper is organized as follows. Section 2 presents the metadata model and query language used for describing and querying resources in the current implementation of P2P-DIET. Section 3 discusses the protocols for processing queries, answers and notifications. Section 4 discusses other interesting functionalities of P2P-DIET. Section 5 discusses the implementation of P2P-DIET using mobile agents. Finally, Section 6 presents our conclusions.

2 Data Models and Query Languages

In [10] we have presented the data model $\mathcal{AWPS}$, and its languages for specifying queries and *textual* resource metadata in SDI systems such as P2P-DIET. $\mathcal{AWPS}$ is based on the concept of *attributes* with values of type *text*. The query language of $\mathcal{AWPS}$ offers *Boolean* and *proximity operators* on attribute values as in the Boolean model of Information Retrieval (IR) [5]. It also allows textual *similarity* queries interpreted as in the vector space model of IR [11].

The current implementation of P2P-DIET supports only *conjunctive* queries in $\mathcal{AWPS}$. The following examples of such queries demonstrate the features of $\mathcal{AWPS}$ and its use in an SDI application for a digital library:

$$AUTHOR \sqsupseteq Smith \ \land \ TITLE \sqsupseteq (peer\text{-}to\text{-}peer \ \lor$$
$$(selective \prec_{[0,0]} dissemination \prec_{[0,3]} information))$$

$$AUTHOR \sqsupseteq Smith \ \land$$
$$ABSTRACT \sim_{0.8} \text{``}Peer\text{-}to\text{-}peer \ architectures \ have \ been...\text{''}$$

The data model $\mathcal{AWPS}$ is attractive for the representation of textual metadata since it offers linguistically motivated concepts such as *word* and traditional IR operators. Additionally, its query language is more expressive than the ones used in earlier SDI systems such as SIFT [11] where documents are free text and queries are conjunctions of keywords. On the other hand, $\mathcal{AWPS}$ can only model resource metadata that has a *flat* structure, thus it cannot support hierarchical documents as in the XML-based models of [4]. But notice that IR-inspired constructs such as proximity and similarity *cannot* be expressed in the query languages of [4] and are also *missing* from W3C standard XML query languages

XQuery/XPath. The recent W3C working draft[3] is expected to pave the way for the introduction of such features in XQuery/XPath. Thus our work on $\mathcal{AWPS}$ can be seen as a first step in the introduction of IR features in XML-based frameworks for SDI.

3   Routing and Query Processing

P2P-DIET targets content sharing applications such as digital libraries [10], networks of learning repositories [12] and so on. Assuming that these applications are supported by P2P-DIET, there will be a stakeholder (e.g., a content provider such as Akamai) with an interest in building and maintaining the super-peer subnetwork. Thus super-peer subnetworks in P2P-DIET are expected to be more stable than typical pure P2P networks such as Gnutella. As a result, we have chosen to use routing algorithms appropriate for such networks.

P2P-DIET implements routing of queries (ad-hoc or continuous) by utilizing *minimum weight spanning trees* for the super-peer subnetwork, a *poset* data structure encoding continuous query subsumption as originally suggested in [1], and *data* and *query indexing* at each super-peer node. Answers and notifications are unicasted through the shortest path that connects two super-peers.

3.1   Ad-hoc Querying

P2P-DIET supports the typical *ad-hoc query scenario*. A client A can post a query q to its access point AP. AP broadcasts q to all super-peers through its minimum weight spanning tree. *Answers* are produced for all matching network resources and are returned to the access point AP that originated the query through the shortest path that connects the super peer that generated the answer with AP (unicasting). Finally, AP passes the answers to A for further processing. Answers are produced for all matching resources regardless of whether owning resource clients are on-line or not, since super-peers do not erase resource metadata when clients disconnect (see Section 4).

Each super-peer can be understood to store a relation

$$resource(ID, A_1, A_2, \ldots, A_n)$$

where ID is a resource identifier and $A_1, A_2, \ldots, A_n$ are the attributes known to the super-peer network. In our implementation, relation *resource* is implemented by keeping an *inverted file index* for each attribute A_i. The index maps every word w in the vocabulary of A_i to the set of resource IDs that contain word w in their attribute A_i. Query evaluation at each super-peer is then implemented efficiently by utilizing these indices in the standard way.

---

[3] http://www.w3.org/TR/xmlquery-full-text-use-cases

3.2   Continuous Queries

SDI scenarios are also supported. Clients may *subscribe* to their access point with a *continuous query* expressing their information needs. Super-peers then *forward* posted queries to other super-peers. In this way, matching a query with metadata of a published resource takes place at a super-peer that is *as close as possible* to the origin of the resource.

Whenever a resource is published, P2P-DIET makes sure that all clients with continuous queries matching this resource's metadata are notified. Notifications are generated at the access point where the resource was published, and travel to the access point of every client that has posted a continuous query matching this notification following the *reverse path* that was set by the propagation of the query.

We expect P2P-DIET networks to *scale* to very large numbers of clients, published resources and continuous queries. To achieve this, we utilize the following data structures at each super-peer:

- A *partially ordered set* (called the *continuous query poset*) that keeps track of the subsumption relations among the continuous queries posted to the super-peer by its clients or forwarded by other super-peers. This poset is inspired by SIENA [1]. We can also have it in P2P-DIET because the relation of subsumption in $\mathcal{AWPS}$ is reflexive, anti-symmetric and transitive i.e., a *(weak) partial order*. Like in SIENA, P2P-DIET utilizes the continuous query poset to to minimize network traffic: in each super-peer no continuous query that is less general than one that has already been processed is actually forwarded.
- A sophisticated *index* over the continuous queries managed by the super-peer. This index is used to solve the *filtering problem*: Given a database of continuous queries db and a notification n, find all queries $q \in db$ that match n and forward n to the neighbouring super-peers or clients that have posted q.

4   Stored Notifications and Rendezvous at Super-peers

Clients may not be online all the time, thus we can not guarantee that a client with a specific continuous query will be available at the time that matching resources are added to the network and relevant notifications are generated. Motivated by our target applications (e.g., digital libraries or networks of learning repositories), we do not want to ignore such situations and allow the loss of relevant notifications.

Assume that a client A is off-line when a notification n matching its continuous query is generated and arrives to its access point AP. AP checks if A is on the active client list. If this is true then n is forwarded to A, otherwise n is stored in the *stored notifications directory* of AP. Notification n is delivered to A by AP next time A connects to the network.

A client may request a resource at the time that it receives a notification n, or later on using a saved notification n on his local *notifications directory*.

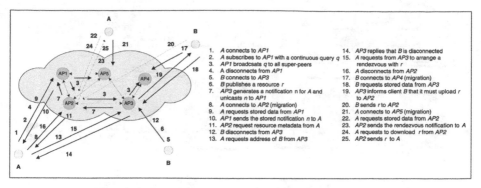

Fig. 2. A stored notification and rendezvous example

Consider the case when a client A requests a resource r, but the resource owner client B is not on-line. A requests the address of B from $AP2$ (the access point of B). A may request a *rendezvous* with resource r from $AP2$ with a message that contains the identifiers of A and B, the address of AP and the path of r. When B reconnects, $AP2$ informs B that it must upload r to AP as a *rendezvous file* for A. Then, B uploads r. AP checks if A is on-line and if it is, AP forwards r to A or else r is stored in the *rendezvous directory* of AP and when A reconnects, it receives a rendezvous notification from AP.

The features of stored notifications and rendezvous take place even if clients *migrate* to different access points. For example, let us assume that A has migrated to $AP3$. The client agent understands that, and requests from AP any rendezvous or notifications. A updates the variable *previous access point* with the address of $AP3$. AP deletes A form its client list, removes all resource metadata of A from the local resource metadata database and removes the continuous queries of A from the poset. Finally, A sends to $AP3$ its resource metadata and continuous queries. A complete example is shown in Figure 2.

5   Agents of P2P-DIET

The implementation of P2P-DIET makes a rather simple use of the DIET Agents concepts *environment, world* and *infohabitant*. Each super-peer and each client occupy a different world, and each such world consists of a single *environment*. All the worlds together form the *P2P-DIET universe*. However, the P2P-DIET implementation makes heavy use of all the capabilities of lightweight mobile agents offered by the platform to implement the various P2P protocols. Such capabilities are agent creation, cloning and destruction, agent migration, local and remote communication between agents etc.

5.1   The Super-peer Environment

A world in a super-peer node consists of a single *super-peer environment*, where 10 different types of agents live. A super-peer environment is shown in Figure 3(a).

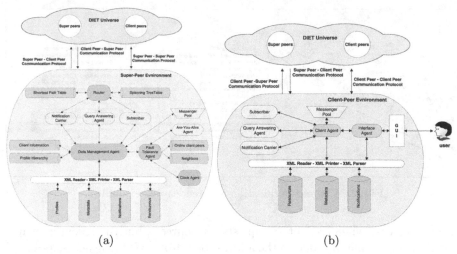

Fig. 3. A Super-Peer Environment and a Client Peer Environment

The *data management agent* is the agent with the greatest number of responsibilities in the P2P-DIET universe. This agent manages the local database of peer meta-data, resource meta-data, continuous queries and their indices. Moreover, it arranges rendezvous and stores notifications and rendezvous files. The data management agent can create notification carriers and messengers (these agents will carry out the tasks discussed below).

The *router* is responsible for the correct flow of messages in the network. It holds the shortest path table and the spanning tree table of the local superpeer. Mobile agents travel around the network using information from the local Router on each super-peer environment where they arrive. The *make routing paths scheduler* is a very lightweight agent that decides when it is the right time for the router to update its routing paths when the network is in an unstable condition.

A *subscriber* is a mobile agent that is responsible for subscribing continuous queries of clients to super-peers. To subscribe a continuous query q of client C, a subscriber S starts from the environment of C. Then, it migrates to all super-peers of the network to subscribe q and to find any resource meta-data published earlier that match q. S will start from the super-peer environment of the access point A of C and it will reach all super-peers through the minimum-weight spanning tree of A. Whenever a subscriber finds any resource metadata matching its continuous query in a super-peer environment B, it clones itself. The clone returns to the environment of C to deliver the notification by travelling towards super-peer A through the shortest path that connects B and A. The original subscriber will continue in order to visit the rest of the super-peers of the network. A subscriber agent destroys itself when it returns to the client-peer environment with a notification. A subscriber can also destroy itself away from its starting client environment when it is on a remote super-peer environment with no notifications to deliver and no more super-peers to visit.

A *notification carrier* is a mobile agent that is responsible for delivering notifications. A notification carrier may start from a super-peer environment SP and travel along the shortest path to the environment of super-peer AP and from there migrates to the environment of client C if C is online. Note, that it is not possible for the notification carrier to travel directly to the client environment for two reasons. First, the super-peer SP does not know the IP address of C. Second, the notification must arrive to environment AP because more than one clients may have continuous queries that match the notification. A notification carrier destroys itself after it has delivered the notification to the client or when it arrives to the access point of the client and the client is not online.

A *query answering agent* is a mobile agent that answers queries. The query-answering agent that finds the answers to query q of client C starts from the environment of C. Then, it migrates to all super-peers of the network to search for answers to q. It will start from the super-peer environment of the access point A of C and it will reach all super-peers through the minimum-weight spanning tree of A. Each time, it finds any resource metadata matching q in a super-peer environment B, it clones itself. The clone returns to the environment of client C to deliver the answer by travelling towards super-peer A through the shortest path that connects B and A. The original query-answering agent will continue in order to visit the rest of the super-peers of the network to search for answers to q. A query-answering agent destroys itself when it returns to the client-peer environment with an answer. A special case that a query-answering agent will destroy itself away from its starting client-peer environment, is when it is on a remote super-peer environment with no answers and no more super-peers to visit.

A *messenger* is a mobile agent that implements remote communication between agents in different worlds. A messenger is a very lightweight agent that will migrate to a remote environment and deliver a message to a target agent. We need Messengers to support simple jobs i.e, just send a message to a remote agent. For example, consider the case that a client agent sends a `connect` or `disconnect` message to its access point. In this way, we do not create a new type of agent for each simple job that is carried out by our system. Messengers can be used to support new simple features that require remote communication. Each environment has a messenger pool. When a messenger arrives at an environment, it delivers the message and stays in the pool, if there is space. In this way, when an agent wants to send a remote message, it assigns the message to a messenger from the pool unless the pool is empty, in which case a new messenger will be created.

Subscribers, notification carriers, query-answering agents and messengers use information from the local router on each super-peer environment that they arrive in order to find the address of their next destination. They use shortest paths and minimum weight spanning trees to travel in the pure peer-to-peer network of super-peers. In this way, they may ask two types of questions to a router:

– I want to migrate to all super-peers and I started from super-peer X. The answer of the local router to this question are the IP addresses of remote the super-peers that are children in the minimum weight spanning tree of the local super-peer.

– I want to migrate to super-peer X. The answer of the local router to this question is the IP address of the remote super-peer that is its neighbor and is in the shortest path from the local super-peer to the destination super-peer X.

The *fault-tolerance agent* is responsible for periodically checking the clients agents, that are supposed to be alive and are served by this super-peer. The agents of the neighbor super-peers are checked too, to guarantee connectivity. The fault-tolerance agent can create are-you-alive agents. A useful heuristic in P2P-DIET, is that a fault-tolerance agent does not check a node x (client or super-peer) if x has sent any kind of message during the last period of checks (there is no need to ensure that x is alive in this case). An *are-you-alive agent* is a mobile agent that is sent by the fault-tolerance agent to a remote client-peer environment or super-peer environment to check whether the local agents are alive or not. An are-you-alive agent will return to its original environment with the answer. In each super-peer environment there is an are-you-alive agent pool where agents wait for the local fault-tolerance agent to assign them a remote environment to check. All are-you-alive agents return to their original environment to inform the local fault-tolerance agent on the status of the remote environment that they checked and then they stay in the local are-you-alive agent pool. The *clock agent* is the scheduler for the fault-tolerance agent. It decides when it is the right time to send messages or to check for replies.

5.2   The Client-Peer Environment

The world in the client-peer nodes has a *client-peer environment*. The *client agent* is the agent that connects the client-peer environment with the rest of the P2P-DIET universe. It communicates, through mobile agents, with the super-peer agent that is the access point or any other remote client agents. The client agent sends the following data to the remote super-peer agent of the access point: the continuous query of the client, the metadata of the resources, the queries, the requests for rendezvous etc. The client agent can create Subscribers, query-answering agents and messengers. Figure 3 (b), shows all the agents in the client-peer environment. Additionally, an *interface agent* is responsible for forwarding the demands of the user to the client agent and messages from the client agent to the user. A *messenger, query-answering agent, notification carrier* and *subscriber* may inhabit a client-peer environment and are exactly the same as the agents that inhabit the super-peer environments.

6   Conclusions

We have presented the design of P2P-DIET, a resource sharing system that unifies ad-hoc and continuous query processing in P2P networks with super-peers. P2P-DIET has been implemented using the mobile agent system DIET Agents and has demonstrated the use of mobile agent systems for the implementation of P2P applications. Currently we are working on implementing the query and SDI functionality of P2P-DIET on top of a distributed hash table like Chord [7] and compare this with our current implementation. We are also working on more expressive resource description and query languages e.g., such as the ones based on RDF and currently used in EDUTELLA [12].

References

1. Antonio Carzaniga and David S. Rosenblum and Alexander L Wolf. Design and evaluation of a wide-area event notification service. *ACM Transactions on Computer Systems*, 19(3):332–383, August 2001.
2. B. Yang and H. Garcia-Molina. Designing a super-peer network. In *Proceedings of the 19th International Conference on Data Engineering (ICDE 2003)*, March 5–8 2003.
3. C. Hoile and F. Wang and E. Bonsma and P. Marrow. Core specification and experiments in diet: a decentralised ecosystem-inspired mobile agent system. In *Proceedings of the 1st International Joint Conference on Autonomous Agents & Multiagent Systems (AAMAS 2002)*, pages 623–630, July 15–19 2002.
4. C.-Y. Chan, P. Felber, M. Garofalakis, and R. Rastogi. Efficient Filtering of XML Documents with XPath Expressions. In *Proceedings of the 18th International Conference on Data Engineering*, pages 235–244, February 2002.
5. C.-C. K. Chang, H. Garcia-Molina, and A. Paepcke. Predicate Rewriting for Translating Boolean Queries in a Heterogeneous Information System. *ACM Transactions on Information Systems*, 17(1):1–39, 1999.
6. S. Idreos and M. Koubarakis. P2P-DIET: A Query and Notification Service Based on Mobile Agents for Rapid Implementation of P2P Applications. Technical Report TR-TUC-ISL-2003-01, Intelligent Systems Laboratory, Dept. of Electronic and Computer Engineering, Technical University of Crete, June 2003.
7. Ion Stoica and Robert Morris and David Karger and M. Frans Kaashoek and Hari Balakrishnan. Chord: A scalable peer-to-peer lookup service for internet applications. In *Proceedings of the ACM SIGCOMM '01 Conference*, San Diego, California, August 2001.
8. M. J. Franklin and S. B. Zdonik. "Data In Your Face": Push Technology in Perspective. In *Proceedings ACM SIGMOD International Conference on Management of Data*, pages 516–519, 1998.
9. M. Koubarakis and C. Tryfonopoulos and S. Idreos and Y. Drougas. Selective Information Dissemination in P2P Networks: Problems and Solutions. *ACM SIGMOD Record, Special issue on Peer-to-Peer Data Management, K. Aberer (editor)*, 32(3), September 2003.
10. M. Koubarakis and T. Koutris and P. Raftopoulou and C. Tryfonopoulos. Information Alert in Distributed Digital Libraries: The Models, Languages and Architecture of DIAS. In *Proceedings of the 6th European Conference on Research and Advanced Technology for Digital Libraries (ECDL 2002)*, volume 2458 of *Lecture Notes in Computer Science*, pages 527–542, September 2002.
11. T.W. Yan and H. Garcia-Molina. The SIFT information dissemination system. *ACM Transactions on Database Systems*, 24(4):529–565, 1999.
12. W. Nejdl and B. Wolf and Changtao Qu and S. Decker and M. Sintek and A. Naeve and M. Nilsson and M. Palmer and T. Risch. Edutella: A P2P Networking Infrastructure Based on RDF. In *Proc. of WWW-2002*. ACM Press, 2002.

Taxonomy-Based Annotation of XML Documents: Application to eLearning Resources*

Birahim Gueye, Philippe Rigaux, and Nicolas Spyratos

Laboratoire de Recherche en Informatique
Université Paris-Sud Orsay, France
{gueye,rigaux,spyratos}@lri.fr

Abstract. In this paper we propose an automatic mechanism for annotating XML documents. This mechanism relies on a simple data model whose main features are: (1) a modeling of XML documents as *trees* composed of elements that are possibly distributed over a network, (2) a *composition* operator to create new documents from existing ones, and (3) an inference algorithm for automatically deriving the annotation of composite documents from the annotations of their components.
We illustrate the features of the model with an application to eLearning resources. We also describe a prototype which allows to create a new document from eLearning fragments collected over the Web, and generates an RDF-based annotation of the document's content. The RDF output can then be used as a support for browsing and querying, by users wishing to create new documents.

1 Introduction

In the present paper we focus on the requirements of applications that search, access and integrate resources disseminated over the Internet. More specifically we consider the management of *metadata* related to a specific knowledge domain, and propose a conceptual model that allows to develop search, retrieval and integration functionalities based on *annotations*, i.e., content descriptions. Moreover we consider the effective support of these functionalities in the context of a distributed repository of XML documents.

Our model is based on the following approach. First, a document is represented as a graph of *components*, which are themselves other documents available over a network. Second, we associate with each document a taxonomy-based description, or *annotation*; such annotations allow users to find documents of interest, retrieve them, and use them as components of a new, composite document. Finally, the main contribution of the paper is a mechanism for the automatic derivation of the appropriate annotation for a newly created document, based on the annotations of its components. The conceptual model that we propose can be instantiated in various environments, and this feature is illustrated by a case study concerning the management of distributed eLearning documents.

* Research supported by the EU DELOS Network of Excellence in Digital Libraries and the EU IST Project (Self eLearning Networks), IST-2001-39045.

G.A. Vouros and T. Panayiotopoulos (Eds.): SETN 2004, LNAI 3025, pp. 33–42, 2004.

In Section 2 we discuss the motivations of this work. Our formal data model is presented in Section 3, and the case study in Section 4. Section 5 concludes the paper. Proofs are omitted, due to space restrictions. The interested reader is referred to the report [14], available at *http://www.lri.fr/ rigaux/DOC/RS03b.pdf.*

2   Motivation

Let us develop briefly the motivation of this work and position it in the context of the semantic web [16]. A major effort of the semantic web is devoted to the development of the XML language in order to bring new solutions regarding some major limitations of HTML. If we focus on the specific metadata-management applications considered in this paper, first, we note that XML allows the creation of well-structured documents whose "fragments" can be identified and extracted. Second, new XML documents can be created by assembling fragments, and moreover this can be done in a distributed setting where the referred fragments do not necessarily reside at the same site. This provides a quite powerful mechanism to reuse existing content in a new context or, put differently, to view and manipulate a set of distributed XML documents as if it were a single (huge) digital library.

Unfortunately, although XML meets the needs for extraction and restructuring of documents, it provides very little support for the *description* of their content. This widely acknowledged weakness constitutes one of the major challenges of the Semantic Web, namely adding information to web documents in order to access *knowledge* related to the contents of documents. This external semantic description constitutes the document's *metadata*. A lot of efforts have been devoted recently to develop languages and tools to generate, store and query metadata. Some of the most noticeable achievements are the RDF language [12] and RDF schemas [13], query languages for large RDF databases [8,2] and tools to produce RDF descriptions from documents [7,4]. Generation of metadata remains however essentially a manual process, possibly aided by acquisition software (see for instance Annotea [7]). The fully automatic generation of metadata is hardly addressed in the literature, with few exceptions [10,18,5]. A representative work is the Semtag system described in [5] which "tags" web pages with terms from a standard ontology, thanks to text analysis techniques. This is different – and essentially complementary – to our approach, which relies on the structure of composite objects (or documents) to infer new annotations.

Several metadata standards exist today, such as the Dublin Core [6], or the IEEE Learning Object Metadata [11]. However, if one considers the full set of metadata that these standards propose to attach to a document, it seems indeed quite difficult to produce them automatically. In this paper, we focus only on *semantic* metadata, i.e., the part of metadata which describes the content of the document [3], hereafter called *annotation*. The key idea is to exploit the structure of the document in order to infer its annotation from the annotations ot its components. The inference mechanism that we propose relies on a tree-structured taxonomy whose terms are used by *all* authors to annotate their documents (at least those documents that they wish to make sharable by other authors). An annotation is actually a set of terms from that taxonomy. To make a document sharable by other users, its author must register the document with a coordinator, or *syndicator*, and users that search for documents matching their needs must address their queries to the syndicator.

A suitable application for illustrating the usefulness of our approach is the management of eLearning resources available in a distributed environment. In the context of the SeLeNe project [15], we have implemented a prototype to help authors create their own pedagogical documents, based on existing resources. Fragments of these resources can be collected and aggregated, resulting in a new document which can in turn be made available to the community of users. The authoring tool also generates an RDF description of the content of the document which can then be used to inform the network of the document's content, and also as a support for querying functionalities.

3   The Annotation Model

In our model, we adopt a high-level view, whereby an XML document is represented by an *identifier* together with a *composition graph* showing how the document is constructed from other simpler documents. In practice the identifier can be any URI-based mechanism for addressing the internal structure of XML documents and allowing for traversal of the document's structure and for the choice of internal parts (see the XPointer recommandation [19]). The composition graph reflects the structure commonly obtained by nesting XML elements.

Definition 1 (The representation of a document) *A* document *is represented by an identifier d together with a possibly empty set of document identifiers* $d_1, \ldots, d_n$, *called the* parts *of d and denoted as parts(d), i.e., parts(d)* $= \{d_1, \ldots, d_n\}$. *If parts(d)* $= \emptyset$ *then d is called* atomic, *else it is called* composite.

Hereafter, we shall confuse a document and its representation, i.e., we shall use the term "document" to mean its representation. For notational convenience, we shall write $d = d_1 + d_2 + \ldots + d_n$ to stand for $parts(d) = \{d_1, d_2, \ldots, d_n\}$.

A composite document is recursively composed of other documents that can be either atomic or composite. It follows that a document d can be represented as a graph with d as the single root. We shall refer to this graph as the *composition graph* of d. We restrict the composition graph to be a directed acyclic graph (*dag*). This reflects the reasonable assumption that a document cannot be an element of itself. Note that our definitions ignore the ordering of the parts. As we shall see shortly, deriving the annotation of a composite document from the annotations of its parts does not depend on any ordering.

As we mentioned in the introduction, annotations are built based on a controlled vocabulary, or *taxonomy*. A taxonomy consists of a set of terms together with a subsumption relation between terms. An example of taxonomy is the well known ACM Computing Classification System [1].

Definition 2 *A* taxonomy *is a pair* $(T, \preceq)$ *where* T *is a* terminology, *i.e., a finite and non-empty set of names, or* terms, *and* $\preceq$ *is a reflexive and transitive relation over* T *called* subsumption.

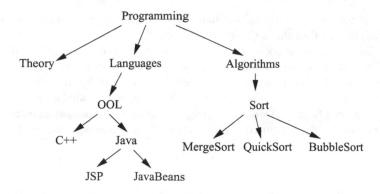

Fig. 1. A taxonomy

Figure 1 shows an example of a taxonomy. The term Object-Oriented Languages (OOL) is subsumed by Languages (OOL $\preceq$ Languages) and JavaBeans is subsumed by Java (JavaBeans $\preceq$ Java). We note that a taxonomy is not necessarily a tree. However, most taxonomies used in practice (including the ACM Computing Classification System mentioned earlier) are in fact trees. For the purposes of this report we shall assume that the taxonomy used by the authors to describe the contents of their documents is a tree.

When creating a document, its author chooses one or more terms of the taxonomy to annotate its content. For example, if the document concerns the Quick Sort algorithm written in java then its author most likely will choose the terms QuickSort and Java to annotate it. Then the set of terms {QuickSort, Java} will be the annotation of the document.

Definition 3 (Annotation) *Given a taxonomy* $(T, \preceq)$ *we call* annotation *in* T *any set of terms from* T.

However, a problem arises with annotations: an annotation can be redundant if some of the terms it contains are subsumed by other terms. For example, the annotation {QuickSort, Java, Sort} is redundant, as QuickSort is subsumed by Sort, whereas the annotations {QuickSort, Java} and {Sort, Java} are not redundant. Clearly, redundant annotations are undesirable as they can lead to redundant computations during query evaluation. We shall limit our attention to *reduced annotations*, defined as follows:

Definition 4 (Reduced Annotation) *An annotation A in* T *is called* reduced *if for any terms s and t in A, s $\not\preceq$ t and t $\not\preceq$ s.*

Following the above definition one can reduce a description in two ways: removing all but the minimal terms, or removing all but the maximal terms. In this paper we adopt the first approach, i.e., we reduce a description by removing all but its minimal terms. The reason for choosing this definition of reduction is because we want to describe as precisely as possible the contents of a LO. Thus, of the two possible reductions of

{QuickSort, Java, Sort}, we shall keep {QuickSort, Java}. and we will denote $\mathcal{A}(d)$ the reduced annotation of a document d.

In the case of an atomic document its annotation can be provided either by the author or by the system via a semi-automatic analysis. In the case of a composite document, though, we would like the annotation to be derived automatically from the annotations of its parts. We shall refer to this derived annotation as the *implied annotation* of the document. To get a feeling of what the derived annotation of a document is, consider a document $d = d_1 + d_2$, composed of two parts with the following annotations:

$$\mathcal{A}(d_1) = \{\texttt{QuickSort, Java}\} \qquad \mathcal{A}(d_2) = \{\texttt{BubbleSort, C++}\}$$

Then the derived annotation of d would be {Sort, OOL}, that summarizes what the two components contain, collectively. We shall come back to this example after the formal definition of derived annotation. Intuitively, we would like the implied annotation of a document d to satisfy the following criteria:

- it should be reduced, for the reasons explained earlier;
- it should describe what the parts of d have in common, as in our previous example;
- it should be a minimal annotation, i.e., as close as possible to the annotation of each and every part of d (see again our previous example).

To illustrate points 2 and 3 above, suppose that a composite document has two parts with annotations {QuickSort} and {BubbleSort}. The term Sort is a good candidate for being the implied annotation, as it describes what the two parts have in common. Moreover Sort is the minimal term with this property. On the other hand, the term Algorithm is not a good candidate because, although it describes what the parts have in common, it is not minimal as it subsumes the term Sort. In order to formalize these intuitions, we introduce the following relation on annotations.

Definition 5 (Refinement Relation on annotations) *Let A and A' be two annotations. We say that A is finer than A', denoted $A \sqsubseteq A'$, iff for each $t' \in A'$, there exists $t \in A$ such that $t \preceq t'$*

For example, the annotation $A=\{\texttt{QuickSort, Java, BubbleSort}\}$ is finer than $A' = \{\texttt{Sort, Java}\}$, whereas A' is not finer than A. Clearly, $\sqsubseteq$ is a reflexive and transitive relation, thus a pre-ordering over the set of all annotations. However, $\sqsubseteq$ is *not* antisymmetric, as the following example shows. Consider $A_1 = \{\texttt{OOL, Java, Sort}\}$ and $A_2 = \{\texttt{Java, Sort, Algorithms}\}$. It is easy to see that $A_1 \sqsubseteq A_2$ and $A_2 \sqsubseteq A_1$, although $A_1 \neq A_2$. If we restrict our attention to reduced annotations then $\sqsubseteq$ becomes also antisymmetric, thus a partial order.

Proposition 1 *The relation $\sqsubseteq$ is a partial order over the set of all reduced annotations.*

Now, using this ordering, we can define formally the implied annotation of a composite document so as to satisfy the criteria for a "good" implied annotation, given earlier. First, we need the following result:

Proposition 2 (Least Upper Bound of a Set of Reduced Annotations) *Let* $\mathcal{D} = \{A_1,$
.., $A_n\}$ be any set of reduced annotations. Let $\mathcal{U}$ be the set of all reduced annotations
S such that $A_i \sqsubseteq S, i = 1, 2, ..., n$, i.e., $\mathcal{U} = \{S | A_i \sqsubseteq S, i = 1, ..., n\}$. Then $\mathcal{U}$ has a
unique minimal element, that we shall denote as $lub(\mathcal{D}, \sqsubseteq)$.

We call *implied annotation* of d, denoted $\mathcal{A}_{imp}(d)$, the least upper bound of $\{A_1, ..,$
$A_n\}$ in $\sqsubseteq$, i.e., $\mathcal{A}_{imp}(d) = lub(\{A_1, .., A_n\}, \sqsubseteq)$ The following algorithm computes the
implied annotation of a document d.

Algorithm IMPLIEDANNOTATION
Input: A composite document $d = d_1 + d_2 + ... + d_n$
Output: The implied annotation $\mathcal{A}_{imp}(d)$
begin
  Compute $P = \mathcal{A}(d_1) \times \mathcal{A}(d_2) \times ... \times \mathcal{A}(d_n)$
  for each tuple $L_k = [t_1^k, t_2^k, ..., t_n^k]$ in P, compute $T_k = lub_{\preceq}(t_1^k, t_2^k, ..., t_n^k)$
  Let $A' = \{T_1, ..., T_l\}$
  Reduce A' [i.e., eliminate all but its minimal terms]
  return A'
end

In the algorithm, the function $lub_{\preceq}(t_1, ..., t_n)$ returns the least upper bound of the
terms $t_1, ..., t_n$ with respect to $\preceq$. Note that, as $(T, \preceq)$ is a tree, this least upper bounds
exists. To see how this algorithm works, consider again the document $d = d_1 + d_2$ that
we have seen earlier, composed of two parts with the following annotations:

$$\mathcal{A}(d_1) = \{\texttt{QuickSort, Java}\} \qquad \mathcal{A}(d_2) = \{\texttt{BubbleSort, C++}\}$$

The cross-product $\mathcal{A}(d_1) \times \mathcal{A}(d_2)$ yields the following set of tuples:

$$P = \begin{cases} L_1 = \texttt{<QuickSort, BubbleSort>} \\ L_2 = \texttt{<QuickSort, C++>} \\ L_3 = \texttt{<Java, BubbleSort>} \\ L_4 = \texttt{<Java, C++>} \end{cases}$$

For each tuple L_i, $i = 1, ..., 4$, one computes then the *lub* of the terms in L_i, and
one obtains respectively $T_1 = \texttt{Sort}$, $T_2 = \texttt{Programming}$, $T_3 = \texttt{Programming}$
and $T_4 = \texttt{OOL}$. The set A' is therefore $\{\texttt{Sort, Programming, OOL}\}$ which, once
reduced, becomes $\{\texttt{OOL, Sort}\}$ (see the taxonomy of Figure 1). The result can be interpreted as follows: the composite document is devoted, *in all its parts*, both to sorting
and to object-oriented languages.

Here is a second example to illustrate that the implied annotation retains only what
is common to *all* parts. Consider the document $d' = d_1 + d_3$, composed of two parts
with the following annotations:

$$\mathcal{A}(d_1) = \{\texttt{QuickSort, Java}\} \qquad \mathcal{A}(d_3) = \{\texttt{BubbleSort}\}$$

Applying the algorithm, we find first the cartesian product:

$$P = \begin{cases} L_1 = \texttt{<QuickSort, BubbleSort>} \\ L_2 = \texttt{<Java, BubbleSort>} \end{cases}$$

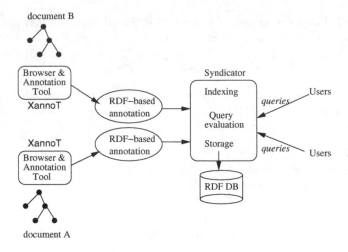

Fig. 2. Overview of the system's architecture

Therefore $A' = \{\texttt{Sort, Programming}\}$ from which one eliminates, during the reduction phase, the term $\texttt{Programming}$ as it subsumes $\texttt{Sort}$. As a consequence, the implied annotation is $\{\texttt{Sort}\}$. Intuitively, both parts concern sorting algorithms, and this is reflected in the implied description. Two comments are noteworthy:

1. No loss of information results from the elimination of the term $\texttt{Java}$ from the implied annotation. Indeed, if a user searches for documents related to java, d_1 will be in the answer and d' will not, which is consistent.
2. If we had put $\texttt{Java}$ in the implied annotation of d', this would give rise to the following problem: when one searches for documents related to java, the system will return both d_1 and d'. Clearly, this answer is at the same time redundant (because d_1 is part of d'), and partially irrelevant as only a part of d' concerns java.

4   Application to eLearning Resources

We describe in this section a prototype, XANNOT (*XML Annotation Tool*) which instanciates in a practical setting the functionalities of our model and illustrates its usefulness. In this prototype the documents and their components are XML documents, and the system relies on XML tools and languages for addressing and transformation tasks.

The architecture of XANNOT system is summarized in Figure 2. Composite documents are represented in this specific implementation by XML *documents* which are *valid* with respect to the DocBook DTD [17]. A program can be used at the client's side to browse and annotate the elements (i.e., subtrees) in these documents. Annotations are then represented in RDF and sent to the syndicator which stores them in a repository, and proposes querying services.

We now embark in a detailed description of the browser and annotation tool.

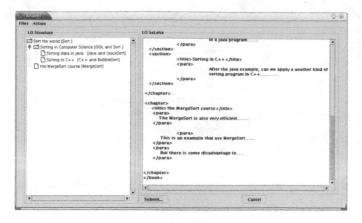

Fig. 3. Infering annotation in XANNOT

Documents

DocBook is a DTD for writing structured documents using SGML or XML. It is particularly well-suited to books and papers about computer hardware and software, though it is by no means limited to them. DocBook is an easy-to-understand and widely used DTD: dozens of organizations use DocBook for millions of pages of documentation, in various print and online formats, worldwide.

It is worth mentioning however that any other DTD would do, the important assumption here being that *all* authors in the system provide their document content in a common format. This assumption is mostly motivated by practical considerations. Indeed the exchange of fragments and their integration is greatly facilitated by the homogeneity of the representation. In particular, it is easy with minimal effort to ensure that inserting a DocBook fragment in a DocBook document keeps the whole document valid with respect to the DTD.

We distinguish in a DocBook document the following tags that identifiy the *structure* of the document: `book`, `chapter`, and `section`. Elements of type `section` are considered to form the leaves of the composition graph, to which annotations must be associated. The inference mechanism described in Section 3 is then used to create the annotations for the upper-level elements `book`, `chapter` and `section`[1].

Browsing and Annotating Documents

The XANNOT tool proposes a graphical interface to browse a DocBook document and to create annotations. When a document is loaded, its structure is analysed and represented with a tree-like menu on the left size, while the content of the document is displayed in the main window (Figure 3).

---

[1] Note that `section` is recursive in the DocBook DTD: a `section` element can be part of another `section`.

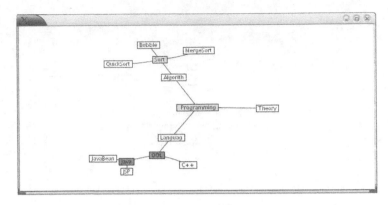

Fig. 4. Term selection in the taxonomy

The role of the author, before submitting such a document to the syndicator, is to annotate the elements located at the lower level in the structure (here <section>) with terms from the common taxonomy to which all authors adhere. In order to facilitate this task, the terms of the taxonomy can be picked up from a graphical window which displays the tree-structure using a hyperbolic representation which compactly displays a tree by projecting it on to an hyperbolic plane [9]: see Figure 4.

Whenever all the atomic elements located under a composite node n are annotated, XANNOT applies the IMPLIEDANNOTATION algorithm to infer the annotation of n. This is shown in Figure 3: two nodes have been manually annotated with, respectively, {Java, QuickSort} and {C++, BubbleSort}. The implied annotation {OOL, Algorithms} has been correctly inferred and associated to the composite node.

Finally the composition graph together with the annotations of the nodes are represented in RDF and sent to the syndicator who stores, with each term of the terminology, the path to the XML subtree(s) that relate(s) to this term.

5 Concluding Remarks

We have presented a model for composing documents from other simpler documents, and automatically deriving annotations during the process of creating new documents from existing ones. In our model, a document is represented by an identifier together with a composition graph which shows the structure of the document. The annotation of a document is a set of terms from the taxonomy, and we distinguish *atomic* documents whose annotation is provided by the author, from *composite* documents whose annotation is derived from the annotations of their parts.

Work in progress mainly aims at designing and implementing the *syndicator* module which collects and exploits the annotations. We plan to embed our model in the RDF Suite [2] developed by ICS-FORTH, a SeLeNe partner. A taxonomy will be represented as a RDF scheme, and annotations will be represented as a RDF database. In this respect, we note that RQL facilities include browsing and querying facilities that cover the requirements identified so far, as well as primitives for expressing that a set of resources constitute parts of a given resource.

References

1. The ACM Computing Classification System. ACM, 1999. http://www.acm.org/class/.
2. S. Alexaki, V. Christophides, G. Karvounarakis, D. Plexousakis, and K. Tolle. The ICS-FORTH RDFSuite: Managing Voluminous RDF Description Bases. In *Proc. Intl. Conf. on Semantic Web*, 2001.
3. R. Baeza-Yates and B. Ribeiro-Neto, editors. *Modern Information Retrieval*. Addison-Wesley, 1999.
4. F. Ciravegna, A. Dingli, D. Petrelli, and Y. Wilks. User-System Cooperation in Document Annotation based on Information Extraction. In V. Richard Benjamins A. Gomez-Perez, editor, *Proc. of the Intl. Conf. on Knowledge Engineering and Knowledge Management (EKAW02)*, Lecture Notes in Artificial Intelligence 2473, Springer Verlag, 2002.
5. S. Dill, N. Eiron, D. Gibson, D. Gruhl, R. Guha, A. Jhingran, T. Kanungo, S. Rajagopalan, and A. Tomkins. SemTag and seeker: bootstrapping the semantic web via automated semantic annotation. In *Proc. Intl. World Wide Web Conference (WWW)*, pages 178–186, 2003.
6. Dublin Core Metadata Element Set. Technical Report, 1999. http://dublincore.org/.
7. J. Kahan and M.-. Koivunen. Annotea: an Open RDF Infrastructure for Shared Web Annotations. In *Proc. Intl. World Wide Web Conference (WWW)*, pages 623–632, 2001.
8. G. Karvounarakis, S. Alexaki, V. Christophides, D. Plexousakis, and M. Scholl. RQL: A Declarative Query Language for RDF. In *Proc. Intl. World Wide Web Conference (WWW)*, pages 623–632, 2002.
9. J. Lamping and R. Ramana. The Hyperbolic Browser: A Focus+Context Technique for Visualization Large Hierarchies. In *Proc. ACM Intl. Conf. on Human Factors in Computing Systems*, pages 401–408, 1995.
10. E. D. Liddy, E. Allen, S. Harwell, S. Corieri, O. Yilmazel, N. E. Ozgencil, A. Diekema, N. McCracken, J. Silverstein, and S.A. Sutton. Automatic Metadata Generation and Evaluation. In *Proc. ACM Symp. on Information Retrieval*, Tempere, Finland, 2002.
11. Draft Standard for Learning Objects Metadata. IEEE, 2002.
12. Resource Description Framework Model and Syntax Specification. World Wide Web Consortium, 1999.
13. Resource Description Framework Schema (RDF/S). World Wide Web Consortium, 2000.
14. P. Rigaux and N. Spyratos. Generation and Syndication of Learning Object Metadata. Technical Report 1371, Laboratoire de Recherche en Informatique, 2003.
15. SeLeNe: Self eLearning Networks. www.dcs.bbk.ac.uk/ ap/projects/selene/.
16. The Semantic Web Community Portal. Web site, 2003. http://www.semanticweb.org.
17. N. Walsh and Leonard Muellner. *DocBook, the definitive guide*. O'Reilly, 1999.
18. J. Wang and F.H. Lochovsky. Data extraction and label assignment for web databases. In *Proc. Intl. World Wide Web Conference (WWW)*, pages 187–196, 2003.
19. The XML Pointer Language. World Wide Web Consortium, 2002. http://www.w3c.org/TR/xptr/.

Precise Photo Retrieval on the Web with a Fuzzy Logic\Neural Network-Based Meta-search Engine

Ioannis Anagnostopoulos, Christos Anagnostopoulos,
George Kouzas, and Vergados Dimitrios

School of Electrical and Computer Engineering,
Heroon Polytechneiou 9, Zographou, 15773, Athens, Greece
janag@telecom.ece.ntua.gr

Abstract. Nowadays most web pages contain both text and images. Nevertheless, search engines index documents based on their disseminated content or their meta-tags only. Although many search engines offer image search, this service is based over textual information filtering and retrieval. Thus, in order to facilitate effective search for images on the web, text analysis and image processing must work in complement. This paper presents an enhanced information fusion version of the meta-search engine proposed in [1], which utilizes up to 9 known search engines simultaneously for content information retrieval while 3 of them can be used for image processing in parallel. In particular this proposed meta-search engine is combined with fuzzy logic rules and a neural network in order to provide an additional search service for human photos in the web.

1 Introduction

Since the web is growing exponentially search engines cannot spider all the new pages at the same time due to the fact that they use different algorithms in order to index their 'attached' web pages. As a result they have different response time in updating their directories and the user may lose some useful information resources in case that he use the returned results from only one search service [1]. To overcome this problem most users try to expand their results with the help of meta-search engines. Using such search-tools, additional information is provided, without having to know the query language for all search services, which, some of them offer the ability for image/picture search. However, in this kind of retrieval a large amount of inappropriate and useless information is often returned to the user. Therefore, the same problem occurs when using a meta-search engine since the returned merged results depend on the respective result of each used search service. Especially in case of inquiring human photos the ratio of accurate information is very low, due to the fact that face images are highly variable and difficult to be interpreted. Hence, in order to minimize the information noise this paper suggests a meta-search engine, which combines fuzzy logic rules for human skin recognition joint with a probabilistic neural network for face detection. The innovation in using the proposed machine stands in the fact that the user after a multiple image/picture query can work off-line and bound his search for retrieving human photos.

G.A. Vouros and T. Panayiotopoulos (Eds.): SETN 2004, LNAI 3025, pp. 43–53, 2004.

2 Inquiring Photos in the Web

This section presents an example of using the proposed meta-search engine in order to reveal all possible results for an image query. It must be noted that the web search services used are depicted in Table 1, where AlltheWeb, AltaVista and Excite support image search.

Table 1. HML search sources

SEARCH SERVICES		
Image and Text Search	Text Search	
AlltheWeb	DMOZ	Lycos
AltaVista	DirectHit	Northern Light
Excite	HotBot	Yahoo!

Figure 1 presents the GUI of the proposed engine in case of image query submission. As it is shown AltaVista, Excite and AlltheWeb are engaged in the search while the rest are inactive, since they do not support queries for images. The meta-search interface also supports Boolean queries for both textual and image search. However, even if the search engines used support the Boolean retrieval model, their query syntax differs. In addition, the query-translation problem also presents a barrier from the different stemming algorithms or the stop-word lists that are involved in the query model of each search engine. As a result of all this inconsistency, the proposed meta-search engine translates the user query before submitting it in parallel to the selected search engines. A unified syntax is proposed and it is presented in Table 2. This syntax allows the user to submit more complicated queries such as "term1*#Exact Phrase# - term2". In this case the proposed meta-search engine asks to get results from the selected search engines, having both term1 and an exact matching string, excluding term2. As presented in Figure 1, the user wants to collect all possible images concerning the query "Georgatos AND Inter", seeking photos of a football player of Italian team Inter. The system simultaneously translates the query and submits it to the three selected search services, respectively. Table 3 holds all the returned results in terms of returned images that contain the player and other images that are irrelevant to photos of the football player. After merging the results and removing the duplicate fields the meta-search engine returned 27 images, from which only 14 of them are actually photos that fulfill the submitted query.

Table 2. Unified query syntax

Boolean Operator	Symbol	Example
AND	*	term1*term2
OR	+	term1+term2
NOT	-	term1-term2
EXACT	##	#term1 term2#

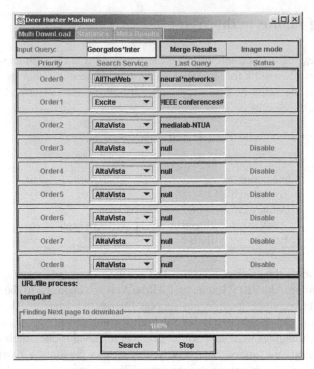

Fig. 1. Image query interface

Table 3. Unified query syntax

Search service	Photos	Other images
AlltheWeb	8	11
AltaVista	9	5
Excite	5	4
Total returned results excluding duplicate images	14	13

As it is obvious a significant amount of information is actually not relevant according to the respective query. The innovation in this paper stands in the fact that the user can further investigate among all the returned results in order to restore photos that include human faces. The existence of a human face in the proposed tool is crucial since it is implies a human presence in the image. The "PhotoSearch" button initiates a two-step off-line mechanism, which it briefly explained in the followings.

3 The Proposed System

In this section the major subsystems as well as the overall architecture of the proposed meta-search machine is presented. Concerning the web interface and the respective technologies the meta-search engine was created using JDK 1.4, while C++ was used for the applied fuzzy rules and the neural network implementation. Figure 2 presents the overall architecture of the proposed system and how its major parts interact, in order to collect, store evaluate and present the meta-results to the user. All the main sub-systems and functions are briefly explained in [1]. However, an additional function ('PhotoSearch' mode) employs a probabilistic neural network fed by Fuzzy Logic rules, aiming to offer a more precise search through image information analysis and retrieval.

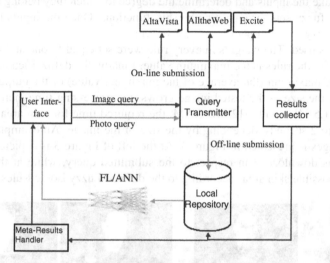

Fig. 2. System architecture

3.1 Fuzzy Logic Rules for Human Skin Detection

By pressing the "PhotoSearch" button, a sequence of a two-step procedure is initiated. Firstly, every candidate image is analyzed according to fuzzy logic rules for chromatic analysis in order to distinguishing web pages with possible human presence. This arise due to the fact that the color of human skin is distinctive from the color of many other objects and, therefore, the statistical measurements of this attribute are of great importance for the problem addressed [2],[3]. Evaluating the skin tone statistics, it is expected that the face color tones will be distributed over a discriminate space in the RGB color plane, respectively. Thus, the first step of the proposed system is the location of potential skin areas in the image, using RGB color and chrominance (CbCr) information [4], [5] In the proposed system, the skin-masking algorithm is partially used along with RGB cluster groups that represent skin color extracted from experimental tests in a large database of images with human presence [6]. The above measurements and the skin-masking algorithm formed the basis for the definition of the fuzzy logic rules. The aforementioned if-then rule statements are used to formulate the conditional statements that comprise the fuzzy logic-based skin color detector. A basic rule, of significant importance to the application of the proposed system, is resulted from the experimental in [7]. In this method, the chromatic field YCbCr is used, since it was proved to be more representative for the choice of regions that suit human skin [8], [9], [10], [11]. Through the application of Fuzzy Logic rules, the proposed system decides whether a specified window in the inspected image contains a potential skin region. However, a skin region does not represent always a face, and therefore the candidate area should be further normalized and checked in order to discern whether it represent a face or not. For defining the fuzzy logic rules applied for skin area discrimination the work described in [7] and [11] was taken under consideration. The first step is to take the inputs and determine the degree to which they belong to each of the appropriate fuzzy sets through membership functions. Once the inputs have been fuzzified, the fuzzy logical operations must be implemented. For this application the OR operator was used. The weights in every rule were set equal to one and the aggregation method for the rules is the maximum value. Finally, the defuzzification method is the middle of maximum (the average of the maximum value) of the output set. It is evident that, as the size of the tested image grows, the processing time increases. In a Pentium IV at 1.5 MHz with 512 MB RAM, the required time for skin area detection varied from 1 to 2 seconds, depending by the size of the image. An example of input and output images is presented in Figure 3. At the left of Figure 3 is depicted a tested image as it was downloaded in respect to the submitted query, while at the right is presented the possible skin areas according to the defined Fuzzy Logic Rules.

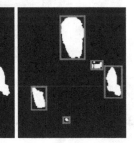

Fig. 3. Human skin detection   **Fig. 4.** Definition of the RoIs

3.2 The ANN for Image Classification

Having collected images with possible skin areas, the next step involves the correct identification of images with human faces (photos). This requires further image processing steps in order to properly feed the image classifier. The image-processing operations consist of four distinct parts.

Firstly, potential skin areas are clustered to form the Region of Interest (RoI), roughly describing its shape, on the basis of the FL output. Every image is transformed in gray scale and in the specific size of 100x100 pixels. Then two morphological operations, which help to eliminate some of the noise in the tested image, are involved. In particular, simple erosion with a 10x10 matrix of ones is performed followed by dilation. Further on, the created image is parsed through a skeletonisation technique, removing simultaneously all the areas that are considered as 'holes'. As a result of the previously described image processing steps, the RoIs of all the possible skin areas are depicted in Figure 4.

Having defined the RoI in the previous part, in the second step the algorithm is applied to the initial tested image, merging objects that belong to one defect, performing a simple dilation once again, with a structural element, which is a 5x5 matrix of ones. With this technique, segmented pixels in the same neighborhood, are merged in one region. All the image parts that are included in the defined RoIs, are then transformed to gray scale. In the following part all the segmented images are resizing to a specific size of 225x225 pixels. Finally, the 225x225 pixel images are divided into non-overlapping sub-images of size 15x15 and the mean value for each is calculated, followed by histogram equalization, which expands the range of intensities in the window [12]. During this procedure, a lower resolution image in respect to the RoI is created, forming in parallel a descriptor vector that consists of 225 gray scale values from 0 to 255. Figure 5 presents the input for the proposed neural network.The proposed ANN is trained to identify which of the skin regions detected from the FL system represent facial photos. The training set of the ANN consists of a large group of images of the size 15x15, representing face regions or other skin areas. The idea of this approach was motivated by the observation that human faces present a high degree of resemblance when they are sampled in low-resolution [13]. This is quite natural, since all faces have darker areas, which represent the eyes and the mouth. It is undoubtedly easier for an ANN to recognize the presence or absence of a face, judging from a low quality image. Additionally, the numbers of the computational units are significantly smaller for a low quality image.

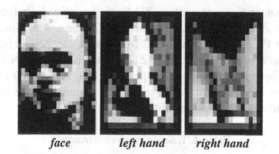

face   *left hand*   *right hand*

Fig. 5. Candidate inputs for classification

The ANN is a two layer Probabilistic Neural Network with biases and Radial Basis Neurons in the first layer and Competitive Neurons in the second one. Training a neural network for the face detection task is quite challenging due to the difficulty in characterizing prototypical "non-face" images. Unlike in face recognition, where the classes to be discriminated are different faces, in face detection, the two classes to be discriminated are "face area" and "non-face area". Figure 6 depicts the topology of the proposed PNN as well as the transformation of a face image in the appropriate input vector form, which consists of 225 gray scale values.

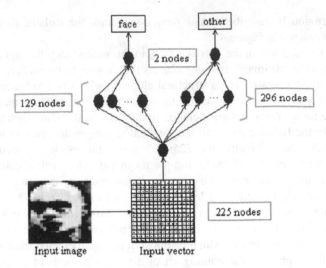

Fig. 6. PNN's architecture

A sample of 129 frontal view face images was used as training set for the class 'Face', as well as a large sample of 296 images corresponding to other correct or erroneously detected skin areas, such as hands, legs and other objects. Table 4 presents the confusion matrix percentages in terms of the learning ability during the training epoch. The training set consists of 425 sub-images of size 15x15 in a vector form, as these were extracted from 103 color images according the proposed image processing steps. In other words, the neural network 'learned' to identify 128 from the 129 sub-images corresponding to human faces as well as 293 from the 296 sub-images corresponding to other skin areas and objects. The time needed for the completion of one training epoch in a Pentium IV at 1.5 MHz with 512 MB RAM, was 22 seconds. The topology of the proposed neural network is 225-425-2. This means that the PNN has a 225-input vector (the 15x15 input image) and a 2-output vector corresponding to the decision of the system (whether it is a face or not). Finally, the system has 425 nodes in the middle layer corresponding to the total training set.

Table 4. Training confusion matrix

	Face	Other skin area – object
Face	99.22% (128/129)	0.88% (1/129)
Other skin area - Object	1.01% (3/296)	98.99% (293/296)

3.3 Image Analysis Performance

The performance of the add-in system for photo recognition was tested using 317 color images of various extensions, types and size containing human faces. More specifically, the sample of 317 color images contained 482 faces. The system implementing the fuzzy logic rules segmented totally 841 skin areas. However, 30 faces were not selected and therefore the performance of this system is 93.77% (452/482). Following the fuzzy logic system, the ANN received the 841 skin areas and decided that 397 of them represent faces. Thus, the performance of the ANN is 87.83% (397/452). Finally, the overall system performance is 82.36%, since 397 from a total of 482 faces were identified. All the results are shown analytically in Table 5.

Table 5. System's Performance

Training Set		
Total color images	**Number of faces**	**Skin areas - Other objects**
103	129	296
Testing Set		
Total images		**Number of faces**
317		482
FL rules		
Segmented areas	841	**452 faces + 389 possible skin areas**
FL Rules performance	452/482	93.77%
Artificial Neural Network (ANN)		
Faces	397	
No faces	444	
ANN Performance	397/452	87.83%
Total System Performance	397/482	82.36%

4   The Meta-search Engine Performance

In the specific submitted query, which is described in section 2 at least half of the returned images are irrelevant to photos of the soccer player. In particular some of them represented stadium images, t-shirts of the team, or logos. Having removed the duplicated fields the returned meta-results were 27. Initiating the FL/ANN photo search sub-system the user narrows his search in retrieving only photos. After analyzing the tested images with the FL rules, 21 images were sent for further identification. However 13 of them were indeed photos of the player, while 8 were images with possible human appearance. Finally, the PNN returned 12 images in respect to the submitted query, recognizing correctly the human face among the first candidate group (12 of 13 images), excluding successfully the rest 8 images, which included regions of interest with potential skin areas but not human face. The time needed for all the above procedure was 41 seconds. Consequently, the meta-search engines returned 12 photos collected from AltaVista, AlltheWeb and Excite, while 2 of them erroneously excluded. Nevertheless, the user got a significantly precise amount of information concerning the Boolean image query "Georgatos AND Inter". Table 6 holds some results over a large sample from more than 300 mixed Boolean image queries collected by the three search services. Therefore, over 14857 images from which 8932 are indeed photos, the FL rules successfully identified 8552 of them. It was evaluated that the failure in this step occurred due to the fact that the chrominance fuzzy logic rules do not cover sufficiently all the variation in terms of the human skin color. Other reasons come from the area of image processing involving limitations in illumination conditions or image texture and inconsistency. The ANN further processed the above set of images and decided that 8039 are actually photos that contain human faces, while 513 images were erroneously excluded from this class. On the other hand, this was expected since many images depict human faces in different angle positions and not only frontal or slightly rotated. For similar reason and in accordance with the images that indeed present human faces, the procedure added erroneously 176 images, which are unrelated to the photo query submissions. However, using the 'SearchPhoto' meta-search procedure a significant large amount of irrelevant information was excluded as depicted in Table 6. Figure 7 shows the information reduction in case of irrelevant results as well as the information loss in case of the relevant results for the photos, the other retrieved images and the total returned meta-results.

Table 6. PhotoSearch Performance

Submitted image queries	324	
Total returned meta-results	Photos	Other
14857	8932	5925
FL Rules		
Human skin identification	8552	2271
ANN		
Face recognition	8039	176
'PhotoSearch' returned meta-results		
8215		
Excluded meta-results		
6642		
	Excluded Relevant	Excluded Irrelevant
FL rules	380	3654
ANN	513	2095

5 Conclusions

This paper proposes a meta-search engine, aiming to provide precise and accurate search for image queries with a fusion search mode, which uses both text/content analysis and image processing. For the purposes of this work an additional sub-system was implemented in complement to the previous work in [1], involving Fuzzy Logic rules for tracking possible human presence and an artificial neural network for further authentication. The user gets enhanced amount of information in respect to the submitted query, records his search preferences in parallel and narrows his search when seeking photos in the web. Despite the limitations confronted in terms of different image types, sizes and illumination conditions, the procedure is effective enough since it excludes a large amount of irrelevant and useless information in image search. In order to further reduce the response time and increase the accuracy of the proposed meta-search engine, a possible implementation, which embraces more than one neural network with enhanced FL rules, is considered as an interesting issue left for future work.

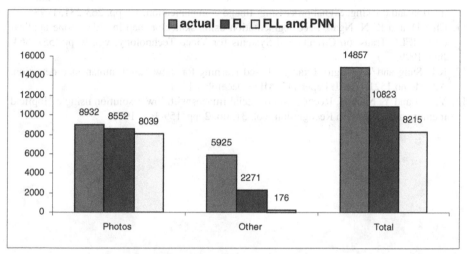

Fig. 7. Information Reduction/Loss

References

1. Anagnostopoulos I., Psoroulas I., Loumos V. and Kayafas E., Implementing a customised meta-search interface for user query personalisation, 24th International Conference on Information Technology Interfaces, ITI 2002 June 24-27, pp. 79-84, Cavtat/Dubrovnik, CROATIA, 2002.
2. S. Belongie, C. Carson, H. Greenspan and J. Malik, Color – and texture-based image segmentation using EM and its application to content-based image retrieval, Proceedings of the 6th IEEE International Conference in Computer Vision, pp. 675–682, 1998.
3. Murase and Nayar, Learning and Recognition of 3D Object from Appearance, Technical Report of IEICE, PRU93-120, 1994, pp. 31-38.
4. C. Garcia and G. Tziritas, Face detection using quantized skin color regions merging and wavelet packet analysis, IEEE Trans. on Multimedia, vol. 1, no. 3, pp. 264-277, 1999.
5. H. Wang and S.-F. Chang, "A highly efficient system for automatic face region detection in MPEG video," *IEEE Trans. Circuits Syst. VideoTechnol.*, vol. 7, no. 4, pp. 615–628, 1997.

6. Scott E. Umbaugh, Computer Vision and Image Processing, pp. 334, Prentice Hall International, NJ, 1998.
7. Chai D. and K. N. Ngan, Locating facial region of a head-and-shoulders color image, Third IEEE International Conference on Automatic Face and Gesture Recognition (FG'98), Nara, Japan, pp. 124-129, Apr. 1998.
8. Menser Bernd and Michael Brünig, Locating human faces in color images with complex background. In Proc. IEEE Int. Symposium on Intelligent Signal Processing and Communication Systems ISPACS '99, pp. 533-536, Phuket, Thailand, December 1999.
9. Saber A. and A. M. Tekalp, Frontal-view face detection and facial feature extraction using color, shape and symmetry based cost functions, Pattern Recognition Letters, vol. 19, pp. 669–680, June 1998.
10. K. Sobottka, I. Pitas, A novel method for automatic face segmentation, facial feature extraction and tracking, Signal processing: Image communication, 12, pp. 263-281, 1998.
11. Chai D. and K. N. Ngan, Face segmentation using skincolor map in videophone applications, IEEE Trans. on Circuits and Systems for Video Technology, vol. 9, pp. 551–564, June 1999.
12. K.K Sung and T. Poggio, Example-based learning for view-based human face detection. A.I. Memo 1521, CBCL Paper 112, MIT, December 1994.
13. Y. Dai and Y. Nakano, Recognition of facial images with low resolution using a Hopfield memory model, Pattern Recognition, vol. 31, no. 2, pp. 159-167, 1998.

Intelligent Web Prefetching Based upon User Profiles – The WebNaut Case

George Kastaniotis, Nick Zacharis,
Themis Panayiotopoulos, and Christos Douligeris

Department of Informatics, University of Piraeus, Piraeus, 18534 Greece
{gskast78,nzach,themisp,cdoulig}@unipi.gr

Abstract. The timely provision of content to the clients strictly according to their interests is one of the key factors for the success and wider acceptance of World Wide Web technologies. Intelligent Assistants, such as WebNaut, belong to a class of innovative technologies proposed for use by the Web. The main objective of these technologies is the retrieval of information that interest the client. WebNaut is able to integrate with a web browser and 'build' user profiles that form the base for Web content selection from keyword search engines or meta-search engines. This ability to recognize users' information interests and to constantly adapt to their changes makes WebNaut and all intelligent agents a potential source of information for supporting prefetching algorithms that can be used by Web Cache applications. In this paper, we examine to what extent intelligent assistants, such as WebNaut, are able to contribute to the reduction of the user – perceived latency. An ideal algorithm is proposed for the WebNaut case and basic conclusions are extracted that are favorable for the utilization of this type of the intelligent agents in prefetching.

1 Introduction

The World Wide Web constitutes the largest source of information on a wide range of topics and is able to serve clients with various interests. This large information system is constantly expanding, as new sites are added to the existing ones at an extremely high rate. The addition of these sites continuously strengthens the ability of the Web to cover clients' information needs. Taking into account the vastness of the Web nowadays, two problems of utmost importance to the users are the finding of contents strictly according to personal interests, and the perception of the least latency possible when downloading these contents.

Even during the first stages of the Web's evolution, the need for a better management of this extraordinary bulk of information led to the development and implementation of the keyword search – e.g. Google ([2], [4]), AltaVista [1], etc. – and meta-search engines – e.g. SpiderServer [10], SavvySearch[5]. Nowadays, intelligent web agents and assistants, products of artificial intelligence, belong to a new class of innovative technologies that contribute to a better use of the search and meta-search engines on the user's behalf. Their main aim is to facilitate clients to find Web content of their interest, by discarding or avoiding all useless and/or irrelevant results of a keyword search – e.g. On-line Ads, E-Commerce Sites.

In this paper, we are concerned with intelligent web assistants that undertake the building of a user profile, which represents his/her information universe of interest. This profile is used as a basis for filtering the search or meta-search engine results.

G.A. Vouros and T. Panayiotopoulos (Eds.): SETN 2004, LNAI 3025, pp. 54–62, 2004.
© Springer-Verlag Berlin Heidelberg 2004

The primary objective of this research is to extract basic conclusions on how this class of web agents is able to encourage data prefetching techniques and web cache applications. All these conclusions are extracted through the study of a representative intelligent web assistant, namely the WebNaut [9].

2 Motivation

It is widely accepted that the possibility of a Web Cache application to support content prefetching algorithms requires the ability to successfully predict the web content that the user/client intends to download to his/her browser. Incorrect predictions result in unnecessary waste of bandwidth to transfer data of no use to the user. In general, successfully predicting users' preferences when visiting Web sites could be considered as an extraordinary complex and hard-to-solve problem, especially in cases that the users' information interests are fleeting.

There are some particular cases in which prediction of a web user's sequence of actions is feasible. One special case is that of a user trusting an intelligent assistant, such as WebNaut, for accomplishing the difficult task of seeking for Web content of interest. These assistants were especially developed to serve this purpose and promise the best results possible, according to user's information needs. Employing intelligent assistants that operate according to WebNaut standards and mostly the subsequent strong dependence on such applications is a powerful incentive to prefetch the Web content the assistants explicitly or implicitly propose.

The remainder of this paper outlines the architecture and operation features of WebNaut (based on [9]), in order to understand how it interacts and cooperates with the user. A brief survey follows as to which extend WebNaut is able to assist Web caching and prefetching ([6], [7], [8]). The operation features of an ideal prefetching algorithm are also analyzed. Finally, conclusions are extracted and proposals are made as to how the functionality of WebNaut could be enhanced or extended to thoroughly support Web caching on a user's local machine.

Fig. 1. The Webnaut Toolbar that appears on the top of each web page opened by the web browser

3 The WebNaut Intelligent Assistant

The WebNaut intelligent assistant [9] integrates with the client's web browser. In its default operating mode the assistant is idle. WebNaut creates a command toolbar that uses the same window with the web browser (see figure 1). This format enables the user to insert a command when viewing web pages. Consequently, triggering Web-Naut's operation is up to the user's will.

3.1 Architecture

Most web assistants of this kind are implemented over an agent-based architecture. In particular, WebNaut's operation is based on a six-agent architecture (see figure 2). Nominally, these agents are the following:

- *Proxy Server Agent.* The proxy server agent is central operational unit of the Web-Naut. Its main task is to serve the Web browser's request and to coordinate the communication with the other agents. Thus, the users must configure their browsers to use the Proxy Server Agent (PSA). PSA is also responsible for incorporating the command toolbar into web browser's window.
- *SiteMirror Agent.* This agent is used for replicating interesting web sites at the local machine.
- *MetaSearch Agent.* The MetaSearch agent is a simple meta-search engine. It helps the client to create queries in the form of keywords separated with logical operators. These queries are introduced into five different search engines (AltaVista, Excite, Lycos, HotBot and Yahoo).
- *WWWServer Agent.* The Web Server Agent (WSA) meets all the needs of the local system for producing HTML documents corresponding to the interfaces for the SiteMirror and MetaSearch agents. It satisfies the need for creating HTML local error, setup and help messages as well. The utilization of WSA gives the impression of a continuous connection to the Internet, even while the web browser is working offline.
- *Learning Agent.* Its main task is to create user profiles. After bookmarking a web page as 'very interesting', the Learning Agent (LA) uses a Text Information Extractor (TIE) to distinguish between common words and keywords depicting users' personal information interests. LA is also responsible for collecting, organizing and recommending to users new web documents close to their personal profiles.
- *Genetic Algorithm Agent.* It is the WebNaut's module that mobilizes Artificial Intelligence techniques to find web documents close to user profiles. In particular, this agent calls two algorithms, the Primary Genetic Algorithm (PGA) and the Secondary Genetic Algorithm (SGA), which generate populations of keywords related to user interests and logic operators, respectively. Both populations are combined with each other in order to create queries, which are then introduced into the MetaSearch agent. Both PGA and SGA apply special genetic operators – crossover, inversion and mutation – to renew the populations. This procedure is repeated for a user-defined number of times.

3.2 Operation

Users must run the WebNaut engine to bring the intelligent assistant into operation. This means that each web page visited is accompanied by the WebNaut's toolbar on the user's browser. Clicking on the appropriate tool, the user bookmarks a document of his/her interest. The process following triggers the learning agent to parse this document, which results in creating a dictionary of the keywords describing the client's profile. The genetic algorithm agent combines sets of keywords with sets of logical operators in order to build queries which are served by the meta-search agent. The results are evaluated and filtered according to the keywords dictionary. The learning agent recommends the URLs that are close to the client's profile (see figure 3). Finally, the client's feedback leads to the renewal of the profile and the overall procedure starts from scratch based upon the updated profile.

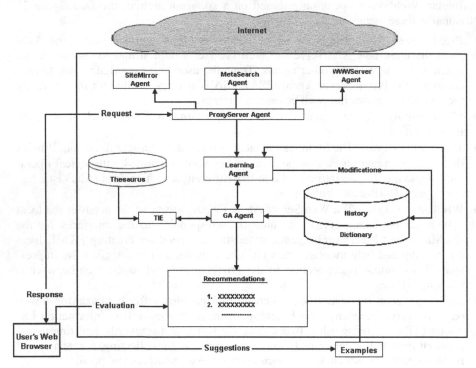

Fig. 2. The WebNaut agent-based architecture

4   Using WebNaut's Functionality to Support Prefetching

The main question that arises and constitutes our main point of interest in this section is how the WebNaut assistant is able to support prefetching and caching techniques in order for the client to perceive the least possible latency when downloading web documents. The cacheability problem is of high interest only in the case that the user clicks on the special tool to see the learning agent's recommendations and responds with the appropriate feedback to each of them. In our attempt to obtain a clear view on prefetchability, we examine two different aspects of the problem that are analyzed in the following subsections.

4.1   Prefetching of Web Documents Recommended by the Learning Agent

As mentioned above, the learning agent presents a list of URLs to the user and then waits for the user's feedback. The system knows that the user's next step, after loading the LA, is to visit the web documents corresponding to the URLs of the list. Thus, prefetching them on the user's behalf is a matter of substance.

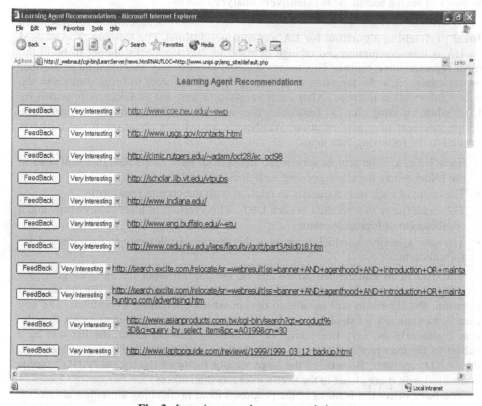

Fig. 3. Learning agent's recommendations

Utilizing a dummy process. One first approach to prefetching the LA recommendations is to use a dummy process, even from the initial stage of their similarity evaluation to the user's profile. This process could save all documents with the highest score to a cache folder on the local hard disk. Instead of downloading them, when visiting the corresponding sites, the system could redirect the request to that folder.

A solution such as the one above would be too easy to illustrate, but is not devoid of serious disadvantages. First and foremost, the period of time between saving the documents onto the local disk and presenting the list of the corresponding URLs may be too long so as to consider them as stale. Thus, while bringing back the local copies, WebNaut must first check for new versions in the remote server. Furthermore, due to a not very representative user profile, the user may decide not to visit a site, considering it as irrelevant beforehand. This means that local resources are wasted for useless documents, which a user may select not to download at all.

For the reasons stated above, the idea of utilizing the dummy process described must be abandoned. A more evolutionary technique is needed that will be able to utilize the learning agent's recommendations and information, the user profile and the recommended web documents' HTTP header in a better manner. The basic operation features of such a technique is extensively analyzed below.

Ideal prefetching algorithm for LA's recommendations. The learning process used by LA is time-consuming and of high demand in user feedbacks aiming to build the most representative profile. This means that the process may include a large number of iterations, each one targeting to update the profile in order to bring it close to the user's information interests. After each iteration, a new list of URLs is provided by LA, while waiting for a feedback. the arrival of the feedback triggers the commencement of a new iteration. WebNaut's knowledge about the listed URLs is limited to the following data items:

- Each URL, i.e. the remote server and the special path on its disk that will lead to the folder where the corresponding web document resides.
- The score of each web document in relation with the current user profile.
- The exact query that resulted in each URL. This consists of a set of keywords and a combination of logical operators.
- The user's feedback, which represents the degree of relevance to the personal information interests.

The data items enumerated above can be used as an input for an intelligent prefetching algorithm during each iteration of the LA's learning process. During the next iteration, the algorithm will be able to decide which documents to prefetch. The key idea is to maintain a list of keywords of the queries resulting in documents that the user bookmarks as 'very interesting' or 'interesting'. In particular, the list will be a subset of the user profile that contains all the keywords connected in the queries with the 'AND' operator. Because of the large weight factor of the logical 'AND', words connected with it are closer to the user's interests than others.

The basic operation features of the proposed ideal prefetching algorithm are as follows (see Figure 4): During the commencement of the learning process the list is empty. When the first results are delivered to the client, the algorithm waits for the user's feedback. For those URLs that client responds with a positive bookmark, the keywords of the relative query will be added to the list. In the next iteration of the learning process, the list will form the base for the evaluation of recommendations to be prefetched on the client's behalf. The algorithm will continue to update the list in the same way at each iteration.

The algorithm must prevent the list from growing without control and must also ensure that it will faithfully follow the client's interests. This can be achieved by holding metrics for each keyword in the list, which represent its current weight in the prefetching task. The client's feedback will keep these metrics informed and if their value falls to a lower bound, the keyword will be expelled from the list. A measure that can be taken against the out-of-control expansion of the list is the use of an aging factor. Each time the client responds with a negative feedback, the aging factor of all keywords participating in the query and residing in the list must be reduced. In cases of a positive feedback, an increase must occur. When the aging factor of a keyword reaches a predefined lower level, the keywords must be expelled from the list. Taking into account that other keywords in the list may be in close relationship with the expelled one when forming queries, multiple expulsions are possible.

Finally, another factor that must be taken into consideration by the algorithm is the web caching hints provided by HTTP 1.1 headers. This is to ensure that no web document stored in the local cache is to become out-of-date. This factor is crucial for deciding which web pages to store even from the phase of the evaluation with the client's profiles and which ones to prefetch at the phase of the presentation of the learning agent's recommendations.

4.2 Prefetching Based on HTML Anchors

Apart from just prefetching LA's recommendations another matter of interest is prefetching web pages linked to the recommended ones and having the same or related content to them. According to [3] the likelihood of linked web pages to have similar content is high. Moreover, titles, descriptions and anchor text represent at least part of the target page. Keeping this in mind, we could modify WebNaut's learning agent to focus around or in HTML anchors of the web documents recommended by LA. Finding there a rich collection of profile keywords is a good reason for prefetching the target web pages.

Prefetching based on HTML anchors should be triggered at the time a client visits a web document of the LA's recommendation list. While loading this document to the browser, WebNaut could scrutinize the anchors in order to prefetch to the local cache pages they point at. Because clients tend to revisit previous pages to click on other hyperlinks, the recommended documents should also be stored in the local cache for a while.

The above prefetching scheme could be extended to the point that enables prefetching support when clients surf through a sequence of web pages. This means that WebNaut may scrutinize anchors of target pages to prefetch new targets.

In an alternative approach, instead of using the overall profile for making decisions about anchor tags, the keyword list supporting the ideal algorithm described in the previous subsection could be used as well. This results in limiting the set of keywords and in further reducing the total number of web content to be prefetched. Consequently, the waste of local resources on web caching needs is minimized.

5   Illustration of a Prefetching Agent

Extending WebNaut's functionality to fulfill prefetching tasks is our future research goal. Illustrating the ideal prefetching algorithm is the first step towards this goal. The key idea is to build a new agent (called the *Prefetching Agent*) and add it to the Web-Naut's backbone. The prefetching agent's operation is going to follow the iterative procedure shown in figure 4. It will continuously parse the text files provided by the WebNaut's main operation.

The text file mentioned above is the output of the learning agent. The text is organized into three fields: the URL field, the similarity field – e.g. a number between 0 and 1 depicting the degree of similarity between the web page behind the URL and the current user profile – and the queries that leaded to the URL. The question is a sting of keywords separated by logical operators.

The prefetching agent will use an algorithm which will bring pages to the local cache according to whether or not some conditions are met. For example, a condition could be a lower bound in the similarity factor – e.g. prefetch those pages whose similarity to the current user is more or equal to 0.6. More complex algorithms that take into account the unique question for each URL can be used instead.

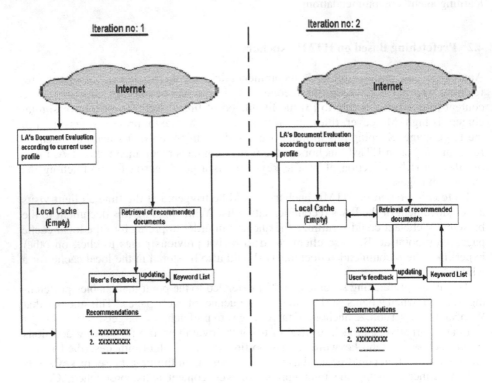

Fig. 4. Prefetching of the learning agent's recommendations. The procedure is repeated in the same way for more than two iterations

The prefetching agent will present the prefetched web pages to the user as shown in figure 3. The user will respond with a feedback representative of his interests about each page. The feedback will trigger an aging factor which will be then responsible for the updating of the user profile. The aging factor used by WebNaut [9] can also be used.

At first, the prefetching agent will be created as a standalone program and tested with manually created inputs. After the debugging procedure, it will be converted to use as an input to the learning agent's output files.

6 Conclusions and Future Work

The WebNaut intelligent assistant was developed and illustrated to help web clients to find documents according to their information interests. Apart from fulfilling its main duties, it is also able to support web cache applications due to the way it works and the technology utilized behind its operation. The user profile WebNaut builds and the information provided by its learning agent can become the base for developing a pre-fetching algorithm that could support client's local cache. The operation features of an ideal algorithm for prefetching web documents that WebNaut recommends to clients were highlighted. Ways to improve WebNaut's functionality in order to extent its prefetching ability were also discussed. It was deduced that web clients using intelligent assistants such as WebNaut could perceive reduced latencies.

Developing a testbed environment with suitable evaluation criteria and methodologies for the proposed algorithm are also a main priority. Employing artificial intelligence techniques to support web caching and content prefetching at proxy servers is also a worth-to-study subject.

Acknowledgement

This work has been partially supported by the university of Piraeus research center.

References

1. AltaVista Company, AltaVista – The search company, http://www.altavista.com/about/, 2003.
2. Brin Sergey, Page Lawrence: The anatomy of a large-scale hypertextual Web search engine. In Proceedings of the Seventh International World Wide Web Conference, Brisbane, Australia, April 1998.
3. Davison Brian D.: Topical locality in the Web. In Proceedings of the 23rd Annual ACM International Conference on Research and Development in Information Retrieval (SIGIR 2000), Athens, Greece, July 2000.
4. Google Inc., Google home page, http://www.google.com/about.html/, 2003.
5. Howe Alede, Dreilinder Daniel: SavvySearch: A metasearch engine that learns which search engines to query. AI Magazine, 18 (2), 1997.
6. Kroeger Thomas M., Long Darrell D.E., Mogul Jeffrey C.: Exploring the bounds of Web latency reduction from caching and prefetching. In Proceedings of the USENIX Symposium on Internet Technologies and Systems (USIT'S 97), December 1997.
7. Padmanabhan Venkata N., Mogul Jeffrey C.: Using predictive prefetching to improve World Wide Web latency. Computer Communication Review, 26 (3): 22-36, July 1996.
8. Vander Wiel Steven P., Lilja David J.: When caches aren't enough: Data prefetching techniques. Computer, 30 (7), July 1997.
9. Zacharis N. Z., Panayiotopoulos T.: Web Search Using a Genetic Algorithm. Internet Computing, IEEE Computer Press, vol. 5, no 2, pp. 18-26, 2001.
10. Zacharis N. Z., Panayiotopoulos T.: SpiderServer: the MetaSearch engine of WebNaut. 2nd Hellenic Conference on Artificial Intelligence, SETN-02, Thessaloniki, Greece, April 11-12, 2002, pp. 475-486, February 2002.

An Intelligent System
for Aerial Image Retrieval and Classification

Antonios Gasteratos[1], Panagiotis Zafeiridis[2], and Ioannis Andreadis[2]

[1] Laboratory of Robotics and Automation, Section of Production Systems,
Department of Production and Management Engineering, Democritus University of Thrace
Building of University's Library, Kimmeria, GR-671 00 Xanthi, Greece
agaster@pme.duth.gr
http://utopia.duth.gr/~agaster
[2] Laboratory of Electronics, Section of Electronics and Information Systems Technology,
Department of Electrical and Computer Engineering, Democritus University of Thrace
Vassilisis Sophias 12, GR-671 00 Xanthi, Greece
{pzafirid,iandread}@ee.duth.gr

Abstract. Content based image retrieval is an active research area of pattern recognition. A new method of extracting global texture energy descriptors is proposed and it is combined with features describing the color aspect of texture, suitable for image retrieval. The same features are also used for image classification, by its semantic content. An exemplar fuzzy system for aerial image retrieval and classification is proposed. The fuzzy system calculates the degree that a class, such as sea, clouds, desert, forests and plantations, participates in the input image. Target applications include remote sensing, computer vision, forestry, fishery, agricultures, oceanography and weather forecasting.

Keywords: CBIR, Machine intelligence, Fuzzy systems, Data fusion

1 Introduction

The recent improvements in network technologies lead to higher data transmission rates. Consequently this leads to faster internet connections around the globe. On the other hand one might say that the vast number of internet users necessitated the high speed internet connections and pushed the research to faster networks. No matter which comes first, the fast internet connections along with today's powerful computers and the proliferation of the imaging devices (scanners, digital cameras etc) moved forward a relatively new branch of *pattern recognition*; the so-called *content-based image retrieval* (CBIR). This is the retrieval of images on the basis of features automatically derived from the images themselves. The features most widely used are texture [1-3], color [4-6] and shape [7-9]. A plethora of texture features extraction algorithms exists, such as wavelets [10-12], mathematical morphology [13] and stochastic models [14], to mention few. A simple but efficient method to represent textures is using signatures based on texture energy [15, 16]. Energy images result from the convolution of the original image with special kernels representing specific texture properties. An attempt to describe the texture by means of color information was carried out in [17]. This method allows an effective evaluation of texture similarity in terms of color aspect and, therefore, to attribute textures to classes based on their color composition.

G.A. Vouros and T. Panayiotopoulos (Eds.): SETN 2004, LNAI 3025, pp. 63–71, 2004.

A review of the existing image retrieval techniques is presented in [18]. These are categorized into three groups: automatic scene analysis, model-based and statistical approaches and adaptive learning from user feedback. Conclusively, it is said that the CBIR is in its infancy and that, in order to develop truly intelligent CBIR systems, combination of techniques from the image processing and artificial intelligence fields should be tried out. In the present paper such an algorithm is proposed. It combines texture and color features by means of a least mean square (LMS) technique. The texture features of the images are extracted using the Laws convolution method [15, 16]. However, instead of extracting a new image each of its pixels describing the local texture energy, a single descriptor is proposed for the whole image. Each class of scenes corresponds to a certain band in the descriptor space. The color similarity is examined by means of its characteristic colors [17]. The same feature set can be used also for image classification, by its semantic content. The classification is performed by a fuzzy system. The membership functions (mf) of the proposed method are constructed by statistical analysis of the training features. As an example, a system that classifies aerial images is described. Experiments demonstrate the high efficiency of the proposed system. The use of these particular texture and color texture descriptors is attempted for the first time. The redundancy of texture information decreases the classification uncertainty of the system.

2   Algorithm Description

2.1   Texture Feature Extraction

The texture feature extraction of the proposed system relies on Laws texture measures [15], where the notion of "local texture energy" is introduced. The idea is to convolve the image with 5x5 kernels and then to apply a nonlinear windowing operation over the convolved image. In this way a new image results, each pixel of which represents the local texture energy of the corresponding pixel of the original image. Laws have proposed 25 individual zero-summing kernels, each describing a different aspect of the local texture energy. These kernels are generated by the one-dimensional kernels, shown in Figure 1. As an example of how the 2-dimensional kernels are generated, L5S5 results by multiplying the 1-dimensional kernel L5 with S5. Experiments with all the 25 kernels showed that, as far as our application is concerned, the most potent ones are R5R5, E5S5, L5S5 and E5L5. More specifically, applying each of these four masks to images of a certain class (sea, forest, etc.) the global texture descriptors were more concentrated than with the rest of the masks. These kernels were used to extract the four texture descriptors of the proposed system.

L5 = [	1	4	6	4	1	]
E5 = [	-1	-2	0	2	1	]
S5 = [	-1	0	2	0	-1	]
W5 = [	-1	2	0	-2	1	]
R5 = [	1	-4	6	-4	1	]

Fig. 1. 1-dimensional kernels; the mnemonics stand for Level, Edge, Spot, Wave and Ripple, respectively.

The first texture descriptor of the image is extracted by convolving it with the first kernel (R5R5). The descriptor is the absolute average of the convolved image pixels. Thus, instead of measuring local texture descriptors, by averaging over local windows (typically 15x15), as it is proposed in Laws original work, we keep one global texture descriptor by averaging over the whole image. This descriptor is normalized by the maximum one, found among a database of 150 training images. If, for a sought image, the absolute average of the convolved image is greater than maximum value, then the descriptor is 1:

$$d_1 = \begin{cases} \dfrac{\left(\dfrac{1}{m \times n} \sum\limits_{i=1}^{m} \sum\limits_{j=1}^{n} |I(i,j) * R5R5| \right)}{d_{1max}} & \text{if} \left(\dfrac{1}{m \times n} \sum\limits_{i=1}^{m} \sum\limits_{j=1}^{n} |I(i,j) * R5R5| \right) \leq d_{1max} \\ 1 & \text{otherwise} \end{cases} \tag{1}$$

The same procedure is followed to extract the other three texture descriptors d_2, d_3 and d_4, by replacing in eqn (1) kernel R5R5 with the kernels E5S5, L5S5 and E5L5, respectively.

2.2 Color Feature Extraction

According to [17], in order to extract the characteristic colors of an image the following steps are followed:

1. On each color appearing in the image, its frequency of appearance is assigned.
2. Colors are sorted in descending order according to their frequency of appearance.
3. Given a color and a certain radius, a spherical volume is constructed in the RGB color space. The first color in the descending order comprises the first characteristic color of the image. Starting with the second color it is examined whether it lies within the volume of any color above it. If so, then the examined color is merged with the color in the volume where it lies. Otherwise it comprises a new characteristic color of the image.

Considering the set of the characteristic colors as a vector, the color similarity of two images is computed by means of the angle between these two vectors. More specifically, the ratio of the inner product to the product of the measures of the two vectors corresponds to the cosine of the angle of these two vectors. The greater the value of the cosine, the smaller the angle and the more similar the two images (in terms of their color prospect). Therefore, the cosine could be used as the color descriptor of similarity. However, because of the fact that the angle is the absolute descriptor and the cosine is a nonlinear function, the descriptor used in the proposed system is:

$$d_5 = \frac{2}{\pi} \arccos \frac{\overline{C}_1 \cdot \overline{C}_2}{\|\overline{C}_1\| \cdot \|\overline{C}_2\|} \tag{2}$$

where: $\overline{C}_1$ and $\overline{C}_2$ the set of the characteristic colors of images 1 and 2, respectively.

2.3 Image Retrieval

After extracting the descriptors both for the input and the sought images, the retrieval is performed by minimizing the following distance:

$$m = \frac{1}{\sum_{i=1}^{5} w_i} \sqrt{\sum_{i=1}^{4} w_i (din_i - ds_i)^2 + w_5 (d_5)^2} \qquad (3)$$

where: din_i ($i=1,...4$) are the four texture descriptors of the input image, resulting according to eqn (1) and ds_i is the corresponding texture descriptor of the sought image; d_5 is the color descriptor according to eqn (2) and w_i is a weight tuning the retrieval process according to the importance of each descriptor. By comparing eqns (1) and (2) it can be observed that though d_5 is a differential descriptor, i.e. it presents the difference of two images by means of their color aspect, $d_1,...d_4$ are absolute ones. This is the reason why the difference of the last ones appears in eqn (3).

2.4 Image Classification

The same feature set described above and used for CBIM may be used to classify images according to their texture and color properties. In this section a fuzzy system for the data fusion of the different descriptors is proposed. The system is tailored to meet the needs of the target application, i.e. the categorization of aerial images into five different classes. However, with slight variations it might be applied to other applications of image classification as well. The inputs of the fuzzy system are the five descriptors presented in the previous paragraphs. In order to construct the mfs for the inputs a statistical analysis was carried out. More specifically, there were used five different classes of photographs named: sea, clouds, desert, forests and plantations. As training data, 100 images of each class were used. For each image the four texture descriptors were extracted. In Figure 2 the histograms of the distribution of the four descriptors for the class of the sea, are presented. As it can be seen, the distribution can be approximated by a trapezoidal or even a triangular mf. However, a Gaussian function is also a good approximation, far better than the two latter. The reason is that its curve is not as steep as these of a triangular or a trapezoidal one and, therefore, it includes also the sided values. Experiments with several mfs proved this intuition. For each descriptor and for each image class the mean value and the standard deviation were calculated. The mf were computed as the normal distribution, for the previous values (see Figure 2). In Figure 3 the membership functions for the descriptor d_1 are depicted, as an example of the four first inputs of the fuzzy system.

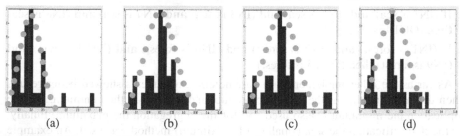

(a)   (b)   (c)   (d)

Fig. 2. The histogram of the global texture energy distribution for the training images belonging to the class of the sea. Graphs (a), (b), (c) and (d) show the histograms of descriptor d_1,... d_4, respectively.

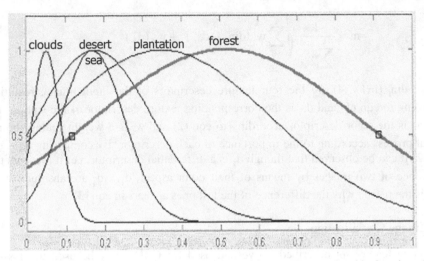

Fig. 3. The first input of the fuzzy system is the descriptor d_1. The membership functions from left to right are: Clouds, desert, sea, plantations and forests.

For the color descriptor five different inputs were used. The characteristic colors of the 100 training images of each class were merged in the same way as described in section 2.2 for a single image. The result is a color codebook [17] containing the characteristic colors of the whole image class. Eqn (2) is used to compute the similarity between the characteristic colors of the input image and the codebook of each of the classes. The result of each of the color similarity values is used as an input to the fuzzy system (inputs from five to ten). Similarly, five sigmoid mfs outputs, one for each class, were used. Having defined the inputs and the output of the system, the following set of if-then rules was used:

1. **If** (IN1 is clouds) **and** (IN2 is clouds) **and** (IN3 is clouds) **and** (IN4 is clouds) **and** (IN5 is clouds) **then** (OUT1 is clouds)

2. **If** (IN1 is plantation) **and** (IN2 is plantation) **and** (IN3 is plantation) **and** (IN4 is plantation) **and** (IN6 is plantation) **then** (OUT2 is plantation)

3. **If** (IN1 is desert) **and** (IN2 is desert) **and** (IN3 is desert) **and** (IN4 is desert) **and** (IN7 is desert) **then** (OUT3 is desert)

4. **If** (IN1 is sea) **and** (IN2 is sea) **and** (IN3 is sea) **and** (IN4 is sea) **and** (IN8 is sea) **then** (OUT4 is sea)

5. **If** (IN1 is forest) **and** (IN2 is forest) **and** (IN3 is forest) **and** (IN4 is forest) **and** (IN9 is forest) **then** (OUT5 is forest)

As far as the other implementation parameters, experiments showed better results when the "*and*" method is the algebraic product and the "*or*" is the minimum. For the implication the minimum is also used and for the aggregation the maximum. Finally, for the defuzzification the *som* (smallest of maximum) method was used. An example of how the system operates is shown in Figure 4. The input image in Figure 4a does not clearly belong to a certain class. The system perceives this fact and gives output for almost each of the classes.

3 Experiments

In order to evaluate the performance of both the retrieval and the classification systems, several experiments were carried out:

3.1 Image Retrieval

The first experiments were carried out, in order to assign the weights of eqn (3), that gives optimum results. Each time the six more relevant images were asked to be retrieved. The precision, i.e. the ratio of the correctly retrieved images over the total retrieved images, was used to measure the efficiency of the retrieval system. It has been observed that the best results occurred when $w_1=w_2=w_3=w_4=1$ and $w_5=11$. In particular, the retrieval precision was measured in the range of 35% to 100%, whilst no other combination of weights had ever resulted to precision 100%. This is to say that the color information plays dominant role in the image retrieval process, as the ratio of color to texture coefficients in the minimization of eqn (3) is 11/4.

(a)

(b)

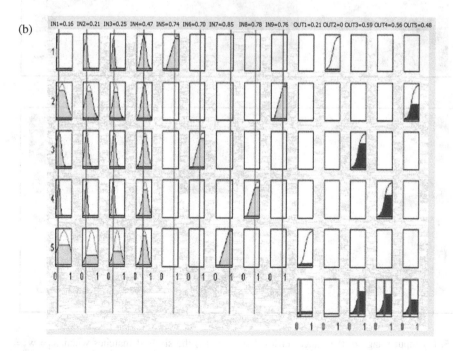

Fig. 4. An example of system's operation: (a) An input image and (b) system's outputs, corresponding to forest, clouds, desert, sea and plantation, respectively.

An example of how weights affect the retrieval is shown in Figure 5. In Figure 5a the input image is show. The six best matches of the retrieval procedure with $w_1=w_2=w_3=w_4=w_5=1$ are presented in Figure 5b. Figure 5c illustrates the six best matches, after having altered w_5 to 11. Comparing Figure 5b to Figure 5c, one can see that the retrieved images belonging to a different class than plantations where now reduced to one. Therefore, the improvement in performance is obvious when the weight corresponding to color descriptor is high.

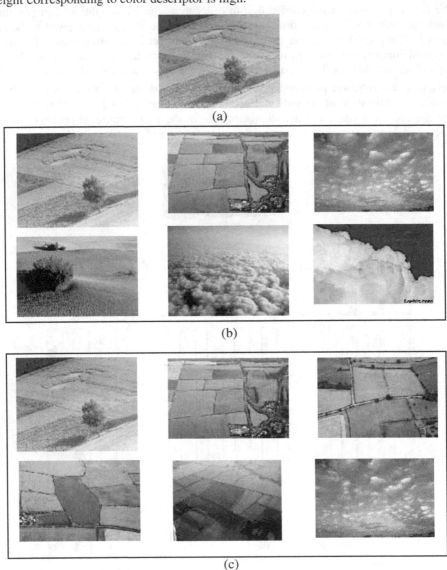

(a)

(b)

(c)

Fig. 5. (a) Input image to the image retrieval system; (b) the six best matches when $w_1 = w_2 = w_3 = w_4 = w_5 = 1$ and (c) the six best matches when $w_1=w_2=w_3=w_4=1$ and $w_5=11$.

3.2 Image Classification

As independent test data, a set of 500 landscapes were used. In many of them, that exhibit a mixture of the 5 different classes, the corresponding outputs were activated. We considered a classification to be correct if the output corresponding to the dominant class has the largest value. In this way, a winner-takes-it-all procedure can result to a single output. As an example for the image of dessert in Figure 6 the outputs are: forest: 0.07, clouds: 0, desert: 0.37, sea: 0.16, and plantation: 0.34, which is correct, as the desert output results the largest value. The high values in other outputs are due to the existence of a range of bushes in the picture. The bushes have the same characteristic colors with the class of forests and plantations. The quite high value of the output corresponding to the sea class is justified as the desert and the sea comprise the same texture characteristics, but their characteristic colors are extremely dissimilar. Therefore, to conclude neither the texture itself nor the color itself is adequate for reliable classification, but the combination of these two could lead to efficient and reliable classification. The Empirical Error Rate (EER) of the classification system, which is the number of errors made on independent test data over the number of classifications attempted, was measured over 500 independent test data and it was found 18.02%.

Fig. 6. The outputs of the fuzzy classification system for this dessert image are: forest: 0.07, clouds: 0, desert: 0.37, sea: 0.16, and plantation: 0.34.

4 Conclusions

The extraction of global texture and color descriptors was presented in this paper. Laws' local texture energy method was modified to extract four different global texture descriptors. The color descriptor extraction was based on a method for describing the color aspect of texture images. It has been shown that the same descriptors can be combined for the construction of an image-retrieval and an image classification system, providing good results. Target applications of such a system include remote sensing, computer vision, forestry, fishery, agricultures, oceanography and weather forecasting.

References

1. Manjunath, B.S. and Ma, W.Y.: Texture Features for Browsing and Retrieval of Large Image Data. *IEEE Trans. Pattern Anal. Mach. Intell.*, **18**, (1996) , 837-842.
2. Gimelfarb, G.L. and Jain, A.K.: On Retrieving Textured Images From an Image Database. *Pattern Recognition*, **29**, (1996), 1461-1483.
3. Carkacloglu, A and Yarman-Vural, F.: SASI: a generic texture descriptor for image retrieval. *Pattern Recognition*, **36**, (2003), 2615-2633.
4. Gevers, T. and Smeulders, A.W.M.: Color-based Object Recognition. *Pattern Recognition*, **32**, (1999), 453-464.
5. Konstandinidis, K. and Andreadis, I.: On the Use of Color Histograms for Content Based Image Retrieval in Various Color Spaces. *Int. Conf. of Computational Methods in Sciences and Engineering*, Kastoria, Greece, (2003).
6. Eftekhari-Moghadam, A.M., Shanbehzadeh, J., Mahmoudi, F. and Soltanian-Zadeh, H.: Image Retrieval Based on Index Compressed Vector Quantization. *Pattern Recognition*, **36**, (2003), 2635-2647.
7. Mechrotra, R. and Gary, J.E.: Similar Shape Retrieval in Shape Data Management. *IEEE Computer*, **28**, (1995) , 57-62.
8. Del Bimbo, A., Pala, P. and Santini, S.: Image Retrieval by Elastic Matching of Shapes and Image Patterns. *Proc. IEEE Int. Conf. Multimedia Systems and Computing*, Hiroshima, Japan, (1996), 215-218.
9. Oonincx, P.J. and de Zeeuw, P. M.: Adaptive Lifting for Shape-based Image Retrieval. *Pattern Recognition*, **36**, (2003), 2663-2672.
10. Zhang, D. S. and Lu, G.: Content-based Image Retrieval Using Gabor Texture Features. *Proc. First IEEE Pacific-Rim Conference on Multimedia*, Sydney, Australia, (2000), 392-395.
11. Kam, A.H., Ng, T.T., Kingsbury, N.G. and Fitzgerald, W.J.: Content Based Image Retrieval Through Object Extraction and Querying. *Proc. IEEE Workshop on Content-based Access of Image and Video Libraries*, Hilton Head Island, S. Carolina, (2000), 91-95.
12. Wang, J.Z. and Li, J. and Wiederhold, G.: SIMPLIcity: Semantics-sensitive integrated matching for picture libraries. *IEEE Transactions on PAMI*, **23**, (2001), 947-963.
13. Soille, P.: Morphological Texture Analysis: a survey. *Workshop on Texture Analysis 1998*, Albert-Ludwigs-Universitat Freiburg, Germany, (1998), 193-207.
14. Cross, G.R. and Jain, A.K.: Markov Random Field Texture Models. *IEEE Trans. Pattern Anal. Mach. Intell.*, **18**, (1983) , 25-39.
15. Laws, K.: *Textured Image Segmentation*, Ph.D. Dissertation, University of South California, (1980).
16. Laws, K.: Rapid Texture Identification. *SPIE Vol 238, Image Processing for Missile Guidance*, (1980), 376-380.
17. Scharcanski, J., Hovis, J.K. and Shen, H.C.: Representing the Color Aspect of Texture Images. *Pattern Recognition Letters*, **15**, (1994) , 191-197.
18. Eakins, J. P.: Towards Intelligent Image Retrieval. *Pattern Recognition*, **35**, (2002) , 3-14.

Computationally Intelligent Methods
for Mining 3D Medical Images

Despina Kontos[1], Vasileios Megalooikonomou[1], and Fillia Makedon[2,3]

[1] Department of Computer and Information Sciences,
Temple University, 1805 N.Broad St., Philadelphia, PA 19122, USA
{dkontos,vasilis}@temple.edu
[2] Department of Computer Science, Dartmouth College, Hanover, NH, USA
[3] University of the Aegean, Greece
makedon@cs.dartmouth.edu

Abstract. We present novel intelligent tools for mining 3D medical images. We focus on detecting discriminative Regions of Interest (ROIs) and mining associations between their spatial distribution and other clinical assessment. To identify these highly informative regions, we propose utilizing statistical tests to selectively partition the 3D space into a number of hyper-rectangles. We apply quantitative characterization techniques to extract k-dimensional signatures from the highly discriminative ROIs. Finally, we use neural networks for classification. As a case study, we analyze an fMRI dataset obtained from a study on Alzheimer's disease. We seek to discover brain activation regions that discriminate controls from patients. The overall classification based on activation patterns in these areas exceeded 90% with nearly 100% accuracy on patients, outperforming the naïve static partitioning approach. The proposed intelligent tools have great potential for revealing relationships between ROIs in medical images and other clinical variables assisting systems that support medical diagnosis.

Keywords: data mining, diagnosis, information extraction, knowledge discovery, applications.

1 Introduction

Developing intelligent tools in order to extract information that supports decision-making has been of critical importance in fields such as knowledge discovery, information retrieval, artificial intelligence, and databases. Initially, mining problems have been grouped in three categories: identifying classifications, finding sequential patterns, and discovering associations [1]. Intelligent solutions for such problems are application-dependent and different applications usually require different mining techniques. A field where artificial intelligence (AI) has the potential of introducing challenging developments is medicine [2]. Systems developed under a pure AI perspective in the early years, such as MYCIN [3], Internist-1 [4] and DXplain [5] inspired a lot of hope for leveraging diagnosis by means of technological tools.

Unfortunately, this initial esperance surrounding the deployment of intelligent diagnostic systems has been followed by the general lapse in funding for AI projects. Today, expert systems of this kind are more likely to be found in clinical laboratories and educational settings. On the other hand, subfields of AI such as data mining and

G.A. Vouros and T. Panayiotopoulos (Eds.): SETN 2004, LNAI 3025, pp. 72–81, 2004.

machine learning have witnessed profound advancement. Tools developed under these disciplines have the ability to analyze large amounts of medical data and learn the underlying patterns, leading to the discovery of new phenomena and the extraction of medical knowledge. Looking for complex patterns within large medical data repositories and discovering previously unexpected associations can be of particular interest for understanding the development of several diseases.

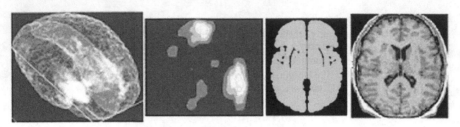

Fig. 1. Examples of Regions of Interest (ROIs) in medical images

2 Background

In this work we are interested in developing intelligent medical imaging tools that can support diagnosis. We focus particularly in brain imaging. We are interested in mining functional associations in the brain, focusing on highly informative Regions of Interest (ROIs). Figure 1 shows examples of such regions. Several techniques have been proposed for this particular purpose and large brain image data repositories have been developed [6], [7] that consist of 3-D images from different medical imaging modalities. These capture structural (e.g., MRI[1]) and/or functional/physiological (e.g., PET[2], fMRI[3]) information about the human brain. Techniques combining findings from several disciplines, such as AI, machine learning, pattern recognition, and data mining have been employed [8], [9] to analyze this vast amount of imaging data.

Two kinds of functional associations in the human brain are of particular interest when developing intelligent brain imaging tools. The first kind refers to associations between lesioned structures and concomitant neurological or neuropsychological deficits. The second includes associations between brain activation patterns and tasks performed. For this case, experiments are designed where subjects are asked to perform a certain task and their brain activation level is measured. A current obstacle in this type of analysis is the lack of intelligent tools to assist in diagnosis and medical decision making using methods that automatically classify such patterns (i.e., activation regions) and quantitatively measure levels of their similarity.

The tools we present in this paper focus on analyzing 3D functional Magnetic Resonance Imaging (fMRI) that shows functional activity of the human brain. Current popular techniques employed for this purpose can be computationally expensive when analyzing activation levels or they do not model activation patterns entirely.

---

[1] Magnetic Resonance Imaging: shows soft-tissue structural information.

[2] Positron Emission Tomography: shows physiological activity.

[3] Functional-Magnetic Resonance Imaging: shows physiological activity.

More specifically, *statistical parametric mapping* (SPM) [10] analyzes each voxel's changes independently of the others and builds a corresponding map of statistical values. The significance of each voxel is ascertained statistically by means of Student's t-test, F-test, correlation coefficient, or other univariate statistical parametric tests. The multiple comparison problem (which occurs when computing a statistic for many pairwise tests) is usually handled by estimating corrected p-values for clusters. Although approaches have been proposed that seek to overcome the multiple comparison problem [11], they are based on a linearization of the 3D domain that might fail to preserve 100% the spatial locality of the ROIs.

Another approach to detect functional associations in the human brain is to model (estimate) their underlying distributions when distinct classes are present (controls vs. patients) [12], [13], utilizing parametric, non-parametric or semi-parametric techniques. EM and k-means algorithms [14] have been employed for this purpose, and statistical distance based methods have been used to distinguish among distributions. The Mahalanobis distance [15] and the Kullback-Leibler divergence [14] are most often employed. The main problem of these techniques is that real data are not accurately modeled using a simple mixture of Gaussian components, since they correspond to highly non-uniform distributions.

We seek to develop intelligent brain imaging tools that can provide decision-making support for diagnosis. We propose a unified framework for analyzing functional activity in the human brain. Our approach consists of two basic steps. The first is based on an adaptive recursive partitioning of the 3D domain to discover discriminative areas. This technique reduces the multiple comparison problem encountered in voxel-based analysis by applying statistical tests to groups of voxels. Compared with [11] this step of analysis is performed directly on the 3D domain (hyper-rectangles) without any loss of spatial locality. For classification, to avoid problems with distribution estimation techniques that are not suitable for non-uniform real datasets, we use neural networks having as inputs measurements obtained from highly discriminative ROIs. The second step is to further characterize these highly informative ROIs by extracting k-dimensional feature vectors (signatures) the uniquely represent them. As a case study we look at a group of patient and control subjects from a study on Alzheimer's disease (AD) [16]. Our intention is to develop intelligent tools that can provide both good classification and in depth quantitative analysis of discriminative activation patterns expressed by ROIs. In the context of the proposed framework we want to support diagnosis when the fMRI image of a new subject is presented. In other words, we seek to determine the group to which it belongs, i.e., control versus patient.

3 Methodology

The tools we propose combine methodologies initially presented in the field of data mining and image-processing. We focus on mining associations between fMRI activation and other non-spatial attributes (i.e. clinical assessment). Furthermore we provide an efficient characterization mechanism for representing and compacting highly informative ROIs such that classification, indexing and similarity searches are feasible under the perspective of a medical imaging repository. In the discussion that follows we present the method for a two-class problem although it can be easily extended to more than two classes.

For the first step of the analysis we employ *Adaptive Recursive Partitioning* (ARP) that has been so far applied mainly to realistic and synthetic 3D region datasets of discrete (binary) voxel values [17]. Some initial results from attempts to apply the technique on real fMRI datasets have been presented in [18]. The main idea of this technique is to treat the initial 3D volume as a hyper rectangle and search for informative regions by partitioning the space into sub-regions. The intelligence of the tool lies in the selectivity of partitioning the hyper rectangles in an adaptive way. Only hyper rectangles that do not exhibit statistically significant discriminative power are selected to be partitioned recursively. More specifically, for each sample, we use the mean V_{mean} of all voxel values belonging to the volume (hyper-rectangle) under consideration as a measurement of activation/deactivation level. The adaptive partitioning of the 3D space continues in the following way: A hyper-rectangle is partitioned only if the corresponding attribute V_{mean} does not have a sufficient discriminative power to determine the class of samples. To decide this, we can apply statistical parametric (e.g. t-test [19]) or non-parametric tests (e.g. Wilcoxon rank sum [20]). The procedure progresses recursively until all remaining sub-regions are discriminative or a sub-region becomes so small that cannot be further partitioned. For this purpose, we define the maximum number of partitioning steps (depth) that the partitioning can go through. If the splitting criterion is satisfied, the spatial sub-domain (or hyper-rectangle) corresponding to the node of the oct-tree is partitioned into 8 smaller sub-domains. The corresponding tree node becomes the parent of eight children nodes, each corresponding to a subdomain and the new measurements V_{mean} corresponding to the region data in the sub-domains become new candidate attributes. Observe that the proposed method effectively reduces the multiple comparison problem encountered when using voxel-based analysis. The number of times a statistical test is applied is significantly reduced since we selectively deal with groups of voxels (hyper rectangles).

After detecting ROIs of highly discriminative activation we propose a second step of detailed quantitative characterization of these regions, aiming to extract unique signatures. We apply a method that efficiently extracts a k-dimensional feature vector using concentric spheres in 3D (or circles in 2D) radiating out of the ROI's center of mass, initially presented in [21] and applied on artificially generated data. Here we demonstrate the potential of the technique to be utilized for characterizing real ROIs. The proposed technique extends the original idea of Sholl's analysis [22] (i.e. the use of concentric circles radiating out of the root of the tree to partition a tree-like structure) to non-tree like structures. The process is described by the following steps: (i) estimate the center of mass, *m,* of the region (for non-homogeneous regions this is calculated using a weighted contribution based on each voxel's value), (ii) construct a series of 1,...,k concentric spheres in 3D (or circles in 2D) radiating out of *m*, using regular increments of radius, and (iii) construct the feature vectors f_s and f_r of size k measuring respectively at each increment the fraction of the sphere (or circle) occupied by the region and the fraction of the region occupied by the sphere (circle).

Fig. 2. Intersecting concentric circles with the ROI being characterized

The feature vectors obtained are of the form (a) $f_s = [f_{1s}, f_{2s},...., f_{ks}]$ or (b) $f_r = [f_{1r}, f_{2r},..., f_{kr}]$ respectively. The features f_{is} or f_{ir} (where $i=1,..,k$), obtained at each increment of radius, express the sum of voxels belonging to the intersection of the sphere (or circles in 2D) with the ROI, divided by (a) the total number of voxels belonging to the sphere or (b) the total number of voxels belonging to the ROI. The sum of voxels for the non-homogeneous ROIs are calculated by a weighted contribution of each voxel, based on its value. Figure 2 illustrates a snapshot of the characterization process for a ROI in 2D. This technique has been shown to be two orders of magnitude faster than mathematical morphology (namely the "pattern spectrum") although it achieves comparable to or even better characterization results [21].

The purpose of extending these two approaches to be applicable on real data and combining them in the context of a unified approach is to create an intelligent brain informatics tool. This can be useful for mining associations between spatial patterns and clinical assessment as well as providing compact characterization for interesting ROIs, overall assisting diagnosis with classification and similarity searches. One of the computational advantages of the proposed tool is that it operates on groups of voxels (hyper-rectangles) significantly reducing the multiple comparison problem encountered when applying statistical tests on a voxel wise basis (SPM). Finally, the selectivity that the system exhibits when partitioning the space in an adaptive recursive manner guides the analysis to focus only on highly informative ROIs, avoiding unnecessary processing.

4   Experimental Evaluation

Our dataset consisted of 3D activation contrast maps of 9 controls and 9 Alzheimer's disease (AD) patients. The task was designed to probe semantic knowledge of categorical congruence between word pairs, exploring neuroanatomical correlates in AD [16]. Figure 3 shows sample views of these contrast activation maps. Preprocessing of the data included spatial normalization, i.e. registration to a standard template. Each subject's task-related activation was analyzed individually versus the subject's rest condition, resulting in individual contrast maps giving a measurement of fMRI signal change at each voxel. Background noise was removed by subtracting the signal value measured in representative background voxels from all the voxels of the 3D volume. Finally, we masked the data using a binary mask extracted from the T1 canonical atlas that was used as the template for the registration. Only signal within the binary mask was included in the analysis.

4.1   Mining Informative Patterns

As a first step of mining informative patterns and associations we applied ARP using as splitting criterion the t-test with threshold levels for the p-value 0.05 and 0.01. A p-value reflects the probability of observing a test statistic as extreme as or more extreme than the observed value, assuming that the null hypothesis is true. In our case, the null hypothesis is that the two groups do not differ significantly with respect to activation levels. The values of 0.05 and 0.01 are the typical values used in the literature for such statistical tests. The maximum allowed tree depth was set to either 3 or 4. ARP uses these parameters to refrain from further partitioning a 3D hyper-rectangle. The above values for the tree depth were determined based on the resolution of the original images and a trade-off between the size of the discovered regions and the number of tests performed. Due to space limitations, in Figure 4, we present the indicated ROIs for a significance threshold of 0.05 and a maximum tree depth of 3, overlaid on the T1 canonical atlas template. The significance of each region is annotated using a color coding (colorbar). The majority of significant regions determined by the proposed approach that could discriminate Alzheimer patients from controls were within the medial temporal lobe. The findings of multiple distributed regions in this area that differentiate patients and controls, as detected by ARP, is consistent with atrophy observed in widespread cortical and subcortical areas in AD [23] and may be consistent with a distributed reorganization of networks subserving the semantic memory task [16].

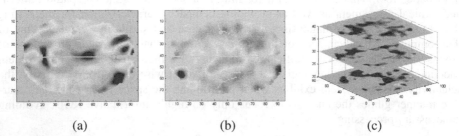

(a)   (b)   (c)

Fig. 3. Sample views of the contrast activation maps in our dataset. 2D slices of (a) a control and (b) a patient sample. 3D view of 2D slices for a sample fMRI activation volume (c)

To further verify the validity of these results we include the following classification experiments that can be viewed as building a model for assisting in diagnosis. More specifically, for the classification model we used Neural Networks. To avoid overfitting due to a small training dataset we applied one-layer perceptron networks trained by the Pocket algorithm [24]. As inputs to the classifier we used the attributes V_{mean} of the discovered regions (after being standardized to have zero mean and unit standard deviation), and a binary class label indicating the class of the samples (control vs. patient). The leave-one-out approach was employed to evaluate out of sample classification performance [14],[15]. More specifically, the training set consisted of patients and controls with indices 1,2,3,...,i-1,i+1,...9, and the method was tested on patient and control with index i, where i=1,...,9. Taking into account the stochastic nature of the Pocket algorithm, we repeated the process of training and testing the model in each of the leave-one-out loops for 5 times and averaged the percentage of the correct predictions to obtain the reported accuracy. Table 1 shows the overall classification accuracies as well as those obtained separately for controls and patients. These results support the argument that the regions discovered by ARP in the specific study are indeed associated with AD, thus providing significant discriminative information.

To provide a comparison basis for the proposed tools we implemented as well a static partitioning approach. This approach is naïve (as compared to the adaptive partitioning of the space) and simply partitions the space into equal length hyper-rectangles. Each dimension is actually split in l equal length bins, resulting in a total partitioning of the space of $l \times l \times l$ hyper-rectangles for the 3D domain. Again the V_{mean} of each sub-region is used as a representative attribute and the same classification model is employed. Table 2 demonstrates the classification accuracies for this scenario. It is clear that the adaptive approach outperforms the static partitioning approach, being able to indicate as well specific patterns (ROIs) where discriminative activation is observed.

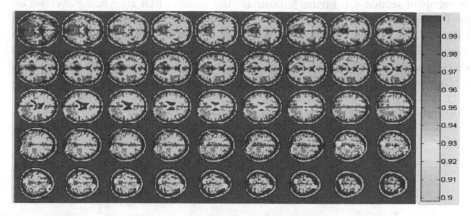

Fig. 4. Transaxial view of the T1 canonical atlas showing the areas discovered by ARP when applied with parameters: significance threshold = 0.05, maximum tree depth = 3

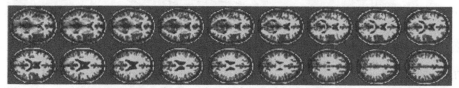

Fig. 5. The ROI used for applying the proposed feature selection technique, shown in consecutive 2D slices after being overlaid on the T1canonical brain atlas

Table 1. Classification accuracy based on the discriminative regions detected by ARP

Criterion	Threshold	Depth	Accuracy		
			Controls	Patients	Total
	0.05	3	89%	100%	94%
t-test	0.05	4	84%	100%	92%
	0.01	4	87%	100%	93%

Table 2. Classification accuracy based on the static partitioning

l	Accuracy		
	Controls	Patients	Total
2	58.89%	71.11%	65%
3	57.78%	78.89%	68.33%
4	100%	0%	50%

4.2 Characterizing Highly Informative Regions

Here, we demonstrate an example of applying the proposed quantitative characterization technique described in Section 3 in order to extract unique signatures from the highly informative regions. The ROI that we focus on was constructed by two neighboring sub-regions within the medial temporal lobe of the human brain. These sub-regions have p-values of 0.0012 and 0.0025 respectively when using a t-test to determine the significance of their association with Alzheimer's disease in the experiments of section 4.1. Figure 5 illustrates the selected ROI after being overlaid on the T1 canonical atlas. We experimented with a radius increment of 0.02 extracting feature vectors of length 40. Figure 6 shows the obtained f_s feature vectors. As we can observe, signatures of subjects of the same class tend to cluster following similar behavior and the two classes barely overlap. The curvature of the signatures conveys information about the activation patterns of the original data. As demonstrated initially in [21] with synthetic data, using morphological operators for such an analysis is two orders of magnitude slower than the approach employed here.

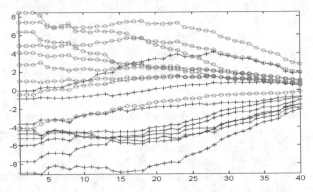

Fig. 6. The obtained f_s characterization signatures from the highly discriminative ROI. Signatures with '+' correspond to controls (blue), 'o' to patients (red)

As illustrated, patient samples exhibit positive activation in the specific ROI, whereas the control subjects have lower negative activation (deactivation) levels. This information is highly discriminative and the proposed characterization technique has the ability to represent the initial ROI in a compact form. These signatures provide both quantitative and qualitative information and can be utilized for indexing and similarity searches in the framework of a medical imaging data repository that can assist clinical decision-making and diagnosis.

5   Conclusions

We proposed a framework for constructing computationally intelligent medical informatics tools. These tools combine data mining and image processing techniques, extending them to be applied on real fMRI data. The focus is to mine associations between spatial patterns and other non-spatial clinical assessment, employing an adaptive partitioning of the space guided with statistical tests. At the same time we seek to characterize highly informative regions, providing compact signatures that uniquely identify the ROIs. These can be utilized for indexing and similarity searches in the context of a medical imaging data repository. As a case study, we analyzed an fMRI dataset obtained from a study that explores neuroanatomical correlates of semantic processing in Alzheimer's disease. We evaluated the validity of our findings providing classification experiments with neural networks. The overall classification based on activation patterns in these areas exceeded 90% with nearly 100% accuracy on patients outperforming the naïve static partitioning approach. The proposed intelligent tools have great potential for elucidating relationships between ROIs in medical images and other clinical variables assisting in medical decision-making.

Acknowledgement

The authors would like to thank A. Saykin for providing the fMRI data set and clinical expertise and J. Ford for performing some of the preprocessing of this data set. This work was supported in part by the National Science Foundation (NSF) under grants IIS-0237921 and IIS-0083423. NSF specifically disclaims responsibility for any analyses, interpretations and conclusions.

References

1. Agrawal, R., Imielinski, T., and Swami, A.: Database Mining: A performance Perspective. IEEE Transactions on Knowledge and Data Engineering, 5(6) (1993) 914-925
2. Coiera, E., Editorial: Artificial Intelligence in Medicine - The Challenges Ahead. Journal American Medical Informatics Association, 3(6) (1996) 363-366
3. Buchanan, B. G. and Shortliffe, E. H., editors. Rule-based expert systems: The MYCIN experiments of the Stanford Heuristic Programming Project. Addison-Wesley, Reading, MA, (1984)
4. Miller, R.A., Pople, H.E., Myers, J.D.: INTERNIST-1: An experimental computer-based diagnostic consultant for general internal medicine. New Eng. J. Med., 307 (1982) 468-476
5. Barnett, O., Cimino, J.J, Hupp, J. A. and Hoffer, E.P.: DXplain: An evolving diagnosis decision-support system. Journal of the American Medical Association, 258 (1987) 67-74
6. Arya, M., Cody, W., Faloutsos, C., Richardson, J., and Toga, A.: A 3D Medical Image Database Management System. Int. Journal of Computerized Medical Imaging and Graphics, Special issue on Medical Image Databases, 20(4) (1996) 269-284
7. Letovsky, S., Whitehead, S., Paik, C., Miller, G., Gerber, J., Herskovits, E., Fulton, T., and. Bryan, R.: A brain-image database for structure-function analysis. American Journal of Neuroradiology, 19(10) (1998) 1869-1877
8. Megalooikonomou, V., Ford, J., Shen, L., Makedon, F., Saykin, F.: Data mining in brain imaging. Statistical Methods in Medical Research, 9(4) (2000) 359-394
9. Megalooikonomou, V., Davatzikos, C., Herskovits, E.: Mining lesion-deficit associations in a brain image database. In Proceedings of the ACM SIGKDD International Conference on Knowledge Discovery and Data Mining, San Diego, CA, (1999) 347-351
10. Friston, KJ., Holmes, AP., Worsley, KJ., Poline, JP., Frith, CD., Frackowiak, RSJ.: Statistical parametric maps in functional imaging: a general linear approach. Human Brain Mapping, (1995) 189–210
11. Kontos, D., Megalooikonomou, V., Ghubade, N., Faloutsos, C., Detecting discriminative functional MRI activation patterns using space filling curves. In Proceedings of the 25th Annual International Conference of the IEEE Engineering in Medicine and Biology Society (EMBC), Cancun, Mexico, (2003) 963-967

12. Lazarevic, A., Pokrajac, D., Megalooikonomou, V., Obradovic, Z.: Distinguishing Among 3-D Distributions for Brain Image Data Classification. In Proceedings of the 4th International Conference on Neural Networks and Expert Systems in Medicine and Healthcare, Milos Island, Greece, (2001) 389-396
13. Pokrajac, D., Lazarevic, A., Megalooikonomou, V., Obradovic, Z.: Classification of brain image data using meaasures of distributional distance, 7th Annual Meeting of the Organization for Human Brain Mapping (OHBM01), Brighton, UK, (2001)
14. Duda, R., Hart, P., Stork, D.: Pattern Classification, John Wiley and Sons, NY, (2000)
15. Fukunaga, K.: Introduction to Statistical Pattern Recognition, Academic Press, San Diego, (1990)
16. Saykin, A.J., Flashman, L.A., Frutiger, S.A., Johnson, S.C., Mamourian, A.C., Moritz, C.H., O'Jile, J.R., Riordan, H.J., Santulli, R.B., Smith, C.A., Weaver, J.B.: Neuroanatomic substrates of semantic memory impairment in Alzheimer's disease: Patterns of functional MRI activation. Journal of the International Neuropsychological Society, 5 (1999) 377-392
17. Megalooikonomou, V., Pokrajac, D., Lazarevic, A., V., Obradovic, Z.:, Effective classification of 3-D image data using partitioning methods. In Proceedings of the SPIE 14th Annual Symposium in Electronic Imaging: Conference on Visualization and Data Analysis San Jose, CA, Jan. (2002), 62-73
18. Megalooikonomou, V., Kontos, D., Pokrajac, D., Lazarevic, A., Obradovic, Z., Boyko, O., Saykin, A., Ford, J., Makedon, F.: Classification and Mining of Brain Image Data Using Adaptive Recursive Partitioning Methods: Application to Alzheimer Disease and Brain Activation Patterns", presented at the *Human Brain Mapping Conference (OHBM'03)*, New York, NY, Jun. (2003)
19. Devore, J.L.:Probability and Statistics for Engineering and the Sciences, 5th edn., International Thomson Publishing Company, Belmont, (2000)
20. Conover, W.J.: Practical Nonparametric Statistics, Wiley, New York, (1999)
21. Megalooikonomou, V., Dutta, H., Kontos, D.: Fast and Effective Characterization of 3D Region Data. In Proc. of the IEEE International Conference on Image Processing (ICIP), Rochester, NY, (2002) 421-424
22. Sholl, D.: Dendritic Organization in the Neurons of the Visual and Motor Cortices of the Cat. Journal of Anatomy, 87 (1953) 387-406
23. Flashman, L.A., Wishart, H.A., Saykin, A.J.: Boundaries Between Normal Aging and Dementia: Perspectives from Neuropsychological and Neuroimaging Investigations, in: Emory VOB and Oxman TE, editors. Dementia: Presentations, Differential Diagnosis and Nosology. Baltimore: Johns Hopkins University Press, (2003) 3-30
24. Gallant, S.I.: Perceptron-Based Learning Algorithms. IEEE Transactions on Neural Networks, 1(2) (1990) 179-191

Text Area Identification in Web Images

Stavros J. Perantonis[1], Basilios Gatos[1], Vassilios Maragos[1,3],
Vangelis Karkaletsis[2], and George Petasis[2]

[1] Computational Intelligence Laboratory,
Institute of Informatics and Telecommunications,
National Research Center "Demokritos",
153 10 Athens, Greece
{sper,bgat}@iit.demokritos.gr
http://www.iit.demokritos.gr/cil
[2] Software and Knowledge Engineering,
Institute of Informatics and Telecommunications,
National Research Center "Demokritos",
153 10 Athens, Greece
{vangelis,petasis}@iit.demokritos.gr
http://www.iit.demokritos.gr/skel
[3] Department of Computer Science,
Technological Educational Institution of Athens,
122 10 Egaleo, Greece

Abstract. With the explosive growth of the World Wide Web, millions of
documents are published and accessed on-line. Statistics show that a significant
part of Web text information is encoded in Web images. Since Web images
have special characteristics that sometimes distinguish them from other types of
images, commercial OCR products often fail to recognize Web images due to
their special characteristics. This paper proposes a novel Web image processing
algorithm that aims to locate text areas and prepare them for OCR procedure
with better results. Our methodology for text area identification has been fully
integrated with an OCR engine and with an Information Extraction system. We
present quantitative results for the performance of the OCR engine as well as
qualitative results concerning its effects to the Information Extraction system.
Experimental results obtained from a large corpus of Web images, demonstrate
the efficiency of our methodology.

1 Introduction

With the explosive growth of the World Wide Web, millions of documents are published and accessed on-line. The World Wide Web contains lots of information but
even modern search engines just index a fraction of this information. This issue poses
new challenges for Web Document Analysis and Web Content Extraction. While there
has been active research on Web Content Extraction using text-based techniques,
documents often include multimedia content. It has been reported [1][2] that of the

G.A. Vouros and T. Panayiotopoulos (Eds.): SETN 2004, LNAI 3025, pp. 82–92, 2004.
© Springer-Verlag Berlin Heidelberg 2004

total number of words visible on a Web page, 17% are in image form and those words are usually the most semantically important.

Unfortunately, commercial OCR engines often fail to recognize Web images due to their special key characteristics. Web images are usually of low resolution, consist mainly of graphic objects, are usually noiseless and have the anti-aliasing property (see Fig. 1). Anti-aliasing smoothes out the discretization of an image by padding pixels with intermediate colors.

Several approaches in the literature deal with text locating in color images. In [3], characters are assumed of almost uniform colour. In [4], foreground and background segmentation is achieved by grouping colours into clusters. A resolution enhancement to facilitate text segmentation is proposed in [5]. In [6], texture information is combined with a neural classifier. Recent work in locating text in Web images is based on merging pixels of similar colour into components and selecting text components by using a fuzzy inference mechanism [7]. Another approach is based on information on the way humans perceive colour difference and uses different colour spaces in order to approximate the way human perceive colour [8]. Finally, approaches [9][10] restrict their operations in the RGB colour space and assume text areas of uniform colour.

(a)   (b)

Fig. 1. A Web image example (a) and a zoom in it (b) to demonstrate the web image key characteristics.

In this paper, we aim at two objectives: (a) Development of new technologies for extracting text from Web images for Information Extraction purposes and (b) Creation of an evaluation platform in order to measure the performance of all introduced new technologies.

Recently, some of the authors have proposed a novel method for text area identification in Web images [11]. The method has been developed in the framework of the EC-funded R&D project, CROSSMARC, which aims to develop technology for extracting information from domain-specific Web pages. Our approach is based on the transitions of brightness as perceived by the human eye. An image segment is classified as text by the human eye if characters are clearly distinguished from the background. This means that the brightness transition from the text body to the foreground exceeds a certain threshold. Additionally, the area of all characters observed by the human eye does not exceed a certain value since text bodies are of restricted thickness. These characteristics of human eye perception are embodied in our approach. According to it, the Web color image is converted to gray scale in order to record the transitions of brightness perceived by the human eye. Then, an edge extraction technique facilitates the extraction of all objects as well as of all inverted objects. A conditional dilation technique helps to choose text and inverted text objects among all objects. The criterion is the thickness of all objects that in the case of characters is of restricted value. Our approach is mainly based on the detected character edges and character thickness that are the main human eye perception characteristics.

The evaluation platform used in order to assess the performance of the proposed method for text area location was based on the Segmentation Evaluation Tool v.2 of the Computational Intelligence Laboratory (NCSR "DEMOKRITOS") [12]. We measured the performance of the proposed scheme for text area identification and recorded a significant facilitation in the recognition task of the OCR engine. Our methodology for text area identification has been fully integrated with an OCR engine and with an Information Extraction system (NERC module [13]). We present quantitative results for the performance of the OCR engine as well as qualitative results concerning its effects to the Information Extraction system. Experimental results obtained from a large corpus of Web images, demonstrate the efficiency of our methodology.

2 Text Area Location Algorithm

2.1 Edge Extraction

Consider a color Web image I. First, we covert it to the gray scale image Ig. Then, we define as e and e^{-1} the B/W edge and invert edge images that encapsulate the abrupt increase or decrease in image brightness:

$$e(x,y) = \begin{cases} 1, & \text{if } \exists (m,n): Ig(m,n) - Ig(x,y) > D \ \wedge \\ & \quad |m-x| <= d \ \wedge \ |n-y| <= d \\ 0, & \text{otherwise} \end{cases} \qquad (1)$$

$$e^{-1}(x,y) = \begin{cases} 1, & \text{if } \exists (m,n): Ig(m,n) - Ig(x,y) < D \ \wedge \\ & \quad |m-x| <= d \ \wedge \ |n-y| <= d \\ 0, & \text{otherwise} \end{cases} \qquad (2)$$

where D is the gray level contrast visible by the human eye and d defines the window at x,y in which we search for a gray level contrast. Fig. 2 shows an example for e and e^{-1} calculation.

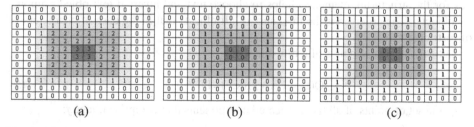

Fig. 2. (a) Gray scale image Ig, (b) edge image e and (c) invert edge image e-1 (parameters used: D=2, d=2).

2.2 Object Identification

Objects are defined as groups of pixels that neighbor with edge pixels and have similar gray scale value. To calculate image objects, we proceed to a conditional dilation of edge images. A pixel is added only if it has a similar gray scale value in the original image Ig. The dimension of the structuring element defines the expected maximum thickness of all objects. Objects O_s and inverted objects O_s^{-1} are defined as follows:

$$O_s(x, y) = \begin{cases} 1, & \text{if } \exists\,(m,n) : e(m,n) = 1 \wedge |m\text{-}x| <= s \wedge |n\text{-}y| <= s \\ & \wedge |Ig(x,y)\text{-}Ig(m,n)| < S \\ 0, & \text{otherwise} \end{cases} \qquad (3)$$

$$O_s^{-1}(x, y) = \begin{cases} 1, & \text{if } \exists\,(m,n) : e^{-1}(m,n) = 1 \wedge |m\text{-}x| <= s \wedge |n\text{-}y| <= s \\ & \wedge |Ig(x,y)\text{-}Ig(m,n)| < S \\ 0, & \text{otherwise} \end{cases} \qquad (4)$$

where s the dimension of the structuring element and S is the expected maximum difference in gray scale values within the same object. Fig. 3 shows an example for O_s and O_s^{-1} calculation.

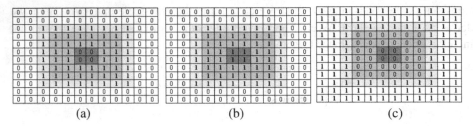

$\qquad\qquad$ (a) $\qquad\qquad\qquad\qquad\qquad$ (b) $\qquad\qquad\qquad\qquad\qquad$ (c)

Fig. 3. For the example of fig. 2 we calculate object O_1 (a), object O_n, $n>1$ (b) and object O_1^{-1} (c) (parameters used: $S=1$).

2.3 Text Identification

The above conditional dilation technique applied with several iterations (several values for the structuring elements) helps to choose text and inverted text objects among all objects. The criterion is the thickness of all objects that in the case of characters is of restricted value.

Let $P(f)$, the set of points of a b/w image f:

$$O(f) = \{(x,y):f(x,y)=1\} \qquad (5)$$

$p_i(f)$, the set of points of all the connected components that comprise image f:

$$P(f) = \cup\, p_i(f) \qquad (6)$$

$S(p_i(f))$, the number of pixels of the connected component, $E(p_i(f))$, the set of background points that have a 4-connected relation with the connected component, $S(E(p_i(f)))$, the number of pixels of $E(p_i(f))$, and $C(p_i(f))$, the category a connected component belongs to:

$$C(p_i(f)) = \text{TEXT or OTHER CATEGORY} \tag{7}$$

A connected component of image object O_n is classified as text region if while increasing n the set of background pixels that have a 4-connected relation with the connected component remains almost the same (see the example of Fig. 3b where object O_n remains the same for $n>1$):

$$C(p_i(O_n)) = \text{TEXT if } \exists j: (\, p_i(O_n) \subseteq p_j(O_{n+1}) \text{ AND}$$
$$S(E(p_i(O_n)) \cap E(p_j(O_{n+1}))) / S(E(p_i(O_n))< s) \text{ AND } n<N \tag{8}$$

where N depends on the maximum expected letter thickness and s is the allowed tolerance in changes of the 4-connected background pixel set. The reason we trace the changes to the 4-connected background pixels and not to the foreground pixels is that due to dilation with a larger structuring element, the connected components may be joined together. In the same way, we define the condition for locating inverse text objects.

At Fig. 4 the flowchart of the proposed method is demonstrated.

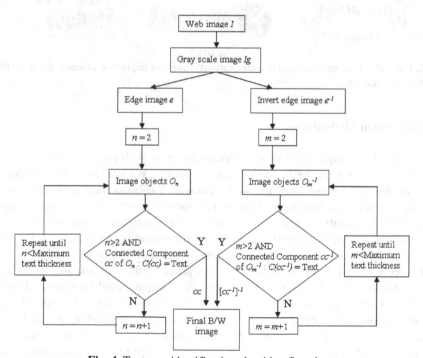

Fig. 4. Text area identification algorithm flowchart.

3 System Evaluation

3.1 Corpus Preparation

The corpus for the evaluation of the proposed technique was prepared by selecting more than 1100 images from English, French, Greek and Italian Web pages. These images contain text, inverse text and graphics and concern laptop offers and job offers. In order to record the performance of the proposed method for text area location we annotated the text areas for all images (see Fig.5) using the Ground Truth Maker v.1 of the Computational Intelligence Laboratory (NCSR "DEMOKRITOS") [11].

(a)

(b)

Fig. 5. Example of the ground truth text annotations: (a) From the laptop offers domain (b) from the job offers domain.

3.2 Evaluation Methodology

The proposed technique for text area identification in Web images has been implemented and tested with the large Web image corpus. We compared the results obtained by the well-known OCR engine FineReader 5 (FineReader) with and without applying our text area location technique. FineReader which has come out on top in major OCR comparative tests, can recognize the structure of a document including columns, graphic inserts and table formatting and can readily retain the page layout. It is also very effective in recognizing characters in different languages.

In order to record the performance of the proposed method for text area location we used the Segmentation Evaluation Tool v.2 of the Computational Intelligence Laboratory. We created a ground truth set with the annotations of the text areas. The performance evaluation method used is based on counting the number of matches between the text areas detected by the algorithm and the text areas in the ground truth. We calculated the intersection of the ON pixel sets of the result and the ground truth images.

Let I be the set of all image points, G the set of all points inside the ground truth text regions, R the set of all points of the result text regions and T(s) a function that counts the elements of set s. For every ground truth region we exclude all points that have approximate the same color with the surrounding of the annotation area. Detection rate and recognition accuracy are defined as follows:

$$DetectionRate = \frac{T(G \cap R \cap I)}{T(G)} \tag{9}$$

$$RecognitionAccuracy = \frac{T(G \cap R \cap I)}{T(R)} \tag{10}$$

A performance metric for text location can be extracted if we combine the values of detection rate and recognition accuracy. We used the following Text Detection Metric (TDM):

$$TDM = \frac{2 DetectionRate\ RecognitionAccuracy}{DetectionRate + RecognitionAccuracy} \tag{11}$$

The evaluation strategy we followed concerns three main tasks: (a) Evaluation of the text locating module (b) evaluation of the OCR result after applying our text locating module, and (c) evaluation of the performance of an information extraction system using the OCR results.

3.3   Evaluation of the Text Locating Module

The evaluation results concerning the performance of the text location module for the laptop offers and the job offers domains are shown in tables 1 and 2.

3.4   Evaluation of the OCR Result after Applying Our Text Locating Module

In almost all cases, the recognition results were improved after applying our text area identification technique. A list of OCR results with and without the text extraction tool are presented in Table 3.

Table 1. Text location evaluation results for the laptop offers domain.

	Detection Rate	Recognition Accuracy	Text Detection Metric
English web image corpus	85,08	61,53	71,41
French web image corpus	84,32	61,61	71,20
Greek web image corpus	80,93	61,73	70,03
Italian web image corpus	78,41	61,50	68,93
TOTAL	**83,58**	**61,58**	**70,91**

Table 2. Text location evaluation results for the job offers domain.

	Detection Rate	Recognition Accuracy	Text Detection Metric
English web image corpus	72,67	61,84	66,81
French web image corpus	78,50	74,16	76,27
Greek web image corpus	79,58	64,83	71,46
Italian web image corpus	78,33	66,95	72,19
TOTAL	77,31	66,57	71,54

Table 3. OCR results with and without the text extraction tool.

	FineReader	Text extraction + FineReader
340S2	-	340S2
dabs©com Buy a SONY EXCLUSIVE! VPL-CS3 Projector	SONY 1VPL-CS3 Projector	da*sOc*m exclusive! Buy a SONY VPL-CS3 Projector
PC WORLD THE COMPUTER SUPERSTORE	• ι π «*-):^·	PC WORLD THE COMPUTER SUPER-STORE
Il tuo partner per l'e-business	jmrfc flrηsm &wtm	il tuo partner per l'e-business
Consultation des offres d'emploi	-	.Consultation des offres d'emploi
MEDIA BEAT® Information Technology	MEDIA BEAT» I riformatici n Ttch nalóg y	MEDIA BEAT* Information Technology

A quantitative evaluation of the performance of the text extraction and preprocessing tool in combination with the OCR engine in terms of detection rate and recognition accuracy is shown in table 4.

Table 4. Evaluation of the performance of the text extraction and preprocessing tool in combination with the OCR engine in terms of detection rate and recognition accuracy.

Laptop offers domain			
Detection Rate		Recognition Accuracy	
FineReader	Text extraction + FineReader	FineReader	Text extraction + FineReader
19.11%	22.09%	75.03%	74.13%
Job offers domain			
Detection Rate		Recognition Accuracy	
FineReader	Text extraction + FineReader	FineReader	Text extraction + FineReader
27.06%	33.63%	71.13%	70.28%

3.5 Evaluation of the Performance of the Information Extraction System Using the OCR Results

The evaluation results concerning the performance of the information extraction system (NERC module [13]) after adding to the web text information the OCR results show that:

- For the words added by the OCR procedure, 30% are correctly classified by the NERC module while the 70% of it are misclassified.
- If we had the perfect OCR engine with 100% recognition rate, then we would have a 45% correct classification by the NERC module while the 55% of it would be misclassified.
- From the above two remarks, we can state that the proposed text extraction and preprocessing module working with an OCR engine adds textual information to the NERC module and produces 66% of the correct results we would have if we used an 100% correct OCR scheme.

Some examples of correct classification results and misclassifications of the information extraction system (NERC module) are shown in figure 5.

COMPAQ. = <MANUF,manufacturerName> Market Hellas = <MANUF,manufacturerName>

(a)

AVIA = <CAPACITY.hdCapacity>   ALFA = <CAPACITY.hdCapacity>

(b)

Fig. 6. Results from the information extraction system (NERC module). (a) Correct classification results (b) Misclassifications.

4   Concluding Remarks

The evaluation results show that many cases, where text is present as part of an image, are recovered by our text location algorithm. Moreover, it must be stressed that our method not only locates text areas, but it also preprocesses the characters present in them, so that the OCR engines are significantly facilitated in their recognition task.

The quantitative evaluation of the performance of the text extraction and preprocessing tool in combination with the OCR engine in terms of detection rate and recognition accuracy shows an approximate 20% increase in Recognition Rates. On the other hand, the evaluation results concerning the performance of text locating after applying our extraction and preprocessing tool module show that we have satisfactory results with more that 70% success. The main reason we did not achieve higher recognition rates is that we used the well-known OCR engine FineReader that is not oriented to work with low resolution images. Our future work concerning the improvement of our text extraction tool involves integration with a low resolution oriented OCR engine.

References

1. Antonacopoulos, A., Karatzas, D., Ortiz Lopez, J.: Accessing Textual Information Embedded in Internet Images. SPIE Internet Imaging II, San Jose, USA (2001) 198-205
2. Lopresti, D., Zhou, J.: Document Analysis and the World Wide Web. Workshop on Document Analysis Systems, Marven, Pennsylvania (1996) 417-424
3. Jain, A. K., Yu, B.: Automatic Text Location in Images and Video Frames. Pattern Recognition, Vol. 31, No. 12 (1998) 2055-2076
4. Huang, Q., Dom, B., Steele, D., Ashley, J., Niblack, W.: Foreground/background segmentation of color images by integration of multiple cues. Computer Vision and Pattern Recognition (1995) 246-249
5. Li, H., Kia, O., Doermann, D.: Text enhancement in digital video. Doc. Recognition & Retrieval VI (IS&SPIE Electronic Imaging'99), San Jose, Vol. 3651 (1999) 2-9
6. Strouthopoulos, C., Papamarkos, N.: Text identification for document image analysis using a neural network, Image and Vision Computing, Vol. 16 (1998) 879-896
7. Antonacopoulos, A., Karatzas, D.: Text Extraction from Web Images Based on Human Perception and Fuzzy Inference. 1st Int'l Workshop on Web Document Analysis (WDA 2001), Seattle, USA (2001) 35-38
8. Antonacopoulos, A., Karatzas, D.: An Anthropocentric Approach to Text Extraction from WWW Images. 4th IAPR Workshop on Document Analysis Systems (DAS2000), Rio de Janeiro (2000) 515-526
9. Antonacopoulos, A., Delporte, F.: Automated Interpretation of Visual representations: Extracting textual Information from WWW Images. Visual Representations and Interpretations, R. Paton and I. Neilson (eds.), Springer, London (1999)
10. Lopresti, D.,Zhou, J.: Locating and Recognizing Text in WWW Images. Information Retrieval, Vol. 2 (2/3) (2000) 177-206

11. Perantonis, S. J., Gatos, B., Maragos, V.: A Novel Web Image Processing Algorithm for Text Area Identification that Helps Commercial OCR Engines to Improve Their Web Image Recognition Efficiency. Second International Workshop on Web Document Analysis (WDA2003), Edinburgh, Scotland (2003).
12. Antonacopoulos, A., Gatos, B., Karatzas, D.: ICDAR 2003 Page Segmentation Competition. 7th International Conference on Document Analysis and Recognition (ICDAR'03), Edinburgh, Scotland (2003)
13. Petasis G., Karkaletsis V and Spyropoulos C. D: Cross-lingual Information Extraction from Web pages: the use of a general-purpose Text Engineering Platform. 4th International Conference on Recent Advances in Natural Language Processing (RANLP 2003), Borovets, Bulgaria (2003)

A Mixed Reality Learning Environment for Geometry Education

George Nikolakis, George Fergadis, Dimitrios Tzovaras, and Michael G. Strintzis

Informatics and Telematics Institute / Centre for Research and Technology Hellas
1st Km Thermi-Panorama Road, 57001 (PO Box 361), Thermi-Thessaloniki, Greece
{gniko,Dimitrios.Tzovaras}@iti.gr

Abstract. This paper presents a mixed reality environment for geometry education. The proposed system consists of three main sub-components: The Geometry construction agent, which allows users to create objects in the 3D scene, a
Collision Detection algorithm, which calculates the collisions between the virtual hand and the dynamical geometrical objects and the haptic interaction agent
which is responsible for the haptic feedback returned to the user. The user can
perform actions in the virtual environment using a haptic glove and create a
scene out of geometrical objects. Stereoscopic view is supported and actions are
visualized on a large screen so that many users can observe the actions. The
system has been evaluated in secondary schools in Thessaloniki, Greece and the
results have shown that users consider it very satisfactory in terms of providing
a more efficient learning approach.

Introduction

Nowadays, there has been a growing interest in developing force feedback interfaces
that allow people to access information presented in 3D virtual reality environments
(VEs). It is anticipated that VEs will be the most widely accepted, natural form of
information interchange in the near future [1]. The greatest potential benefits from
VEs, built into current virtual reality (VR) systems, exist in such applications as design, planning, education, training, and communication of general ideas and concepts.

Recently, virtual reality has become a very efficient tool for implementing novel
training and educational approaches. The use of advanced techniques for human-
computer interaction and realistic three-dimensional graphics has proved to increase
the student interest and provide significantly better perception. A learning environment for teaching three-dimensional geometry named "Construct3D" has been recently developed by H. Kaufmann[2]. The system is based on the Studierstube system
described by Schmalstieg et al. in [3], which uses augmented reality to allow multiple
users to share a virtual space. See-through HMDs are used, achieving a combination
of virtual and real world. The user of Construct3D can interact with the scene using a
personal interaction panel and a tracked pen. There is no haptic feedback send to the
user. Another approach, VRMath is an open, online VRLE (Virtual Reality Learning
Environment), in which users can use a Logo like language to construct three-
dimension virtual worlds [4]. In [5], an edutainment environment based on geometry
visualization is proposed. The main aim is to teach effectively and promote the reflec-

G.A. Vouros and T. Panayiotopoulos (Eds.): SETN 2004, LNAI 3025, pp. 93–102, 2004.
© Springer-Verlag Berlin Heidelberg 2004

tive cognition necessary for learning mathematical concepts while providing an enjoyable computer environment for children to play. CyberMath [6] is a 3D learning environment for the interactive exploration of mathematics in a CAVE environment. Also, work in [7] presents and evaluates a virtual reality system for descriptive geometry teaching.

The present work proposes the use of a haptic device named Cybertouch™ [8], [9] to provide with a tangible picture of complex three-dimensional objects and scenes. In contrast to traditional geometry education with two-dimensional views, the proposed setup allows a haptic three-dimensional representation of the exercise construction and solution process. The users can study a variety of training cases such as: (i) Surface intersections of cone, cylinder and sphere, (ii) Conic Sections, (iii) Vector algebra and (iv) Visualizing three-dimensional geometric theorems.

Dynamic geometry is used to experiment with geometrical problems and to support a constructive approach for finding own solutions to problems. The proposed system consists of three main sub-components: The Geometry construction agent, which allows users to create objects in the 3D scene, a Collision Detection algorithm, which calculates the collisions between the virtual hand and the dynamical geometrical objects and the haptic interaction agent, which is responsible for the haptic feedback returned to the user.

These components provide the user with the ability to create and modify constructive solid geometry objects (spheres, cones, cylinders and parallelepipeds) using a variety of ways. The user can draw lines in the scene and insert points on any surface. The user can also perform Boolean operations between any couple of objects in the scene. The environment supports different layers in order to provide an easier way of interaction to the user. The user can select one layer as active and multiple layers as visible or invisible. Haptic interaction occurs only when the hand is in contact to objects that belong to visible layers. The user can move objects or groups of objects from one layer to another. In order to increase the immersion in the virtual environment, stereoscopic view is implemented. The scene is displayed on a large screen (64'') where many students can view realistic 3d representation of the scene. This is accomplished using shutter glasses and placing a synchronization emitter on the screen.

The paper is organized as follows: The first section presents the application environment and the following sections present the Geometry Contraction Agent, the collision detection algorithm and the Haptic Interaction Agent, respectively. Finally, the user interface, the stereo view and the application test cases are discussed.

Learning Environment

The proposed application allows the user to create a scene that consists of three-dimensional geometrical objects. The procedure can be implemented using virtual hands in the virtual environment. A position tracker (MotionStar™ Wireless Tracker of Ascension Technologies Inc. (2000)[10]) with a position sensor installed, is used to detect the position and orientation of the user hand in the workspace. Cybertouch® haptic glove of Immersion technologies is used to obtain the hand gesture and to return tactile force feedback to the user.

An important element of the proposed virtual environment is that of VE agents. The VE agents are sophisticated software components with the capability to control dynamic virtual environment and take actions based on a set of aims and rules. There are two kinds of agents implemented in the proposed learning environment: a) the Geometry Construction Agent (GCA) and b) Haptic Interaction Agent (HIA). The GCA agent is responsible for the creation and modification of the geometries in the scene. It receives input from the HIA. The HIA is responsible for the haptic feedback send to the user and for the communication of data to the GCA. The HIA uses as input the hand gesture, the tracker position and the results of the collision detection algorithm. The user interface is based on a toolbar like haptic menu and stereoscopic view. The geometrical objects are presented semi-transparent. This allows the user to view geometries that lie behind other objects (Fig. 1).

Fig. 1. Application Screenshot and testing the interface in the laboratory

Geometry Construction Agent

The geometry construction agent is responsible for the construction of the geometrical objects in the scene. The agent allows the user to insert a variety of objects. Default size geometrical objects can be used in order to construct an environment rapidly. The shape of inserted objects can be modified using one or more modifier points. To activate the modifier points, the user selects from the toolbar the modify option and then touches the object with the index fingertip. The user may also insert an object using a number of points or lines that reside on the scene. The geometrical objects supported by the GCA follow:

1. *Point:* A point can be inserted in the coordinate center or in an object surface. In order to insert a point on a surface, the user selects the function "insert point" from the toolbar and touches the object with the index fingertip. The point is inserted at the contact point.
2. *Line:* The default line is inserted on Y-axis. The user can insert a line using two points. The user can modify the length of a line by moving the modifier point on the edge of the line.
3. *Plane:* The default plane is inserted on the XZ plane. The user can insert a plane out of three points, a plane perpendicular to a line (crossing the middle point of the line) or a plane perpendicular to a line defined from two points (the line crosses the edge of the line).

4. *Sphere:* The center of the default sphere is placed at coordinate center and has a radius of 10 cm. The user can construct a sphere out of two points. The first point is assumed to be the center of the sphere and the second is considered a point on the surface of the sphere. The modifier point is a point on the surface of the sphere. When the user moves this point the radius of the sphere changes so that the point is always on the surface of the sphere.

5. *Cone:* The base of the default cone is on the XZ plane (radius: 10 cm – height: 5 cm). The user can insert a cone out of a line and a point. The line defines the height of the cone and the selected point is considered as a point on the surface of the cone. There are two modifier points, the first lies on the top of the cone and the other on the side of it. Moving the first point results to change of the height of the cone and moving the second point changes the radius of the cone (Fig. 2).

6. *Cylinder:* The center of the default cylinder lies on the coordinate center (radius: 5 cm – height: 10 cm). The user can insert a cylinder out of a line and a point. The line defines the height of the cylinder and the selected point is considered as a point on the surface of the cylinder. There are two modifier points, the first lies on the top of the cylinder and the other on the side of it. Moving the first point results to change of the height of the cylinder and moving the second point changes its radius.

7. *Parallelepiped:* The center of the default parallelepiped is on the coordinate center. The default parallelepiped is a cube and each side has 20 cm length. The user can insert a parallelepiped from two points. The inserted parallelepiped sides are parallel to the XZ, XY and ZY planes. The one point is the lower front left point and the second the upper back right point. There is one modifier point, on a vertex of the box. The user moves the point in order to change the size of the sides of the box. The point is always attached to the corner of the box.

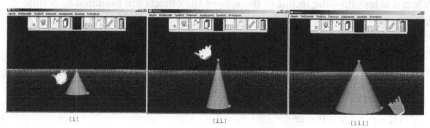

Fig. 2. Object Reshaping: (i) initial Cone, (ii) change the height of the cone, (iii) change the radius of the cone base.

The parametric representation of the shapes and the geometry axioms impose constrains during interaction. The GCA is responsible to appropriately check and modify the user's actions in order to allow only admissible modifications to the objects.

Collision Detection

Collision detection is performed between the fingertips and the geometrical objects. The fingertips are assumed as small spheres for the collision detection algorithm. The fact that all the objects in the scene have well-defined geometrical properties allows the implementation of direct collision detection between the fingertips and the objects. This allows real-time collision detection while the geometrical object shape changes.

In order to detect collision between the fingertip and an object, the fingertip transformation is calculated relatively to the transformation of the object. Thus, all objects are assumed to be located in the center of the new coordinate system. Four cases are examined separately in the proposed collision detection algorithm:

1. *Sphere to sphere*: Collision detection is simple in this particular case. The distance d between the centers of the spheres is compared to the sum of their radiuses in order to examine collision.
2. *Sphere to parallelepiped*: In this specific case, the value of the distance d is calculated using equations (1):

$$xd = \max(|Cx| - \frac{w}{2}, 0), yd = \max(|Cy| - \frac{h}{2}, 0), zd = \max(|Cz| - \frac{l}{2}, 0)$$

$$d = \sqrt{xd^2 + yd^2 + zd^2}$$

(1)

where Cx, Cy, Cz are the coordinates of the center of the sphere, w, l, h are the width, length and height of the parallelepiped, respectively. When d is less than the radius of the sphere, the objects are assumed to collide.

3. *Sphere to cylinder*: The distance d is calculated using equations (2):

$$xzd = \max(\sqrt{Cx^2 + Cz^2} - r_{cyl}, 0), yd = \max(|Cy| - \frac{h}{2}, 0),$$

$$d = \sqrt{xzd^2 + yd^2}$$

(2)

When d is less than the radius of the sphere the objects are assumed to collide.

4. *Sphere to cone*: In this case, the set of inequalities (3) has to be checked in order to examine collision.

$$Cxz = \sqrt{Cx^2 + Cz^2}, a = \frac{h}{r_c}, \vartheta = \arctan(a), h_2 = \frac{r_s}{\cos(\vartheta)} + h,$$

$$b = \tan(90 - \vartheta), h3 = r \cdot b$$

$$(1) - r_s < Cy < 0, Cxz < r_c$$

$$(2)\sqrt{(Cxz - r_c)^2 + Cy^2} < r_s.$$

$$(3)\sqrt{Cxz^2 - (Cy - h)^2} < r_x$$

$$(4)Cy > 0, Cy + a \cdot Cxz < h$$

$$(5)Cy > 0, Cy + a \cdot Cxz < h_2, Cy + b \cdot Cxz < h, Cy + b \cdot Cxz > h3$$

(3)

where r_s the radius of the sphere, r_{cyl} the radius of the cylinder and r_c the radius of the cone. In case that any of the five conditions (1),..,(5) is true, the objects are assumed to collide.

Points, lines and planes are examined separately as special cases. Specifically, a point is assumed to be a sphere of 3 cm radius, a line is assumed to be a cylinder of 2 cm radius and a plane is assumed as a parallelepiped of 2 cm height.

Haptic Interaction Agent

The (Haptic Interaction Agent) HIA is responsible for returning force feedback to the user, providing sufficient data to the Geometry Construction Agent and triggering the appropriate actions according to the user input. Thus the HIA is responsible to allow the users draw lines, insert points on surfaces, and perform Boolean operations between couples of objects. The environment supports different layers in order to provide an easier way of interaction to the user. The user can select one layer as active and multiple layers as visible. The HIA returns feedback only when the hand is in contact to objects of visible layers and actions of the user modify the active layer. The user can move objects or groups of objects from one layer to another.

The HIA receives collision information from the collision detection sub-component and is responsible to trigger actions in the haptic environment and send haptic feedback to the user. Feedback is send to the fingers that touch any visible geometry in the scene or a button of the toolbar menu. Geometries that belong to an invisible layer cannot be touched or modified by the user. Especially, interaction with the toolbar exists only for the index finger. The HIA decides when geometries in the scene are grasped or released by the user hand. To grasp an object the user must touch the object with the thumb and index fingertips. To release an object the index and thumb fingers should retain from touching the object. In order to support easier grasping of Points, lines and planes, these are treated as special cases. As already mentioned, the point is assumed as a sphere of 3cm radius, the line as a cylinder of 3cm radius and the plane as a parallelepiped with 2cm height. Additionally, points have increased priority in terms of grasping, so that when a point resides close to or at a larger object's surface the user can grasp the point and not the object.

Boolean operations are performed between objects selected by the user. The operations are performed using rendering techniques for contractive solid geometry [11] based on the stencil buffer functionality. Thus, the result of a Boolean operation does not change the geometries but only the visualization result. This allows the user to change the relative position of an object (part in the Boolean operation) and view correctly the changes in the screen.

User Interface – Stereo View

The user interface is based on haptic interaction with the environment. The toolbar resides on the top of the visible area. The user can touch it and press any button on it. Depending on the working mode, the user can touch, grasp and move, reshape or select geometries. There are four working modes: The 'Move mode', where the user can grasp and move visible objects, the 'Reshape mode', where the user can grasp modifier points and reshape the geometry, the 'Delete mode', where the user select an object to delete and the 'Select mode' where the user can select multiple objects in the scene in order to perform an action

Toolbar Menu

The user can select a variety of options from the Toolbar using the index fingertip. When the fingertip collides with a button for a period longer than 600msec a sound is produced and the function of the button is activated. The supported functions and the toolbar menu structure follow (Fig. 3).

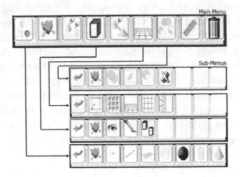

Fig. 3. Toolbar menu and first order submenus

The main menu has the following options: (i) Insert Object, (ii) Move Object, (iii) Multiple Select, (iv) Layer, (v) Reshape Object, (vi) Grid, (vii) Boolean operation, (viii) Measure and (ix) Delete Object. All submenus contain a "Back" button so that the user can move to a higher-level menu and the "Move Object" button.

1. *Insert Object:* the button enables a submenu that contains all the supported primitives and each of the primitive buttons enables a submenu that contains all the supported ways to construct the primitives as they were described in the "Geometry Construction Agent" section.
2. *Move Object:* Allows the user to grasp and move visible objects. Changes the working mode to 'Move'.
3. *Multiple Select:* Allows the user to select objects from the scene. Changes the working mode to 'Select'.
4. *Layer Menu:* Enables a submenu that allows the user to select the active layer, the visible layers and to move objects from one layer to another. The software supports eight predefined layers. This is due to the interface restrictions (number of buttons on the toolbar).
5. *Reshape:* The user can select an object using the index finger and then modify its shape using the "modifier points" as described in the "Geometry Construction Agent" section (Fig. 2).
6. *Grid:* Enables a submenu that allows the user to activate or deactivate snapping to grid and show or hide grid on the coordinate planes, or a three-dimension grid.
7. *Boolean Operation:* Allows the user to select the Boolean operation to be performed between selected objects. Supported operations are: 'or', 'and' and 'subtraction'. The user can cancel the Boolean operation.
8. *Measure:* Measures the distance between two points. The user presses the measurement button and selects the two points. The result is shown to the left bottom of the screen. The mode is set to 'Select'.
9. *Delete:* Allows the user to delete an object. The user presses the button on the toolbar and selects the object to delete. The working mode is initially set to 'Delete'. When the user deletes an object the mode is set to 'Move'.

Stereo View

In order to increase the immersion of the user, the system supports also stereoscopic vision. Shutter glasses and a Head Mounted Display (HMD) are used providing stereoscopic visual feedback. The stereoscopic view helps the user understand the exact position of the hand and the geometries in the scene. Thus, it helps the user to avoid mistakes that may occur from illusions and occlusions while working on a perspective 2D graphical environment. Using the shutter glasses in combination with a large projection screen, allows many users to view the working scenario. In this way, while one user is working on a scene others can view the actions and intervene. The geometrical objects are drawn semi-transparent so that the user can view all the objects at the same time. This makes the use of the environment easier, because users do not need to change the angle of view or hide objects in the scene in order to manipulate objects placed at the rear part of the scene. The students can walk around the large screen table any time during the session, and perceive the displayed objects in real 3D on the projection table using special shutter glasses, which is an attractive and spectacular way.

Test Cases

The Learning Environment for Geometry Teaching has been evaluated with students of secondary school in Greece. Two relatively simple scenarios were tested in order to identify the interest of the students and the overall performance of the system. The aim of the scenarios was not to teach the students three-dimensional Euclidian geometry, but to identify the feasibility of such a system in secondary school education and the acceptance of the system by the target users. In both cases shutter glasses and large projection screen were used. The test setup configuration is presented in Fig. 4. In the following the two test scenarios used in the experiment are described in detail.

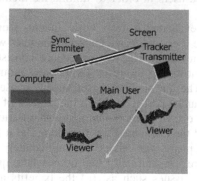

Fig. 4. Test case setup configuration

In the *first scenario* the user is asked to create an environment following a number of instructions. Initially the user is asked to insert two points into a layer and then hide it. Then they should insert a Sphere into a different layer and create a plane tangent to the sphere. In the following the user is asked to check if the line that connects the two points intersects with the plane and to measure the distance between the points.

This scenario lets the user understand the concept of layers. The user must hide a layer, change the active layer, create the sphere and the plane, and makes the layer visible again in order to create a line and check if it intersects with the plane.

In order to perform all the operations the user needs to understand and use the haptic interface and have basic knowledge on three-dimensional Euclidian geometry. Furthermore in order to create the tangent plane, the user must insert a point on the surface of the sphere and make a plane perpendicular to the line that connects the center of the sphere and the point on the surface.

The aim of the first scenario used is to assist the students to understand the usefulness of layers in order to create scenes in a three dimensional environment and to examine the usability of the introduced haptic user interface.

According to the *second scenario* a tutorial presented as an interactive animation introduces elliptic, hyperbolic and parabolic intersections of the cone. The user selects the objects and performs Boolean operations between the geometrical objects. This is a demonstration scenario were everyone can see the shape of a plane cutting a cone or a cylinder.

The aim of this scenario is to assist students understand Boolean operations, which are used in CAD packages nowadays, to learn about intersection curves of surfaces of second order and to experiment with intersections in order to understand how a) Boolean operations work, b) to construct surface intersections and c) to learn and experiment with the mathematical theory behind intersections of second order surfaces.

Discussion and Conclusions

All aforementioned steps were deemed necessary in order to develop a realistic virtual environment for the education of three-dimensional geometry, which can offer adequate functionality for end-users in order to familiarize themselves with the technology.

The system has been evaluated in tests with students from secondary schools in Thessaloniki, Greece. The users that participated in the tests were interviewed using a two-part structured questionnaire. The test procedure consisted of two phases. The first phase was carried out during the tests. Users were inquired to reply to specific questions for each test. The questionnaire used in this phase consisted of a part focused on usability issues and a part focused on the interest of the user in participating to the particular test. The questionnaire contained also questions to the test observers, e.g. if the user performed the task correctly, how long did it take him/her to perform the task, etc. The second phase was carried out immediately after the tests using the "After Tests Questionnaire". Specifically, the users where questioned after finishing all the tests about general issues such as: (a) the benefits and limitations that they foresee on this technology, (b) the usability of the system for training applications, (c) other tests and applications that they would like to experiment with the technology, if any, etc.

The system evaluation results have shown that users consider it very innovative and satisfactory in terms of providing a more efficient learning approach (constructive learning) to solve well-known geometry problems. The percentage of the satisfied students was reported to be 87%. The evaluation procedure has revealed the need of a multi-user training system in order to enhance the collaboration between students. This need is expected to drive our future plans for the improvement of the usability of the system.

References

1. Burdea, G. C. (1994). Force and touch feedback for virtual reality, Wiley-Interscience Publication.
2. Kaufmann Hannes, Dieter Schmalstieg, Michael Wagner, "Construct3D: A Virtual Reality Application for Mathematics and Geometry Education, Education and Information Technologies", January 2001.
3. Schmalstieg, D., Fuhrmann, A., Hesina, G., Szalavari, Z., Encarnação, M., Gervautz, M., and Purgathofer, W. The Studierstube AR Project. PRESENCE: Teleoperators and Virtual Environments 11(1), pp. 32-54, MIT Press, 2002.
4. VRMath: http://cobia.ed.qut.edu.au/~andy/vrmath/index.php
5. Annie Tat, "Edutainment through Geometry Visualization", October 26, 2001
   http://pages.cpsc.ucalgary.ca/~annie/502/proposal.htm
6. Taxén G. & Naeve, A., "CyberMath – A Shared 3D Virtual Environment for Exploring Mathematics", Geometric Algebra - New Foundations, New Insights, Siggraph2000, New Orleans July 2000.
7. Teixeira F., Silva R. and Silva T., "The Use of Virtual Reality in Virtual Learning Environment", Proc. ICEE 2000, 2000.
8. Immersion Technologies Inc., CyberGlove Haptic Device,
   http://www.immersion.com/3d/support/documentation.php
9. Immersion Technologies Inc. (2000), Virtual Hand Suite 2000 user & programmers guide,
   http://www.immersion.com/3d/support/documentation.php
10. Ascension Technologies Corp., MotionStar Wireless™ Installation and Operation Guide, 2000.
11. SGI http://www.sgi.com/software/opengl/advanced96/node33.html

A Multi-criteria Protocol for Multi-agent Negotiations

Nikolaos F. Matsatsinis and Pavlos Delias

Technical University of Crete
Decision Support Systems Laboratory
University Campus, 73100, Chania, Greece
{nikos,mirouvor}@ergasya.tuc.gr

Abstract. Negotiation processes are often characterized by conflicts of interests of the negotiating parts. However, it is possible to mitigate these conflicts, if we support the negotiation process with a well-structured model. This area of interest has large occupied the scientists of Group Decision Support Systems (GDSS) and particularly those who focus on the Negotiation Support Systems (NSS). In this paper, we propose an experimental multi-criteria prototype negotiation protocol which allows agents to follow a process, in order to end up with an optimal decision. The proposed model is able to estimate agents' preferences and suggest a convenient solution.

1 Introduction – Background

Scientists from intelligent agents' scientific area as well as those from distributed artificial intelligence area postulate that autonomy is one of the fundamental constituent parts of agents. This is the way that agents are able to develop a particular attitude towards their goals. However, in many cases, agents interact with other agents, who, in their turn, have similar autonomy; indeed this interaction is necessary because of the limitations – constraints in agents' skills or resources. So, whenever agents try to communicate, a negotiation process takes place.

Kersten et al. [10] have defined negotiation as a form of a decision-making involving two or more parties who cannot make decisions independently and are required to make concessions to achieve agreement. D. G. Pruit [6] describes negotiation as a process by which a joint decision is made by two or more parties. The parties first verbalize contradictory demands and then move towards agreement by a process of concession making or search for new alternatives. Research on negotiating suggests that face-to-face parties have difficulty in bargaining in ways that allow them to identify tradeoffs and that this leads to inefficient outcomes and lost opportunities. Most realistic negotiations are not well structured and therefore require an well-defined context to guide the negotiation process. To address this problem, under negotiation analysis, efforts have been undertaken to search for tools to help negotiators achieve integrative outcomes.

Interest in using computers to enhance negotiations has lead to the development of a field commonly referred to as Negotiation Support Systems (NSS). They are a subset of group decision support systems (GDSS) and include an electronic communication component and a decision support system (DSS) module. Therefore, the core elements of a NSS provide a comprehensive system to support the entire negotiation process [1],[9]. The field of NSS is rapidly developing from specialized expert sys-

G.A. Vouros and T. Panayiotopoulos (Eds.): SETN 2004, LNAI 3025, pp. 103–111, 2004.

tems that help in preparing for negotiation to mediation and interactive systems that restructure the way negotiations occur [2].

In the context of the current study, we propose an innovative methodology based on multi-agent technology. This methodology meditates on three broad and very important areas (Jennings et al. [14]):

1. What negotiation protocol will be used?
2. What are the issues over which negotiation takes place?
3. What reasoning model will the agents employ?

In section 2.1 we declare the rationale of the protocol as well as the variables that it uses, while in paragraph 2.2 we explain the steps of the negotiation's process. Section 2.3 is devoted to the negotiators' evaluation model. At the end of this study, we criticize the model and figure out its perspectives.

2 The Negotiation Protocol

2.1 Defining the Method and Making the Concessions

The method describes an iterative process which works towards a consensus among the negotiators. The negotiation protocol we suggest is based on a multi-criteria approach. There are still some requirements:

1. The decision that has to be made is the choice of one of the predefined alternatives. This is the fact that will lead us to a guided solution on an ill-structured problem. However, this case imposes the following requirement: The final choice has to be one of the predefined alternatives. Negotiators do not have the ability to combine each alternative's best characteristics in order to shape a new one. So, the final solution is certainly the best among the already formulated alternatives, but we can not be sure if this solution is also globally optimal.
2. As the method is based in a multi-criteria approach, the decision criteria have to fulfill the three fundamental principles as declared by Roy [4]: Monotony, exhaustively and non-pleonasm. In addition, the protocol we propose demands these criteria to be the same for all the negotiators. All the negotiators have to utilize the same scale to evaluate each criterion. Namely, the margin utility functions for each criterion are explicitly defined before the beginning of the process. Of course, each negotiator can construe the importance and the purpose of each criterion according to his beliefs.
3. We consider that negotiators act in a reasonable and rational way. This attitude should dominate in their decisions about the ranking of the alternatives, in their definitions of the criteria thresholds and generally, in the entire negotiation process. The final objective must be to reach consensus.

Holding in mind the constraints – requirements of the method, let us define the variables that the method employs: Let

M   to be the number of the negotiators
A   the set of the alternatives
k   number of the alternatives
G   the evaluation criteria set
n   the total of the criteria

c_{ij} alternative's i performance in criterion j   , $i \in A$, $j \in G$

b_{jm} weight of the criterion j as declares by negotiator m   , $j \in G$, $m \in M$

$\overline{b}_j$ mean weight of the criterion j

σ_j standard deviation of the criterion j

R_i alternative's i score   , $i \in A$

2.2 The Proposed Methodology

The negotiation protocol's flow chart is illustrated in Figure 1. This paragraph explains step by step the negotiation process:

- **Step 1:** *Input Data.* Data needed as input consist of the criteria data, the alternatives' data and the negotiators' preferences data. Analyzing these requirements, we end up with the final data categories: As far as it is concern the criteria, the process demands their scales (one scale can be either quantitative or qualitative) and their marginal utility functions. While the criteria scales are the same for every negotiator, their marginal utility functions can vary according to the decision makers' attitude. As regards the alternatives' data, each alternative must have a certain performance (grade) in every criterion. Moreover, the negotiators should declare an indicative ranking of the alternatives. This ranking is used by the protocol to evaluate negotiators' preferences and should indicate preference or indifference between the alternatives. Finally, the negotiators should also declare the criteria thresholds. These thresholds reveal the minimum (if the criterion monotony is ascending) or the maximum (if the criterion monotony is descending) accepted value for every criterion.

- **Step 2:** *Implementing UTA II method to estimate criteria weights.* The method implements UTA II [13], [19] once for each negotiator. This way, the method estimates each negotiator's criteria weights. Hence, by the end of this step, a table dimensioned [M+2,n] (where M is the total of the negotiators and n the number of the evaluation criteria) is available to the protocol. The rows of this table represent the negotiators and each column denotes a criterion. Thereby, cell m_j includes the weight for the criterion j, as it was estimated by UTA, for the negotiator m. Obviously, the sum for each row is 1. The last two rows contain the mean weight for each criterion and its standard deviation.

- **Step 3:** *Formulation of the global aggregative function to evaluate the alternatives.* In this step we use the results of the Step 2. We are able therefore to express the global function as follows :

$$R_i = \sum_{j=1}^{n} \left(\overline{b}_j - \sigma_j \right) c_{ij} \qquad i \in A, j \in G \tag{1}$$

This score displays in a way how commonly accepted is every alternative.

- **Step 4:** *Ranking the alternatives.* The method ranks the alternatives according to the score R_i that they achieved during the previous step. The final ranking is a descending order of the alternatives, so that the alternative with the biggest score is first in this rank.

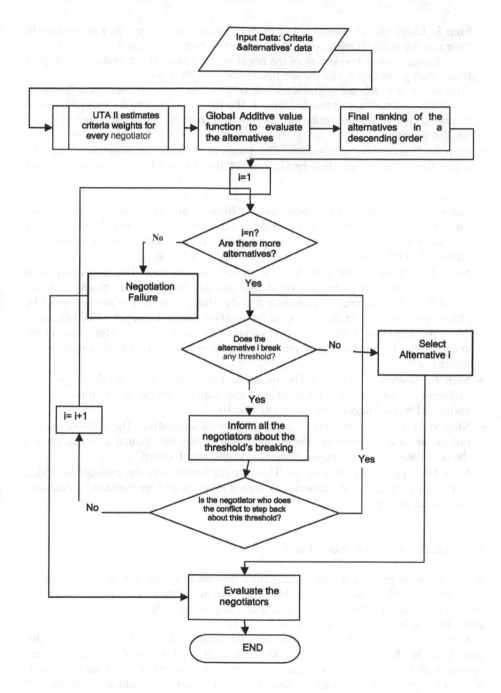

Fig. 1. Negotiation's Protocol Flow Chart.

– **Step 5:** *Check the alternatives*. The model checks one by one every alternative in their ranking order. If there is no other alternative then go to step 8
  Does the alternative breaks any of the negotiators' thresholds as declared in step 1? If not, then go to step 9, else the method keeps on with step 6.
  The protocol check the negotiators one by one, therefore, if there is a threshold breaking, that means that this breaking is the first met. If there are many threshold breakings about the same criterion, these will be met during the next step of the iterative process.
– **Step 6:** *Negotiators' information*. The protocol informs the negotiators that the alternative currently checked breaks one of the thresholds. This communication process is implemented through a message that contains the following fields: Which alternative is currently checked, what was the rank of this alternative, the negotiator that broke the threshold and his history (history means here how many times has this particular negotiator brake criteria threshold before), the negotiator's criterion threshold that was violated and finally the distance between negotiator's threshold and the alternative's performance in this criterion.
– **Step 7:** *Negotiate with the decision maker (negotiator)*. The negotiator who blocked the process (being informed that his threshold was the block) is being asked if he is attainable to reconsider that threshold's value. The answer could be either "yes" or "no". In the "no" case the method returns to step 5 while in case of "yes" the negotiator's threshold is set equal to the alternative's performance in the criterion that the breaking took place. The process reveals its iterative style by returning to step 5.
– **Step 8:** *Negotiation Failure*. The model is not capable to solve the negotiation problem. Actually, there is no alternative that satisfies all the negotiators' requirements. Inform the negotiators and go to step 10.
– **Step 9:** *Select the alternative*. Select the current alternative. The method worked out the negotiation problem. The protocol has chosen the optimal solution. Inform the negotiators about the negotiation success and step forward.
– **Step 10:** *Negotiators' evaluation*. The process implements the evaluation model. The results are sent to the negotiators with a message and are posted to a database. End of the process.

2.3 Negotiators' Evaluation Model

In a negotiation process, its outcome is fully dependent on the negotiators, no matter what the protocol is. Moreover, in this study, the negotiation takes place among humans, so it is not a great sin to suppose that a negotiator would behave the same way every time he is involved in a negotiation process.

Consider the above, and we realize how important is to evaluate the humans that participate in the negotiation. Such an evaluation method should reveal how cooperative or how reactive a negotiator is. The method should reward the negotiators who let the process flow towards a consensus but the method should also "punish" the negotiators who obstruct the process and keep the negotiation away from a final (optimal) solution. This model could be used in future negotiations processes as it provides an actual "preference" of the negotiators. So, humans that stand against consensus should have fewer possibilities to join a future negotiation process.

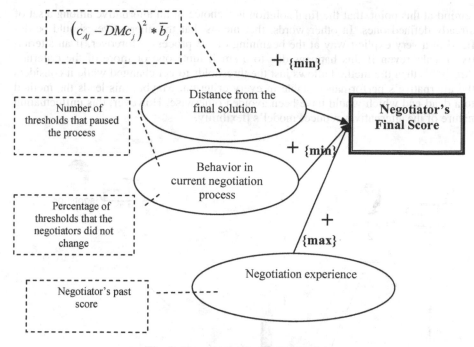

Fig. 2. Negotiators' Evaluation Model.

The model we propose is illustrated in figure 2. Three main aspects configure the final score for each negotiator, these are: the distance between the negotiator's preferences from the final solution, the will for co-operation that the negotiator demonstrated through this process and finally, his negotiating behavior during past processes. These aspects participate to the final score's definition by certain weights. In order to estimate these weights, it is possible to implement once again UTA II method, or just any other analytical regression's method.

3 Conclusions

This study tried to adjust a multi-criteria model into a negotiation process. This model utilizes an analytical – synthetic approach, since it implements UTA II method [13], [19]. The methodology proposed could be implemented through the internet and work efficiently.

However, there are some constraints that this model imposes. First of all, the negotiators (decision makers) must agree to a multi-criteria view of the problem. In such a view, the most critical step is to define the decision's criteria. Hence, the negotiators should only agree to these criteria but they do not have to also agree to the criteria's marginal utility functions, since the methodology allows these functions to vary. Usually, the decision's criteria are globally accepted when they are imposed by some extraneous factors (e.g. real world's demands). This is a fact that limits system's independency. One constraint added, is the way of the alternatives' definition. We shall remind at this point, that the final solution is a choice of an alternative among a set of already defined ones. In other words, that means that the alternatives should be defined in a very explicit way at the beginning of the process. Moreover, if an alternative breaks (even if this happens due to a small hint) one or more of the criteria's thresholds then the method allows just the thresholds to get changed while it considers the alternative's performance stable in every criterion. Maybe, this leads the method to a dead-end which would have been avoided otherwise. However, this unfluctuating nature of the alternatives reduces model's flexibility.

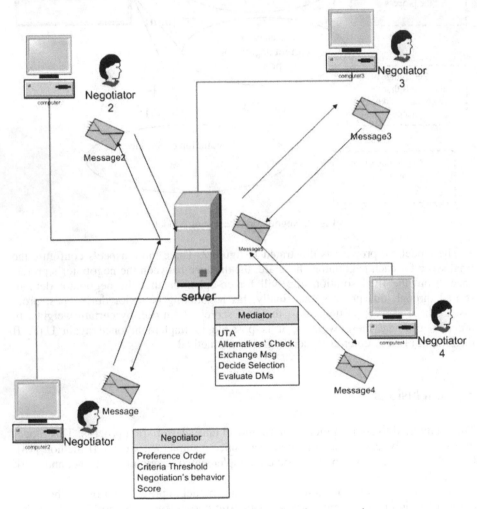

Fig. 3. Multi-agent Implementation through an internet environment.

Furthermore, the protocol proposed, demands a mediator. The mediator's role is a really important one as the mediator is responsible for the communication among agents (negotiators), the final choice as well as for the negotiators' evaluation. He is the supervisor of the process, so it is necessary for him to be fair and reliable. If this is not what happens, then we can certainly doubt about the model's efficiency and functionality. Besides, if the mediator is absent, the process can not function.

The model was designed to support two kinds of problems as they are defined by the decision making theory. To be more specific, the model actually arrives to a solution by choosing one alternative among a set of them (so choice is the first kind of problem) but, in a less direct way, it provides a ranking of the alternatives according to the score that they achieved. This ranking of course could be considered as an indicative solution, since we should never forget that each negotiator has the right to declare his own veto through criteria's thresholds.

Concluding, we should insist on how interesting is to implement this model through internet's technology. This would lead the method to a great functionality and usefulness. This vision's diagram is illustrated in figure 3. Multi-agent technology is one of the most applicable technologies that could be used to design and implement this protocol, since the protocol's design was keeping in mind such an approach. In case, since the model has not been tested yet, the results of the implementation and the use of such a negotiation protocol are yet to come.

References

1. A. Anson, M.T. Jelassi, A developmental framework for computer-supported conflict resolution, European Journal of Operational Research 46 (2). 1990, pp. 181-199.
2. A.Rangaswamy, G.R. Shell, Using computers to realize joint gains in negotiations: toward an electronic bargaining table, Management Science 43 (8), 1997, pp. 1147-1163.
3. B. Espinasse, G. Picolet, E. Chouraqui, Negotiation Support Systems: A multi-criteria and multi-agent approach, European Journal of Operational Research 103, pp. 389-409, 1997.
4. B. Roy, Méthodologie Multicritère d'Aide a la Decision, Economica, Paris, 1985.
5. Corkill, D.D. and Lesser, V.R., 1983. The use of meta-level control for coordination in a distributed problem solving network. Proc. Int. Jt. Conf. Artif. Intell, 8th, Karlsruhe, Germany: 784-756.
6. D.G. Pruit, Negotiation Behaviour, Academic Press 1981
7. D. Zeng and K. Sycara. How can an agent learn to negotiate. In J. Mueller, M.Wooldridge, and N. Jennings, editors, Intelligent Agents III. Agent Theories, Architectures, and Languages, number 1193 in LNAI, pages 233{244. Springer Verlag, 1997.
8. Despotis, D.K., Yannacopoulos D., Zopounidis C., A review of the UTA multicriteria method and some improvements, Decision Support Systems Laboratory, working paper 90-04, 1990.
9. E. Carmel, B. Herniter, J.F. Nunamaker Jr., Labor management contract negotiations in an electronic meeting room: a case study, Group Decision and Negotiation 2 (1), 1993, pp. 27-60.
10. G. Kersten, W. Michalowski, S. Szpakowicz, Z. Koperzac, Restructurable representations of negotiation, Management Science 37 (10), 1991, pp. 1269-1290.
11. H. Wang, S. Liao, L. Liao, Modeling constraint based negotiating agents, Decision Support Systems 33, pp. 201-217, 2002.
12. J. Lim, A conceptual framework on the adoption of negotiation support systems, Information and Software Technology 45,pp. 469–477, 2003.
13. Jacquet-Lagrèze, E. and J.Siskos (1982), Assessing a set of additive utility functions for multicriteria decision making: The UTA method, European Journal of Operational Research, no. 10(151-164).
14. Jennings, N.R., Sycara, K., Wooldridge, M.. 1998 A Roadmap of Agent Research and Development. Int Journal of Autonomous Agents and Multi-Agent Systems 1 (1):7-38.

15. J-P. Brans, B. Mareschal, Ph. Vincke, PROMETHEE : A new family of outranking methods in multi-criteria analysis, in: J-P. Brans (Ed.), Operational Research '84, North-Holand, 1984, pp. 408-421.
16. K. Sycara, Problem restructuring in negotiation, Management Science 37 (10), pp.1248–1268, 1991.
17. L.A. Busch, I.J. Horstmann, The game of negotiations: ordering issues and implementing agreements, Games and Economic Behavior 41 (2002) 169–191
18. P. Faratin, C. Sierra, N.R. Jennings, Negotiation Decision Functions for Autonomous Agents, preprint submitted to Elsevier Science, 1997.
19. Siskos, Y. (1980), Comment modéliser les préférences au moyen de functions d'utilité additives, RAIRO Recherche opérationnelle, 14, 53-82.

Clustering XML Documents by Structure

Theodore Dalamagas[1], Tao Cheng[2], Klaas-Jan Winkel[3], and Timos Sellis[1]

[1] School of Electr. and Comp. Engineering
National Technical University of Athens, Greece
{dalamag,timos}@dblab.ece.ntua.gr
[2] Dept. of Computer Science
University of California, Santa Barbara, USA
taocheng@cs.ucsb.edu
[3] Faculty of Computer Science
University of Twente, the Netherlands
winkel@cs.utwente.nl

Abstract. This work explores the application of clustering methods for grouping structurally similar XML documents. Modeling the XML documents as rooted ordered labeled trees, we apply clustering algorithms using distances that estimate the similarity between those trees in terms of the hierarchical relationships of their nodes. We suggest the usage of tree structural summaries to improve the performance of the distance calculation and at the same time to maintain or even improve its quality. Experimental results are provided using a prototype testbed.

Keywords: XML, structural similarity, tree distance, structural summary, clustering

1 Introduction

The XML language is becoming the standard Web data exchange format, providing interoperability and enabling automatic processing of Web resources. While the processing and management of XML data are popular research issues [1], operations based on the structure of XML data have not yet received strong attention. Applying structural transformations and grouping together structurally similar XML documents are examples of such operations. Structural transformations are the basis for using XML as a common data exchange format. Grouping together structurally similar XML documents refers to the application of clustering methods using distances that estimate the similarity between tree structures in terms of the hierarchical relationships of their nodes.

There are many cases where clustering by structure can assist application tasks. Many XML documents are constructed from data sources without DTDs. XTRACT [2] and DDbE[1] are systems that automatically extract DTDs from XML documents. Identifying groups of XML documents of similar structure can be useful for such systems, where a collection of XML documents should be

---

[1] http://www.alphaworks.ibm.com/tech/DDbE

G.A. Vouros and T. Panayiotopoulos (Eds.): SETN 2004, LNAI 3025, pp. 112–121, 2004.
© Springer-Verlag Berlin Heidelberg 2004

first grouped into sets of structurally similar documents and then a DTD can be assigned to each set individually. Moreover, since the XML language can encode hierarchical data, clustering XML documents by structure can be exploited in any application domain that needs management of hierarchical structures. For example, the discovery of structurally similar macromolecular tree patterns, encoded as XML documents, is a critical task in bioinformatics [3, 4].

The main contribution of this work is a methodology for grouping structurally similar XML documents. Modeling XML documents as rooted ordered labeled trees, we face the 'clustering XML documents by structure' problem as a 'tree clustering' problem. We propose the usage of tree structural summaries that have minimal processing requirements instead of the original trees representing the XML documents. We present a new algorithm to calculate tree edit distances and define a structural distance metric to estimate the structural similarity between the structural summaries of two trees. Using this distance, we perform clustering of XML data sets. Experimental results indicate that our algorithm for calculating the structural distance between two trees, representing XML documents, provides high quality clustering and improved performance. Also, the usage of structural summaries to represent XML documents instead of the original trees, improves further the performance of the structural distance calculation without affecting its quality.

This paper is organized as follows. Section 2 presents background information on tree-like representation of XML data and analyzes tree editing issues. Section 3 suggests the tree structural summaries. Section 4 presents a new algorithm to calculate the tree edit distance between two trees and introduces a metric of structural distance. Section 5 analyzes the clustering methodology. Section 6 presents the evaluation results, and, finally, Section 7 concludes our work.

2   Tree Editing

The *XML data model* is a graph representation of a collection of atomic and complex objects, that without the IDREFS mechanism becomes a *rooted ordered labeled tree* [1]. Since we use such rooted ordered labeled trees to represent XML data, we exploit the notions of *tree edit sequence* and *tree edit distance* originating from editing problems for rooted ordered labeled trees [3]:

Definition 1. *Let T_1, T_2 be rooted ordered labeled trees. A tree edit sequence is a sequence of tree edit operations (insert node, delete node, etc) to transform T_1 to T_2.*

Definition 2. *Let T_1, T_2 be rooted ordered labeled trees. Assuming a cost model to assign costs for every tree edit operation, the tree edit distance between T_1 and T_2 is the minimum cost between the costs of all possible tree edit sequences that transform T_1 to T_2.*

All of the algorithms for calculating the edit distance for two ordered labeled trees are based on dynamic programming techniques related to the string-to-string correction problem [5]. [6] was the first work that defined the tree edit distance and provided algorithms to compute it, permitting operations anywhere in the tree. Selkow's [7] and Chawathe's (II) [8] algorithms allow insertion and deletion only at leaf nodes, and relabel at every node. The former has exponential complexity, while the latter is based on the model of edit graphs which reduces the number of recurrences needed. Chawathe's (I) algorithm [9] starts using a pre-defined set of matching nodes between the trees, and is based on a different set of tree edit operations than Chawathe's (II). It allows insertion and deletion only at leaf nodes. Zhang's algorithm [10] permits operations anywhere in the tree. We believe that using insertion and deletion only at leaves fits better in the context of XML data. For example it avoids deleting a node and moving its children up one level. The latter destroys the membership restrictions of the hierarchy and thus is not a 'natural' operation for XML data. In this work, we consider Chawathe's (II) algorithm as the basic point of reference for tree edit distance algorithms, since it permits insertion and deletion only at leaves and is the fastest available.

3   Tree Structural Summaries

Nesting and repetition of elements is the main reason for XML documents to differ in structure although they come from a data source which uses one DTD. A *nested-repeated node* is a non-leaf node whose label is the same with the one of its ancestor. Following a pre-order tree traversal, a *repeated node* is a node whose path (starting from the root down to the node itself) has already been traversed before. Figure 1 has an example of redundancy: trees T_1 and T_3 differ because of nodes A (nested-repeated) and B (repeated). We perform *nesting reduction* and *repetition reduction* to extract structural summaries for rooted ordered labeled trees which represent XML documents. Both kind of reductions need only a pre-order traversal each on the original tree.

Nesting reduction reduces the nesting in the original tree so that there will be no nested-repeated nodes. We traverse the tree using pre-order traversal to detect nodes which have an ancestor with the same label in order to move up their subtrees. This process may cause non-repeating nodes to be repeating nodes. This is why we deal first with the nesting reduction and then with the repetition reduction. Repetition reduction reduces the repeated nodes in the original tree. We traverse the tree using pre-order traversal, too, ignoring already existed paths and keeping new ones, using a hash table.

Figure 1 presents an example of structural summary extraction from T_1. Applying the nesting reduction phase on T_1 we get T_2, where there are no nested-repeated nodes. Applying the repetition reduction on T_2 we get T_3 which is the structural summary tree without nested-repeated and repeated nodes.

4   Tree Structural Distance

Our approach for the tree edit distance between structural summaries of rooted ordered labeled trees uses a dynamic programming algorithm which is close

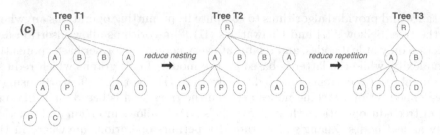

Fig. 1. Structural summary extraction.

to Chawathe's algorithm (II) [8] in terms of the tree edit operations that are used. However, the recurrence that we use does not need the costly edit graph calculation of the latter (see the timing analysis in Section 6.1). Permitted tree edit operations are:

1. *insertion*: Let n be a node with label l to be inserted as the i_{th} child of node p in tree T. After the insertion operation $ins(n, i, p, l)$, n is a new leaf node with label l. We assign cost $cost\_ins = 1$ to the insertion operation.
2. *deletion*: Let n be a leaf node in tree T. The deletion operation $del(n)$ will remove n from T. We assign cost $cost\_del = 1$ to the deletion operation.
3. *update*: Let n be a node with label l. The update operation $upd(n, m)$ will change the label l to m for node n. We assign cost 1 to the update operation if $l \neq m$ or 0 if $l = m$.

$CalculateDistance(r_1, r_2)$ calculates the tree edit distance of T_1 and T_2, with roots r_1 and r_2, respectively:

```
int CalculateDistance(TreeNode s, TreeNode t) {
    int[][] D=new int[numOfChildren(s)+1][numOfChildren(t)+1];
    D[0][0]=UpdateCost(LabelOf(s), LabelOf(t));
    for (int i=1; i≤numOfChildren(s); i++)
        D[i][0]= [i-1][0]+numOfNodes(s_i);
    for(int j=1; j≤numOfChildren(t); j++)
        D[0][j]=D[0][j-1]+numOfNodes(t_j);
    for (int i=1; i≤numOfChildren(s); i++)
        for (int j=1; j≤numOfChildren(t); j++)
            D[i][j]=Min(D[i-1][j-1]+CalculateDistance(s_i,t_j),
                    D[i][j-1]+numOfNodes(t_j),
                    D[i-1][j]+numOfNodes(s_i));
    Return D[numOfChildren(s)][numOfChildren(t)];
}
```

where: s_i (t_j) is the i_{th} (j_{th}) subtree of node s (t), $numOfChildren(s)$ returns the number of child nodes of node s, $numOfNodes(s)$ returns the number of nodes of the subtree rooted at s, $UpdateCost(LabelOf(s), LabelOf(t))$ returns the cost to make the label of node s the same as the label of node t (1 if $LabelOf(s) = LabelOf(t)$ or 0 otherwise).

In the algorithm, $D[i][j]$ keeps the tree edit distance between tree T_1 with only its first i subtrees and tree T_2 with only its first j subtrees. $D[0][0]$ keeps the distance between T_1 and T_2, having only their roots (initially 0, since the examined trees are assume to have same roots). Since the cost of an insert or delete operation is 1, we use $numOfNode(s_i)$ to represent the cost to delete the ith subtree of node s and $numOfNodes(t_j)$ to represent the cost to insert the jth subtree of node t. The main for nested loop first calculates the tree edit distance between tree T_1 with only its first subtree and tree T_2 with only its first subtree, then the distance between T_1 with only its first two subtrees and T_2 with only its first subtree, etc. In the end, the algorithm returns the distance between T_1 with all its subtrees and T_2 with all its subtrees. We call the function CalculateDistance once for each pair of nodes at the same depth in the 2 structural summary trees, so the complexity is $O(MN)$, where M is the number of nodes in the tree rooted at s, and N is the number of nodes in the tree rooted at t.

Let $\mathcal{D}$ be the tree edit distance between two trees T_1 and T_2 calculated from the previous algorithm. Using $\mathcal{D}$, we can now define the *structural distance* $\mathcal{S}$ between two structural summaries for rooted ordered labeled trees which represent XML documents.

Definition 3. *Let T_1 and T_2 be two structural summaries for rooted ordered labeled trees that represent two XML documents, $\mathcal{D}(T_1, T_2)$ be their tree edit distance and $\mathcal{D}_{max}(T_1, T_2)$ be the maximum cost between the costs of all possible sequences of tree edit operations that transform T_1 to T_2. The structural distance $\mathcal{S}$ between T_1 to T_2 is defined as $\mathcal{S}(T_1, T_2) = \frac{\mathcal{D}(T_1, T_2)}{\mathcal{D}_{max}(T_1, T_2)}$.*

To calculate $\mathcal{D}_{max}$, we calculate the cost to delete all nodes from T_1 and insert all nodes from T_2. The $\mathcal{S}(T_1, T_2)$ is low when the trees have similar structure and high percentage of matching nodes and high when the trees have different structure and low percentage of matching nodes (0 (1) is the min (max) value).

5 Clustering Trees

We chose single link hierarchical method [11, 12] to be the basic clustering algorithm for the core part of the experiments for our work since it has been shown to be theoretical sound, under a certain number of reasonable conditions [13]. We implemented a single link clustering algorithm using Prim's algorithm for computing the minimum spanning tree (MST) of a graph [14]. Given n structural summaries of rooted labeled trees that represent XML documents, we form a fully connected graph G with n vertices and $n(n-1)/2$ weighted edges. The weight of an edge corresponds to the structural distance between the vertices (trees) that this edge connects. The single link clusters for a *clustering level* l_1 can be identified by deleting all the edges with weight $w \geq l_1$ from the MST of G. The connected components of the remaining graph are the single link clusters.

A stopping rule is necessary to determine the most appropriate clustering level for the single link hierarchies. C−index [15, 16] exhibits excellent performance. C−index is a vector of pairs $((i_1, n_1), (i_2, n_2), \ldots$, where $i_1, i_2, \ldots$ are the values of the index and $n_1, n_2, \ldots$ the number of clusters in each clustering arrangement. We can calculate i_1 for the first pair (i_1, n_1) of C-index vector as follows: $i_1 = (d_w - min(d_w))/(max(d_w) - min(d_w))$, where

1. $d_w = Sum(d_{w_1}) + Sum(d_{w_2}) + \ldots + Sum(d_{w_{N_1}})$, with $Sum(d_{w_i})$ to be the sum of pairwise distances of all members of cluster $C_i, 1 \leq i \leq n_1$,
2. $max(d_w)$ $(min(d_w))$: the sum of the n_d highest (lowest) pairwise distances in the whole set of data, that is, sort distances, higher first, and take the Top-n_d (Bottom-n_d) sum, given that $n_d = c_1 * (c_1 - 1)/2 + c_2 * (c_2 - 1)/2 + \ldots + c_{n_1} * (c_{n_1} - 1)/2$ (c_i = number of members in cluster C_i).

Similarly we can calculate $i_2, i_3, \ldots$. We adopt $C - index$ in the single link procedure by calculating its values, varying the clustering level in different steps. The number of clusters with the lowest C−Index is chosen [16].

6 Evaluation

We implemented a testbed to perform clustering on synthetic and real data, using structural distances[2]. Two sets of 1000 synthetic XML documents were generated[3] from 10 real-case DTDs[4], varying the parameter *MaxRepeats* to determine the number of times a node will appear as a child of its parent node. For real data set we used 150 documents from the ACM SIGMOD Record and ADC/NASA[5]. We chose single link to be the basic clustering algorithm for the core part of the experiments.

While checking time performance is straightforward, checking clustering quality involves the calculation of metrics based on an a priori knowledge of which documents should be members of the appropriate cluster. Such knowledge, in turn, presumes that we have a mapping between original DTDs and extracted clusters. To get such a mapping, we derived a DTD D_c for every cluster C and mapped it to the most similar of the original DTDs, by calculating the structural distance between the tree derived from D_c and each of the trees derived from the original DTDs[6].

To evaluate the clustering results, we used two metrics quite popular in the research area of information retrieval: *precision PR* and *recall R* [13].For an extracted cluster C_i that corresponds to a DTD DTD_i let (a) a_i be the number of the XML documents in C_i that were indeed members of that cluster (correctly clustered), (b) b_i be the number XML documents in C_i that were not members of that cluster (misclustered) and (c) c_i be the number of XML documents not in C_i, although they should be C_i's members. Then $PR = \frac{\sum_i a_i}{\sum_i a_i + \sum_i b_i}$ and $R = \frac{\sum_i a_i}{\sum_i a_i + \sum_i c_i}$. High precision means high accuracy of the clustering task

---

[2] All the experiments were performed on a Pentium III 800MHz, 192MB RAM.
[3] www.alphaworks.ibm.com/tech/xmlgenerator
[4] from www.xmlfiles.com and http://www.w3schools.com
[5] www.acm.org/sigmod/record/xml and xml.gsfc.nasa.gov respectively.
[6] using www.alphaworks.ibm.com/tech/DDbE

for each cluster while low recall means that there are many XML documents that were not in the appropriate cluster although they should have been. High precision and recall indicate excellent clustering quality.

Notice that there might be the case where there are clusters not mapped to any of the original DTD. We treated all XML documents in such clusters as misclustered documents. Based on the above, we present the timing analysis for calculating structural distances and the clustering results.

6.1   Timing Analysis

We compared (a) the time to derive the 2 structural summaries from 2 rooted ordered labeled trees representing 2 XML documents plus (b) the time to calculate the structural distance between those 2 summaries, vs the time to calculate the structural distance between 2 rooted ordered labeled trees of 2 XML documents.

We tested both Chawathe's algorithm and our algorithm using randomly generated XML documents, with their nodes ranging from 0 to 2000. This timing analysis gives an indication of how fast a file for storing pairwise structural distances is constructed. Such a file can then be used as an input in any clustering algorithm to discover clusters. A clustering algorithm needs to calculate $N * (N - 1)/2$ pairwise structural distances, N the number of documents to be clustered.

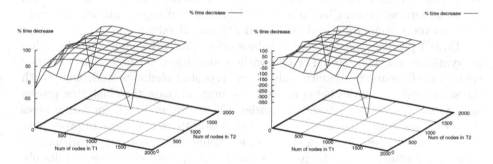

Fig. 2. % time decrease for structural distance calculation using tree summaries instead of using the original trees (Chawathe's algorithm).

Fig. 3. % time decrease for structural distance calculation using tree summaries instead of using the original trees (our algorithm).

Figures 2 and 3 show the % time decrease for calculating the structural distance between 2 XML documents using their summaries instead of using the original trees, for Chawathe's algorithm and our algorithm. Using summaries, the decrease lays around 80% on average for Chawathe's and around 50% on average for our algorithm.

To give a sense about the scaling of the calculations, Figure 4 presents the % time decrease for calculating the structural distance between 2 XML documents, using our algorithm instead of Chawathe's algorithm (52% on average).

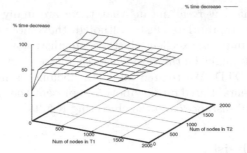

Fig. 4. % time decrease for structural distance calculation using our algorithm instead of Chawathe's.

Chawathe's algorithm is significantly slower than our algorithm due to the pre-calculation of the editgraph (see Section 2). We estimated that the editgraph calculation spends more then 50% of the time needed for the overall distance calculation.

6.2   Clustering Evaluation

We performed single link clustering on synthetic and real data, using structural distances returned from Chawathe's algorithm and our algorithm, with or without structural summaries, and calculated PR and R values.

Table 1 presents the PR and P values using Chawathe's and our algorithm on synthetic and real data. For Chawathe's algorithm, we note that for small trees ($maxRepeats = 3$) with only a few repeated elements and, thus, with the structural summaries being actually the original trees, the clustering results are the same with or without summaries. On the other hand, for larger trees ($maxRepeats = 6$) with many repeated elements there is a clear improvement using summaries, especially in the precision value (PR). For our algorithm, we note that summary usage keeps the already high quality clustering results obtained by clustering without using summaries. In any case, with or without summary, our algorithm shows better clustering quality either with small trees and only a few repeated elements or with larger trees and many repeated elements. We note that PR and R reach excellent values. For real data, summary usage maintains the already high quality clustering results obtained without using summaries.

The evaluation results indicate that structural summaries maintain the clustering quality, that is they do not hurt clustering. Thus, using structural summaries we can clearly improve the performance of the whole clustering procedure, since the decrease on the time needed to calculate the tree distances using summaries is high (see Section 6.1). Furthermore, in any case, with or without summaries, our algorithm shows excellent clustering quality, and improved performance compared to Chawathe's. Prelimianty tests with other clustering algorithms showed similar results.

Table 1. P, PR values for clustering synthetic and real data.

Synthetic data (CH: Chawathe's algorithm, D: our algorithm)	
CH without summaries ($maxRepeats = 3$)	**CH with summaries** ($maxRepeats = 3$)
$NumOfClusters = 11, Cluster. level = 0.37$	$NumOfClusters = 11, Cluster. level = 0.37$
$PR = 0.71, R = 0.90$	$PR = 0.71, R = 0.90$
CH without summaries ($maxRepeats = 6$)	**CH with summaries** ($maxRepeats = 6$)
$NumOfClusters = 11, Cluster. level = 0.51$	$NumOfClusters = 12, Cluster. level = 0.50$
$PR = 0.58, R = 0.89$	$PR = 0.83, R = 0.96$
D without summaries ($maxRepeats = 3$)	**D with summaries** ($maxRepeats = 3$)
$NumOfClusters = 11, Cluster. level = 0.51$	$NumOfClusters = 11, Cluster. level = 0.51$
$PR = 1.00, R = 0.98$	$PR = 1.00, R = 0.98$
D without summaries ($maxRepeats = 6$)	**D with summaries** ($maxRepeats = 6$)
$NumOfClusters = 12, Cluster. level = 0.61$	$NumOfClusters = 11, Cluster. level = 0.56$
$PR = 1.00, R = 0.97$	$PR = 1.00, R = 0.98$
Real data (CH: Chawathe's algorithm, D: our algorithm)	
CH without summaries	**CH with summaries**
$NumOfClusters = 4, Cluster. level = 0.63$	$NumOfClusters = 3, Cluster. level = 0.63$
$PR = 1.00, R = 0.98$	$PR = 1.00, R = 1$
D without summaries	**D with summaries**
$NumOfClusters = 4, Cluster. level = 0.63$	$NumOfClusters = 3, Cluster. level = 0.63$
$PR = 1.00, R = 0.98$	$PR = 1.00, R = 1$

7   Conclusions

This work presented a framework for clustering XML documents by structure, exploiting distances that estimate the similarity between tree structures in terms of the hierarchical relationship of their nodes.

Modeling XML documents as rooted ordered labeled trees, we faced the 'clustering XML documents by structure' problem as a 'tree clustering' problem. We proposed the usage of tree structural summaries that have minimal processing requirements instead of the original trees representing the XML documents. Those summaries maintain the structural relationships between the elements of an XML document, reducing repetition and nesting of elements. Also, we presented a new algorithm to calculate tree edit distances and defined a structural distance metric to estimate the structural similarity between the summaries of two trees. We implemented a testbed to perform clustering on synthetic and real data, using structural distances. We provided timing analysis as well as precision PR and recall R values to evaluate each test case. Our results showed that structural summaries clearly improved the performance of the whole clustering procedure, since the decrease on the time needed to calculate the tree distances using summaries is high. On the other hand, summaries maintained the clustering quality. Moreover, our structural distance algorithm showed improved performance compared to Chawathe's.

To the best of our knowledge, the only work directly compared with ours is [17]. Their set of tree edit operations include two new ones which refer to whole trees rather than nodes. They preprocess the trees to detect whether a subtree is contained in another tree. Their approach requires the same amount of computation with Chawathe's algorithm. There are no results about PR and R values. In our work, we diminish the possibility of having repeated subtrees using structural summaries instead of expanding the tree edit operations. Summaries are used as an index structure to speed up the tree distance calculation. Such an approach has the advantage of being useful to reduce the performance cost in every algorithm that estimates the structural distance between trees.

To conclude, this work successfully applied clustering methodologies for grouping XML documents which have similar structure, by modeling them as rooted ordered labeled trees, and utilizing their structural summaries to reduce time cost while maintaining the quality of the clustering results. As a future work, we will explore properties that tree distances present. Also, we will test how our approach scales using larger data sets of XML documents.

References

1. S. Abiteboul, P. Buneman, D. Suciu, Data on the Web., Morgan Kaufmann, 2000.
2. M. Garofalakis, A. Gionis, R. Rastogi, S. Seshadri, K. Shim, XTRACT: A system for extracting document type descriptors from XML documents, in: Proceedings of the ACM SIGMOD Conference,Texas, USA, 2000.
3. D. Sankoff, J. Kruskal, Time Warps, String Edits and Macromolecules, The Theory and Practice of Sequence Comparison, CSLI Publications, 1999.
4. H. G. Direen, M. S. Jones, Knowledge management in bioinformatics, in: A. B. Chaudhri, A. Rashid, R. Zicari (Eds.), XML Data Management, 2003, Addison Wesley.
5. R. Wagner, M. Fisher, The string-to-string correction problem, Journal of ACM 21 (1) (1974) 168–173.
6. K. C. Tai, The tree-to-tree correction problem, Journal of ACM 26 (1979) 422–433.
7. S. M. Selkow, The tree-to-tree editing problem, Information Processing Letters 6 (1977) 184–186.
8. S. S. Chawathe, Comparing hierarchical data in external memory, in: Proceedings of the VLDB Conference, Edinburgh, Scotland, UK, 1999, pp. 90–101.
9. S. S. Chawathe, A. Rajaraman, H. Garcia-Molina, J. Widom, Change Detection in Hierarchically Structured Information, in: Proceedings of the ACM SIGMOD Conference, USA, 1996.
10. K. Zhang, D. Shasha, Simple fast algorithms for the editing distance between trees and related problems, SIAM Journal of Computing 18 (1989) 1245–1262.
11. E. Rasmussen, Clustering algorithms, in: W. Frakes, R. Baeza-Yates (Eds.), Information Retrieval: Data Structures and Algorithms, Prentice Hall, 1992.
12. M. Halkidi, Y. Batistakis, M. Vazirgiannis, Clustering algorithms and validity measures, in: SSDBM Conference, Virginia, USA, 2001.
13. C. J. van Rijsbergen, Information Retrieval, Butterworths, London, 1979.
14. J. C. Gower, G. J. S. Ross, Minimum spanning trees and single linkage cluster analysis, Applied Statistics 18 (1969) 54–64.
15. L. J. Hubert, J. R. Levin, A general statistical framework for accessing categorical clustering in free recall, Psychological Bulletin 83 (1976) 1072–1082.
16. G. W. Milligan, M. C. Cooper, An examination of procedures for determining the number of clusters in a data set, Psychometrika 50 (1985) 159–179.
17. A. Nierman, H. V. Jagadish, Evaluating structural similarity in xml documents, in: Proceedings of the WebDB Workshop, Madison, Wisconsin, USA, 2002.

Music Performer Verification
Based on Learning Ensembles

Efstathios Stamatatos and Ergina Kavallieratou

Dept. of Audio and Musical Instrument Technology
T.E.I. of Ionian Islands
28200, Lixouri
{stamatat,ergina}@teiion.gr

Abstract. In this paper the problem of music performer verification is introduced. Given a certain performance of a musical piece and a set of candidate pianists the task is to examine whether or not a particular pianist is the actual performer. A database of 22 pianists playing pieces by F. Chopin in a computer-controlled piano is used in the presented experiments. An appropriate set of features that captures the idiosyncrasies of music performers is proposed. Well-known machine learning techniques for constructing learning ensembles are applied and remarkable results are described in verifying the actual pianist, a very difficult task even for human experts.

1 Introduction

The printed score of a musical piece provides a representation of music that captures a limited spectrum of musical nuance. This means that if the exact information represented in the printed score is accurately transformed into music by an ideal performer, the result would sound mechanical or unpleasant. The interpretation of the printed score by a skilled artist always involve continuous modification of important musical parameters, such as tempo and loudness, according to the artist's understanding of the structure of the piece. That way the artist stresses certain notes or passages deviating from the printed score. Hence, *expressive music performance* is what distinguishes one performer from another in the interpretation of a certain musical piece.

Because of its central role in our musical culture, expressive performance is a central research topic in contemporary musicology. One main direction in empirical performance research aims at the development of rules or principles of expressive performance either with the help of human experts [5] or by processing large volumes of data using machine learning techniques [12,13]. Obviously, this direction attempts to explore the similarities between skilled performers in the same musical context. On the other hand, the differences in music performance are still expressed generally with aesthetic criteria rather than quantitatively. The literature in this topic is quite limited. In [8] an exhaustive statistical analysis of temporal commonalities and differences among distinguished pianists' interpretations of a well-known piece is presented and

G.A. Vouros and T. Panayiotopoulos (Eds.): SETN 2004, LNAI 3025, pp. 122–131, 2004.
© Springer-Verlag Berlin Heidelberg 2004

the individuality of some famous pianists is demonstrated. A computational model that distinguishes two pianists playing the same pieces based on measures that represent the deviation of the performer from the score plus measures that indicate the properties of the piece is presented in [10]. Results of limited success in the identification of famous pianists' recordings based on their style of playing have been reported in [14].

This paper is an attempt to quantify the main parameters of expressive performance that discriminate between pianists playing the same musical pieces. Specifically, our aim is to develop a music performer verification system, that is, given a certain performance of a musical piece and a set of candidate pianists the task is to examine whether or not a particular pianist is the actual performer. To this end, machine learning techniques are used for taking advantage of different expressive performance features by combining a number of independent simple 'experts' [2]. The dimensions of expressive variation that will be taken into account are the three main expressive parameters available to a pianist: *timing* (variations in tempo), *dynamics* (variations in loudness), and *articulation* (the use of overlaps and pauses between successive notes).

The data used in this study consist of performances played and recorded on a Boesendorfer SE290 computer-monitored concert grand piano, which is able to measure every key and pedal movement of the artist with very high precision. 22 skilled performers, including professional pianists, graduate students and professors of the Vienna Music University, played two pieces by F. Chopin: the *Etude* op. 10/3 (first 21 bars) and the *Ballade* op. 38 (initial section, bars 1 to 45). The digital recordings were then transcribed into symbolic form and matched against the printed score semi-automatically. Thus, for each note in a piece we have precise information about how it was notated in the score, and how it was actually played in a performance. The parameters of interest are the exact time when a note was played (vs. when it 'should have been played' according to the score) – this relates to tempo and timing –, the dynamic level or loudness of a played note (dynamics), and the exact duration of played note, and how the note is connected to the following one (articulation). All this can be readily computed from our data.

In the following, the term *Inter-Onset Interval* (IOI) will be used to denote the time interval between the onsets of two successive notes of the same voice. We define *Off-Time Duration* (OTD) as the time interval between the offset time of one note and the onset time of the next note of the same voice. The *Dynamic Level* (DL) corresponds to the MIDI velocity of a note. The 22 pianists are referred by their code names (i.e., #01, #02, etc.).

2   Representation of Expressive Music Performance

If we define (somewhat simplistically) expressive performance as 'intended deviation from the score', then different performances differ in the way and extent the artist 'deviates' from the score, i.e., from a purely mechanical ('flat') rendition of the piece, in terms of timing, dynamics, and articulation. In order to be able to compare performances of pieces or sections of different length, we need to define features that characterize and quantify these deviations at a global level, i.e., without reference to individual notes and how these were played.

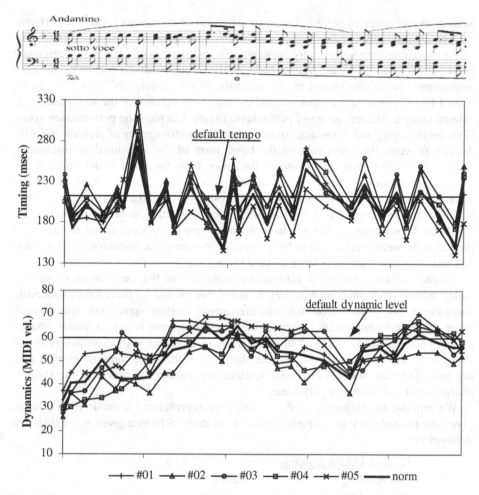

Fig. 1. Timing and dynamics variations for the first 30 soprano notes of the *Ballade* (score above) as performed by pianists #01-#05. Default tempo and dynamic level, and performance norm derived by pianists #06-#10 are depicted as well.

Figure 1 depicts the performances of the first 30 soprano notes of *Ballade* by the pianists #01-#05 in terms of timing (expressed as the inter-onset interval on the sixteenth-note level) and dynamics. The default tempo and dynamic level according to a pre-specified fixed interpretation of the score correspond to straight lines. As can be seen, the music performers tend to deviate from the default interpretation in a similar way in certain notes or passages. In the timing dimension, the last note of the first bar is considerably lengthened (last note of the introductory part) while in the dynamics dimension the first two bars are played with increasing intensity (introductory part) and the 2nd soprano note of the 5th bar is played rather softly (a phrase boundary). Although the deviation of the real performances from the score can capture some general stylistic properties of the performer, it seems likely that it would heavily depend on the structure of the piece (i.e., similar form of deviations for all the performers, presenting peaks and dips in the same notes or passages).

For discriminating successfully between different performers, we need a reference point able to focus on the *differences* between them rather than on *common expressive performance principles* shared by the majority of the performers. This role can be played by the *performance norm*, i.e. the average performance of the same piece calculated using a different group of performers. Figure 1 depicts the performance norm, in terms of timing and dynamics, calculated by the performances of pianists #06-#10. As can be seen, the norm follows the basic form of the individual performances. Therefore, the deviation of a given performance from the norm is not dramatically affected by structural characteristics of the piece. Consequently, the deviations of different performers from the norm are not necessarily of similar form (peaks and dips in different notes or passages) and the differences between them are more likely to be highlighted. Norm-based features have been compared to score-based features and proved to be more reliable and stable especially in intra-piece conditions, i.e., training and test cases taken from the same musical piece [11].

Another valuable source of information comes from the exploitation of the so-called melody lead phenomenon, that is, notes that should be played simultaneously according to the printed score (chords) are usually slightly spread out over time. A voice that is to be emphasized precedes the other voices and is played louder. Studies of this phenomenon [7] showed that melody lead increases with expressiveness and skill level. Therefore, deviations between the notes of the same chord in terms of timing and dynamics can provide useful features that capture an aspect of the stylistic characteristics of the music performer.

We propose the following global features for representing a music performance, given the printed score and a performance norm derived from a given set of different performers:

Score deviation features:

$D(\text{IOI}_s, \text{IOI}_m)$ timing
$D(\text{IOI}_s, \text{OTD}_m)$ articulation
$D(\text{DL}_s, \text{DL}_m)$ dynamics

Norm deviation features:

$D(\text{IOI}_n, \text{IOI}_m)$ timing
$D(\text{OTD}_n, \text{OTD}_m)$ articulation
$D(\text{DL}_n, \text{DL}_m)$ dynamics

Melody lead features:

$D(\text{ON}_{xy}, \text{ON}_{zy})$ timing
$D(\text{DL}xy, \text{DL}zy)$ dynamics

where $D(x, y)$ (a scalar) denotes the deviation of a vector of numeric values x from a reference vector y, IOI_s and DL_s are the nominal inter-onset interval and dynamic-level, respectively, according to the printed score, IOI_n, OTD_n, and DL_n are the inter-onset interval, the off-time duration, and the dynamic-level, respectively, of the performance norm, IOI_m, OTD_m, and DL_m are the inter-onset interval, the off-time duration, and the dynamic-level, respectively, of the actual performance, and ON_{xy}, and DL_{xy} are the on-time and the dynamic-level, respectively, of a note of the x-th voice within the chord y.

3 The Learning Model

The presented problem is characterized by the extremely limited size of training data as well as the instability of some of the proposed features (i.e., score deviation measures). These characteristics suggest the use of an ensemble of classifiers rather than a unique classifier. Research in machine learning [1] has thoroughly studied the construction of meta-classifiers, or learning ensembles. In this study, we take advantage of such techniques, constructing an ensemble of classifiers derived from two basic strategies:

- *Subsampling the input features.* This technique is usually applied when multiple redundant features are available. In our case, the input features cannot be used concurrently due to the limited size of the training set (i.e., only a few training examples per class are available) and the consequent danger of overfitting the training set.
- *Subsampling the training set.* This technique is usually applied when unstable learning algorithms are used for constructing the base classifiers. In our case, a subset of the input features (i.e., the score deviation measures) is unstable – their values can change drastically given a slight change in the selected training segments.

Given the scarcity of training data and the multitude of possible features, we propose the use of a relatively large number of rather simple individual base classifiers or 'experts', in the terminology of [2]. Each expert is trained using a different set of features and/or parts of the training data. The features and sections of the training performances used for the individual experts are listed in table 1. C_{11} is based on the deviation of the performer from the norm. C_{21}, C_{22}, C_{23}, and C_{24} are based on the deviation of the performer from the score and are trained using slightly changed training sets (because the norm features are known to be unstable relative to changes in the data). The training set (see next section) was divided into four disjoint subsets and then four different overlapping training sets were constructed by dropping one of these four subsets (i.e., cross-validated committees). Finally, C_{31}, C_{32}, C_{33}, C_{34}, and C_{35} are based on melody lead features. The last column in table 1 shows the accuracy of each individual expert on the training data (estimated via leave-one-out cross-validation). As can be seen, the classifier based on norm deviation features is by far the most accurate.

The classification method used for constructing the base classifiers is *discriminant analysis*, a standard technique of multivariate statistics. The mathematical objective of this method is to weight and linearly combine the input variables in such a way so that the classes are as statistically distinct as possible [3]. A set of linear functions (equal to the input variables and ordered according to their importance) is extracted on the basis of maximizing between-class variance while minimizing within-class variance using a training set. Then, class membership of unseen cases can be predicted according to the *Mahalonobis distance* from the classes' *centroids* (the points that represent the means of all the training examples of each class). The Mahalanobis distance d of a vector x from a mean vector m is as follows:

$$d^2 = (x - m)' C_x^{-1} (x - m)$$

where C_x is the covariance matrix of x. This classification method also supports the calculation of *posterior probabilities* (the probability that an unseen case belongs to a particular group) which are proportional to the Mahalanobis distance from the classes centroids. In a recent study [6], discriminant analysis is compared with many classification methods (coming from statistics, decision trees, and neural networks). The results reveal that discriminant analysis is one of the best compromises taking into account the classification accuracy and the training time cost. This old and easy-to-implement statistical algorithm performs better than many modern versions of statistical algorithms in a variety of problems.

Table 1. Description of the proposed base classifiers. The third column indicates the number of training examples (and their length in soprano notes) per class. The last column refers to their accuracy on the training data.

Code	Input features	Training examples	Accuracy (%)
C_{11}	$D(\text{IOI}_n, \text{IOI}_m), D(\text{OTD}_n, \text{OTD}_m), D(\text{DL}_n, \text{DL}_m)$	4x40	82.5
C_{21}	$D(\text{IOI}_s, \text{IOI}_m), D(\text{IOI}_s, \text{OTD}_m), D(\text{DL}_s, \text{DL}_m)$	12x10	50.8
C_{22}	$D(\text{IOI}_s, \text{IOI}_m), D(\text{IOI}_s, \text{OTD}_m), D(\text{DL}_s, \text{DL}_m)$	12x10	44.8
C_{23}	$D(\text{IOI}_s, \text{IOI}_m), D(\text{IOI}_s, \text{OTD}_m), D(\text{DL}_s, \text{DL}_m)$	12x10	46.7
C_{24}	$D(\text{IOI}_s, \text{IOI}_m), D(\text{IOI}_s, \text{OTD}_m), D(\text{DL}_s, \text{DL}_m)$	12x10	48.3
C_{31}	$D(\text{ON}_{1m}, \text{ON}_{2m}), D(\text{ON}_{1m}, \text{ON}_{3m}), D(\text{ON}_{1m}, \text{ON}_{4m})$	4x40	57.5
C_{32}	$D(\text{DL}_{1m}, \text{DL}_{2m}), D(\text{DL}_{1m}, \text{DL}_{3m}), D(\text{DL}_{1m}, \text{DL}_{4m})$	4x40	42.5
C_{33}	$D(\text{ON}_{1m}, \text{ON}_{2m}), D(\text{DL}_{1m}, \text{DL}_{2m})$	4x40	25.0
C_{34}	$D(\text{ON}_{1m}, \text{ON}_{3m}), D(\text{DL}_{1m}, \text{DL}_{3m})$	4x40	35.0
C_{35}	$D(\text{ON}_{1m}, \text{ON}_{4m}), D(\text{DL}_{1m}, \text{DL}_{4m})$	4x40	47.5

The combination of the resulting simple classifiers or experts is realized via a weighted majority scheme. The prediction of each individual classifier is weighted according to its accuracy on the training set. Both the first and the second choice of a classifier are taken into account. Specifically, the weight w_{ij} of the classifier C_{ij} is as follows:

$$w_{ij} = \frac{a_{ij}}{\sum_{xy} a_{xy}}$$

where a_{ij} is the accuracy of the classifier C_{ij} on the training set (see table 3). $a_{ij}/2$ is used to compute the weight for the second choice of a classifier. The classes can be ordered according to the votes they collect. Specifically, if $c_{ij}(x)$ is the prediction of the classifier C_{ij} for the case x and P is the set of possible classes (i.e., pianists) then the score for a class p is calculated as follows:

$$s_p(x) = \sum_{ij} w_{ij} \| c_{ij}(x) = p \| \quad p \in P$$

where $\|a=b\|$ is 1 if a is equal to b and 0 otherwise. The greater the score the more probable the pianist as the actual performer. Since both the first and second choices of each base classifier are taken into account, the highest possible score is 0.66 (first choice of all the classifiers) and the lowest is 0 (no first nor second choice of any classifier).

4 Music Performer Verification

In the following experiments, pianists #01-#12 will be used as the set of reference pianists to compute the 'norm performance', that is the average performance. The task will be to learn to distinguish pianists #13-#22. Chopin's *Ballade* op. 38 will be used as the training material, and the *Etude* op.10/3 as the test piece. Specifically, the training piece was divided into four non-overlapping segments, each including 40 soprano notes providing four training examples per class for the norm-based and the melody lead classifiers. As concerns the score-based classifiers, the training piece was divided into 16 non-overlapping segments, each including 10 soprano notes. These segments were grouped into four overlapping sets of training examples, leaving out four different segments each time (see table 1).

The task of music performer verification can be viewed as a two-class classification problem. Given a certain performance of the test piece (*Etude*) and a particular pianist (of the set #13-#22) the output of the proposed system will be either 1, i.e., the pianist in question is the actual performer, or 0, i.e., the pianist in question is not the actual performer. The implementation of a music performer verification system requires:

- The definition of a response function for a given pianist. For a given performance, this function should provide an indication of the degree at which the pianist is the actual performer. In this study, the output of the ensemble of classifiers, defined in the previous section is used as response function.
- The definition of a threshold value for this function. For a given performance, any pianist with score lower than the threshold is rejected.

Additionally, for measuring the accuracy of a music performer verification method as regards a certain pianist, False Rejection (FR) and False Acceptance (FA) can be used. These measures have been defined in and applied to areas of similar characteristics, such as speaker verification [4] and author verification [9] and are defined as follows:

FR = rejected performances of the pianist / total performances of the pianist
FA = accepted performances of other pianists / total performances of other pianists

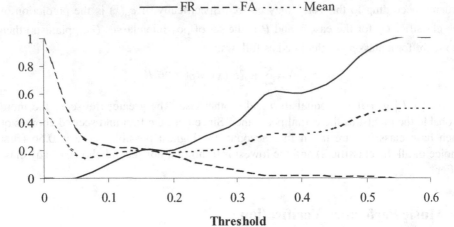

Fig. 2. FR, FA, and Mean error of the ensemble model for different threshold values.

For the appropriate selection of the threshold value, the mean error, i.e., (FR+FA)/2, is used. Figure 2 depicts the variation of the average FR, FA, and the mean error values for the performances of the test piece by pianists #13-#22 using threshold values ranging from 0 to 0.6. Since these pianists were taken into account for calculating the discriminant functions and consequently the score function, this evaluation is considered to be a closed-set one. As can be seen, low values of threshold correspond to minimal FR while high values of threshold correspond to minimal FA. The minimal mean error corresponds to the threshold value 0.1 corresponding to FR and FA values of 0.1 and 0.23, respectively.

The results of the method based on the ensemble of classifiers can be compared to the results of the individual base classifiers. In that case, each base classifier is used alone and the response function is the Mahalanobis distance from the centroids of each class. Table 2 shows the FR and FA values for each individual base classifier for a threshold value that minimizes the mean error. As can be seen, the model coming from the learning ensemble is much better as concerns both FR and FA.

5 Conclusion

We have proposed a computational approach to the problem of distinguishing music performers playing the same pieces focusing on the music performer verification task. A set of features that capture some aspects of the individual style of each performer is presented. Due to the limited available data and certain characteristics of the discriminating features, we proposed a classification model that takes advantage of machine learning techniques for constructing meta-classifiers.

The results show that the proposed learning model performs much better than any of the constituent base classifiers and provides another supporting case for the utility of ensemble learning methods, specifically, the combination of a large number of independent simple 'experts'. Moreover, it is demonstrated that the differences between music performers can be objectively quantified. While human experts use mostly aesthetic criteria for distinguishing different performers, it is shown that the individuality of each performer can be captured using machine-interpretable features.

Table 2. Average FA and FR values of the base classifiers and the ensemble model. In each model, a threshold value that minimizes mean error is used.

Classifier	FR	FA
Ensemble	0.10	0.23
C_{11}	0.30	0.31
C_{21}	0.40	0.34
C_{22}	0.60	0.40
C_{23}	0.40	0.33
C_{24}	0.50	0.37
C_{31}	0.40	0.31
C_{32}	0.30	0.33
C_{33}	0.40	0.38
C_{34}	0.50	0.36
C_{35}	0.50	0.32

The proposed system copes with a difficult musical task, displaying a remarkable level of accuracy. Imagine you first hear 10 different pianists performing one particular piece (and that is all you know about the pianists), and then you have to verify the hypothesis that a particular pianist is (or is not) the actual performer of a certain performance of another (and quite different) piece[1]. The comparison with human experts performing the same task is not straightforward. This is because it is very difficult to define what the similar conditions would be. How many times would the human-expert be allowed to listen to each of the training/test recordings? What would be the level of expertise of the listener? What would be the human-expert's prior knowledge of the piece? Would such a procedure be meaningful?

The reliability of our current results is still severely compromised by the very small set of available data. Substantial effort is required in order to collect and precisely measure a larger and more diverse set of performances by several pianists (on a computer-controlled piano). Studying famous pianists with this approach would require us to be able to precisely measure timing, dynamics, and articulation from sound recordings, which unfortunately still is an unsolved signal-processing problem.

Acknowledgement

This work was supported in part by the EU project HPRN-CT-2000-00115 (MOSART). Many thanks to Gerhard Widmer and Werner Goebl for preparing and providing the music performance data used in this study.

---

[1] The interested reader can attempt to follow this procedure. The digital recordings used in this study can be accessed at: http://www.ai.univie.ac.at/~wernerg/mp3.htm

References

1. Bauer, E., Kohavi, R.: An Empirical Comparison of Voting Classification Algorithms: Bagging, Boosting, and Variants. Machine Learning 39:1/2 (1999) 105-139
2. Blum, A.: Empirical Support for Winnow and Weighted-Majority Based Algorithms: Results on a Calendar Scheduling Domain. Machine Learning, 26:1 (1997) 5-23
3. Eisenbeis, R., Avery, R.: Discriminant Analysis and Classification Procedures: Theory and Applications, Lexington, Mass.: D.C. Health and Co. (1972)
4. Fakotakis, N., Tsopanoglou, A., Kokkinakis, G.: A Text-independent Speaker Recognition System Based on Vowel Spotting. Speech Communication 12 (1993) 57-68
5. Friberg, A.: Generative Rules for Music Performance: A Formal Description of a Rule System. Computer Music Journal, 15:2 (1991) 56-71
6. Lim, T., Loh, W., Shih, Y.: A Comparison of Prediction Accuracy, Complexity and Training Time of Thirty-Three Old and New Classification Accuracy. Machine Learning 40:3 (2000) 203-228
7. Palmer, C.: On the Assignment of Structure in Music Performance. Music Perception 14 (1996) 23-56
8. Repp, B.: Diversity and Commonality in Music Performance: An Analysis of Timing Microstructure in Schumann's 'Träumerei'. Journal of the Acoustical Society of America, 92:5 (1992) 2546-2568
9. Stamatatos E., Fakotakis, N., Kokkinakis, G.: Automatic Text Categorization in Terms of Genre and Author. Computational Linguistics 26:4 (2000) 471-495
10. Stamatatos, E.: A Computational Model for Discriminating Music Performers. Proc. of the MOSART Workshop on Current Research Directions in Computer Music (2001) 65-69
11. Stamatatos, E.: Quantifying the Differences Between Music Performers: Score vs. Norm. Proc. of the International Computer Music Conference (2002) 376-382
12. Widmer, G.: Using AI and Machine Learning to Study Expressive Music Performance: Project Survey and First Report. AI Communications 14 (2001) 149-162
13. Widmer, G.: Discovering Simple Rules in Complex Data: A Meta-learning Algorithm and Some Surprising Musical Discoveries. Artificial Intelligence 146:2 (2003) 129-148
14. Zanon, P., Widmer, G.: Recognition of Famous Pianists Using Machine Learning Algorithms: First Experimental Results. Proc. of the 14th Colloquium of Musical Informatics (2003)

Using the k-Nearest Problems
for Adaptive Multicriteria Planning

Grigorios Tsoumakas, Dimitris Vrakas, Nick Bassiliades, and Ioannis Vlahavas

Department of Informatics, Aristotle University of Thessaloniki
54124 Thessaloniki, Greece
{greg,dvrakas,nbassili,vlahavas}@csd.auth.gr
http://lpis.csd.auth.gr/

Abstract. This paper concerns the design and development of an adaptive planner that is able to adjust its parameters to the characteristics of a given problem and to the priorities set by the user concerning plan length and planning time. This is accomplished through the implementation of the k nearest neighbor machine learning algorithm on top of a highly adjustable planner, called HAP. Learning data are produced by running HAP offline on several problems from multiple domains using all value combinations of its parameters. When the adaptive planner HAP_{NN} is faced with a new problem, it locates the k nearest problems, using a set of measurable problem characteristics, retrieves the performance data for all parameter configurations on these problems and performs a multicriteria combination, with user-specified weights for plan length and planning time. Based on this combination, the configuration with the best performance is then used in order to solve the new problem. Comparative experiments with the statistically best static configurations of the planner show that HAP_{NN} manages to adapt successfully to unseen problems, leading to an increased planning performance.

1 Introduction

In domain independent heuristic planning there is a number of systems that their performance varies between best and worse on a number of toy and real-world planning domains. No planner has been proved yet to be the best for all kinds of problems and domains. Similar instability in their efficiency is also noted when different variations of the same planner are tested on the same problem, when the value of one or more parameters of the planner is changed. Although most planners claim that the default values for their options guarantee a stable and averagely good performance, in most cases fine tuning the parameters by hand improves the performance of the system for the given problem.

Few attempts have been made to explain which are the specific dynamics of a planning problem that favor a specific planning system and even more, which is the best setup for a planning system given the characteristics of the planning problem. This kind of knowledge would clearly assist the planning community in producing flexible systems that could automatically adapt themselves to each problem, achieving best performance.

G.A. Vouros and T. Panayiotopoulos (Eds.): SETN 2004, LNAI 3025, pp. 132–141, 2004.

Some promising past approaches towards this goal, followed the methodology of utilizing Machine Learning in order to infer rules for the automatic configuration of planning systems [1],[2]. However, these approaches exhibited two important problems. The first one is that they used a fixed policy for what can be considered as a good solution to a planning problem and didn't allow users to specify their own priorities concerning the speed of the planner and the quality of the plans, which are frequently contradictious. The second one is that learning is very computationally expensive and thus extending the knowledge base of the planner is a non-trivial task.

This paper presents a different approach to adaptive planning that is based on instance-based learning in order to deal with the two aforementioned problems. Specifically, the k nearest neighbor machine learning algorithm is implemented on top of the HAP highly adjustable planner. Learning data are produced by running HAP offline on 30 problems from each one of 15 domains (i.e. 450 problems) using 864 combinations of values for its 7 parameters. When the adaptive planner HAP_{NN} is faced with a new problem, it retrieves the steps and time performance data for all parameter configurations of the k nearest problems and performs a multi-criteria combination, with user-specified weights. The best configuration is then used for running the planner on the new problem. Most importantly, the planner can store new problems and train incrementally from them, making the system highly extensible.

The performance of HAP_{NN} was thoroughly evaluated through experiments that aimed at showing the behavior of the adaptive system in new problems. The results showed that the system managed to adapt quite well and the use of different weights for steps and time had the expected effect on the resulting plan length and planning time of the adaptive planner.

The rest of the paper is organized as follows: Section 2 overviews related work combining Machine Learning and Planning. The planning system used for the purposes of our research and the problem analysis done for deciding the problem attributes are presented in Section 3 and 4 respectively. Section 5 describes in detail the methodology we followed for designing the adaptive planner. The experimental results are presented and discussed in the Section 6 and finally, Section 7 concludes the paper and poses future research directions.

2 Related Work

Machine learning has been exploited extensively in the past to support Planning systems in many ways. There are three main categories of approaches based on the phase of planning that learning is applied to and the consequent type of knowledge that is acquired.

Domain knowledge is utilized by planners in pre-processing phases in order to either modify the description of the problem in a way that will make it easier for solving it or make the appropriate adjustments to the planner to best attack the problem [1].

Table 1. The seven planning parameters and their valuesets

Name	Value Set
Direction	$\{0, 1\}$
Heuristic	$\{1, 2, 3\}$
Weights (w_1 and w_2)	$\{0, 1, 2, 3\}$
Penalty	$\{10, 100, 500\}$
Agenda	$\{10, 100, 1000\}$
Equal Estimation	$\{0, 1\}$
Remove	$\{0, 1\}$

Control knowledge can be utilized during search in order to either solve the problem faster or produce better plans. For example, the knowledge extracted from past examples can be used to refine the heuristic functions or create a guide for pruning non-promising branches [3].

Finally, optimization knowledge is utilized after the production of an initial plan, in order to transform it in a new one that optimizes certain criteria, e.g. number of steps or resources usage [4].

A concise survey of related work on learning-powered adaptive planners can be found in [2]. Furthermore, a very detailed and analytical survey of past approaches on Machine Learning and Planning has been presented in [5].

3   The HAP Planner

The proposed methodology has been applied to HAP (Highly Adjustable Planner), a customizable planning system, embodying the search modules of the BP planner [6], the heuristics of AcE [7] and several add-ons that improve the speed and the accuracy of the planner. The customization of the system is feasible through the 7 planning parameters, outlined in Table 1, which can be set by the user.

The first one refers to the planning direction, which can be either backward (0) or forward (1). The second parameter allows the user to select one of the three available heuristic functions in order to use it as a guide during the search. The third parameter sets the values for the weights used during planning in the weighted $A*$ search technique. The fourth parameter sets the penalty put on states violating pre-computed fact orderings, while the next one sets the size of the planning agenda (maximum number of states in the frontier set). The last two parameters enable or disable techniques for overcoming plateaus in the search space and simplifying the definition of subproblems, respectively. More details about the planning parameters and their possible setups can be found in [2].

4   Problem Characteristics

The purpose of this research effort was to discover interesting knowledge that associates the characteristics of a planning problem with the parameters of HAP and leads to good performance. Therefore, a first necessary step that we performed was a theoretical analysis of a planning problem, in order to discover salient features that could influence the choice of parameters of HAP.

Our main concern was to select attributes that their values are easily calculated and not complex attributes that would cause a large overhead in the total planning time. Therefore, most of the attributes come from the PDDL files, which are the default input to planning systems, and their values can be calculated during the standard parsing process. We also included a small number of attributes which are closely related to specific features of the HAP planning system such as the heuristics or the fact-ordering techniques. In order to calculate the values of these attributes, the system must perform a limited search but the overhead is negligible compared to the total planning time.

A second concern which influenced the selection of attributes was the fact that the attributes should be general enough to be applied to all domains and their values should not depend so much on the size of the problem. Otherwise the knowledge learned from easy problems would not be applied effectively to difficult ones. For example, instead of using the number of mutexes (mutual exclusions between facts) in the problem as an attribute that strongly depends on the size of the problem (larger problems tend to have more mutexes), we divide it by the total number of dynamic facts and this attribute (mutex density) identifies the complexity of the problem without taking into account whether it is a large problem or a not. This is a general solution followed in all situations where a problem attribute depends nearly linearly on the size of the problem.

Taking all the above into consideration we resulted in a large set of 35 measurable characteristics, which can be divided in three categories: The first category refer to simple and easily measured characteristics of planning problems, e.g. number of actions per operator, that source directly from the input files. The second category consists of more sophisticated characteristics that arise from features of modern planners, such as mutexes or orderings (between goals and initial facts). The last category contains attributes that can be instantiated after the calculation of the heuristic functions, such as the estimated distance between the initial state and the goals. The list of the attributes and a more detailed analysis on their purpose can be found in [2].

5 The HAP$_{\text{NN}}$ Adaptive Multi-criteria Planner

HAP$_{\text{NN}}$, is an extension of HAP that implements the k Nearest Neighbor (kNN) machine learning algorithm in order to learn the necessary knowledge for auto-tuning its planning parameters to best fit the morphology of each planning problem. This section presents the process of preparing the learning data for the kNN algorithm, the adaptation functionality of the planner when faced with a new problem and its offline incremental training capability.

5.1 Preparing the Training Data

Training data were produced by running the HAP planner on 450 planning problems (30 problems from each one of 15 domains) using all 864 combinations of values for its 7 planning parameters. For each run of HAP, we recorded the features of the problem, the performance of the planner (steps of the resulting plan and required planning time) and the configuration of parameters. This process is illustrated in Figure 1.

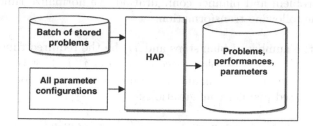

Fig. 1. Preparing the training data

The training data were organized as a multi-relational data set, consisting of 2 primary tables, problems (450 rows) and parameters (864 rows), and a relation table performances (450*864 rows), in order to save storage space and enhance the search for the k nearest neighbors and the retrieval of the corresponding performances. The tables were implemented as binary files, with the performances table being sorted on both the problem id and the parameter id.

One issue that had to be dealt is how to record the cases where HAP failed to find a solution due to memory or time limitations. Note here that an upper limit of 60 seconds was imposed on all runs of the planner. In such cases a special number (999999), was recorded for both plan steps and planning time.

5.2   Online Planning Mode

Given a new planning problem, HAP_{NN} first calculates the values of the problem characteristics. Then the kNN algorithm is engaged in order to retrieve the ids of the k nearest problems from the problems file. k is an input parameter of HAP_{NN} whose default value is set to 7 (see section 6.1). In the implementation of kNN we use the Euclidean distance measure with the normalized values of the problem attributes to calculate the nearest problem.

Using the retrieved ids and taking advantage of the sorted binary file, HAP_{NN} promptly retrieves the performances for all possible configurations in a k*864 2-dimensional matrix. The next step is to combine these performances in order to suggest a single parameter configuration with the optimal performance, based on past experience of the k nearest problems.

Optimal is however susceptible to user preferences, i.e. a shorter plan is usually preferred than a longer one, but there are cases (e.g. real time systems) where the planner must respond promptly even if the plan isn't very good. Since, these two criteria (fast planning, short plans) are contradicting, it is up to the domain expert to set up his/her priorities. HAP_{NN} has the advantage of letting the user express his/her priorities through two parameters: w_s (weight of steps) and w_t (weight of time). The overall planner performance is calculated as a multi-criteria combination of the steps and time based on these weights. Specifically, the straightforward Weighted Average method is used to obtain an overall score from steps and time. This requires the normalization of the criteria. For each problem and planner configuration, we normalize time and steps according to the following transformation:

- Let S_{ij} be the number of plan steps and T_{ij} be the required time to build it for problem i ($i=1..k$) and planner configuration j ($j=1..864$).
- First, we find the shortest plan and minimum planning time for each problem among the tested planner configurations:

$$S_i^{min} = \underset{i}{argmin} S_{ij} \qquad T_i^{min} = \underset{i}{argmin} T_{ij}$$

- Then, we normalized the results by dividing the minimum plan length and minimum planning time of each run with the corresponding problem value. For the cases where the planner had not managed to find a solution, the normalized values of steps and time were set to zero.

$$S_{ij}^{norm} = \begin{cases} 0 & \text{if } S_{ij} = 999999 \\ \frac{S_i^{min}}{S_{ij}} & \text{otherwise} \end{cases} \qquad T_{ij}^{norm} = \begin{cases} 0 & \text{if } T_{ij} = 999999 \\ \frac{T_i^{min}}{T_{ij}} & \text{otherwise} \end{cases}$$

- Subsequently HAP$_{\text{NN}}$ calculates an overall score as the average of the normalized criteria weighted by the user-specified weights:

$$Score_{ij} = ws * S_{ij}^{norm} + wt * T_{ij}^{norm}$$

We can consider the final $k*864$ 2-dimensional matrix as a classifier combination problem, consisting of k classifiers and 864 classes. We can combine the decisions of the k classifiers, using the average Bayes rule, which essentially comes down to averaging the planner scores across the k nearest problems and selecting the decision with the largest average. Thus, HAP uses the parameter configuration j ($j=1..864$) with the largest C:

$$C_j = \frac{1}{k} \sum_{i=1}^{k} Score_{ij}$$

The whole process for the online planning mode of HAP$_{\text{NN}}$ is depicted in Figure 2. It is worth noting that HAP$_{\text{NN}}$ actually outputs an ordering of all parameter configurations and not just one parameter configuration. This can be exploited for example in order to output the top 10 configurations and let the user decide amongst them. Another useful aspect of the ordering, is that when the first parameter configuration fails to solve the problem within certain time, then the second best could be tried. Another interesting alternative in such a

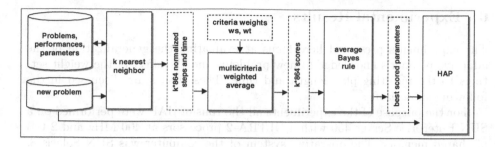

Fig. 2. Online planning mode

case is the change of the weight setting so that time has a bigger weight. The effect of the weights in the resulting performance is empirically explored in the experimental results section that follows.

The computational cost of training the HAP$_{NN}$ planner is zero, as no training is involved in lazy learning approaches such as the kNN algorithm. However, there is some cost involved during classification, which is however negligible (1 second on a typical Pentium III system at 1Ghz), and can be reduced using a suitable data indexing structure. In contrast, past rule learning approaches [1], [2] exhibit a very large training time (a few hours on a typical Pentium III system at 1Ghz) and a negligible classification time (20 milliseconds on a typical Pentium III system at 1Ghz). Our approach sacrifices a small amount of response time, but gains tremendously in training performance. This way it solves the impractical problems of rule learning approaches, like incremental training and training with user-specified weights for steps and time.

5.3   Offline Incremental Mode

HAP$_{NN}$ can be trained incrementally with each new planning problem that arises. Specifically, the planner stores each new planning problem that it examines, so that it can later train from it offline. As in the training data preparation phase, training consists of running the HAP planner on the batch of newly stored problems using all 864 value combinations of the 7 parameters. For each run, the features of the problem, the performance of the planner (steps of the resulting plan and required planning time) and the configuration of parameters are recorded as before.

The incremental training capability is an important feature of HAP$_{NN}$, stemming from the use of the kNN algorithm. As the generalization of the algorithm is postponed for the online phase, learning actually consists of just storing past experience. This is an incremental process that makes it possible to constantly enhance the performance of the adaptive planner with the advent of new problems. In comparison, rule-based adaptive planning approaches, require the recomputation of the rule-base, which is a computationally expensive task.

6   Experimental Results

The experiments presented here focus at evaluating the generalization of the adaptive planner's knowledge to new problems and the effect of the weight settings to the resulting plan length and time. These issues are discussed in the following subsections.

For the purpose of the experiments all the runs of HAP were performed on a SUN Enterprise Server 450 with 4 ULTRA-2 processors at 400 MHz and 2 GB of shared memory. The operating system of the computer was SUN Solaris 8. For all experiments we counted CPU clocks and we had an upper limit of 60 sec, beyond which the planner would stop and report that the problem is unsolvable.

6.1   Evaluating the Adaptation of the Planner

Examining the problem of learning to adapt HAP to new problems from the viewpoint of a machine learner we notice that it is quite a hard problem. The number of available problems (450) is small, especially compared to the number of problem attributes (35). Since the training data were limited, a proper strategy should be followed for evaluating the planner performance.

For the above reason, we decided to perform 10-fold cross-validation. We split the original data into 10 cross-validation sets, each one containing 45 problems (3 from each of the 15 domains). Then we repeated the following experiment 10 times: In each run, one of the cross-validation sets was withheld for testing and the 9 rest (405 problems) were merged into a training set. The training set was used for finding the k nearest problems, and the test set for measuring the adaptive planner's performance. Specifically, we calculated the sum of the average normalized steps and time. In order to evaluate the learning approach, we calculated the same metric for all 864 static planner configurations based on the training set and chose the one that performs best for comparison on the test set. This is even better than having an expert choose the default parameter configuration for the planner. We also calculated the same metric with the best configuration that an "oracle" adaptive planner could achieve if it would always use the best configuration on the test set. 3 sets of weights were used at each run: a) ws=1, wt=1, b) ws=2, wt=1 and c) ws=1, wt=2. The results of each run, were averaged and thus a proper estimation was obtained, which is presented in Figure 3.

We notice that for all sets of weights and all numbers of nearest neighbors the adaptive planner exceeded the best static planner configuration. The average difference for all three settings and for the best average adaptive planner (k=7) was 0.274 which can be translated as an approximate 14% average gain combining both steps and time. If we notice the performance of the oracle planner we can see that the adaptive planner has still the potential to improve with the use of more training problems, but it managed to reach approximately half the gain in performance of an "oracle" planner.

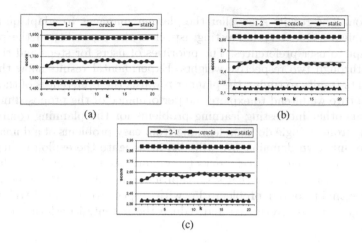

Fig. 3. Average score of static, adaptive and oracle HAP for a) $w_s=1$ and $w_t=1$, b) $w_s=1$ and $w_t=2$, and c) $w_s=2$ and $w_t=1$

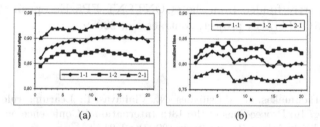

Fig. 4. Average normalized steps (a) and time (b) for three different weight settings

6.2   Evaluating the Effect of Weights

In order to evaluate the effect that the change of weights have in the resulting plans we produced the graphs depicted in Figure 4 that show the average normalized steps and time respectively for the three different weight settings.

Figure 4a shows that giving more weight to steps (2-1), reduces the average steps of the adaptive planner, in comparison with giving equal weights to both steps and time (1-1). In addition giving more weight to time, further increases the steps in comparison to equal weight setting. Similar conclusions can be drawn from Figure 4b, which concerns planning time. These graphs empirically show that tuning the weights has the user-desired effect on the planner behavior.

7   Conclusions and Future Work

This work has presented a methodology for multicriteria adaptive planning, using the k nearest neighbor algorithm on top of a highly adjustable planner. The planner consults past runs on similar problems and selects the most promising configuration. The results show that the planner manages to adapt quite well to new problems. One very interesting aspect is the capability of the planner to also adapt to user preferences. The priorities of users for steps and time are quantified through two respective weights. Experimental results show that the use of weights results to tuning the planner towards the preferences of the users.

In the future we intend to explore the performance of the proposed methodology various other interesting learning problems for the planning community, like learning from a single domain, learning from easy problems of a domain and adapting to unknown domains. We will also investigate the exploitation of feature selection and weighting techniques to enhance the performance of the kNN algorithm. It is widely known that kNN is prone to irrelevant attributes and the large dimensionality of our problem (35) with respect to the small training set (450) may give rise to overfitting and reduce the potential performance of our methodology.

Acknowledgements

This work is partly funded from the eCONTENT FP5 European Programme under the EUROCITIZEN project, contract No. 22089.

References

1. Vrakas, D., Tsoumakas, G., Bassiliades, N., Vlahavas, I.: Learning rules for Adaptive Planning. In: Proceedings of the 13th International Conference on Automated Planning and Scheduling, Trento, Italy (2003) 82–91
2. Vrakas, D., Tsoumakas, G., Bassiliades, N., Vlahavas, I.: Rule Induction for Automatic Configuration of Planning Systems. Technical report, Dept. of Informatics, Aristotle University of Thessaloniki (2003)
3. Carbonell, J., Knoblock, C.A., Minton, S.: PRODIGY: An integrated architecture for planning and learning. In: Architectures for Intelligence. Volume K. VanLehn, ed. Lawrence Erlbaum Associates (1991) 241–278
4. Ambite, J., Knoblock, C., Minton, S.: Learning Plan Rewriting Rules. In: Proceedings of the 5th International Conference on Artificial Intelligence Planning and Scheduling Systems, AAAI Press (2000) 3–12
5. Zimmerman, T., Kambhampati, S.: Learning-Assisted Automated Planning: Looking Back, Taking Stock, Going Forward. AI Magazine **24** (2003) 73–96
6. Vrakas, D., Vlahavas, I.: Combining progression and regression in state-space heuristic planning. In: Proceedings of the 6th European Conference on Planning. (2001) 1–12
7. Vrakas, D., Vlahavas, I.: A heuristic for planning based on action evaluation. In: Proceedings of the 10th International Conference on Automated Planning and Scheduling. (2002) 61–70

Focused Crawling
Using Temporal Difference-Learning

Alexandros Grigoriadis[1,2] and Georgios Paliouras[1]

[1] Software and Knowledge Engineering Laboratory
Institute of Informatics and Telecommunications,
National Centre for Scientific Research "Demokritos"
153 10 Ag. Paraskevi, Athens, Greece
{grigori,paliourg}@iit.demokritos.gr
[2] Language Technology Group
Human Communication Research Centre
University of Edinburgh, Edinburgh, UK

Abstract. This paper deals with the problem of constructing an intelligent Focused Crawler, i.e. a system that is able to retrieve documents of a specific topic from the Web. The crawler must contain a component which assigns visiting priorities to the links, by estimating the probability of leading to a relevant page in the future. Reinforcement Learning was chosen as a method that fits this task nicely, as it provides a method for rewarding intermediate states to the goal. Initial results show that a crawler trained with Reinforcement Learning is able to retrieve relevant documents after a small number of steps.

Keywords: Machine learning, reinforcement learning, web mining, focused crawling.

1 Introduction

World Wide Web can be considered as a huge library of every kind of information, accessible to many people throughout the world. However, it lacks a global indexing system that would consist of an explicit directory of all the information found in the Web. In order to deal with this problem, many Web tools have been constructed that mostly try either to construct a Web directory a priori, or respond to a user's query about keywords contained in a Web page.

These methods usually require exhaustive crawling, an effort to traverse as many Web pages as possible in order to maintain their database updated. However, this procedure is very resource consuming and may take weeks to be completed. On the other hand, "Focused Crawling" [3] is the effort to retrieve documents relevant to a predefined topic, trying to avoid irrelevant areas of the Web. Therefore it is more effective in finding relevant documents faster and more accurately.

A "Focused Crawler" searches the Web for relevant documents, starting with a base set of pages. Each of these pages contains usually many outgoing hyperlinks and a crucial procedure for the crawler is to follow the hyperlinks that are

G.A. Vouros and T. Panayiotopoulos (Eds.): SETN 2004, LNAI 3025, pp. 142–153, 2004.

more probable to lead to a relevant page in the future. Therefore, the crawler must include a component that evaluates the hyperlinks, usually by assigning a numerical "score" to each one of them. The highest the score is, the more probable it is that this hyperlink will lead to a relevant page in the future.

This component, the "Link Scorer" is implemented here by a reinforcement learning (R.L.) agent. An R.L. agent can recognize different states of the environment and for each of these *states* $s \in S$ it is able to choose an *action* α from a set of actions A. The choice of the action that the agent will perform in a specific state, is based on the *policy* π of the agent and can be represented simply as a look-up table.

Except for the agent, another important factor of an R.L. scheme, is the environment. The environment "judges" each of the agent's choices (actions) by providing a numerical *reward*. The reward is indicative of what we want the agent to perform, but not how it will perform it.

Based on the rewards it receives, the agent's policy is rearranged towards the optimal policy π^*. When a reward is given, the course of actions that the agent has followed so far gets credit. The way this credit is distributed backwards to the actions is determined by the specific R.L. method adopted. Moreover, the environment makes the transition to the next state s_{t+1}, given the current state s_t and the action a_t, chosen by the agent.

Reinforcement learning seems to fit nicely to the task of focused crawling. Indeed, the environment can tell the agent when it has done a good job (found a relevant page), but not how to do it - this is its own responsibility. Moreover, when the agent receives a reward the whole course of actions followed is affected, and not only the last one as would be the case in a supervised learning approach. This is a promising solution to the central problem of focused crawling, which is to assign credit to all the pages of the path that leads to a relevant document.

Our aim is to construct a focused crawler that uses an R.L. agent to train the "link scoring" component. This crawler should have increased ability to identify good links, because of the R.L. scheme, and therefore become more efficient and faster than a baseline crawler.

The next section presents a survey of the most important related work on Focused Crawling. Special attention is paid to methods engaging machine learning and the different aspects of dealing with this problem are illustrated. Section 3 is devoted to our own approach and the issues of representing the entities of the problem in an R.L. scheme. Section 4 describes our implementation of the R.L. agent and section 5 presents experimental results. These results are analyzed, in order to draw conclusions on our method, which are presented in the last section.

2   Related Work

The first attempts to implement focused crawling were based on searching the Web using heuristic rules that would guide the choices of the crawler. These rules are usually based on keywords found near the link and in the rest of the page that contains it. The crawler performs a search strategy combined with the heuristic rules in order to follow successful paths leading to relevant pages. Such implementations are "Fish-Search" [6] and "Shark-Search" [8].

More recent methods use information related to the structure of the Web graph, in order to perform more efficient focused crawling. Some of these methods take advantage of the "Topical Locality" of the Web (the property of pages with similar topic being connected with hyperlinks [2]) and use it to guide the focused crawler [3]. Moreover, the "backlink" information (pages that link to a certain document), provided by search engines like Google or Altavista, can be used to generate a model of the Web-graph near a relevant page, such as in the case of "Context Graphs" [7]. Finally, information such as contents of in-linking pages, tokens in the URL, and contents of sibling pages, can be extracted in order to train an agent to recognize the "linkage structure" for each topic [1].

There are also some methods that use R.L. in order to deal with focused crawling. In [9], the crawling component is based on R.L., although some simplifying assumptions are made. More specifically, in this approach the state space has been omitted, due to high dimensionality of the data. Therefore, the agent examines only the value of the possible actions to be taken, irrespective of the state of the environment. The actions are represented by the different hyperlinks that exist in a Web page, and the value of each action is estimated by a "bag-of-words" mapping of the keywords in the neighborhood of the hyperlink to a scalar value.

3 Problem Representation

In order to analyze the issues that arise in the representation of the focused crawling task as an R.L. task, we should examine a small part of the Web graph, like the one depicted in **Figure 1**. Each node ①..⑨ represents a Web page and each arc represents a link from a Web page to another. Web page ⑨ is relevant and there is only one path, following the nodes ①→④→⑧→⑨ leading to that page.

The aim of Focused Crawling, is to be able to recognize promising links early on, in order to follow the right path. Assume that an agent is in node ④ and has to choose between two links to follow, link 1 and link 3. It should be able to evaluate those links and choose the best, which is the one that is more promising in leading to a relevant page. In this case it should be link 1. By following this link, the agent will now be in node ⑧, which is one step closer to the relevant page.

Reinforcement learning seems to fit this task nicely. When the agent finds the target, which in this case is the relevant page, all the actions that lead to this take credit, allowing the agent to learn patterns of paths leading to relevant pages in the Web. However, a great deal of attention must be paid to the design of the reinforcement learning approach, in order to determine the most suitable problem representation, the role of each unit and the environment's behaviour.

In our approach, every Web page represents a different state $s_t \in S$. The set of actions contains the hyperlinks that exist in each page. Therefore, the agent

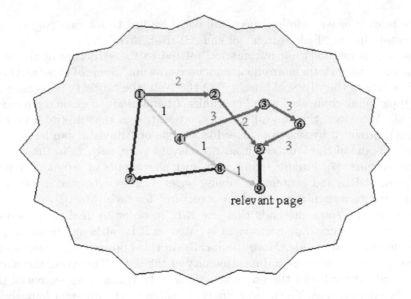

Fig. 1. A small part of the Web graph

being in state s_t (Web page), must choose among the actions that exist for this state $\alpha \in A(s_t)$, i.e. the hyperlinks found in this Web page. This action leads to another state s_{t+1} and a numerical reward, r_{t+1}, is given to the agent. This reward is +1 in case the Web page the agent has moved to is relevant, and 0 otherwise.

The aim of the R.L. agent is to maximize the reward it accumulates over the long run. This quantity is called the *Return*, and is defined as follows:

$$R_t = r_{t+1} + \gamma r_{t+2} + \gamma^2 r_{t+3} + \ldots = \sum_{k=0}^{\infty} \gamma^k r_{t+k+1}, \tag{1}$$

where γ is a discount factor, denoting the importance of recent rewards compared to older ones.

In order to find a policy, i.e. a mapping from states to actions, that would maximize the *Return*, the agent must be able to evaluate each state according to that criterion, as follows:

$$V^{\pi}(s) = E_{\pi}\{R_t | s_t = s\} = E_{\pi}\{\sum_{k=0}^{\infty} \gamma^k r_{t+k+1} | s_t = s\} \tag{2}$$

which is called the state-value function for policy π. In our case, the state-value function represents the possibility of a Web page being on a path to a relevant page. Therefore, a page with high state-value is preferable to a page with a lower one. When the agent must make a decision upon which hyperlink to be followed, it needs to estimate the state-value of the page pointed to by the hyperlink, termed the *outlink* page here. In other words, being in state s_t the agent needs to find the action a_t that leads to the state s_{t+1} with maximum value:

$$\arg\max_{a_t} V(s_{t+1}) \tag{3}$$

This estimation can be achieved either by estimating the values of all the possible next states, e.g. by fetching and evaluating all the outlink pages, or by estimating the value of the actions themselves, i.e. evaluating the hyperlinks, rather than the pages they point to.

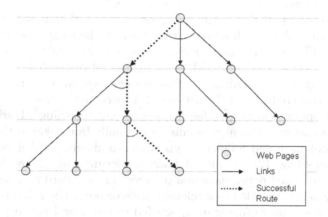

Fig. 2. A search tree of Web pages

This process is illustrated schematically in **Figure 2**, which depicts the out-link structure by a tree and our purpose is to find the best search strategy for relevant pages. The successful route is denoted by a dotted line. Starting from the root page (level 0) the agent needs to evaluate the pages on the next level and choose the best, according to the value function. Being in a node at level n it evaluates only the children of this node at level $n + 1$. As the experience of the agent grows it will become easier to find the right path in an efficient and cost-effective way.

4   Implementation

In order for an R.L. agent to be implemented, there are many practical issues that need to be considered. One is the dimensionality of the state-space. In our case, each state (Web page) is represented by a feature vector of 500 binary values. Each value corresponds to the existence or not of a specific keyword, which is important for the classification of a page as relevant or not. This makes up a space of approximately $3 \cdot 10^{150}$ different states, that can not be examined separately in a tabular policy format. Therefore, a function approximation method must be employed, where the features of each state are used as the input, and the estimation of the state-value as the output of the function.

The method chosen for our experiments was Temporal Difference Learning with eligibility traces $TD(\lambda)$ and gradient descent function approximation [11]. Temporal Difference is a very commonly used method for R.L. Eligibility traces are used to implement $TD(\lambda)$, a faster version of TD, where a fewer number of episodes is required to train the agent.

Moreover, a neural network is trained to estimate the values of different states, since their dimensionality does not allow a direct mapping. This neural network receives a training instance at each step of the crawling process. The input vector represents the features of the current Web page and the output the estimated state-value of that page, based on the reward that is received. The reward takes the value 1 or 0 according to whether the page is relevant or not. Implementing $TD(\lambda)$, each synapse is associated with its weight and its *eligibility trace*, which captures the discounted reward provided by the R.L. policy. These parameters, weights and eligibility traces, are updated, in order to ensure that the network gives credit to all the actions of a successful course.

The agent operates in two modes: "training" and "crawling". During "training" the agent executes a number of episodes, usually from 1000 to 10000, starting from a root page and following hyperlinks randomly, until it completes a number of steps (e.g. 10), or until it finds a relevant page. At each step, the agent is in state s_t and performs action α_t, receiving a reward r_{t+1} according to how good the action was (led to a relevant page or not). The reward r_{t+1} along with the features representing state s_t are fed to the neural network. Since the neural network is enhanced with eligibility traces, it gradually learns to evaluate a state's potential of leading to a relevant page, not only immediately but also in the future.

In the "crawling" mode, the agent is embedded in a crawler, which maintains a list of hyperlinks and their scores. Starting from a "root" page, the crawler evaluates all the outlinks using the trained neural network. These hyperlinks with their scores are added to the list. The crawler selects the hyperlink with the highest score, examines whether it is relevant or not, and extracts and evaluates their outlinks in order to store them in the list. The process ends when a predefined number of pages have been visited.

In order to evaluate outgoing links at each step, there are two alternative approaches that can be followed. The first is to fetch all the outlink pages and estimate their state-values. This is referred to hereafter as the "original lookahead method". However, this one-step lookahead causes a computational overhead, because the crawler is obliged to fetch all the outlink pages, even though it may decide not to follow most of them. Since the performance of a crawler is usually measured according to the number of pages that have to be visited until the relevant pages are found, this overhead cannot be ignored. Therefore, it would be desirable to have a variant of the original method, that is able to assign scores to links without having to visit them first.

This is realised by using the score of the current page as an approximation of the score of the pages that it links to. The crawler first examines the root page and assigns a score to it using the same procedure as in the original method. However, it does not fetch outlink pages and examine their contents. Instead, they immediately inherit their parent's score before being added to the list. Then, the crawler chooses the page with the highest score and visits it. When a page is found that has already been scored and needs to inherit a new value (multiple inheritance from more than one parents), the average of all the previous scores is used. This approach is referred to hereafter as the "variant without lookahead".

5   Experiments

5.1   Setup

The data used for the experiments are those used in the 2nd domain of the multilingual information integration project CROSSMARC [4,10], for the English and Greek language. CROSSMARC examined two thematic domains: "laptop product descriptions" and "job adverts on corporate Web sites". The latter domain is considered here.

The datasets used in the experiments represent Web sites containing pages of the specific domain for the two languages. The characteristics of the datasets are shown in **Table 1** and **Table 2**.

Table 1. Datasets used in experiments – English

#	Name	Web Pages	Hyperlinks	Average Outlinks	Relevant Pages
1	ApcInc	24	342	14	1
2	En-Vivo	24	88	4	1
3	Rowan	10	60	6	1
4	Harmonia	241	3332	14	1
5	Quarry	92	1712	19	9

Table 2. Datasets used in experiments - Greek

#	Name	Web Pages	Hyperlinks	Average Outlinks	Relevant Pages
1	Abc	194	1544	8	11
2	Forthnet	1907	4480	2	18
3	Intracom	555	15599	28	11
4	Marac	87	1249	14	3
5	Sena	102	2074	20	1

One characteristic of the domain that makes it particularly challenging for a focused crawler is the small proportion of relevant pages in each dataset. This situation, however, is very realistic, given the vastness of the Web, in which a crawler operates. Furthermore, it should be noted that the Greek datasets are generally larger and contain more relevant pages.

In order to present objective and comparative results, cross-validation is used according to the following procedure:

- Given n different datasets, a separate Neural Network with eligibility traces is trained on each one of them.
- After the training has been performed, each dataset passes through the crawling phase as follows:
  - The selected dataset is crawled, using an average of the value functions of the $n-1$ remaining Neural Networks.
  - The crawler's performance is calculated as a cumulative count of the number of relevant pages found at each navigation step.
- The procedure continues until all the datasets have been tested.

5.2   Experimental Results

The experiments were run for 1000 episodes with a maximum of 10 steps each. **Figures 3 to 6** depict the percentage of the relevant pages that were found by the algorithm against the percentage of the pages visited, for the various methods. Each point represents the number of pages that have been examined so far (x-axis) and the number of relevant pages that were discovered until then (y-axis). Therefore, lines positioned in the left side of the graph represent better performance (more relevant pages found earlier). Also, the fewer relevant pages a dataset has, the steeper the line is, since there are less points in the graph that denote the discovery of a relevant page.

Figures 3 and 4 present the results for the English sites. Both methods perform better in the "Quarry" dataset, followed by "En-vivo", "ApcInc", "Harmonia" and finally "Rowan". Although the variant method performed worse in the "Quarry" dataset than the original one, it was better in the other datasets. However, since "Quarry" was the only dataset containing more than one relevant pages, it represents a more realistic situation, while the other datasets can be considered problematic.

Figures 5 and 6 present the graphs for the Greek sites. The original method performed better for the "Forthnet" dataset, while the variant in all the other datasets. Moreover, the Greek datasets are much larger, with various graphical structures (number of outlinks) and thus pose a more realistic evaluation scenario.

Using the same datasets used in CROSSMARC, which is a variant of the method presented in [9], produced the results shown in **Figures 7 and 8**. In the English datasets, CROSSMARC's crawler performed better on large datasets, such as 'Harmonia", and "Quarry", while its performance was worse in the rest of the datasets, being worst in the "En-Vivo" case. For the Greek datasets, the performance of the CROSSMARC's crawler is similar to our method, being better in some datasets and worse in others.

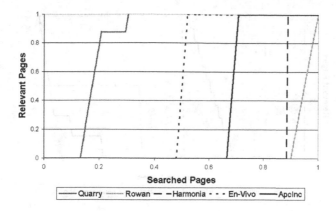

Fig. 3. Results for the original lookahead method – English

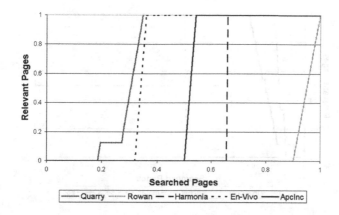

Fig. 4. Results for the variant without lookahead – English

It should be noted that the results for the original lookahead method are not directly comparable with the other two methods. This is because the lookahead method has to visit more pages en route to the relevant page.

Despite this fact the lookahead method seems to be worse than the other two methods in most cases. Therefore, the additional computation is not justified. Among the other two methods, no clear conclusion can be drawn about which of the two is better. However, the fact that the two methods are based on the R.L. principle, combined with the fact that they seem to complement each other in terms of performance, indicates a potential synergy among them.

6   Conclusion

This paper dealt with the problem of Focused Crawling using an intelligent crawling agent based on Reinforcement Learning. A crawler must be able to recognize patterns within the Web graph and make the right choices in order to

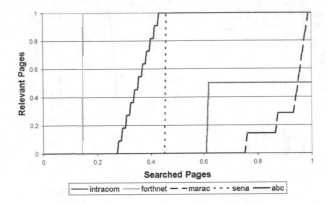

Fig. 5. Results for the original lookahead method – Greek

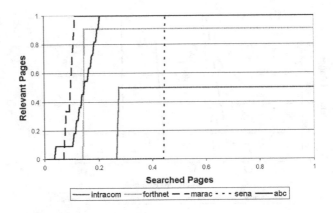

Fig. 6. Results for the variant without lookahead – Greek

be efficient and cost-effective. Reinforcement learning was chosen because it is a method that allows an agent to accumulate knowledge by experimenting with the environment, without using direct supervision. It seems to be appropriate for the task of Focused Crawling where success can be recognised but detailed guidance to this success cannot be provided, as would be required by a supervised learning approach.

The results of the experiments show that reinforcement learning is a good choice for this task. Indeed, in most of the cases only a small number of steps was required in order to retrieve all the relevant pages.

Further work includes further experimentatin and potential extension of the method, incorporating features of the method used in CROSSMARC's crawler.

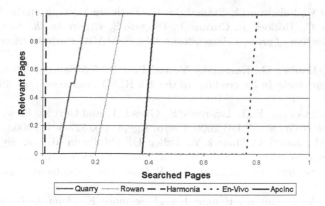

Fig. 7. CROSSMARC's Crawler – English

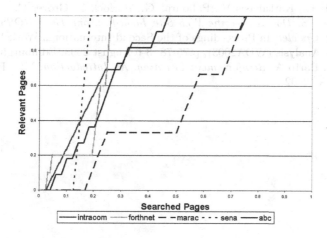

Fig. 8. CROSSMARC's Crawler – Greek

References

1. Aggarwal C., Al-Garawi F. and Yu P. *Intelligent Crawling on the World Wide Web with Arbitrary Predicates.* In Proceedings of the 10th International WWW Conference, pp. 96-105, Hong Kong, May 2001.
2. Brin S. and Page L. *The Anatomy of a Large-Scale Hypertextual Web Search Engine.* In the Proceedings of the Seventh International WWW Conference, pp. 107-117, Brisbane, April 1998.
3. Chakrabarti S., van den Berg M. and Dom B. *Focused Crawling: A New Approach to Topic-Specific Web Resource Discovery.* In Proceedings of the 8th International WWW Conference, pp. 545-562, Toronto, Canada, May 1999.
4. CROSS-lingual Multi Agent Retail Comparison. http://www.iit.demokritos.gr/skel/crossmarc.

5. Karkaletsis V., Paliouras G., Stamatakis K., Pazienza M.-T., Stellato A., Vindigni M., Grover C., Horlock J., Curran J., Dingare S. *Report on the techniques used for the collection of product descriptions*, CROSSMARC Project Deliverable D1.3, 2003.
6. De Bra P., Houben G., Kornatzky Y. and Post R. *Information Retrieval in Distributed Hypertexts*. In Proceedings of the 4th RIAO Conference, pp. 481-491, New York, 1994.
7. Diligenti M., Coetzee F.M., Lawrence S., Giles C.L. and Gori M. *Focused Crawling Using Context Graphs*.VLDB 2000, Cairo, Egypt, pp. 527-534, 2000.
8. Hersovici M., Jacovi M.,Maarek Y., Pelleg D., Shtalhaim M. and Sigalit U. *The Shark-Search Algorithm - An Application: Tailored Web Site Mapping*. In Proceedings of the Seventh International WWW Conference, Brisbane, Australia, April 1998.
9. McCallum A., Nigam K., Rennie J. and Seymore K. *Building Domain-Specific Search Engines with Machine Learning Techniques*. In AAAI Spring Symposium on Intelligent Agents in Cyberspace, Stanford University, USA, March 1999.
10. Stamatakis K., Karkaletsis V., Paliouras G., Horlock J., Grover C., Curran J.R. and Dingare S. *Domain-specific Web Site Identification: The CROSSMARC Focused Web Crawler*. In Proceedings of the Second International Workshop on Web Document Analysis (WDA2003), p.75-78. 3-6 August 2003, Edinburgh, Scotland.
11. Sutton R., Barto A. *Reinforcement Learning. An Introduction*. MIT Press, Cambridge, MA (2002).

A Meta-classifier Approach for Medical Diagnosis

George L. Tsirogiannis, Dimitrios Frossyniotis,
Konstantina S. Nikita, and Andreas Stafylopatis

School of Electrical and Computer Engineering
National Technical University of Athens
Zographou 157 80, Athens, Greece

Abstract. Single classifiers, such as Neural Networks, Support Vector Machines, Decision Trees and other, can be used to perform classification of data for relatively simple problems. For more complex problems, combinations of simple classifiers can significantly improve performance. There are several combination methods, like Bagging and Boosting that combine simple classifiers. We propose, here, a new meta-classifier approach which combines several different combination methods, in analogy to the combination of simple classifiers. The meta-classifier approach is employed in the implementation of a medical diagnosis system and evaluated using three benchmark diagnosis problems as well as a problem concerning the classification of hepatic lesions from computed tomography (CT) images.

Keywords: machine learning, neural networks, diagnosis

1 Introduction

It is well known, that classifier combination approaches can provide solutions to tasks which either cannot be solved by a single classifier, or which can be more effectively solved by a multi-classifier combination scheme. The problem is that we do not know from the beginning which is the best classifier combination method for a particular classification task. In this work, we try to solve this problem by developing a new methodology that combines different combination methods in order to get better performance compared to each individual method. More specifically, in analogy to the combination methods considered, which combine simple classifiers, the proposed meta-classifier approach combines these methods at a higher level aiming at the best classification performance.

For the evaluation of our approach, we created a medical diagnosis system to classify medical data that have been collected and appropriately inserted into a knowledge base. The basic components used in the system are classifiers such as Neural Networks [18], Support Vector Machines [15, 21, 22] and C4.5 Decision Trees [5, 16, 17] along with different combination methods, such as Bagging [4] and Boosting [6, 7, 8, 9]. The key feature of the system, from a technical point of view, is that it involves an extra level above the combination of simple classifiers. Specifically, the lowest level consists of simple classifiers, whereas in the middle level there are combination methods that combine the classifiers of the level below. Such methods are Bagging, Boosting and a fuzzy multi-classifier algorithm (FuzzMCS) [10]. The upper

G.A. Vouros and T. Panayiotopoulos (Eds.): SETN 2004, LNAI 3025, pp. 154–163, 2004.
© Springer-Verlag Berlin Heidelberg 2004

level represents the proposed meta-classifier approach that combines different methods of the middle level. The final decision of the system may be a class label with the corresponding reliability measure or a class probability. Four combination schemes of the combination methods are tested, namely, simple and weighted voting each using class labels or class probabilities. A different meta-classifier module is created for each diagnosis problem.

The meta-classifier is composed of the three levels mentioned above and operates in two phases. The first is the training phase during which the system is trained on known data for the problem. Additional parameter adaptation is embedded in the training phase which enables the system to select its parameters by its own and, thus, work autonomously without any intervention. Moreover, this feature allows the system to work properly for different medical diagnosis problems in a dynamic way. After training, the main working phase follows during which the system operates for the classification of new unlabeled data. The system has been empirically evaluated on known benchmark diagnosis problems as well as on the classification of hepatic lesions from computed tomography (CT) images [11].

As for relevant work done before, an example of an automatic diagnosis system is reported in [13]. This system tries to adapt the ECG processing and classification according to the patient. It uses a Mixture-of-Experts approach in which a Global Expert classifier is trained on a big ECG database and a Local Expert classifier is trained on a special recording of the patient's ECG. The adaptation in this case is based on the wide experience acquired by the database. Another system [23] is proposed as a general structure which allows the rule extraction of a decision. This is done by ensemble combining of Neural Networks (generalization ability) and C4.5 Decision Trees (rule readability). After experimentation, the performance of this system proved to be not reliable.

2   Meta-classifier

The meta-classifier approach extends the notion of multi-classifier combination schemes by combining methods instead of simple classifiers. While, in other words, combination methods such as Bagging and Boosting, take into consideration the decisions of different simple classifiers, such as Neural Networks, Support Vector Machines or Decision Trees, the meta-classifier combines the decisions of several different combination methods.

From an operational point of view, a specific method creates and trains a population of classifiers using training data for a particular problem. Then, for each new pattern presented to the system, each classifier assigns it to a class and, finally, the method reaches its decision by estimating which is the most probable class for the pattern, according to the decisions of the classifiers [2, 12, 14, 19]. If we consider this procedure as a compact module referred to as combination method, then the meta-classifier repeats the latter steps using combination methods instead of classifiers.

The motivation for the development of a meta-classifier approach is twofold. On the one hand, it is well known that, for complex problems, combination methods perform better than simple classifiers. Thus, it might be possible to further enhance performance by proceeding one step beyond that and combine combination methods. On the other hand, for a particular problem, there can be no prior knowledge of which is the best method to use. It must be noted here that the selection of the best method for a particular classification problem is a time-consuming procedure and sometimes yields only indicative results. By using the combination of these methods in a meta-classifier approach, we might be able to eliminate this difficulty and obtain good performance without needing to select the best method.

3 Combination of Combination Methods

Let us consider a classification task with C classes. First, we apply M different methods to solve the problem, each of which points to one of the C classes, thus providing an output vector with elements y_i, $i=1,...,C$, where $y_i \in [0,1]$ or $y_i \in \{0,1\}$ depending on the method. In the first case, each y_i can be considered as a probability measure for the corresponding class, whereas,. in the latter case, the y_i values correspond to class labels (as $y_i=1$ only when the pattern x belongs to class i).

In what concerns the combination of the methods, four different schemes are considered depending on the type of the output, as above, as well as on the voting/averaging technique, simple or weighted.

In weighted schemes, the weights correspond to a reliability measure assigned to each method, extracted from the error made on test data. We have selected this reliability to be calculated as 1 - *test error rate*. As the error rate falls into the [0,1] range, the reliability will be in the same range (the smaller the test error rate, the higher the reliability of the method).

Simple or crisp voting is a simple majority voting based on the decisions of the methods. The class with most votes will be selected as the class for the corresponding pattern.

In weighted voting, we assign a weight to each method, corresponding to its reliability as described above, and count the votes taking into account the weights

For simple averaging, the final decision will be computed by the relation

$$y_i = \sum_{m=1}^{M} y_i^m / M$$. For weighted averaging, a normalized weighted sum is computed

using the weight w^m, $m=1,...,M$, for each method: $y_i = \sum_{m=1}^{M} y_i^m w^m / \sum_{m=1}^{M} w^m$.

So, we have four different combination schemes, crisp voting (class labels without weights), weighted voting (class labels with weights), average class probabilities (class probabilities without weights) and class probabilities weighted sum (class probabilities with weights).

4 Medical Diagnosis System

In this section, we describe the medical diagnosis system based on the meta-classifier approach. The system is designed to receive pre-processed arithmetic data. More specifically, the data are row vectors and each row corresponds to a pattern with the values of the features and the label of the class. In the following, we present some special features of the system, pertaining to its hierarchical organization, automatic adaptation to the problem and parallel operation.

4.1 Hierarchical Organization

The system includes three types of modules that perform classification. The first type concerns simple classifier modules, like MultiLayered Perceptrons (MLPs), Support Vector Machines (SVMs) with RBF kernel, SVMs with polynomial kernel and C4.5 Decision Trees. The second type concerns combination methods that combine the above simple classifiers. Three algorithms are used in this system, namely Bagging, AdaBoost.M2 [9] and the FuzzMCS method that uses both supervised and unsupervised learning. Totally, ten methods are formed (each algorithm with each classifier type, excluding the use of SVMs of both types with AdaBoost.M2). The most complex module of the system is the meta-classifier that combines the ten methods. Generally, the modules of each level are controlled by those of the immediately upper level and control those of the lower level. This hierarchical organization allows simplicity of operation and easiness of expansion to use more methods or classifier types.

4.2 Automatic Adaptation to the Problem

A very attractive feature of the system is its ability to adapt itself to the problem for which it is created. This means that some parameters are chosen automatically, according to the performance on a validation set. For tuning the values of these parameters, the system uses half of the patterns of its training set as a validation set. Each classifier and each method are validated by selecting different values for their parameters. At the end, the set of parameters giving the best performance is selected. The range of parameter values that are going to be tested is properly predefined so as to cover most cases. After selection of parameter values, the system is supposed to have adapted itself to the problem and it is ready to be trained. Due to automatic adaptation, the system does not need an expert's opinion to tune it before putting it to work. So, a doctor can use the system without necessitating technical knowledge and is able to create anytime a new system for a new diagnosis problem.

Specifically, for the simple classifiers, the parameters concern their structure or their training algorithms. We chose to have only one parameter undefined for each type of classifier. For Multilayered Feed-forward Neural Networks it is their training epochs, for Support Vector Machines with polynomial kernel it is the degree of the polynomial, for Support Vector Machines with RBF kernel it is the dispersion of the exponential. The exception is the C4.5 Decision Trees that are completely defined irrelevantly of the problem. For the methods, there is only one parameter to tune and this is the number of sub-classifiers combined by the method. Originally, values that lead to small training times are selected. After the initialization, the values are gradually increased. The number of trials allowed is limited. Once this number is reached, no more trials are performed and the best values until then (with the lowest validation error) are kept.

Now, for the combination methods, we start with 2 classifiers in the ensemble (the lowest possible) and on each trial we increase the population by 1 until a maximum of

30 (according to experimental results reported in [3], 20 to 25 classifiers are usually enough) classifiers is reached.

4.3 Parallel Operation

The system has been constructed in such a way so as to have the ability of parallel operation from the upper to the lower level of hierarchy. In a parallel environment, all methods are trained simultaneously and independently, so the training time will be that of the slowest method. The same is the case when the system classifies new patterns, after training is completed. The third level of hierarchy (simple classifiers) also supports parallelism. Each classifier used by a method works independently of the others. The only exception is in the case of the AdaBoost.M2 method, where the training of the classifiers must be done in a serial way. With parallel organization we have significant reduction in time complexity, particularly in training, which is the most time-consuming phase. The trade-off for this gain is the increased computational resources needed. The implementation of this operation has been done using Java threads. However, the experiments that we present later were held on a single-processor system that does not take advantage of the parallelization abilities. On a multi-processor system the time needed would be severely reduced.

5 Experimental Results

We evaluated the system on three well-known benchmark medical problems from the UCI data repository [20], namely diabetes, breast-cancer and new-thyroid. Also, we tested the system on a problem concerning the classification of hepatic lesions from computed tomography (CT) images. The goal of this experimental study is to discover whether the meta-classifier approach exhibits better performance than the best single combination method or, at least, if we can use it in order to avoid searching for the best method for a particular problem. The comparisons are based on the test data available for each problem and the evaluation of the performance concerns the errors made in the classification of the test data.

More specifically, for each of the four problems, we create and train ten different meta-classifier systems. In the beginning of the training, the data sets are shuffled and divided into two parts. The first two thirds will compose the training set while the remaining one third will form the test set. Due to the shuffling originally done, these sets are different for each trial. At the end of training, the test error is extracted for each method used. As described in Section 3, four different combination schemes are considered and at each trial the test error is estimated for each scheme. By that, at the end, representative average error rates are formed, so as to compare not only the performance of the methods but the different combination schemes as well. Also, as described in Section 4, each meta-classifier system combines ten different combination methods.

In the next sub-sections, we briefly describe each problem and present experimental results. In the tables, we are using the numbering (1, 2, ...,10) to denote the methods as follows: 1-Bagging with MLPs, 2-Bagging with SVMs having polynomial kernels, 3-Bagging with SVMs having polynomial kernels, 4-Bagging with C4.5

Decision Trees, 5-AdaBoost.M2 with MLPs, 6-AdaBoost.M2with C4.5 Decision Trees, 7-FuzzMCS with MLPs, 8-FuzzMCS with SVMs having RBF kernels, 9-FuzzMCS with SVMs having polynomial kernels, 10-FuzzMCS with C4.5 Decision Trees. Similarly, the combination schemes will be denoted by the letters (A, B, C, D) as follows: A-Crisp voting, B-Weighted voting, C-Average class probabilities, D-Class probabilities weighted sum.

5.1 The Diabetes Problem

The first benchmark problem concerns diabetes diagnosis in female members of the Pima Indian tribe of America. The data of the problem consists of 768 different patterns. Each of them has 8 arithmetic features (there are no missing values) and one class label, diabetic or not. Out of the 768 patterns, the 500 are for not diabetic behavior. The two thirds of the original data will compose the training set and the rest will be the testing data. The original data set is shuffled for each of the ten trials and the error rate is computed. Table 1 presents the results (mean, min and max values) for each of the ten methods combined and for each of the four combination schemes. The numbers presented are per cent rates.

Table 1. Results for the diabetes problem

	1	2	3	4	5	6	7	8	9	10	A	B	C	D
Min	21.9	19.9	21.1	20.7	20.7	20.3	26.6	22.3	22.3	23.8	18.8	20.3	19.5	19.5
Max	28.9	27.7	27.7	27.7	28.9	28.9	33.2	32	32	34	27.3	27.3	27.3	27.3
Mean	25.4	23.7	24	24.3	24.7	25.5	30.1	25.6	27	27.6	23.6	23.7	24.2	24

We first observe that Bagging with SVMs having RBF kernel has the best performance with an error rate of 23.7%. On the other hand, the best combination scheme for this problem is crisp voting with 23.6% error rate. We can observe that, in this case, the combination of the methods (meta-classifier) performs better than the best method by 0.1%.

5.2 The Breast-Cancer Problem

The breast-cancer problem is about the diagnosis of malignance of breast tumors. The data come from the University of Wisconsin. There are in total 699 patterns, each having 10 integer features (values between 1 and 10) and a class label (malignant or benign tumor). Out of 699 patterns, 458 are benign whereas the remaining 241 are malignant. The trials are performed in the same way as for the previous problem and the results are presented in Table 2.

Table 2. Results fort he breast-cancer problem

	1	2	3	4	5	6	7	8	9	10	A	B	C	D
Min	3	3	3	3	3	3	3.4	3	3.4	3	2.6	2.6	2.6	2.6
Max	5.6	5.2	6.4	6.9	5.2	7.7	6.9	5.2	6.9	6.4	5.6	5.2	4.7	4.7
Mean	4.1	4.1	4.7	4.3	4	4.6	4.8	4	5.2	4.6	3.6	3.6	3.5	3.5

We can observe that, in this case, the best methods are AdaBoost.M2 with MLPs and FuzzMCS with SVMs having RBF kernel, each yielding 4% average error rate. The best combination schemes are those that use class probabilities with 3.5% error rates. This means that the performance of the best combination scheme is better by 0.5% than the best method. This is a considerable improvement since the error rates for this problem are generally small and it is difficult to decrease them significantly.

5.3 The New-Thyroid Problem

The third benchmark problem used to evaluate the meta-classifier is the so called new-thyroid. This problem concerns the characterization of the functionality of the thyroid under three possible states: normal, hypothyroid and hyperthyroid. The data set includes 215 patterns each of which has 5 continuous arithmetic features. Out of them, 150 are normal, 35 are hyperthyroid and 30 are hypothyroid. The results of the ten trials are shown in Table 3.

Table 3. Results for the new-thyroid problem

	1	2	3	4	5	6	7	8	9	10	A	B	C	D
Min	1.4	5.6	6.9	1.4	1.4	2.8	0	0	0	0	0	0	0	0
Max	5.6	16.7	13.9	15.3	16.7	12.5	4.2	4.2	4.2	4.2	4.2	4.2	4.2	4.2
Mean	3.2	10.4	10.3	7.7	5.1	7.6	2.1	1.7	2.1	1.4	1.5	1.6	2.5	2.5

The FuzzMCS method with C4.5 Decision Trees is the best for this problem with an 1.4% error rate. The best combination technique is crisp voting with 1.5% average error rate. In this case, the meta-classifier approach is slightly worse than the best method but achieves performance very close to that.

5.4 Classification of Hepatic Lesions from Computed Tomography (CT) Images

Apart from the three benchmark problems on which we have tested the system so far, another problem concerning classification of hepatic lesions is used to evaluate the meta-classifier. The data for this problem come from Computed Tomography (CT) images, acquired at the Second Department of Radiology, Medical School, University of Athens [11] and they are not widely available with responsibility of the source. A total number of 147 images were acquired corresponding to 147 different patients. Out of them, 76 are healthy, 19 have cysts, 28 hemangiomas and 24 hepatocellular carcinomas. So, it is a problem with four classes and 147 different patterns. Each pattern has originally 89 features, but, by using genetic algorithms for dimensionality reduction (the procedure for this is described in [11]), 12 features are selected and used. The results of the experiment are presented in Table 4.

Table 4. Results for the problem of classification of hepatic lesions

	1	2	3	4	5	6	7	8	9	10	A	B	C	D
Min	22.4	22.4	12.2	22.4	22.4	18.3	16.3	22.4	22.4	22.4	18.3	16.3	18.3	16.3
Max	32.6	48.9	38.7	42.8	38.7	40.8	38.7	42.8	40.8	46.9	34.6	34.6	38.7	36.7
Mean	27.3	35.5	28.7	31.4	30.4	30.6	26.7	32.2	30.2	33.2	25.9	24.0	25.7	24.9

The best method for this problem is FuzzMCS with MLPs as classifiers yielding 26.7% error rate. As long as the combinations are concerned, the best one is weighted voting having 24% error rate. This performance is significantly better than that of the best method, pointing that the use of the meta-classifier is beneficial to the classification. Moreover, we observe that every combination scheme is better than the best method, which means that whatever is our combination choice, the performance of the meta-classifier will be high. We underline that, in general, the performance of the classification for this problem can be better if we use all 89 features or at least a more representative subset than the 12 finally used. However, having in mind that the comparison was our objective in this experiment, the use of 12 features was considered adequate.

6 Conclusions

In this work, a new methodology has been developed which combines several different combination methods, in analogy to the combination of simple classifiers by these methods, in an attempt to get better performance results than the best individual method. The aim of this meta-classifier approach is to combine combination methods in an efficient way improving performance and to avoid the selection of the best combination method - as we do not know in advance which the best one is. The latter involves time-consuming experimentation and depends on the complexity of the problem.

The proposed meta-classifier approach was implemented in a medical diagnosis system and evaluated on three benchmark diagnosis problems and a problem concerning the classification of hepatic lesions from computed tomography (CT) images. The first conclusion is that on average, the best combining method out of the four tested for the combination of the methods in the meta-classifier is the second in turn, the weighted voting. Despite the fact that it is outperformed by the first method (crisp voting) in the diabetes and the new-thyroid problem by 0.1%, it is considerably better in the hepatic lesions problem. These two methods are slightly worse than crisp and weighted averaging only in the breast cancer problem, a fact indicating that voting performs better than averaging. Generally, however, the best combination method depends each time on the particular classification problem. Comparing the performance of the weighted voting with that of the best method each time, in the diabetes problem the error rates are equal, in the breast cancer problem there is an enhancement of 0.4%, in the new-thyroid problem the combination is worse by 0.2% and in the hepatic lesions problem a significant improvement of 2.7% is observed. So, the main conclusion is that the combination of the combination methods enhances performance. In some data sets, the test error rate is on average lower than that of the best individual method used. When this is not the case, the combination exhibits performance analogous to that of the best method. Practically, this implies that -in the worst case- the combination of combination methods has almost the same performance as the best method. This allows us to avoid the search for the best method and directly use the meta-classifier method expecting to obtain the best performance. Ultimately, the system is a medical diagnosis aiding tool which provides to the doctor a suggestion-opinion along with a degree of reliability.

As for the future work that can be done, first of all we can test the system on a multi-processing environment, which is expected to severely reduce the time needed for training. Also, we can try to expand the range of types of simple classifiers used in the lower level of the system (for example we can use RBF Neural Networks). The same can be done for combining methods (for example we can use Mixture-of-Experts approaches). Another issue that might be possible to study would be the effect of the combination through a gating network properly trained instead of the voting or averaging combination methods used so far.

References

1. Alpaydin, E.: Multiple networks for function learning. Proceedings of the 1993 IEEE International Conference on Neural Networks, vol. I, pp. 27-32,1993.
2. Alpaydin, E.: Techniques for combining multiple learners. Proceedings of Engineering of Intelligent Systems, vol. 2, ICSC Press, pp. 6-12, 1998.
3. Bauer, E., Kohavi, R.: An Empirical Comparison of Voting Classification Algorithms: Bagging, Boosting and Variants. Machine Learning, Vol. 36, pp. 105-139, 1999.
4. Breiman, L.: Bagging Predictors. Technical report 421. Department of Statistics, University of California, Berkeley, 1994.
5. Breiman, L., Friedman, J., Olshen, R., Stone, C.: Classification and Regression Trees. Chapman and Hall, New York, 1994.
6. Drucker, H.: Boosting using Neural Networks. Springer-Verlag, 1998.
7. Drucker, H., Cortes, C., Jackel, L., LeCun, Y., Vapnik, V.: Boosting and other machine learning algorithms. Proceedings on the Eleventh International Conference on Machine Learning, pp. 53-61, New Brunswick, NJ, 1994.
8. Freund, Y.: Boosting a weak learning algorithm by majority. Information and Computation 121, vol. 2, pp. 256-285, 1996.
9. Freund, Y., Schapire, R.E.: Experiments with a new boosting algorithm. Proceedings on the Thirteenth International Conference on Machine Learning, pages 148-156, 1996
10. Frosyniotis, D., Stafylopatis, A., Likas, A. : A divide-and-conquer method for multi-net classifiers. Pattern Analysis and Applications, Vol. 6, pp. 32-40. Springer-Verlag. 2003
11. Gletsos, M., Mougiakakou, S.G., Matsopoulos, G., Nikita, K.S., Nikita, A.S.: A Computer-Aided Diagnostic System to Characterize CT Focal Liver Lesions: Design and Optimization of a Neural Network Classifier. IEEE Transactions on Information Technology in Biomedicine, Vol. 7, No. 3, September 2003.
12. Hansen, L., Salamon, P.: Neural Network Enembles. IEEE Transactions on Pattern Analysis and Machine Intelligence, vol. 12, pp. 993-1001, 1990.
13. Hu, Y.H., Palreddy, S., Tompkins, W.J.: A Patient-Adaptable ECG Beat Classifier Using a Mixture-of-Experts Approach. IEEE Transactions on Biomedical Engineering, Vol. 44, No. 9, September 1997.
14. Maclin, R., Opitz, D.: Popular Ensemble Methods: An empirical study. Journal of Artificial Intelligence Research 11, 169-198, 1999.
15. Platt, J.: Fast Training of Support Vector Machines using Sequential Minimal Optimization. Advances in Kernel Methods - Support Vector Learning, MIT Press, 1998.
16. Quinlan, J.R. : Bagging, Boosting and C4.5. Proceedings on the Thirteenth National Conference on Artificial Intelligence. AAAI Press and the MIT Press, 725-730. 1996
17. Quinlan, J.R.: C4.5: Programs for Machine Learning. Morgan Kaufmann, San Mateo, California, 1993.
18. Rumelhart, D.E., Hinton,G.E., Williams, R.J.: Learning representations of backpropagation errors. Nature (London), vol. 323, pp. 533-536, 1986.

19. Sharkey, A.J.C.: Combining Artificial Neural Nets: Ensemble and Modular Multi-Net Systems. Springer Press, 1999.
20. UCI Machine Learning Databases Repository, University of California-Irvine, Department of Information and Computer Science. [ftp://ftp.ics.edu/pub/machine-learning-databases]
21. Vapnik, V.N.: Principles of risk minimization for learning theory. Advances in Neural Information Processing Systems, vol. 4, pp. 831-838, San Mateo, CA, Morgan Kaufmann, 1992.
22. Vapnik,V.N.: The Nature of Statistical Learning Theory. Wiley, New York, 1998.
23. Zhou, Z.H., Jiang, Y.: Medical Diagnosis With C4.5 Rule Preceded by Artificial Neural Network Ensemble. IEEE Transactions on Biomedical Engineering, Vol. 7, No. 1, March 2003.

Learning In-between Concept Descriptions Using Iterative Induction*

George Potamias[1] and Vassilis Moustakis[1, 2]

[1] Institute of Computer Science, Foundation for Research and Technology-Hellas (FORTH),
Science and Technology Park of Crete, P.O. Box 1385, 71110 Heraklion, Crete, Greece
{potamias,moustaki}@ics.forth.gr
[2] Department of Production and Management Engineering, Technical University of Crete, University Campus, Kounoupidiana, 73100 Chania, Crete, Greece

Abstract. Post and prior to learning concept perception may vary. Inductive learning systems support learning according to concepts provided and miss to identify concepts, which are hidden or implied by training data sequences. A training instance, known to belong to concept 'A' either participates in the formation of rule about concept 'A' or indicates a problematic instance. A test instance known to belong to concept 'A' is either classified correctly or misclassified. Yet an instance (either training or test) may be pointing to a blurred description of concept A and thus may lie in between two (or more) concepts. This paper presents a synergistic iterative process model, SIR, which supports the resolution of conflict or multi-class assignment of instances during inductive learning. The methodology is based on two steps iteration: (a) induction and (b) formation of new concepts. Experiments on real-world domains from medicine, genomics and finance are presented and discussed.

1 Introduction

Equivocal association of a training example with a rule during inductive learning spots vagueness about the concept the example manifests. The rule points to a class, which covers examples that belong also to other classes. A majority metric is often used to tag the rule to a single concept (or class). Majority often refers to the number of examples (or cases) covered by the rule. Thus a rule that covers 10 cases known to belong to class A and one example known to belong to class B would be tagged as a rule associated with class A. Although equivocal rule(s) – case(s) association may happen for a variety of reasons it may also point out to the existence of concepts, which lie in-between the concepts steering learning in the first place. Equivocal rule learning may also be attributed to data inconclusiveness (this means that some essential features are missing from concept and case representation), tuning of generalization heuristics used in learning, or noisy training cases. Attempts to rectify multi-class assignment include addition or deletion of attributes, attribute-values and training cases, [2], [14].

---

* Work reported herein was partially supported via the INTERCARE Health Telematics project, funded by the European Commission (HC 4011). Responsibility for results reported lies with the authors and do not represent official INTERCARE views.

G.A. Vouros and T. Panayiotopoulos (Eds.): SETN 2004, LNAI 3025, pp. 164–173, 2004.

In between concepts may reflect a tacit property of the domain over which learning is directed. For example, in a medical domain in-between concepts may either reflect uncertainty about the status of the patient at some point of clinical decision making, or because of a wealth of data (such as the gene-expression data), which point to in-between concepts for molecular-based disease characterization [5], [9]). In financial decision making in-between concepts may point to a firm, which is neither excellent nor very good, but it is in between excellent and very good.

Literature has focused more on accuracy and rule comprehensibility and has not addressed in-between class resolution. Borderline concepts are discussed in [7], yet no formal procedure has been established to support identification and modeling. In [8] it is suggested the use of a dummy feature to resolve borderline concept conflict in medical decision making; however, his approach sheds light on the cause of learned rule ambivalence, but does not support identification and modeling of the intrinsic features of in-between concepts and cases.

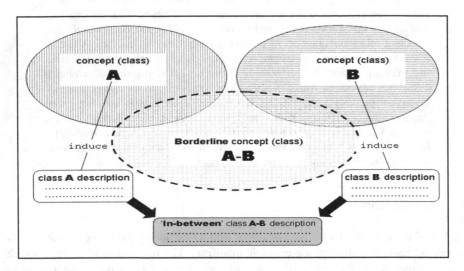

Fig. 1. The diagram presents an in-between or borderline concept, which lies between concepts A and B. The shaded area corresponds to the new concept description. SIR supports learning of the "in-between" concept description.

In the present article we elaborate on an iterative learning process, which copes with equivocal (or multi-class) rule(s) – case(s) association. Objectives are twofold: (a) to present, and demonstrate a methodology for inventing in-between hidden classes that could explain and model multi-class assignment; and, (b) to identify representative and borderline cases. We support our approach by coupling the learning process with multi-class resolve heuristics reflecting respective domain dependent background knowledge. Work reported herein conceptually links with earlier research by [17] and practically focuses on the identification of in-between concept description along lines suggested in Figure 1.

Section 2 overviews the methodology Synergistic Iterative Re-assignment (SIR) learning process principles and SIR heuristics. Section 3 summarizes the implementation of SIR to two learning frameworks: rule induction and similarity based learning. Section 4 presents results from extensive experimentation using medical and financial decision-making domains. We conclude the paper in section 5 by discussing the importance of our work for vague concept modeling and decision support, and by suggesting areas for future work.

2   Methodology: The SIR Process

To present our methodology in a formal way we adopt special notation and introduce definitions, which are presented in the lines that follow.

Definition 1. Let $E = \{1, 2, ..., n\}$, $C = \{c_1, c_2, ..., c_k\}$ be the sets of cases and classes, with cardinality $|E| = n$, and $|C| = k$, respectively. The combined or, in-between classes of C are all the members (c_i, cj) of $CC = C \times C$, denoted with c_{ij}; for $i=j$, (c_i, c_i) represents the original single-class c_i. Note that c_{ij}, and c_{ji} represent different combined classes. Furthermore, $\varnothing$ as a member of CC, represents the *null-class*, denoted with $c_\varnothing$. A default rule equalizes the null class with a class from CC. Thus, the set CC contains a total of k^2 combined classes.

Definition 2. Let E, n, k, and CC as defined in Definition 1. A *state*, $s(E)$, is a n places ordered vector: $s(E) = <cv_1, cv_2, ... , cv_n>$, where, $cv_i \in CC$, is the class (original or combined) assigned to case i, $1 \leq cv_i \leq k^2$. Each case may be assigned to one of the k^2 classes, concluding into a set, $S(E)$, of <u>at most</u> k^{2n} states for E.

Definition 3. Algorithm function, α, is defined as follows: $\alpha: S(E) \rightarrow S(E)$ with values, $\alpha(s(E)) = s'(E)$.

Function α encodes both induction and *execution* (deduction) phases of a learning algorithm and operates (runs) over the set of training cases. We execute learning outcome over the same set of cases in order to classify them. So, from a state $s(E)$, a new state $s'(E)$ is reached. In-between class invention follows from the intuitive observation that the user will tend to solve the puzzle. This intuition supports class invention strategically. It also positions it as a post-processing operation coupling learning outcome with background knowledge specifics that the learning system is unable to exploit in the first place. The operation ends either when the user achieves a desired learning aspiration threshold or when further improvement is not possible.

Definition 4. The resolve function ε over the set of combined class CC is defined as follows: $\varepsilon: CC \times CC \rightarrow CC$ with values, $\varepsilon(c_{xy}, c_{x'y'}) = c_{zw}$

Function ε takes as input two single- or, combined-classes form set CC, and outputs a respective class from CC. For example, $\varepsilon(c_1, c_2) = c_{12}$, resolves between classes c_1 and c_2 by inventing and forming a new combined class c_{12}, to be assigned to a multi-classified case. As a further example, $\varepsilon(c_1, c_{12}) = c_1$, takes as input one single-, c_1, and one combined-class c_{12}, and resolves them to the single-class c_1. Function α operates on a set of cases E to generate a state $s(E)$ of E. Application of ε on $s(E)$, may result to a new resolve state of E, namely: $\varepsilon(s(E))$.

The instantiation of the resolve function is totally dependent on domain specifics and user's requirements. For example, $\varepsilon(c_1 c_{12})=c_1$, presupposes some form of background knowledge that resolves multi-class assignment in favor of their common class assignment (i.e., c_1 is a common part for both c_1 and c_{12}). Note that only *2-place* combined classes are allowed. Furthermore, CC is defined to hold all the 2-place combined classes from C. As it will be shown in the sequel, the user is allowed to consider and define just a subset of these classes. In the current version of the SIR process a simple default rule strategy is followed. As an example assume a 4 class domain where, class c_{34} is not declared as a valid combined class. When a case is pre-assigned to class c_3 and the learning outcome classifies it as c_4, the adopted *default resolve rule* operation assigns to the case its incoming (original) class, c_3. In a medical domain where, two or more diseases share common symptoms, an in between concept formed by the combination of two or more diseases is conceptually valid in the early stages of the diagnostic process, manifests lack of knowledge, and may be interpreted as a domain dependent heuristic steering the diagnostic process. On the contrary, an in between concept, formed by the combination of completely separable diseases may not be considered as valid and should not be declared as a conceptually valid class.

Now we are in the position to define the core function of the SIR process which, encompasses the consecutive application of both α, and ε -- see Figure 2.

```
Let E the given training set of cases
 Set i=0, s_i=s(E),and S(E)={s_i}
   repeat
   apply the algorithm function a on s_i and derive a(s_i);
   apply the resolve function e on a(s_i) and derive
    e(a(s_i))=m(s(0))=s_i+1
     if s_i+1 ∈ S(E) then Stop
     else
     set i=i+1 and S(E)=S(E)U{s_i+1}
```

Fig. 2. The Synergistic Iterative Re-assignment (SIR) algorithmic process.

Definition 5. Transform function μ is defined as follows: $\mu = \varepsilon \bullet \alpha : S(E) \to S(E)$ with values, $\mu(s(E)) = \varepsilon(\alpha(s(E))) = \varepsilon(s'(E)) = s''(E)$, the resolve state of E after applying algorithm α on state $s(E)$, producing state $s'(E)$, and then applying ε on state s'(E).

Function μ implements the kernel of the SIR process. Applying it *iteratively*, a sequence of ordered resolved states, s_j, is generated where, $\mu(s_j) = s_{j+1}$, and s_{j+1} represents the transform of s_j. By definition 2, a maximum of k^{2n} states of a set of cases E could be generated. Without loss of generality, we may assume that the starting state, s_0, corresponds to the given training set of cases. Then, after at most k^{2n} application of

μ, the original state will repeat again and from that point an identical sequence of states will be generated. We consider the state before the repeated one as the terminating or, the final state. Each of the subsequent generated states encompasses invented in-between classes, which are linked to respective cases. Then follows induction over the new set of classes, rules are induced and cases are mapped to rules. At the final state the remaining in-between classes are not only explainable but, could be also considered as the only combined classes that are conceptually valid for the modeling of the application domain. In Figure 2, above, the pseudo-code of the SIR process is shown.

3 SIR and Learning Algoritms

The generality in the definition of the algorithm function allows for different implementations of the SIR process itself. That is, different inductive learning algorithms could be used as the base framework for implementing the SIR process. Up to now we have used the CN2 rule induction system [3], and a simple instance-based learning (IBL) process [1], as our base frameworks.

- **CN2/SIR:** SIR can really operate and proceed to "in-between" class invention only if the inductive algorithm allows for borderline case identification and induction of respective multi-class rules. CN2/SIR coupling is most suitable for domains where, the classes themselves are ordered. For example, consider a domain with three classes, c_1, c_2, and c_3, where, $c_1 < c_2 < c_3$, is a conceptually valid ordering of classes. Then the following valid combined classes are defined, accompanied with respective ground resolve function heuristics:

$$c_1 \& c_2 \rightarrow c_{12} \quad c_2 \& c_3 \rightarrow c_{23} \quad c_1 \& c_3 \rightarrow c_2 \quad c_1 \& c_{12} \rightarrow c_1 \quad c_1 \& c_{23} \rightarrow c_2$$
$$c_{12} \& c_2 \rightarrow c_2 \quad c_{12} \& c_{23} \rightarrow c_2 \quad c_{12} \& c_3 \rightarrow c_2 \quad c_2 \& c_{23} \rightarrow c_3 \quad c_2 \& c_3 \rightarrow c_{23}$$
$$c_{23} \& c_3 \rightarrow c_2$$

- **IBL/SIR:** Assume a domain with m attribute-values and C class-values. Then, a number of C, m-places ordered class-vectors is formed, one for each class-value. Each place of the class-vector holds a weight for the respective attribute-value; e.g., *Class Weighted Relevant Vector* (CWRV). An ordered case vector is formed. The case vector is also an M-places vector, but now the value for each place is binary, i.e., in {0,1}, depending on the occurrence or not, of the specific attribute-value in the case. Various techniques exist for computing attribute-value weights. Here we rely on a well known, and widely used, metric borrowed from information retrieval [12], which is based on a separation between relevant and non-relevant collections of documents. Cases assigned to one class correspond to the relevant documents and all other cases correspond to non-relevant documents -- see contingency matrix in Table 1, and the class attribute weight value $w_{ij}(c)$ is assessed – see formula (1) and a class-weighted vector (CWRV) is formed for each of the relevant classes. Classification is based on similarity match between the binary vector representative of the case and the respective CWRVs.

$$w_{ij}(c) = \frac{(r_{ij} + 0.5)(E - n_{ij} - (E_c - r_{ij}) + 0.5)}{(n_{ij} - r_{ij} + 0.5)(E_c - n_{ij} + 0.5)} \quad (1)$$

Table 1. Occurrence characteristics for an attribute-value v_{ij} (v_{ij}: value j of attribute i ; E: total number of cases; r_{ij} cases, from the total E_c cases assigned to class Cc , contain attribute-value v_{ij} ; n_{ij} - r_{ij} cases assigned to a class c', different from c, contain attribute-value v_{ij}).

	C_c	$C_{c', c \neq c'}$	
$v_{i,j}$ present	$r_{i,j}$	$N_{i,j}$ - r_{ij}	$n_{i,j}$
$v_{i,j}$ absent	E_c - $r_{i,j}$	E - $n_{i,j}$ - $(E_c$ - $r_{i,j})$	E - $n_{i,j}$
	E_c	E - E_c	E

4   Experiments and Results

In this section we examine and demonstrate the behavior and utility of the SIR process. First, we demonstrate the use of SIR on three real world domains: (i) venture capital assessment (VCA), (ii) treatment of acute abdominal pain in children (AAPC), and (iii) diagnosis of leukemia types (LEUK). The VCA domain is representative of a diverse range of such domains all of which belong to the area of financial decision-making and share a basic characteristic, their concept classes are ordered. The AAPC is an indicative medical decision-making domain where, the alternative therapeutic decisions cannot be clearly distinguished in the early stages of the diagnostic process. The LEUK domain is a domain from molecular biology; the classification task concerns the ability to predict the disease-type class of patients' tissue-samples based on their gene-expression profiles.

Venture Capital Assessment (VCA): Venture capital decision-making represents a complex, ill-structured decision-making task, [15]. The exemplar presented in this section draws from a real world venture capital assessment discussed in [13]. The task is to rank order 25 firms, seeking venture capital by using nine criteria. Firms are evaluated each with respect to the nine criteria and placed into one of nine classes, see Table 2. Assignment of firms to the nine classes was carried out by domain experts and presents the initial state of the firms' data set.

The ranking of firms to ordered solutions validates the introduction and consideration of in-between solutions. So, instead of the given nine rank classes we may introduce all the ranks between two alternative solutions (see Table 2). The CN2/SIR framework was used for our experimentation and reached a final state after three iterations. Results are summarized in Table 3. Accuracy was assessed using the C5 system (an offspring of the c4.5 system [11]; www.rulequest.com) and the final set of explainable classes includes an additional class. The result gives a better understanding to the ranking of firms because finer distinctions between them are now available. Although classes (original and in-between) are by definition ordered, use of a logistic regression approach was not considered because it would not support the explicit learning of symbolic knowledge in concept description.

Table 2. Venture capital assessment representation.

Criterion (attribute)	Values
Information security	1, 2, 3
Market trend	1, 2, 3
Market niche/position	1, 2, 3
Conjecture sensibility	1, 2, 3
Result trend	1, 2, 3
Expected dividend rate	1, 2, 3
Quality of management	1, 2, 3
R & D	1, 2, 3, 4
Accessibility to financial markets	1, 2, 3
Initial Ranks	1, 2, 3, 4, 5, 6, 7, 8, 9
Conceptually Valid Ranks	**12, 23, 34, 45, 56, 67, 78, 89**
	Rank 12 indicates a new concept, lying in-between" the original 1 and 2 concepts,

Table 3. CN2/SIR results on the VCA domain.

	#Rules	#Ranks	Ranks	Accuracy
Initial state	12	9	See Table 2	80 %
Final CN2/SIR state	11	10	1-2, 2, 2-3, 4, 4-5, 5, 5-6, 7, 8, 9	92 %

Acute Abdominal Pain in Children (AAPC): AAPC encompasses a set of symptoms that cause severe pain, discomfort and increased tenderness in the abdomen of the child. AAPC originates from disorders either in the intra-abdominal or, extra-abdominal areas, [4]. In the current case study we rely on a set of 81 attributes to represent AAPC patient cases. Selected attributes cover demographic, clinical and laboratory results. In total 300 AAPC patient cases were selected randomly from a database, installed and running in the Pediatric Surgery Clinic, University Hospital at Heraklion, Crete, Greece – the database is part of the HYGEIANet [6].

Management of AAPC patients is based on the De Dombal protocol [4]. Using the protocol, the attending physician needs to diagnose the cause of pain and then, make one of the following decisions, either "discharge" the child (in case the cause of the pain is not pathologic), or, to proceed to immediate "operation", or, to "follow-up" the case for a period of six to eight hours at the end of which, patient condition is re-assessed and the child is either discharged or admitted for operation. AAPC background knowledge, provided by experts in the field achieved an overall accuracy of about 70%, when applied on the given set of cases [10]. Poor accuracy has been attributed to uncertainty and domain clinical complexity [4, 10]. Often the physician cannot clear-cut the situation and finds ambivalent. We used SIR, based on the IBL/CRWV procedure to model physician decision-making ambivalence. The following conceptual valid combined classes were suggested by domain experts and incorporated into the respective resolve function (f: `'f'ollow_up`, o: `'o'peration`, d: `'d'ischarge`):

```
f & d → f_d    f & o → f_o    f & f → d_f    o & f → f_o    o & d → o_d
```

CWRV/SIR reached a final state after five iterations, and the following (single and in-between) concepts were induced: `d`, `o_d`, `f_d`, `f_o`, and `d_f`. The final state fed the C5 system, and the learning outcome was executed over the original set of cases. Inspecting the classification results the following was observed: most (over 80 %) of the `'follow_up'` (`f`) and `'operate'` (`o`) cases, were miss-classified as `'follow_up OR discharge'` (`f_d`), and `'operate OR discharge'` (`o_d`), respectively. The result is not disappointing. The combined therapeutic decisions, or `'o_d'` could be utilized and support the medical decision-making into the early phases of the diagnostic process. For instance, `'f_d'` excludes operation and `'o_d'` may indicate to an acute status that may be real or not – if real, the patient should be immediately taken to surgery, if not the patient should be sent back home. Pediatric Surgery Clinic personnel validated, from a semantic point of view, the learned, in-between, set of concepts. Accuracy improved slightly, e.g., 94% over an original 92% estimate. Accuracy assessment was not based on randomized testing. To assess accuracy we used the same cases, which were used to derive learning output. Because in between concepts essentially exclude on class it may seem that binary classification would be appropriate. Indeed, concept `'f_d'` excludes operation. So, from a classification point of view results should be identical and indeed they were (binary classification was examined during randomized testing with V-fold validation using a 80%/20% split between training and test sets, respectively.) However, SIR does not aim on improving accuracy; rather it focuses on identifying new classes, hidden and implied by the original class definitions.

Gene-Expression Based Diagnosis of Leukemia Types (LEUK): Histochemical analyses provided the first basis for classification of acute leukemias into those arising from lymphoid precursors (acute lymphoblastic leukemia, ALL) or from myeloid precursors (acute myeloid leukemia, AML). Although the distinction between AML and ALL has been well established, no single test is currently sufficient to establish the diagnosis. Accurate, leukemia classification remains imperfect and errors do occur. Distinguishing ALL from AML is critical for successful treatment [5]. In the original study, [8], a total of 6817 genes are studied for 27 *ALL*, and 11 *AML* training samples.

Here we concentrate on the same dataset with the difference that we use just 50 genes (i.e., features). These genes were selected as the *most discriminant* and *descriptive* for the two classes (ALL and AML) by the study presented in [5]. Furthermore, following a two-interval descrisation process, the continuous feature-values were assigned to respective 'high' and 'low' nominal values (the discretisation process, as well the background to gene-expression profiling and analysis, are presented in [9].)

We initiated the IBL(CRWV)/SIR process. A new 'in-between' class was invented, the *ALL_AML* class. When the revised data were fed to C5 the following ALL_AML rule was induced,

```
gene_M19045 = high → ALL_AML
```

The gene 'M19045' discriminates between the two leukemia types, and is associated with the AML leukemia type (as reported in the original study [5]). Based on this observation, we decided to re-assign the *ALL_AML* case to the *AML* class. Using C5 and running a fitness test (i.e., train vs. train dataset) a 100% accuracy figure was achieved, as compared with the respective 97.4% figure for the original dataset (the class-reassigned case is missed). So, with the SIR process we were able to discover *hidden irregularities*, and (based on domain background knowledge) to rectify them.

5 Conclusions, Remarks and Future Work

We presented, in a formal manner, a Synergistic Iterative Re-assignment (SIR) process for tackling the multi-class assignment problem in a inductive learning. The synergistic nature of SIR is drawn from the use of learning from examples induction algorithm coupled with specially devised heuristics for resolving between the classes of multi-class assigned cases. SIR output is inductive and thus the domain expert(s) should assess semantics.

The SIR process operates iteratively between the different states of a given set of cases. Given a set of classes then, we can form the set of all possible combinations of them. Of course domain depended, or other, restrictions of this set may apply, concluding into domain dependent and conceptually valid in-between classes. All the different combinations of assigning the cases to the single- or, combined-classes realize the different states of a given set of cases. SIR is robust and computational complexity depends only on the complexity of the learning algorithm over which SIR it is used. SIR does not impose further computations other than the computations (and corresponding complexity). SIR carries a framework, which supports the iterative implementation of a learning algorithm.

The SIR process receives as input one of these states and transforms it to a different one. The transformation is realized by three basic iterative operations: (a) application of the induction algorithm on the set of cases, (b) execution of the learning outcome on the cases, and application of heuristics for resolving between the classes of multi-class assigned cases, and (c) termination of the process when a newly formed state of cases was already generated into a previous iteration.

The instantiation of the SIR process by different types of learning algorithms and resolve heuristics, presents a general enough framework for tackling diverse sets of domains where *hidden* similarities between concept classes are obscured and need to be revealed. The SIR process realizes this need by properly inventing classes able to capture class similarities and by that, explain and model vague concepts. Especially, in domains where the set of classes receives an ordering interpretation, the concept of in-between class and the corresponding resolve heuristics are naturally defined. In the current study we presented the coupling of the SIR process with the CN2 algorithm, and an IBL classification method based on information retrieval metrics and techniques.

Putting SIR in a more general perspective, we can envisage a set of pre-established domain rules as a form of (potentially) incomplete and inconclusive background knowledge. In that sense, the given set of rules plays the role of the resolve function and its elaboration in the SIR process will result to an amalgam of pure theoretical domain knowledge (reflected in the rule set) with case based knowledge. Such a setting of the SIR process acts as a knowledge refinement or, revision process, a critical aspect with increasing interest in machine learning research.

References

1. Aha, D., Kibler, W.D., Albert, M.K.: Instance-based learning algorithms. Machine Learning 6 (1991) 37-66
2. Baim, P.W.: A method for attribute selection in inductive learning systems. Pattern Analysis and Machine Intelligence 10:6 (1988) 888-896
3. Clark, P., Niblett, T.: The CN2 induction algorithm. Machine Learning 3 (1989) 261-283
4. De Dombal, F.T.: Diagnosis of Abdominal Pain. Churchill Livingstone (1991)
5. Golub, T.R., Slonim, D.K., Tamayo, P., Huard, C., Gaasenbeek, M., Mesirov, J.P., Coller, H., Loh, M.L., Downing, J.R., Caligiuri, M.A., Bloomfield, C.D., Lander, E.S.: Molecular classification of cancer: class discovery and class prediction by gene expression monitoring. Science 286 (199) 531-537
6. HygeiaNet: Integrated Health Telematics Network of Crete. http://www.hygeianet.gr/ (2003)
7. Michalski, R.S.: Inferential Theory of Learning as Conceptual Basis for Multi-strategy Learning. Machine Learning 11:2/3 (1993) 111-152
8. Moustakis, V.: CEG: A case based decision modeling architecture. European Journal of Operational Research 84 (1995) 170-191
9. Potamias, G., Koumakis, L., Moustakis, V.: Gene Selection via Discretized Gene-Expression Profiles and Greedy Feature-Elimination. In Proceedings: 3rd Hellenic Conference on Artificial Intelligence, Samos, Greece (2004) – this volume.
10. Potamias, G., Moustakis, V., Charissis, G.: Interactive knowledge based construction and maintenance. Applied Artificial Intelligence 11 (1997) 697-717
11. Quinlan, J.R.: C4.5: Programs for Machine Learning. Morgan Kaufmann, San Mateo, California (1993)
12. Salton, G., McGill, M.G.: Introduction to Modern Information Retrieval. New York: McGraw-Hill Book Company (1983)
13. Siskos, J., Zopounidis, C.: The evaluation criteria for the venture capital investment activity: an interactive assessment. European Journal of Operational Research (EJOR) 31 (1987) 304-313
14. Spangler, S., Fayyad, U.M, Uthurusamy, R.: Induction of decision trees from inconclusive data. In Proceedings of the 6th International Conference on Machine Learning (ICML '89) Morgan Kaufmann (1989) 146-150.
15. Tyebjee, T, Bruno, A.: A Model of Venture Capitalist Investment Activity. Management Science 30:9 (1984) 1051-1066
16. Wrobel, S.: On the proper definition of minimality in specialization and theory revision. In P.B. Brazdil (Ed.), Machine Learning: ECML-93, Proceedings of the European Conference on Machine Learning, pp. 65-82. Berlin: Springer-Verlag (1993)
17. Zytkow, J.M., (1993). Cognitive autonomy in machine discovery. Machine Learning 12:1-3 (1993) 7-16

Splitting Data in Decision Trees Using the New *False-Positives* Criterion

Basilis Boutsinas[1] and Ioannis X. Tsekouronas[2]

[1] Dept. of Business Administration
University of Patras Artificial Intelligence Research Center (UPAIRC)
University of Patras, Greece
vutsinas@upatras.gr
[2] Department of Mathematics
University of Patras, Greece
tsekos@math.upatras.gr

Abstract. Classification is a widely used technique in various fields, including data mining and statistical data analysis. Decision trees are one of the most frequently occurring knowledge representation schemes used in classification algorithms. Decision trees can offer a more practical way of capturing knowledge than coding rules in more conventional languages. Decision trees are generally constructed by means of a top down growth procedure, which starts from the root node and greedily chooses a split of the data that maximizes some cost function. The order, in which attributes are chosen, according to the cost function, determines how efficient the decision tree is. Gain, Gain ratio, Gini and Twoing are some of the most famous splitting criteria used in calculating the cost function. In this paper, we propose a new splitting criterion, namely the *False-Positives* criterion. The key idea behind the *False-Positives* criterion is to consider the instances having the most frequent class value, with respect to a certain attribute value, as true-positives and all the instances having the rest class values, with respect to that attribute value, as false positives. We present extensive empirical tests, which demonstrate the efficiency of the proposed criterion.

Keywords: decision trees, data mining, machine learning

1 Introduction

Classification is a widely used technique in various fields, including data mining [8] and statistical data analysis. Recently, due to the explosive growth of business and scientific databases, an increasing number of researchers has concentrated on various classification methodologies. Classification algorithms aim at extracting knowledge from large databases using supervised learning methods. The extracted knowledge can be used to classify data into predefined classes, described by a set of concepts (attributes). Pure symbolic machine learning algorithms are the most common, such as decision trees algorithms (eg. ID3 [11] and C4.5 [12]) and rule based algorithms (eg. CN2 [5]). There are, also, pure statistic

G.A. Vouros and T. Panayiotopoulos (Eds.): SETN 2004, LNAI 3025, pp. 174–182, 2004.

algorithms, such as CART [3], adaptive spline methods [9] and graphical models [4], to mention some of them. Nonlinear algorithms based on neural networks (eg. back–propagation networks [13] and Radial Basis Function networks) and nonlinear regression are, also, used. Finally, there are example-based algorithms (eg. PEBLS [6]) and algorithms based on inductive logic programming [10,7] and hybrid systems [2].

Decision trees are one of the most frequently occurring knowledge representation schemes used in classification algorithms. Decision trees can offer a more practical way of capturing knowledge than coding rules in more conventional languages. Decision trees are generally constructed from a set of instances, which are represented by attribute-value pairs. In general, decision trees represent a disjunction of conjunctions of constraints on the attribute-values of instances. Each path from the tree root to a leaf corresponds to a conjunction of attribute tests, and the tree itself to a disjunction of these conjunctions. A decision tree assigns a classification to each instance. More specifically, decision trees classify instances by sorting them down the tree from the root node to some leaf node, which provides the classification of the instance. Each node in the tree specifies a test of some attribute of the instance, and each branch descending from that node corresponds to one of the possible values for this attribute. An instance is classified by starting at the root node of the decision tree, testing the attribute specified by this node, then moving down the tree branch corresponding to the value of the attribute. This process is then repeated at the node on this branch and so on until a leaf node is reached. Decision trees are generally learned by means of a top down growth procedure, which starts from the root node and greedily chooses a split of the data that maximizes some cost function. After choosing a split, the subsets of data are then mapped to the children nodes. This procedure is then recursively applied to the children, and the tree is grown until some stopping criterion is met. Then, usually, a pruning of the tree is performed in a bottom-up order. The pruning eliminates nodes that are overspecialized. The order, in which attributes are chosen, according to the cost function, determines how efficient the decision tree is. Gain, Gain ratio, Gini and Twoing are some of the most famous splitting criteria used in calculated the cost function. In this paper, we propose a new splitting criterion, namely the *False-Positives* criterion. The key idea behind the *False-Positives* criterion is to consider the instances having the most frequent class value, with respect to a certain attribute value, as true-positives and all the instances having the rest class values, with respect to that attribute value, as false positives.

In the rest of the paper, we first briefly present the most widely used splitting criteria, in Section 2. Then, we present the proposed *False-Positives* criterion, in Section 3. Then, in Section 4, we present extensive empirical tests, which demonstrate the efficiency of the proposed criterion. Finally, Section 5 concludes.

2   Widely Used Splitting Criteria

The Gain splitting criterion is used by the ID3 classification algorithm [11]. ID3 is the algorithm with the greatest impact on classification research during the last years. The ID3 algorithm tries to split the training set T into a number of subsets according to a test X, that is an attribute of the training set. For each of the n possible values a_i of chosen attribute X, a subset T_i is defined by those instances of the initial set T that carry the a_i value at the attribute X. This process continues, recursively, for all subsets that derive from partitioning the initial training set T, until all defined splits consist of instances that belong to only one class and thus they will be named after it. Early versions of the ID3 algorithm generate descriptions for two class values, but this restriction has been removed in later systems.

The best test/attribute is selected by ID3 by using the Gain criterion. The Gain criterion is based on the information theory that suggests: The information conveyed by a message depends on its probability and can be measured in bits as minus the logarithm to base 2 of that probability. At first the algorithm scans the training set and enumerates, for each possible value a_i of every attribute X, the number of positive, negative and total appearances (instances that carry the x_i value at the X attribute) in T.

Then it calculates the entropy of the set T with the equation:

$$info(T) = -\sum_{j=1}^{k} \left(\frac{freq(C_j, T)}{|T|} \times log_2 \frac{freq(C_j, T)}{|T|} \right) \tag{1}$$

where $|T|$ is the number of instances in T and $freq(C_j, T)$ is the number of instances in T than belong to the C_j class. At the third step the Gain criterion calculates for each attribute X the information requirements if the set had been separated by X, by calculating the weighted sum over the subsets:

$$info_x(X) = -\sum_{i=1}^{n} \left(\frac{|T_i|}{|T|} \times info(T_i) \right) \tag{2}$$

Finally the quantity $gain(X) = info(T) - info_x(T)$ is the information gain, if T is partitioned using attribute X. The Gain criterion selects the test/attribute with the maximum information gain. Then, the same procedure is used in all the recursively defined splits.

The C4.5 classification algorithm [12] is widely used in classification software systems. It is an extension of the ID3 algorithm. C4.5 follows the same steps with the ID3 algorithm. Instead, it uses the Gain ratio criterion, which is similar to the Gain criterion with the addition of two more calculations at the end. The Gain ratio criterion aims at removing the preference of the Gain criterion to tests/attributes with the greater number of possible values. According to Gain criterion, a test/attribute with a different value for each instance in the training set, (e.g. an identification attribute), always has the maximum information gain. Choosing such test/attribute to partition the initial training set, results to a large number of useless subsets, since each of them has only one instance.

The additional step in calculating Gain ratio criterion concerns the normalization of the results of the Gain criterion. There are two more calculations:

$$split\ info(X) = -\sum_{i=1}^{n} \left(\frac{|T_i|}{|T|} \times log_2 \frac{|T_i|}{|T|} \right) \tag{3}$$

$$gain\ ratio(X) = \frac{gain(X)}{split\ info(X)} \tag{4}$$

where *gain ratio(X)* is the normalized *gain(X)*. Of course, C4.5 also selects the test/attribute with the maximum normalized information gain.

The CART classification system is also widely used. It is, also, trying to divide the initial training set into subsets so that, at the end of the process, a subset can be assigned to a single class. Yet, CART splits a set always into two subsets. CART includes various single variable splitting criteria for classification trees, namely the *Gini, symmetric Gini, Twoing, ordered Twoing* and *class probability*. The default *Gini* criterion typically performs best, but, given specific circumstances, other criteria can generate more accurate results.

Gini and *Towing* criteria choose a test/attribute in order to split a set into two subsets, according to the attribute values. They both try to split the instances of a set in such a way that as much instances carrying the same class value as possible to be assigned to the same subset. They differ in the way they try to split a set. *Gini* criterion calculates the largest of the classes and splits the set trying to separate it from the others. *Twoing* criterion tries to split a set into two subsets so that each of them includes instances with some specific class value but, at the same time, includes half of the total instances within this set. There are a great number of classification algorithms, most of them being variations and extensions of some standard algorithms like ID3. Note that, most of them use the criteria mentioned above (e.g. ID4, ID5, ID5R, C5, SLIQ, CMP, Sprint, e.t.c.).

3   The Proposed *False-Positives* Criterion

The key idea behind the *False-Positives* criterion is to consider those instances of the training set TS having the most frequent class value, with respect to a certain attribute value, as true-positives and all the instances having the rest class values, with respect to that attribute value, as false-positives. Thus, the *False-Positives* criterion considers that the class value that classifies the majority of the instances having a certain attribute value (true-positives) should classify all the instances having that certain attribute value. Consequently, it considers as noise (false-positives) those instances classified by a different class value.

Therefore, for each attribute value a_{i_j} of an attribute a_i, true-positives TP are calculated as a function (see the formal representation of the algorithm, later in this section) of the maximum number of instances having that attribute value and classified by the same class value c_k:

$$TP: \ _k^{max} \left(|\{x|x \in TS, a_{i_j} = a_i, class = c_k\}| \right).$$

False-positives FP are calculated as the number of the rest instances having that attribute value:

$$FP : |\{x|x \in TS, a_{i_j} = a_i, class = c_l, l \neq k\}|.$$

Then, for each attribute value a_{i_j} of an attribute a_i, an attribute value norm $NV(a_{i_j})$ is calculated by detracting FP from TP. Next, an attribute norm $NA(a_i)$ is calculated by summing the attribute value norms $NV(a_{i_j})$ of every attribute value a_{i_j}.

Thus, the larger is the attribute value norm $NV(a_{i_j})$ for a certain attribute value a_{i_j} the safer is to consider false-positives as noise. Additionally, the larger is the attribute norm $NA(a_i)$ the less is the noise introduced in classification using the test/attribute a_i.

The *False-Positives* criterion for each attribute a_i is calculated by:

$$NA(a_i) \times MaxNA \times Countzero + MaxNV(a_i),$$

where $NA(a_i)$ is the attribute norm for a_i, $MaxNA$ is the maximum attribute value norm among all attributes, $MaxNV(a_i)$ is the maximum attribute value norm among all attribute values of a_i and $Countzero$ is a measure of noise, to be explained later.

Since, it is likely that the maximum value norm can be obtained by more than one attributes, we add $MaxNV(a_i)$ to an attribute norm in order to give precedence to those attributes with the higher maximum classification accuracy, with regard to a certain attribute value. Adding $MaxNV(a_i)$ to attribute norms may disturb the order obtained by the key idea of the *False-Positives* criterion which is represented by the magnitude of the attribute norms themselves. Therefore, we first multiply attribute norms by the maximum attribute norm among all attributes ($MaxNA$), so that to preserve that order.

$Countzero$ is calculated by:

$$Countzero = number\ of\ attribute\ values\ having\ FP = 0)-$$
$$2 * (number\ of\ attribute\ value\ norms\ that\ equals\ to\ zero) + 1.$$

The attribute norms are multiplied by the $Countzero$ in order to give precedence to those attributes with the lower noise, expressed as a linear function of zero false-positives (only true-positives) and of zero attribute value norms (true-positives equal to false positives).

The algorithm to calculate the *False-Positives* criterion is formally given below:

Input: a training set $TS = x|x = (C, a_1, \ldots, a_n)$ of records/instances, each described by n attributes
Step 1. for each instance of the training set TS
           where $|dom(c)| = L$
          for each attribute a_i
          do
            if $a_i = a_{i_j}$
            then
               if $c = c_k$
                  then $P_{i_j}^k + +$

Step 2. for each attribute a_i
　　　　do
　　　　for each possible attribute value a_{i_j} of a_i
　　　　　　do
　　　　　　　　if $P_{i_j}^d = {}_k^{max}\left(P_{i_j}^k\right)$
　　　　　　　　then
　　　　　　　　　　$TP_{i_j} = (L-1) \times P_{i_j}^d$
　　　　　　　　　　$FP_{i_j} = \sum_{i=1}^{L}\left(P_{i_j}^k\right) - P_{i_j}^d$
　　　　　　　　　　$NV(a_{i_j}) = TP_{i_j} - FP_{i_j}$
$MaxNV(a_i) = {}_j^{max}\left(NV(a_{i_j})\right)$
$Countzero = (sumof FP_{i_j} zeros) - 2*(sumof NV(a_{i_j} zeros) + 1$
$NA(a_i) = \sum_j NV(a_{i_j})$
$MaxNA = {}_i^{max}\left(MaxNV(a_i)\right)$
Step 3. $FPC_i = NA(a_i) \times MaxNA \times Countzero + MaxNV(a_i)$
Output: $max(FPC_1, \cdots, FPC_i)$

During Step 1 the algorithm scans the training set and, for each combination of each possible value a_{i_j} with each possible class value, enumerates instances carrying that combination.

Based on these calculations, during Step 2, first calculates false-positives and true-positives and stores them in an $L \times M$ array, where M is the total number of possible values of all attributes and L is the total number of possible values of class attribute. The time complexity is $O(XN)$, where X is the numbers of instances and N is the number of attributes in the training set.

Then it calculates FP and TP and, from them, calculates the value attribute norms. It stores them in a $3 \times M$ array. The time complexity is $O(M)$.

Finally, the attribute norms and parameters are calculated and stored in a $4 \times N$ array, where N is the number of attributes. The time complexity is $O(N)$.

During the last step, the algorithm assigns to each attribute the final score and selects the test/attribute with the highest one. Thus, the total space needed is $L \times M + 3 \times M + 4 \times M + 1$, which is $O(LM + N)$ and the time complexity is $O(XN) + O(M) + O(N) = O(XN + M + N) = O(XN)$, since $M << N$.

4   Empirical Tests

We have used the proposed *False-Positives* criterion, in order to construct decision trees both from a real-world data set and from test databases supplied by the UCI Machine Learning Repository [1]. The real-world data set comes from the domain of Molecular Biology, especially that of DNA sequence analysis, namely the "*promoter recognition*" problem [15], having 106 instances described by 58 attributes. Notice that DNA sequence analysis problems are used as benchmarks for comparing the performance of learning systems. The test databases are "Mushrooms", "MONK" and the "1984 United States Congressional Voting Records data sets supplied by [1]. The "Mushrooms" data set, having 8124 instances described by 23 attributes, classifies mushrooms as poisonous or edible, in terms of their physical characteristics. The MONK's Problem data set, having 432 instances described by 8 attributes, describes an artificial domain over the same attribute space. It was the basis of a first international comparison of learning algorithms. The "1984 United States Congressional Voting Records data set includes votes for each of the U.S. House of Representatives Congressmen on the 16 key votes identified by the Congressional Quarterly Almanac.

We compared the results obtained by the *False-Positives* criterion with those obtained by the Gain criterion. A first measure of comparison is the number of times that the two criteria agree on what attribute to choose. Instead of calculating this measure using a great number of different data sets, we used 100 different subsets of each of the *"promoter recognition"* and "Mushrooms" data sets. All subsets of each data set have the same size, that is carefully chosen. If the size is large enough, then always the same attribute is chosen by both criteria. If it is small enough, then there would be no remarkable classification accuracy to be observed. The size of subsets of *"promoter recognition"* and "Mushrooms" data sets is chosen to be 64 and 25, respectively. The two criteria agree in 62% cases for the *"promoter recognition"* data set and 77% cases for the "Mushrooms" data set.

A second measure of comparison concerns the classification accuracy of decision trees obtained by the two criteria. Using four different subsets of each the above data sets, we built four decision trees for each one of the two criteria. We used the standard steps of the ID3 algorithm to build the decision trees:

Step 1 Select the best test/attribute as the root. Make branches for all different values the selected test/attribute can have;

Step 2 If all instances at a particular leaf node belong to the same class, this leaf node is labelled with this class. If all leaves are labelled with a class the algorithm terminates;

Step 3 otherwise, the node is labelled with the best test/attribute that does not occur on the path to the root. Make branches for all different values the selected test/attribute can have. Continue with Step 2.

The best test/attribute is selected according to the Gain and *False-Positives* criteria. As far as the *False Positive* criterion is concerned, given as input the instances included in a node, the algorithm of the previous section:

1 enumerates the positive and negative instances for each possible value of every attribute;

2 calculates the true-positive (TP) and the false-positives (FP) values for each possible value of every attribute by setting TP and FP the maximum of the numbers of positive and negative instances respectively;

3 calculates the NA value, through the calculation of $NV = TP - FP$ and then the sum of the NV values of every possible value of each attribute. It also calculates the $MaxNA$ and $MaxNV$ values;

4 calculates the FPC (False Positive Criterion) value for each attribute;

5 outputs the test/attribute with the highest FPC value.

Table 1. Mean classification accuracy for various subsets

	promoter	Mushrooms	MONK 1984	US C.V.R.
Gain	71,8%	82,5%	82,9%	92,2%
False-Positives	74,2%	83,7%	81,7%	91,5%

Then we measured the classification accuracy obtained by each of the eight decision trees on the same test set. The mean classification accuracy for each criterion applied to the four data sets is shown in Table 1.

5 Conclusion

We presented a new splitting criterion for constructing Decision Trees, the *False-Positives* criterion. Based on the presented experimental tests, we can conclude that the proposed criterion is almost so accurate as the Gain criterion. Thus, the proposed *False-Positives* criterion is rather a minimal improvement of the very famous Gain criterion, as far as the classification accuracy is concerned.

The time complexity of selecting the best test/attribute using the Gain criterion is $O(XN)$, where X is the number of instances and N is the number of attributes in the training set. The same time complexity has the step of selecting the best test/attribute using the proposed criterion. Also, in order to build a decision, there are $O(B^N)$ calculations, in the worst case, where B is the maximum number of possible values for an attribute. However, in the case of the Gain criterion, these calculations are logarithmic calculations. Since $O(B^N) > N(X-1)$ [14], the Gain criterion is based on extended logarithmic calculations, especially when deep decision trees are going to be constructed. Thus, the proposed criterion has a better time complexity, due to lack of logarithmic calculations.

We are currently working on extending the proposed criterion, in order to remove its preference to tests/attributes with the greater number of possible values, analogously to Gain ratio criterion. Of course, one can always attack this problem removing such attributes in a preprocessing phase.

We are also investigating the type of training data for which the proposed criterion outperforms other criteria. Thus, we can detect certain type of applications where the proposed criterion can be used instead of other known criteria.

We are also working on improving the proposed criterion through a heuristic improvement of its parameters, like the *Countzero* parameter. However, although such heuristics may improve the accuracy, the basic strategy, presented in this paper, performs well on numerous different data sets.

References

1. Blake C. L., Merz C. J.: UCI Repository of machine learning databases. [http://www.ics.uci.edu/~mlearn/MLRepository.html], Irvine, CA: University of California, Department of Information and Computer Science.

2. Boutsinas B., Vrahatis M.N.: Artificial Nonmonotonic Neural Networks. Artif. Intelligence, Elsevier Science Publishers B.V., **132(1)**, (2001) 1–38.
3. Breiman L., Friedman J. H., Olshen R. A., C. J. Stone: Classification and Regression Trees. Wadsworth & Brooks, Calif., (1984).
4. W. Buntine: Graphical Models for Discovering Knowledge. In Fayyad U.M., Piatetsky-Shapiro G. and Smyth P., editors, Advances in Knowledge Discovery and Data Mining, (1996) 59–82.
5. Clark P., Niblett T.: The CN2 Induction Algorithm. Machine Learning, **3(4)**, (1989) 261–283.
6. Cost S., Salzberg S.: A Weighted Nearest Neighbor Algorithm for Learning with Symbolic Features. Machine Learning, **10**, (1993) 57–78.
7. Dzeroski S.: Inductive Logic Programming and Knowledge Discovery in Databases. In U. M. Fayyad U.M., Piatetsky-Shapiro G. and Smyth P., editors, Advances in Knowledge Discovery and Data Mining, (1996) 117–152.
8. Fayyad U.M., Piatetsky-Shapiro G., Smyth P.: Advances in Knowledge Discovery and Data Mining. AAAI Press/MIT Press, (1996).
9. Friedman J. H.: Multiple Adaptive Regression Splines. Annals of Statistics, **19**, (1991) 1–141.
10. Muggleton S.: Inductive Logic Programming. vol. **38** of A.P.I.C. series, Academic Press, London, (1992).
11. Quinlan J.R.: Induction of Decision Trees. Machine Learning, **1**, (1986) 81–106.
12. Quinlan J.R.: C4.5: Programs for Machine Learning. Morgan Kaufmann, CA, (1993).
13. Rumelhart D. E., Hinton G. E., Williams R. J.: Learning internal representations by error propagation. In D.E. Rumelhart and J.L. McClelland, editors, Parallel Distributed Processing: Explorations in the Microstructure of Cognition, MIT Press, (1986) 318–363.
14. Utgoff P. E.: Incremental Induction of Decision Trees. Machine Learning, **4**, (1989) 161–186.
15. Watson J.D., Hopkins N.H., Roberts J.W., Steitz J.A., Weiner A.M.: Molecular Biology of the Gene. Benjamin Cummings: Menlo Park, **1**, (1987).

Efficient Training Algorithms for the Probabilistic RBF Network

Constantinos Constantinopoulos and Aristidis Likas

Dept. of Computer Science
Univ. of Ioannina
GR 45110, Ioannina, Greece
{ccostas,arly}@cs.uoi.gr

Abstract. The Probabilistic RBF (PRBF) network constitutes an a-daptation of the RBF network for classification. Moreover it extends the typical mixture model by allowing the sharing of mixture components among all classes, in contrast to the conventional approach that suggests mixture components describing only one class. The typical learning method of PRBF for a classification task employs the Expectation – Maximization (EM) algorithm. This widely used method depends strongly on the initial parameter values. The Greedy EM algorithm is a recently proposed method that tries to overcome this drawback, in the case of the density estimation problem using mixture models. In this work we propose a similar approach for incremental training of the PRBF network for classification. The proposed algorithm starts with a single component and incrementally adds more components. After convergence the algorithm splits all the components of the network. The addition of a new component is based on criteria for detecting a region in the data space that is crucial for the classification task. Experimental results using several well-known classification datasets indicate that the incremental method provides solutions of superior classification performance.

Keywords: Machine Learning, Neural Networks, Probabilistic Reasoning, Mixture Models, Classification.

1 Introduction

An efficient method to tackle the classification problem is to construct a model that estimates the class conditional densities $p(x|k)$ of the data and the respective prior probabilities $P(k)$ for each class. Using Bayes theorem, we can compute the posterior probabilities $P(k|x)$ according to:

$$P(k|x) = \frac{p(x|k)P(k)}{\sum_\ell p(x|\ell)P(\ell)}. \tag{1}$$

In order to classify an unknown pattern, according to Bayes decision rule, we select the class with the higher posterior probability. In the traditional statistical approach each class density $p(x|k)$ is estimated using a separate mixture model

G.A. Vouros and T. Panayiotopoulos (Eds.): SETN 2004, LNAI 3025, pp. 183–190, 2004.

and considering only the data points of the specific class, therefore the density of each class is estimated independently from the other classes. We will refer to this approach as the *separate mixtures* model.

The probabilistic RBF network [6,7] constitutes an alternative approach for class conditional density estimation. It is an RBF-like neural network [4] adapted to provide output values corresponding to the class conditional densities $p(x|k)$. Since the network is RBF [4], the kernels (hidden units) are shared among classes and each class conditional density is evaluated using not only the corresponding class data points (as in the traditional statistical approach [5]), but using all the available data points. In order to train the PRBF network, an Expectation - Maximization (EM) algorithm can be applied [1,2,3,7]. In addition, it has been found [8] that the generalization performance is improved if after training the kernels are split, so that new kernels are not shared among classes. Considering the problem of EM initialization and its influence on the performance of the algorithm, we propose a incremental training method for the probabilistic RBF network, where components are sequentially added to the network at appropriately selected positions. Adopting the incremental training and the split method offers significant improvement in generalization. The effectiveness of the proposed method is demonstrated using several data sets and the experimental results indicate that the method leads to performance improvement over the classical PRBF training method.

2   The Probabilistic RBF Network (PRBF)

Consider a classification problem with K classes. We are given a training set $X = \{(x^{(n)}, y^{(n)}), n = 1, \ldots, N\}$ where $x^{(n)}$ is a d-dimensional pattern, and $y^{(n)}$ is a label $k \in \{1, \ldots, K\}$ indicating the class of pattern $x^{(n)}$. The original set X can be easily partitioned into K independent subsets X_k, so that each subset contains only the data of the corresponding class. Let N_k denote the number of patterns of class k, ie. $N_k = |X_k|$.

Assume that we have a number of M kernel functions (hidden units), which are probability densities, and we would like to utilize them for estimating the conditional densities of all classes by considering the kernels as a common pool [6,7]. Thus, each class conditional density function $p(x|k)$ is modelled as

$$p(x|k) = \sum_{j=1}^{M} \pi_{jk} p(x|j), \quad k = 1, \ldots, K \tag{2}$$

where $p(x|j)$ denotes the kernel function j, while the mixing coefficient π_{jk} represents the prior probability that a pattern has been generated from kernel j, given that it belongs to class k. The priors take positive values and satisfy the following constraint:

$$\sum_{j=1}^{M} \pi_{jk} = 1, \quad k = 1, \ldots, K. \tag{3}$$

It is also useful to introduce the posterior probabilities expressing our posterior belief that kernel j generated a pattern x given its class k. This probability is obtained using the Bayes' theorem

$$P(j|x, k) = \frac{\pi_{jk} p(x|j)}{\sum_{i=1}^{M} \pi_{ik} p(x|i)}. \tag{4}$$

In the following, we assume that the kernel densities are Gaussians of the general form

$$p(x|j) = \frac{1}{(2\pi)^{d/2} |\Sigma_j|^{1/2}} \exp\left\{ -\frac{1}{2}(x - \mu_j)^T \Sigma_j^{-1} (x - \mu_j) \right\} \tag{5}$$

where $\mu_j \in \Re^d$ represents the center of kernel j, while Σ_j represents the corresponding $d \times d$ covariance matrix. The whole adjustable parameter vector of the model consists of the priors and the component parameters (means and covariances), and we denote it by Θ, while we use θ_j to denote the parameter vector of component j.

It is apparent that the PRBF model is a special case of the RBF network [4], where the outputs correspond to probability density functions and the second layer weights are constrained to represent prior probabilities. Furthermore, it can be shown that the separate mixtures model [5] can be derived as a special case of PRBF.

The typical training method of the network computes the Maximum Likelihood estimates of the parameters using the EM algorithm [1,2,6,7], and split the kernels according to [8]. At the same time is widely known that the convergence of the EM depends on the initial conditions. To avoid this we propose an *incremental* training method. It is a deterministic two stage algorithm that overcomes the initialization problem of EM. During the first stage we incrementally add components to the network, and during the second stage we split all its components.

3   The Incremental Training Method

Consider a PRBF network with M components. In order to construct a network with $M + 1$ components, we utilize the given network and add to this another component. The procedure of component addition involves global and local search in the parameter space, for each new component. During global search the algorithm searches among a set of positions to place a new component, and selects the most appropriate candidate according to some criteria. During local search the algorithm optimizes the parameters of the resulting network with $M + 1$ components. This procedure starts with one component and is repeated until a maximum number of components has been added.

3.1   Component Addition

Assuming a network with M components and parameter vector Θ_M, the conditional density of class k is $p(x|k; \Theta_M)$. In order to add a new component

$j = M + 1$ with density $p(x|j = M + 1)$, the new class conditional density $p(x|k; \Theta_{M+1})$ yields as a mixture of $p(x|k; \Theta_M)$ and $p(x|j = M + 1)$

$$p(x|k; \Theta_{M+1}) = (1 - \alpha_k)p(x|k; \Theta_M) + \alpha_k p(x|j = M + 1) , \qquad (6)$$

where α_k is the mixing weight of the new component, following the approach suggested in [9]. This way the resulting network is again PRBF. Assuming i.i.d. data, the log-likelihood $\mathcal{L}$ is

$$\begin{aligned}
\mathcal{L} &= \log p(X|k; \Theta_{M+1}) \\
&= \log \prod_{k=1}^{K} \prod_{x \in X_k} p(x|k; \Theta_{M+1}) \\
&= \sum_{k=1}^{K} \sum_{x \in X_k} \log \left\{ (1 - \alpha_k)p(x|k; \Theta_M) + \alpha_k p(x|j = M + 1) \right\} .
\end{aligned} \qquad (7)$$

Given a fixed parameter vector Θ_M, in order to optimize the mean, the covariance and the mixing weights of the new component we find the ML estimates applying partial EM. During the *Expectation* step we compute the posterior probabilities $P^{(t)}(j = M + 1|x, k)$ using the current estimates of $\alpha_k^{(t)}$, $\mu_{M+1}^{(t)}$ and $\Sigma_{M+1}^{(t)}$, according to:

$$P^{(t)}(j = M + 1|x, k) = \frac{\alpha_k^{(t)} p(x|j = M + 1)}{(1 - \alpha_k^{(t)})p(x|k; \Theta_M) + \alpha_k^{(t)} p(x|j = M + 1)} . \qquad (8)$$

During the *Maximization* step we compute the new estimates of the parameters, according to:

$$\mu_{M+1}^{(t+1)} = \frac{\sum_{k=1}^{k} \sum_{x \in X_k} P^{(t)}(j = M + 1|x, k)x}{\sum_{k=1}^{k} \sum_{x \in X_k} P^{(t)}(j = M + 1|x, k)} \qquad (9)$$

$$\Sigma_{M+1}^{(t+1)} = \frac{\sum_{k=1}^{k} \sum_{x \in X_k} P^{(t)}(j = M + 1|x, k)(x - \mu_{M+1}^{(t+1)})(x - \mu_{M+1}^{(t+1)})^T}{\sum_{k=1}^{k} \sum_{x \in X_k} P^{(t)}(j = M + 1|x, k)} \qquad (10)$$

$$\alpha_k^{(t+1)} = \frac{1}{|X_k|} \sum_{x \in X_k} P^{(t)}(j = M + 1|x, k), \quad k = 1, \ldots, K . \qquad (11)$$

For a detailed derivation of the update equations see [6,7]. However we have to initialize somehow the estimates, in order to apply EM. To resolve this problem we resort to a clustering method, namely the *kd-tree*, following the approach in [10]. We partition the data in M subsets $X_j = \{x | P(j|x) > P(i|x), \forall i \neq j\}$, where the posterior probability of each component is computed according to:

$$P(j|x) = \sum_{k=1}^{K} P(j|x, k)P(k). \qquad (12)$$

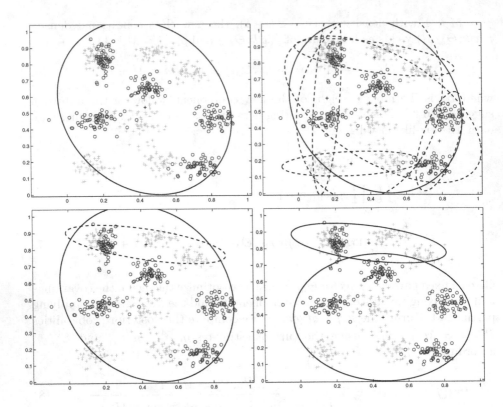

Fig. 1. Addition of the first two components. The components of the network are drawn with solid lines, and the candidate components with dotted lines.

Employing the kd-tree we repartition each of X_j is six subsets, and use the statistics of the resulting clusters as initial estimates. In this way we create $6M$ candidate initial values for the component, and after partial EM optimization using Eq. (8) - (11), we select the most appropriate according to some criteria that we present in the next section. This procedure constitutes the global search for the parameters of the new component. Then local search is applied, where we optimize all the parameters of the network with $M + 1$ components using EM, as in the typical training. The training procedure of a network with two components is depicted in Fig 1.

3.2   Selection Criteria for Component M+1

An obvious criterion for the determination of the appropriate candidate is the increase in log-likelihood of the data. Nevertheless in a classification problem we are interested in the generative model of each class individually. For this reason we introduce two more criteria that refer to the log-likelihood of each class. We are interested in the change of log-likelihood for each class, as we add a new component according to (6). So we define the change $\Delta\mathcal{L}_k$ for class k as:

$$\Delta \mathcal{L}_k = \mathcal{L}_k(\Theta_{M+1}) - \mathcal{L}_k(\Theta_M)$$
$$= \sum_{x \in X_k} \log \left\{ 1 + \alpha_k \left[\frac{p(x|j = M + 1)}{p(x|k; \Theta_M)} - 1 \right] \right\} \tag{13}$$

and suggest search between candidate components to find the one that mostly increases the log-likelihood of two classes. Such a candidate lies in a region containing data of both classes, consequently on the decision boundary.

Experimental results revealed that, after the incremental addition of few initial components, there are no candidates that simultaneously increase the log-likelihood of two classes. We can explain this attitude studying the first and second partial derivatives of ΔL_k with respect to α_k. We observe that:

$$\text{if } \frac{1}{|X_k|} \sum_{x \in X_k} \frac{p(x|k; \Theta_M)}{p(x|j = M + 1)} < 1, \text{ then } \Delta \mathcal{L}_k > 0, \tag{14}$$

independently of the mixing weight. According to (14), the log-likelihood of one class increases if the mean value of the likelihood ratio is less than one. In other words if the likelihood $p(x|j = M +1)$ according to the new component is higher than the likelihood $p(x|k; \Theta_M)$ according to the current model, then component addition increases likelihood. In a similar way we can prove that:

$$\text{if } \frac{1}{|X_k|} \sum_{x \in X_k} \frac{p(x|j = M + 1)}{p(x|k; \Theta_M)} < 1, \text{ then } \Delta \mathcal{L}_k < 0. \tag{15}$$

Consequently there is a limit in the number of components that can be added, so that the log-likelihood of two classes increases simultaneously. Beyond this limit we need a less strict criterion.

The next criterion we introduce, in order to continue the addition of components, searches for the candidate that mostly increases the log-likelihood of all data. This is a natural choice, in accordance with the Maximum Likelihood estimates we are looking for.

If there are no candidates that increase the log-likelihood of all data, we search for the candidate that mostly increases the log-likelihood of a single class. Such candidates lie away from the decision boundary, but are important for describing the generative model of the class. We can not assure that the addition of such components in the model increases the log-likelihood of the data compared to the previous model. If this is the case we stop the addition of components.

3.3   Component Splitting

After the completion of the first stage of the training algorithm, there may be components of the network located to regions with overlapping among classes. This happens if we have underestimated the maximum allowed number of components. In order to increase the generalization performance of the network we follow the approach suggested in [8], and split each component. This means that we evaluate the posterior probability $P(j|x, k)$ for a component and define if it is responsible for patterns of more than one class. If this is true, then we remove it from the network, and add a separate component for each class. So finally each component describes only one class. Splitting a component $p(x|j)$, the resulting component of class k is a Gaussian probability density function $p(x|j,k)$, with mean μ_{kj}, covariance matrix Σ_{kj} and mixing weight π_{jk}. These parameters are estimated according to:

$$\pi_{jk} = \frac{\sum_{x \in X_k} P(j|x,k)}{|X_k|} \tag{16}$$

$$\mu_{kj} = \frac{\sum_{x \in X_k} P(j|x,k)x}{\sum_{x \in X_k} P(j|x,k)} \tag{17}$$

$$\Sigma_{kj} = \frac{\sum_{x \in X_k} P(j|x,k)(x - \mu_{kj})(x - \mu_{kj})^T}{\sum_{x \in X_k} P(j|x,k)} , \tag{18}$$

where $P(j|x,k)$ is the posterior probability of component $p(x|j)$ and computed according to (4).

4 Experimental Results

The proposed training method for the PRBF network is compared with the standard EM training followed by a split stage [8]. We considered six benchmark data sets from the UCI repository, namely Bupa Liver Disorder (bld), Pima Indian Diabetes (pid), Phoneme (phon), Clouds (cld), Ionosphere (ion) and Cleveland Heart Disease (clev) data sets. For each data set, in order to obtain an estimation of the generalization error, we employed 10-fold cross–validation. For each of the ten experiments we evaluated the number of components of the network using a validation set containing the 10% of the training data. An important feature of the proposed incremental method, is that for the training of a network with M components the method constructs all the intermediate models with $j = 1, \ldots, M$ components. Consequently the model selection procedure is very fast, compared to the conventional approach, where a separate run is needed for every value of $j = 1, \ldots, M$. Table 1 provides the obtained generalization error for both methods. For four of the data sets the two methods gave similar generalization error, but for these the typical approach exhibits already near optimal performance and the incremental method also provides similar results. As regards the other data sets the proposed incremental training algorithm clearly exhibits better generalization performance. It must also be noted that results are comparable with those obtained by other state–of–the–art methods, such as Support Vector Machines [11].

5 Future Work

We presented an incremental training of the PRBF network, that overcomes the initialization problem of the standard EM algorithm, and provides networks with

Table 1. The generalization error of incremental training compared to the typical training approach.

	bld	pid	phon	cld	ion	clev
PRBF & Split	0.31	0.23	0.15	0.10	0.07	0.23
Incremental PRBF	0.28	0.23	0.14	0.10	0.06	0.18

superior generalization performance. In our future work we are going to extend the experiments, and systematically compare the incremental PRBF network with Support Vector Machines [11]. Also we are especially interested in Bayesian methods for estimating the number of components that the network utilizes. Finally we are going to examine the use of Probabilistic Principal Component Analyzers [12] instead of Gaussian components.

References

1. A. P. Dempster, N. M. Laird and D. B. Rubin, "Maximum Likelihood Estimation from Incomplete Data via the EM Algorithm", *Journal of the Royal Statistical Society B*, vol. 39, pp. 1-38, 1977.
2. G. McLachlan, T. Krishnan, *The Em Algorithm and Extensions*, Wiley, 1997.
3. T. Mitchell, *Machine Learning*, McGraw-Hill, 1997.
4. C. M. Bishop, *Neural Networks for Pattern Recognition*, Oxford University Press, 1995.
5. G. McLachlan, D. Peel, *Finite Mixture Models*, Wiley, 2000.
6. M. Titsias, A. Likas, "A Probabilistic RBF network for Classification", *Proc. of International Joint Conference on Neural Networks*, Como, Italy, July 2000.
7. M. Titsias, A. Likas, "Shared Kernel Models for Class Conditional Density Estimation", *IEEE Trans. on Neural Networks*, vol. 12, no. 5, pp. 987-997, Sept. 2001.
8. M. Titsias, A. Likas, "Mixture of Experts Classification Using a Hierarchical Mixture Model", *Neural Computation*, vol. 14, no. 9, Sept. 2002.
9. N. A. Vlassis and A. Likas, "A Greedy-EM Algorithm for Gaussian Mixture Learning", *Neural Processing Letters*, vol. 15, pp. 77-87, 2002.
10. J. J. Verbeek, N. Vlassis and B. Krose, "Efficient Greedy Learning of Gaussian Mixtures", *Neural Computation*, vol.15, no. 2, 2003.
11. C. Cortes and V. Vapnik, "Support–vector Networks", *Machine Learning*, vol. 20, no. 3, 1995.
12. M. Tipping and C. Bishop, "Mixtures of Probabilistic Principal Component Analysers", *Neural Computation*, vol. 11, no. 2, 1999.

Using k-Nearest Neighbor and Feature Selection as an Improvement to Hierarchical Clustering

Phivos Mylonas, Manolis Wallace, and Stefanos Kollias

School of Electrical and Computer Engineering
National Technical University of Athens
9, Iroon Polytechniou Str., 157 73 Zographou, Athens, Greece
{fmylonas,wallace}@image.ntua.gr
stefanos@cs.ntua.gr

Abstract. Clustering of data is a difficult problem that is related to various fields and applications. Challenge is greater, as input space dimensions become larger and feature scales are different from each other. Hierarchical clustering methods are more flexible than their partitioning counterparts, as they do not need the number of clusters as input. Still, plain hierarchical clustering does not provide a satisfactory framework for extracting meaningful results in such cases. Major drawbacks have to be tackled, such as curse of dimensionality and initial error propagation, as well as complexity and data set size issues. In this paper we propose an unsupervised extension to hierarchical clustering in the means of feature selection, in order to overcome the first drawback, thus increasing the robustness of the whole algorithm. The results of the application of this clustering to a portion of dataset in question are then refined and extended to the whole dataset through a classification step, using k-nearest neighbor classification technique, in order to tackle the latter two problems. The performance of the proposed methodology is demonstrated through the application to a variety of well known publicly available data sets.

1 Introduction

The essence of clustering data is to identify homogeneous groups of objects based on the values of their attributes. It is a problem that is related to various scientific and applied fields and has been used in science and in the field of data mining for a long time, with applications of techniques ranging from artificial intelligence and pattern recognition to databases and statistics [1]. There are different types of clustering algorithms for different types of applications and a common distinction is between hierarchical and partitioning clustering algorithms. But although numerous related texts exist in the literature, clustering of data is still considered an open issue, basically because it is difficult to handle in the cases that the data is characterized by numerous measurable features. This is often referred to as the curse of dimensionality.

Although hierarchical clustering methods are more flexible than their partitioning counterparts, in that they do not need the number of clusters as an input, they are less

G.A. Vouros and T. Panayiotopoulos (Eds.): SETN 2004, LNAI 3025, pp. 191–200, 2004.

robust in some other ways. More specifically, errors from the initial steps of the algorithm tend to propagate throughout the whole procedure to the final output. This could be a major problem, with respect to the corresponding data sets, resulting to misleading and inappropriate conclusions. Moreover, the considerably higher computational complexity that hierarchical algorithms typically have makes them inapplicable in most real life situations, due to the large size of the data sets.

Works in the field of classification focus in the usage of characterized data, also known as training data, for the automatic generation of systems that are able to classify (characterize) future data. This classification relies on the similarity of incoming data to the training data. The main aim is to automatically generate systems that are able to correctly classify incoming data [1].

Although the tasks of classification and clustering are closely related, an important difference exists among them. While in the task of classification the most important part is the distinction between classes, i.e. the detection of class boundaries, in the task of clustering the most important part is the identification of cluster characteristics. The latter is usually tackled via the selection of cluster representatives or cluster centroids).

Typically, in order to achieve automatic classification systems generation, one first needs to detect the patterns that underlie in the data, in contrast to simply partitioning data samples based on available labels [7], and then study the way these patterns relate to meaningful classes. Efficient solutions have been proposed in the literature for both tasks, for the case in which a unique similarity or dissimilarity measure is defined among input data elements [6]. When, on the other hand, multiple independent features characterize data, and thus more than one meaningful similarity or dissimilarity measures can be defined, both tasks become more difficult to handle. A common approach to the problem is the lowering of input dimensions, which may be accomplished by ignoring some of the available features (feature selection) [2].

In the case when input features are independent, or when the relation among them is not known a priori, which is often the case with real data, a decrease of space dimensions cannot be accomplished without loss of information. The proposed algorithm of this work is an extension of agglomerative clustering in this direction and is based on a soft selection of features to consider when comparing data. The results of the initial clustering, performed on a small amount of the original data set, are then refined via a classification step; this step, although unsupervised, is based on the principles of the k-nearest neighbour classification scheme and is applied to the whole data set. In this way we overcome two major drawbacks that dominate agglomerative clustering; the one of initial error propagation and the one regarding complexity issues. This important step also contributes to the experimental evaluation of the method's efficiency.

The structure of the paper is as follows: in section 2, after a short introduction to agglomerative clustering, we present the main problems that are related to our task and the proposed method for initial clustering. In section 3 we explain how a k-nearest neighbour classifier can be used to refine, as well as to experimentally verify the efficiency of the algorithm. Finally, in section 4, we present experimental results for the proposed algorithm and in section 5, we present our concluding remarks.

2   Agglomerative Clustering and Soft Feature Selection

Most clustering methods belong to either of two general methods, partitioning and hierarchical. Partitioning methods create a crisp or fuzzy clustering of a given data set, but require the number of clusters as input. When the count of patterns that exist in a data set is not known beforehand, partitioning methods are inapplicable; an hierarchical clustering algorithm needs to be applied.

Hierarchical methods are divided into agglomerative and divisive. Of those, the first are the most widely studied and applied, as well as the most robust. Their general structure is as follows [4]:

1. Turn each input element into a singleton, i.e. into a cluster of a single element.
2. For each pair of clusters c_1, c_2 calculate their distance $d(c_1, c_2)$.
3. Merge the pair of clusters that have the smallest distance.
4. Continue at step 2, until the termination criterion is satisfied. The termination criterion most commonly used is the definition of a threshold for the value of the distance.

The two key points that differentiate agglomerative methods from one another, and determine their efficiency, are the distance and the termination criterion used. Major drawbacks of agglomerative methods are their high complexity and their susceptibility to errors in the initial steps, that propagate all the way to their final output.

The core of the above generic algorithm is the ability to define a unique distance among any pair of clusters. Therefore, when the input space has more than one dimensions, an aggregating distance function, such as Euclidean distance, is typically used [9]. This, of course, is not always meaningful and there are cases where a selection of meaningful features needs to be performed, prior to calculating a distance [8]. In other words, it may not be possible to select a single distance metric, which will apply in all cases, for a given data set. Moreover, one feature might be more important than others, while all of the features are useful, each one to its own degree.

In this paper we tackle feature weighting based on the following principle: while we expect elements of a given meaningful set to have random distances from one another according to most features, we expect them to have small distances according to the features that relate them. We rely on this difference in distribution of distance values in order to identify the context of a set of elements, i.e. the subspace in which the set is best defined.

More formally, let c_1 and c_2 be two clusters of elements. Let also r_i, $i \in \mathbb{N}_F$ be the metric that compares the i-th feature, and F the overall count of features (the dimension of the input space). A distance measure between the two clusters, when considering just the i-th feature, is given by:

$$f_i(c_1, c_2) = \sqrt[\kappa]{\frac{\sum_{a \in c_1, b \in c_2} [r_i(a_i, b_i)]^\kappa}{|c_1||c_2|}} \tag{1}$$

where the subscript i denotes the i-th feature of an element, $|c|$ is the cardinality of cluster c and $\kappa \in \mathbb{R}$ is a constant. Typical value used for κ is 2. The overall distance between c_1 and c_2 is calculated as:

$$d(c_1,c_2) = \sum_{i=1}^{F} [x_i(c_1,c_2)]^{\lambda} f_i(c_1,c_2) \tag{2}$$

where x_i is the degree to which i, and therefore f_i, is included in the soft selection of features, $i \in N_F$ and $\lambda \in \mathbb{R}$ is a constant. Typical value used for λ is 2. Based on the principle presented above, values of vector x are selected through the minimization of distance d [12]. The features that relate c_1 and c_2 are "most probably" the ones that produce the smallest distances f_i.

3   Refinement and Classification through k-Nearest Neighbor Classification

As stated in preceding sections, the primary aim of clustering algorithms is not to correctly classify data, but rather to identify the patterns that underlie in it and produce clusters of similar data samples. Therefore, 'wrong' elements in clusters may be acceptable, as long as the overall cluster correctly describes an existing and meaningful pattern: in fact, we have established in our previous work that clusters with wrongfully assigned data samples may be better than perfect data set partitionings in describing the underlying patterns and thus may lead to better classifier initialization [7]. This implies that if we feed labelled data to the algorithm and measure the classification rate may not be enough to evaluate the actual efficiency of the algorithm.

In order for a clustering algorithm to be properly evaluated, the patterns described by the clusters in its output need to be evaluated; their application towards the generation of a classifier and the evaluation of the resulting classifier is a means towards this direction. In this paper we examine whether the specific results of such an algorithm, applied to several well known machine learning data sets, are meaningful by evaluating the results from a k-nearest neighbours classifier that is created by using them.

Undoubtfully, several classification schemes exist in the literature [3]. We have chosen to work with the k-nearest neighbours (kNN) classifier, although others could have been chosen as well, mainly because of the nature of the instance-based learning method itself and its straightforward approach [11]. The kNN algorithm is extremely simple, yet powerful, used in many applications and can be safely applied in all sorts of data sets, real life and artificial ones, independently of size or time compromises, resulting into high quality scientific observations. kNN is also extremely suitable to use in cases where instances map to points in $\mathbb{R}^n$, there are lots of training data into consideration and – after performing soft feature selection – less than 20 attributes per instance.

Possible disadvantages to the kNN method, acknowledging the fact that it typically considers *all* the attributes from *all* the elements, are easily overcome by applying the initial clustering procedure on a small subset of the available data, thus reducing the number of elements that the classification scheme will need to consider in order to classify each incoming sample. The aforementioned approach is extremely suitable and appropriate for online classification.

Specifically, the kNN algorithm assumes that all elements correspond to points in the n-dimensional space R^n. The neighbours of an element are defined in form of some distance measurement. A variety of metrics can be used as distances in the algorithm, like Euclidean square distance:

$$d(a,b) = \sqrt{\sum_{i \in N_F} (a_i - b_i)^2} \qquad (3)$$

Minkowsky distance:

$$d(a,b) = \sum_{i \in N_F} |a_i - b_i| \qquad (4)$$

minimax distance:

$$r(a,b) = \max \sum_{i \in N_F} |a_i - b_i| \qquad (5)$$

Mahalanobis distance and others.

Specifically, we tackle each initial element and calculate its distance from every other element in the data set. We define a priori the number of the nearest to the element under consideration neighbours, k, that are going to play a significant role in the cluster characterization of the element at the latest stage, thus using a suitable threshold regarding the precision of the classification. Clearly if k becomes very large, then the classifications will become all the same. Generally, there is some sense in making k > 1, but certainly little sense in making k equal to the number of training elements.

Formally, let e_q be each given query element to be classified and e_1, e_2 ,...e_k denote the k elements that are nearest to e_q. Let also c(a) be defined as:

$$c(a, j) = \begin{cases} 1 & \text{, a belongs to class j} \\ 0 & \text{, otherwise} \end{cases}$$

Then, e_q is classified as follows:

$$c(e_q) = z : \sum (e_i, z) = \max(\sum_{j=1}^{countofclasses} c(e_i, j)) \qquad (6)$$

where e_i is the training instance (element) nearest to e_q. In other words, e_q is classified to the class to which most of its k closest neighbors belong.

Obviously, in order to apply the kNN classification scheme, a small set of labelled data samples are needed. In this work, we describe the unsupervised classification of data, and thus we assume such information to be unavailable; we only use data labels in our experiments in order to measure the classification rate and thus the performance of the algorithm. Therefore, we assume that each one of the clusters detected during the step of hierarchical clustering corresponds to a distinct class.

Using the classification scheme described above, and the cluster assignments of the clustered data samples as class labels, we may proceed to classify all available data elements. If the initial clustering was successful in revealing the patterns that underlie in the data, then this process will refine the output and improve the classification rate by removing some of the clusters' members that were a result of errors in the initial steps. Thus, this process offers an indication of the hierarchical clustering's true performance. Moreover, it makes the overall algorithm more robust, as opposed to simple hierarchical clustering, as it is more resilient to errors in the initial steps.

Finally, it is this step of classification that extends the findings of the initial clustering to the whole data set, thus allowing for the former to be applied on just a portion of the data set. This is very important, as without this it would not be possible to have the benefits of hierarchical clustering when dealing with larger data sets. Furthermore, a significant role in the classification process plays the iterative nature of the algorithm, which rises from the fact that the input is the same as the output, thus allowing several iterative applications of the algorithm, until the cluster assignments of the elements remain unchanged.

4 Experimental Results

In this section we list some indicative experimental results of the proposed methodology from application to real data sets from the well-known machine learning databases. In all consequent experiments we have used the Euclidean distance for the estimation of the k nearest neighbours. Values of κ, λ and k differ from case to case and are thus mentioned together with each reported result.

In all experiments the proposed clustering algorithm that is described in section 2 has been applied on a small portion of the data set, while the whole data was consequently classified based on the output of this step and applying kNN classification, as described in section 3.

Iris Data

The iris data set contains 150 elements, characterized by 4 features, that belong to three classes; two of these classes are not linearly separable from each other. The labels of the elements were not used during clustering and classification; there were used, though, for the estimation of the classification rates; specifically, each cluster was assigned to the class that dominated it. Results are shown in Tables 1 and 2, whereas the numbers inside parenthesis separated by commas denote the elements belonging to its one of the three classes in each step.

For the application of the proposed methodology a portion of the dataset, specifically 20% of it, was separated and submitted to the clustering procedure. The classification rate on this portion of the dataset (63.3%) is not impressive. Still, the application of the classification step on the whole data set produces a considerably better classification rate, which indicates that the initial clustering process had successfully detected the patterns and the kNN classification process successfully clustered the remaining data.

We can also observe that the proposed methodology, although applying the computationally expensive step of hierarchical clustering to only 20% of the dataset (initial clustering for 30 elements), does not produce inferior results to the approach that applies an hierarchical clustering algorithm to the whole dataset. Comparing them to simple agglomerative clustering with no feature selection and no recursive classification (i.e. classification rate ~ 74%), proves its very good overall performance.

Table 1. Classification rates for Iris data (constants: $\kappa = \lambda = 1.3$, neighbours k = 5).

Method	cluster 1	cluster 2	cluster 3	Classification rate
Initial clustering	(2,0,4)	(6,1,4)	(2,9,2)	63,3%
Knn classification	(7,0,31)	(43,0,19)	(0,50,0)	82,7%

Table 2. Comparison of proposed classification approach to plain clustering.

Method	Classification rate
Clustering of the whole dataset	74,7%
Proposed approach	82,7%

Wisconsin Breast Cancer Database

The Wisconsin breast cancer database contains 699 elements, which are characterized by the following attributes: clump thickness, uniformity of cell size, uniformity of cell shape, marginal adhesion, single epithelial cell size, bare nuclei, bland chromatin, normal nucleoli, mitoses. All these attributes assume integer values in [9]. Elements are also accompanied by an id, and class information; possible classes are benign and malignant. 65.5% of the elements belong to the benign class and 34.5% to the malignant class. 16 elements are incomplete (an attribute is missing) and have been excluded from the database for the application of our algorithm.

Detailed results acquired using the proposed methodology are available in Tables 3 and 4, whereas the numbers inside parenthesis separated by comma denote the elements belonging to its one of the two classes in each step. It is worth noting that, similarly to the case of iris data, although the classification rate of the initial clustering procedure, which was performed on a 7,32% subset of the original data set (50 data samples), is not extremely high, the classification step on the whole database refines it considerably. This indicates that the proposed clustering approach was efficient in revealing the patterns in the small portion of the data set, and the kNN process successfully utilized this information for the refinement of the clustering and the extension to the remaining dataset.

Additionally, performing the initial clustering on a mere 7,32% subset is not only more efficient computationally wise, it is also better in the means of quality and performance, as indicated by the results in Table 4, when compared to the approach of applying the hierarchical process to the whole data set.

Finally, it is worth noting that the small computational needs of the kNN classification process allow for its repeated / recursive application on the data. Such reclassification steps also induce an increase to the classification rate, as is evident in Table 3, thus further stressing the efficiency of the proposed approach in revealing the patterns that underlie in the data. The classification rate of 93.1% that is reported is extremely high for this data set for an unsupervised clustering algorithm.

Table 3. Classification rates for Wisconsin data (constants: $\kappa = 1.3, \lambda = 1.3, k = 3$).

Method	cluster 1	cluster 2	cluster 3	Classification rate
Initial clustering	(21,2)	(9,10)	(0,8)	78,0%
Knn classification	(341,24)	(100,50)	(3,165)	88,7%
Knn reclassification 1	(348,21)	(91,31)	(5,187)	91,7%
Knn reclassification 2	(349,20)	(90,23)	(5,196)	93,0%
Knn reclassification 3	(349,20)	(90,22)	(5,197)	93,1%

Table 4. Comparison of proposed classification approach to plain clustering.

Method	Classification rate
Clustering of the whole dataset	86,1%
Proposed approach	88,7%
Proposed approach with recursive kNN	93,1%

This performance is not far from that of trained classification systems that utilize the same dataset. This is indicative of the method's efficiency, considering that we are referring to the comparison of an unsupervised method to a supervised ones. Best results may be presented in our work in [12], but there was undoubtfully more information used, mainly because a Gaussian distribution of the dataset was assumed, which is not the case in this work. Furthermore, we must also note that number k of the nearest neighbours is obviously chosen based on observed relative statistics and is subject to further improvements.

5   Conclusions

In this paper we developed an algorithm for the detection of patterns in unlabelled data in the means of agglomerative clustering improvement, using the k-nearest neighbours classification scheme. The first step of the algorithm consists of an hierarchical clustering process, applied only to a subset of the original data set. This process performs a soft feature selection in order to determine the subspace within which a set of elements is best defined and thus it is suitable for data sets that are characterized by high dimensionality. The second part of the algorithm performs a k-nearest neighbours classification. This process considers initial clusters to be labels and uses this information to build a classifier, through which to classify all data. Thus, errors from the hierarchical algorithm's initial steps are corrected; moreover, as the computational complexity of this classification step is considerably smaller that that of the complexity of the clustering process, it may be applied to the entire dataset. In addition to making the overall algorithm more efficient and resilient to errors, it also serves as a means for its evaluation.

The efficiency of the proposed algorithm has been demonstrated through application to a variety of real data sets. Experiments on the iris dataset indicated the method's ability to perform as well as simple hierarchical clustering having a much better complexity. Application on the Wisconsin breast cancer database which is a multi – dimensional data set, on the other hand, was indicative of the method's performance in such environments: the results of the application of the proposed methodology to less than 10% of the available data exceed those obtained by application of the computationally expensive hierarchical clustering process to the entire dataset.

In our future work we aim to extend on our work on improvement of the hierarchical clustering process by providing guidelines for the automatic selection of the thresholds used in this work, namely parameters κ and λ of the clustering process and k of the kNN classification. On a more practical side, we are already working towards the application of the methodology presented herein for the clustering of usage history and the extraction of low level and semantic user preferences, in the framework of the EU funded IST-1999-20502 FAETHON project.

Acknowledgments

This work has been partially funded by the EU IST-1999-20502 FAETHON project.

References

1. Hirota, K., Pedrycz, W. (1999) Fuzzy computing for data mining. Proceedings of the IEEE 87:1575–1600.
2. Kohavi, R., Sommerfield, D. (1995) Feature Subset Selection Using theWrapper Model: Overfitting and Dynamic Search Space Topology. Proceedings of KDD-95.
3. Lim, T.-S., Loh, W.-Y., Shih, Y.-S. (2000) A Comparison of Prediction Accuracy, Complexity, and Training Time of Thirty-three Old and New Classification Algorithms. Machine Learning 40:203–229.
4. Miyamoto, S. (1990) Fuzzy Sets in Information Retrieval and Cluster Analysis. Kluwer Academic Publishers.
5. Swiniarski, R.W., Skowron, A. (2003) Rough set methods in feature selection and recognition. Pattern Recognition Letters 24:833–849.

6. Theodoridis, S. and Koutroumbas, K. (1998) Pattern Recognition, Academic Press.
7. Tsapatsoulis, N., Wallace, M. and Kasderidis, S. (2003) Improving the Performance of Resource Allocation Networks through Hierarchical Clustering of High – Dimensional Data. Proceedings of the International Conference on Artificial Neural Networks (ICANN), Istanbul, Turkey.
8. Wallace, M., Stamou, G. (2002) Towards a Context Aware Mining of User Interests for Consumption of Multimedia Documents. Proceedings of the IEEE International Conference on Multimedia and Expo (ICME), Lausanne, Switzerland.
9. Yager, R.R. (2000) Intelligent control of the hierarchical agglomerative clustering process. IEEE Transactions on Systems, Man and Cybernetics, Part B 30(6): 835–845 Tsapatsoulis, N., Wallace, M. and Kasderidis, S.
10. Wallace, M., Mylonas, P. (2003) Detecting and Verifying Dissimilar Patterns in Unlabelled Data. 8th Online World Conference on Soft Computing in Industrial Applications, September 29th - October 17th, 2003.
11. Tom M. Mitchell. Machine Learning. McGraw-Hill Companies, Inc., 1997.
12. Wallace, M. and Kollias, S., "Soft Attribute Selection for Hierarchical Clustering in High Dimensions", Proceedings of the International Fuzzy Systems Association World Congress(IFSA), Istanbul, Turkey, June-July 2003.

Feature Deforming
for Improved Similarity-Based Learning

Sergios Petridis and Stavros J. Perantonis

Computational Intelligence Laboratory,
Institute of Informatics and Telecommunications,
National Center for Scientific Research "Demokritos",
153 10 Aghia Paraskevi, Athens, Greece
{petridis,sper}@iit.demokritos.gr

Abstract. The performance of similarity-based classifiers, such as K-NN, depends highly on the input space representation, both regarding feature relevence and feature interdependence. Feature weighting is a known technique aiming at improving performance by adjusting the importance of each feature at the classification decision. In this paper, we propose a non-linear feature transform for continuous features, which we call feade. The transform is applied prior to classification providing a new set of features, each one resulting by deforming in a local base the original feature according to a generalised mutual information metric for different regions of the feature value range. The algorithm is particularly efficient because it requires linear complexity in respect to the dimensions and the sample and does not need other classifier pre-training. Evaluation on real datasets shows an improvement in the performance of the K-NN classifier.

1 Introduction

The K-NN classifier is one of the earliest classifiers used for pattern recognition tasks. Its popularity stems from its conceptual simplicity and from the fact that it does not require elaborate training, since it stores training instances and performs evaluations only on queries (*lazy learning*). However, its performance and efficiency depend highly on the feature input space and on the number of training instances. A large number of variations of K-NN have been proposed to solve these problems. In this paper, we focus on the feature input space representation and propose an algorithm that aims at suitably transforming input features to improve classification performance. The algorithm is novel in that it integrates local relevance information *on* the features, by means of a deforming transform. The algorithm is thus decoupled from K-NN and can be viewed as a useful preprocesing of features and used with other classifiers as well.

2 Background

Adapting the feature space to increase performance of similarity – based classification is not a new idea. The reader is refered to [1] and [2] for an extended organ-

G.A. Vouros and T. Panayiotopoulos (Eds.): SETN 2004, LNAI 3025, pp. 201–209, 2004.
© Springer-Verlag Berlin Heidelberg 2004

ised survey of such methods. In this section we describe plain *feature weighting* for continuous features and stress its equivalence to a simple feature pre-scaling transform. In the literature, feature weighting is closely tied to the distance function used for classification. Let $x \in \mathcal{X} \subseteq \mathbb{R}^n, x = [x_1, \ldots, x_n]^\top$ be a stored observation vector and $q \in \mathcal{X}$ a "target" observation vector, the class of which we wish to determine. The feature-weighted distance is defined as

$$d(x, q) = \left(\sum_{i \in n} w_i \cdot |x_i - q_i|^r \right)^{1/r}, r = 1 \ldots \infty \tag{1}$$

where w_i, $i = 1 \ldots n$ are the non-negative feature–specific weights. Most commonly $r = 2$ which yields the feature–weighted euclidean distance. In words, (1) has the following interpretation: The weights w_i denote "importance". The more important a feature, the larger its contribution to the overall distance. Now, by a minor rearrangement of terms,

$$d(x, q) = \left(\sum_{i \in n} |w_i^{1/r} \cdot x_i - w_i^{1/r} \cdot q_i|^r \right)^{1/r} \tag{2}$$

$$= \left(\sum_{i \in n} |x_i' - q_i'|^r \right)^{1/r}, \quad \text{where}$$

$$x' = w^\top x, \quad \text{and}$$

$$q' = w^\top q$$

i.e. feature weighted distance can be viewed as a common L^r distance, where the feature has been previously linearly transformed by the weight vector $w = [w_1^{1/r}, \ldots, w_n^{1/r}]^\top$. Equation (2) gives rise to a slightly different view of feature weighting: to emphasize one feature in relation to the others, one can simply stretch it out, i.e. scale it by a factor larger than the others. This view has the advantage of completely dissociating weighting from distance computation and therefore the K-NN algorithm.

A crucial issue in the above is the definition of feature "importance" and, consequently, the evaluation of the weight (or scaling) vector. Since our concern is to increase classification accuracy, the importance measure has to be related to the relevance of features to the classification task. In this paper, we make use of a flexible family of mutual information metrics derived from the generalised Harvda-Chavrat entropy (see [3]). Mutual information metrics have the advantage of not making any a-priori assumptions about the probability density underlying the data.

Formally, the *generalised Harvda-Charvat (HC) entropy of order b* for the continous feature X_i is defined as

$$\mathcal{H}_b(X_i) = \frac{1}{1 - 2^{1-b}} \int_{\mathcal{X}_i} p(x)(1 - p(x)^{b-1}) dx, \quad b > 0, b \neq 1 \tag{3}$$

At the limit $b \to 1$, $\mathcal{H}_b$ coincides with Shannon's differential entropy, whereas for $b = 2$ it is known as quadratic entropy. Similarly, one defines the *generalised*

HC class-conditional entropy of a feature, i.e. the entropy of the feature when the value of the class random variable, C, is known

$$\mathcal{H}_b(\mathsf{X}_i|C = c) = \frac{1}{1 - 2^{1-b}} \int_{\mathcal{X}_i} p(x|c)(1 - p(x|c)^{b-1}) dx \qquad (4)$$

and, by averaging over all feature values, the *generalised HC feature equivocation*

$$\mathcal{H}_b(\mathsf{X}_i|C) = \sum_{c \in |\mathcal{C}|} p(c) \mathcal{H}_b(\mathsf{X}_i|C = c) \qquad (5)$$

Taking the difference of the generalised HC feature entropy and the generalised HC feature equivocation we obtain a form of the generalised HC feature information gain:

$$\mathcal{I}_b(\mathsf{X}_i \parallel C) = \mathcal{H}_b(\mathsf{X}_i) - \mathcal{H}_b(\mathsf{X}_i|C) \qquad (6)$$

$$= \frac{1}{1 - 2^{1-b}} \int_{\mathcal{X}_i} \left[p(x)(1 - p(x)^{b-1}) - \sum_{c \in |\mathcal{C}|} p(c)p(x|c)(1 - p(x|c)^{b-1}) \right] dx$$

which can be used to measure the dependence between X_i and C and thus the overall pertinence of X_i for deciding upon variable X_i. In the limit $b \rightarrow 1$, $\mathcal{I}_b(\mathsf{X}_i \parallel C)$ is symmetric with respect to C and X_i and is widely known as *mutual information* between the variables [4].

3   The Algorithm

Equivocation and mutual information, as seen in (6), are evalutated as averages over the entire feature value range. However, the term inside the integral contains localised information about the relevance of each feature, which in general varies as a function of the feature value. In other words, it may be the case that within some range the feature is relevant for classification (i.e classification boundaries depend on that feature), whereas within some other range the feature is less relevant, or even completely irrelevant. By taking the average, this local-type information is lost.

The idea underlying the feade algorithm is that instead of taking the average we can keep the local relevence information and *integrate* it to the feature by defining *local stretching factors*. Since these factors are in general different, the feature will be stretched in a non-homogeneous way and thus it can be thought of as *deformed*. In section 3.1 we define in mathematical terms the feature deforming transform and in section 3.2 we describe the method by which stretching factors are evaluated.

3.1   The Feature Deforming Transform

To formally define the deforming transform, consider first a single feature x taking values at the range $[\underline{x},\ \overline{x})$. Let also m be a strictly positive integer.

The feature is then split in m consequitive regions r^j, each one having length $\delta = |r^j| = (\overline{x} - \underline{x})/m$, as follows:

$$r^j = [(j-1) \cdot \delta + \underline{x}, \quad j \cdot \delta + \underline{x}), \quad j \in \{1, m\} . \tag{7}$$

The region index j is denoted with a superscript to avoid confusion with the feature index, which is denoted with a subscript throughout the presentation. The process of spliting in regions, here, should not be mistaken as quantisation of the continuous variable. The number of regions of x correspond merely to the finesse of the analysis. i.e more regions allow for a more precise definition of the transform.

Now, to each one of these regions, we attribute a *stretching factor* w^j. The evaluation of the stretching factors is based on local mutual information and will be the topic of the next section. For convenience, we also define the *cumulative stretched length* v^j as

$$v^j = \begin{cases} \sum_{k=1}^{j} w^k \cdot \delta, & j \in \{1, m\} \\ 0, & j = 0 \end{cases} \tag{8}$$

Then, the *feature deforming transform* is defined as

$$x' = g(x, \{w^j\}) = v^{\lfloor (x-\underline{x})/\delta \rfloor} + ((x - \underline{x}) \text{ rmod } \delta) \, w^{\lceil (x-\underline{x})/\delta \rceil}$$

where $\lfloor \cdot \rfloor$ and $\lceil \cdot \rceil$ are used to denote the maximum lower and minum higher integers indexes respective and the operator $(\alpha \text{ rmod } \beta)$ has been used to denote $\alpha - \lfloor \frac{\alpha}{\beta} \rfloor \beta$.

By applying the above transform, the range $[\underline{x}, \overline{x}]$ is un-homogenously mapped to the range $[0, v^m]$. In practice, the domain of x is deduced through training samples, and thus the bounds $\underline{x}$ and $\overline{x}$ may not be known exactly. In this case, one can extend the transform in the whole $(-\infty, +\infty)$ axis, assuming that the stetching factor w^1 applies also to the region $(-\infty, \underline{x})$ and the stretching factor w^m applies also to the $[\overline{x}, +\infty)$ region, as follows:

$$x' = g(x, \{w^j\}) = \begin{cases} (x - \underline{x}) \cdot w^1, & x \in (-\infty, \underline{x}) \\ v^{\lfloor (x-\underline{x})/\delta \rfloor} + ((x - \underline{x}) \text{ mod } \delta) \, w^{\lceil (x-\underline{x})/\delta \rceil}, & x \in [\underline{x}, \overline{x}) \\ v^m + (x - \overline{x}) \cdot w^m, & x \in [\overline{x}, +\infty) \end{cases} \tag{9}$$

The above deforming transform is defined independently for all n features, i.e. for each feature x_i, we attribute the feature–specific stretching factors w_i^j and define the feature–specific cumulative stretched lengths v_i^j. Thus the deformed feature vector can be evaluated as

$$\boldsymbol{x}' = g(\boldsymbol{x}, W) \tag{10}$$

where W is the stretching factors matrix $W = \{w_i^j\}$, $i = 1 \ldots n, j = 1 \ldots m$ and

$$\mathbf{g}(\boldsymbol{x}, W) = [g(x_1, \{w_1^j\}), \ldots, g(x_n, \{w_n^j\})]^\top \tag{11}$$

In terms of complexity, during its testing phase the algorithm requires storing the $m \times n$ matrices $W = \{w_i^j\}$ and $V = \{v_i^j\}$ and making $O(n)$ computations for each transform. As noted earlier m is a free parameter corresponding to the finesse of the transform, allowing for a trade-off between the memory required and the performance of the algorithm. In practice, for maximum perfomance, m is sometimes required to be larger than 500 although in most cases a value of 100 is enough.

3.2   Stretching Factor's Definition

In this section we discuss stretching factors learning. This topic is largely covered in litterature and includes two issues: the definition of a suitable metric for stretching factors and its evaluation through the training set. Regarding the first issue, as stated in Sect.2, we make use of a family of metrics derived from the generalised Harvda-Chavrat entropy. Looking back at (6), notice that the feature information gain can be written as

$$\mathcal{I}(X_i \parallel C) = \int_{\mathcal{X}_i} i(x \parallel C)dx \ , \tag{12}$$

where

$$i_b(x \parallel C) = \frac{1}{1 - 2^{1-b}} \left(p(x)(1 - p(x)^{b-1}) - \sum_{c \in |\mathcal{C}|} p(c)p(x|c)(1 - p(x|c)^{b-1}) \right) \tag{13}$$

The last quantity, $i_b(x \parallel C)$ is a measure of the feature relation with the class, when the feature takes the value x. Thus, it can be directly used to define the stretching factors w_i^j for all regions r_i^j. This is done by assuming that the probability is constant inside each region. Namely, consider a feature i and the region r_i^j as defined in (7) and let x_i^j be the mean value of the feature in this region:

$$x_i^j = (j - \frac{1}{2}) \cdot \delta + \underline{x} \tag{14}$$

Then the stretching factor w_i^j is defined as

$$w_i^j = i_b(x_i^j \parallel C) \cdot \delta \tag{15}$$

3.3   Stretching Factors' Evaluation

Unfortunately, evaluating $i_b(X_i = x_i^j; C)$, and thus w_i^j, requires the knowledge of probabilities $p(c|x_i^j)$ for all classes, which have to be estimated from the training set. Although the probability densities to be estimated are one-dimensional, this is still a crucial part for the success of the algorithm. In this version of the algorithm, we use a flexible kernel – smoothed histogram – based approach with a bias-correction term, allowing for a trade-off between accuracy and speed as well as compensation for noisy samples and overfitting. In general terms, it is a variant of parzen estimate with gaussian kernel [5], [6].

To begin with, consider first a window of width l around x_i^j.

$$s_i^j = [x_i^j - \frac{l}{2}, x_i^j + \frac{l}{2}] \tag{16}$$

The window width is not necessarily related to the region length δ, even though a larger value is recommended, so that the window covers at least the whole region. Furthermore, by using a kernel, the optimal window width is also dissociated from the specific sample set: larger values for l allow a more precise probability estimate. Finally, consider a *gaussian kernel* centered at x_i^j as

$$\kappa_i^j(x) = \frac{1}{\sqrt{2\pi}\sigma} e^{-\frac{(x-x_i^j)^2}{2\sigma^2}}, \quad \sigma \in \mathbb{R}^+ \tag{17}$$

The probabilities are then estimated by a training sample set $\{x\}$ as follows:

$$\hat{p}(c) = \frac{P_c}{P}, \quad \forall c \in \mathcal{C}, \tag{18}$$

$$\hat{p}(x_i^j|c) = \frac{1}{P_c} \sum_{\left\{ \substack{x:x_i \in s_i^j \\ x \mapsto c} \right\}} \kappa_i^j(x_i) \quad \text{and} \tag{19}$$

$$\hat{p}(x_i^j) = \sum_{c \in \mathcal{C}} \hat{p}(c) \cdot \hat{p}(x_i^j|c) \tag{20}$$

where, P is the total number of samples and P_c is the number of samples mapped to class c. Notice that the sums involve only samples whose projection on features lies inside the considered window s_i^j. This "approximate" parzen-density relies on the fact that, due to the kernel, distant features will not contribute essentially to the sum and thus can be ignored.

As it is known,(see,for instance,[7]), the width of the kernel σ is crucial for the evaluation of probabilities. A large value tends to reduce the estimation variance but increases its bias. To partially compensate for this defficiency, we make use of two techniques:

1. By making use of an adaptive kernel width, as suggested by Abramson [8]. The kernel width is set for each window as $p(x|c)^{-1/2}$, where the probabilities estimates are done using a fixed kernel width.
2. By adding a bias-correction term, as suggested in [9], to each of the local entropies that contribute to local mutual information. This term has the form

$$\lambda_{q,r} = \frac{1 - \frac{q}{r}}{2r},$$

where q is the number of samples in the window under consideration and r the total number of windows.

Both these techniques have been shown to improve algorithm performance.

Table 1. Generalisation accuracy of the K-NN: The columns correspond to: dataset name, number of input features, number of classes, number of samples, K-NN performance (K) and K-NN performance after the feade preprocessing

Dataset	N	C	P	K-NN (K)	feade +K-NN
diab	8	2	384	74.2 (15)	76.7 (15)
glass	9	6	214	68.2 (3)	76.4 (1)
indians	8	2	384	74.3 (15)	75.8 (15)
ionosph	33	2	351	86.3 (1)	90.7 (1)
iris	4	3	149	96.3 (11)	96.8 (9)
sonar	60	2	208	85.5 (1)	89.5 (1)

4   Experiments

4.1   Overall Performance

To evaluate the feade algorithm, we applied it to a number of benchmark tests, taken from the UC Irvine Machine Learning Repository. The evaluation aimed at comparing the generalisation performance of the K-NN algorithm, with and without the feade preprocessing. Table 1 presents the classificication accuracies achieved with plain K-NN vs feade + K-NN, as the average correct rates of 100 cross validation sets, using 80% of the data for training and the remaining 20% for testing. The scores concern the best performance, for varying numbers of neighbors.

As it is seen, feade manages to increase generalisation performance in all cases. The result is quite interesting, considering that the feade transform adapts dimensions independently from one an other. However it should be stressed that theses scores are the optimal scores obtained for varying configurations of the feade parameters. In particular, the kernel width seems to play an important role, even though special care has been taken for an automatic adjustement. Moreover, the entropy order also affects the performance. The results above have been obtained by setting the order to either $b = 1$ or $b = 2$.

4.2   The "Glass" Dataset

As a particular study case, we present the effect of the feade algorithm when applied to the "glass" benchmark test. The dataset, taken from the UC Irvine Machine Learning Repository, consists of 214 instances of glasses, grouped in 6 classes: float and non-float -processed building windows, non-float processed vehicle windows, containers, tableware and headlamps. Each instance is identified by 9 attributes (refractive index, Sodium, Magnesium, Aluminum, Silicon, Potassium, Calcium, Barium and Iron). Performing classification in this feature space has been proved to be difficult since there is a high overlapping of classes, with non-linear optimal borders and few number of instances.

Figure 1 shows a projection along the magnesium and silicon plane, before and after applying the feade transform. See that different regions of both the axes

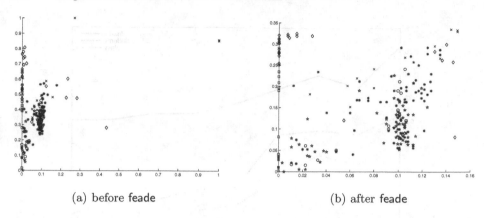

(a) before feade   (b) after feade

Fig. 1. Projection of the "glass" dataset along the "magnesium" and "silicon" axes

have been given different weights. Thus the feade space is a deformed version of the original space. Regions with no pertinent classification information have been "erased". Notice in particular, at the left half of the plane, instances marked with "x", corresponding to "containers", as well as instances marked with a diamond, corresponding to "headlamp", have approached each other, in comparison to the original space.

An evaluation of the improvement of the K-NN classifier generalisation is shown in Fig. 2. The curves correspond to the average classification over 30 trials, using 80% of the sample to adjust both the pre-processing step and the K-NN. The curves correspond to feade preprocesing, uniform weighting and non-preprocesing. As it is shown, optimal performance in all cases is achieved for $K = 1$. However, feade manages to achieve an increase on the generalisation accuracy by $\sim 8\%$ over no-preprocessing. Especially, notice that performance continues to be superior to the best no-preprocessing score even with increased number of neighbors.

5   Conclusions and Prospects

A novel algorithm has been presented which performs a non–linear transform of continuous one–dimensional features. The algorithm is efficient in that it has linear complexity with respect to the sample size and dimension. It has also been shown to significantly improve the generalisation accuracy of the K-NN algorithm. The algorithm performance has been shown to depend on two parameters, the kernel width and the order of the entropy, and a more thorough investigation is underway for their automatic setting.

By integrating local classification-pertinent information on the features, feade is dissociated from the classification algorithm. This amounts to a novel view of local feature weighting algorithms, since it allows for more flexibility in the design of a pattern recognition system. In particular, the authors intend to explore its behavior when combined with other preprocessing techniques and/or other classification methods.

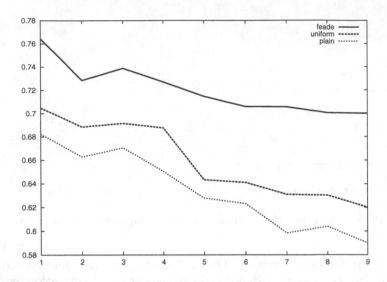

Fig. 2. Classification Accuracy of the K-NN algorithm for the "glass" dataset as a function of the number of nearest neighbors

References

1. Aha, D.W.: Feature weighting for lazy learning algorithms. In Motoda, H.L..H., ed.: Feature Extraction, Construction and Selection: A Data Mining Perspective. Norwell MA: Kluwer (1998)
2. Toussaint, G.: Proximity graphs for neares neighbor decision rules:recent progress. In: Proceedings of INTERFACE-2002, 34th Symposium on Computing ans Statistics. (2002)
3. Tsallis, C.: Entropic nonextensivity: A possible measure of complexity. Technical Report 00-08-043, Santa-Fe Institute (2000)
4. Cover, T.M., Thomas, J.A.: Elements of Information Theory. John Wiley & Sons, inc (1991)
5. Fukunaga, K.: Introduction to Statistical Pattern Recognition. Academic Press Limited (1990)
6. Wilson, D., R.Martinez, T.: Improved heterogeneous distance functions. Journal of Artificial Intelligence Research (1997)
7. J.Brewer, M.: A bayesian model for local smoothinh in kernel density estimation. Statistics and Computing **10** (2000) 299–309
8. Abramson, I.: On bandwidth variation in kernel estimates — a square root law. Annals of Statistics (1982)
9. Paninski, L.: Estimation of entropy and mutual information. Neural Computation **15** (2003) 1191–1253

Incremental Mixture Learning
for Clustering Discrete Data

Konstantinos Blekas and Aristidis Likas

Department of Computer Science, University of Ioannina, 45110 Ioannina, Greece
{kblekas,arly}@cs.uoi.gr

Abstract. This paper elaborates on an efficient approach for clustering discrete data by incrementally building multinomial mixture models
through likelihood maximization using the Expectation-Maximization
(EM) algorithm. The method adds sequentially at each step a new multinomial component to a mixture model based on a combined scheme of
global and local search in order to deal with the initialization problem
of the EM algorithm. In the global search phase several initial values
are examined for the parameters of the multinomial component. These
values are selected from an appropriately defined set of initialization candidates. Two methods are proposed here to specify the elements of this
set based on the agglomerative and the kd-tree clustering algorithms.
We investigate the performance of the incremental learning technique on
a synthetic and a real dataset and also provide comparative results with
the standard EM-based multinomial mixture model.

1 Introduction

Clustering of discrete (or categorical) data is an important problem with many
significant applications [1,2,3,4]. Although several methods have been proposed
for clustering continuous (real) data, the clustering of discrete data seems to
be more difficult mainly due to the nature of the discrete data: discrete values
cannot be ordered, it is not straightforward to define 'distance' measures and it
is also more difficult to specify appropriate differentiable objective functions and
apply continuous optimization methods to adjust the clustering parameters.

Nevertheless, several techniques have been proposed for clustering discrete
data [1,2,3]. Some of them transform the discrete features into continuous using
some type of encoding, most of them 1-of-K encoding for a feature assuming K
discrete values [2]. A disadvantage of such methods is that the dimensionality of
the input space becomes very large. Other techniques are simply based on the
definition of a distance measure (e.g. Hamming distance) which is exploited to
construct hierarchical clustering solutions (e.g. agglomerative) [1,3].

In this work we focus on *statistical model-based* methods for clustering discrete data [5,3]. Such methods are based on the *generative model* paradigm and
assume that the data have been generated by an appropriate mixture model
whose parameters can be identified through the maximization of a likelihood
function.

G.A. Vouros and T. Panayiotopoulos (Eds.): SETN 2004, LNAI 3025, pp. 210–219, 2004.
© Springer-Verlag Berlin Heidelberg 2004

More specifically we consider a *mixture of multinomials* model and assume that each data point has been generated through sampling from some multinomial component of the mixture model [3]. It is well-known that the EM algorithm can be employed to adjust the parameters of the model. Once the model has been trained, a data point is assigned to the cluster (multinomial component) with the highest posterior probability. An additional advantage of this approach is that it allows for soft clustering solutions based on the values of the posterior probabilities.

The main problem with EM is the dependence on the initial parameter values. An effective incremental solution has been recently proposed for the multinomial mixture model, which has been successfully applied in a bioinformatics context [4]. This method starts with one component and each time attempts to optimally add a new component to the current mixture through the appropriate use of global and local search procedures. As it will be described later, the application of the incremental approach requires the specification of set C of candidate parameter vectors for the new component to be added at each step. In [4] the set C was considered to contain as many elements as the training set. In this work we propose and evaluate two other methods for constructing the set C of initialization candidates, based on the methods *kd-tree* and *agglomerative clustering*. Comparative experimental results indicate that the integration of the agglomerative clustering approach into the incremental multinomial mixture learning method leads to a very powerful method for clustering discrete data.

2   An Incremental Scheme for Multinomial Mixture Models

2.1   The Mixture of Multinomials Model

Consider a dataset $X = \{\mathbf{x}^1 \ldots \mathbf{x}^N\}$, where each data point $\mathbf{x} = x_1, \ldots, x_d$ contains features with discrete values. More specifically, we assume that each feature x_i $(i = 1, \ldots, d)$ can take values from a finite set Ω_i of L_i discrete values, i.e. $x_i \in \Omega_i = \{\alpha_1^i, \ldots, \alpha_{L_i}^i\}$. We also assume that each feature x_i can be modeled with a multinomial distribution

$$P(x_i = \alpha_l^i) = p_{il} \text{ , with } |\mathbf{p}_i| = \sum_{l=1}^{L_i} p_{il} = 1 \text{ .} \tag{1}$$

The probabilistic vectors $\mathbf{p}_i$ $(i = 1, \ldots, d)$ define a multinomial parameter vector θ, i.e. $\theta = [\mathbf{p}_1 \ldots \mathbf{p}_d]$. Assuming that the features are independent, the density function $\phi(\mathbf{x}^n | \theta)$ for an arbitrary observation $\mathbf{x}^n = (x_1^n \ldots x_d^n)$ is given by

$$\phi(\mathbf{x}^n | \theta) = \prod_{i=1}^{d} \prod_{l=1}^{L_i} p_{il}^{\mathbf{I}(x_i^n, l)} \text{ ,} \tag{2}$$

where $\mathbf{I}(x_i^n, l)$ is a binary indicator function such that $\mathbf{I}(x_i^n, l) = 1$ if $x_i^n = \alpha_l^i$ and 0 otherwise.

A *mixture of multinomials* model $f(\mathbf{x}^n|\Psi_k)$ with k components is defined as:

$$f(\mathbf{x}^n|\Psi_k) = \sum_{j=1}^{k} \pi_j \phi_j(\mathbf{x}^n|\theta^j), \tag{3}$$

where Ψ_k is the vector of all unknown parameters, i.e. $\Psi_k = [\pi_1 \ldots \pi_k, \theta^1 \ldots \theta^k]$ and the mixing proportion π_j ($\pi_j \geq 0$) satisfy that $\sum_{j=1}^{k} \pi_j = 1$.

The log-likelihood of the dataset $X = \{\mathbf{x}^1, \ldots, \mathbf{x}^N\}$ given the above model is

$$\mathcal{L}(\Psi_k) = \sum_{n=1}^{N} \log f(\mathbf{x}^n|\Psi_k). \tag{4}$$

The EM algorithm provides a straightforward, convenient approach for maximum likelihood (ML) estimation of the parameters of the component densities based on the iterative application of the following update equations for each component $j = 1, \ldots, k$ [6,3,4]:

$$z_j^{n\,(t+1)} = \frac{\pi_j^{(t)} \phi_j(\mathbf{x}^n|\theta^{j^{(t)}})}{\sum_{j=1}^{k} \pi_j^{(t)} \phi_j(\mathbf{x}^n|\theta^{j^{(t)}})}, \tag{5}$$

$$\pi_j^{(t+1)} = \frac{1}{N} \sum_{n=1}^{N} z_j^{n\,(t+1)}, \tag{6}$$

$$p_{il}^{j\,(t+1)} = \frac{\sum_{n=1}^{N} z_j^{n\,(t+1)} \mathbf{I}(x_i^n, l)}{\sum_{n=1}^{N} \sum_{r=1}^{L_i} z_j^{n\,(t+1)} \mathbf{I}(x_i^n, r)}. \tag{7}$$

After training the multinomial mixture model, we can assign to a data point $\mathbf{x}^n$ a cluster label corresponding to the highest posterior probability value z_j^n ($j = 1, \ldots, k$).

It is well-known that the quality of the solutions provided by the EM algorithm depend highly on the initialization of the model parameters. To overcome the problem of poor initialization for the multinomial mixture model, an incremental learning scheme [4] has been proposed based on an appropriate adaptation of the greedy-EM algorithm for Gaussian mixtures [7].

2.2   Incremental Mixture Learning

Assume that a new component $k+1$ with density $\phi_{k+1}(\mathbf{x}^n|\theta^{k+1})$ is added to a k-component mixture model $f(\mathbf{x}^n|\Psi_k)$. This new component corresponds to a new cluster in the discrete domain modeled by a parameter vector θ^{k+1} containing the multinomial parameters. The resulting mixture with $k+1$ components can be represented as

$$f(\mathbf{x}^n|\Psi_{k+1}) = (1-a)f(\mathbf{x}^n|\Psi_k) + a\phi_{k+1}(\mathbf{x}^n|\theta^{k+1}), \tag{8}$$

where $a \in (0, 1)$. The new parameter vector Ψ_{k+1} consists of the parameter vector Ψ_k of the k-component mixture, the weight a and the vector θ^{k+1}. Then, the log-likelihood for Ψ_{k+1} is given by

$$\mathcal{L}(\Psi_{k+1}) = \sum_{n=1}^{N} \log f(\mathbf{x}^n | \Psi_{k+1})$$

$$= \sum_{n=1}^{N} \log\{(1-a)f(\mathbf{x}^n|\Psi_k) + a\phi_{k+1}(\mathbf{x}^n|\theta^{k+1})\}. \tag{9}$$

The above formulation proposes a two-component likelihood maximization problem, where the first component is described by the old mixture $f(\mathbf{x}^n|\Psi_k)$ and the second one is the new component with density $\phi_{k+1}(\mathbf{x}^n|\theta^{k+1})$, where $\theta^{k+1} = [\mathbf{p}_1^{k+1} \ldots \mathbf{p}_d^{k+1}]$. If we consider that the parameters Ψ_k of $f(\mathbf{x}^n|\Psi_k)$ remain fixed during maximization of $\mathcal{L}(\Psi_{k+1})$, the problem can be treated by applying searching techniques to optimally specify the parameters a and θ^{k+1} which maximize $\mathcal{L}(\Psi_{k+1})$. An efficient technique for the specification of θ^{k+1} and a is presented in [7] that follows a combination of global and local searching.
Global Search: It has been shown that a local maximum of $\mathcal{L}(\Psi_{k+1})$ with respect to a for a given parameter vector $\theta^{k+1} = \vartheta^m$, is given by [7]

$$\hat{\mathcal{L}}(\Psi_{k+1}) = \hat{\mathcal{L}}(\vartheta^m) = \sum_{n=1}^{N} \log \frac{f(\mathbf{x}^n|\Psi_k) + \phi_{k+1}(\mathbf{x}^n|\vartheta^m)}{2} + \frac{1}{2} \frac{[\sum_{n=1}^{N} \delta(\mathbf{x}^n|\vartheta^m)]^2}{\sum_{n=1}^{N} \delta^2(\mathbf{x}^n|\vartheta^m)},$$

$$\tag{10}$$

and is obtained for

$$\hat{a} = \frac{1}{2} - \frac{1}{2} \frac{\sum_{n=1}^{N} \delta(\mathbf{x}^n|\vartheta^m)}{\sum_{n=1}^{N} \delta^2(\mathbf{x}^n|\vartheta^m)}, \tag{11}$$

where

$$\delta(\mathbf{x}^n|\vartheta^m) = \frac{f(\mathbf{x}^n|\Psi_k) - \phi_{k+1}(\mathbf{x}^n|\vartheta^m)}{f(\mathbf{x}^n|\Psi_k) + \phi_{k+1}(\mathbf{x}^n|\vartheta^m)}. \tag{12}$$

The above formulation has the benefit of making the problem of likelihood maximization (Equation 9) independent of a. Therefore, it restricts global searching for finding good initial values ϑ^m for the multinomial distribution of the newly inserted component. To this end, the problem is now to define a proper set $\mathcal{C} = \{\vartheta^m, m = 1, \ldots, M\}$ of initialization *candidates*. Then, the candidate $\hat{\theta}_{k+1} \in \mathcal{C}$ that maximizes Equation 10 is identified and the corresponding $\hat{a}$ value is computed using Equation 11.
Local Search: The EM algorithm can be used to perform local search for the maximum of the likelihood with respect to parameters a and θ_{k+1} only, starting from the values $\hat{a}$ and $\hat{\theta}_{k+1}$ identified in the global search phase. In analogy to Equations 5-7, the following update equations called *partial EM* can be derived for maximizing $\mathcal{L}(\Psi_{k+1})$:

$$z_{k+1}^{n^{(t+1)}} = \frac{a^{(t)} \phi_{k+1}(\mathbf{x}^n|\theta^{k+1^{(t)}})}{(1-a^{(t)})f(\mathbf{x}^n|\Psi_k) + a^{(t)}\phi_{k+1}(\mathbf{x}^n|\theta^{k+1^{(t)}})}, \tag{13}$$

$$a^{(t+1)} = \frac{1}{N} \sum_{n=1}^{N} z_{k+1}^{n^{(t+1)}}, \tag{14}$$

$$p_{il}^{k+1^{(t+1)}} = \frac{\sum_{n=1}^{N} z_{k+1}^{n^{(t+1)}} \mathbf{I}(x_i^n, l)}{\sum_{n=1}^{N} \sum_{r=1}^{L_i} z_{k+1}^{n^{(t+1)}} \mathbf{I}(x_i^n, r)}. \tag{15}$$

The performance of the above incremental algorithm highly depends on the 'quality' of the initialization candidates included in set $\mathcal{C}$. In the following sections we describe and evaluate several methods for candidate specification.

3   Methods for the Specification of Initialization Candidates

3.1   Exhaustive Search over the Training Set

A reasonable and straightforward strategy to define the set $\mathcal{C}$ of candidates is to consider the whole training set $X = \{\mathbf{x}^1, \ldots, \mathbf{x}^N\}$, and directly associate each discrete data point $\mathbf{x}^m$ with a multinomial distribution $\vartheta^m = [\rho_1^m \ldots \rho_d^m]$ constructed as follows:

$$\rho_{il}^m = \lambda^{\mathbf{I}(x_i^m, l)} \left(\frac{1-\lambda}{L_i - 1}\right)^{1 - \mathbf{I}(x_i^m, l)}, \tag{16}$$

It is easy to show that $\sum_{l=1}^{L_i} \rho_{il}^m = 1$ for each feature i ($i = 1, \ldots, d$). The parameter λ has a fixed value in the range $(0, 1)$, and should satisfy $\lambda \geq 1/L_i$ ($\forall i$). In such way a set with $M = N$ candidates is created. We will refer to this method as ES (Exhaustive Search).

The drawback of this method is that all the N data points of X must be examined each time a new component has to be inserted. Alternatively, we can use data partitioning schemes that lead to the identification of much less candidates ($M << N$) and more informative.

3.2   The kd-Tree Algorithm for Partitioning Discrete Data

The first partitioning scheme we have used is based on the notion of kd-trees. Initially, kd-trees [8] were proposed in the case of continuous data, as an attempt to speed-up the execution of nearest neighbor queries. A kd-tree defines a recursive binary partitioning of a k-dimensional dataset, where the root node contains all data. A subset of the original dataset is assigned to each tree node and the tree construction procedure proceeds by partitioning the subset of a node into two subsets using a hyperplane perpendicular to the direction for which the subset data demonstrate the highest variance.

In order to deal with discrete features we have used the following entropy-based procedure to partition the data points corresponding to a node. In particular, for a node m that contains N^m data points, we first calculate its multinomial parameters $\rho_{il}^m = N_{il}^m/N^m$, based on the sufficient statistics N^m and

$N_{il}^m = \sum_{n=1}^{N^m} \mathbf{I}(x_i^n, l)$. Then, the entropy H_i^m of each feature i ($i = 1, \ldots, d$) for the data of node m can be computed as follows

$$H_i^m = -\sum_{l=1}^{L_i} \rho_{il}^m \log \rho_{il}^m \ . \tag{17}$$

Then, we can identify the feature $i^\star$ that exhibits the largest entropy value, i.e. $i^\star = \arg\max_i H_i^m$. The partitioning procedure is based on the values $x_{i^\star}$ of the data points belonging to node m. First the $L_{i^\star}$ different values of the feature $i^\star$ are sorted according to the probabilities $\rho_{i^\star l}^m$ and then each value is marked in turn as *odd* or *even*. In this way, two new nodes m_1 and m_2 are created, where the m_1 (m_2) node contains the node m data for which the value of feature $i^\star$ is marked as odd (even).

One last observation that must be made concerns the selection of the leaf node m that will be partitioned at each step. This is done by selecting among the current leaf nodes of the tree the one that exhibits the minimum likelihood value. Following the definition in Equation 2, the log-likelihood that characterizes a node m is

$$\mathcal{L}_m(\vartheta^m) = \sum_{n=1}^{N_m} \sum_{i=1}^{d} \sum_{l=1}^{L_i} \mathbf{I}(x_i^n, l) \log \rho_{il}^m$$

$$= \sum_{i=1}^{d} N^m \sum_{l=1}^{L_i} \rho_{il}^m \log \rho_{il}^m = -\sum_{i=1}^{d} N^m H_i^m \ . \tag{18}$$

The above top-down procedure builds a tree with several nodes and the partitioning of a leaf node is not allowed when the number of included data points is lower than a fixed value T. The kd-tree construction procedure terminates either when there exist no leaf nodes that can be splitted, or when a predetermined number M of leaf nodes have been constructed.

In our experiments in order to specify a candidate initialization set $\mathcal{C}$ with M vectors ϑ^m, a kd-tree was first constructed with M leafs. Then each vector ϑ^m was determined from the sufficient statistics of the data points assigned to the corresponding leaf m ($m = 1, \ldots, M$). We will refer to this method as KD.

3.3   Agglomerative Clustering

In contrast to the kd-tree method, the Agglomerative clustering (AC) is a synthetic clustering scheme [3]. The method starts with a set of N clusters, each containing one data point $\mathbf{x}^n$. At each step the AC method searches among the set of current clusters to identify the two closest clusters (m_1, m_2) that are subsequently merged into one cluster by assigning all data points of clusters m_1, m_2 to the newly formed cluster $< m_1, m_2 >$. To apply the AC algorithm, an intercluster distance measure $d(m_1, m_2)$ is needed, defined as

$$d(m_1, m_2) = \mathcal{L}_{m_1}(\vartheta^{m_1}) + \mathcal{L}_{m_2}(\vartheta^{m_2}) - \mathcal{L}_{<m_1, m_2>}(\vartheta^{<m_1, m_2>}) \ , \tag{19}$$

where the $\mathcal{L}_m(\vartheta^m)$ is calculated, as in the kd-tree case, according to Equation 18. The algorithm terminates when a specified number M of clusters have been found. An implementation of the AC algorithm for discrete data is presented in [3] that requires nearly $\mathcal{O}(N^2)$ runtime.

Once the AC algorithm has terminated with M clusters, we specify the elements ϑ^m $(m = 1, \ldots, M)$ of $\mathcal{C}$ using exactly the same procedure with the kd-tree approach described previously.

4   Experimental Results

We have conducted a series of experiments to evaluate how the different procedures for candidate specification influence the performance of the incremental algorithm. Using each method (ES, KD, AC) three sets of candidates were specified and the incremental scheme was then applied for initializing the parameters of each added component k.

Moreover, two additional standard EM-based multinomial mixture models were created, where their parameters were initialized by the agglomerative and the kd-tree clustering algorithms, respectively. More specifically, we first applied both algorithms until a number of K clusters were created. Then, the statistics of each cluster k were used for initializing the mixture model parameters and the EM algorithm was applied to adjust them. We will refer to these two models as AC-EM and KD-EM, respectively. Two evaluation criteria have been used, the first being the likelihood of each obtained mixture model on a test set and the second the test set classification accuracy (although class labels were not used in training).

4.1   Experiments with a Synthetic Dataset

In the synthetic dataset used in our experiments each true cluster (called class) j $(j = 1, \ldots, K)$ was associated with a unique *generator* string of length d containing letters from an alphabet $\Omega = \{A, B, \ldots, I\}$, ie. $\Omega_i = \Omega, \forall i = 1, \ldots, d$. In this way, $K = 10$ different data generators with $d = 20$ features were selected, where some of them present high degree of similarity and thus the discrimination among the corresponding clusters is difficult.

The data points of each class j were created as noisy copies of generator string j by randomly deciding whether to mutate each generator feature i with mutation probability $\varrho = 0.4$ $(0 \leq \varrho \leq 1)$, where mutation means that the value of a feature i changes by randomly selecting a value from the corresponding alphabet Ω_i. In this way, 10000 discrete data points were sampled (1000 for each class) and 3000 of them (300 for each class) were selected for training, while the rest 7000 data were used for testing.

Table 1 presents the results for the synthetic dataset. The AC and KD clustering algorithms were run until $M = 200$ subsets were discovered, which are subsequently used to specify the multinomial parameter vectors included in the set $\mathcal{C}$ of initialization candidates. As the results indicate, the exhaustive search

(ES) method for defining the set $\mathcal{C}$, although considering the whole training set, does not provide as good results as the other two approaches AC and KD which illustrate the best (and similar) performance for both criteria.

It is also interesting to note that the proposed incremental schemes compare favorably to both AC-EM [3] and KD-EM, ie. stand-alone EM with the K components, initialized from the statistics of K subsets obtained using either AC or kd-tree. Since the AC-EM approach is considered one of the most effective approaches for clustering discrete data[3], it can be concluded that the proposed methods are very powerful. These conclusions are also supported from the experiments on a real dataset described below.

Table 1. Performance of the incremental approach using three methods for specifying initialization candidates as well as of the AC-EM and KD-EM models on the synthetic dataset.

Performance criteria	Incremental mixture			AC-EM	KD-EM
	Initialization methods				
	AC	KD	ES		
log-Likelihood (training)	-92612	-92612	-94108	-92715	-93209
log-Likelihood (test)	-220067	-220067	-223676	-220276	-221574
Classification rate (%)	98.21	98.21	72.09	97.33	90.66

4.2   Experiments with the Mushrooms Dataset

We have also conducted experiments with a real dataset, namely the mushrooms dataset from the UCI Machine Learning repository. It consists of $d = 22$ discrete features that describe physical attributes of mushrooms taking between 2 and 12 values. Totally there are 8124 discrete data labeled as either class 0 (poisonous mushrooms) or class 1 (eligible mushrooms), which were equally divided into a training and testing set (4062 cases in each dataset). In all experiments the class labels were ignored in the training phase. We first applied the AC algorithm to construct a set $\mathcal{C}$ of $M = 200$ initialization candidates for the incremental mixture learning method. The kd-tree algorithm was also applied to create another set $\mathcal{C}'$ of $M = 200$ candidates. The incremental learning scheme using either $\mathcal{C}$ or $\mathcal{C}'$ was compared to AC-EM method.

Figure 1 displays the log-likelihood value $\mathcal{L}(\Psi_K)$ on the test set as a function of the number of clusters (components) K. The superiority of the incremental approach when initialized with the AC algorithm is clear for all values of K ($2 \leq K \leq 12$). In contrast to the synthetic dataset, the kd-tree algorithm did not offer so good values for initializing the multinomial components, and thus the corresponding model provided worse results for this dataset. Moreover, the superiority of the incremental AC scheme can also be seen in Table 2 providing the class distribution in the clusters obtained for $K = 10$.

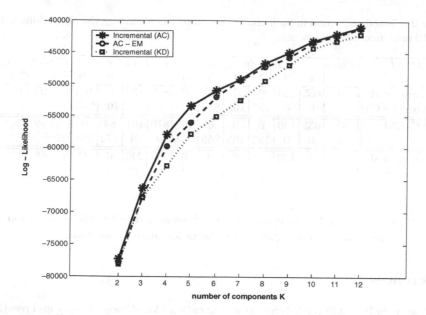

Fig. 1. The test set log likelihood values for several values of the number of multinomial components K.

5   Conclusions

In this paper we elaborated on an incremental scheme for model-based clustering of discrete data, where a multinomial model is constructed by sequentially adding new components. An exploration mechanism based on global and local search ensures the fine tuning of the parameter vector of the added multinomial component. To solve the problem of specifying the set C of initialization candidates two clustering methods have been examined based on kd-trees and agglomerative clustering. The experiments conducted on a synthetic and a real dataset have shown the incremental training method, coupled with a powerful technique for the specification of initialization candidates, constitutes a very effective approach for clustering discrete data.

In cases of very large datasets, the application of the AC algorithm to the whole training set is time consuming [3]. A solution to this problem is to apply the AC method to a randomly selected portion of the dataset. On the other hand, the size of the dataset does not constitute a problem for the proposed kd-tree algorithm, therefore, the use of kd-tree for the specification of initialization candidates may lead to better results in the case of very large datasets. It is also possible to develop hybrid schemes combining the AC and kd-tree methods. An approach of this type would first divide the dataset into a number of subsets using the kd-tree method and then would apply the AC algorithm to the data of each subset. Finally, it must be noted that in this work we do not address the problem of assessing the optimal number of multinomial components K. This

Table 2. Class distribution in each cluster obtained when running the algorithms with $K = 10$ multinomial components.

Model	Class	Class distribution in every cluster										Classification rate (%)
		1	2	3	4	5	6	7	8	9	10	
Incremental mixture (AC)	0	655	130	0	0	0	0	870	139	0	185	95.44
	1	0	0	127	105	855	338	0	0	102	556	
AC-EM	0	655	130	0	0	0	139	870	101	84	0	92.27
	1	0	0	127	105	855	338	0	91	172	395	
Incremental mixture (KD)	0	655	130	0	0	0	0	934	240	0	20	86.32
	1	0	0	127	105	855	338	508	48	102	0	

constitutes one of our future research directions and requires the adaptation of several well-known methodologies and criteria for model selection [5].

References

1. Cheeseman P. and Stutz J. Bayesian classification (AutoClass): Theory and resutls. In U. Fayyad, G. Piatesky-Shapiro, P. Smyth, and R. Uthurusamy, editors, *Advances in Knowledge Discovery and Data Mining*, pages 153–180. CA: AAAI Press, 1995.
2. Bengio Y. and Bengio S. Modeling high-dimensional discrete data with multi-layer neural networks. In S.A. Solla, T.K. Leen, and K.-R. Móller, editors, *Advances in Neural Processing Systems 12*, pages 400–406. MIT Press, 2000.
3. Meilǎ M. and Hecherman D. An experimental comparison of model-based clustering methods. *Machine Learning*, 42:9–29, 2001.
4. Blekas K., Fotiadis D.I., and Likas A. Greedy mixture learning for multiple motif discovering in biological sequences. *Bioinformatics*, 19(5):607–617, 2003.
5. Chickering D. and Heckerman D. Efficient approximations for the marginal likelihood of Bayesian networks with hidden variables. *Machine Learning*, 29:181–212, 1997.
6. Render R.A. and Walker H.F. Mixture densities, maximum likelihood and the EM algorithm. *SIAM Review*, 26(2):195–239, 1984.
7. Vlassis N. and Likas A. A greedy EM algorithm for Gaussian mixture learning. *Neural Processing Letters*, 15:77–87, 2002.
8. Bentley J.L. Multidimensional binary search trees used for associative searching. *Commun. ACM*, 18(9):509–517, 1975.

A Cost Sensitive Technique
for Ordinal Classification Problems

Sotiris B. Kotsiantis and Panagiotis E. Pintelas

Educational Software Development Laboratory, Department of Mathematics
University of Patras, Hellas
{sotos,pintelas}@math.upatras.gr

Abstract. A class of problems between classification and regression, learning to predict ordinal classes, has not received much attention so far, even though there are many problems in the real world that fall into that category. Given ordered classes, one is not only interested in maximizing the classification accuracy, but also in minimizing the distances between the actual and the predicted classes. This paper provides a systematic study on the various methodologies that have tried to handle this problem and presents an experimental study of these methodologies with a cost sensitive technique that uses fixed and unequal misclassification costs between classes. It concludes that this technique can be a more robust solution to the problem because it minimizes the distances between the actual and the predicted classes, without harming but actually slightly improving the classification accuracy.

1 Introduction

Machine learning methods for classification problems commonly assume that the class values are unordered. However, in many practical applications the class values do exhibit a natural order. Ordinal classification refers to an important category of real world problems, in which the attributes of the instances to be classified and the classes are linearly ordered. Ordinal classification may be viewed as a bridging problem between the two standard machine-learning tasks of classification and regression.

In a standard classification problem the input instances are associated with one of k unordered sets of labels denoting the class membership. Since the target values are unordered, the metric distance between the prediction and the correct output is the non-metric 0-1 indicator function. In a standard regression problem target values range over the real numbers therefore the loss function can take into account the full metric structure. In ordinal classification, the target values are in a finite set (like in classification) but there is an ordering among the elements (like in regression, but unlike classification).

Settings in which it is natural to rank or rate instances arise in many fields such as information retrieval, visual recognition, collaborative filtering, econometric models and classical statistics. In collaborative filtering for example, the goal is to predict a person's rating on new items such as learning material given the person's past ratings on similar items and the ratings of other people of all the items (including the new

G.A. Vouros and T. Panayiotopoulos (Eds.): SETN 2004, LNAI 3025, pp. 220–229, 2004.

item). The ratings are ordered, such as "highly recommended", "good",..., "very bad" thus collaborative filtering falls naturally under the domain of ordinal classification. In another domain such as the prediction of the therapeutic success, the outcome will be also ordered, e.g. (1) good recovery, (2) moderate disability, (3) severe disability, (4) vegetative survival, and (5) dead.

Although machine learning algorithms for ordinal classification are rare, there are many statistical approaches to this problem. However, they all rely on specific distributional assumptions for modeling the class variable and also assume a stochastic ordering of the input space [7]. The machine learning community has mainly addressed the issue of ordinal classification in two ways. One is to apply classification algorithms by discarding the ordering information in the class attribute [3]. The other is to apply regression algorithms by transforming class values to real numbers [8] This paper proposes a cost-sensitive technique that takes into account matrices of misclassification costs. The cost matrices express relative and unequal distances between classes. Experimental results show that this technique minimizes the distances between the actual and the predicted classes, without harming but actually slightly improving the prediction accuracy.

This paper is organized as follows: The next section discusses the different techniques that have been proposed for handling ordinal classification problems. In section 3, we describe the proposed cost sensitive technique. In Section 4, we present the experimental results of our methodology using different distribution algorithms and compare these results with those of other approaches. In the final section of the paper we discuss further work and some conclusions.

2 Techniques for Dealing with Ordinal Problems

Standard classification algorithms for nominal classes can be applied to ordinal prediction problems by discarding the ordering information in the class attribute. However, some information that could improve the predictive performance of a classifier is lost when this is done.

The usage of regression algorithms to solve ordinal classification problems has been examined in [8]. In this case each class needs to be mapped to a numeric value. However, if the class attribute represents a truly ordinal quantity, which, by definition, cannot be represented as a number in a meaningful way, there is no principled way of devising an appropriate mapping and this procedure is necessarily ad hoc.

Another approach is to reduce the multi-class ordinal classification problem to a set of binary classification problems using the one-against-all approach. In the one-against-all approach, we train a classifier for each of the classes using as positive examples the training examples that belong to that class, and as negatives all the other training examples. We then couple the estimates given by each binary classifier in order to obtain class probability membership estimates for the multi-class problem [3].

A more sophisticated approach that enables standard classification algorithms to make use of ordering information in ordinal class attributes is presented in [5]. Similarly with previous method, this method converts the original ordinal class problem

into a series of binary class problems that encode the ordering of the original classes. However, to predict the class value of an unseen instance this algorithm needs to estimate the probabilities of the k original ordinal classes using our $k - 1$ models. For example, for a three class ordinal problem, estimation of the probability for the first ordinal class value depends on a single classifier: Pr(*Target* < *first value*) as well as for the last ordinal class: Pr(*Target* > *second value*). Whereas, for class value in the middle of the range, the probability depends on a pair of classifiers and is given by
    Pr(*Target* > *first value*) * (1 − Pr(*Target* > *second value*)).

3 Proposed Technique

Given ordered classes, one is not only interested in maximizing the classification accuracy, but also in minimizing the distances between the actual and the predicted classes. Thus, we want a bias in favor of the middle class. An approach is to incorporate costs in decision-making defining fixed and unequal misclassification costs between classes. Cost model takes the form of a cost matrix, where the cost of classifying a sample from a true class j to class i corresponds to the matrix entry λ_{ij}. This matrix is usually expressed in terms of average misclassification costs for the problem. The diagonal elements are usually set to zero, meaning correct classification has no cost. We may define conditional risk for making a decision α_i as:

$$R(a_i \mid x) = \sum_i \lambda_{ij} P(v_j \mid x)$$

The equation states that the risk of choosing class i is defined by fixed misclassification costs and the uncertainty of our knowledge about the true class of x expressed by the posterior probabilities. The goal in cost-sensitive classification is to minimize the cost of misclassification, which can be realized by choosing the class (v_j) with the minimum conditional risk. Thus, a cost matrix for a three-class ordinal classification problem could be:

$$\begin{bmatrix} 0 & 1 & 2 \\ 1 & 0 & 1 \\ 2 & 1 & 0 \end{bmatrix}$$

whereas for n-class problem it would be:

$$\begin{bmatrix} 0 & 1 & 2 & \ldots & n-1 \\ 1 & 0 & 1 & \ldots & n-2 \\ \ldots & \ldots & \ldots & \ldots & \ldots \\ n-2 & \ldots & 1 & 0 & 1 \\ n-1 & \ldots & 2 & 1 & 0 \end{bmatrix}$$

A key feature of our method is that it does not require any modification of the underlying learning algorithm; it is applicable as long as the classifier produces class probability estimates. In the following section, we empirically evaluate the performance of our approach with the other well known techniques.

4 Experiments

To test the hypothesis that the above method improves the generalization performance on ordinal prediction problems, we performed experiments on real-world datasets. We used well-known datasets from many domains from the UCI repository [4]. The used datasets represented numeric prediction problems and thus we converted the numeric target values into ordinal quantities using equal-size binning. This unsupervised discretization method divides the range of observed values into three equal size intervals. The resulting class values are ordered, representing variable-size intervals of the original numeric quantity. This method was chosen because of the lack of benchmark datasets involving ordinal class values.

All accuracy estimates were obtained by averaging the results from 10 separate runs of stratified 10-fold cross-validation. It must be mentioned that we used the free available source code for our experiments by the book [14]. We have tried to minimize the effect of any expert bias by not attempting to tune any of the algorithms to the specific data set. Wherever possible, default values of learning parameter were used. This naïve approach results in lower estimates of the true error rate, but it is a bias that affects all the learning algorithms equally.

In the following subsections we present the empirical results obtained using a decision tree algorithm, a rule-based algorithm and an instance-based learning algorithm. All of them produce class probability estimates.

4.1 Decision Trees

A recent overview of existing work on decision trees and a taste of their usefulness to the newcomers in the field of machine learning are provided in [9]. Decision trees are trees that classify instances by sorting them based on feature values. Each node in a decision tree represents a feature in an instance to be classified, and each branch represents a value that the node can take. Instances are classified starting at the root node and sorting them based on their feature values. Most well-known decision tree algorithm is the C4.5 [11]. Model trees are the counterpart of decision trees for regression tasks. They have the same structure as decision trees, with one difference: they employ a linear regression function at each leaf node to make a prediction. The most well known model tree inducer is the M5´[12].

Table 2 shows the results for the C4.5 algorithm in the three-class situation, applied (a) without any modification of C4.5, (b) in conjunction with the ordinal classification method presented in Section 2 (C45-ORD), (c) using classification via regression (M5´) and (d) using the proposed cost-sensitive technique (C4.5-COST).

Table 1. Transforming a decision tree algorithm for ordinal classification tasks.

Dataset		C4.5-COST	C4.5	M5´	C4.5-ORD
auto93	accuracy	79.71	80.83	81.24	78.31
	MeanError	0.13	0.16	0.15	0.17
autoHorse	accuracy	96.78	96.78	94.74	96.93
	MeanError	0.02	0.03	0.06	0.03
autoMpg	accuracy	82.24	82.09	82.36	82.79
	MeanError	0.12	0.17	0.16	0.17
autoPrice	accuracy	89.25	89.25	89.5	89.68
	MeanError	0.07	0.08	0.11	0.08
baskball	accuracy	71.29	70.64	71.46	67.9
	MeanError	0.19	0.26	0.26	0.27
bodyfat	accuracy	98.37	98.37	99.12	98.37
	MeanError	0.01	0.02	0.06	0.02
cleveland	accuracy	69.5	69.57	75.09	68.9
	MeanError	0.2	0.23	0.22	0.23
cloud	accuracy	90.53	90.54	88.76	91.12
	MeanError	0.06	0.08	0.11	0.07
cpu	accuracy	97.19	96.95	97.14	97.42
	MeanError	0.02	0.02	0.03	0.02
echoMonth	accuracy	63.46	62.46	66.08	65.54
	MeanError	0.24	0.29	0.31	0.31
fishcatch	accuracy	97.72	97.65	96.84	97.91
	MeanError	0.02	0.02	0.06	0.01
housing	accuracy	80.34	78.22	82.33	79.07
	MeanError	0.15	0.17	0.17	0.16
hungarian	accuracy	80.22	80.22	82.44	80.22
	MeanError	0.13	0.2	0.17	0.2
lowbwt	accuracy	60.09	60.09	61.3	60.04
	MeanError	0.27	0.3	0.3	0.3
pbc	accuracy	55.25	55.53	57.4	54.27
	MeanError	0.3	0.34	0.34	0.35
pharynx	accuracy	70.52	69.4	43.97	73.59
	MeanError	0.2	0.26	0.39	0.25
pwLinear	accuracy	78.05	76.55	78.3	78.5
	MeanError	0.16	0.18	0.23	0.17
sensory	accuracy	64.24	64.24	64.24	64.05
	MeanError	0.24	0.35	0.33	0.35
strike	accuracy	99.21	99.21	99.21	99.21
	MeanError	0.01	0.01	0.01	0.01
veteran	accuracy	91.26	91.26	91.26	91.26
	MeanError	0.06	0.11	0.11	0.11
AVERAGE	accuracy	80.76	80.49	80.14	80.75
	MeanError	0.13	0.16	0.18	0.16

In Table 2, for each data set the algorithms are compared according to classification accuracy (the rate of correct predictions) and to mean absolute error:

$$\frac{|p_1 - a_1| + \ldots + |p_n - a_n|}{n}$$, where p: predicted values and a: actual values.

As one can see from the aggregated results in Table 2, the proposed cost-sensitive technique is slightly better in classification accuracy than the remaining approaches. However, it manages to minimize the distances between the actual and the predicted classes. The reduction of the mean absolute error is about 19% (1-0.13/0.16) compared to the simple C4.5 and the C4.5-ORD, while it exceeds the 27% compared to M5′ It must be mentioned that the C4.5-ORD technique [5] outperforms the simple C4.5 only in classification accuracy. It does not manage to minimize the distance between the actual and the predicted class. Moreover, the M5′ seems to give the worst average results according to our experiments even though in several data sets its performance is much better than the performance of the remaining algorithms.

It must also be mentioned that a decision tree learning algorithm for monotone learning problems has been presented in [10]. In a monotone learning problem both the input attributes and the class attribute are assumed to be ordered. This is different from the setting considered in this paper because we do not assume that the input is ordered.

4.2 Rule Based Learning

Classification rules represent each class by disjunctive normal form (DNF). A k-DNF expression is of the form: $(X_1 \wedge X_2 \wedge \ldots \wedge X_n) \vee (X_{n+1} \wedge X_{n+2} \wedge \ldots X_{2n}) \vee \ldots \vee (X_{(k-1)n+1} \wedge X_{(k-1)n+2} \wedge \ldots \wedge X_{kn})$, where k is the number of disjunctions, n is the number of conjunctions in each disjunction, and X_n is defined over the alphabet $X_1, X_2, \ldots, X_j. \cup {\sim}X_1, {\sim}X_2, \ldots, {\sim}X_j$ The general goal is to construct the smallest rule-set that is consistent with the training data. A large number of learned rules are usually a sign that the learning algorithm tries to "remember" the training set, instead of discovering the assumptions that govern it. PART algorithm forms rules from pruned partial decision trees in an attempt to avoid over-prune. Once a partial tree has been build, a single rule is extracted from it [6]. M5rules implements routines for generating a decision list using M5′ model trees and the approach used by the PART algorithm [14].

Table 6 shows the accuracy and the mean absolute error estimates for the rule based algorithm PART in the three-class situation, applied (a) without any modification PART, (b) in conjunction with the ordinal classification method presented in Section 2 (PART-ORD), (c) using classification via regression (M5rules) and (d) using the proposed cost-sensitive technique (PART-COST).

As one can see from the aggregated results in Table 3, the proposed cost-sensitive technique is not extraordinarily better in classification accuracy than the remaining techniques. However, it manages to minimize the distances between the actual and the predicted classes. The reduction of the mean absolute error is about 12% compared to the simple PART and the PART-ORD, while it overcomes the 17% compared to M5 rules.

Table 2. Transforming a rule-based algorithm for ordinal classification tasks.

Dataset		PART-COST	PART	M5rules	PART-ORD
auto93	accuracy	81.31	80.23	79.9	78.2
	MeanError	0.13	0.14	0.15	0.15
autoHorse	accuracy	96.78	96.78	93.9	96.93
	MeanError	0.02	0.03	0.06	0.03
autoMpg	accuracy	81.99	80.03	82.14	80.76
	MeanError	0.13	0.15	0.16	0.15
autoPrice	accuracy	89.38	89.38	90.5	90.44
	MeanError	0.07	0.08	0.09	0.07
baskball	accuracy	67.96	66.6	70.72	60.39
	MeanError	0.22	0.26	0.26	0.28
bodyfat	accuracy	98.37	98.13	98.41	98.37
	MeanError	0.01	0.02	0.04	0.02
cleveland	accuracy	69.69	69.73	75.02	68.91
	MeanError	0.2	0.21	0.22	0.22
cloud	accuracy	90.86	89.75	88.97	90.84
	MeanError	0.07	0.08	0.1	0.08
cpu	accuracy	97.57	97.05	97.42	97.42
	MeanError	0.02	0.02	0.02	0.02
EchoMonth	accuracy	63.69	62.77	65.69	63.38
	MeanError	0.24	0.28	0.31	0.29
fishcatch	accuracy	97.79	97.65	97.08	97.91
	MeanError	0.02	0.02	0.04	0.01
Housing	accuracy	81.27	78.74	82.07	79.68
	MeanError	0.14	0.15	0.16	0.15
hungarian	accuracy	81.07	81.11	82.4	80.9
	MeanError	0.13	0.17	0.17	0.17
lowbwt	accuracy	56.66	56.66	61.51	56.34
	MeanError	0.29	0.31	0.3	0.31
pbc	accuracy	52.74	52.86	57.62	52.45
	MeanError	0.32	0.34	0.34	0.34
pharynx	accuracy	70.56	70.61	43.38	71.45
	MeanError	0.2	0.25	0.38	0.25
pwLinear	accuracy	79.55	76.55	76.9	77.8
	MeanError	0.16	0.16	0.23	0.16
sensory	accuracy	60.99	57.92	64.38	60.41
	MeanError	0.28	0.33	0.33	0.32
strike	accuracy	99.21	99.21	99.11	99.21
	MeanError	0.01	0.01	0.01	0.01
veteran	accuracy	88.78	87.18	90.82	87.34
	MeanError	0.09	0.11	0.11	0.11
AVERAGE	accuracy	80.31	79.45	79.90	79.46
	MeanError	0.14	0.16	0.17	0.16

It must be mentioned that the ordinal technique [5] does not manage to outperform the simple PART. On the contrary, the M5rules seems to give better classification accuracy but worse mean absolute error according to our experiments than plain PART.

4.3 Instance Based Learning

One of the most straightforward instance-based algorithms is the nearest neighbour algorithm [1]. K-Nearest Neighbour (kNN) is based on the principal that the instances within a data set will generally exist in close proximity with other instances that have similar properties. If the instances are tagged with a classification label, then the value of the label of an unclassified instance can be determined by observing the class of its nearest neighbours. The kNN locates the k nearest instances to the query instance and determines its class by identifying the single most frequent class label. The absolute position of the instances within this space is not as significant as the relative distance between instances. This relative distance is determined using a distance metric. Many different metrics are presented in [13].

Locally weighted linear regression (LWR) is a combination of instance-based methods and linear regression [2]. Instead of performing a linear regression on the full, unweighted dataset, it performs a weighted linear regression, weighting the nearest training instances according to their distance to the test instance at hand. This means that a linear regression has to be done for each new test instance, which makes the method computationally quite expensive. However, it also makes it highly flexible, and enables it to approximate non-linear target functions.

Table 3 shows the accuracy and the mean absolute error estimates for the 3NN in the three-class situation, applied (a) without any modification 3NN, (b) in conjunction with the ordinal classification method presented in Section 2 (3NN-ORD), (c) using classification via regression (LWR) and (d) using the proposed cost-sensitive technique (3NN-COST).

As one can see from the aggregated results in Table 3, the proposed cost-sensitive technique has similar results to 3NN-ORD However, the reduction of the mean absolute error is about 12% compared to the simple 3NN and the LWR.

It must be mentioned that the LWR seems to give the worst average results according to our experiments even though in several data sets its performance is much better than the performance of the remaining algorithms.

5 Conclusion

This paper is devoted to the problem of learning to predict ordinal (i.e., ordered discrete) classes. We study various ways of transforming a simple algorithm for ordinal classification tasks. The cost-sensitive ordinal classification method discussed in this paper uses fixed and unequal misclassification costs between classes and is applicable in conjunction with any learning algorithm that can output class probability estimates.

Table 3. Transforming an instance based algorithm for ordinal classification tasks.

Dataset		3NN-COST	3NN	LWR	3NN-ORD
auto93	accuracy	78.46	78.36	84.01	78.46
	MeanError	0.14	0.15	0.12	0.14
autoHorse	accuracy	88.33	88.33	93.56	88.33
	MeanError	0.08	0.09	0.05	0.08
autoMpg	accuracy	82.41	82.41	81.44	82.41
	MeanError	0.12	0.14	0.14	0.12
autoPrice	accuracy	86.93	86.23	88.94	86.23
	MeanError	0.09	0.1	0.09	0.09
baskball	accuracy	60.36	59.52	60.66	60.36
	MeanError	0.26	0.29	0.29	0.26
bodyfat	accuracy	86	86	79.72	86
	MeanError	0.09	0.12	0.15	0.09
cleveland	accuracy	71.12	72.32	69.2	71.12
	MeanError	0.19	0.2	0.21	0.19
cloud	accuracy	81.93	81.93	85.69	81.93
	MeanError	0.12	0.12	0.12	0.12
cpu	accuracy	96.42	97.05	98.48	97.05
	MeanError	0.02	0.02	0.01	0.02
echoMonths	accuracy	64.15	56.31	55	64.15
	MeanError	0.24	0.31	0.32	0.24
fishcatch	accuracy	95.84	94.83	94.44	95.84
	MeanError	0.03	0.05	0.06	0.03
Housing	accuracy	78.34	78.04	78.2	78.34
	MeanError	0.14	0.17	0.17	0.14
hungarian	accuracy	82.33	82.33	78.84	82.33
	MeanError	0.12	0.14	0.15	0.12
lowbwt	accuracy	56.13	55.81	58.67	56.13
	MeanError	0.29	0.31	0.3	0.29
pbc	accuracy	51.36	50.78	49.53	51.36
	MeanError	0.32	0.35	0.35	0.32
pharynx	accuracy	62.88	63.43	58.53	64.26
	MeanError	0.25	0.26	0.33	0.24
pwLinear	accuracy	72.15	70.45	62.65	71.1
	MeanError	0.19	0.24	0.25	0.19
sensory	accuracy	62.54	60.63	52.57	62.21
	MeanError	0.25	0.33	0.32	0.25
strike	accuracy	99.21	99.21	98.77	99.21
	MeanError	0.01	0.01	0.01	0.01
veteran	accuracy	88.08	88.08	87.05	88.08
	MeanError	0.08	0.12	0.11	0.08
AVERAGE	accuracy	77.25	76.60	75.80	77.24
	MeanError	0.15	0.17	0.17	0.15

According to our experiments in synthetic ordinal data sets, it manages to minimize the distances between the actual and the predicted classes, without harming but actually slightly improving the classification accuracy in conjunction with C4.5, PART and 3-NN algorithms. Drawing more general conclusions from these synthetic experimental data seems unwarranted. Our results so far show that cost-sensitive methodology for predicting ordinal classes can be naturally derived from classification algorithms, but more extensive experiments with real ordinal data sets from diverse areas will be needed to establish the precise capabilities and relative advantages of this methodology.

References

1. Aha, D.: Lazy Learning. Dordrecht: Kluwer Academic Publishers (1997).
2. Atkeson, C. G., Moore, A.W., & Schaal, S.: Locally weighted learning. Artificial Intelligence Review 11 (1997) 11–73.
3. Allwein, E. L., Schapire, R. E., and Singer, Y.: Reducing multiclass to binary: A unifying approach for margin classifiers. Journal of Machine Learning Research 1 (2000) 113–141.
4. Blake, C.L. & Merz, C.J.: UCI Repository of machine learning databases. Irvine, CA: University of California, Department of Information and Computer Science. [http://www.ics.uci.edu/~mlearn/MLRepository.html] (1998).
5. Frank, E. and Hall M.: A simple approach to ordinal prediction, L. De Raedt and P. Flach (Eds.): ECML 2001, LNAI 2167, pp. 145-156, 2001, Springer-Verlag Berlin.
6. Frank E. and Witten I.: Generating Accurate Rule Sets Without Global Optimization. In Shavlik, J., ed., Machine Learning: Proceedings of the Fifteenth International Conference (1998), Morgan Kaufmann Publishers, San Francisco, CA.
7. Herbrich R., Graepel T., and Obermayer K.: Regression models for ordinal data: A machine learning approach. Technical report, TU Berlin, 1999.
8. S. Kramer, G. Widmer, B. Pfahringer, and M. DeGroeve. Prediction of ordinal classes using regression trees. Fundamenta Informaticae (2001).
9. Murthy (1998), Automatic Construction of Decision Trees from Data: A Multi-Disciplinary Survey, Data Mining and Knowledge Discovery 2 (1998) 345–389, Kluwer Academic Publishers.
10. Potharst R. and Bioch J.C.: Decision trees for ordinal classification. Intelligent Data Analysis 4(2000) 97-112.
11. Quinlan J.R.: C4.5: Programs for machine learning. Morgan Kaufmann, San Francisco (1993).
12. Wang, Y. & Witten, I. H.: Induction of model trees for predicting continuous classes, In Proc. of the Poster Papers of the European Conference on ML, Prague (1997) 128–137. Prague: University of Economics, Faculty of Informatics and Statistics.
13. Wilson, D., Martinez, T.: Reduction Techniques for Instance-Based Learning Algorithms Machine Learning 38 (2000) 257–286,. Kluwer Academic Publishers.
14. Witten I. & Frank E.: Data Mining: Practical Machine Learning Tools and Techniques with Java Implementations, Morgan Kaufmann, San Mateo (2000).

Pap-Smear Classification Using Efficient Second Order Neural Network Training Algorithms

Nikolaos Ampazis[1], George Dounias[1], and Jan Jantzen[2]

[1] Department of Financial and Management Engineering, University of the Aegean,
82100 Chios, Greece
[2] Technical University of Denmark, Oersted-DTU Automation,
DK-2800 Kongens Lyngby, Denmark

Abstract. In this paper we make use of two highly efficient second order neural network training algorithms, namely the LMAM (Levenberg-Marquardt with Adaptive Momentum) and OLMAM (Optimized Levenberg-Marquardt with Adaptive Momentum), for the construction of an efficient pap-smear test classifier. The algorithms are methodologically similar, and are based on iterations of the form employed in the Levenberg-Marquardt (LM) method for non-linear least squares problems with the inclusion of an additional adaptive momentum term arising from the formulation of the training task as a constrained optimization problem. The classification results obtained from the application of the algorithms on a standard benchmark pap-smear data set reveal the power of the two methods to obtain excellent solutions in difficult classification problems whereas other standard computational intelligence techniques achieve inferior performances.

1 Introduction

The medical task of classifying and daily diagnosing several pap-smear images is a time-consuming process, which is done manually for the moment. A faster computer-assisted technique able to perform classification and diagnosis, somewhat automatically and competitively to human experts, would represent a great advancement for cytologists in the future. In this paper we utilize two very efficient feedforward neural network training techniques recently proposed in [1, 2], to the pap-smear image classification problem. The utilized techniques achieve superior performance compared to several previous classification attempts, especially when the task is to discriminate between normal and abnormal cell images. Comparative results of competitive approaches are given within the paper. The Pap-Test data consist of measurements that correspond to the acquisition of a specimen from the uterine cervix, which is then stained using the widely known "Papanikolaou method" [22]. This procedure enables the observation of the cells using a microscope. The clinical database includes 500 cases each of them described in terms of various morphological characteristics of cells. Recent work in the domain of pap-smear classification, demonstrates the application of neuro-fuzzy systems for classification [5], nearest neighbour methods [5], supervised and

G.A. Vouros and T. Panayiotopoulos (Eds.): SETN 2004, LNAI 3025, pp. 230–245, 2004.

unsupervised hard and fuzzy c-means techniques [20], Gustafson-Kessel clustering [20], genetic programming and entropy information-based machine learning
approaches [28].

2   Overview of the LMAM and OLMAM Algorithms

The Levenberg Marquardt with Adaptive Momentum (LMAM) and the Optimized Levenberg Marquardt with Adaptive Momentum (OLMAM) algorithms
are two very efficient second-order algorithms for training feedforward neural
networks and, in some cases, they have been shown to achieve the best training
results on standard benchmark datasets ever reported in the neural networks
literature[1, 2]. The main idea in the formulation of the algorithms is that a
one-dimensional minimization in the direction dw_{t-1} followed by a second minimization in the direction dw_t does not guarantee that the neural network's cost
function has been minimized on the subspace spanned by both of these directions. For a feedforward neural network with K output units and a set of P
training patterns, the Mean Square Error (MSE) cost function is defined as

$$E(\boldsymbol{w}) = \frac{1}{2} \sum_{p=1}^{P} \sum_{i=1}^{K} (d_i^{(p)} - y_i^{(p)})^2 \tag{1}$$

where $y_i^{(p)}$ and $d_i^{(p)}$ denote the output activations and desired responses respectively, and $\boldsymbol{w}$ is the column vector containing all the weights and thresholds of
the network.

A solution to the problem of simultaneous subspace minimization is to choose
minimization directions which are non-interfering and linearly independent. This
can be achieved by the selection of *conjugate* directions which form the basis of
the Conjugate Gradient (CG) method [8]. Two vectors dw_t and dw_{t-1} are non-
interfering or mutually conjugate with respect to $\nabla^2 E(\boldsymbol{w}_t)$ when

$$dw_t^T \nabla^2 E(\boldsymbol{w}_t) dw_{t-1} = 0 \tag{2}$$

Therefore, the objective is to reach a minimum of the cost function of equa-
tion (1) with respect to $\boldsymbol{w}$ and to simultaneously maximize $\Phi_t = dw_t^T \nabla^2 E(\boldsymbol{w}_t)$
dw_{t-1} without compromising the need for a decrease of the cost function. The
strategy adopted for the solution of this problem follows the methodology for
incorporating additional knowledge in the form of constraints in neural network
training originaly proposed in [23].

At each iteration of the learning process, the weight vector $\boldsymbol{w}_t$ is incremented
by dw_t, so that

$$dw_t^T \nabla^2 E(\boldsymbol{w}_t) dw_t = (\delta P)^2 \tag{3}$$

where δP is a constant. Thus, at each iteration, the search for an optimum new
point in the weight space is restricted to a small hyperellipse centered at the
point defined by the current weight vector. The shape of such a hyperellipse
reflects the scaling of the underlying problem, and restricts the assignment of

undeserved weight to certain directions. If δP is small enough, the changes to $E(\boldsymbol{w}_t)$ induced by changes in the weights can be approximated by the first differential $dE(\boldsymbol{w}_t)$. At each iteration, it is desirable to achieve the maximum possible change in Φ_t, so that (3) is respected, and the change $dE(\boldsymbol{w}_t)$ in $E(\boldsymbol{w}_t)$ is equal to a predetermined quantity $\delta Q_t < 0$ i.e.

$$dE(\boldsymbol{w}_t) = \delta Q_t \tag{4}$$

This is a constrained optimization problem which can be solved analytically by introducing two Lagrange multipliers λ_1 and λ_2 to take account of equations (4) and (3) respectively. The function ϕ_t is introduced, which is defined as follows:

$$\phi_t = \Phi_t + \lambda_1(\delta Q_t - dE(\boldsymbol{w}_t)) + \lambda_2[(\delta P)^2 - d\boldsymbol{w}_t^T\nabla^2 E(\boldsymbol{w}_t)d\boldsymbol{w}_t] \tag{5}$$

On evaluating the differentials involved in the right hand side, and substituting Φ_t we readily obtain:

$$\phi_t = d\boldsymbol{w}_t{}^T\nabla^2 E(\boldsymbol{w}_t)d\boldsymbol{w}_{t-1} + \lambda_1(\delta Q_t - \nabla E(\boldsymbol{w}_t)^T d\boldsymbol{w}_t)$$
$$+\lambda_2[(\delta P)^2 - d\boldsymbol{w}_t^T\nabla^2 E(\boldsymbol{w}_t)d\boldsymbol{w}_t] \tag{6}$$

To maximize ϕ_t at each iteration, we demand that:

$$d\phi_t = d^2\boldsymbol{w}_t^T \cdot (\nabla^2 E(\boldsymbol{w}_t)d\boldsymbol{w}_{t-1} - \lambda_1\nabla E(\boldsymbol{w}_t) - 2\lambda_2\nabla^2 E(\boldsymbol{w}_t)d\boldsymbol{w}_t) = 0 \tag{7}$$

and

$$d^2\phi_t = -2\lambda_2[d^2\boldsymbol{w}_t^T\nabla^2 E(\boldsymbol{w}_t)d^2\boldsymbol{w}_t] < 0 \tag{8}$$

Hence, from equation (7) we obtain:

$$d\boldsymbol{w}_t = -\frac{\lambda_1}{2\lambda_2}[\nabla^2 E(\boldsymbol{w}_t)]^{-1}\nabla E(\boldsymbol{w}_t) + \frac{1}{2\lambda_2}d\boldsymbol{w}_{t-1} \tag{9}$$

The above equation constitutes the weight update rule for the neural network. Due to the special form of the cost function (equation (1)), the Hessian matrix can be also approximated by the following equation [2]:

$$\nabla^2 E(\boldsymbol{w}_t) = (J_t^T J_t + \mu_t \boldsymbol{I}) \tag{10}$$

This approximation yields the following weight update rule for the neural network

$$d\boldsymbol{w}_t = -\frac{\lambda_1}{2\lambda_2}[(J_t^T J_t + \mu_t \boldsymbol{I})]^{-1}\nabla E(\boldsymbol{w}_t) + \frac{1}{2\lambda_2}d\boldsymbol{w}_{t-1} \tag{11}$$

Equation (11) is similar to the Levenberg-Marquard (LM) weight update rule with the important differences that in equation (11) there is an additional adaptive momentum term (Levenberg-Marquardt with Adaptive Momentum - LMAM) and that the LM step is multiplied with an adaptive factor which controls its size. The quantity μ_t can be selected as in [12]: If a successful step is taken (i.e. $E(\boldsymbol{w}_t + d\boldsymbol{w}_t) < E(\boldsymbol{w}_t)$) then μ_t is decreased by a factor of 10 biasing, therefore, the iteration towards the Gauss-Newton direction. On the other hand if for the current μ_t the step is unsuccessful ($E(\boldsymbol{w}_t + d\boldsymbol{w}_t) > E(\boldsymbol{w}_t)$) then μ_t is increased by the same factor until a successful step can be found (since the increase of μ_t drives $d\boldsymbol{w}_t$ to the negative gradient).

Equation (11) is useful provided that λ_1 and λ_2 can be evaluated in terms of known quantities. This can be done as follows: From equations (4) and (9) we obtain:

$$\delta Q_t = \frac{1}{2\lambda_2}(I_{GF} - \lambda_1 I_{GG}) \tag{12}$$

with I_{GG} and I_{GF} are given by

$$I_{GG} = \nabla E(\boldsymbol{w}_t)^T [\nabla^2 E(\boldsymbol{w}_t)]^{-1} \nabla E(\boldsymbol{w}_t), \quad I_{GF} = \nabla E(\boldsymbol{w}_t)^T d\boldsymbol{w}_{t-1} \tag{13}$$

with $\nabla^2 E(\boldsymbol{w}_t)$ given by equation (10).

Eqn (12) can be readily solved for λ_1, giving :

$$\lambda_1 = \frac{-2\lambda_2 \delta Q_t + I_{GF}}{I_{GG}} \tag{14}$$

It remains to evaluate λ_2. To this end, we substitute (9) into (3) to obtain:

$$4\lambda_2^2 (\delta P)^2 = I_{FF} + \lambda_1^2 I_{GG} - 2\lambda_1 I_{GF} \tag{15}$$

where I_{FF} is given by

$$I_{FF} = d\boldsymbol{w}_{t-1}^T \nabla^2 E(\boldsymbol{w}_t) d\boldsymbol{w}_{t-1}, \tag{16}$$

Finally, we substitute (14) into (15) and solve for λ_2 to obtain :

$$\lambda_2 = \frac{1}{2}\left[\frac{I_{GG}(\delta P)^2 - (\delta Q_t)^2}{I_{FF}I_{GG} - I_{GF}^2}\right]^{-1/2} \tag{17}$$

where the positive square root value has been chosen for λ_2 in order to satisfy equation (8) for a positive definite Hessian matrix. Note also the bound $|\delta Q_t| \leq \delta P \sqrt{I_{GG}}$ set on the value of δQ_t by equation (17). We always use a value $\delta Q = -\xi \delta P \sqrt{I_{GG}}$ where ξ is a constant between 0 and 1. Thus, the final weight update rule has only two free parameters, namely δP and ξ. The value chosen for the free parameter ξ determines the contribution of the constraints to the weight update rule. A large value of ξ means that the weight update rule is biased towards the LM step, while a small value of ξ has the opposite effect. In our experiments the values recorded for δP and ξ are those giving the best performance. However, similar performances were recorded with $0.85 < \xi < 0.95$ and $0.6 < \delta P < 0.1$. The range of optimal values for ξ indicates that it is a good practice not to deviate much from the LM step which actually predicts the maximum possible decrease in the error function, whereas the range of optimal δP values shows that the size of the trust region should be conservatively selected.

The LMAM algorithm has two free parameters δP and ξ that should be externally determined for the evaluation of the adaptation of the weights according

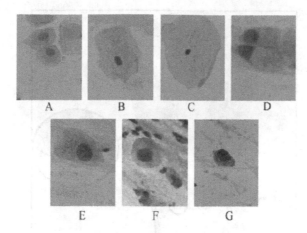

Fig. 1. Some of the cells found in cervix: (A) parabasal, (B) intermediate, (C) super-ficial squamous epithelia, (D) columnar epithelium, (E-F) mild, moderate and severe non-keratinizing dysplasia (Source: Byriel, 1999)

to equation (11). The OLMAM (Optimized Levenberg-Marquardt with Adaptive Momentum) implements exactly the same weight update rule of equation (11) but is a modification of the LMAM algorithm in order to achieve independency from the externaly provided parameter values δP and ξ. This independency is achieved by automaticaly regulating analytical mathematical conditions that should hold in order to ensure the constant maintenance of the conjugacy between weight changes in successive epochs. Further details on the OLMAM algorithm can be found in [2].

3   Description of the Pap-Smear Problem

Using a small brush, a cotton stick or wooden stick, a specimen is taken from the uterine cervix and transferred onto a thin, rectangular glass plate (slide). The specimen (smear) is stained using the Papanikolaou method. This makes it possible to see characteristics of cells more clearly in a microscope. The purpose of the smear screening, is to diagnose pre-malignant cell changes before they progress to cancer. Smears contain mainly two types of cells: squamous epithelial cells and columnar epithelial cells (Figure 1). The columnar epithelium is found in the upper part of cervix, and the squamous epithelium in the lower part (Figure 2). The screening of smears is done by a cyto-technologist and/or cyto-pathologist. It is time consuming, as each slide may contain up to 300,000 cells. The columnar epithelium consists of a single layer of cells, resting on the basal membrane. Underneath the columnar epithelium are the reserve cells, which can multiply to produce squamous metaplasia. The nucleus is located at the bottom of the cytoplasm. When viewed from the top, the area of the nucleus will seem large when compared to the area of its cytoplasm. Viewed from the side, the

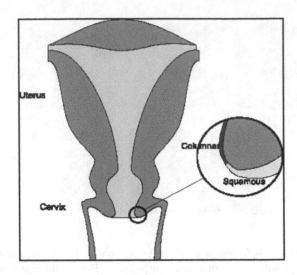

Fig. 2. Schematic drawing of the uterus and the cervix. The drawing also shows the transformation zone where the exocervicas squamous epithelium meets the endocervical columnar epithelium. (Source: Byriel, 1999)

cytoplasm will seem larger (Figure 1(d)) . The area of the nucleus is $\sim 50\mu m^2$ and it is darker than the surrounding cytoplasm. The squamous epithelium is divided into four layers; the basal, parabasal, intermediate and superficial layer. The cells of the basal layer lie on the basal membrane, and they produce the cells of the overlying layers. The most mature cells are found in the superficial layer. Cells of the basal and parabasal layers are round, with nuclei of $\sim 50\mu m^2$ and cytoplasm of $200-300\mu m^2$ (Figure 1(a)). Cells of the intermediate and superficial layers have small nuclei of $20 - 35\mu m^2$ and large cytoplasm of $800 - 1600\mu m^2$ (Figure 1(b-c)). Dysplastic cells are cells that have undergone pre-cancerous changes. They generally have larger and darker nuclei and have a tendency to cling together in large clusters. Squamous dysplasia is divided into three classes: mild, moderate and severe (Figure 1(e-g)). Mild dysplastic cells have enlarged and light nuclei. For moderate dysplastic cells, the nuclei are larger and darker. The nuclei may have begun to deteriorate, which is seen as a granulation of the nuclei. In the last stage of precancerous changes, severe dysplasia, the nuclei are large, dark and often deformed. The cytoplasm of severe dysplasia is dark and small when compared to the nuclei. More details on the pap-smear problem can also be found in [16] and [21].

4   The Data Set

The complete data set consists of 500 cases. Occasionally, we split this data set into training and testing sub-sets in different ways per approach. The complete data set consists of the following cases:

Class Number	General diagnosis of cells	Detailed description of the type of cells	Number of cases
1	Normal	*Columnar* epithelial	50
2	Normal	*Parabasal* squamous epithelial	50
3	Normal	*Intermediate* squamous epithelial	50
4	Normal	*Superficial* squamous epithelial	50
5	Abnormal	*Mild* squamous non-keratinizing dysplasia	100
6	Abnormal	*Moderate* squamous non-keratinizing dysplasia	100
7	Abnormal	*Severe* squamous non-keratinizing dysplasia	100

For describing the main characteristics of the examined pap-smear images, we use 20 numerical attributes, which represent typical cell measurements, such as nucleus area, cytoplasm area, nucleus and cytoplasm brightness, nucleus and cytoplasm shortest and longest diameter, nucleus and cytoplasm perimeter, nucleus and cytoplasm x- and y- locations, maxima and minima in nucleus and cytoplasm, etc., see [5] and [20] for more details.

5 Previously Applied Methodologies

Several intelligent classification approaches have been previously attempted for the pap-smear classification problem. The neuro-fuzzy architecture called ANFIS (Adaptive Neuro Fuzzy Inference System) introduced by Jang [14, 13], has been used to implement fuzzy rules for classification of cells [5]. ANFIS is a methodology for tuning a fuzzy inference system by implementing it as an adaptive network (see also [15]). Regarding the pap-smear problem, ANFIS reached its best performance (95.5% overall correct classification of cells) when used to produce a model for discriminating between normal and abnormal cells (2 classes). The c-means clustering algorithm is a clustering algorithm that finds natural (spherical) clusters in the data. C-means clustering has relatively few parameters to tune and the used data has no limit on how many dimensions it can have (i.e. the number of features). There are two versions of the c-means algorithm, hard c-means (HCM) and fuzzy c-means (FCM), see ([4] and [10]). Hard c-means assigns for each case the membership value of 1 to the nearest cluster center and a membership of 0 to all others, while fuzzy c-means modifies in fact HCM, by allowing the data points to belong to all clusters, with membership degrees in the interval [0,1]. Another competitive clustering method is the Gustafson-Kessel (GK) approach, by which a cluster could adapt from spherical to hyperellipsoidal shapes. All clustering techniques can be either supervised, or unsupervised. Supervised is called the clustering by which an expert somehow guides the process (i.e. predefines the number of clusters to be formed). Sometimes, feature selection is desirable prior to the application of a clustering technique, so better discriminating attributes are used to form clusters and complexity also reduces. All the above mentioned clustering approaches, are described in detail within [20], both in theory and presentation of results for the pap-smear problem. The most important and representative results of all techniques (HCM, FCM, GK) under various settings are shown in Table 1. Most of the approaches perform

Table 1. Results for separation accuracy between normal and abnormal cells, using various supervised and unsupervised clustering techniques, such as fuzzy c-means, hard c-means, and the Gustafson-Kessel method (Byriel, 1999), (Martin 2003)

Method	Nr. of Cases used & Classes to Discriminate	Division of the Data Set to Train & Test Data	Testing Accuracy
Unsupervised GK (Gustafson -Kessel) Clust. Method	500 (2) (classes 1+2+3+4 vs 5+6+7)	90 - 10 % (cross. val. 10-folds)	88.66 %
Supervised GK Clustering Method	500 (2) (classes 1+2+3+4 vs 5+6+7)	90 - 10 % (cross. val. 10-folds)	95.56 %
Feature Selection & Unsupervised GK Clust. Method	500 (2) (classes 1+2+3+4 vs 5+6+7)	90 - 10 % (cross. val. 10-folds)	90.08 %
Feature Selection & Supervised GK Clust. Method	500 (2) (classes 1+2+3+4 vs 5+6+7)	90 - 10 % (cross. val. 10-folds)	97.11 %
Unsupervised FCM (Fuzzy C-Means)	500 (2) (classes 1+2+3+4 vs 5+6+7)	90 - 10 % (cross. val. 10-folds)	96.69 %
Supervised FCM	500 (2) (classes 1+2+3+4 vs 5+6+7)	90 - 10 % (cross. val. 10-folds)	96.94 %
Feature Selection & Unsupervised FCM	500 (2) (classes 1+2+3+4 vs 5+6+7)	90 - 10 % (cross. val. 10-folds)	98.19 %
Feature Selection & Supervised FCM	500 (2) (classes 1+2+3+4 vs 5+6+7)	90 - 10 % (cross. val. 10-folds)	98.36 %
Unsupervised HCM (Hard C-Means)	500 (2) (classes 1+2+3+4 vs 5+6+7)	90 - 10 % (cross. val. 10-folds)	94.01 %
Supervised HCM	500 (2) (classes 1+2+3+4 vs 5+6+7)	90 - 10 % (cross. val. 10-folds)	95.97 %
Feature Selection & Unsupervised HCM	500 (2) (classes 1+2+3+4 vs 5+6+7)	90 - 10 % (cross. val. 10-folds)	96.12 %
Feature Selection & Supervised HCM	500 (2) (classes 1+2+3+4 vs 5+6+7)	90 - 10 % (cross. val. 10-folds)	97.20 %

well when called to discriminate among two classes, whereas their performance reduces considerably when a discrimination of the data set to all 7 classes is requested. The best performance is obtained for the application of supervised fuzzy c-means classification, after the application of an initial feature selection based on simulated annealing. The method separates normal from abnormal cells (2 class discrimination) obtaining accuracy of 98.36% in the test set according to 10-fold cross-validation. If FCM and GK clustering methods assume that clusters are spherical or cigar-shaped, the Nearest NeighbourHOOD algorithm (NNH) is able to handle cluster of more complex schemes, see [10] and [5]. According to the NNH method, the separation of two pap-smear classes (normal and abnormal cells) is comparatively high, reaching 96.3%. Entropy information-based machine learning techniques attempt to split the data into smaller subsets using the divide-and-conquer principle through entropy measurements, aiming at forming a decision tree or a set of rules that classifies all data into a category [26]. The C4.5 algorithm is the most famous approach, mainly among experts, for its comprehensibility rather than its accuracy level. For example, the application of C4.5 on the pap-smear data gave meaningful rules, recognized by medical experts as very close to their practice, as the following:

Rule 8: (cover 45) :
$K/C \leq 0.044$ AND *KerneLong*>8.23 AND *CytoLong*>52.39 AND *KernePeri*>27.56
THEN class-3 [0.979]

Table 2. Results of C4.5

C4.5	Pruning Level	Items to form a rule	Training Acc.	Testing Acc.
Standard	0 %	1	97.8 - 99.8 %	67.2 - 67.4 %
Boost	0 %	1	99.8 - 100 %	68.0 - 69.4 %
Standard	0 %	2	94.6 - 95.4 %	67.0 - 70.0 %
Boost	0 %	2	100 %	70.6 - **73.0** %
Standard	25 %	2	94.6 - 95.4 %	66.8 - 67.8 %
Boost	25 %	2	100 %	71.4 %

The above rule covers nearly 10% of the training data, no negative instances and there is a prospect for 97.9% probability of correct classification of new cases in the future. The meaning of the symbolic names are as follows: K/C is the ratio between nucleus area and cytoplasm area, KerneLong is the nucleus longest diameter, CytoLong is the cytoplasm longest diameter, and KernePeri is the nucleus perimeter. The measurement unit is 1 micron or 10^{-6} meters. The entropy-based technique described above obtains quite low performance on the test set, when used to discriminate among all 7 classes (70% of correct classification) using 10-fold cross validation. Some advances in entropy information-based machine learning techniques suggest the use of boosting techniques [27, 24, 25, 7], i.e. the simultaneous incorporation of several decision tree classifiers instead of one for building more robust and less over-fitting classification models. Classification accuracy on new data is then somewhat increased, approaching 73%, but comprehensibility is not there any longer. The most representative results obtained from standard and boosting C4.5 experimentation are given below, in Table 2. Finally, there are several genetic programming (GP) approaches applied to pap-smear diagnosis, the most representative of which are summarized in [28]. Genetic programming initially introduced by Koza [18, 17, 19], later enriched and extended by Gruau [11], Angeline & Kinnear [3], etc., consists in fact an extension of the well-known genetic algorithms [9]. In GP the Darwinian principal of the survival of the fittest is followed, in the form of auto-evolving programming code. The output can be generalized mathematical formulas, decision trees, (grammar-guided) fuzzy-genetic rule based systems, etc. GP solutions evolve slowly due to high complexity, but on the other hand they seem to generalize adequately over difficult real-world problems. Previous attempts of GP for pap-smear data classification include (a) the production of standard GP symbolic regression formulas obtaining a satisfactory classification accuracy (80.7%) on the test set for discriminating among all 7 classes, which increases to 88.9% when all categories of dysplasic (i.e. abnormal) cells are all unified into one single class, and (b) the production of a crisp rule-based system which also performs well on new data (accuracy of 91.6%) again if all abnormal cases are treated as one. When discrimination is requested among all 7 classes through any GP approach, the rules that are produced for discriminating among abnormal classes (i.e. class 5, 6, 7) are of low accuracy, a fact that indicates the existence of unclear boundaries in the characteristics of dysplasic cells of different types.

Comprehensibility of the GP outcomes is characterized medium to low, with a few exceptions of really good generalization. For example the request for a rule that discriminates among normal cells belonging to class 4 and abnormal cells belonging to classes 5, 6, 7 leads to a surprisingly high accuracy (100%), and simplicity (KA/CS: nucleus area divided by cytoplasm shortest diameter). This rule is not unknown to medical staff, while it is already used to characterize Class #4 cells (SUPER - Superficial) between other types of cells and thus, the genetic programming procedure just revealed this criterion. The rules of the GP approach that produces a crisp rule based system, is also somewhat comprehensible:

If *KerneY>CytoMin & KernePeri<28 & KerneMax>CytoShort THEN class is INTER (class3), else...*

All the intelligent classification approaches previously attempted, as well as their main settings and their classification accuracy, are summarized in Table 3.

Some additional remarks that we can make for the results of the previously applied computational intelligence approaches are the following:

- Most misclassification errors (more than 80% of the total) in standard and boosting C4.5 approaches occur in discrimination between classes 5, 6, and 7.
- Data are collected in a quite uniform way for all classes, a hypothesis which does not necessarily correspond to reality. Nevertheless, where a unique (and not a randomly created) testing data set has to be formed, it is supposed that it follows a similar uniform distribution of all classes contained within the set (i.e. in genetic programming approaches, where repeated experimentations are not possible due to time restrictions).
- Feature selection in all the above mentioned experiments, was performed with simulated annealing.
- The idea for performing feature selection prior to the application of an intelligent clustering method was first introduced by Byriel [5]. The results were encouraging and thus, the best classification performance was obtained by Martin [20], when trying to discriminate between normal and abnormal cells. In fact the previous best performing attempt of [20] consisted a good example for the application of a hybrid intelligent scheme towards data classification.
- Previous analysis of different pap-smear data sets in respect to the classification performance, showed that (a) the abnormal cells are hard to separate from each other (also for the cyto-technicians) and that (b) columnar cells are sometimes wrongly classified as severe dysplastic cells [20].

6   Classification Results of LMAM and OLMAM

In our experiments we used two different pap-smear datasets. The first was the standard pap-smear dataset described in section 4 which consists of 500 samples each of which is represented by 20 numerical attributes and by a label which indicates whether it is abnormal (positive) or normal (negative). The second

Table 3. Comparison of accuracy and comprehensibility of selected results of various computational intelligence methods for the problem of pap-smear diagnosis (entropy-based machine learning, genetic programming, c-means clustering)

Method	Nr. of Cases used & Classes to Discriminate	Division of the Data Set to Train & Test Data	Training Accuracy	Testing Accuracy	Compre-hensibility of the Outcome
Entropy Based ML-Results (C4.5 Standard)	500 cases (7 classes)	90 - 10 % (cross. val. 10-folds)	95.4 %	70.0 %	HIGH
Entropy Based ML-Results (C4.5 Boost)	500 (7)	90 - 10 % (cross. val. 10-folds)	100 %	73.0 %	LOW
Neuro-Fuzzy Classification (ANFIS Method)	500 (2)	Swap-random tests were used for validation	~100 %	95.5 %	MEDIUM
Nearest Neighbour Classification (NNH-Method)	500 (2)	Swap-random tests were used for validation	~ 100 %	96.3 %	LOW
Standard GP Method for all classes	500 (7)	90 - 10 % (single split)	~ 100 %	80.7 %	LOW
Standard GP for abnormal vs all types of normal cells	500 (5) (5+6+7 unified)	90 - 10 % (single split)	~ 100 %	88.9 %	LOW
PST-GP: GP-derived Crisp Rule-Based Syst	450 (5) (5+6+7 unified)	50 - 50 % (single split)	95.6 %	91.6 %	MEDIUM
(Un)supervised HCM/FCM/GK Direct Classification	500 (7)	90 - 10 % (cross. val. 10-folds)	~ 100 %	72.3 - 77.0 %	LOW
(Un)supervised HCM/FCM/GK Hierarch. Classification	500 (7)	90 - 10 % (cross. val. 10-folds)	~ 100 %	79.7 - 80.5 %	LOW
Supervised FCM	500 (2) (classes 1+2+3 +4 vs 5+6+7)	90 - 10 % (cross. val. 10-folds)	~ 100 %	96.94 %	LOW
Feature Selection & Supervised FCM	500 (2) (classes 1+2+3 +4 vs 5+6+7)	90 - 10 % (cross. val. 10-folds)	~ 100 %	98.36 %	LOW

pap-smear dataset consists also of 500 samples, labeled as normal or abnormal, but each sample was represented by 9 numerical attributes selected by simulated annealing as described in [5] since it was reported that this particular feature selection combined with ANFIS classification provided the best False-Negative (see below) rate of 0.7%.

Each of the pap-smear datasets was divided into train and test data using 90% and 10 % of the samples respectively using 10-folds cross-validation. For each network configuration (i.e. for each different selection of hidden nodes) we performed a total of 100 training trials resulting from training the network 10 times for each of the 10 folds of the dataset. Each different training trial was performed by initializing the network's weights in the range [-0.1, 0.1]. In each trial the maximum number of epochs was set to 500 and training was considered successful whenever Fahlman's "40 − 20 − 40" criterion was satisfied [6]. All experiments were carried in MATLAB using the LMAM/OLMAM Neural Network Toolbox which is publically available at "http://www.iit.demokritos.gr/~abazis/toolbox".

In order to test the performance of the algorithms for the two category classification problem (i.e. classes 1+2+3+4 vs 5+6+7) we use five criteria: Testing Accuracy, False-Negative rate (FN%), False-Positive rate (FP%), Positive-Predictive rate (PP%) and Negative-Predictive rate (NP%). These criteria are defined as follows: Testing Accuracy referes to the percentage of cells in the test dataset that are classified correctly by the trained neural network. We denote by N the number of normal/negative and by P the number of dysplastic/positive cells in the test dataset. TP is the number of cells which are correctly classified as positive and FN is the number of cells falsely classified as negative. Obviously it holds that

$$P = TP + FN \tag{18}$$

TN is the number of cells which are correctly classified as negative and FP is the number of cells falsely classified as positive. It follows that

$$N = TN + FP \tag{19}$$

An obviously very important criterion for the performance and reliability of the classifier is the False-Negative rate FN% which is equal to the rate of cells that are classified as normal, but should have been classified as dysplastic.

$$FN\% = \frac{FN \times 100\%}{TP + FN} \tag{20}$$

Accordingly, the False-Positive rate FP% is equal to the rate of cells that are classified as dysplastic, but should have been classified as normal:

$$FP\% = \frac{FP \times 100\%}{TN + FP} \tag{21}$$

Furthermore, the positive predictive rate PP% measures the overall ability of the classifier to recognize positive cells, and is defined as the rate of cells classified as positive that are truly dysplastic. In a similar way, the negative predictive rate NP% measures the overall ability of the classifier to discriminate negative cells and is defined as the rate of cells classified as negative that are truly negative:

$$PP\% = \frac{TP \times 100\%}{TP + FP} \tag{22}$$

$$NP\% = \frac{TN \times 100\%}{TN + FN} \tag{23}$$

Tables 4 and 5 show the results obtained for different neural network architectures (all utilizing a single hidden layer of neurons) trained on the two datasets with LMAM and OLMAM respectively. The classification accuracy reported for each neural network configuration is the average over the 10 training trials for all 10-folds of the datasets. From these tables we can observe that the classification accuracy in all cases exceeds 98% and that better results are obtained with the standard (20 features) dataset. The best overall classification accuracy (98.86%)

Table 4. Results for separation accuracy between normal and abnormal cells (classes 1+2+3+4 vs 5+6+7), using LMAM with various number of features and hidden nodes

Number of Used Features	Number of Hidden Nodes	Testing Accuracy
9	0	98.00 %
9	2	98.12 %
9	3	98.14 %
9	4	98.26 %
9	5	98.06 %
9	6	98.18 %
20	0	98.02 %
20	2	98.34 %
20	3	98.28 %
20	4	98.40 %
20	5	98.34 %
20	6	98.36 %
20	7	98.42 %
20	8	98.34 %
20	9	98.34 %
20	10	98.42 %

Table 5. Results for separation accuracy between normal and abnormal cells (classes 1+2+3+4 vs 5+6+7), using OLMAM with various number of features and hidden nodes

Number of Used Features	Number of Hidden Nodes	Testing Accuracy
9	0	98.10 %
9	2	98.20 %
9	3	98.28 %
9	4	98.26 %
9	5	98.34 %
9	6	98.40 %
20	0	98.38 %
20	2	98.54 %
20	3	98.52 %
20	4	98.72 %
20	5	98.68 %
20	6	98.68 %
20	7	98.80 %
20	8	98.80 %
20	9	98.86 %
20	10	98.58 %

was obtained with a neural network with 9 hidden nodes trained with OLMAM on the standard 20 features pap-smear dataset.

Figures 3(a), 3(b), 3(c), and 3(d) show the FN%, FP%, PP% and NP% values obtained for the same set of neural network training trials. Each point on the graphs has been calculated as the average over the 10 training trials for all 10-folds of each dataset. From figure 3(a) we can see that the best FN% value (0.7921) was obtained on the standand 20 features dataset with the 10 hidden nodes neural network trained with OLMAM. This observation combined with the fact that the best classification accuracy was also obtained with the standard 20 features pap-smear dataset indicates that the proposed algorithms are able to achieve very good classification results on the original dataset without the need to turn into sophisticated feature selection techniques (e.g. simulated annealing).

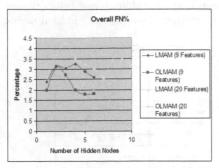

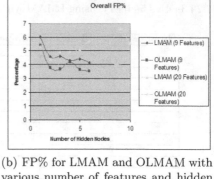

(a) FN% for LMAM and OLMAM with various number of features and hidden nodes. OLMAM with 20 features and 10 hidden nodes achieves the best FN% value of 0.7921

(b) FP% for LMAM and OLMAM with various number of features and hidden nodes.

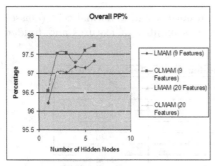

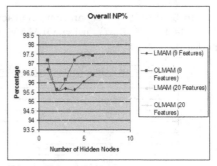

(c) PP% for LMAM and OLMAM with various number of features and hidden nodes.

(d) NP% for LMAM and OLMAM with various number of features and hidden nodes.

Fig. 3. Results of FN%, FP%, PP%, and NP% values for LMAM and OLMAM with various number of features and hidden nodes

7   Conclusions

In this paper we utilized two highly efficient second order neural network training algorithms, namely LMAM and OLMAM, for the construction of an efficient pap-smear test classifier. Performance comparisons were included in the paper between the proposed LMAM / OLMAM methodologies and previously attempted computational intelligence approaches, such as Gustafson-Kessel clustering techniques, hard c-means, fuzzy c-means, entropy-based intuctive machine learning, genetic programming and finally, hybrid intelligence methods combining feature selection and clustering techniques. The proposed algorithms manage to build very efficient pap-smear classifiers under various parameter settings, when attempting to discriminate among normal and abnormal pap-smear cells (i.e. for the two class category problem), minimizing the false negative error in

0.79%. The best performance of the proposed approach is obtained when OL-MAM methodology with 10 hidden nodes is applied, with all (20) features used to build the classifier. For the case of the OLMAM methodology applied with 9 hidden nodes and 20 features used (see Table 5), the overall classification accuracy for the two class category problem becomes the maximum obtained ever, reaching up to 98.86%. The most competitive approach in literature for the same problem (see Table 1) is the application of a hybrid intelligent approach consisting of feature selection and supervised fuzzy c-means, which obtains an overall classification accuracy of 98.36%. Further experimentation is underway, in order to test and compare the efficiency of the proposed LMAM and OLMAM methodology when discriminating among all 7 diagnostic classes of the pap-smear problem. Best performance for the full-problem classification are (a) the application of standard genetic programming with an overall accuracy of 80.7% and (b) the application of a hybrid intelligent scheme, consisting of feature selection and hierarchical classification as suggested in [20], with an overall correct classification accuracy of 80.5%. Concluding, a clear trade-off seems to exist between the classification accuracy and the comprehensibility of the acquired output of different computational intelligence methodologies in the pap-smear diagnosis problem.

Acknowledgement

The data were collected at the Herlev University Hospital, Denmark, thanks to Beth Bjerregaard. They are available on the Internet at http://fuzzy.iau.dtu.dk/smear/download.html.

References

1. Ampazis N., Perantonis S. J.: Levenberg-Marquardt Algorithm with Adaptive Momentum for the Efficient Training of Feedforward Networks. Proceedings of International Joint Conference on Neural Networks IJCNN'00 , Como, Italy, 2000.
2. Ampazis N., Perantonis S. J.: Two Highly Efficient Second Order Algorithms for Training Feedforward Networks, IEEE Transactions on Neural Networks, 13 (5) (2002) 1064–1074.
3. Angeline P. J .and Kinnear,Jr K.E.: Advances in Genetic Programming, 2 (1996) MIT Press
4. Babuska R.: Fuzzy Modeling for Control, (1998), Kluwer Academic Publishers.
5. Byriel J.: Neuro-Fuzzy Classification of Cells in Cervical Smears. MSc Thesis, Technical University of Denmark, Dept. of Automation, (1999), http://fuzzy.iau.dtu.dk/download/byriel99.pdf.
6. Fahlman S. E.: Faster-Learning Variations on Back-Propagation: An Empirical Study. Proceedings of the 1988 Connectionist Models Summer School, Morgan Kaufmann, (1988).
7. Johannes Furnkranz: Pruning Algorithms for Rule Learning. Machine Learning 27 (1997) 139–171.
8. Gilbert J. C. Nocedal J.: Global convergence properties of conjugate gradient methods for optimization. SIAM J. on Optimization 2 (1) (1992).

9. Goldberg D.E.: Genetic Algorithms in Search, Optimization.and Machine Learning, (1989) Addison-Wesley.
10. Gonzalez R. C., Woods R. E.: Digital Image Processing, (1993) Addison-Wesley.
11. Gruau F.: On Using Syntactic Constraints with Genetic Programming, P.J.Angeline, K.E.Jinnear,Jr.. eds., Advances in Genetic Programming, (1996) MIT Press.
12. Hagan M. T., Menhaj, M.: Training feedforward networks with the Marquardt algorithm. IEEE Transactions on Neural Networks 5 (6) (1994) 989–993.
13. Jang J-S. R.: Neuro-fuzzy modeling for nonlinear dynamic system identification. E.H. Ruspini, P.P. Bonissone, W. Pedrycz, eds., Handbook of Fuzzy Computation, (1998) Institute of Physics Publishing, Dirak House, Temple Back, Bristol BS1 6BE UK.
14. Jang J-S. R.: ANFIS: Adaptive-Network-based Fuzzy Inference Systems. IEEE Transactions on Systems, Man and Cybernetics, 23 (3) (1993) 665–685.
15. Jantzen J.: Neurofuzzy Modelling. Technical University of Denmark: Oersted-DTU, Tech report no 98-H-874 (nfmod), (1998).
    URL http://fuzzy.iau.dtu.dk/download/nfmod.pdf.
16. Koss L.: The Application of PAPNET to Diagnostic Cytology. P. Lisboa, E. Ifeachor, P. Szczepaniak (Eds.), Artificial Neural Networks in Biomedicine, (2000) 51–68 Springer.
17. Koza J. R: Genetic Programming II - Automatic Discovery of Reusable Programs (1994) MIT Press.
18. Koza J. R.: Genetic Programming - On the Programming of Computers by Means of Natural Selection (1992) MIT Press.
19. Koza J.R., Forrest H. Bennett III, David Andre, Martin A. Keane: Genetic Programming III, , (1999) Morgan Kaufmann Publishers, Inc.
20. Martin Erik: Pap-Smear Classification, MSc Thesis, Technical University of Denmark, Oersted-DTU, Automation (2003).
21. Matthews, B.W.: Comparison of the predicted and observed secondary structure of T4 phage lysozyme. Biochemica et Biophysica Acta, 405 (1975) 442–551.
22. Meisels A., Morin C.: Cytopathology of the Uterus 2nd edition (1997) ASCP Press.
23. Perantonis S. J., Karras D. A.: An efficient constrained learning algorithm with momentum acceleration. Neural Networks 8 1995 237–249.
24. Quinlan J.R.: Boosting First Order Learning. Conf. on Algorithmic Learning Theory, 7th Int. Workshop ALT'96, Sydney, Australia, (1996) 1–11 Springer Verlag.
25. Quinlan J.R.: Boosting, Bagging, and C4.5. Proc. of the 13th National Conf. on AI, Portland, Oregon, USA, (1996) 725–730, AAAI Press.
26. Quinlan, J.R.: C4.5: Programs for Machine Learning (1993) San Mateo: Morgan Kaufmann.
27. Schapire R.: The strategy of weak learnability. Machine Learning 5 (2) (1990) 197–227.
28. Tsakonas A., Dounias G., Jantzen J., Axer H, Bjerregaard B., von Keyserlingk D.G.: Evolving Rule Based Systems in two Medical Domains Using Genetic Programming. AIM Journal, (2003) (to appear) Artificial Intelligence in Medicine, Elsevier.

Towards an Imitation System
for Learning Robots

George Maistros and Gillian Hayes

Institute of Perception, Action and Behaviour,
School of Informatics, The University of Edinburgh,
Edinburgh, EH9 3JZ, UK
georgem@dai.ed.ac.uk, gmh@inf.ed.ac.uk

Abstract. This paper proposes an imitation system for learning robots
that attempts to model the functional role of pre-motor brain areas and
in particular *mirror neurons, i.e.* neurons that are believed to form the
fundamental basis for imitation in primates [27]. Mirror neurons were
found in the *macaque* monkey brain and are active during both observation and manual execution of an interaction [24].
The mirror system (previous work) is concerned with the activation of
structures in response to both the observation and the execution of interactions. Previous experiments show that observed interactions are represented, learnt, and in turn reproduced. These interactions however remain limited due to a rather crude modelling of neighbouring brain areas
outwith the mirror system. The imitation system (current work) is an
extension to the mirror system that brings neighbouring areas into play
to exploit the learning capacity and diversity of the premotor cortex.

Keywords: robotics; cognitive robotics; perception; adaptive systems;
imitation learning

1 Introduction

Considering the time it takes to program a robot (for a single task alone) and
the resulting performance, traditional approaches to robot programming are far
from satisfying [29]. Programmers usually attempt to predict perceptual stimuli
and at the same time program appropriate reactions or behaviours; a process
that is both time consuming and potentially error prone. Further, minor changes
to the robot, or to its environment usually result in unpredictable and potentially
undesirable behaviours.

Imitation, or programming by demonstration, offers an alternative approach;
firstly, robots are able to learn a variety of tasks, and secondly, they learn directly through their own sensors and actuators, and are therefore less sensitive
to changes or variations in their environment.

Our approach to imitation is inspired from Biology. Experiments on the
macaque monkey brain (area F5) exposed the presence of *mirror* and *canonical* neurons that, in addition to the common motor properties of F5 neurons,

G.A. Vouros and T. Panayiotopoulos (Eds.): SETN 2004, LNAI 3025, pp. 246–255, 2004.

have visual properties as well [24, 9]. More importantly however there is a relationship between these two modalities. Single neurons studies exposed a strong relationship between the perceptual and motor discharge of F5 neurons, as well as a high grasp (and finger configuration) selectivity [8, 26].

For example, the same mirror neurons that discharge during the manual execution of a particular type of grasp, also discharge when the monkey observes another monkey (or the experimenter) perform the same grasp. Similarly, the canonical neurons that discharge during manual execution of a particular type of grasp, also discharge when the monkey observes a 3D object (fixation) that affords[1] this interaction. A more detailed description of F5 neurons and their properties is beyond the scope of this paper[2].

The discharge characteristics of F5 neurons (individually or in small populations) suggest that they provide the motor coding of *specific* interactions (they are highly selective), and that they are *also* used to perceive/recognise the interaction that they code [8, 26].

Our earlier work implements the *mirror system* and is primarily concerned with the functional role of F5 mirror neurons. Previous experiments [13, 16] show that the mirror system is able to observe and reproduce demonstrated interactions. These interactions however remain limited due to a rather crude modelling of neighbouring brain areas outwith the mirror system.

This paper gives an overview of the mirror system (previous work), and proposes the imitation system (current work); a model that brings neighbouring brain areas into play to more closely express F5 neuron properties, and exploits the learning capacity and diversity of the monkey premotor cortex.

2   The Mirror System

This section provides an overview of the mirror system, and is intended to illustrate the platform and scenarios that we are using in our research. This section also exposes the limitations of the mirror system that led to our current work, described in subsequent sections. For a detailed description of the mirror system and its application the interested reader is referred to the literature [16, 15].

The mirror system, shown in Figure 1, consists mainly of two tightly coupled components: a perceptual and a motoric component. The perceptual component is a Self-Organising-Feature-Map (SOFM, left) [14], and the motoric component is a set of motor schemas (right) [12]. The output of the mirror system is then sent to the motor system for execution.

The mirror system operates in two modes, a learning phase, and a recall phase. In the learning phase, perceptual and motoric components are trained on the input to the mirror system and no output is produced. In the recall phase,

---

[1] Gibson defined perception of a physical entity (object) in terms of *affordances*, *i.e.* the actions that one may apply to that object [10]. A mug, for example, affords various hand grasps, as a chair affords sitting.

[2] The interested reader is referred to available literature [24, 4, 8, 26, 25].

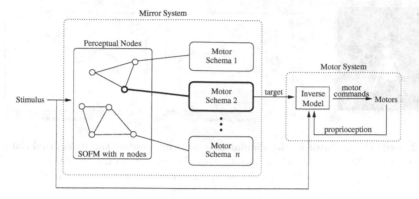

Fig. 1. The mirror system. In the recall phase (bold font), the Self-Organising-Feature-Map handles the stimulus and finds the best matching node at each time; its hard-wired motor schema sends motor targets to the motor system for execution.

the SOFM is employed to recognise the input and trigger the appropriate motor schema, which in turn produces the output that is sent to the motor system.

The SOFM[3] is a topology-preserving network of nodes and edges that grows from experience as and when required. It receives continuous input and essentially forms clusters in the multi-dimensional input space.

Motor schemas can be thought of as motor primitives [3, 29, 18] that store actions in a representation that can be readily used by the motor system. The motor system consists mainly of an inverse model that given the robot's current state and the target desired state, calculates the motor commands that best achieve that target state. Therefore, the representation of actions in motor schemas is in terms of targets that are handled by the inverse model.

The nature of the perceptual input to the SOFM, the representation of actions stored within motor schemas, and the implementation of the inverse model are all platform-dependent. As part of collaborative work with Dr Marom, the mirror system has been extensively and successfully implemented on three different platforms (for a detailed account see [15]): a simulated mobile robot learning from another how to follow walls; a physical mobile robot learning from a human how to follow walls; and a simulated humanoid robot learning from another how to interact with objects. The following section considers the simulated humanoid platform as an example to further explain the implementation of platform-dependent issues.

2.1 A Simulated Humanoid Experiment

This section provides an overview of an experiment that simulates the dynamics of two eleven degrees of freedom robots (waist upwards): a demonstrator and an

---

[3] Dr. Marom has adopted and suited to our purposes a variation of the SOFM algorithm originally developed by [17], which incorporates notions of habituation, novelty detection, and forgetting [14].

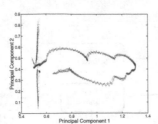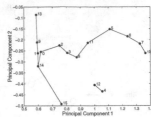

Fig. 2. Left: the imitator in the simulation platform. Centre: the perceptual data the SOFM is typically exposed to in a learning episode, projected onto their first 2 principal components. Right: the SOFM produced by the attention system for this data.

imitator (Figure 2(left)). Each robot has three degrees of freedom at the neck, three at each shoulder, and one at each elbow. The robots are allowed to interact with one object each. The objects are identical and have six degrees of freedom. The kinematics of each robot (*e.g.* torque, joint friction, etc.) and the dynamics of their interaction with the environment (*e.g.* gravity, slip/friction, collision detection, etc.) are simulated in DynaMechs, a collection of C++ libraries [19].

The demonstrator performs a fixed behaviour that the imitator observes in the learning phase and is expected to reproduce in the recall phase. The behaviour of the imitator is governed by the mirror system. The input to the mirror system comes from a crude approximation to vision, while its output is in terms of postural targets that are sent to the inverse model, a Proportional-Integral-Derivative (PID) controller. The PID controller considers these postural targets (desired state) together with proprioception (current state) and calculates the torque values (motor commands) for each joint.

Our approximation to visual input is a multi-dimensional vector that consists of a noisy version of the joint angles and joint velocities of the demonstrator, extended by a noisy version of object coordinates and orientation. Similarly, the proprioception vector consists of a noisy version of the joint angles and joint velocities of the imitator.

Our approach to vision or proprioception may appear to be crude but it is well justified. Firstly, we are not concerned with computational vision; our focus lies on the premotor area rather than the visual cortex. Secondly, recent advances suggest that the perceptual information that our approach assumes is often available by the use of a variety of techniques; from extensive colour coding, to motion capture, and to specialised hardware[4]. Finally, any approach towards real vision would have little to offer towards the understanding of the mirror system, or the premotor area in general; premotor brain areas appear to provide the mirror system with perceptual data similar to those of our approach.

In the learning phase, the SOFM receives continuous visual input and develops to better represent the input space (*i.e.* a multi-dimensional joint angle

---

[4] For example, the Sarcos SenSuit, is a wearable exoskeleton that reads the joint angles and joint velocities of its owner.

space). Figure 2(centre) shows the perceptual data that a SOFM receives in a typical learning episode phase, while Figure 2(right) shows the resulting SOFM.

Since the dimensionality of the input space is quite high (34), we used Principal Component Analysis (PCA) to reduce the number of dimensions to two, for display and analysis purposes only. Figure 2(centre) is the projection of the perceptual data onto the first 2 principal components found by PCA, while Figure 2(right) is the projection of the resulting SOFM network. The principal components used in the figure account for approximately 80% of the variance.

Each SOFM node essentially represents a segment of the observed behaviour. For instance if the behaviour involves grasping a container and drinking its contents, some node represents moving towards the container, another grasping it, etc. While SOFM nodes are added to the existing network and moved to better represent the input space, motor schemas are created and updated in synchrony to SOFM nodes.

Each motor schema receives the continuous input vector through its hard-wired SOFM node and, in its simplest form, stores a sequence of these vectors. Since this sequence of vectors is a part of the observed demonstrator postures, it is considered to represent the postural targets that, if achieved, the imitator would effectively reproduce that part of the observed behaviour. In practice, a more principled heuristic update is employed to ensure better generalisation and learning of the observed sequence.

2.2 Mirror System Limitations

There are several implementations that rely on the pre-existence of perceptuo-motor structures, *i.e.* structures are either hand coded arbitrarily (as in our earlier work [12]), or generated automatically, yet off-line or in batches [23, 6]. Our approach [16] differs from those above in that perceptuo-motor structures grow on-line from experience; each observed interaction is treated as novel, and structures are automatically clustered (primarily in the joint angle space).

However, our system is limited in that motor structures are internally inflexible and non-parameterised; *i.e.* structures are sensitive to changes in object size, translation, orientation, etc. Although, selectivity is supported by experimental data, such un-intuitive selectivity is not; F5 neurons *are* selective to such object characteristics *yet* in a rather principled way. The selectivity of F5 neurons is mostly concerned with the affordances of objects (*i.e.* the graspable characteristics of objects), rather than with their geometrical properties. For instance, the same F5 neuron would discharge for the apprehension of a small cylinder, as it would for a small sphere, or even a small cuboid.

3 Neurophysiological Background

Mirror and premotor neuron studies offer a good understanding about the discharge of these neurons, yet not about their development. When it comes to infusing a robot with mechanisms that provide similar behaviour, the understanding of the development and training of those neurons becomes essential.

We believe that neighbouring brain areas that provide input or triggers to the mirror system play a key role in the development and shaping of the mirror system itself. This section summarises experimental data [7, 28, 11, 20] that investigate further the roles of brain areas that are thought to be primarily involved in the functioning of the mirror system.

The caudal IntraParietal Sulcus (*cIPS*) receives input from the visual cortex and is primarily responsible for the binocular detection of the orientation of the axis of objects (AOS), and for the surface orientation of objects (SOS). It is believed that these hyper-features describe most of the necessary information (although without structure) for the apprehension and manipulation of objects.

The Anterior IntraParietal area (*AIP*) imposes and provides structure on object hyper-features. Structured hyper-features are termed affordances. Consider for example the object features of a cuboid, *e.g.* usually five visible surfaces (SOS), grouped into affordances, *e.g.* pairs of opposite and parallel surfaces.

The Superior Temporal Sulcus (*STS*) is mainly involved with the detection and tracking of biological limbs in a translation, scale, and rotation invariant way. STS is also somatotopically organised, and thus offers the representation of biological articulation structures in a variety of limb centred frames of reference. In fact, STS is able to detect even biological-like limbs. We argue that STS could in principle be replaced by a motion capture system whereby markers are placed in a humanoid articulation fashion — which is indeed often the case.

By *VIP* we conceptualise all the Lateral, Medial, and Ventral IntraParietal (LIP/MIP/VIP) areas. These areas are involved in the representation of the location of objects in an egocentric (from eye, to head, to body centred) frame of reference. Such a representation (*e.g.* distance between object and wrist) is thought to play a key role in reaching and preshaping.

Although there is an intense controversy on the role of Parietal areas *7a* and *7b*, experimental data suggest that area 7a provides a motor encoding of the visual space (MEVS) in a variety of frames of reference, while 7b integrates further information about observed limb motion, object affordances, and MEVS. The motor encoding of the visual space refers to the limb centred representation of objects in the space projecting outwards from (and anchored to) the tactile receptive fields of that limb. In other words, area 7a encodes the object location with respect to the individual limbs, while area 7b first relates this encoding with object affordances and then associates it with current limb motion.

4   Towards an Imitation System

The previous section described the Biological roles of some of the brain areas involved in the development and functioning of the mirror system. This section proposes a schematic implementation of these areas to promote the behaviour that is readily observed in primates and that we wish to infuse our system with.

Figure 3 shows our schematic implementation of the imitation system. Our implementation is inspired by and in many ways resembles the work of Demiris [2], Fagg and Arbib [5] and Oztop [21, 1, 22]. However, most related work makes

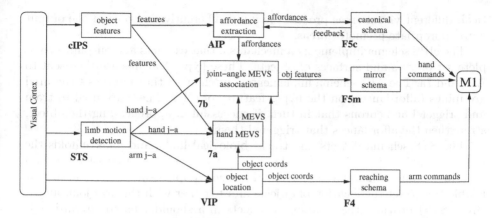

Fig. 3. The schematic implementation of the proposed imitation system.

extra assumptions on the interconnectivity of premotor areas and propose that mirror neurons are not actively involved in grasping. It is also hypothesised that mirror neurons elaborate on visual feedback for visually guided grasping. Our work makes no extra assumptions on the interconnectivity and propose an alternative hypothesis, namely that both mirror and canonical neurons are actively involved in grasping, while mirror neurons elaborate on visual (among other forms of) feedback for the finer control of grasping.

We believe that during the development of area F5, neurons that receive input from and send feedback to AIP become canonical neurons (F5c), while neurons that receive input (of mostly perceptual nature) from area 7b become mirror neurons (F5m). Our hypothesis is that, as AIP and F5c neurons are refined and shaped by each other (mutual activation and feedback), more coherent affordances are coded by AIP neurons; this enables area 7b to form more stable associations that F5m can use to constructively develop distinct populations of neurons for the finer control of distal movements.

In other words, canonical neurons provide the motor control for basic affordances (*e.g.* location of the axis of a banana, for grasping), while mirror neurons monitor and encode the distance between limbs and basic affordances (*e.g.* distance between fingers and a banana stem, for peeling).

4.1 Implementation

Figure 3 illustrates the proposed implementation of the premotor brain areas described previously that comprise the imitation system. Perceptual input arrives from the Visual Cortex and motor output is sent to the Primary Motor Cortex. Note that for clarity's sake, kinaesthetic and tactile feedback (from the Second Somatosensory Cortex) is omitted since nearly all of the brain areas receive such feedback. Also note, that the Visual Cortex is involved with much preprocessing of the perceptual input and its projections to cIPS, STS, and VIP are not identical; different visual areas process the input differently and project the output onto appropriate premotor areas.

The cIPS schema implements a mechanism that extracts and outputs a complete set of axes and surfaces of objects. These hyper-features are then sent to AIP and 7a. The AIP schema implements a mechanism that imposes structured groupings (affordances) on the hyper-features of cIPS. These are used to train and trigger F5c neurons that in turn, if successful in apprehending the object, strengthen the affordances that triggered them.

The STS schema detects and tracks biological limbs and folds/unfolds the biological articulation[5] into arm (shoulder to wrist) and hand (wrist to fingers) joint angles and joint velocities. The VIP schema implements a mechanism that is able to extract the location of objects and together with the arm joint angles (from STS) provides the location of objects in a shoulder-based (towards F4) and in a wrist based (towards 7a and 7b) frame of reference.

Schema 7a calculates the distance between end effectors (fingers) and object hyper-features for objects located within the 'visual' space near each limb. Schema 7b employs a SOFM (similar to that of Section 2) to segment any observed (from STS) or executed behaviour (from kinaesthetics) into clusters. Affordances (from AIP) are then combined with the MEVS (from 7a) and associated with these clusters. These associations are formed and updated in synchrony to the creation and update of clusters (or SOFM nodes, similar to the hardwiring in the SOFM of Section 2). Schema 7b also employs the distance from the object (from VIP) to continuously adapt the velocity profile for preshaping purposes.

The canonical schema is a collection of canonical motor schemas (similar to motor schemas of Section 2) that encode the motor aspects of an affordance. For instance as F5c receives input from AIP, say a pair of surfaces of an object, the corresponding schema controls the end effectors towards these surfaces. The mirror schema is a collection of mirror motor schemas (similar to motor schemas of Section 2) that encode the means to an end goal affordance. For instance as F5m receives continuous input from 7b, say the distances of the end effectors from a location on an object, the corresponding schema controls the end effector to match the MEVS projected from 7b, approach, and manipulate the object accordingly. Note, however that a schema may not necessarily follow the same trajectory while matching the same MEVS. The output of either canonical or mirror schemas is executed by the motor system (similar to the one of Section 2).

5   Conclusion and Future Work

This paper provides a brief description of previous work (mirror system), and demonstrates how our current work (the proposed imitation system) provides a more intuitive and adaptive learning framework. Our schematic implementation towards an imitation system aims to shift the focus away from solely F5 neurons and onto F5 neurons together with neighbouring brain areas. We believe that the

---

[5] we are only concerned with object manipulation from the upper body, thus focusing only on arms and hands.

current system implements representations and transformations that are present in the brain, and essentially infuse the mirror system with the potential for a more flexible and adaptive learning framework.

Our hypothesis is that both mirror and canonical neurons are actively involved in grasping, while mirror neurons elaborate on visual (among other forms of) feedback for the finer control of grasping.

The imitation system is intended to be tested on the same platform as in our previous work. Our aim is to show that canonical neurons only encode basic affordances (*e.g.* simple apprehension of, say, fruit objects), while mirror neurons encode an intimate relationship between hands (or fingers) and affordances (*e.g.* object manipulation, say, tearing or peeling a fruit).

References

1. M. A. Arbib, A. Billard, M. Iacoboni, and E. Oztop. Synthetic brain imaging: grasping, mirror neurons and imitation. *Neural Networks*, 13(8–9):975–997, 2000.
2. J. Demiris and G. M. Hayes. Active and passive routes to imitation. In Kerstin Dautenhahn and Chrystopher Nehaniv, editors, *Proceedings of the AISB Symposium on Imitation in Animals and Artifacts*, pages 81–87, Edinburgh, UK, 1999.
3. J. Demiris and M. J. Matarić. Perceptuo-motor primitives in imitation. In K. Dautenhahn and G. Hayes, editors, *Working Notes, Autonomous Agents '98 Workshop on Agents in Interaction - Acquiring Competence Through Imitation*, MN, 1998.
4. G. di Pellegrino, L. Fadiga, L. Fogassi, V. Gallese, and G. Rizzolatti. Understanding motor events: a neurophysiological study. *Exp. Br. Research*, 91(1):176–180, 1992.
5. A. H. Fagg and M. A. Arbib. Modeling parietal-premotor interactions in primate control of grasping. *Neural Networks*, 11(7–8):1277–1303, Oct–Nov 1998.
6. Ajo Fod, Maja J. Matarić, and Odest Chadwicke Jenkins. Automated derivation of primitives for movement classification. *Autonomous Robots*, 12(1):39–54, 2002.
7. L. Fogassi, V. Gallese, G. di Pellegrino, L. Fadiga, M. Gentilucci, G. Luppino, M. Matelli, A. Pedotti, and G. Rizzolatti. Space coding by premotor cortex. *Experimental Brain Research*, 89(3):686–690, 1992.
8. V. Gallese, L. Fadiga, L. Fogassi, and G. Rizzolatti. Action recognition in the premotor cortex. *Brain*, 119:593–609, April 1996. Part 2.
9. M. Gentilucci, L. Fogassi, G. Luppino, M. Matelli, R. Camarda, and G. Rizzolatti. Functional organization of inferior area 6 in macaque monkey .1. Somatotopy and the control of proximal movements. *Exp. Brain Research*, 71(3):475–490, 1988.
10. J. J. Gibson. *The Senses Considered as Perceptual Systems*. MA, 1966.
11. M. S. A. Graziano, G. S. Yap, and C. G. Gross. Coding of visual space by premotor neurons. *Science*, 226(5187):1054–1057, 1994.
12. G. Maistros and G. M. Hayes. An imitation mechanism for goal-directed actions. In U. Nehmzow and C. Melhuish, editors, *Proceedings of Towards Intelligent Mobile Robots (TIMR) 2001*, Manchester University, 2001.
13. G. Maistros, Y. Marom, and G. M. Hayes. Perception-action coupling via imitation and attention. In *AAAI Fall Symposium on Anchoring Symbols to Sensor Data in Single and Multiple Robot Systems*, 2001.
14. Y. Marom and G. M. Hayes. Attention and social situatedness for skill acquisition. In C. Balkenius, J. Zlatev, H. Kozima, K. Dautenhahn, and C. Breazeal, editors, *Proceedings of the First International Workshop on Epigenetic Robotics: Modeling Cognitive Development in Robotic Systems*, pages 105–114. 2001.

15. Y. Marom, G. Maistros, and G. Hayes. Experiments with a social learning model. *Adaptive Behavior*, 9(3–4):209–240, 2001.
16. Y. Marom, G. Maistros, and G. M. Hayes. Towards a mirror system for the development of socially-mediated skills. In C. G. Prince, Y. Demiris, Y. Marom, H. Kozima, and C. Balkenius, editors, *Proceedings of the Second International Workshop on Epigenetic Robotics: Modeling Cognitive Development in Robotic Systems*, 2002.
17. S. Marsland, U. Nehmzow, and J. Shapiro. Novelty detection in large environments. In U. Nehmzow and C. Melhuish, editors, *Proceedings of Towards Intelligent Mobile Robots (TIMR) 2001*, Manchester University, 2001.
18. M. J. Matarić. Getting humanoids to move and imitate. *IEEE Intelligent Systems*, 14(4):18–24, July 2000.
19. S. McMillan, D. E. Orin, and R.B. McGhee. Dynamechs: An object oriented software package for efficient dynamic simulation of underwater robotic vechicles. In J. Yuh, editor, *Underwater Vechicles: Design and Control*, pages 73–98, 1995.
20. A. Murata, L. Fadiga, L. Fogassi, V. Raos V. Gallese, and G. Rizzolatti. Object representation in the ventral premotor cortex (area F5) of the monkey. *Journal of Neurophysiology*, 78(4):2226–2230, 1997.
21. E. Oztop. *Modeling the Mirror: Grasp Learning and Action Recognition*. PhD thesis, University of Southern California, 2002.
22. E. Oztop and M. A. Arbib. Schema design and implementation of the grasp-related mirror neuron system. *Biological Cybernetics*, 2002. In press.
23. M. Pomplun and M. J. Matarić. Evaluation metrics and results of human arm movement imitation. In *Proceedings of the First IEEE-RAS International Conference on Humanoid Robotics (Humanoids-2000)*, 2000.
24. G. Rizzolatti, R. Carmada, L. Fogassi, M. Gentilucci, G. Luppino, and M. Matelli. Functional organization of inferior area 6 in macaque monkey .2. Area F5 and the control of distal movements. *Experimental Brain Research*, 71(3):491–507, 1988.
25. G. Rizzolatti and L. Fadiga. Grasping objects and grasping action meanings: the dual role of monkey rostroventral premotor cortex (area F5). *Novartis Foundation Symposium*, 218:81–103, 1998. In book: Sensory Guidance of Movement.
26. G. Rizzolatti, L. Fadiga, V. Gallese, and L. Fogassi. Premotor cortex and the recognition of motor actions. *Cognitive Brain Research*, 3(2):131–141, March 1996.
27. G. Rizzolatti, L. Fogassi, and V. Gallese. Cortical mechanisms subserving object grasping and action recognition: A new view on the cortical motor functions. In M. Gazzaniga, editor, *The New Cog. Neurosci.*, pages 539–552. MIT Press, 2000.
28. H. Sakata., M. Taira, A. Murata, V. Gallese, Y. Tanaka, E. Shikata, and M. Kusnunoki. Parietal visual neurons coding three-dimensional characteristics of objects and their relation to hand action. In P. Their and H.-O. Karnath, editors, *Parietal lobe contributions to orientation in 3D space*, pages 237–254. Heidelberg, Germany: Springer-Verlag, 1997.
29. S. Schaal. Is imitation learning the route to humanoid robots? *Trends in Cognitive Sciences*, 3(6):233–242, June 1999.

Gene Selection via Discretized Gene-Expression Profiles and Greedy Feature-Elimination

George Potamias[1], Lefteris Koumakis[1], and Vassilis Moustakis[1,2]

[1] Institute of Computer Science, Foundation for Research and Technology-Hellas (FORTH),
P.O. Box 1385, 71110 Heraklion, Crete, Greece
{potamias,koumakis,moustaki}@ics.forth.gr
[2] Department of Production and Management Engineering, Technical University of Crete,
University Campus, Kounoupidiana, 73100 Chania, Crete, Greece

Abstract. Analysis and interpretation of gene-expression profiles, and the identification of respective molecular- or, gene-markers is the key towards the understanding of the genetic basis of major diseases. The problem is challenging
because of the huge number of genes (thousands to tenths of thousands!) and the
small number of samples (about 50 to 100 cases). In this paper we present a
novel gene-selection methodology, based on the discretization of the continuous
gene-expression values. With a specially devised gene-ranking metric we measure the strength of each gene with respect to its power to discriminate between
sample categories. Then, a greedy feature-elimination algorithm is applied on
the rank-ordered genes to form the final set of selected genes. Unseen samples
are classified according to a specially devised prediction/matching metric. The
methodology was applied on a number of real-world gene-expression studies
yielding very good results.

1 Introduction

As the physical mapping of the Human Genome Project (http://www.genome.gov)
comes to completion, the respective R&D agenda moves from static structural genomics activities to dynamic *functional genomics*. The vision is to compact major diseases
on an *individualized* diagnostic, prognostic and treatment manner [7], [9], and the
whole endeavor is based on the synergy between *Medical Informatics* and *Bioinformatics* [13], [16], [19].

With the recent advances in *microrray* technology [6], the potential for molecular
diagnostic and prognostic tools seem to come in reality. The last years, microarray-
chips have been devised and manufactured in order to measure the *expression-profile*
of thousands of genes. In this context a number of pioneering studies have been conducted that profile the expression-level of genes for various types of cancers such as
breast, colon, lymphoma, leukemia and other tumors [8], [11], [15], [18]. The aim is to
add molecular characteristics to the classification of cancer so that diagnostic procedures are enhanced and prognostic predictions are improved [1]. These studies demonstrate that gene-expression profiling has great potential in identifying and predicting

G.A. Vouros and T. Panayiotopoulos (Eds.): SETN 2004, LNAI 3025, pp. 256–266, 2004.
© Springer-Verlag Berlin Heidelberg 2004

various targets and prognostic factors of cancer. *Gene-expression* data analysis is heavily depended on Gene Expression Data Mining (GEDM) technology, and the involved data analysis is based on two approaches: (a) hypothesis testing- to investigate the induction or perturbation of a biological process that leads to predicted results, and (b) *knowledge discovery-* to detect underlying *hidden-regularities* in biological data. For the later, one of the major challenges is *gene-selection*. The selected genes, after tested for their reliability (e.g., via appropriately conducted clinical trials) present molecular or, *gene-markers* to be used for the classification of new samples into respective disease-type classes.

In this paper we present a novel gene-selection methodology form gene-expression data, accompanied by a novel and intuitive method for predicting the class of unseen samples. The methodology relies on: (i) the discretization of gene-expression values, (ii) a metric that ranks the genes relatively to their power to discriminate between the classes, (iii) a greedy feature elimination process that selects the most discriminant genes, and (iv) on a metric that predicts the class of samples.

2 Microarrays: Basics and Experimental Set-up

Microarray technology targets to identify the genes that are expressed in particular cells of an organism at particular time or, at particular conditions (e.g., disease-states or, disease-types). A microarray is typically a glass (or some other material) slide, on to which DNA molecules are attached at fixed locations (spots). There may be tens of thousands of spots on an array, each containing a huge number of identical DNA molecules (or fragments of identical molecules), of lengths from twenty to hundreds of nucleotides. For gene expression studies, each of these molecules ideally should identify one gene in the genome (even if this is not always possible) [4].

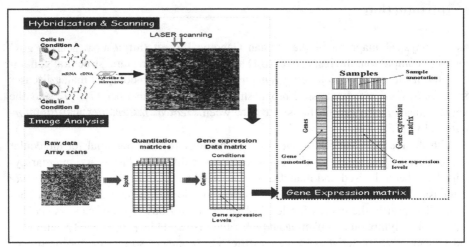

Fig. 1. Microarrays: Experimental set-up.

The spots are either printed on the microarrays by a robot, or synthesized by photo-lithography (similarly as in computer chip productions) or, by ink-jet printing. See Figure 1, above, for the general schema of a microarray experimental set-up. After *hybridization* and *scanning* the total mRNA from the samples in two different conditions is extracted and labeled. The final product is a microarray image (in most cases the '.tiff' format is followed).

Each spot on the array image is identified, its intensity measured and compared to the background (the *image quantization* process, conducted by dedicated image analysis software). To obtain the final *gene-expression matrix* from spot quantization, all the quantities related to some gene are combined and the entire matrix is scaled to make different arrays comparable. In the resulted gene-expression matrix, *rows* represent genes, *columns* represent samples, and each cell contains a number characterizing the expression level of a gene in the particular sample. Introductory material related to microarray technology and gene-expression profiling may be found at http://www.ebi.ac.uk/microarray/biology_intro.html. For material on the techniques followed during the fabrication of microarray-chips and the related protocols refer to http://www.imbb.forth.gr/facilities/genomic.html.

3   Gene Selection and Class Prediction

Gene selection is crucial for gene-expression based disease classification problems. Methods for selecting informative genes for sample classification have been recently proposed [3], [8], [17].

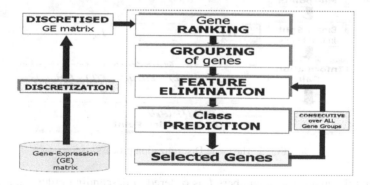

Fig. 2. The Gene-Selection process.

Here we present a novel gene-selection methodology composed by four main modules: (i) gene ranking; (ii) grouping of genes; (iii) consecutive feature elimination; and (iv) class prediction. A data pre-processing step is also performed that takes as input the gene-expression matrix and outputs a discretised transform of it (Figure 2).

3.1 Dicretization of Gene-Expression Data

In many gene-expression profiling studies the researchers decide to visualize the potential clustering of the genes (or, the samples), as well as the final selected set of genes in a discretized manner (see for example the work in [8]). We decide to utilize discretization of the gene-expression continuous values into the core of the gene-selection process. Discretization of a given gene's expression values means that each value is assigned to an interval of numbers that represents the expression-level of the gene in the given samples.

A variable set of such intervals may be utilized and assigned to naturally interpretable values e.g., `low, high`. Given the situation that, in most of the cases, we are confronted with the problem of selecting genes that discriminates between two classes (i.e., disease-states) it is convenient to follow a *two-interval* discretization of gene-expression patterns. The multi-class (i.e., more than two classes) problem may be tackled by splitting it into a series of two-class discrimination problems and then combining the results, as it is done in various gene-expression studies [21]. Below we give a general statement of the two-interval discretization problem followed by an algorithmic two-step process to solve it (Figure 3).

<u>Given:</u> A set of number $L = \{n_1, n_2 \dots n_m\}$ where, each number in L is assigned to one of two classes c_i, c_j. <u>Find:</u> A binary split of L into two sets H_k and L_k, that best discriminates between the classes.

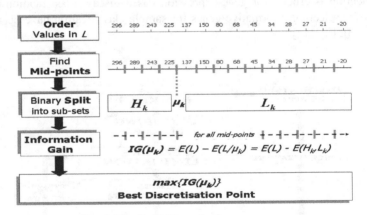

Fig. 3. The Gene Discretization process.

Step 1. First the given set of numbers L is ordered in descending order (an ascending order arrangement it could be also followed), resulting in an order vector of numbers $L' = <n'_1, n'_2 \dots n'_k>$, $n'_i < n'_j$, and $k \leq m$ ($k = m$ when there are not repeated numbers in L). For all consecutive pair of numbers n'_i, n'_{i+1} in L' their midpoint, $\mu_i = (n'_i, n'_{i+1})/2$ is computed, and the corresponding ordered vector of midpoint numbers is formed, $M = <n'_1, n'_2 \dots n'_{k/2}>$.

Step 2. For each $\mu_k \in M$ two subsets of L are formed, $H_k = \{n_i \in L / n_i > \mu_k\}$, and $L_k = \{n_i \in L / n_i \le \mu_k\}$, and the well-known information-gain formula, [20], is utilized and computed, $IG(\mu_k) = E(L) - E(L/\mu_k) = E(L) - E(H_k, L_k)$. In this formula, $E(L)$ stands for the entropy of the system, i.e., the original set of numbers L, with respect to their assignment to classes c_i and c_j; and $E(L/\mu_k) = E(H_k, L_k)$ for the entropy of the system when the set of numbers L is split into the disjoint sets H_k and L_k. The midpoint that exhibits the maximum information-gain is selected as the split of the numbers in L that best discriminates between the two classes. The discretization procedure is applied to each gene separately. Assuming that H_k, and L_k values are assigned the natural interpretation of 'h' (high) and 'l' (low), respectively, the result is a pattern of 'h's and 'l's, as it is shown below (an example from the leukemia domain, see section 4).

Gene / Sample-class →	ALL	ALL	ALL	ALL	ALL	ALL	ALL	AML	AML	AML	AML	AML	AML	AML
M77142- original	296	225	243	137	289	-20	150	27	28	45	34	68	80	21
M77142- *discretized*	h	h	h	h	h	l	h	l	l	l	l	l	l	l

The overall discretisation process is visually presented in Figure 3, above. The introduced process resembles the one introduced by Fayyad and Irani, [5], with two fundamental differences (recently, the same approach was also utilized in a gene-expression profiling study, see ref. [15]). Because we use the sorted list of numbers for the selection of midpoints, all the points are 'boundary values' (in Fayyad's terminology). Furthermore, in [5] and [15], the discretization process is recursively applied to each of the formed binary-splits until an appropriately devised stopping criterion is met. So, with this approach the fundamental demand for a two-interval discretization is not guaranteed, as it is done by our approach.

3.2 Ranking and Selection of Genes

The problem now is how to select the genes that best discriminate between the different disease states. The problem is well-known in the machine learning community as the problem of feature-selection (with its dual 'feature-elimination') [10], and various 'wrapper-based' [14], or, 'filtering' [2], approaches have been proposed. Traditionally, in machine learning research the number of features, m, is quite smaller than the number of cases, k (samples in the case of gene-expression studies) that is, $m \ll k$. In contrast, gene-expression studies refer to a huge number of features and quite few samples. In most gene-expression domains the number of genes is in the range of 2000 – 35000 (= the estimated number of human genes), and the number of samples in the range of 50 – 200, that is $k \ll m$. In this context it is questionable if a 'wrapper' based feature-selection approach could help, especially because of its high-computational cost and so, a 'filtering' approach seems more appropriate.

Our filtering-based gene-selection approach unfolds into two layers: (a) the genes are *ranked* with respect to their power to distinguish between the different disease-states (classes), and (b) a *greedy gene-groups elimination* process is consecutively applied on the ordered list of grouped genes in order to select the most discriminant.

3.2.1 Gene Ranking

For each discretized gene we count the number of 'h's and 'l's that occur in the respective samples. Assume that each sample is assigned to one of two classes, i.e., P, and N. The following quantities are computed: $H_{g,P}$ = number of 'h' values for gene g assigned to class P; $L_{g,P}$ = number of 'l' values for gene g assigned to class P; $H_{g,N}$ = number of 'h' values for gene g assigned to class N; and $L_{g,N}$ = number of 'h' values for gene g assigned to class N. Formula (1), below, computes a *rank* for each gene that measures the power of the gene to distinguish between the two classes:

$$r_g = (H_{g,P} \times L_{g,N}) - (H_{g,N} \times L_{g,P}) \tag{1}$$

For a completely distinguishing gene where, <u>all</u> of its values for class P are 'h', and <u>all</u> of its values for class N are 'l', $H_{g,N} = L_{g,P} = 0$ and, r_g, takes its maximum *positive* value. In this case the gene is considered as descriptive for (or, associated with) class P.

The gene remains completely distinguishing in the inverse case where, $H_{g,P} = L_{g,N}$ = 0 and, r_g, takes the minimum *negative* value. In this case the gene is associated with class N. In other words the gene ranking formula encompasses and expresses a *polarity* characteristic that represents the descriptive power of the gene with respect to the present disease-state classes. So, ordering the positive ranks in descending order and the negative ranks in ascending order we may identify the most discriminant genes for class P and N, respectively. Formula 1 could be considered as a 'discrete analog' of the respective signal-to-noise formula presented in [8].

3.2.2 Feature-Elimination and Gene-Selection

Rank-ordering of the genes does not solve the problem of 'how many genes' should be considered as the most discriminant. In most of the published gene-expression studies the researchers decide on an 'ad hoc' basis for a threshold cut-off value for this (for an example refer to the study presented in [8]). Here we introduce a more careful and sound method that selects the most discriminant genes from the two rank-ordered lists. It consists of two processes.

Grouping of genes. We present the case for the positively ranked genes (i.e., genes associated with class P) where, $<n_1, n_2 \dots n_p>$ the descending ordered vector of class's P gene ranks. The mean difference between all consecutive numbers in the vector, $\delta = (n_1 - n_p)/(n-1)$, is computed. We start by forming the top group $O_{P;1} = \{n_1\}$. Then, the difference of each of the next consecutive pair of numbers, $\delta_i = n_i - n_{i+1}$, is computed and tested against δ. If $\delta_i \leq \delta$ then, n_i and n_{i+1} are grouped together forming the group $O_{P;i} = \{n_i, n_{i+1}\}$, otherwise they are split and a new singleton group $O_{P;i+1} = \{n_{i+1}\}$ is formed. The process continuous till all ranks are examined.

The final outcome is an ordered vector of *groups of genes* starting from the latest formed group, $O_p = <O_{P;f}, O_{P;f-1} \dots O_{P;1}>$, $f \leq P$ ($P = f$ when each positively ranked gene is grouped in a separate group). The same procedure is applied on the negatively ranked genes, and the respective ordered-vector of gene-groups is formed, $O_N = <O_{n;f}$ $O_{n;f-1} \dots O_{n;1}>, f \leq N.$

Greedy gene-groups elimination. We are presented with the two vectors of groups of genes, $O_P = <O_{p;f}, O_{p;f-1} \dots O_{p;1}>$ and $O_N = <O_{n;f}, O_{n;f-1} \dots O_{n;1}>$. Note that the beginning elements in the two vectors contain groups of genes that are less distinguishing between the two classes. In contrast, the ending elements contain genes that are most discriminant. So, it is rational to consider a procedure that eliminates groups from the beginning of the two vectors.

We consider three situations: (i) deleting a group from O_P, (ii) deleting a group from O_N, and (iii) deleting a group from both O_P and O_N. In all cases, the accuracy of the remaining genes on the training samples is assessed. The accuracy is computed based on a specially devised *predictor* metric (presented in the next section). The accuracy figure and the respective list of remaining genes are recorded. The deletion that exhibits the highest accuracy is performed.

The group-elimination process continues till all the groups in the two lists are considered. The list of remaining genes with the highest accuracy is selected as the final set of most discriminant genes.

3.3 Samples Class Prediction

The vision of functional genomics, at least for the human case, is the devise of diagnostic and prognostic kits for various major diseases. With the utilization of microarray chip technology the target is to devise microarray *chip-based diagnostic and prognostic kits* dedicated to specific diseases. In the core of the process for devising such a kit are gene-selection methods, much in the sense presented above. Having on our disposal such a kit the question is how a new patient (i.e., its pathologic sample-tissue) is classified to a disease-state class or, how its prognosis is predicted.

Assume that the sample is presented as a vector of gene-expression values for the genes that are present in the diagnostic/prognostic kit. We introduce a novel matching procedure, and a respective metric, that predicts the class of a sample. Denote with $H_{g,P}, L_{g,P}$, and $H_{g,N}, L_{g,N}$, the number of 'h' and 'l' values of gene g in classes P and N, respectively. We assign the integer values '1' and '-1' to the respective discretized genes' expression-levels of the new sample. The integer values '1' and '-1' stands for the 'h' and 'l' assignments, respectively and is denoted with $sign(s_g)$. The matching formula 2, below, is used to predict the class of a sample s.

$$class(s) = sign(s_g) \times \left[\sum_{g \in P} \frac{H_{g;P} - L_{g;P}}{|P|} - \sum_{g \in N} \frac{H_{g;N} - L_{g;N}}{|N|} \right] \qquad (2)$$

As with the gene-ranking formula (section 3.2.1), formula (2) also encompasses a polarity characteristic. If the outcome of the formula is positive then the new sample is assigned to class P, and if it is negative then it assigned to class N. In addition, the strength with which the sample is predicted to belong to one of the two classes is also provided so that, *strong* (or, *weak*) predictions could be made. Take as an example the extreme case were $L_{g;P} = H_{g;N} = 0$ for all selected genes (i.e., all the genes have *'high'* values for all class P samples, and *'low'* values for all class N samples; in other words all selected genes are ideally associated with the respective classes). Then, in formula 2 the bracketed factor receives its maximum positive value which equals the total number of training samples, S. Now, if the incoming unseen sample have *'high'* values (i.e., $sign(s_g) = 1$) for all genes associated with class P, and *'low'* values (i.e., $sign(s_g) = -1$) for all genes associated with class N (i.e., an ideal class P sample) then, formula 2 receives its maximum positive value which equals to $2S$. So, the sample is strongly predicted to belong to class P. All the above holds for the inverse case where, the incoming sample is an ideal class N sample- the outcome of formula 2 will be $-2S$, and the sample will be strongly predicted to belong to class N. Under suitable assumptions (based on an analysis of all prediction figures) a 'weak' prediction could leave the sample *unclassified*.

4 Experiments and Results

4.1 Domains and Datasets

We applied the introduced gene-selection and samples classification methodology on five real-world gene-expression domain studies that are pioneering in their fields. A total of five biomedical domains were investigated and respective tasks are posted: *CC* (Colon Cancer) [12] - the task is to distinguish between *normal* and *tumor* samples; *LEUK* (Leukemia) [8] - to distinguish between two leukemia classes: *ALL* and *AML*; *LYMPH* (Lymphoma) [1] – to distinguish between two lymphoma-characteristic classes: *DLBCL* and *GC;* *HBC* (Hereditary Breast Cancer) [11] – two tasks are tackled, *HBC-1*: to distinguish between *BRCA1* and *not-BRCA1* mutated samples, and *HBC-2*: to distinguish between *BRCA2* and *not-BRCA2* mutated samples; and *CNS* (Central Nervous System) [18] – to distinguish between *failed* and *succeed* treatment outcome. Table 1 gives a summarized description of the selected biomedical domains, accompanied with links to the original published references and the respective studies' sites (from where the respective datasets may be retrieved).

Table 1. Experimental domain studies: Comparison references and datasets.

Domain Study (Data access[+])	CR*	#Genes	TD*		tD*	
			#c$_1$	#c$_2$	#c$_1$	#c$_2$
CC	[15]	2000	27	13	10	7
LEUK	[8]	6817	27	11	21	14
LYMPH	[15]	4026	19	15	5	8
HBC-1	[11]	5361	7	15	NP*	NP
HBC-2	[11]	5361	8	14	NP	NP
CNS	[18]	7129	21	39	NP	NP

Index to the table. **CR**: Comparison Reference; **TD**: Training Data; **tD**: test Data; **#c$_i$**: number c$_i$ samples; **NP**: Not provided. [+]Data access: *CC*: http://www.sph.uth.tmc.edu/hgc/Downloads.asp - *LEUK*: http://www-genome.wi.mit.edu/cgi-bin/cancer/publications/pub_paper.cgi?mode=view&paper_id=43 - *LYMPH*: http://llmpp.nih.gov/lymphoma/data.shtml - *HBC-1,-2*: http://research.nhgri.nih.gov/microarray/NEJM_Supplement/ - *CNS*: http://www-genome.wi.mit.edu/mpr/CNS/

4.2 Results and Discussion

Table 2, summarizes the results of applying the introduced gene-selection and sample classification methodology. The bold figures indicate superior performance with respect: (a) to the number of selected genes (i.e., the less the better), and (b) to accuracy assessment results.

Table 2. Compasrison results: Our results vs. the Comparison References (CR) results. Bold figures indicate superior performance (better accuracy or, less number of selected genes).

		CC	*LEUK*	*LYMPH*	*HBC-1*	*HBC-2*	*CNS*	Average
CR* Results	#SG[1]	50	50	50	**9**	11	**8**	29.7
	CV%[2]	100.0[a]	94.7	84.6[a]	95.5[a]	81.8[a]	78.3	87.6
	Tt%[3]	**100.0**	85.3	**84.6**	95.5	81.8	78.3[b]	89.4
Our Results	#SG	**14**	**10**	**12**	23	**10**	14	**13.8**
	CV%	100.0	**100.0**	**97.1**	**100.0**	**95.5**	**91.7**	**97.4**
	Tt%	94.1	**97.1**	84.6	**100.0**	**100.0**	**95.0**	**95.1**

Index to the table: *CR: Comparison Reference; [1]#SG: number of Selected Genes; [2]CV: leave-one-out Cross-Validation accuracy; [3]Tt: Train vs test accuracy; [a]Not-provided and replaced by the respective Tt figure; [b]Not provided and replaced by respective CV figure.

As it can be observed, the introduced gene-selection methodology outperforms, in most of the cases, the ones in the comparison-references. At an average, the leave-one-out cross-validation accuracy (CV) achieved with our method is 97.4 % as compared with the respective average figure of 87.6% for the comparison references. The difference of the results are statistically significant on the P>99.9% level (applying a two-tail t-test). For the training vs. test (Tt) accuracy levels, our method shows an average accuracy of 95.1% as compared with the respective 89.4% figure of the comparison-references. The results are statistically significant on the P>90% level.

Furthermore, our methodology results in a smaller number of selected genes (SG), an average of 13.8 over all domains, as compared with the average of 29.7 of the comparison-references (a statistically significant difference on the P>90% level, applying a one-tail t-test on the number of genes over all domains). This result is quite satisfactory because a small number of disease associated genes gives the opportunity for more complete and better biological interpretation (e.g., for the involved disease-related biochemical pathways).

The results show the reliability of the introduced gene-selection and sample classification methodology. The performance is high, not only because of the introduced gene-selection approach (i.e., discretization, gene-ranking and gene-selection) but also because of the introduced prediction metric. In some preliminary experiments where we used the list of selected genes reported in the comparison references, we were able to exhibit higher (than the originally published) accuracy results by using the introduced formula 2 as the prediction/matching metric.

5 Conclusion and Future Work

Recent advances in microarray technology provide the basis for understanding the genetic mechanisms of specific diseases. The sophisticated analysis and interpretation of the respective gene-expression data is the key. The problem is quite challenging because of the huge number of genes and the small number of samples.

In this context we presented a novel approach to the problem of gene-selection from gene-expression data. It is based on a method enabled by the careful application of an information-theoretic metric, which discretize the continuous gene-expression values. With a specially devised gene-ranking metric we measure the strength of each gene with respect to its power to discriminate between the present samples' categories (i.e., disease-states or, types). Then, a greedy feature-elimination algorithm is applied on the rank-ordered genes. The output is the final set of selected genes. Unseen cases (i.e., left-out test samples) are predicted to belong to a specific category with the application of a novel prediction/matching metric.

The whole approach was applied on five indicative real-world gene-expression domain-studies with very good results. In most of the cases the introduced gene-selection methodology compares, and in some cases outperforms the published comparison-references results.

The future R&D agenda includes: (a) further experimentation with other gene-expression profiling domains, especially with multi-class (more than two) domains, (b) biological interpretation of the results (e.g., how many of the selected genes are common in our results and the original comparison references), and (c) inclusion of the gene-selection and samples classification methodology in an Integrated Clinico-Genomics Environment [19].

References

1. Alizadeh, A.A., et al.: Distinct types of diffuse large B-cell lymphoma identified by gene expression profiling. Nature 403:3 (2000) 503-511.
2. Baim, P.W.: A Method for Attribute Selection in Inductive Learning Systems. IEEE PAMI, 10: 6 (1988) 888-896.
3. Bassett, D.E., Eisen, M.B., Boguski, M.S.: Gene expression informatics: it's all in your mine. Nature Genetics 21, Supplement 1 (1999) 51-55.
4. Brazma, A., Parkinson, H., Schlitt, T., Shojatalab, M.: A quick introduction to elements of biology - cells, molecules, genes, functional genomics, microarrays. EMBL- European Bioinformatics Institute (EBI), (October 2001).
   [http://www.ebi.ac.uk/microarray/biology_intro. html; accessed October 2003]
5. Fayyad, U., Irani, K. Multi-interval discretization of continuous-valued attributes for classification learning. Procs of the 13th Inernational Joint Conference of Artificial Intelligence. Morgan Kaufmann, San Francisco, CA (1993) 1022-1029.
6. Friend, H.F.: How DNA microarrays and expression profiling will affect clinical practice. Br Med J 319 (1999) 1-2.

7. Ginsburg, G.S., McCarthy, J.J.: Personalized medicine: revolutionizing drug discovery and patient care. Trends Biotechnol 19:12 (2001) 491-496.
8. Golub, T.R., Slonim, D.K., Tamayo, P., Huard, C., Gaasenbeek, M., Mesirov, J.P., Coller, H., Loh, M.L., Downing, J.R., Caligiuri, M.A., Bloomfield, C.D., Lander, E.S.: Molecular classification of cancer: class discovery and class prediction by gene expression monitoring. Science 286 (199) 531-537.
9. Guttmacher, A.E., Collins, F.S.: Genome Medicine. Special issue of N Engl Med 349 (2003).
10. Hall, M.A.: Correlation-based Feature Selection for Machine Learning. PhD thesis, University of Waikato (1999).
11. Hedenfalk, I., et al.: Gene-expression profiles in hereditary breast cancer. N Engl J Med. 344:8 (2001) 539-548.
12. Kinzler, K.W., Vogelstein, B.: Lessons from hereditary colorectal cancer. Cell 87:2 (1996) 159-170.
13. Kohane, I.S.: Bioinformatics and Clinical Informatics: The Imperative to Collaborate. JAMIA 7 (2000) 512–516.
14. Kohavi, R., John, G.: Wrappers for feature subset selection. Artificial Intelligence (special issue on Relevance) 97:1-2 (1996) 273-324.
15. Li, L., Weinberg, C.R., Darden, T.A., Pedersen, L.G.: Gene selection for sample classification based on gene expression data: study of sensitivity to choice of parameters of the GA/KNN method. Bioinformatics 17:12 (2001) 1131-1142.
16. Maojo, V., Iakovidis, I., Martín-Sánchez, F., Crespo, J., Kulikoswki. C.: Medical Informatics and Bioinformatics: European efforts to facilitate synergy. Journal of Biomedical Informatics 34:6 (2001) 423-427.
17. Nadon, R., Shoemaker, J.: Statistical issues with microarrays: Processing and analysis. Trends in Genetics, 15 (2002) 265-271.
18. Pomeroy, S.L., et al.: Prediction of central nervous system embryonal tumour outcome based on gene expression. Nature 415 (2002) 436-442.
19. Potamias, G.: Utilizing Gene Functional Classification in Microarray Data Analysis: a Hybrid Clustering Approach. 9th Panhellenic Conference in Informatics, 21-23 November, Thessaloniki, Greece (2003).
20. Quinlan, J.R.: Induction of decision trees. Machine Learning, 1:81 (1986) 81-106.
21. Su, A.I., et al.: Molecular Classification of Human Carcinomas by Use of Gene Expression Signatures. Cancer Research 61 (2001) 7388-7399.

Automatic Detection of Abnormal Tissue in Bilateral Mammograms Using Neural Networks

Ioanna Christoyianni, Emmanouil Constantinou, and Evangelos Dermatas

WCL, Electrical & Computer Engineering Dept., University of Patras
26100 Patras, Hellas
ioanna@ios.wcl2.ee.upatras.gr

Abstract. A novel method for accurate detection of regions of interest (ROIs) that contain circumscribed lesions in X-rays mammograms based on bilateral subtraction is presented. Implementing this method requires left and right breast images alignment using a cross-correlation criterion followed by a windowing analysis in mammogram pairs. Furthermore, a set of qualification criteria is employed to filter these regions, retaining the most suspicious for which a Radial-Basis Function Neural Network makes the final decision marking them as ROIs that contain abnormal tissue. Extensive experiments have shown that the proposed method detects the location of the circumscribed lesions with accuracy of 95.8% in the MIAS database.

1 Introduction

Despite the important development of screening programs in the last years, breast cancer is still a leading cause of fatality among all cancers for women, with approximately 1 out of 12 women being affected by the disease during their lifetime. Currently, X-ray mammography is the single most effective, low-cost, and highly sensitive technique for detecting small lesions [1] resulting in at least a 30 percent reduction in breast cancer deaths. The radiographs are searched for signs of abnormality by expert radiologists but complex structures in appearance and signs of early disease are often small or subtle. That's the main cause of many missed diagnoses that can be mainly attributed to human factors [1,2]. However, the consequences of errors in detection or classification are costly. Since the advent of mass screening, there has been a considerable interest in developing methods for automatically detecting mammography abnormalities, as means of aiding radiologists and improving the efficacy of screening programs.

Among the various types of breast abnormalities, which are visible in mammograms, clustered microcalcifications (or "calcifications") and mass lesions are the most important ones. Masses and clustered microcalcifications often characterize early breast cancer [3] that can be detectable in mammograms before a woman or the physician can palp them. Masses appear as dense regions of varying sizes and properties and can be characterized as circumscribed, spiculated, or ill defined. The emphasis of

G.A. Vouros and T. Panayiotopoulos (Eds.): SETN 2004, LNAI 3025, pp. 267–275, 2004.

this paper is given to the detection of the regions of interest that contain circumscribed masses in digitized mammograms.

The use of computer-aided diagnosis (CAD) as a "second opinion" strategy for detecting masses in mammograms or microcalcifications, has been widely used [4-7]. In particular, neural network based CAD systems have already been applied to a variety of pattern recognition tasks such as microcalcifications detection and specification and have proven as a potentially powerful tool [4,7-9]. The detection of masses in mammograms is a difficult task because of the similarity between many of radiopacities and breast tissue and the low contrast of many cancerous lesions. Two general approaches have been explored in mammographic mass detection and analysis: single image segmentation and bilateral image subtraction. In the first case several techniques that incorporate knowledge about lesions have already been employed [8,9].The second approach which uses bilateral subtraction of corresponding left-right matched image pairs, is based on the symmetries between both images [3], with asymmetries indicated possible masses [10,11,12].

In this paper, we present a complete method for the detection of one or several regions which are suspicious of containing circumscribed mass lesions in mammograms based on bilateral subtraction with an accuracy higher than 95%. The implementation of this method requires both left and right breast images or recent mammograms from the same breast to be aligned using a cross-correlation criterion followed by a windowing analysis in mammogram pairs. Then with the implementation of a set of *qualification criteria*, only a small subset of regions remains that are fed into a Radial-Basis Function Neural Network (RBFNN). The result is a number of regions that are considered to be the most suspicious and they are marked as regions of interest (ROIs) for further examination by the radiologist.

The structure of this paper is as follows: In the next section a detailed description of the proposed method is given. In section 3 we present the data set and our experimental results and finally in section 4 some conclusions are drawn.

2 Overall Proposed Method

The basic scheme of the proposed method is shown in Figure 1. It consists of a preprocessing step that registers the two corresponding mammograms, a windowing breast image analysis in the two views of the left and the right breast of the same woman, a set of qualification criteria and a neural network classifier for marking ROIs containing circumscribed mass. All the above steps are important for the method's effectiveness. The preprocessing step is of great importance in order to compensate for some normal differences between the images which share local characteristics with the masses and cause high false positive rates. The windowing analysis and the implementation of the proposed qualification criteria result in a significant reduction of the suspicious regions to be fed to the neural network. Finally, the classifier is making the final decision regarding the ROIs that have to be further examined by an expert radiologist.

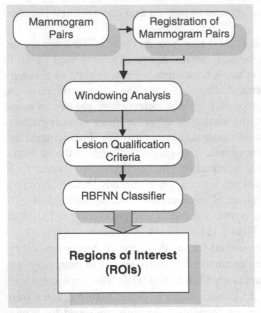

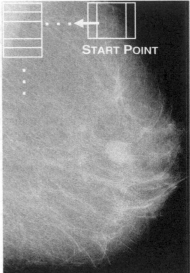

START POINT

Fig. 1. Basic scheme of the proposed method.   **Fig. 2.** The "S Path".

2.1 Registration of Mammogram Pairs

The registration of the mammogram pairs is very complicated procedure due to their structure that depends on the mammogram acquisition accuracy and the differences between the size of the two mammograms. In the proposed method, we align the mammogram pairs using the maximum coefficient of a cross-correlation criterion.

In case of left/right mammogram, the first step in order to align the mammogram pairs is to mirror the right mammogram with respect to its vertical axis. Then, both mammograms are thoroughly examined for similarities by scanning the right mammogram with a region-mask extracted from the left. The region-mask is moved horizontally/vertically, one pixel at a time to scan the whole right mammogram. In each iteration the cross correlation coefficient is computed between the region-mask and the corresponding region of the right mammogram, using the following equation:

$$p = \frac{\sum\limits_{r=1c=1}^{R}\sum\limits^{C}(g_1(r,c)-\mu_1)(g_2(r,c)-\mu_2)}{\sqrt{\sum\limits_{r=1c=1}^{R}\sum\limits^{C}(g_1(r,c)-\mu_1)^2\sum\limits_{r=1c=1}^{R}\sum\limits^{C}(g_2(r,c)-\mu_2)^2}} \tag{1}$$

where $g_1(r,c)$ is the region-mask's gray-level pixel intensity, μ_1 is the mean intensity of the region-mask, $g_2(r,c)$ is the gray-level pixel intensity of the corresponding window of the right mammogram, μ_2 is the mean intensity of the region-mask corresponding window of the right mammogram and RxC is the size of the region-mask.

The displacement that we need in order to align the mammograms results from the location where the cross correlation coefficient becomes maximum. The appropriate mask is important to contain part of the breast tissue and the border line of the mammogram that carries out information about the size and shape of the mammogram.

2.2 Windowing Analysis

The alignment is of great importance in order to highlight the regions that appear in only one of the same view left and right breast digitised mammograms of the same patient, taken at approximately the same time. Therefore, a successive windowing analysis is performed in both left and right mammograms that have already been aligned by moving a testing window in 5-pixel increments.

The size of the aforementioned window plays an important role to the efficacy of the comparing procedure. As extensive experiments have shown the size of the window is strongly associated with the size of the smallest central tumor that will be detected. Experimentally, we have selected a window size of 30 pixels, which permits even very small tumor lesions to be successfully located. The window on the tested mammogram follows the "S-path" (Figure 2) performing the windowing analysis at the same time in both mammograms.

2.3 Lesion Qualification Criteria

The main goal of the implemented criteria is to select the most important candidate regions that strongly resemble a circumscribed mass in terms of their area and their statistical characteristics such as their pixel's intensity and higher order moments. This comes out progressively as a result of the evaluation of three acceptance/rejection criteria.

Qualification Criterion 1. Each pair of regions is considered to be suspicious if the Euclidian distance between the first and the third moment is higher than a threshold value.

The first and the third gray-level sensitive histogram moments highlight the existence of a circumscribed mass and are extracted from the pixel value histogram of each region and are defined as follows:

$$\text{Mean: } \mu = \sum_{k=1}^{N} f_k p_f(f_k) \ , \ \text{Skewness: } \mu_3 = \frac{1}{\sigma^3} \sum_{k=1}^{N} (f_k - \mu)^3 p_f(f_k) \tag{2}$$

where: N denotes the number of gray levels in the mammogram, f_k is the k-th gray-level and $p_f(f_k) = n_k / n$, where n_k is the number of pixels with f_k gray-level and n is the total number of pixels in the region.

The *threshold value* was chosen experimentally to be 15 in order to reject most of the healthy regions but to retain at the same time all the suspicious ones.

Qualification Criterion 2. Each remaining pair of regions is still considered as suspicious candidate regions (SCRs) if its third order moment (skewness) is negative.

The choice of negative skewness is justified by the fact that nearly all the circumscribed masses in the MIAS Database have negative skewness, as extensive statistical studies have proven. For a random variable x, the skewness is a measure of the symmetry of the distribution and is defined as in [12]

$$\mu_3 = \frac{E\left[\left(x - E[x]\right)^3\right]}{\left(E\left[\left(x - E[x]\right)^2\right]\right)^{3/2}} \tag{3}$$

This qualification step is posed as a hypothesis testing problem in which the hypothesis H1, corresponds to the case that the candidate regions still remain to be suspicious (SCRs) against the alternative null hypothesis H0 where the regions are rejected:

- H1 : the candidate regions still remain to be suspicious
- H0 : the candidate regions are rejected

The hypothesis testing problem is reduced to the following decision rule H based on the skewness:

$$H(\mu_3(R_i)) = \begin{cases} 0 & \text{if } \mu_3(R_i) \geq 0 \\ 1 & \text{if } \mu_3(R_i) < 0 \end{cases} \tag{4}$$

Qualification Criterion 3. Each remaining pair of regions is still considered as SCRs if their mean intensity is higher than a threshold value Tm. The regions that do not validate this last qualification criterion are rejected. The threshold value is chosen according to the various types of the background tissue as shown in Table 1.

Table 1. Threshold values for the various types of background tissue.

Background Tissue	Threshold value
Fatty	> 160
Fatty-Glandular	> 170
Dense-Glandular	> 170

2.4 Neural Network Classifier

Neural networks have been widely used in situations where the knowledge is not explicitly defined and cannot be described in terms of statistically independent rules. A radial-basis-function neural network (RBFNN) is employed as proposed in [4].

The implemented feature extraction procedure relies on the texture, which is the main descriptor for all kinds of mammograms. Therefore, statistical descriptors that depend on averages, standard deviations, and higher-order statistics of intensity values are used for texture description. Specifically, the mean, variance, skewness and the kurtosis statistical features employed in our method are estimated for each remaining SCRs [4]. All extracted features are normalised by their sample means and standard deviations.

The RBFNN input layer handles the four features extracted from each SCRs. Two output units denote the presence or absence of a lesion. A hidden layer with five nodes is located between the input and the output layer. The number of hidden nodes was estimated experimentally for the optimal classification of the circumscribed lesions. In our implementation, the k-means unsupervised algorithm was used to estimate the hidden layer weights from a set of training data containing statistical features from both circumscribed masses and normal tissue. After the initial training and the estimation of the hidden layer weights, the weights in the output layer are computed by minimizing the mean square error (MSE) between the actual and the desired filter output over the set of examples.

3   Experimental Results

3.1   The MIAS Data Set

In our experiments the MIAS MiniMammographic Database [13], provided by the Mammographic Image Analysis Society (MIAS), was used. The mammograms are digitized at 200-micron pixel edge, resulting to a 1024x1024-pixel resolution.

There are a total of 20 bilateral mammograms containing circumscribed lesions. The smallest lesion extends to 18 pixels in radius, while the largest one to 198 pixels. For the training procedure 22 groundtruthed abnormal regions from the 22 mammograms, along with 22 randomly selected normal regions were used. This resulted in a training data subset of 44 regions.

For the evaluation of the proposed method we used all the abnormal mammograms from the MIAS database that contain circumscribed masses (20 mammogram pairs with 24 abnormal regions).

The MIAS database provides groundtruth for each abnormality in the form of circles; an approximation of the center and the radius of each abnormality. Since the abnormal tissues are rarely perfectly circular, and the MIAS policy was to err on the side of making the groundtruth circles completely inclusive rather than too small, these regions often contain a substantial amount of normal tissue as well.

3.2   Classification Results

For the validation of the circumscribed lesion detection method we employed an objective 50% overlap criterion. In particular, if the area of the groundtruth circle, approximated with a square region for reasons of compatibility with our region of interest form, overlaps the area of the detected window by at least 50%, then the detection is considered as a true positive (TP), otherwise the detection is a false positive (FP). This is similar to the validation strategy employed by Woods [14] and Kegelmeyer [15].

For the case of the abnormal mammogram pairs, the proposed method detected correctly 19 out of 20 (19/20) mammograms with circumscribed lesions that satisfied the above validation criterion resulting to 95% True Positive Rate (TPR). On the other hand, the method failed to detect the abnormality in the remaining mammogram; it was left out after the qualification criteria step. Specifically, the 20 mammograms consist of 24 abnormal regions where the proposed method detected correctly 23 out of 24 (23/24). The false positive ROIs, which is the number of the regions that were misclassified as abnormal although they were healthy tissue, was found to be 9.6 ROIs per image. Table 2 shows analytically the experimental results for the testing set of the 24 regions in the 20 mammograms pairs for each type of background tissue.

Table 2. Recognition results.

Type of background tissue	True Positive Rate	False Positive per Image
Fatty (13 regions)	92.3 %	8.5
Glandular (8 regions)	100 %	10.1
Dense (3 regions)	100 %	12
TOTAL (24 regions)	**95.8 %**	**9.6**

In addition, our method achieved to detect successfully the abnormalities, even in cases that were *hard-to-diagnose* (Figure3-case2). However, a significant factor that affects the performance of the overall method is the character of the mammogram's background tissue. Particularly, in the case of fatty background tissue our method achieved a minimum number of FPs per image while in the *hard-to-diagnose* cases the

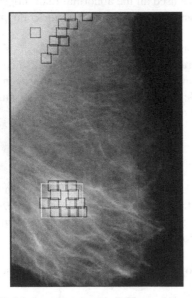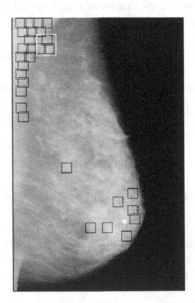

Fig.3. Mammograms with ROIs as detected by the proposed method (The white window is a circumscribed mass as determined by expert radiologists).

method's effectiveness reached very high levels although the number of FPs increased too. The number of FPs in the case of dense background can be attributed to the small number of the dense tissue mammograms with circumscribed masses in the MIAS Database.

4 Conclusion

In this paper we presented a novel method based on the RBFNN classifier and a set of qualification criteria capable of detecting automatically regions of interest that contain circumscribed masses in any given bilateral mammogram. The experimental results show a very high True Positive Rate. Furthermore, by setting less stringent criteria we can increase the sensitivity of the detector to the expense of the detected FPs per image the number of which will increase at the same time. In this case, using a well trained RBFNN with a great number of mammograms (more than 20) would be necessary along with extending and refining the utilized qualification criteria in order to minimize the misdetected cases.

References

1. Martin, J., Moskowitz, M. and Milbrath, J.: Breast cancer missed by mammography. AJR, Vol. 132. (1979) 737.
2. Kalisher, L.: Factors influencing false negative rates in xero-mammography. Radiology, Vol.133. (1979) 297.
3. Tabar, L. and Dean, B.P.: Teaching Atlas of Mammography.2nd edition, Thieme, NY (1985).
4. Christoyianni, I., Dermatas, E., and Kokkinakis, G.: Fast Detection of Masses in Computer-Aided Mammography. IEEE Signal Processing Magazine, vol. 17, no 1. (2000) 54-64.
5. Chan, H., Wei, D., Helvie, M., Sahiner, B., Adler, D., Goodsitt, M. and Petrick, N.: Computer-Aided Classification of Mammographic Masses and Normal Tissue: Linear Discriminant analysis in Texture Feature Space. Phys. Med. Biol.,Vol.40 (1995) 857-876.
6. Meersman, D., Scheunders, P. and Dyck, Van D.: Detection of Microcalcifications using Neural Networks. Proc. of the 3rd Int. Workshop on Digital Mammograph, Chicago, IL (1996) 97-103.
7. Dhawan, P.A., Chite, Y., Bonasso, C. and Wheeler K.: Radial-Basis-Function Based Classification of Mammographic Microcalcifications Using Texture Features. IEEE Engineering in Medicine and Biology & CMBEC (1995) 535-536.
8. Sonka, M., Fitzpatrick, J. : Handbook of Medical Imaging. SPIE Press (2000).
9. Doi, K., Giger, M., Nishikawa, R., and Schmidt, R. (eds.): Digital Mammography 96. Elsevier Amsterdam (1996).
10. Méndez, A.J., Tahoces, P.G., Lado, M.J., Souto, M., Vidal, J.J.: Computer-aided diagnosis: Automatic detection of malignant masses in digitized mammograms. Medical Physics 25 (1998) 957-964.

11. Bovis, K.J. and Singh, S. : Detection of Masses in Mammograms using Texture Measures, Proc.15th International Conference on Pattern Recognition, IEEE Press, vol. 2, (2000) 267-270.
12. Wiles, S., Brady, M. and Highnam, R. : Comparing mammogram pairs for the detection of lesions, International Workshop on Digital Mammography, Kluwer (1998).
13. Bickel, P.J., Doksum, K.A. : Mathematical statistics, Holden- Day California (1997).
14. http://peipa.essex.ac.uk/info/mias.html.
15. Woods, K.S. : Automated Image Analysis Techniques for Digital Mammography, Ph.D. Dissertation, University of South Florida, (1994).
16. Kegelmeyer, W., Pruneda, J., Bourland, P., Hillis, A., Riggs, M. and Nipper, M. : Computer-Aided mammographic screening for spiculated lesions, Radiology, vol. 191 (1994) 331-337.

Feature Selection for Robust Detection of Distributed Denial-of-Service Attacks Using Genetic Algorithms

Gavrilis Dimitris[1], Tsoulos Ioannis[2], and Dermatas Evangelos[1]

[1] Department of Electrical Engineering and Computer Technology, University of Patras,
Patras, Hellas
[2] Department of Computer Science, University of Ioannina, Hellas

Abstract. In this paper we present a robust neural network detector for Distributed Denial-of-Service (DDoS) attacks in computers providing Internet services. A genetic algorithm is used to select a small number of efficient features from an extended set of 44 statistical features, which are estimated only from the packet headers. The genetic evaluation produces an error-free neural network DDoS detector using only 14 features. Moreover, the experimental results showed that the features that best qualify for DDoS detection are the SYN and URG flags, the probability of distinct Source Ports in each timeframe, the number of packets that use certain port ranges the TTL and the window size in each timeframe.

Keywords: Genetic Algorithms, Neural Networks, Denial of Service.

1 Introduction

In recent years there has been a sudden increase of DDoS attacks in computers providing Internet services [1,2,8,10,13]. Especially, after the year 2000 the DDoS attacks cost of losses come up to even billions of US dollars. Major commercial web sites have been disabled for several hours due to such attacks. A DDoS attack uses network flooding, but is harder to defend against because the attack is launched from hundreds or even thousands of hosts simultaneously. Rather than appearing as an excess of traffic coming from a single host, a DDoS attack appears instead as a normal traffic coming from a large number of hosts. This makes it harder to be identified and controlled [21].

Furthermore, continuous monitoring of a network domain for preventing DDoS attacks poses several challenges [17-20]. In high-speed networks real-time monitoring and detection of DDoS attacks cannot be implemented using a huge amount of data or complex pattern recognition methods. Extended studies in specific tools [2,7,8] have been published, and neural networks [3,4,5,9,12] have already been used to detect intrusions and DDoS attacks.

2 Neural Network DDoS Detector and Features Selection

Taking into account that the introduction of network encryption technologies such as IPSec, renders the traditional Network Intrusion Detection Systems useless, we present a robust neural network based DDoS detector, where statistical features are esti-

G.A. Vouros and T. Panayiotopoulos (Eds.): SETN 2004, LNAI 3025, pp. 276–281, 2004.

mated from non-encrypted data such as a network packet header. Moreover, in the direction of detecting the most efficient features, a genetic solution to the features selection problem is implemented.

The proposed DDoS detector consists of three sequentially connected modules:

- The Data Collector: A sniffer captures the appropriate data fields for each packet. The timestamp for each packet is also recorded in order to group the packets into timeframes. Sequential timeframes are also overlapping with each other.
- Features estimator: The frequency of occurrences for various data encoded in the captured packet headers is estimated.
- The Detector: The features vector is passed onto a two-layer feed-forward neural network that determines if an attack is in progress.

The complete set of 44 statistical features estimated in each timeframe consists of statistical probabilities or distinct values normalized by the total number of frame packets transferred in the timeframe:

- Features 1-5. The probabilities of the SYN, ACK, FIN, URG, RST flag to be raised.
- Feature 6. The distinct SEQ values.
- Features 7-8. The distinct values of the source and destination port.
- Feature 9. The probability of the source port to be within the first 1024 values.
- Features 10-25. The sixteen probabilities of the source port value in 1024-65535 divided in groups of 4032 ports.
- Feature 26. The probability of the destination port to be within the first 1024 values.
- Features 27-42. The sixteen probabilities of the destination port value in 1024-65535 divided in groups of 4032 ports.
- Features 43. The distinct values of the window size.
- Features 44. The distinct TTL values.

From experiments, it is has been established that the nature of features plays an important role in the DDoS detection efficiency. In general, the optimum set of features remains an unsolved problem, but a sub-optimum solution can be obtained by a natural selection mechanism known as genetic algorithm [6].

A general description of genetic algorithms theory and application details can be found elsewhere [14-16]. In this paper the main variance of the genetic algorithms is implemented [16], where the chromosomes are selected using a tournament method. In the experiments, the mutation probability varies from 0.05-0.1 and the selection probability varies from 0.25-0.9. The mean square error between the DDoS detector output and the desired values is used as the genetic algorithm's evaluation function.

3 Simulation Environment and Data Collection

A computer network was used to gather information. The attacks were launched from an attack host using the Tribe Flood Network 2000 (TFN2k). The clients were simulated from a single host using the Web Application Stress Tool from Microsoft Corp. that sends HTTP requests on a web server using actual user profiles. The profiles were recorded from an actual user that browsed through the web server's contents. Each request is an actual session that takes into consideration time delays and follows links on the server's contents. The mean rate of the HTTP request is about 3169 in a time frame of 30 secs. The traffic was recorded using a sniffer placed on a monitoring host. It is possible that the sniffer could "miss" some packets but can be implemented easily without the use of special hardware or by reducing the network's efficiency. Furthermore, it is a passive monitoring device that can reside in any system on a network. Different scenarios were created using normal traffic only, traffic produced only by the TFN2k and a combination of the above. More specifically, three types of traffic were recorded:

- Normal traffic of 2400 connections for 5 minutes.
- Pure DDoS traffic in TCP flooding mode for 5 minutes.
- Combined traffic for 5 minutes from multiple clients; the DDoS attack is started after the first second and lasted for about 3 minutes. Then for another minute, the traffic is normal.

A Linux based sniffer (developed using the popular libpcap library) was used to gather the data. From the data that were collected, the client's SEQ number was replaced with a random one, one for each distinct connection, because the Web Application Stress Tool use only two real clients to simulate all the other clients. Therefore the original SEQ numbers produced by the tool were complete unreliable. This modification was verified from a great number of experiments carried out in the same network configuration.

The maximum number of neurons in the input layer was 44. The number of neurons in the hidden layer varies from 1-3 and for each network configuration the features from a 4, 16 and 32 seconds timeframe window was established. The well-known BFGS optimization method is used to estimate the neural network weights.

4 Genetic Optimization

The genetic algorithm is implemented in gnu C++ language and the experiments were carried out in a Linux cluster consisting of 48 computers. The genetic algorithm for the features selection is implemented as follows:

1 A population of 100 randomly defined chromosomes defines the initial generation. Each chromosome is 44-bits long. The selection (ps) and mutation (pm) probabilities were set.

2 The Genetic fitness of each chromosome is evaluated using the neural DDoS detector, after a proper training. The 44-bits chromosome controls the configuration of the feature vector used in the neural DDoS detector. Only the features with the activated bit are used to activate the detector. The neural network weights are estimated by minimization of the least-square-error for the set of training data using the BFGS optimization method. The Genetic fitness is estimated by the mean-square-error between the neural network output and the expected data in the testing set. The data in the test and the training set are mutually exclusive.

3 A selection procedure is applied to the population. The population is sorted according to the fitness of each chromosome. The worst fitting individuals ((1-ps)*number of individuals) are removed from the generation pool. The eliminated chromosomes are replaced in the crossover procedure. The result of this phase is a reduced set of chromosomes called mating pool.

4   The crossover procedure is applied to the mating pool, producing the new generation: Two chromosomes are selected from the mating pool with tournament selection, which is the fastest algorithm for selecting parents. Two offsprings from the
selected chromosomes with one point crossover are produced. The crossover repeated until the chromosome pool is completed.

5   The mutation procedure is applied to the new generation chromosomes: For every
bit in the generation pool, if a random number in the range of (0,1) is lower than the
mutation probability, the corresponding bit is inverting.

The steps 2-5 are repeated 1000 times.

Table 1. The best Genetic fitness and the number of activated features for various neural network configurations, timeframe size, selection and mutation probabilities

	Hidden Nodes	Selection Probability	Mutation Probability	Timeframe Size 4	16	32	
1	1	0.50	0.10	0.0494	0.0002	0.01	Best fitness
				21	27	25	Active features
2	1	0.90	0.10	0.0354	0.0007	0.01	Best fitness
				30	26	19	Active features
3	2	0.50	0.05	0.000	0.0000	0.0	Best fitness
				22	23	27	Active features
4	2	0.50	0.10	0.0000	0.0000	0.0	Best fitness
				22	23	20	Active features
5	2	0.90	0.10	0.0000	0.0000	0.0	Best fitness
				23	25	17	Active features
6	3	0.25	0.05	0.0000	0.0000	0.0	Best fitness
				14	17	23	Active features
7	3	0.25	0.10	0.0000	0.0000	0.0	Best fitness
				18	17	23	Active features
8	3	0.50	0.05	0.0000	0.0000	0.0	Best fitness
				20	17	23	Active features
9	3	0.90	0.05	~0	0.0000	0.0	Best fitness
				23	17	23	Active features
10	3	0.90	0.10	0.0000	0.0000	0.0	Best fitness
				22	17	23	Active features

5   Experimental Results

In table 1, the best Genetic fitness and the number of activated features for various
selection and mutation probabilities are displayed. In all experiments if more than two
neurons in the hidden layer are used, the genetic algorithm and the neural network
training process produces a suitable features vector and an error-free DDoS neural
detector. The minimum number of 14 active features was obtained in the case of three
hidden neurons, selection and mutation probability settings in 0.25 and 0.05 corre-
spondingly, and features estimation in 4 seconds timeframe. It is also shown that the
selection and mutation probabilities do not influence the classification rate of the
DDoS detector but lead to different features vector.

An objective definition of the best features set was a difficult task. In this direction the number of times where each feature was setting active in the set of the best fitting ten chromosomes for 4,16 and 32 seconds timeframes is showed in table 2.

Table 2. Number of times a feature is active in the ten best chromosomes for various Time-frames.

Window Size	1	2	3	4	5	6	7	8	9	10	11	12	13	14	15
4	8	8	7	3	8	5	6	5	8	1	2	5	5	5	6
16	5	6	3	10	4	3	9	5	1	2	6	4	4	5	6
32	7	1	2	9	6	2	7	2	1	1	0	7	6	7	8

Window Size	16	17	18	19	20	21	22	23	24	25	26	27	28	29	30
4	7	6	5	1	3	1	5	2	7	5	7	4	7	4	6
16	9	7	2	4	7	4	4	10	10	4	3	1	3	10	3
32	8	9	4	6	5	6	9	7	7	9	10	2	3	9	2

Window Size	31	32	33	34	35	36	37	38	39	40	41	42	43	44
4	6	7	5	5	6	1	8	5	5	5	5	4	3	3
16	7	6	6	1	4	8	1	3	1	4	3	8	2	1
32	3	3	0	3	8	1	4	8	3	9	7	7	2	3

In general and for all timeframe sizes, the experimental results produced by the genetic algorithm, showed that the SYN and URG Flag, the distinct values of the source and destination port, four probabilities of the groups from the upper set of source ports (features 16,17,23,24), and two probabilities of the groups for the destination ports (features 29 and 42) were used very frequently by the best ten chromosomes.

On the other hand, the probability of the source port to be within the first 1024 values (feature 9), two probabilities of the groups from the upper set of source ports (features 10 and 18), eight probabilities of the groups for the destination ports (features 27,28,30,33,34,36,37,39), the distinct values for the window size, and the TTL distinct values are the less frequent features.

From additional experiments that were carried out it is verified that SYN and URG flags do play significant role in the identification of those kinds of attacks, and also that TTL and Window size provide almost no information.

The role of the source port classes was significantly reduced, because the Web Application Stress Tool did not simulate correctly the clients' source port assignment. This fact was confirmed by further experiments with real clients.

References

1. Mell, P., Marks, D., McLarnon.: A denial-of-Service, Computer Networks. 34, (2000) 641.
2. Ditrich, S.: Analyzing Distributed Denial of Service Tools: The Shaft Case. Proc of the 14th Systems Administration Conference-LISA 2000, New Orleans, USA, (2000) 329-339.
3. J. Ryan, M.J. Lin, R. Miikkulainen, "Intrusion Detection with Neural Networks", in: Advances in Neural Information Processing Systems 10, M. Jordan et al., Eds., Cambridge, MA: MIT Press, 1998 pp. 943-949.

4. Mukkamala, S., Janoski, G., Sung, A.: Intrusion Detection using Neural Networks and Support Vector Machines. Proc. IJCNN, 2 (2002) 1702-1707.
5. Bonifacio, J., Casian, A., CPLF de Carvalho, A., Moreira E.: Neural Networks Applied in Intrusion Detection Systems. Proc. Word Congress on Computational Intelligence - WCCI, Anchorage, USA, (1998) 205-210.
6. Helmer, G., Wong, J., Honavar, V., Miller, L.: Feature Selection Using a Genetic Algorithm for Intrusion Detection. Proceedings of the Genetic and Evolutionary Computation Conference, 2, (1999) 1781.
7. Chen, Y.W.: Study on the prevention of SYN flooding by using traffic policing. IEEE Symposium on Network Operations and Management (2000) 593-604.
8. Schuba, C., Krsul, I., Kuhn, M., Spafford, E., Sundaram, A., Zamboni, D.: Analysis of a denial-of-service attack on TCP. Proc. IEEE Computer Society Symposium on Research in Security and Privacy, USA, (1997) 208-223.
9. Lippmann, R., Cunnigham, R.: Improving intrusion detection performance using Keyword selection and neural networks, Computer Networks, 34 (2000) 596-603.
10. Lau, F., Rubin, S., Smith, M., Trajkovic, L.: Distributed denail-of-service attacks. Proc. IEEE Inter. Conference on Systems, Man and Cybernetics, 3 (2000) 2275-2280.
11. Cabrera, J., Ravichandran, B., Mehra, R.: Statistical Traffic Modeling for network intrusion detection. IEEE Inter. Workshop on Modeling, Analysis, and Simulation of Computer and Telecommunication Systems (2000) 466-473.
12. Bivens, A., Palagiri, C., Smith, R., Szymanski, B., and Embrechts M.: Network-Based Intrusion Detection using Neural Networks. Artificial Neural Networks In Engineering Nov. 10-13, St. Louis, Missouri, (2002).
13. Narayanaswamy, K., Ross, T., Spinney, B., Paquette, M., Wright, C.: System and process for defending against denial of service attacks on network nodes. Patent WO0219661, Top Layer Networks Inc. (USA), (2002).
14. Fletcher, R.: Practical methods of optimization. John Wiley & Sons (1980) 38-45.
15. Back, T., Schwefel, H.: An overview of evolutionary algorithms for parameter optimization, Evolutionary Computation, 1 (1993) 1-23.
16. Goldberg, D.: Genetic algorithms in Search, Optimization and Machine Learning. Addison-Wesley, Reading, Massachusetts, (1989).
17. Branch, J., Bivens, A., Chan, C., Lee, T., Szymanski, B.: Denial of Service Intrusion Detection Using Time-Dependent Finite Automata, http://www.cs.rpi.edu/~brancj/ research.htm.
18. Cox, D., McClanahan, K.: Method for Blocking Denial of Service and Address spoofing attacks on a private network. Patent WO9948303, Cisco Tech Ind (USA), (1999).
19. Belissent, J.: Method and apparatus for preventing a denial of service (DOS) attack by selectively throttling TCP/IP requests. Patent WO0201834, Sun Microsystems Inc (USA), (2002).
20. Maher, R., Bennett V.: Method for preventing denial of service attacks. Patent WO0203084, Netrake Corp (USA), (2002).
21. Scwartau W.: Surviving denial-of-service. Computers & Security, 18, (1999) 124-133.

An Intelligent Tool for Bio-magnetic Signal Processing

Skarlas Lambros[1,2], Adam Adamopoulos[3],
Georgopoulos Stratos[1,2], and Likothanassis Spiridon[1,2]

[1] Department of Computer Engineering and Informatics,
University of Patras, GR-26500, Rio, Patras, Hellas
Tel:(+30) 2610 997755, Fax:(+30) 2610 997706
{skarlas,georgops}@ceid.upatras.gr
[2] Research Academic Computer Technology Institute,
61 Riga Feraiou Str., 26221, Patras, Hellas
likothan@cti.gr
[3] Laboratory of Medical Physics, Department of Medicine
Democritus, University of Thrace
GR-68100 Alexandroupolis, Hellas
adam@med.duth.gr

Abstract. In this contribution we present a novel software tool that can be used to implement intelligent signal processing techniques. BSPS which stands for (Bio magnetic Signal Processing Software) is either a standalone application, or it can be embedded in the kernel of an Artificial Intelligence tool, since it performs signal classification. It can be used to analyze both linear and non linear time series, deterministic and stochastic processes. We used our application in order to analyze and predict the behavior of fetal heart during several phases of women pregnancy. By using evolutionary techniques like genetic algorithms, the theory of Kalman filtering, the Multi-model Partitioning Theory, the Approximate Entropy and other approaches we managed the accomplishment of our objectives.

Keywords: Prediction, genetic algorithms, applications, probabilistic reasoning, diagnosis.

1 Introduction

Bio magnetic signal analysis is a very appealing scientific field. The complexity of these bio-signals source, together with the extraction of useful information of usually large amounts of data, is being examined. Recent software applications deal with classical signal analysis, which is not of particular usefulness when someone is involved with complex sources and stochastic processes. Therefore, BSPS has a variety of classical methods for analysis as well as new evolutionary algorithms and methods taken from the Computational Intelligence Theory. We also want to mention that BSPS is platform independent software and it has been tested both under Unix and Windows environment.

G.A. Vouros and T. Panayiotopoulos (Eds.): SETN 2004, LNAI 3025, pp. 282–290, 2004.

The material considered for analysis with the BSPS is consisted of f-MCG (fetal MagnetoCardioGram) signals. In order to obtain these signals the pregnant women referred to the Laboratory of Medical Physics of the University of Thrace by their special gynecologists of the University Hospital Clinic of Gynecology and Obstetrics [14]. These signals represent recordings of the magnetic component of time-varying electromagnetic fields which are generated from the ionic micro-currents at the fetal heart; these ionic movements are originated at the cellular level. It is believed that, under the proper analysis and interpretation of the f-MCG signals, useful information for the underlying fetal heart dynamics can be obtained. The f-MCG signals [1] are recorded using specific Superconductive Quantum Interference Devices (SQUIDs). SQUIDs are very sensitive superconductive magnetometers with the ability to detect and measure very weak magnetic fields, of the order of fT (= 10^{-15}T). Each f-MCG recording consisted of 32 seconds and was digitized and stored with a sampling frequency of 256 Hz.

2   Classical Signal Analysis

As it can be seen in figure 1, BSPS can be easily used to plot the data in the plain, to find the standard deviation, the mean value, the variance, the distribution of the measured data and the lag plot. The histogram of the statistical distribution of the data is depicted at the bottom left, the lag plot where the lag factor equals one is shown at the bottom left. The upper plot is the data plot for the selected file. The respective filename can be seen in the upper left corner with bold letters.

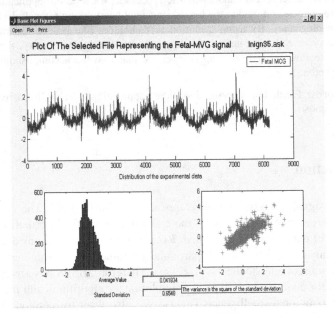

Fig. 1. One instance of the BSPS concerning the classical signal analysis for the file lnign33.ask.

Moreover, an implementation of the Fast Fourier Transform is available in the proposed software tool. In all the aforementioned cases, there is the choice of selecting the portion of the signal to be analyzed by putting the start and the end time points in special text boxes.

2.1 Autocorrelation Plot

The autocorrelation plots [3] are commonly-used tools for checking randomness in a data set. This randomness is ascertained by computing autocorrelations for data values at varying time lags. If random, such autocorrelations should be near zero for any and all time-lag separations. If non-random, then one or more of the autocorrelations will be significantly non-zero. In addition, autocorrelation plots are used in the model identification stage for autoregressive, moving average time series models.

The correlation function computation is also provided with the BSPS tool as shown in figure 2 for the selected signal lnign33.ask. The line plotted in figure 2 also contains several horizontal reference lines. The middle line is at zero. The other four lines are 95% and 99% confidence bands. Note that there are two distinct formulas for generating the confidence bands.

If the autocorrelation plot is being used to test for randomness (i.e., there is no time dependence in the data), the following formula is recommended:

$$\pm \frac{z_1 - a/2}{\sqrt{N}} \tag{1}$$

where N is the sample size, z is the percent point function of the standard normal distribution and α is the significance level. In this case, the confidence bands have fixed width that depends on the sample size. This is the formula that was used to generate the confidence bands in the above plot.

Autocorrelation plots are also used in the model identification stage for fitting ARMA (AutoRegressive Moving Average) models. In this case, a moving average model is assumed for the data and the following confidence bands should be generated:

$$\pm z_1 - \frac{a}{2} \sqrt{\frac{1}{N} (1 + 2 \sum_{i=1}^{K} y_i^2)} \tag{2}$$

where K is the lag, N is the sample size, z is the percent point function of the standard normal distribution and α is the significance level. In this case, the confidence bands increase as the lag increases. The autocorrelation plot is therefore an important tool because, if the analyst does not check for randomness, then the validity of many of the statistical conclusions becomes suspect. The autocorrelation plot is an excellent way of checking for such randomness.

The plots below depict the Fourier transform of the power spectrum which is known, that is the autocorrelation function. In applications where the full autocorrelation function is needed it may be faster to use this method that the direct computation.

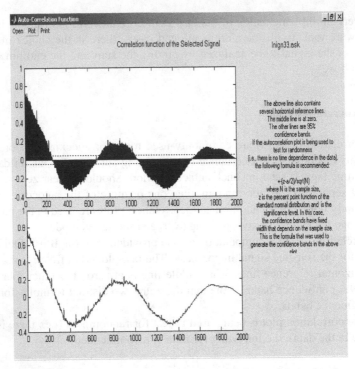

Fig. 2. The auto-correlation plot together with the confidence bands.

2.2 Approximate Entropy

The "approximate entropy" was introduced by Pincus [4],[5],[6] in order to quantify the creation of information in a time series. A low value of the entropy indicates that the time series is deterministic; a high value indicates randomness. The above function has been used to compute the approximate entropy in BSPS:

```
entropy = approxentropy ( pre, post, r );
```

where pre is an embedding of data, post represents the images of the data in the embedding and r is the filter factor, which sets the length scale over which to compute the approximate entropy. The "filter factor" r is an important parameter. In principle, with an infinite amount of data, it should approach zero. With finite amounts of data, or with measurement noise, it is not always clear what is the best value to choose. Past work [7],[8] on heart rate variability has suggested setting r to be 0.2 times the standard deviation of the data.

Another important parameter is the "embedding dimension." Again, there is no precise means of knowing the best such dimension, but the work mentioned above uses a dimension of 2. The final parameter is the embedding lag, which is often set to 1, but perhaps more appropriately is set to be the smallest lag at which the autocorrelation function of the time series is close to zero.

The approxentropy function expects the data to be presented in a specific format. Working with time series, BSPS computes the approximate entropy, with an embedding dimension of 2 and a lag of 1.

3 Evolutionary Signal Analysis

Despite the classical signal analysis, BSPS uses the flexibility and the robustness of computational intelligence methods like genetic algorithms. After testing each measurements file by plotting the autocorrelation and computing the value of the approximate entropy, BSPS responds like an intelligent decision system, since it suggests in an on-line time (without further preprocessing), which should be the most appropriate method or technique one could use to analyze the given time series. For example, for the same measurements file when the approximate entropy value is not significantly high (usually smaller than 1) then an ARMA model (see equation 3) should work well because it is able to capture and to use the dependencies of the data over the time domain. When this is not the case, (the approximate entropy has relatively high value usually greater than 1) BSPS suggests a different model (see equation 4) that is more suitable by means of being able to handle the adaptability which is required when the time series are non linear.

More specific, the models that BSPS uses, are:

For the NAR (Non linear AutoRegressive) processing:

$$x(n) = \sum_{i=1}^{m_1} \alpha_i(n)x(n-i)e^{-(x^2(n-i)/4)} + \varepsilon(n) \tag{3}$$

And for the Genetic Algorithm processing:

$$x(n) = \sum_{i=1}^{m_1} a_i \cdot x(n-i) + \sum_{j=1}^{m_2} b_j \cdot x(n-j)e^{-x^2(n-1)} + \varepsilon(n) \tag{4}$$

Where in both of the above equations x(n) is the n th sample of the f-MCG time series, $\varepsilon(n)$ is a non-necessary Gaussian white noise with variance R, a_i, b_j are the model coefficients (to be calculated) and m_1, m_2 are the orders of the model.

3.1 Genetic Algorithm

An especially designed Genetic Algorithm (GA) was utilized in order to investigate the most suitable values of the model order. The order of each model is a couple of positive integers m = (i, j), where I = 0,.., m_1 and j = 0,.., m_2. Binary codification [2] is used for the representation of the order m of each model. For example when the bits used for binary representation are 5 then the order of the model described by the equation (4) is i=13 and j=25:

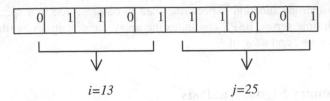

$$i=13 \qquad\qquad j=25$$

As fitness function the GA uses the following:

$$A(m)=100 \cdot \frac{\log\left(1+\dfrac{1}{N}\cdot\sum_{l=1}^{N}p(m/l)\right)}{1+\log\left(1+\dfrac{1}{2\cdot N}\cdot\sum_{l=1}^{N}(x(l)-\hat{x}(l;m))\right)} \tag{5}$$

where:

$$\frac{1}{N}\cdot\sum_{l=1}^{N}p(m/l) \tag{6}$$

is the mean a posteriori probability for the total number of the patterns of the training data set.

The sum:

$$\frac{1}{2\cdot N}\cdot\sum_{l=1}^{N}(x(l)-\hat{x}(l;m)) \tag{7}$$

is calculated after the training of the filters is over and gives an expression of the mean square error of the prediction that the filters can provide.

When genetic algorithm run is completed the user of BSPS can choose the relative report file and evaluate the results in a straightforward manner. Figure 3 presents the latter.

3.2 Non-linear Autoregressive Process

By using the extended Kalman filtering and the Multi Model Partitioning Theory [10], [11], [12], [13] BSPS manages not only to classify the given bio-signals but to predict their often changing behavior, at least in short future time intervals. An example of NAR process is given in figure 4. The user can put the desired values in the text boxes (*right corner*) and by pushing the "*Begin Compute*" button the process starts. Even if the user doesn't put the appropriate values in the text boxes, BSPS has the ability to show the results in the upper right plot where the parameters of the model (see equation 3) are estimated and the real model order is computed in an autonomous way based on probabilistic reasoning. In the above example, the parameter with the blue color indicates that the model order is not 4, as the user suggested, but is equal to 3. The values of those parameters which can be time varying or time invariant are computed with the extended Kalman filtering procedure.

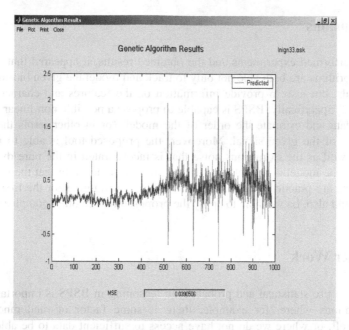

Fig. 3. The genetic algorithm successfully captured the changes over the time for the measurements file lnign33.ask. The Mean Square Error was relatively low as it can be viewed in the gray text box below. In this example there were used 1000 samples as training pattern, the GA population was 10, the execution time was 20 generations, the mutation probability was 0.2 and the crossover probability was 0.5.

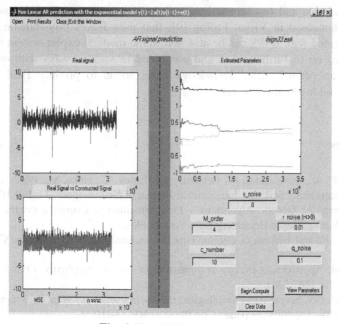

Fig. 4. The NAR processing.

4 Conclusions

From the performed experiments and the obtained results, it appeared that the implemented algorithms are both able not only to track and model the given bio-magnetic f-MCG signals, but also to provide information on the features and characteristics of these signals. Specifically, BSPS is capable to propose a possible non-linear model for the given data and estimate the order of the model, (or in other terms the order of complexity), of the given signal. Moreover, the proposed tool is able to model the ambient as well as the extraneous noise that is incorporated in the pure dynamics of the system. The modeling of both signal and noise is so accurate that the real and the modeled data are practically indistinguishable (i.e. See figure 3 for the first 500 samples). It would also, be valuable to apply the proposed tool to other complex signals.

5 Further Work

Being able to use statistical and probabilistic reasoning in BSPS is important in real-world situations where, for example, there is some factor of randomness in the situation itself, or where we do not have access to sufficient data to be able to know with any real certainty that our conclusions are correct. Medical diagnosis is a clear instance of such a class of problems: a complex domain in which medical knowledge is incomplete, and in which the diagnostician may not have all the data needed.

Often, inexact reasoning is necessary if the doctor is to make any diagnosis at all. Various methods exist for estimating the certainty of conclusions. We are trying to establish a reliable and fast interaction in real time, with a medical diagnosis expert system, implemented in Visual Prolog [9], that uses Bayes probabilistic reasoning. Values computed with BSPS can be attached to the medical expert system rules. They can be passed on to further rules, and combined in various ways with other values taken from an often updated knowledge base, so as to produce final values for conclusions and medical diagnosis.

References

1. Anninos, P. A., Anogianakis, G., Lenhertz, K., Pantev, C.; Hoke, M., 1987, "Biomagnetic measurements using SQUID", International Journal of Neuroscience, 37, 149-168.
2. Michalewicz, Z.: Genetic Algorithms + Data Structures = Evolution Programs. 3rd edn. Springer-Verlag, Berlin Heidelberg New York (1996).
3. Box, G. E. P., and Jenkins, G. (1976), Time Series Analysis: Forecasting and Control, Holden-Day.
4. Pincus SM. Approximate entropy as a measure of system complexity. *Proc Natl Acad Sci USA* 1991;88:2297-2301.
5. Pincus SM, Goldberger AL. Physiological time-series analysis: What does regularity quantify? *Am J Physiol* 1994;266(Heart Circ Physiol):H1643-H1656.

290 Skarlas Lambros et al.

6. Ryan SM, Goldberger AL, Pincus SM, Mietus J, Lipsitz LA. Gender and age-related differences in heart rate dynamics: Are women more complex than men? *J Am Coll Cardiol* 1994;24:1700-1707.

7. Ho KKL, Moody GB, Peng CK, Mietus JE, Larson MG, Levy D, Goldberger AL. Predicting survival in heart failure case and control subjects by use of fully automated methods for deriving nonlinear and conventional indices of heart rate dynamics. *Circulation* 1997 (August);96(3):842-848.

8. Richman JS, Moorman JR. Physiological time-series analysis using approximate entropy and sample entropy. *Am J Physiol Heart Circ Physiol* 278(6):H2039-H2049 (2000).

9. Prolog Development Center A/S H.J. Holst Vej 3-5 C DK-2605 Broendby, Copenhagen Denmark Phone +45 3636 0000 Fax +45 3636 0001

10. Katsikas S. K., Likothanassis S. D., Beligiannis G. N., Berketis K. G. and Fotakis D. A., "Genetically Determined Variable Structure Multiple Model Estimation", IEEE Transactions on Signal Processing, Volume 49, No. 10, October 2001, pp. 2253-2261.

11. G. Beligiannis, E. Demiris and S. Likothanassis, "Evolutionary Non-Linear Multimodel Partitioning Filters", International Journal of Advanced Computational Intelligence, Vol. 5, No. 1, pp. 8-14, 2001.

12. Haykin S. S., "Adaptive Filter Theory", (3rd Edition), Prentice Hall, 1995.

13. L. V. Skarlas, G. N. Beligiannis and S. D. Likothanassis "Evolutionary Multi-Model Estimators for ARMA System Modeling and Time Series Prediction", *Lectures Notes in Computer Science*, Vol. 2687, pp. 409-416, Springer – Verlag Heidelberg, 2003.

14. A.Kotini, P. Anninos, A. Adamopoulos, K. Avgidou, G. Galazios and P. Anastasiadis, "Linear analysis of fetal magnetocardiogram recordings in normal pregnancies at various gestational ages", Journal of Obstetrics and Gynaecology, 21, 2, pp. 154-157 (2001).

Hierarchical Bayesian Networks: An Approach to Classification and Learning for Structured Data

Elias Gyftodimos and Peter A. Flach

Machine Learning Group, Department of Computer Science, University of Bristol, UK
{E.Gyftodimos,Peter.Flach}@bristol.ac.uk

Abstract. Bayesian Networks are one of the most popular formalisms for reasoning under uncertainty. Hierarchical Bayesian Networks (HBNs) are an extension of Bayesian Networks that are able to deal with structured domains, using knowledge about the structure of the data to introduce a bias that can contribute to improving inference and learning methods. In effect, nodes in an HBN are (possibly nested) aggregations of simpler nodes. Every aggregate node is itself an HBN modelling independences inside a subset of the whole world under consideration. In this paper we discuss how HBNs can be used as Bayesian classifiers for structured domains. We also discuss how HBNs can be further extended to model more complex data structures, such as lists or sets, and we present the results of preliminary experiments on the mutagenesis dataset.

1 Introduction

Bayesian Networks [16] are a popular framework for reasoning under uncertainty. However, inference mechanisms for Bayesian Networks are compromised by the fact that they can only deal with propositional domains. Hierarchical Bayesian Networks (HBNs) extend Bayesian Networks, so that nodes in the network may correspond to (possibly nested) aggregations of atomic types. Links in the network represent probabilistic dependences the same way as in standard Bayesian Networks, the difference being that those links may lie at any level of nesting into the data structure [8].

An HBN is a compact representation of the full joint probability distribution on the elements of a structured domain. In this respect, HBNs share some similarities with Stochastic Logic Programs (SLPs) [2, 15]. One of the main differences between the two approaches is that SLPs take clausal logic as a starting point and extend it by annotating clauses with probabilities, whereas HBN rather begin from a probabilistic reasoning formalism (standard Bayesian Networks) and extend it to structured domains. Bayesian Logic Programs [9] are also based on clausal logic, but differ from SLPs in that their probabilistic part corresponds to *degrees of belief* of an agent. Probabilistic Relational Models (PRMs) [10], that are a combination of Bayesian Networks and relational models, are also closely related to HBNs. PRMs are based on an instantiation of a relational schema in order to create a multi-layered Bayesian Network, where layers are derived from different entries in a relational database, and use particular aggregation functions in order to model conditional probabilities between elements of different tables. HBNs adopt a method that is more closely related to the particular data structure, by redefining

G.A. Vouros and T. Panayiotopoulos (Eds.): SETN 2004, LNAI 3025, pp. 291–300, 2004.

the probability distribution on the structured domain. Object-oriented Bayesian Networks [11] also combine Bayesian inference with structured data, exploiting data encapsulation and inheritance.

The outline of the paper is as follows. We begin by presenting preliminary terminology and definitions on HBNs in section 2. In section 3 we present our perspective for the extension of HBNs to first-order and higher-order structures. Section 4 shows an adaptation of a popular algorithm for learning standard Bayesian Networks for the case of HBNs. Section 5 discusses Bayesian classification based on HBNs and presents experimental results on the mutagenesis domain. Finally, we summarise our main conclusions and discuss directions for further work.

2 Hierarchical Bayesian Networks: Preliminaries

A standard Bayesian Network is a graphical model that is used to represent conditional independences among a set of variables. It consists of two parts: the *structural* part, a directed acyclic graph in which nodes stand for random variables and edges for direct conditional dependences between them; and the *probabilistic* part that quantifies the conditional dependences, and in the case of discrete variables is a set of *conditional probability tables* (CPTs), each specifying the conditional probability of each value of a variable given the values of its parents in the graph.

The key property in a Bayesian Network is that a variable is independent of its non-descendants given the values of its parents in the graph. This property can be exploited to decompose the full joint probability of all the variables using the chain rule of probabilities: $P(x_1, x_2, \ldots, x_n) = \prod_{i=i}^{n} P(x_i | \pi_i)$, where π_i denotes the set of parents of x_i in the graph.

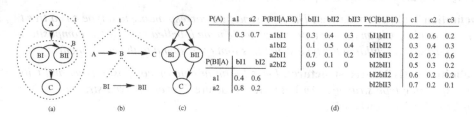

Fig. 1. A simple Hierarchical Bayesian Network. (a) Nested representation. (b) Tree representation. (c) Standard BN expressing the same dependences. (d) Probabilistic part.

Hierarchical Bayesian Networks are a generalisation of standard Bayesian Networks, defined over structured data types. An HBN consists of two parts: the *structural* and the *probabilistic* part. The former (also referred to as the *HBN-tree structure* or simply *HBN structure*) describes the *part-of* relationships and the *probabilistic dependences* between the variables. The latter contains the quantitative part of the conditional probabilities for the variables that are defined in the structural part. In this paper we will restrict our analysis to discrete domains, so the probabilistic part will be a set of conditional probability tables. Figure 1 presents a simple Hierarchical Bayesian Network. The structural part consists of three variables, A, B and C, where B is itself a pair (BI, BII). This may be represented either using nested nodes (a), or by a tree-like type hierarchy (b). We use the symbol t to denote a top-level composite node that includes all the variables of our world. In (c) it is shown how the probabilistic dependence links unfold if we flatten the hierarchical structure to a standard Bayesian Network.

In an HBN two types of relationships between nodes may be observed: relationships in the type structure (called *t-relationships*) and relationships that are formed by the probabilistic dependence links (*p-relationships*). We will make use of everyday terminology for both kinds of relationships, and refer to *parents, ancestors, siblings* etc. in the obvious meaning. In the previous example, B has two t-children, namely BI and BII, one p-parent (A) and one p-child (C). The scope of a probabilistic dependence link is assumed to "propagate" through the type structure, defining a set of *higher-level* probabilistic relationships. Trivially, all p-parents of a node are also considered its higher-level parents. For example, the higher-level parents of C are B (as a trivial case), BI and BII (because they are t-children of B and there exists a p-link $B \rightarrow C$).

We will now provide more formal definitions for HBNs. We begin by introducing hierarchical type aggregations, over which Hierarchical Bayesian Networks are defined. Types are recursively defined, in order to represent nested structures, e.g. "a 5-tuple of pairs of booleans". Currently, the only aggregation operator that we allow for composite types is the Cartesian product, but we plan to extend composite types to include aggregations such as lists and sets, as we discuss in section 3. This will demand a proper definition of probability distribution over these constructs, such as the ones used in the 1BC2 first-order naive Bayesian classifier [12].

Definition 1 (Type). *An atomic type is a domain of constants. If $\{\tau_1, \tau_2, ..., \tau_n\}$ is a set of types, then the Cartesian product $\tau = \tau_1 \times \tau_2 \times ... \times \tau_n$ is a composite type. The types $\tau_1, \tau_2, ..., \tau_n$ are called the component types of τ.*

Definition 2 (Type structure). *The type structure corresponding to a type τ is a tree t such that: (1) if τ is an atomic type, t is a single node labelled τ; (2) if τ is composite, t has root τ and as children the type structures that correspond to the components of τ.*

Definition 3 (HBN-tree structure). *Let τ be an atomic or composite type, and t its corresponding type structure. An HBN-tree structure T over the type structure t, is a triplet $< R, \mathcal{V}, \mathcal{E} >$ where*

- *R is the root of the structure, and corresponds to a random variable of type τ.*
- *$\mathcal{V}$ is a set of HBN-tree structures called the t-children of R. If τ is an atomic type then this set is empty, otherwise it is the set of HBN-tree structures over the component-types of τ. R is also called the t-parent of the elements of $\mathcal{V}$.*
- *$\mathcal{E} \subset \mathcal{V}^2$ is a set of directed edges between elements of $\mathcal{V}$ such that the resulting graph contains no directed cycles. For $(v, v') \in \mathcal{E}$ we say that v and v' participate in a p-relationship, or more specifically that v is a p-parent of v' and v' is a p-child of v.*

If τ is an atomic type, an *HBN-tree structure* over t will be called an *HBN-variable*. We will use the term *HBN-variable* to refer also to the random variable of type τ that the root of the structure is associated to.

Definition 4 (Higher-level parents and children). *Given an* HBN-tree structure $T = <R, \mathcal{V}, \mathcal{E}>$ *and a* t-child *of R*, $<R', \mathcal{V}'', \mathcal{E}'> \in \mathcal{V}$, *then for any* v_P, v_C, v_i *such that* $(v_P, v) \in \mathcal{E}, (v, v_C) \in \mathcal{E}, v_i \in \mathcal{V}'$, *we say that* v_P *is a* higher-level parent *of* v_i, *and that* v_i *is a* higher-level parent *of* v_C. *Furthermore, if* v_{HLP} *is a* higher-level parent *of* v, *then* v_{HLP} *is also a* higher-level parent *of* v_i, *and if* v *is a* higher-level parent *of* v_{HLC} *then* v_i *is also a* higher-level parent *of* v_{HLC}.

For an HBN structure we can construct a standard Bayesian Network that maps the same independences between variables. The nodes in the Bayesian Network correspond to variable nodes of the HBN, and links in the Bayesian Network correspond to higher-level links of the HBN. We will call the resulting structure the *corresponding Bayesian Network* of the original HBN.

Definition 5. *The* HBN-Probabilistic Part *related to an* HBN-structure T *consists of: (1) a probability table for each HBN-variable in T that does not have any p-parents or higher-level parents; (2) a conditional probability table for each other HBN-variable, given the values of all HBN-variables that are its p-parents or higher-level parents.*

Definition 6. *A* Hierarchical Bayesian Network *is a triplet* $<T, \mathcal{P}, t>$ *where*

- t *is a type structure*
- $T = <R, \mathcal{V}, \mathcal{E}>$ *is an HBN-tree structure over* t
- $\mathcal{P}$ *is the HBN-Probabilistic Part related to* T

Definition 7 (Probability distributions over types). *If* τ *is an atomic type,* $P_\tau(x), x \in \tau$, *is the probability distribution over* τ. *If* $\tau = \tau_1 \times \ldots \times \tau_n$ *and* $x \in \tau$, *then* $P(x) = P(x_1, \ldots, x_n)$, *where* $x_i \in \tau_i$ *are the components of x.*

An HBN maps the conditional independences between its variable nodes, in a way that the value of an atomic variable is independent of all atomic variables that are not its higher-level descendants, given the value of its higher-level parents. The independences that an HBN describes can be exploited using the chain rule of conditional probability, to decompose the full joint probability of all the atomic types into a product of the conditional probabilities, in the following way:

$$P(x) = \begin{cases} P_{\tau_X}(x) & \text{if } x \in \tau_X \text{ is atomic} \\ \prod_{i=1}^{n} P(x_i | \pi_i) & \text{otherwise} \end{cases} \tag{1}$$

where $x_1, x_2, \ldots, x_n$ are the components of x and π_i are the p-parents of x_i in the structure.

Example 1. For the HBN structure of Figure 1, we have:

$$
\begin{aligned}
P(t) &= P(A, B, C) && \text{by Definition 7} \\
&= P(A)P(B|A)P(C|B) && \text{by the chain rule of probability} \\
&= P(A)P(BI, BII|A)P(C|BI, BII) && \text{by Definition 7} \\
&= P(A)P(BI|A)P(BII|BI, A)P(C|BI, BII) && \text{by Equation (1)}
\end{aligned}
$$

3   Extending HBNs to First-Order and Higher-Order Structures

So far, we have only considered tuples as type aggregations. We will now discuss how more complex type constructors can be embedded into HBNs to allow for handling first-order and higher-order structures, such as lists, trees, sets, etc. We address this issue from the perspective of typed higher-order logics[14]. Intuitively, a composite type is defined over a number of simpler component types, and a number of aggregation operators (tuples, functors or λ-abstractions). E.g., the type of integers *Int* is a component of the type of lists of integers *List Int*, while a set of integers can be described by the λ-abstraction of type *Int* $\rightarrow$ *Boolean* that defines the membership function of that set. In order to deal with a particular domain in HBNs, one needs to define first a specific composite type that represents the domain, and second a probability distribution on the domain, possibly based on the probability distributions of the component types. Here follows an example of how such definitions could be provided for lists and sets. The λ-abstraction definition of a set (actually, this defines a finite subset of a possibly infinite domain) is adapted from [14] and the distribution on the set type comes from [3].

Example 2. Let A be a type and $P_A(x)$ a probability distribution over its elements.

Lists The set of lists of elements of A is a type $\tau_{[A]}$ such that
1. $[] \in \tau_{[A]}$
2. $\forall m \in \mathbb{N}, m > 0$,
   $x_1, x_2, \ldots x_m \in A \rightarrow [x_1, x_2, \ldots x_m] \in \tau_{[A]}$
A probability distribution over the elements of $\tau_{[A]}$ is given by

$$P_{[A]}([x_1, x_2, \ldots, x_l]) = P_{len}(l) \times \prod_i P_A(x_i)$$

where P_{len} is a distribution over integers, that stands for the probability over the lengths of a list (for example, the geometric distribution $P_{len}(l) = p_0(1 - p_0)^l$, where p_0 determines the probability of the empty list).

Sets The set of finite sets of elements of A is a type $\tau_{\{A\}}$ such that for all $m \in \mathbb{N}$,

$$\lambda.x(if\ x \in \{x_1, x_2, \ldots x_m\}\ then\ TRUE\ else\ FALSE)$$

is a member of $\tau_{\{A\}}$. A probability distribution over the elements of $\tau_{\{A\}}$ is given by

$$P_{SS}(S) = \sum_{S' \subseteq S} (-P_{A'}(S'))^{l - l'} \varepsilon \frac{P_{A'}(S')^l}{1 - P_{A'}(S')}$$

where l is the cardinality of S, l' is the cardinality of S', $P_{A'}(S) = \sum_{x \in S} P_A(x)$, and ε is a parameter determining the probability of the empty set.

The definition of such probability distributions for composite domains shows also how, under certain additional independence assumptions, conditional probabilities can be computed. Different cases of conditional probabilities may occur in an HBN, with a composite structure conditioned upon another variable, or being on the conditional part itself.

Example 3. Consider a domain of lists labeled according to a class, where the distribution on lists is defined as above and $P_C(c)$ is the distribution on the class attribute, and an HBN modelling that domain with two nodes *List* and *Class*. In case of the p-link *Class→List*, we have (assuming independence for the different elements given c):

$$P_{[A]}([x_1, x_2, \ldots, x_l] | c) = P_{len}(l | c) \times \prod_i P_A(x_i | c)$$

For the conditional probability that corresponds to the link *List→Class*, we use Bayes theorem to obtain:

$$P_C(c | [x_1, x_2, \ldots, x_l]) = \frac{P_{[A]}([x_1, x_2, \ldots, x_l] | c) \times P_C(c)}{P_{[A]}([x_1, x_2, \ldots, x_l])}$$

$$= \frac{P_{len}(l | c) \times \prod_i P_A(x_i | c) \times P_C(c)}{P_{len}(l) \times \prod_i P_A(x_i)}$$

4   Learning HBNs

One important area of concern is the problem of learning HBNs, i.e., given a database of observations, to construct an HBN that fits the data in a satisfactory way. In our analysis, we assume that there are no missing values in the database, and that different observations in the database occur independently. Learning the probabilistic part can be achieved in a straightforward manner, using the relative frequencies of events in the database in order to estimate the values of the respective conditional probabilities. Given the independence of different instances, the relative frequencies will converge to the actual probability values when the database is sufficiently large. We use Laplace estimate to ensure that even unobserved events will be assigned a non-zero probability. Deriving the HBN structure from the database is a more complex task. Knowledge of the type structure is exploited in HBNs as a declarative bias, as it significantly reduces the number of possible network structures. We will discuss two different approaches to the learning problem: a Bayesian scoring criterion, and a minimal description length method.

The first approach to learning the HBN structure is an adaptation of the method described in [1]. We use a Bayesian method to compute the likelihood of a structure given the data, and search for the structure that maximises that likelihood. A restriction of this method is that it requires a set of training data in propositional form, i.e. a single-table database. In [1] a formula is derived to compute $P(B_S, D)$ for a Bayesian Network structure B_S and a database D, depending on the prior $P(B_S)$. That result is based on the assumptions that (a) the variables in the database are discrete, (b) different instances occur independently given the structure, (c) there are no missing values, and (d) that before seeing the database, we consider all the possible conditional probability values setups for a given structure equally likely.

Theorem 1 (Cooper and Herskovits). *Let B_S be a Bayesian Network structure containing n discrete variables x_i, each associated to a domain $(v_{i1}, \ldots, v_{ir_i})$, and π_i be the set of parents of x_i in B_S. Suppose D is a database of m instantiations of the variables*

x_i, and let $(w_{i1}, \ldots w_{iq_i})$ be all the unique instantiations of π_i in D. Let N_{ijk} be the number of cases where $x_i = v_{ik}$ and π_i is instantiated to w_{ij}, and let $N_{ij} = \sum_{k=1}^{r_i} N_{ijk}$. The joint probability of having the structure B_S and the database D is given by:

$$P(B_S, D) = P(B_S) \prod_{i=1}^{n} \prod_{j=1}^{q_i} \frac{(r_i - 1)!}{(N_{ij} + r_i - 1)!} \prod_{k=1}^{r_i} N_{ijk}!$$

Definition 8. Let B_{HS} be an HBN structure, and B_S the corresponding Bayesian Network structure of B_{HS}. We define the joint probability of the structure B_{HS} and the database D as $P(B_{HS}, D) = \alpha P(B_S, D)$, where α is a normalising constant such that $\sum_{HS} P(B_{HS}, D) = 1$.

As mentioned above, the application of the Bayesian scoring function requires the data to be in a single-table propositional form. The introduction of first-order and higher-order aggregation operators, which is a natural extension of HBNs as discussed in Section 3, would introduce a problem since these constructs do not have fixed size and therefore are not representable in a propositional way. For this reason, we discuss another scoring function, based on the minimal description length principle, that deals with data instances regardless from the form of representation. The minimal description length principle (MDL) [17] is based on finding the model that provides the shortest description of the data. The aim is (a) to minimise the size of the model, i.e. the number of parameters needed by the HBN, and (b) find the parameter values that achieve the shortest description of the original data. Here we provide an MDL likelihood function for HBNs, based on a measure used for standard Bayesian Networks [13].

Definition 9. Let B be a Hierarchical Bayesian Network, formed by the HBN structure B_{HS} and probabilistic part $\mathcal{P}$. Suppose $D = u_1, u_2, \ldots, u_n$ is a set of training data instances, and that the conditional probabilities in $\mathcal{P}$ are estimated by the frequencies of events in D. The MDL scoring of the structure B_{HS} and the database is

$$M(B_{HS}, D) = \frac{\log n}{2} |B| - \sum_{i=1}^{n} \log(P_B(u_i))$$

where $|B|$ is the number of parameters in the network and P_B is the distribution over instances that is defined by B.

The first term in the above formula penalises structures with more p-links, while the second is the (negated) log-likelihood measure of the probabilistic part given the data.

5   Classification with HBNs

Bayesian classifiers [7] compute the most likely class of an instance that is described by a vector of attributes $(X_1, X_2, \ldots, X_n)$, i.e. derive the class value that maximises $P(Class|X_1, X_2, \ldots, X_n)$, using Bayes theorem to invert the conditional probability and then applying a series of independence assumptions to decompose the joint probability to a product of simpler probabilities. The most widely known member of this family is the *Naive Bayes* classifier, that assumes that all attributes are independent of each other given the class, and therefore $P(Class|X_1,X_2,\ldots,X_n) = \alpha\prod_i P(X_i|Class)$ (where α is a normalising constant).

Extensions of the Naive Bayes classifier have been proposed in two orthogonal directions: on the one hand, lifting the "naive" independence assumption and using Bayesian Networks in order to model more complex conditional independences (e.g. *tree-augmented naive Bayesian classifiers* [6]), and on the other hand, using first-order and higher-order representations for classification of structured data (e.g. the *first-order naive Bayesian* classifiers 1BC and 1BC2 [5, 12]). Preliminary experiments show that HBNs can successfully combine both these two directions, using similar probability distributions on structured domains as 1BC2, but with independence assumptions that are based on Bayesian Network-like directed acyclic graphs. An HBN based classifier uses the decomposition of the posterior probability $P(X_1,X_2,\ldots,X_n|Class)$ to a product of simpler probabilities according the independences derived from the HBN structure. In the case of composite nodes, the distribution over the composite type needs to be used as well (e.g. as described in Definition 7 and Example 2).

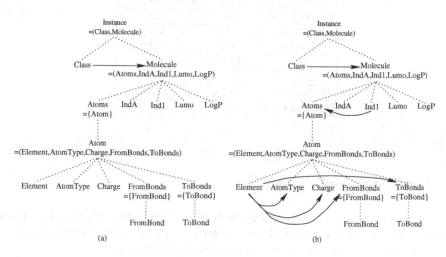

Fig. 2. HBN structures for the mutagenesis domain. (a) Under the naive Bayes assumption. (b) Extended structure.

We have tested our approach on the Mutagenesis dataset [18]. Instances in this domain are molecular structures, and each one is described by four propositional attributes and a set of atoms. The atoms themselves are characterised by three propositional attributes and two sets of "incoming" and "outgoing" chemical bonds. The task is to predict whether particular molecules are mutagenic or not. The data are split in two sets, called "regression friendly" and "regression unfriendly". For our experiments, we have constructed several HBNs based on the same type structure for instances, and tested different sets of p-links between the nodes. We have employed lists as aggregation operators for atoms and bonds, and used the distribution defined in section 3 to compute the respective conditional probabilities. We present here the results for two such structures, one corresponding to the "naive" assumption of attribute independence given the class, and the other containing a set of p-links that achieved a relatively high accuracy (Figure 2). Reported results correspond to accuracy over 10-fold cross validation for the regression friendly data and leave-one-out cross validation for the regression unfriendly data. Table 1 summarises the results achieved by HBNs and some other approaches. Results for regression, Progol, 1BC and 1BC2 are quoted from [4]. At this stage no learning was performed for deriving the HBN structure, so further experiments in this domain will involve the application of the techniques discussed in section 4 in order to determine the optimal structure given the particular datasets. In conclusion, our method gives results comparable to the state of the art algorithms on the domain, combined with the increased expressiveness and interpretability of a probabilistic model.

Table 1. Accuracy on the Mutagenesis regression friendly (r.f.) and unfriendly (r.u.) datasets (regression result is based on the propositional attributes only).

Classifier	Accuracy(r.f.)	Accuracy(r.u.)
Majority class	66.5%	69%
Regression	89%	67%
Progol	88%	88.1%
1BC	87.2%	
1BC2	82.4%	
Naive HBN	77.7%	73.8%
Extended HBN	88.3%	88.1%

6   Conclusions and Further Work

In this paper we have presented Hierarchical Bayesian Networks, a framework for learning and classification for structured data. We have defined a learning method for HBNs based on the Cooper and Herskovits structure likelihood measure.

Presently, we are working towards extending HBNs by introducing more aggregation operators for types, such as lists and sets. Preliminary experiments show that using lists high accuracy can be achieved in comparison to approaches that employ the naive Bayes assumption. Further research is essential in order to create and test more generic type constructors. This will allow the application of our framework to structures of arbitrary form and length, such as web pages or DNA sequences.

Acknowledgements

Part of this work was funded by the EPSRC project *Efficient probabilistic models for inference and learning*. Thanks are due to Mark Crean for designing and implementing an XML interface for HBNs.

References

1. Gregory F. Cooper and Edward Herskovits. A bayesian method for the induction of probabilistic networks from data. *Machine Learning*, 9:309–347, 1992.
2. James Cussens. Parameter estimation in stochastic logic programs. *Machine Learning*, 44(3):245–271, 2001.
3. Peter A. Flach, Elias Gyftodimos, and Nicolas Lachiche. Probabilistic reasoning with terms. *Linkoping Electronic Articles in Computer and Information Science*, 7(011), 2002. Submitted. Available at http://www.ida.liu.se/ext/epa/cis/2002/011/tcover.html.
4. Peter A. Flach and Nicalas Lachiche. Naive bayesian classification of structured data. Submitted, 2003.
5. Peter A. Flach and Nicolas Lachiche. 1BC: a first-order Bayesian classifier. In S. Džeroski and P. Flach, editors, *Proceedings of the 9th International Conference on Inductive Logic Programming*, pages 92–103. Springer-Verlag, 1999.
6. Nir Friedman, Dan Geiger, and Moisés Goldszmidt. Bayesian network classifiers. *Machine Learning*, 29(2-3):131–163, 1997.
7. Ashutosh Garg and Dan Roth. Understanding probabilistic classifiers. In Luc De Raedt and Peter Flach, editors, *Proceedings of the 12th European Conference in Machine Learning (ECML 2001)*, pages 179–191. Springer, 2001.
8. Elias Gyftodimos and Peter A. Flach. Hierarchical bayesian networks: A probabilistic reasoning model for structured domains. In Edwin de Jong and Tim Oates, editors, *Proceedings of the ICML-2002 Workshop on Development of Representations*. University of New South Wales, 2002.
9. Kristian Kersting and Luc De Raedt. Bayesian logic programs. Technical report, Institute for Computer Science, Machine Learning Lab, University of Freiburg, Germany, 2000.
10. Daphne Koller. Probabilistic relational models. In Sašo Džeroski and Peter A. Flach, editors, *Inductive Logic Programming, 9th International Workshop (ILP-99)*. Springer Verlag, 1999.
11. Daphne Koller and Avi Pfeffer. Object-oriented bayesian networks. In *Proceedings of the Thirteenth Conference on Uncertainty in Artificial Intelligence (UAI-97)*, pages 302–313, 1997.
12. Nicolas Lachiche and Peter A. Flach. 1BC2: a true first-order Bayesian classifier. In S. Matwin and C. Sammut, editors, *Proceedings of the 12th International Conference on Inductive Logic Programming*, pages 133–148. Springer-Verlag, 2002.
13. Wai Lam and Fahiem Bacchus. Learning bayesian belief networks: An approach based on the mdl principle. *Computational Intelligence*, 10:269–294, 1994.
14. J.W. Lloyd. *Logic for Learning*. Springer, 2003.
15. Stephen Muggleton. Stochastic logic programs. In Luc de Raedt, editor, *Advances in inductive logic programming*, pages 254–264. IOS press, 1996.
16. Judea Pearl. *Probabilistic Reasoning in Intelligent Systems — Networks of Plausible inference*. Morgan Kaufmann, 1988.
17. Jorma Rissanen. Modeling by shortest data description. *Automatica*, 14:465–471, 1978.
18. A. Srinivasan, S. Muggleton, R.D. King, and M.J.E. Sternberg. Mutagenesis: ILP experiments in a non-determinate biological domain. In S. Wrobel, editor, *Proceedings of the 4th International Workshop on Inductive Logic Programming*, volume 237, pages 217–232. Gesellschaft für Mathematik und Datenverarbeitung MBH, 1994.

Fuzzy Automata for Fault Diagnosis: A Syntactic Analysis Approach

Gerasimos G. Rigatos[1] and Spyros G. Tzafestas[2]

[1] Industrial Systems Institute, University Campus of Patras, Building A',
26500 Rion Patras, Greece
grigat@isi.gr
http://www.isi.gr
[2] National Technical University of Athens,
Dept. of Electrical and Computer Engineering,
Intelligent Robotics and Automation Lab.
Zografou Campus, 15773 Athens, Greece
tzafesta@softlab.ece.ntua.gr
http://www.robotics.ntua.gr

Abstract. Fuzzy automata are proposed for fault diagnosis. The output of the monitored system is partitioned into linear segments which are assigned to pattern classes (templates) with the use of fuzzy membership functions. A sequence of templates is generated and becomes input to fuzzy automata which have transitions that correspond to the templates of the properly functioning system. If the automata reach their final states, i.e. the input sequence is accepted by the automata with a membership degree that exceeds a certain threshold, then normal operation is deduced, otherwise, a failure is diagnosed. Fault diagnosis of a DC motor and detection of abnormalities in the ECG signal are used as case studies.

1 Introduction

Fault diagnosis based on syntactic analysis considers that the output of a dynamic system is a sequence of linear segments of variable length and slope which leads from an initial state to a final one. This sequence of segments is a regular expression and according to Kleene's theorem is equivalent to a finite automaton M [1]-[2]. Thus the output of the system can be described by the five-tuple $M = \{\Phi, B, \delta, s, F\}$ where: i) Φ is the set of states, ii) B is the set of *input* strings b, iii) $\delta : \Phi \times B \to \Phi$ is the transition function, iv) $s \in \Phi$ is the start state, and v) $F \subseteq \Phi$ is the set of final states. The automaton is said to accept the input string b if starting from s and following the permitted transitions a final state is reached. A string of segments leading to a final state of M is a regular expression and is called *pattern*. The language of M is denoted by $L(M)$ and consists of all regular expressions.

To detect system failures the following two strings are compared: i) pattern a which is the segmented output of the properly functioning system, ii) string b which is the segmented output of the monitored system. If b matches a, i.e. b

G.A. Vouros and T. Panayiotopoulos (Eds.): SETN 2004, LNAI 3025, pp. 301–310, 2004.

is accepted by M, then the monitored system operates properly and no fault is detected. If b does not match a, i.e. b is rejected by M, then a fault is deduced. To isolate that fault, pattern matching between b and a set of fault patterns A_f can be attempted. Each fault pattern A_{f_i} is in turn equivalent to an automaton M_{f_i}.

The detection of a fault is based on distance or similarity measures [3]. If the distance between the input string b and pattern a exceeds a certain threshold then a fault is reported, otherwise the system is assumed to work properly. The distance between two strings is related to the sequence of edit operations (substitution, insertion and deletion) required to transform one string into another.

In this paper, to compare a and b, similarity measures are used and the concept of fuzzy automata is employed. Update of the membership value of the state ϕ_j of M, which is connected to state ϕ_i via the transition a_i takes place using the fuzzy inference rule [4]-[5]. After having applied input b, the fuzzy membership of the final state of a provides a measure of the matching between strings b and a. If this measure goes below a certain threshold then fault is deduced.

The structure of the paper is as follows: In Section 2 fuzzy automata are proposed to model uncertainty in discrete state models. In Section 3 the generation of a string of templates from the segmentation of the output signal is explained. In Section 4 the syntactic analysis of the templates string with the use of fuzzy automata is presented. In Section 5 two application examples are given: i) fault diagnosis in the case of a DC-motor. ii) ECG analysis for automated clinical monitoring. Finally, in Section 6 concluding remarks are stated.

2   Modelling of Uncertainty with the Use of Fuzzy Automata

If each linear segment of the output is considered as a state, then the monitored system can be viewed as a discrete- state system. The knowledge of the system states and of the transitions between different states is subject to uncertainty. This uncertainty can be described by a possibilistic model such as a fuzzy automaton. In this case fuzzy states and fuzzy transitions are assumed for the description of the system's condition.

A typical definition of a fuzzy automaton is the five-tuple $\tilde{M} = (\tilde{\Phi}, \tilde{B}, \tilde{\delta}, \tilde{s}, \tilde{F})$, where

- $\tilde{\Phi}$ is the finite set of fuzzy states. A membership value $\mu(\phi_i) \in [0,1]$ is assigned to each state.
- $\tilde{B}$ is the set of inputs where each input has a membership function $\mu(b_i) \in [0,1]$, provided by the classification procedure.
- $\tilde{\delta} : \Phi \times B \to \Phi$ is the set of fuzzy transitions, where a membership function $\mu(\tilde{\delta}) \in [0,1]$ is associated with each transition from state ϕ_i to state ϕ_j.
- $\tilde{s}$ is the fuzzy start state.
- $\tilde{F} \subset \tilde{\Phi}$ is the set of fuzzy final states.

The advantages of fuzzy automata are summarized as follows:

- Fuzzy automata give a measure of similarity between patterns that is tolerant to measurement noise. Fuzzy automata can be used instead of Markov
  models to represent discrete-state systems subject to uncertainty. Unlike
  Markov models where transition probabilities have to be approximated, fuzzy
  automata have transition membership functions which can be provided by
  experts.
- Unlike correlation, syntactic analysis based on fuzzy automata permits to associate changes of certain parts of the output signal with parametric changes
  of the monitored system. Correlation provides a similarity measure between
  signals but does not identify the uneven segments in case of mismatch.
- In fuzzy automata, fault thresholds are defined by experts, thus human
  knowledge about the monitored system can be exploited.

3   Generation of the Templates String

The main concept is to divide the output signal into consecutive linear segments
and to classify each one of them in pattern classes according to a fuzzy membership function. A candidate segment of n points is selected and the line that
connects the first to the last point is calculated. If the distances of all points from
this line are below a certain threshold ϵ then it is considered that all n points belong to the same segment. Otherwise, the first point (x_j, y_j), $j \in \{1, 2, \cdots, n\}$
which exceeds ϵ is found, the candidate segment $(x_1, y_1), \cdots, (x_j, y_j)$ is defined
and a new check is performed to see if points 1 to j can be assigned to the same
segment.

To decompose the output signal into segments, a sliding window is used. The
size of the sliding window determines the number of segments. A classification
algorithm, assigns each segment to a template (pattern class) and provides also
the corresponding fuzzy membership function. The steps of the segmentation
procedure are [6]:

Step 1: Preprocessing of the output signal. First the output signal is filtered
with a low pass filter to remove high frequency noise. The preprocessed signal is
a set of points $\{(x_1, y_1), \cdots, (x_N, y_N)\}$ where x_i is measured in time units and
$y_i (1 \leq i \leq N)$ is the associated output sample.

Step 2: Segmentation of the output signal. A subset of points $X_i^{(0)}$:, (x_1, y_1)
$\cdots (x_n, y_n)$ is collected, and the equation of the line that connects the first to
the last element of $X_i^{(0)}$ is calculated, $L_i : Ax + By + C = 0$. The segment's
end is the last point in $X_i^{(0)}$ which has a distance from L less than ϵ. Thus,
if $\exists (x_j, y_j), j = 1, \cdots, n$ such that the distance D of (x_j, y_j) from L exceeds a
threshold ϵ, i.e.

$$D\{(x_j, y_j), Ax + By + C\} > \epsilon \tag{1}$$

then n is set to $n = min\{j\}$ satisfying Eq. (1) and the calculation of L is
repeated for the subset of data $C_i^{(1)} = \{(x_1, y_1), \cdots, (x_j, y_j)\}$. The segmentation
algorithm can be summarized as follows:

- Inputs: threshold ϵ, $X_i^{(0)} = \{(x_1, y_1), \cdots, (x_n, y_n)\}$
- Output: segments x_h, $h = 1, 2, \cdots$.

1. Set $j = n$, $h = 1$.
2. Examine the last point (x_j, y_j) and calculate $A_h = (y_j - y_1)$, $B_h = (x_j - x_1)$ and $C_h = x_1 y_j - x_j y_1$.
3. For $i = 1, 2, \cdots, j$ calculate the distance of (x_i, y_i) from $L : A_h x + B_h y + C_h$
4. If Eq. (1) is true then set $j = j - 1$ and go to 2.
5. If Eq. (1) is false $\forall i = 1, \cdots, j$ then $X_i^{(1)} = \{(x_1, y_1), \cdots, (x_j, y_j)\}$
6. Set $h = h + 1$, $j = n$, go to 2 and repeat for another candidate segment.

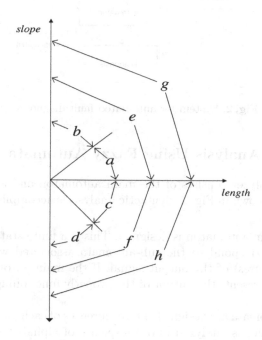

Fig. 1. Class labels for segments of variable slope and length

Step 3: To organise segments in pattern classes (templates), each segment x_i is taken to be a line described by an equation $A_i X + B_i Y + C_i = 0$, $i = 1, \cdots, M$ where M is the number of templates in which the output is segmented. The slope $\frac{-A_i}{B_i}$ of each segment is calculated. The segments are organised in classes according to their slope and length, using algorithms of statistical pattern recognition (e.g. C-Means). An example of class labels is given in Fig. 1.

Once the pattern classes have been found a neural network (e.g. RBF) can be used to memorize the mapping of input segments to classes. By considering membership in multiple pattern classes, more information is provided to the syntactic analyzer. In that case there will be multiple paths that connect the start to the end state of the automaton.

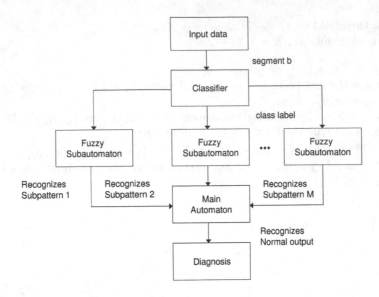

Fig. 2. System for automated fault diagnosis

4 Syntactic Analysis Using Fuzzy Automata

The syntactic analyzer consists of the main automaton and a number of sub-automata and is shown in Fig. 2. Syntactic analysis is accomplished through the following steps:

• *Step 1:* The main automaton is designed. This is a finite state machine where the transitions correspond to the sub-automata associated with the patterns (significant structures) of the output signal. If the main automaton recognizes the string that represents the output of the properly functioning system then no fault exists.

• *Step 2:* Sub-automata are designed. The occurences of each pattern are recorded and every occurence is analyzed into a sequence of alphabet symbols. Next, a path of states is inserted to the sub-automaton and is used to recognize this sequence of symbols. Human experts provide the transition possibilities (transition thresholds). Transition memberships $\mu(\delta_{ij})$ are used as thresholds that enable (prevent) the change of a state in the sub-automaton. If $\mu(b_i) > \mu(\delta_{ij})$ then transition from state ϕ_i to state ϕ_j is permitted.

• *Step 3:* The sequence of templates becomes input to each sub-automaton and if a final state is reached with a membership degree above a certain threshold then a specific pattern is recognized. Update of the states membership takes place using Eq. (2) which denotes that the most possible path between the start and the end state is selected. When a sub-automaton terminates, then transition to another state of the main automaton takes place.

Update of the membership value of the state ϕ_j of M, which is connected to state ϕ_i via the transition a_i takes place using the fuzzy inference rule [4]-[5]:

$$\mu(\phi_j^{k+1}) = \begin{matrix} max_{I_j^k} \; \{\mu(\phi_j^k), min(\mu(\phi_i^k), \mu(b_i^k))\} \;\; if \;\; \mu(\delta_{ij}^k) \le \mu(b_i^k) \\ \mu(\phi_j^k) \;\; otherwise \end{matrix} \qquad (2)$$

where $\mu(\delta_{ij}^k)$ is a fuzzy membership function that shows the possibility of transition between ϕ_i and ϕ_j, and I_j^k is the set of all transitions ending at ϕ_j. This transition is activated if the membership of the input symbol b_i to the fuzzy set associated with symbol a_i exceeds $\mu(\delta_{ij}^k)$.

5   Simulation Examples

5.1   Fault Diagnosis of a DC-Motor

The performance of fuzzy automata for fault diagnosis is first tested in the case of a DC-motor. The transfer function of the DC motor is given by:

$$\frac{\theta_m(s)}{v_f(s)} = \frac{K}{s(1 + s \cdot \tau_f)(1 + s \cdot \tau_m)} \qquad (3)$$

where, $K = \frac{K_f}{\beta R_f}$, $\tau_f = \frac{L_f}{R_f}$ and $\tau_m = \frac{J}{\beta}$ are time constants and θ_m is the motor's output (see Fig. 3). The input v_f is sinusoidal and results into a sinusoidal output. Faults cause a change to the output's amplitude or frequency. Syntactic analysis can identify a change of the output pattern [7].

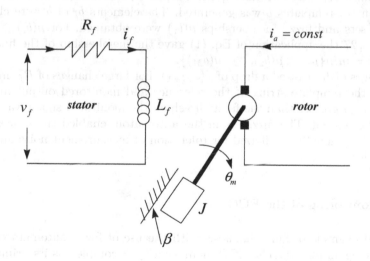

Fig. 3. Model of a DC-motor

The templates string that corresponds to the normal output ($R_f = 100$) is a simple chain $a_1 a_2 \cdots a_n$ (the start to the end point of the automaton are connected through one single path). This is shown in Fig. 4.

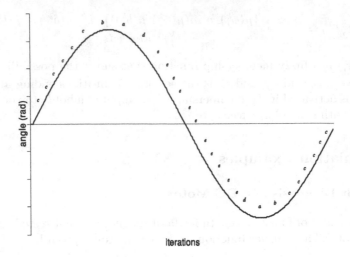

Fig. 4. Language of the normally functioning motor

The segmentation procedure of the reference output resulted into a symmetric chain a of $M = 27$ templates, namely $c^6 bade^{11} dabc^6$. The threshold for each transition was taken to be $\mu(\delta_{ij}) = 0.5$. The initial state memberships were set to $\mu(\phi_1^0) = 1$ and $\mu(\phi_i^0) = 0$, $i = 2, \cdots, M + 1$. Then, a change in resistance R_f was introduced, the output was monitored and the associated string of templates b was generated. The elements b_i of b were classified to fuzzy sets and fuzzy memberships $\mu(b_i)$ were obtained. For $\mu(b_i) \geq \mu(\delta_{ij})$, $i = 1, \cdots, 27$ the application of Eq. (1) gave the membership of the final state $\mu(\phi_{M+1}) = min\{\mu(b_1), \mu(b_2), \cdots, \mu(b_M)\}$.

Changes of R_f caused a drop of $\mu(\phi_{M+1})$. For large changes of R_f mismatch between the template string of the reference and monitored output appeared For $\mu(\phi_{M+1})$ greater than the fault threshold the monitored signal was considered to be normal. The fuzziness in the automaton, enabled the processing of an imperfect signal and allowed for toleration of measurement noise and other ambiguities.

5.2   Monitoring of the ECG

A second example of fault diagnosis with the use of fuzzy automata concerns the ECG signal [8]-[10]. The ECG includes a QRS complex as its primary and most dominant pattern (Fig. 5). Before QRS there is a P wave. After QRS a T wave follows, which is larger than the P wave. The P pattern corresponds to the depolarization of the atria, the QRS complex to the depolarization of the ventricles and the T wave to the repolarization of the ventricles.

To derive a diagnosis, cardiologists study the length and the slope of the segments that constitute the aforementioned patterns. Absence of the P wave

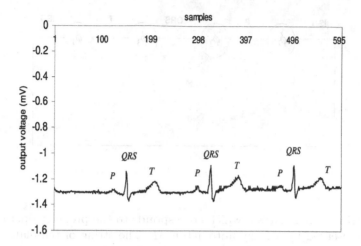

Fig. 5. Stages of a normal ECG

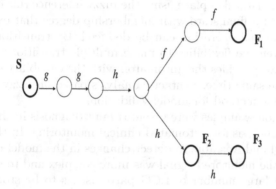

Fig. 6. Sub-automaton that recognizes the P pattern

is an indication of atrial fibrillation. The ECG diagnosis system consists of the main automaton, with transitions which can be analyzed in fuzzy sub-automata.

Using the signal depicted in 5 an automaton that recognizes the P sub-pattern of the normal ECG was derived (Fig. 6). Deformation of the P pattern results in reduced membership values of the final states. Automata for the recognition of the QRS and T pattern can be found in [10].

6 Conclusions

In this paper fuzzy automata and the syntactic analysis approach have been used for fault diagnosis. The main concept is to segment the output of the monitored system and to classify each one of its segments into pattern classes according to a fuzzy membership value.

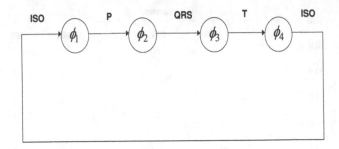

Fig. 7. Main automaton for ECG syntactic analysis

The string of templates a which corresponds to the properly operating system is represented by a fuzzy automaton M. The string of templates b which corresponds to the monitored output, becomes input to the fuzzy automaton M. Update of the membership value of the state ϕ_j of a, which is connected to state ϕ_i via the transition a_i takes place using the fuzzy inference rule of Eq. (2). If the automaton ends at a final state with membership degree that exceeds a certain threshold then normal operation can be deduced. By transition fuzziness, the automaton is given the flexibility to make multiple transitions simultaneously. The state fuzziness provides the automaton with the capability of being at multiple states at the same time. Syntactic analysis based on fuzzy automata is an easily interpretable method for model validation.

Two application examples were given: i) fault diagnosis in the case of a DC-motor, ii) ECG analysis for automated clinical monitoring. In the first case the proposed method and was able to detect changes in the model of the motor. In the second case the monitored signal was more complex and to succeed credible fault diagnosis a large number of ECG patterns has to be stored. The resulting fuzzy automaton has multiple paths connecting the start to the end state. Detection of the deformation of the P pattern was satisfactory.

References

1. Kozen, D.C.: Automata and Computability. (1997) *Springer*
2. Fuzzy Automata and Languages. (2002) *Chapman & Hall*
3. Tzafestas, S.G., Singh, M.G., and G. Schmidt, G.: System fault diagnosis, reliabilty and related Knowledge-based Approaches. vol.1 Fault Diagnostics and Reliability. Knowledge-based and Fault Tolerant techniques, **2** Reidel Dordrecht Holland (1989)
4. Tümer, M., Belfore, L., and Ropella, K.: A Syntactic Methodology for Automatic Diagnosis by Analysis of Continuous Time Measurements Using Hierarchical Signal Representations. IEEE Trans. on Systems, Man and Cybernetics - Part B: Cybernetics (2003)
5. Steimann F. and Adlassnig K.P., Clinical monitoring with fuzzy automata. Fuzzy Sets and Systems. Elsevier. **61**, (1994), pp. 37-42

6. Koski, A., Juhola, M., and Meriste, M.: Syntactic Recognition of ECG signals by attributed finite automata. Pattern Recognition. Elsevier. **28**, (1995), 1927-1940
7. Martins J.F., Pires A.J., Vilela Mendes R. and Dente J.A.: Modelling Electromechanical Drive Systems: A Formal Language Approach. Proc. of 35th IEEE Industry Applications Society Annual Meeting. (Oct. 2000) *(IAS2000)*, Rome, Italy
8. Trahanias, P., Skordalakis, E. and Papakonstantinou G.: A syntactic method for the classification of the QRS patterns. Pattern Recognition Letters. Elsevier. **9** (1989) 13-18
9. Trahanias, P., and Skordalakis, E.: Syntactic Pattern Recognition of the ECG. IEEE Transactions on Pattern Analysis and Machine Intelligence **12** (1990) 648-657
10. Tümer M.B., Belfore L.A., and Ropella K.M.: Applying hierarchical fuzzy automata to automatic diagnosis. *Proc. Mtg. North America Fuzzy Information Process. Syst.*, (1998) Pensacola, FL

A Discussion of Some Intuitions of Defeasible Reasoning

Grigoris Antoniou[1,2]

[1] Institute of Computer Science, FORTH, Greece
antoniou@ics.forth.gr
[2] Department of Computer Science, University of Crete, Greece

Abstract. In this paper we discuss some issues related to the intuitions of defeasible reasoning. Defeasible logic serves as the formal basis for our analysis. We also make some comments on the comparison between defeasible logics and the well-founded semantics of extended logic programs with priorities.

1 Introduction

Nonmonotonic reasoning is concerned with reasoning about incomplete and inconsistent information. Defeasible reasoning is a family of nonmonotonic reasoning approaches which are based on the idea of defeat among rules or arguments. Within defeasible reasoning we distinguish between two kinds of approaches:

First, those which are based on the idea of an extension build full reasoning chains (or arguments) and evaluate their status at a later stage. For example, an argument may be built but may turn out later to be defeated by other arguments. Or a sceptical conclusion may only be drawn if it is included in all extensions of a given theory (knowledge base). Approaches in this category are, among others, default logic [26], stable and answer set semantics [10, 11], Dung semantics [8] and related systems of argumentation [4].

An alternative approach is to evaluate the status of arguments or conclusions during the deductive process, that is, to interleave argument building and argument evaluation. As Horty puts in [15], "arguments are constructed step-by-step and are evaluated in each step of the construction: those that are indefensible . . . are discarded at once, and cannot influence the status of others". Such approaches include [14] and defeasible logics [24, 2]. Often these approaches are called "directly sceptical", or "deeply sceptical".

Usually approaches in the latter category tend to have lower complexity that those in the first category. For example, defeasible logic has, in its simple form, linear complexity [19]. However for a long time it has been commonly accepted that these approaches suffer from certain representational problems, among others regarding floating conclusions and zombie paths [21]. Perhaps many have seen these defeasible reasoning approaches as "quick and dirty".

In two recent articles [15, 16] Horty reinvigoured the discussion about the intuitions and nature of defeasible reasoning by questioning commonly accepted views about certain nonmonotonic reasoning patterns. In particular, he argued that argument reinstatement and floating conclusions may not be reasonable patterns in all instances. We can conclude, that the directly sceptical approaches are not just quick solutions, but have also adequate abstract properties. This argument is certainly encouraging since in the

G.A. Vouros and T. Panayiotopoulos (Eds.): SETN 2004, LNAI 3025, pp. 311–320, 2004.

recent years these approaches have been applied in various application fields, including the modelling of regulations and business rules [22, 13, 1], modelling of contracts [13], and agent negotiations [7]. Of course, there exist other applications for which the traditional, extension-based systems are more suitable (e.g. cognitive robotics, combinatorial problems etc).

Horty's arguments are still subject of a discussion; for example, Prakken responded to his points in [25]. This paper is a contribution towards this discussion. We will reexamine the critical issues of the debate and make some comments.

We will also discuss defeasible reasoning in comparison to the well-founded semantics (WFS) of extended logic programs. In a recent paper [6], Brewka argued that WFS, under a straightforward translation of defeasible theories into extended logic programs, delivers better results than defeasible logic. Here we will investigate and counter his arguments.

2 Basics of Defeasible Logics

2.1 Outline of Defeasible Logics

A *defeasible theory* D is a couple $(R, >)$ where R a finite set of rules, and $>$ a superiority relation on R. In expressing the proof theory we consider only propositional rules. Rules containing free variables are interpreted as the set of their variable-free instances.

There are two kinds of rules (fuller versions of defeasible logics include also defeaters): *Strict rules* are denoted by $A \rightarrow p$, and are interpreted in the classical sense: whenever the premises are indisputable then so is the conclusion. An example of a strict rule is "Emus are birds". Written formally: $emu(X) \rightarrow bird(X)$. Inference from strict rules only is called *definite inference*. Strict rules are intended to define relationships that are definitional in nature. Thus defeasible logics contain no mechanism for resolving inconsistencies in definite inference.

Defeasible rules are denoted by $A \Rightarrow p$, and can be defeated by contrary evidence. An example of such a rule is $bird(X) \Rightarrow flies(X)$ which reads as follows: "Birds typically fly".

A *superiority relation* on R is an acyclic relation $>$ on R (that is, the transitive closure of $>$ is irreflexive). When $r_1 > r_2$, then r_1 is called *superior* to r_2, and r_2 *inferior* to r_1. This expresses that r_1 may override r_2.

2.2 The Defeasible Logic Meta-program

In this section we introduce a meta-program $\mathcal{M}$ in a logic programming form that expresses the essence of defeasible logic. $\mathcal{M}$ consists of the following clauses. We first introduce the predicates defining classes of rules, namely

`supportive_rule`$(Name, Head, Body)$`:- strict`$(Name, Head, Body)$.

`supportive_rule`$(Name, Head, Body)$`:- defeasible`$(Name, Head, Body)$.

Now we present clauses which define provability of literals. Initially we distinguish between two levels of proof: definite provability which uses only the strict rules, and defeasible provability.

c1   definitely(X):-
    strict($R, X, [Y_1, \ldots, Y_n]$),
    definitely(Y_1),...,definitely(Y_n).

Now we turn to defeasible provability. If a literal X is definitely provable it is also defeasibly provable.

c2   defeasibly(X):- definitely(X).

Otherwise the negation of X must not be strictly provable, and we need a rule R with head X which fires (that is, its antecedents are defeasibly provable) and is not overruled.

c3   defeasibly(X):-
    not definitely($\sim X$),
    supportive_rule($R, X, [Y_1, \ldots, Y_n]$),
    defeasibly(Y_1),...,defeasibly(Y_n),
    not overruled(R, X).

A rule R with head X is overruled if there is a rule S with head $\sim X$ which fires and is not defeated.

c4   overruled(R, X):-
    supportive_rule($S, \sim X, [U_1, \ldots, U_n]$),
    defeasibly(U_1),...,defeasibly(U_n),
    not defeated($S, \sim X$).

And a rule S with head $\sim X$ is defeated if there is a rule T with head X which fires and is superior to S.

c5   defeated($S, \sim X$):-
    sup(T, S),
    supportive_rule($T, X, [V_1, \ldots, V_n]$),
    defeasibly(V_1),...,defeasibly(V_n).

Given a defeasible theory $D = (R, >)$, the corresponding program $\mathcal{D}$ is obtained from $\mathcal{M}$ by adding facts according to the following guidelines:

1. strict($r_i, p, [q_1, \ldots, q_n]$).   for each rule $r_i : q_1, \ldots, q_n \rightarrow p \in R$
2. defeasible($r_i, p, [q_1, \ldots, q_n]$). for each rule $r_i : q_1, \ldots, q_n \Rightarrow p \in R$
3. sup(r_i, r_j).   for each pair of rules such that $r_i > r_j$

Of course we still have not laid down which logic programming semantics to use for the negation operator. In [20] it was shown that $\mathcal{D}$, under the Kunen semantics [18], is equivalent to the defeasible logic of [2].

2.3 Support

Support for a literal p consists of a chain of reasoning that would lead us to conclude p in the absence of conflicts. In addition, in situations where two conflicting rules can be applied and one rule is inferior to another, the inferior rule should not be counted as supporting its conclusion. These ideas are encoded in the following clauses:

c6   supported(X):- definitely(X).

c7   supported(X):-
        supportive_rule($R, X, [Y_1, \ldots, Y_n]$),
        supported(Y_1),...,supported(Y_n),
        not beaten(R, X).

c8   beaten(R, X):-
        supportive_rule($S, \sim X, [W_1, \ldots, W_n]$),
        defeasibly(W_1),...,defeasibly(W_n),
        sup(S, R).

2.4 Ambiguity Propagation

A literal is *ambiguous* if there is a chain of reasoning that supports a conclusion that p is true, another that supports that $\neg p$ is true, and the superiority relation does not resolve this conflict.

A preference for ambiguity blocking or ambiguity propagating behaviour is one of the properties of non-monotonic inheritance nets over which intuitions can clash [28]. Stein [27] argues that ambiguity blocking results in an unnatural pattern of conclusions. Ambiguity propagation results in fewer conclusions being drawn, which might make it preferable when the cost of an incorrect conclusion is high. For these reasons an ambiguity propagating variant of DL is of interest.

Defeasible logic, as introduced above, is ambiguity blocking. We can achieve ambiguity propagation behaviour by making a minor change to clause *c4* so that it now considers support to be sufficient to allow a superior rule to overrule an inferior rule.

c9   overruled(R, X):-
        supportive_rule($S, \sim X, [U_1, \ldots, U_n]$),
        supported(U_1),...,supported(U_n),
        not defeated($S, \sim X$).

2.5 Well-Founded Defeasible Logics

Example 2.1
Consider $\{p \Rightarrow p, \Rightarrow \neg p\}$. Here the logic program $\mathcal{D}$ with Kunen semantics fails to derive $defeasibly(\neg p)$. The reason is that it does not detect that the first rule can never be applied.

However a different logic programming semantics can be used in conjunction with $\mathcal{D}$. For example, [20] proposes to use well-founded semantics [9], the semantics also used in Courteous Logic Programs [12, 13]. Now if WFS is used, then indeed we can derive $defeasibly(\neg p)$ in the above example, as desired.

2.6 Conflicting Literals

So far only conflicts among rules with complementary heads were detected and used. We considered all rules with head L as *supportive* of L, and all rules with head $\sim L$

as *conflicting*. However, in applications often literals are considered to be conflicting, and at most one of a certain set should be derived. For example, the risk an investor is willing to accept may be classified in one of the categories low, medium, and high. The way to solve this problem is to use constraint rules of the form

$low, medium \rightarrow \perp$
$low, high \rightarrow \perp$
$medium, high \rightarrow \perp$

Now if we try to derive the conclusion *high*, the conflicting rules are not just those with head $\neg high$, but also those with head *low* and *medium*. Similarly, if we are trying to prove $\neg high$, the supportive rules include those with head *low* or *medium*.

In general, given a rule $L, M \rightarrow \perp$, we augment $\mathcal{D}$ by:

1. $strict(r_i, \sim L, [q_1, \ldots, q_n])$.   for all rules $r_i : q_1, \ldots, q_n \rightarrow M \in R$
2. $strict(r_i, \sim M, [q_1, \ldots, q_n])$.   for all rules $r_i : q_1, \ldots, q_n \rightarrow L \in R$
3. $defeasible(r_i, \sim L, [q_1, \ldots, q_n])$.   for all rules $r_i : q_1, \ldots, q_n \Rightarrow M \in R$
4. $defeasible(r_i, \sim M, [q_1, \ldots, q_n])$.   for all rules $r_i : q_1, \ldots, q_n \Rightarrow L \in R$
5. $competing\_rule(r_i, L, [q_1, \ldots, q_n])$.
         for all rules $r_i \in R[\sim L] \cup R[M]$ where $A(r_i) = \{q_1, \ldots, q_n\}$
6. $competing\_rule(r_i, M, [q_1, \ldots, q_n])$.
         for all rules $r_i \in R[\sim M] \cup R[L]$ where $A(r_i) = \{q_1, \ldots, q_n\}$

Now the modification of $\mathcal{M}$ is straightforward. For example, clause $c4$ is modified as follows:

```
c10   overruled(R, X):-
          competing_rule(S, X, [U_1, ..., U_n]),
          defeasibly(U_1),...,defeasibly(U_n),
          not defeated(S, ~ X).
```

3 Floating Conclusions

Example 3.1

$r_1 : bornInHolland(X) \Rightarrow dutch(X)$
$r_2 : norwegianName(X) \Rightarrow norwegian(X)$
$r_3 : dutch(X) \Rightarrow likesIceSkating(X)$
$r_4 : norwegian(X) \Rightarrow likesIceskating(X)$
$dutch(X), norwegian(X) \rightarrow \perp$

Here there is an obvious conflct between rules r_1 and r_2 for every person a with a Norwegian name born in Holland. However, regardless of how this conflict is resolved, it is reasonable to conclude $likesIceSkating(a)$. Such conclusions are called *floating*, since they rely on other facts which are themselves not conclusions.

     Examples like the above led to widely accepted view that floating conclusions are always a desired behaviour of defeasible reasoning systems. In his paper [16], Horty shuttered this view. Let us consider an example out of his work. A person (call him

Bob) must quickly decide about a certain investment, and both his parents are terminally ill. Both his parents are rich, but Bob is unsure whether he will inherit a large amount of money. His sister tells him that she has spoken with their parents; his father will not let him inherit anything, but his mother will let him inherit enough to make his investment. But his brother tells him the opposite: his father, not his mother will let him inherit enough for his investment. Horty argues that in this case it is reasonable to withhold judgement on whether the investment is secure, because the conflicting testimonies undermine each other.

In response, Prakken [25] (1) makes the point that floating conclusions *are* often desirable, and a couple of counterexamples are not sufficient to invalidate this reasoning pattern. (2) He proceeds to present a refinement of his system which allows a default rule to directly block other defaults. Then it is possible to allow or disallow floating conclusions, as one wishes.

Regarding the first point, there is not a real disagreement with Horty. Horty simply makes the point that floating conclusions are not *always* reasonable, he does not claim them to be always wrong.

No defeasible logic from those presented in section 2 supports floating conclusions. Following Horty we can say that this behaviour is not a drawback, but rather a *feature* of defeasible logics. Of course, Prakken's alternative approach (point 2) allows one to choose whether one wants this feature or not. This advanced flexibility comes along with a meshing of "knowledge" and "control" (rules stating explicitly that they block other rules), which makes the approach less attractive for practical applications.

4   Zombie Paths

Example 4.1

$r_1 : quaker(X) \Rightarrow pacifist(X)$
$r_2 : republican(X) \Rightarrow \neg pacifist(X)$
$r_3 : pacifist(X) \Rightarrow \neg hasGun(X)$
$r_4 : livesInChicago(X) \Rightarrow hasGun(X)$
$r_3 > r_4$

Suppose a person a is Quaker and Republican and lives in Chicago. We can build the following arguments:

$A^- : quaker(a) \Rightarrow pacifist(a)$
$B : republican(a) \Rightarrow \neg pacifist(a)$
$A : quaker(a) \Rightarrow pacifist(a) \Rightarrow \neg hasGun(a)$
$C : livesInChicago(a) \Rightarrow hasGun(a)$

There seems to be a problem with argument B: on one hand it is not justified, but on the other it is still "alive" to influence the status of other arguments. In our case, it "kills" A, so C prevails and we get the conclusion $hasGun(a)$. In a sense, B is lurking in the dark; some people feel uneasy with this phenomenon. Also note that in this example, Horty's deep sceptical approach derives a conclusion that extension-based approaches would not.

We claim that indeed intuitions clash as to whether such conclusions are warranted or not. However it is easy to choose as one wishes. If we look at the family of defeasible logics in section 2, we note that: the standard defeasible logic derives that a has a gun, while the ambiguity propagating defeasible logic does not.

At this point it may be interesting to look back at the original argument of Makinson and Schlechta on zombie paths [21] in more detail. In that paper they give an interesting argument suggesting that sceptical approaches to defeasible nets cannot deal with zombie paths, even if they use a finite number of "values" which can be assigned to paths. Their argument seems to contradict our claim that ambiguity propagating defeasible logics do not suffer from this drawback, since we use three values (levels of proof): strict, defeasible and suppored.

A closer look reveals that the argument of Makinson and Schlechta does not apply to defeasible logics. On one hand, they evaluate paths, while defeasible logics evaluate single literals. And more importantly, their argument depends critically on the concept of "preclusion", which compares entire paths using implicit criteria. Let us look at a concrete example.

$$r_1 : \Rightarrow a$$
$$r_2 : a \Rightarrow b$$
$$r_3 : b \Rightarrow c$$
$$r_4 : c \Rightarrow d$$
$$r_5 : a \Rightarrow c$$
$$r_6 : b \Rightarrow \neg d$$

Now Makinson and Schlechta argue that the path $a \Rightarrow b \not\Rightarrow d$ may be weaker than $a \Rightarrow c \Rightarrow d$ and this point is indeed central to their argumentation. However defeasible logics use only *explicit comparison criteria*, and *compares only pairs of rules, not entire paths*. Of course, the possibility to compare paths adds expressive power, but it seems that the restricted possibilities are a good compromise between high computational complexity and adequacy in practical applications (in almost all practical cases, the available explicit priority information concerns rules, not reasoning chains).

Overall we hope to have demonstrated that the defeasible logics of section 2 stand up to the current discussion on the intuitions of defeasible reasoning. They follow the "deeply sceptical" ideas of Horty, but avoid zombie arguments, if one regards them as problematic. In the following section we will defend this family of logics against criticism which stems from the logic programming community.

5   Defeasible Logics and Well-Founded Semantics

In his [6] paper, Brewka compared the ambiguity propagating defeasible logic with well-founded semantics (WFS) with priorities [5] under a straightforward translation from defeasible theories to extended logic programs. He derived a soundness result of defeasible logic w.r.t. WFS, and identified some sources of incompleteness. At the end of his formal treatment he interpreted his results as a demonstration that WFS is superior to defeasible logics from the representational perspective, with the latter having the advantage of lower computational complexity. In the following we will investigate this judgement in detail by looking at the examples provided in [6].

Example 5.1 (Cyclic Theories; Brewka)

$$\Rightarrow \neg p$$
$$p \Rightarrow p$$

Indeed we agree that we should be able to derive $\neg p$, by detecting that the second rule cannot be applied. While this result is not derived by the meta- program of section 2 in conjunction with Kunen semantics, it can be derived using well-founded semantics and the meta-program. Thus the defeasible logic framework can easily deal with such situations.

Example 5.2 (The treatment of strict rules; Brewka)

$$\Rightarrow p$$
$$p \rightarrow q$$
$$\Rightarrow \neg q$$

Here q is not defeasibly provable from the defeasible theory D in any of the defeasible logics in section 2, while q is included in the well-founded model of the program $Trans(D)$ obtained from translating D: $\{p \leftarrow not \ \neg p, q \leftarrow p, \neg q \leftarrow not \ q\}$. We believe that the conclusion q is highly counterintuitive because there is no reason to prefer q over $\neg q$: both conclusions are based on the application of a defeasible rule, and there is no information about which rule to prefer. Thus the WFS of $Trans(D)$ gives the wrong answer.

If there is a question regarding this example, then only whether p should be defeasibly provable. The defeasible logic view is to derive p since there is no contrary evidence (note that the rule $\neg q \rightarrow \neg p$ is missing; see next subsection on the situation that would arise if this rule was present).

A more purist view would be to reject p because it comes together with q (strict rule $p \rightarrow q$), and there is evidence against q. This alternative approach would treat strict rules closer to other nonmonotonic reasoning systems like default logic.

However the description logic approach is at least defensible, and is additionally justified by its low computational complexity. It interprets a strict rule of the form $p \rightarrow q$ as: *If p is definitely known, then q is also definitely derived. Otherwise, if p is defeasibly known, then usually q is true.* In our example, p is not definitely known, so we do not jump automatically to the conclusion q once p is (defeasibly) proven, but must consider counterarguments in favour of $\neg q$.

Example 5.3(Conflicting literals; Brewka)

$$r_1 : \Rightarrow p$$
$$r_2 : p \rightarrow \neg q$$
$$r_3 : \Rightarrow q$$
$$r_4 : q \rightarrow \neg p$$
$$r_1 > r_3$$

Brewka is right that p is a desirable conclusion, and that defeasible logic fails to derive this result from the above representation. However we claim that the representation is wrong. What one wishes to say is that there are rules for p and q, that the reason for the former is stronger than that for the latter, *and that p and q are mutually exclusive.* Formally:

$$r_1 :\Rightarrow p$$
$$r_2 :\Rightarrow q$$
$$r_3 : p, q \rightarrow \bot$$
$$r_1 > r_2$$

We have discussed in section 2.6 how a simple extension of defeasible logic by incompatibility statements can easily solve this problem.

6 Conclusion

This paper is part of an ongoing discussion of the intuitions of defeasible reasoning. The paper (a) supports Horty's arguments in favour of a "directly sceptical" approach; (b) showed that the direct use of WFS for extended logic programs leads to counterintuitive results, at least in one (important) instance; and (c) defended the family of defeasible logics against some other criticisms.

As an outcome of our analysis, we hope to have demonstrated that defeasible logics are not just a "quick and dirty" nonmonotonic reasoning approach, but rather that it has reasonable representational properties. Therefore its use in practical areas such as electronic commerce and the semantic web should be pursued, given its combination of reasoning adequacy and low computational complexity.

References

1. G. Antoniou and M. Arief. Executable Declarative Business Rules and Their Use in Electronic Commerce. In *Proc. Symposium on Applied Computing*, ACM Press 2002, 6– 10.
2. G. Antoniou, D. Billington, G. Governatori and M.J. Maher. Representation Results for Defeasible Logic. *ACM Transactions on Computational Logic* 2,2 (2001): 255–287. American
3. D. Billington. 1993. Defeasible Logic is Stable. *Journal of Logic and Computation* 3: 370– 400.
4. A. Bondarenko, P. Dung, R. Kowalski and F. Toni. An abstract, argumentation-theoretic approach to default reasoning. *Artificial Intelligence* 93 (1997): 63–101.
5. G. Brewka. Well-Founded Semantics for Extended Logic Programs with Dynamic Priorities. *Journal of Artificial Intelligence Research* 4 (1996): 19–36.
6. G. Brewka. On the Relation Between Defeasible Logic and Well-Founded Semantics. In *Proc. LPNMR 2001*, Springer LNAI 2173, 2001.
7. M. Dumas, G. Governatori, A. ter Hofstede, and P. Oaks. A formal approach to negotiating agents development. *Electronic Commerce Research and Applications*,1,2 (2002).
8. P. Dung. On the acceptability of arguments and its fundamental role in nonmonotonic reasoning, logic programming, and n-person games. *Artificial Intelligence* 77 (1995): 321–357.

9. A. van Gelder, K. Ross and J. Schlipf. The Well-Founded Semantics for General Logic Programs. *Journal of the ACM* 38,3 (1991): 620–650

10. M. Gelfond and V. Lifschitz. The stable model semantics for logic programming. In *Proc. 5th International Conference and Symposium on Logic Programming*, MIT Press 1988, 1070–1080.

11. M. Gelfond and V. Lifschitz. Logic Programs with Classical Negation. In *Proc. 7th International Conference on Logic Programming*, MIT Press 1990, 579–597.

12. B. Grosof. Prioritized conflict handling for logic programs. In *Proc. International Logic Programming Symposium*, MIT Press 1997, 197–211.

13. B. Grosof, Y. Lambrou and H. Chan. A Declarative Approach to Business Rules in Contracts: Courteous Logic Programs in XML. In *Proc. 1st ACM Conference on Electronic Commerce*, ACM 1999.

14. J. Horty. Some direct theories of nonmonotonic inheritance. In D. Gabbay, C. Hogger and J. Robinson (Eds): *Handbook of Logic in Artificial Intelligence and Logic Programming*, Clarendon Press 1994, 111–187.

15. J. Horty. Argument construction and reinstatement in logics for defeasible reasoning. *Artificial Intelligence and Law* 9 (2001): 1 - 28.

16. J. Horty. Skepticism and floating conclusions. *Artificial Intelligence* 135 (2002): 55 - 72.

17. J.F. Horty, R.H. Thomason and D. Touretzky. A Skeptical Theory of Inheritance in Nonmonotonic Semantic Networks. In *Proc. AAAI-87*, 358–363.

18. K. Kunen. Negation in Logic Programming. *Journal of Logic Programming* 4,4 (1987): 289–308.

19. M.J. Maher. Propositional Defeasible Logic has Linear Complexity. *Theory and Practice of Logic Programming*, 1,6 (2001): 691–711.

20. M.J. Maher and G. Governatori. A Semantic Decomposition of Defeasible Logics. *Proc. American National Conference on Artificial Intelligence (AAAI-99)*, 299–306.

21. D. Makinson and K. Schlechta. Floating conclusions and zombie paths: two deep difficulties in the "directly skeptical" approach to defeasible inheritance nets. *Artificial Intelligence* 48 (1991): 199–209.

22. L. Morgenstern. Inheritance Comes of Age: Applying Nonmonotonic Techniques to Problems in Industry. *Artificial Intelligence*, 103(1998): 1–34.

23. D. Nute. 1987. Defeasible Reasoning. In *Proc. 20th Hawaii International Conference on Systems Science*, IEEE Press, 470–477.

24. D. Nute. 1994. Defeasible Logic. In D.M. Gabbay, C.J. Hogger and J.A. Robinson (eds.): *Handbook of Logic in Artificial Intelligence and Logic Programming Vol. 3*, Oxford University Press, 353–395.

25. H. Prakken. Intuitions and the modelling of defeasible reasoning: some case studies. In *Proc. 9th International Workshop on Nonmonotonic Reasoning*, Toulouse, 2002, 91-99.

26. R. Reiter. A Logic for Default Reasoning. *Artificial Intelligence* 13(1980): 81–132.

27. L.A. Stein. 1992. Resolving Ambiguity in Nonmonotonic Inheritance Hierarchies. *Artificial Intelligence* 55: 259–310.

28. D.D. Touretzky, J.F. Horty and R.H. Thomason. 1987. A Clash of Intuitions: The Current State of Nonmonotonic Multiple Inheritance Systems. In *Proc. IJCAI-87*, 476–482, Morgan Kaufmann, 1987.

Knowledge Representation
Using a Modified Earley's Algorithm

Christos Pavlatos, Ioannis Panagopoulos, and George Papakonstantinou

National Technical University of Athens, Dept. of Electrical and Computer Engineering
Zographou Campus, 157 73 Athens, Greece
{pavlatos,Ioannis,papakon}@cslab.ece.ntua.gr

Abstract. Attribute grammars (AGs) have been proven to be valuable tools in knowledge engineering applications. In this paper, we formalize knowledge representation problems in their AG equivalent form and we extend the Earley's parsing algorithm in order to evaluate simultaneously attributes based on semantic rules related to logic programming. Although Earley's algorithm can not be extended to handle attribute evaluation computations for all possible AGs, we show that the form of AGs created for equivalent logic programs and the related attribute evaluation rules are such that allow their use for knowledge representation. Hence, a fast one-pass left to right AG evaluator is presented that can effectively be used for logic programs. We also suggest a possible software/hardware implementation for the proposed approach based on existing hardware parsers for Earley's algorithm, which work in coordination with a conventional RISC microprocessor and can assist in the creation of small-scale applications on intelligent embedded systems with optimized performance.

1 Introduction

Knowledge engineering and logic programming approaches have extensively been used in many application domains such as medicine, scheduling and planning, control [1] etc. Therefore, the possibility of exploiting such approaches in embedded systems is of crucial importance. Since many of those applications need to conform to very strict real-time margins, one of the key requirements for the efficiency of such systems is that of performance. For that reason designing fast algorithms for logic derivations is one of the key requirements for the efficiency of the implementation of an intelligent embedded system.

There are two approaches for knowledge representation and processing, namely the declarative and procedural approach. The advantage of using Attribute Grammars (AGs) [2] for knowledge representation holds at the fact that they can easily integrate the two approaches in a single tool [3], [4], [5]. Moreover, the technology of AGs' processing is fairly mature and many implementations of compilers and interpreters for such evaluation processes can be used.

AGs were devised by D. Knuth [6] as a tool for formal languages specification as an extension to Context Free Grammars (CFGs). Specifically, semantic rules and attributes have been added to CFGs augmenting their expressional capabilities. Knowledge can be represented in AGs, using syntactic (syntax rules) and semantic (attribute evaluation rules) notation [3], [4], [5]. A specially designed AG evaluator is then used for logic derivations and the unification procedure throughout the inference

G.A. Vouros and T. Panayiotopoulos (Eds.): SETN 2004, LNAI 3025, pp. 321–330, 2004.
© Springer-Verlag Berlin Heidelberg 2004

process. Therefore, the problem of designing fast algorithms for knowledge engineering applications may be transformed to the problem of modifying fast existing parsing algorithms so that they support special evaluation rules for logic programming applications.

In this paper we formalize knowledge representation problems in their AG equivalent form and we extend the Earley's parsing algorithm [7] in order to be able to evaluate simultaneously attributes based on semantic rules related to logic programming. Earley's algorithm is an efficient CFG parser. Moreover, variations of the parser also do exist in literature, which are even more effective [8], [9] and can easily be modified for the purposes of the proposed method. Actually, they are the fastest so far parsing algorithms. Finally, hardware implementations of the parser have already been presented in [9], [11]. Although Earley's algorithm can not be extended to handle attribute evaluation computations for all possible attribute grammars [10], [11], we show that the form of AGs created for equivalent logic programs (right recursive parse trees) and the related attribute evaluation rules (simple constant inherited attribute definitions) for the unification process are such that allow their use for knowledge representation. Consequently, a fast one-pass left to right AG evaluator is presented that can effectively be used for logic programming derivations. We also suggest a possible hardware implementation for the proposed approach based on existing hardware parsers for Earley's algorithm, which work in coordination with a conventional RISC microprocessor that handles the attribute evaluation process following the approach presented in [12]. Such an approach optimizes performance by approximately 70% compared to the conventional approaches using a purely software implementation while preserving design flexibility and data space. Therefore the software/hardware implementation of the proposed extension in the Earley's parser for knowledge representation can assist in the creation of small-scale applications on intelligent embedded systems with optimized performance.

Extensive efforts in the implementation of machines for logic programming have been mainly encountered in the 5th generation computing era which envisioned a number of interconnected parallel machines for Artificial Intelligence applications [13]. Powerful processors have been introduced working on UMA and NUMA computers [13], [14] in the effort of increasing the efficiency and parallelisation of declarative programs implemented for PROLOG inference engines. Although the overall speed-up achieved following such approaches has been satisfactory, the cost for the implementation of such systems along with their size has prevented their use in small scale applications in embedded system environments. Additionally, the implemented machines were solely optimized for the logic programming model, which is not always suited for all application domains. Consequently, the introduction of embedded systems [15] seems to present new challenges and requirements in the implementation of processors with optimized logic inference capabilities. Embedded systems do not target generality since they are oriented for small-scale applications running on dedicated hardware. Additionally, their restricted computational power (required for constraint satisfaction), turns approaches for increasing performance extremely useful for design efficiency. As a result, the effort of designing hardware capable of supporting the declarative programming model for logic derivations can now lead to intelligent embedded designs which are considerably more efficient compared to the traditional procedural ones.

The rest of the paper is organized as follows. In Section 2, the way knowledge representation can be accomplished using AGs is described. In Section 3, the proposed algorithm is analyzed. In Section 4, an illustrative example is presented. In Section 5, we suggest a software/hardware implementation. Section 6 is conclusion and future work.

2 Knowledge Representation with Attribute Grammars

In [4] an effective method based on Floyd's parser [13] is presented that transforms any initial logic programming problem to its attribute grammar equivalent representation. The basic concepts underlying this approach are the following: Every inference rule in the initial logic program can be transformed to an equivalent syntax rule consisting solely of non-terminal symbols. For example: $R_0(...) \leftarrow R_1(...) \wedge ... \wedge R_m(...)$ is transformed to the syntax rule: $R_0 \rightarrow R_1 ... R_m \mid$. ("|." represents the end of the rule). Finally facts of the inference rules are transformed to terminal leaf nodes of the syntax tree referring to the empty string. For example the facts: $R_g(a, b)$, $R_g(c, d)$, $R_g(e, f)$ are transformed to: $R_g \rightarrow \mid\mid\mid$.

For every variable existing in the initial predicates, two attributes are attached to the corresponding node of the syntax tree one synthesized and one inherited. Those attributes assist in the unification process of the inference engine. The attribute evaluation rules are constructed based on the initial logic program. A detailed method for specifying those rules can be found in [5]. Attributes at the leaf nodes of the tree are assigned values from the constants in the facts of the logic program. The inference process is carried out during tree derivations and an *EVAL* function is evaluated at the insertion/visit of a each node that computes the attribute rules performing the unification procedure.

The way knowledge representation can be accomplished using AGs is illustrated in the following example. Consider the case where an application needs to find whether a path exists in a directed acyclic graph (Table 1) between two nodes of the graph and if so how many such paths exist. For a graph of k nodes with each node represented by a number i, where 0<i<k we define the predicate connected (i, j) which is true whenever there is a directed edge leading from i to j. A simple logic program for finding paths from an arbitrary node x to another node z in the directed acyclic graph is provided in Table 1(a). The equivalent attribute grammar syntax rules handling this inference procedure are provided in Table 1 (b) and the attribute evaluation rules for the unification process are shown in Table 1 (c). In syntax rules goal is represented by "G", path by "P" and connected by "C".

3 The Proposed Algorithm

Since, the problem of designing fast algorithms for knowledge engineering applications may be transformed to the problem of modifying fast existing parsing algorithms so that they support special evaluation rules for logic programming applications, we extend the Earley's parsing algorithm in order to be able to evaluate simultaneously attributes based on semantic rules related to logic programming.

Table 1. (a) Directed acyclic graph and Logic Program for finding a path in a directed acyclic graph (b) Equivalent syntax rules for the attribute grammar to be used as the inference engine (c) Semantic Rules.

(a) Logic Program	(b) Syntax Rules	(c) Semantic Rules
	0. $G \rightarrow P \mid$.	$P.ia_1 = 1;$ $P.ia_2 = 4;$
	1. $P_1 \rightarrow C\ P_2 \mid$.	$C_1.ia_1 = P_1.ia_1;$ $P_2.ia_2 = P_1.ia_2;$ $P_2.ia_1 = C_1.sa_2;$
	2. $P \rightarrow C \mid$.	$C.ia_1 = P.ia_1;$ $C.ia_2 = P.ia_2;$
goal(x,y) ← path(1,4) path(x,z) ← path(y,z) ∧ connected(x,y) path(x,z) ← connected(x,z) connected (1,2)	3. $C \rightarrow \mid$.	**if** ($C.ia_1$!= 1 && $C.ia_1$!= nil) **then** flag=0; **else** $C.sa_1$=1; **if** ($C.ia_2$!= 2 && $C.ia_2$!= nil) **then** flag=0; **else** $C.sa_2$=2;
connected (1,5) connected (2,3) connected (2,5) connected (3,4) connected (5,4)	4. $C \rightarrow \mid$. 5. $C \rightarrow \mid$. 6. $C \rightarrow \mid$. 7. $C \rightarrow \mid$. 8. $C \rightarrow \mid$.	...

In order to explain the origin of the algorithm presented, it is convenient to start from Earley's original algorithm and progressively apply modifications in order to reach the desired algorithm. Earley's algorithm [7] is a dynamic programming procedure that in each step computes simultaneously all states that have been used for the recognition of a part of the input string and are possible states to recognize the remaining portion of the input string. Earley's algorithm is based on the use of the symbol "•" $\notin$ V called dot. The use of the dot in a rule (dotted rule) is to divide the right part of the rule in two parts. The algorithm scans the input string $a_1a_2a_3...a_n$ from left to right. As each symbol a_i is scanned, a set of states S_i is constructed. A state is a $4 - tuple$ <p, j, f, a> where p is the number of the rule, j is the position of the dot, f is the set that the state belongs to, a is a k-symbol look ahead string (if k=0 we define state as a 3-tuple <p, j, f>). We consider the latter case in our algorithm since.

At the initialization of the algorithm, we put the state <0, 0, 0> to set S_0. By applying three operations to each set of states, we can decide at the end, if the input string is accepted or not by checking the existence of state <0, 2, 0> at the set S_n. The three operations are *predictor*, *completer* and *scanner*.

Although Earley's algorithm is an efficient top-down parser for CFGs, it cannot be extended to handle attribute evaluation computations for all possible attribute grammars. The reason for that is explained below. As stated in the previous section, top-down parsers start from the root of the tree and progressively (recognizing one by one the symbols in the input string from left to right) try to recognize the whole input string. This tree construction mechanism resembles a top-down left to right traversal in the complete parse tree. This is illustrated in the following example.

Consider the example CFG grammar G = (N, T, R, S) where: N = {E, T, P}, T = {+, a, b, c} and R = {S→E, E→E+T, E→T, T→P, P→a, P→b, P→c} and the input string: $a + b + c$. During parsing the parse tree is constructed in a way illustrated in Fig. 1 (a). The nodes enclosed in circles drawn with a dashed line represent the sequence in which nodes of the parse tree are constructed. The number within the circle defines the corresponding place of the construction of each node in the sequence. The corresponding traversal of the complete parse tree is illustrated in Fig. 1 (b).

When trying to construct the parse tree in accordance with Earley's algorithm state derivations, synthesized attributes can be successfully evaluated. On the contrary inherited attributes can not be evaluated since if an inherited attribute instance in node E (enclosed in circle (1) in Fig. 1 (a)) depends on an attribute instance of E (enclosed in circle (6) in Fig. 1(a)) that attribute can not be evaluated since at the construction of nodes in circle (6) the needed node has been already traversed. This problem occurs only whenever an attribute grammar has a left-recursive rule and only at the attribute instances which are related to the left recurrent non-terminal symbol. If there are no left-recursive rules in the grammar this problem does not appear.

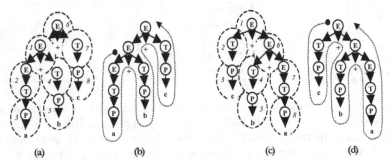

Fig. 1. (a) A tree constructed using Earley's parser for G CFG (b) Equivalent tree traversal for G CFG (c) A tree constructed using Earley' parser for G′ CFG (d) Equivalent tree traversal for G′ CFG.

Consider the CFG grammar G′ = (N, T, R′, S) where: N, T are the sets defined above and R′= {S→E, E→T+E, E→T, T→P, P→a, P→b, P→c}. Note that there are no left-recursive rules in the grammar For the same input string: $a + b + c$ the parse tree is constructed in a way illustrated in Fig. 1 (c,d). In this case both sets of attributes (inherited and synthesized) can successfully be evaluated.

Due to this problem, previous attempts in AG evaluation using the Earley's parser have been restricted only to 1-attribute grammars [10]. Specifically, inherited attributes on left recurrent nodes can only be evaluated if and only if the value of those instances is a constant and is transferred without any computation down in the left recursive nodes. On the contrary if inherited attributes on left recurrent nodes are calculated using a function of the value of their parent's attributes such approach is infeasible since there is no possible way of a priori knowledge of the depth of the recursion.

Although such problems exist, we show that the form of AGs created for equivalent logic programs and the related attribute evaluation rules for the unification process are such that allow their use for knowledge representation, because of the following:

- Since operator conjunction "$\wedge$" has the permutative property and the operator conjunction is used in the logic programming derivations, the equivalent left recursive grammar rules may be transformed to right recursive ones without altering their meaning. For example the inference rules $suc(x,y) \leftarrow suc(x,z) \wedge par(y,z)$ and $suc(x,y) \leftarrow par(y,z) \wedge suc(x,z)$ are equal. Consequently the syntax rule can be $S_1 \rightarrow P\, S_2$ instead of $S_1 \rightarrow S_2\, P$.

- The semantic rules created after the transformation of the logic program to its equivalent AG, evaluate both sets of inherited and synthesized attributes using simple assignment functions (e.g. $P_1.ia_1 = S_1.ia_2$).

Taking into consideration the above observations, Earley's algorithm can be modified in order to simultaneously evaluate the inherited and synthesized attributes. Furthermore the methodology, described in the previous section, of transforming the facts should be modified as well. Since terminal nodes in the equivalent AG evaluation tree represent facts of the initial logic program and are all the same ($R_g \rightarrow |||.$) a way is needed to "force" Earley's algorithm to add those rules to their respective sets even if they all lead to the same dotted rule(distributing the semantic rules). For that reason, the grammar is augmented with a dummy terminal symbol for each fact (dummy$_1$, dummy$_2$ ... dummy$_n$) and we add a syntax rule of the form $P \rightarrow$ dummy$_i$ for each fact.

The modifications made to Earley's algorithm are summarized below.

- There is no input string and there is no need to store the look-ahead symbol therefore states are 3-tuples.
- Every time the operator *predictor* is applied to a state, we can evaluate the inherited attributes of the symbols at the right side of the dotted rule.
- Every time the operator *completer* is applied to a state, we can evaluate the synthesized attributes of the symbols at the left side of the dotted rule. Since there is no input string, the *completer* always succeeds.
- Every time the operator *scanner* is applied to a state, we execute the respective semantic rules. Since there is no input string, the *scanner* always succeeds but adds the dotted rule to the next set after moving the dot over the dummy terminal symbol only if the flag is 1.
- If the attribute instances of a symbol in a state aren't valid then the whole state is deleted (semantically driven parser [17]).
- The creation of state <0, 2, 0> defines the existence of the correct answer to the question (e.g. is Helen successor of George?). The state <0, 2, 0> may be created more than one time since there may be more than one correct answers (successor of George, John and Tom).
- If new states are not created (the *scanner* operation doesn't succeed since flag =0) and the state <0, 2, 0> has not been created then there is no correct answer to the question.
- For every created state, we store the attribute instances of the non-terminals symbols of the dotted rule represented by that state.
- For every operation, a new state is added in the set only if it does not already exist a same state with the same attribute instances in the set.

The proposed algorithm is presented below.

```
add state <0,0,0> to S₀
for (;;)
{
Predictor{Earley's predictor
            evaluate inherited Attributes    }
Completer{Earley's completer
            evaluate synthesized Attributes }
Scanner   {if(there is terminal symbol to the right
            of the dot)
          then execute the respective semantic rules
          if (flag =1)
          add this dotted rule to the next set after
        moving the dot over the dummy terminal symbol}
  if state <0,2,0> is created success
  if new states are not created return failure
}
```

4 An Illustrative Example

A complete run of the algorithm on the grammar of Table 1 is given in Table 2. We want the program to be able to answer questions of the form "path (1, 4)?" that is, "is there a path from 1 to 4?". The correct answers to the question path (1, 4) are three. One can move from node 1 to node 4 through the paths 1→5→4 (path1), 1→2→3→4 (path2)and 1→2→5→4 (path3).

The state is composed of three fields (e.g. 1, G →.P, 0) the first field is the number of the state, the second is the dotted rule and the third is the set where the state was created. This state (1, G →.P, 0) is the 3-tuple <0, 0, 0> since it is the 0 rule, the dot is at the zero position and this state has been created in set 0. The attribute instances of a symbol are in the form $(ia_1, sa_1| ia_2, sa_2)$. For example for symbol P that represents path(x, y) $ia_1 = ia_x$, $sa_1 = sa_x$, $ia_2 = ia_y$, $sa_2 = sa_y$. If the attribute instances of a symbol in a state aren't valid (then the Attribute Instances are written in Italic style. e.g. *C(1 , -|4 , -)* in third state) then this state should be deleted and it is not going to be used any more. There may be more than one valid set of attribute instances for each symbol occurring from different unification processes then all instances are stored in the form $(ia_1, sa_1| ia_2, sa_2)$ or $(ia_1, sa_1| ia_2, sa_2)$. In Table 2 the terminals symbols dummy$_i$ are represented as d$_i$. The symbol (|.) that is used to represent the end in a syntax rule is omitted in this example. Hence the state that indicates the correct answer is <0, 1, 0> (G →P.).

The sequences of states that recognize path1, path2, path3 are 1-2-4-6-7-9-10-14-16-19-20, 1-2-4-5-7-8-11-13-15-16-21-22-25-26-27-28 and 1-2-4-5-7-8-11-14-15-16-21-23-25-26-27-28.

Table 2. A complete run of the algorithm on the AG of the problem of finding a path in a directed acyclic graph.

Set		State		Attribute evaluation
S_0	1	$G \rightarrow .P$	0	$P(1, -\|4, -)$
	2	$P_1 \rightarrow .C\, P_2$	0	$P_1(1, -\|4, -), P_2(-, -\|4, -), C(1, -\|-, -)$
	3	$P \rightarrow .C$	0	$C(1, -\|4, -)$
	4	$C \rightarrow .d_1\|.d_2\|.d_3\|.d_4\|.d_5\|.d_6$	0	$C(1, -\|-, -)$
S_1	5	$C \rightarrow d_1.$	0	$C(1, 1\|-, 2)$
	6	$C \rightarrow d_2.$	0	$C(1, 1\|-, 5)$
	7	$P_1 \rightarrow C.\, P_2$	0	$P_1(1, -\|4, -), P_2(2, -\|4, -)\text{or}(5, -\|4, -),$ $C(1, 1\|-, 2)\text{or}(1, 1\|-, 5)$
	8	$P_1 \rightarrow .C\, P_2$	1	$P_1(2, -\|4, -)\text{or}(5, -\|4, -),$ $P_2(-, -\|4, -), C(2, -\|-, -)\text{ or }(5, -\|-, -),$
	9	$P \rightarrow .C$	1	$P(2, -\|4, -)\text{or}(5, -\|4, -),$ $C(2, -\|4, -)\text{or}(5, -\|4, -)$
	10	$C \rightarrow .d_1\|.d_2\|.d_3\|.d_4\|.d_5\|.d_6$	1	$C(5, -\|4, -)$
	11	$C \rightarrow .d_1\|.d_2\|.d_3\|.d_4\|.d_5\|.d_6$	1	$C(2, -\|-, -)\text{or}(5, -\|-, -)$
S_2	12	$C \rightarrow d_3.$	1	$C(2, 2\|-, 3)$
	13	$C \rightarrow d_4.$	1	$C(2, 2\|-, 5)$
	14	$C \rightarrow d_6.$	1	$C(5, 5\|-, 4)$
	15	$P_1 \rightarrow C.P_2$	1	$P_1(2, -\|4, -)\text{or}(5, -\|4, -),$ $P_2(3, -\|4, -)\text{ or }(4, -\|4, -)\text{ or }(5, -\|4, -)$ $C(2, 2\|-, 3)\text{or}(5, 5\|-, 4)\text{or } C(2, 2\|-, 5)$
	16	$P_1 \rightarrow C.$	1	$P(5, -\|4, -), C(5, -\|4, -)$
	17	$P_1 \rightarrow .C\, P_2$	2	$P_1(3, -\|4, -)\text{ or }(5, -\|4, -),$ $P_2(-, -\|4, -), C(3, -\|-, -)\text{ or } C(5, -\|-, -)$
	18	$P_1 \rightarrow .C$	2	$P(3, -\|4, -)\text{ or }(5, -\|4, -),$ $C(3, -\|4, -)\text{ or } C(5, -\|4, -)$
	19	$P_1 \rightarrow CP_2.$	0	$P_1(1, -\|4, -), P_2(2, -\|4, -)\text{or}(5, -\|4, -),$ $C(1, 1\|-, 2)\text{or}(1, 1\|-, 5)$
	20	$G \rightarrow P.$	0	$P(1, -\|4, -)$
S_3	21	$C \rightarrow .d_1\|.d_2\|.d_3\|.d_4\|.d_5\|.d_6$	2	$C(3, -\|-, -)\text{ or } C(5, -\|-, -)$
	22	$C \rightarrow d_5.$	2	$C(3, 3\|-, 4)$
	23	$C \rightarrow d_6.$	2	$C(5, 5\|-, -4)$
	24	$P_1 \rightarrow C.\, P_2$	2	$P_1(3, -\|4, -)\text{ or }(5, -\|4, -),$ $P_2(-4, -\|4, -), C(3, 3\|-, 4)\text{ or } C(5, 5\|-, 4)$
	25	$P \rightarrow C.$	2	$P(3, -\|4, -)\text{ or }(5, -\|4, -),$ $C(3, 3\|4, -)\text{or}(5, 5\|-, 4)$
	26	$P_1 \rightarrow C.P_2$	1	$P_1(2, -\|4, -)\text{or}(5, -\|4, -),$ $P_2(3, -\|4, -)\text{ or }(5, -\|4, -)$ $C(2, 2\|-, 3)\text{or}(5, 5\|-, 4)\text{or } C(2, 2\|-, 5)$
	27	$P_1 \rightarrow CP_2.$	0	$P_1(1, -\|4, -), P_2(2, -\|4, -)\text{or}(5, -\|4, -),$ $C(1, 1\|-, 2)\text{or}(1, 1\|-, 5)$
	28	$G \rightarrow P.$	0	$P(1, -\|4, -)$

5 The Suggested Hardware/Software Implementation

We also suggest a possible hardware implementation for the proposed approach based on existing hardware parsers [9], [11] for Earley's algorithm, which work in coordination with a conventional RISC microprocessor that handles the attribute evaluation process following the approach presented in [12]. In [12] a hardware parser based on Floyd's parsing algorithm [16] is presented which is attached to a specially designed RISC microprocessor. The parser handles tree derivations while the RISC handles all attribute evaluation rules (Fig. 3 (c)). Such an approach optimizes performance by approximately 70% compared to the conventional approaches using a purely software implementation while preserving design flexibility and data space.

Based on this, it is possible to replace the presented hardware parser in [12] with a hardware implementation of our proposed implementation based on Earley's algorithm. Since efficient hardware implementations of the Earley's parsers already exist (sequential and parallel) in literature such an approach can give even better performance results. The initial logic program (Fig. 3 (a)) is first transformed automatically to its equivalent AG one (Fig. 3 (b)). Then, the syntax rules of the grammar are programmed to the hardware parser while the attribute evaluation rules are programmed to the microprocessor for execution Fig. 3 (c).

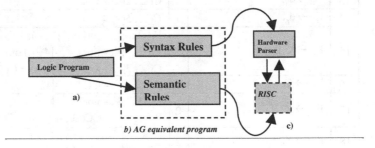

Fig. 2. Overview of the implementation.

6 Conclusion and Future Work

In this paper we transform knowledge representation problems to their AG equivalent forms and we extend the Earley's parsing algorithm in order to create a fast one-pass left to right AG evaluator that is able to evaluate attributes based on semantic rules related to logic programming. We have also suggested a possible software/hardware implementation for the proposed approach based on existing hardware parsers for Earley's algorithm. Future work is planned to present a more efficient hardware implementation that will incorporate the evaluation of the attributes to the hardware parser. This architecture will be implemented in FPGA[18]. In addition, the proposed implementation will be extended to support fuzziness and uncertainty [19], [20].

References

1. Russel, S., Norvig P.: Artificial Intelligence, a modern approach. Prentice Hall, (1995).
2. Paaki, J.: Attribute Grammar Paradigms – A high level methodology in language implementation. ACM Computing Surveys, Vol.27, no.2, (1995).
3. Deransart, P., Maluszynski J.: A grammatical view of logic programming. MIT Press, (1993).
4. Papakonstantinou, G., Kontos J.: Knowledge Representation with Attribute Grammars. The Computer Journal, Vol. 29, No. 3, (1986).
5. Papakonstantinou, G., Moraitis, C., Panayiotopoulos, T.: An attribute grammar interpreter as a knowledge engineering tool. Applied Informatics 9/86, (1986) 382-388.
6. Knuth, D.: Semantics of context free languages. Math. Syst. Theory, Vol.2, No.2, (1971) 127-145.
7. Earley, J.: An efficient context–free parsing algorithm. Communications of the ACM, Vol.13, (1970) 94-102.
8. Graham, S.L., Harrison, M.A., Ruzzo, W.L.: An Improved context – free Recognizer. ACM Trans. On Programming Languages and System, 2(3) (1980) 415-462.
9. Chiang, Y., Fu, K.: Parallel parsing algorithms and VLSI implementation for syntactic pattern recognition". IEEE Transactions on Pattern Analysis and Machine Intelligence, PAMI-6 (1984).
10. Tokuda T., Watanabe Y.: An attribute evaluation of context-free languages. Information Processing Letters 57, (1994) 91-98.
11. Pavlatos, C., Koulouris, A., Papakonstantinou, G.: Hardware Implementation of Syntactic Pattern Recognition Algorithms. IASTED International Conference on Signal Processing and Pattern Analysis (SPPRA), (2003) 360-365.
12. Panagopoulos, I., Pavlatos, C., Papakonstantinou, G.: A hardware extension of the RISC mocroprocessor for attribute grammar evaluation. ACM Conference, SAC 2004, Cyprus (to be published).
13. Gupta, G., Pontelli, E., K.A.M., Carlsson, M., Hermenegildo, M.V.: Parallel execution of prolog programs: a survey. Journal of Programming Languages and Systems, Vol. 23, No 4, (2001), 472-602.
14. Karlsson, R.: A High Performance OR-parallel Prolog System. PhD thesis, The Royal Institute of Technology, Stockholm, (1992).
15. Vahid, F., Givargis, T.: Embedded System Design: A Unified Hardware/Software Introduction. WILEY, (2002).
16. Floyd, R.: The Syntax of Programming Languages-A Survey. IEEE Transactions on Electr. Comp., Vol. EC 13, No 4, (1964).
17. Sideri, M., Efremidis, S., Papakonstantinou, G.: Semantically driven parseing of CFG. The computer Journal, Vol. 32, No.1, (1994) 91-98.
18. Armstrong J., Gray G.: VHDL Design: Representation and Synthesis, Second Edition", Prentice Hall, (2000).
19. Panayiotopoulos, T., Papakonstantinou, G., Stamatopoulos, G.: Attribute Grammar theorem proven. Information and Software Technology, Vol 30, No. 9, (1988) 553-560.
20. Panayiotopoulos, T., Papakonstantinou G., Sgouros N.: An attribute grammar interpeter for inexact reasoning. Information and Software Technology, Vol 32, No. 5, (1990) 347-356.

Fuzzy Causal Maps in Business Modeling and Performance-Driven Process Re-engineering

George Xirogiannis and Michael Glykas

University of Aegean, Department of Financial and Management Engineering
31, Fostini Street, Chios, 82 100, Greece
Tel.: +30-2710-35400 Fax: +30-2710-34499
g.xirogiannis@fme.aegean.gr, mglikas@aegean.gr

Abstract. Despite the rhetoric surrounding performance-driven change (PDC), articulated mechanisms that support intelligent reasoning on the effect of the re-design activities to the performance of a business model are still emerging. This paper describes an attempt to build and operate such a reasoning mechanism as a decision support supplement to PDC exercises. Fuzzy Cognitive Maps (FCMs) are employed as the underlying performance modeler in order to simulate the operational efficiency of complex and imprecise functional relationships and quantify the impact of process re-engineering activities to the business model. Preliminary experiments indicate that the proposed hierarchical and dynamic network of interconnected FCMs forms a sound support aid for establishing performance quantifications that supplement the strategic planning and business analysis phases of typical PDC projects.

Keywords: cognitive modeling, uncertainty, management, reasoning about actions and change.

1 Introduction

Business process re-engineering (BPR) is one general approach widely taken to improve the internal capabilities of an enterprise and implement performance driven internal changes. Since BPR may involve dramatic internal changes, there is a need for monitoring the change initiatives in every organizational level of the enterprise.

This paper proposes a supplement to BPR based on fuzzy cognitive maps (FCM). The proposed decision aid mechanism supplements the strategic planning and business analysis phases of typical PDC projects, by supporting "intelligent" reasoning of the anticipated ("to-be") business performance. The proposed mechanism utilizes the fuzzy causal characteristics of FCMs to generate a hierarchical network of interconnected performance indicators. By using FCM, the proposed mechanism draws a causal representation of dynamic performance principles; it simulates the operational efficiency of complex hierarchical process models with imprecise relationships and quantifies the impact of PDC activities to the hierarchical business model. The proposed FCMs approach fits within the area of decision support systems (e.g. [2]), offering both theoretical and practical benefits. The application of FCMs in modeling the impact of PDC activities is considered to be novel. The fuzzy reasoning capabili-

G.A. Vouros and T. Panayiotopoulos (Eds.): SETN 2004, LNAI 3025, pp. 331–341, 2004.
© Springer-Verlag Berlin Heidelberg 2004

ties enhance the usefulness of the proposed mechanism while reducing the effort for identifying precise performance measurements. Also, the explanatory nature of the mechanism can prove useful in a wider educational setting.

This paper consists of six sections. Section 2 presents a short literature overview of BPR and FCMs. Section 3 discusses the FCM approach in putting realistic and measurable objectives in BPR projects. Section 4 presents the actual FCMs and comments on their characteristics. Section 5 discusses the applicability of the proposed mechanism. Finally, section 6 concludes this paper.

2 Literature Overview

2.1 Fundamentals of BPR Methodologies

BPR implements a critical analysis and radical redesign of existing business processes so as to achieve breakthrough performance improvements. Most BPR methodologies use diagrammatic notations (DFDs, entity relationship attribute techniques, etc.) for modelling business processes. These notations are valuable as informal frameworks, but they lack the semantic content to drive the PDC activities.

Relevant bibliography (e.g. [31, 32]) indicates that most of business analysis is based on subjective rather than objective analytical methods. Graphical notations do not offer a mechanism for verifying the logical consistency and efficiency of the resulting model. The same bibliography analysis shows that there is a big division in the BPR literature between methodologies that concentrate either on process improvement or on process innovation. Other methodologies use automata theory in contrast to graphical representations. Such models usually lead to "state explosion", however, Petri nets [19] were designed to overcome this problem.

2.2 Business Process Modeling Attempts

Among different BPR strategies and methodologies, one common feature is the capturing of business models. The field of knowledge-based systems [7, 23] could fulfil the desire for more accurate predictive models. The research in [20] proposed informal generic modelling structures in an attempt to lower the barriers between process representation and model analysis. The research in [1] built on earlier attempts to use system dynamics but utilized only a small static set of performance factors. It did not cascade relationships; moreover it required the functional definition of causal relationships. Research in [4] reported the development of a tool to quantitatively estimate the potential risk level of a BPR effort based on simple triangular fuzzy approximations. The utilization of uncertainty was also suggested by [9] which proposed a contingency model of quality management practices.

The research in [24] revealed that non-linear science in health care settings offered a practical new frame of reference for BPR initiatives. TCM [14] proposed a cognitive map based method to support process modelling. TCM proposed informal / ambiguous techniques to validate organizational cognitive maps, while causal values were generated by pairwise comparison with no fuzzy definitions allowed.

2.3 FCMs - Definitions and Algorithms

FCMs originated from the combination of Fuzzy Logic and Neural Networks. An FCM describes the behaviour of a system in terms of concepts; each concept represents an entity, a state, a variable, or a characteristic of the system [12]. The graphical illustration of an FCM is a signed fuzzy graph with feedback, consisting of nodes and weighted interconnections (e.g. $\xrightarrow{\text{Weight}}$). Signed and weighted arcs connect various nodes representing the causal relationships that exist among concepts.

Signed weights model the expert knowledge using the causal relationships [13]. The proposed methodology framework assumes that FCMs can have weight values in the fuzzy bipolar interval $[-1,..,1]$. "Bipolarity" is used as a means of representing a positive or negative relationship between two concepts. Concept C_i causally increases C_j if the weight value $W_{ij}>0$ and causally decreases C_j if $W_{ij}<0$, while the value of W_{ij} indicates how strongly concept C_i influences concept C_j. The forward or backward direction of causality indicates whether concept C_i causes concept C_j or vice versa. This paper allows FMCs to utilize fuzzy linguistic weights like strong, medium, or weak, each of these words being a fuzzy set. In contrast, [14] adopted only the "relative weight" representation.

A typical formula for calculating the values of concepts of FCM is the following:

$$A_i^{t+1} = f\left(\sum_{j=1,j\neq i}^{n} W_{ji} A_j^t \right) \tag{1}$$

A_i^{t+1} is the value of concept C_i at the step $t+1$, A_j^t the value of the interconnected concept C_j at step t, W_{ij} is the weighted arc from C_j to C_i and f is a threshold function. Two threshold functions are usually used. The unipolar sigmoid function where $\lambda>0$ determines the steepness of the continuous function $f(x) = \dfrac{1}{1+e^{-\lambda x}}$.

When concepts can be negative and their values belong to $[-1,1]$, function $f(x) = \tanh(x)$ is used.

2.4 Applications of Fuzzy Cognitive Maps

Over the last 10 years, a variety of FCMs have been used for representing knowledge and artificial intelligence in engineering applications, like geographical information systems [22] and fault detection (e.g.[26]). FCMs have been used in modelling the supervision of distributed systems [30]. FCMs have also been used in operation research [3], web data mining (e.g [17]), as a back end to computer-based models and medical diagnosis (e.g. [5]).

Research in [27] has used FCM for representing tacit knowledge in political and social analysis. FCMs have been successfully applied to various fields such as decision making in complex war games [11], strategic information systems planning [10], information retrieval [8] and distributed decision modelling [34]. Research like [15] has successfully applied FCMs to infer implications from stock market analysis results. Research like [16] utilized FCMs to analyse and predict stock market trends. The inference power of FCMs has also been adopted to analyse the competition between two companies [18]. FCMs have been integrated with case-based reasoning techniques in the field of knowledge management [25]. Recent research adopted FCMs to support the core activities of technical operations like urban design [33].

In addition, a few modifications have been proposed. For example, [29] has proposed new forms of combined matrices for FCMs, [6] permitted non-linear and time delay on the arcs, [28] has presented a method for automatically constructing FCMs. More recently, [22] investigated the inference properties of FCMs and applied contextual FCMs to geographical information systems [21].

3   FCMs as a Supplement to BPR Projects

3.1   Performance Modelling Using FCMs

A typical BPR methodology consists of the following re-designing tasks, **Phase 1:** Strategic BPR planning, **Phase 2:** Business modelling, **Phase 3:** Business analysis, **Phase 4:** Process re-design, **Phase 5:** Continuous improvement. The proposed mechanism focuses on supplementing phases 1 and 3. During these phases, a typical BPR methodology defines the strategic level performance metrics and the business analysis performance metrics (operational – tactical level metrics). Such metrics present inherent relationships, in practice, strategic metrics must cascade to operational metrics. Similarly, performance metrics of partial activities must propagate up the overall performance metrics of the parent process itself.

It is the view of this paper that reasoning of the chained impact of PDC initiatives to the overall business performance is not always feasible. Links between metrics at the same level and/or links between metrics of different levels are not always clear and well defined. To resolve this problem, this paper proposes the utilization of the strategic planning and business analysis metrics (Figure 1) to develop FCMs and reason about the performance of existing ("as-is") and desired ("to-be") models.

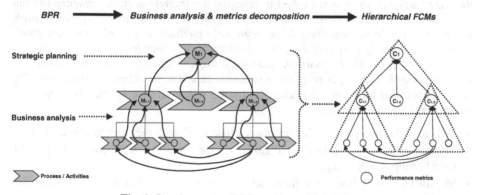

Fig. 1. Supplementing BPR projects with FCMs.

The proposed tool utilizes FCMs to interpret (a) performance metrics as concepts, graphically represented as nodes, (b) decision weights as relationship weights, graphically represented as arrowhead lines, (c) decision variables as concept values, (d) top-down decomposition of metrics as a hierarchy of FCMs. This interpretation allows the re-designers to reason about lower level FCMs first (constituent metrics) before they reason about higher-level metric (affected metrics). In contrast to other approaches (e.g. [14]), the proposed tool builds on hierarchical performance interrelationships utilized by the BPR methodology.

3.2 Development of FCMs

This paper extends the basic FCM algorithm (as discussed in section 2.3 and also used by [14]), by proposing the following new FCM algorithm:

$$A_i^{t+1} = f\,(k_1 A_i^t + k_2 * \sum_{j=1, j\neq i}^{n} W_{ji} A_j^t) \qquad (2)$$

The coefficient k_1 represents the proportion of the contribution of the value of the concept A_i at time t in the computation of the value of A_i at time $t+1$. This is equivalent to assume that $W_{ii}=k_1$. The utilization of k_1 results in smoother variation of concept values during the iterations of the FCM algorithm. The coefficient k_2 indicates the centralized or decentralized importance of the concept A_i in comparison to other concepts. Also, it indicates the sufficiency of the set of concepts A_j $j\neq i$, in the estimation of the value of the concept A_i at time $t+1$. This paper assumes that coefficients k_1 and k_2 can be fuzzy sets as well.

3.3 Assigning Linguistic Variables to FCM Weights and Concepts

Generic concept relationships generate skeleton FCMs. Based on these skeleton FCMs, the re-designer can generate several business cases (scenarios), each modifying the fuzzy weight value of the association rules and coefficients k_1, k_2. To estimate the fuzzy weights, experts are asked to describe the interconnection *influence* of concepts using linguistic notions. Its term set *T(influence) = {negatively very-very high, negatively very high, negatively high, negatively medium, negatively low, negatively very low, negatively very-very low, zero, positively very-very low, positively very low, positively low, positively medium, positively high, positively very high, positively very-very high}*. This paper proposes a semantic rule **M** to be defined at this point. The above-mentioned terms are characterized by the fuzzy sets whose membership functions μ are shown in Figure 2.

- M(zero)= the fuzzy set for "an influence close to 0" with membership function μ_z
- M(positively very-very low)= the fuzzy set for "an influence close to 10%" with membership function μ_{pvvl}
- M(positively very low)= the fuzzy set for "an influence close to 20%" with membership function μ_{pvl}
- M(positively low)= the fuzzy set for "an influence close to 35%" with membership function μ_{pl}

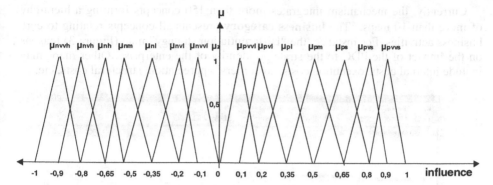

Fig. 2. Membership functions of linguistic variable influence.

- M(positively medium)= the fuzzy set for "an influence close to 50%" with membership function μ_{pm}
- M(positively high)= the fuzzy set for "an influence close to 65%" with membership function μ_{ph}
- M(positively very high)= the fuzzy set for "an influence close to 80%" with membership function μ_{pvh}
- M(positively very-very high)= the fuzzy set for "an influence close to 90%" with membership function μ_{pvvh}

Similarly, for *negatively very-very high, negatively very high, negatively high, negatively medium, negatively low, negatively very low, negatively very-very low.* Different linguistic weights for the same interconnection W_{ij} are integrated using a sum combination method and then the defuzzification method of centre of gravity (CoG) Semantic rules and term sets can be used to define the coefficients k_1 and k_2, as well as the *measurement* of each concept using similar linguistic notions. This approach offers independent reasoning of each weight value, rather than estimation of the relative (i.e. dependent) "strength" as suggested by [14].

4 Presentation of Generic FCMs

4.1 FCM Hierarchies

This paper now introduces generic maps that can supplement the strategic planning and business analysis phases of PDC projects. The hierarchical decomposition of metrics generates a set of dynamically interconnected hierarchical maps. This categorization is compatible with the "process view" of the enterprise, however the "organizational view" can also be portrayed. The model can portray both the overall business model and the targeted BPR exercise following either a holistic or a scalable approach. This is analogous to seeing BPR either as a single, "big bang" event or as an ongoing process of successive BPR sub-projects.

Currently, the mechanism integrates more than 150 concepts forming a hierarchy of more than 10 maps. The **business category** presents all concepts relating to core business activities. For instance, the "Differentiation strategy" map (Figure 3) reasons on the impact of the PDC to the strategic identity of the enterprise. Other maps may include internal costs, execution costs, customers' appreciation, structural costs, etc.

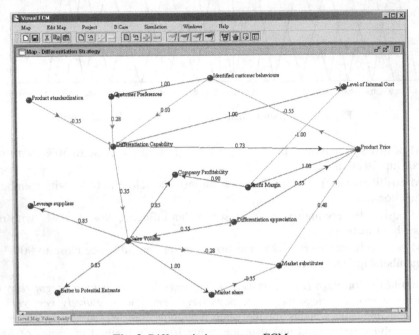

Fig. 3. Differentiation strategy FCMs.

The **HR category** presents all human resources related concepts. For instance, the "Social" map (Figure 4) may support reasoning of the impact of knowledge management, training and employee satisfaction, etc to the business model.

The **infrastructure category** presents all infrastructure related concepts with emphasis on IT. For example, some "Information systems organizational structure" map may support reasoning of the impact of the centralization / decentralization of the IT to the overall business model. The **integrated category** essentially presents all topmost concepts (Figure 5).

Concepts denoted as "↓" expand further to lower level maps, while "↑" denotes bottom-up causal propagation.

5 Discussion

As far as the theoretical value is concerned, the FCM mechanism extends previous research attempts by (a) allowing fuzzy definitions in the cognitive maps, (b) introducing a specific interpretation mechanism of linguistic variables to fuzzy sets, (c) proposing an updated FCM algorithm to suit better the BPR domain, (d) introducing

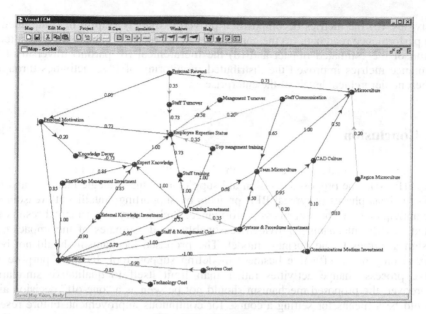

Fig. 4. Social FCM.

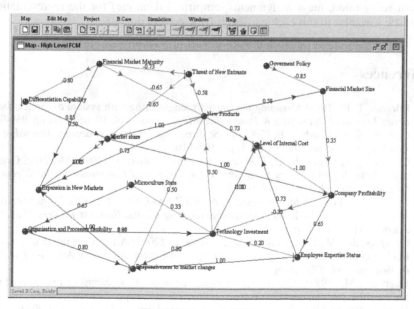

Fig. 5. High level FCM.

the notion of interconnected performance hierarchies, (e) concentrating on the actual BPR activity and its impact on the business model and (f) allowing dynamic map decomposition and reconfiguration. As far as the practical value is concerned, preliminary experimental results indicate that (a) when compared to the expert estimates, the mechanism provides reasonably good approximations of the impact of re-design activities, (b) the metrics decomposition proved extremely helpful in comprehending the performance roadmap, (c) the concept-based approach did not restrict the interpretation of the estimated impact and (d) the hierarchical (or partial) traversal of performance metrics improved the distributed monitoring of PDC activities throughout different hierarchical levels of the enterprise

6 Conclusion

This paper presented a supplement to the BPR methodology based on fuzzy cognitive maps (FCM). The proposed decision aid supplements the strategic planning and business analysis phases of typical BPR projects by supporting "intelligent" reasoning of the anticipated ("to-be") business performance. Preliminary experimental results indicated that the mechanism provided reasonably good estimates of the impact of redesign activities to the business model. The proposed mechanism should not be regarded only as an effective business modeling support tool. Its main purpose is to drive process change activities rather than limit itself to qualitative simulations. Moreover, the proposed mechanism should not be seen as a "one-off" decision aid. It should be a means for setting a course for continuous improvement. Future research will focus on the automatic determination of appropriate fuzzy sets (e.g. utilizing pattern recognition, mass assignments, empirical data, etc) for the representation of linguistic variables to suit each particular BPR project domain.

References

1. Burgess, T. F. (1998) Modeling the impact reengineering with system dynamics, *International Journal of Operations & Production Management,* vol. 18, no. 9/10, pp. 950-963.
2. Carlsson, C. and Turban, E. (2002) DSS: directions for the next decade, *Journal of Decision Support Systems,* vol. 33, no. 1, pp. 105-110.
3. Craiger, J. P., Goodman, D. F., Weiss, R. J. and Butler, A. (1996) Modeling Organizational Behavior with Fuzzy Cognitive Maps, *Journal of Computational Intelligence and Organisations,* vol. 1, no. pp. 120-123.
4. Crowe, T. J., Fong, P. M., Bauman, T. A. and Zayas-Castro, J. L. (2002) Quantitative risk level estimation of business process reengineering efforts, *Business Process Management Journal,,* vol. 8, no. 5, pp. 490-511.
5. Georgopoulos, V., Malandraki, G. and Stylios, C. (2002) A fuzzy cognitive map approach to differential diagnosis of specific language impairment, *Journal of Artificial Intelligence in Medicine,* vol. 679, no. pp. 1-18.
6. Hagiwara, M. (1992). *Extended fuzzy cognitive maps.* Proceedings of the Proceedings of the 1st IEEE International Conference on Fuzzy Systems (pp. 795-801), New York.
7. Harmon, P. and King, D. (1985) *Expert Systems: Artificial Intelligence in Business,* John Wiley & Sons, New York, NY.
8. Johnson, R. J. and Briggs, R. O. (1994). *A model of cognitive information retrieval for ill-structured managerial problems and its benefits for knowledge acquisition.* Proceedings of the 27th Annual Hawaii International Conference on System Sciences (pp. 191-200), Hawaii.
9. Jones, R. T. and Ryan, C. (2002) Matching process choice and uncertainty: Modeling quality management, *Journal of Business Process Management,* vol. 8, no. 2, pp. 161-168.

10. Kardaras, D. and Karakostas, B. (1999) The use of fuzzy cognitive maps to simulate the information systems strategic planning process, *Journal of Information and Software Technology*, vol. 41, no. 1, pp. 197-210.
11. Klein, J. C. and Cooper, D. F. (1982) Cognitive maps of decision makers in a complex game, *Journal of Operation Research Society*, vol. 33, no. pp. 63-71.
12. Kosko, B. (1986) Fuzzy Cognitive Maps, *Journal of Man-Machine Studies*, vol. 24, no. pp. 65-75.
13. Kosko, B. (1991) *Neural networks and fuzzy systems*, Prentice Hall, Englewood Cliffs.
14. Kwahk, K. Y. and Kim, Y. G. (1999) Supporting business process redesign using cognitive maps, *Decision Support Systems*, vol. 25, no. 2, pp. 155-178.
15. Lee, K. C. and Kim, H. S. (1997) A fuzzy cognitive map-based bi-directional inference mechanism: An application to stock investment analysis, *Journal of Intelligent Systems in Accounting Finance & Management*, vol. 6, no. 1, pp. 41-57.
16. Lee, K. C. and Kim, H. S. (1998) Fuzzy implications of fuzzy cognitive map with emphasis on fuzzy causal relationship and fuzzy partially causal relationship, *Journal of Fuzzy Sets and Systems*, vol. 3, no. pp. 303-313.
17. Lee, K. C., Kim, J. S., Chung, N. H. and Kwon, S. J. (2002) Fuzzy Cognitive Map approach to web-mining inference amplification, *Journal of Expert Systems with Applications*, vol. 22, no. pp. 197-211.
18. Lee, K. C. and Kwon, O. B. (1998) A strategic planning simulation based on cognitive map knowledge and differential game, *Journal of Simulation*, vol. 7, no. 5, pp. 316-327.
19. Li, X. and Lara-Rosano, F. (2000) Adaptive fuzzy petri nets for dynamic knowledge representation and inference, *Journal of Expert Systems with Applications*, vol. 19, no. 3, pp. 235-241.
20. Lin, F. R., Yang, M. C. and Pai, Y. H. (2002) A generic structure for business process modeling, *Business Process Management Journal,*, vol. 8, no. 1, pp. 19-41.
21. Liu, Z. Q. (2000) *Fuzzy cognitive maps: Analysis and extension*, Springer, Tokyo.
22. Liu, Z. Q. and Satur, R. (1999) Contexual fuzzy cognitive map for decision support in geographical information systems, *Journal of IEEE Transactions on Fuzzy Systems*, vol. 7, no. pp. 495-507.
23. Metaxiotis, K., Psarras, J. and Samouilidis, E. (2003) Integrating fuzzy logic into decision support systems: current research and future prospects, *Journal of Information Management & Computer Security*, vol. 11, no. 2, pp. 53-59.
24. Murray, M. A., Priesmeyer, H. R., Sharp, L. F., Jensen, R. and Jensen, G. (2000) Nonlinearity as a tool for business process reengineering, *Business Process Management Journal*, vol. 6, no. 4, pp. 304 - 313.
25. Noh, J. B., Lee Lee, K. C., Kim, J. K., Lee, J. K. and Kim, S. H. (2000) A case- based reasoning approach to cognitive map driven -driven tacit knowledge management, *Journal of Expert Systems with Applications*, vol. 19, no. pp. 249-259.
26. Pelaez, C. E. and Bowles, J. B. (1995). *Applying fuzzy cognitive maps knowledge representation to failure modes effect analysis.* Proceedings of the IEEE Annual Reliability Maintainability Symposium (pp. 450-456), New York.
27. Perusich, K. (1996). *Fuzzy cognitive maps for political analysis.* Proceedings of the International Symposium on Technology and Society. Technical Expertise and Public Decisions (pp. 369-373), New York.
28. Schneider, M., Schnaider, E., Kandel, A. and Chew, G. (1995). *Constructing fuzzy cognitive maps.* Proceedings of the IEEE Conference on Fuzzy Systems (pp. 2281-2288), New York.
29. Silva, P. C. (1995). *New forms of combined matrices of fuzzy cognitive maps.* Proceedings of the IEEE International Conference on Neural Networks (pp. 71-776), New York.
30. Stylios, C. D., Georgopoulos, V. C. and Groumpos, P. P. (1997). *Introducing the Theory of Fuzzy Cognitive Maps in Distributed Systems.* Proceedings of the 12 th IEEE International Symposium on Intelligent Control, Istanbul, Turkey.

31. Valiris, G. and Glykas, M. (1999) Critical review of existing BPR methodologies. The need for a holistic approach, *Journal of Business Process Management,* vol. 5, no. 1, pp. 65-86.
32. Valiris, G. and Glykas, M. (2000) A Case Study on Reengineering Manufacturing Processes and Structures, *Journal of Knowledge and Process Management,* vol. 7, no. 1, pp. 20-28.
33. Xirogiannis, G., Stefanou, J. and Glykas, M. (2004) A fuzzy cognitive map approach to support urban design, *Journal of Expert Systems with Applications,* vol. 26, no. 2, pp. 257-268.
34. Zhang, W. R., Wang, W. and King, R. S. (1994) A-pool: An agent-oriented open system for distributed decision process modeling, *Journal of Organisational Computing,* vol. 4, no. 2, pp. 127-154.

Construction and Repair:
A Hybrid Approach to Search in CSPs

Konstantinos Chatzikokolakis, George Boukeas, and Panagiotis Stamatopoulos

Department of Informatics and Telecommunications, University of Athens
Panepistimiopolis, Athens 15784, Greece
{c.chatzikokolakis,boukeas,takis}@di.uoa.gr

Abstract. In order to obtain a solution to a constraint satisfaction problem, *constructive* methods iteratively extend a consistent partial assignment until all problem variables instantiated. If the current partial assignment is proved to be inconsistent, it is then necessary to backtrack and perform alternative instantiations. On the other hand, *reparative* methods iteratively repair an inconsistent complete assignment until it becomes consistent. In this research, we investigate an approach which allows for the combination of constructive and reparative methods, in the hope of exploiting their intrinsic advantages and circumventing their shortcomings. Initially, we discuss a general hybrid method called CR and then proceed to specify its parameters in order to provide a fully operational search method called CNR. The reparative stage therein is of particular interest: we employ techniques borrowed from local search and propose a general cost function for evaluating partial assignments. In addition, we present experimental results on the open-shop scheduling problem. The new method is compared against specialized algorithms and exhibits outstanding performance, yielding solutions of high quality and even improving the best known solution to a number of instances.

Keywords: constraint satisfaction, search, heuristics

1 Introduction

A great number of interesting combinatorial problems can be viewed as constraint satisfaction problems (CSPs), involving a finite set V of variables and a finite set C of constraints between the variables. Given a CSP, the goal is to obtain a *complete consistent assignment*, that is to assign a value to every variable (complete) so that all constraints are satisfied (consistent). Search methods for obtaining solutions to CSPs can be broadly characterized as *constructive* or *reparative*. Constructive (global) methods iteratively extend a consistent partial assignment until a consistent complete assignment is obtained. If the current partial assignment is proved to be inconsistent, it is then necessary to backtrack and explore alternative assignments. On the other hand, reparative (local) methods iteratively modify an inconsistent complete assignment until a consistent complete assignment is obtained. The methods in each category exhibit certain features which are, in fact, complementary. In this research, we investi-

G.A. Vouros and T. Panayiotopoulos (Eds.): SETN 2004, LNAI 3025, pp. 342–351, 2004.

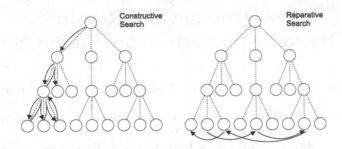

Fig. 1. Constructive methods extend consistent partial assignments or otherwise backtrack. Reparative methods modify inconsistent complete assignments.

gate a framework which allows for the combination of constructive and reparative methods, in the hope of exploiting their intrinsic advantages and circumventing their shortcomings. In the generic CR framework we propose, search is performed in two alternating stages: in the constructive stage a consistent partial assignment is iteratively extended. However, if the current partial assignment is proved to be inconsistent, backtracking is replaced by a reparative stage, in which the inconsistent partial assignment is iteratively modified until it becomes consistent. In order to evaluate the CR framework experimentally, we specify its parameters and provide a fully operational method called CNR-search. The reparative stage therein is of particular interest: we employ techniques borrowed from local search and propose a general cost function for evaluating partial assignments.

The rest of this paper is organized as follows: In Sects. 2 and 3, we examine constructive and reparative search methods separately, identifying some of their most characteristic features. In Sect. 4, we discuss the generic CR search framework. In Sect. 5 we proceed to provide implementations for both the construction and repair operators of the CR framework, thus obtaining a concrete search algorithm called CNR-search. In Sect. 6, we present experimental results from the application of CNR to the *open-shop* scheduling problem. A discussion regarding these excellent results, as well as the method in general, can be found in the concluding Sect. 7.

1.1   Related Work

The notion of merging constructive and reparative features into a hybrid search framework has been investigated in various forms. In some cases, the coupling between the two approaches is loose: constructive and reparative modules exchange information but essentially operate independently [1, 2]. In other frameworks, where the integration is of a higher degree, the reparative process employs constructive methods in order to (systematically) explore the neighborhood [3, 4]. However, our research is more closely related to the approaches described in [5, 6], where repair operators are applied on partial inconsistent assignments, obtained by construction. In both cases, the repair operator undoes previous instantiations, essentially performing some form of non-systematic dynamic backtracking.

Especially in [6], the reparative process is guided by conflict-based heuristics and is coupled with tabu search. Our general CR framework encompasses such approaches while not being restricted to a specific repair operator. In CNR-search, the repair operator does not employ backtracking.

2   Constructive Search

Constructive methods iteratively extend a consistent partial assignment until a consistent complete assignment is obtained. If the current partial assignment is proved to be inconsistent, it is then necessary to backtrack and explore alternative assignments. The fact that search is performed in the space of partial assignments is a defining feature. Proving that a particular partial assignment is inconsistent promptly removes the need to explicitly enumerate all the inconsistent complete assignments in the subtree below it. Consistency techniques can be exploited for reasoning about partial assignments and pruning the search space. On the other hand, operating on partial assignments essentially restricts the search process to a subset of the search space at any given time. Poor search decisions can confine the search process to unproductive branches and are computationally expensive to overcome.

All constructive methods can be described using the generic algorithm of Fig. 2(a). The list L employed therein comprises all partial assignments which remain to be explored and can potentially be backtracked to, in case the current one is proved inconsistent. The use of L allows for a systematic exploration of the search space and endows constructive methods with *completeness*: it is guaranteed that the entire search space will eventually be explored. The extend function generates possible extensions of the current partial assignment α, returns one of them and inserts the rest into L so that they can be backtracked to. The backtrack function selects and returns an assignment out of L.

3   Reparative Search

Reparative methods iteratively modify an inconsistent complete assignment until a consistent complete assignment is obtained. Because of the fact that search is performed exclusively in the space of complete assignments, the features of reparative methods are complementary to those of constructive ones. The search process is endowed with flexibility, since it is possible to perform arbitrary leaps to complete assignments throughout the search space. However, systematic exploration of the search space and completeness are forsaken, consistency techniques can no longer be exploited and the search process is particularly sensitive to the existence of local optima.

All reparative methods can be described using the generic algorithm of Fig. 2(b). The repair function applies a repair operator on assignment α and returns the resulting modified assignment.

```
constructive-search (α) {              reparative-search (α) {
    L ← ∅                                  while (not solution(α))
    while (not solution(α)) {                  α ←repair(α)
        if (consistent(α))                 return α
            α ←extend(α, L)            }
        else if (L ≠ ∅)
            α ←backtrack(α, L)
        else
            return no-solution
    }
    return α
}
                (a)                                    (b)
```

Fig. 2. General algorithms for (a) constructive and (b) reparative search.

4 Search by Construction and Repair

In this section, we discuss a generic search framework which incorporates both construction and repair operators. Intuitively, search is to be performed in two alternating stages:

Constructive Stage. A construction operator is iteratively applied on the current consistent partial assignment, extending it until it becomes inconsistent or until a complete consistent assignment is obtained.

Repair Stage. A repair operator is iteratively applied on the current inconsistent assignment, modifying it until it becomes consistent.

The exploration of the search space using the hybrid CR-search algorithm, is depicted in Fig. 3(b), where the alternating search stages are apparent. Search with CR is performed in the space of both partial and complete assignments. In the constructive stage, it is possible to employ consistency techniques in order to prune the search space and discover inconsistencies. The repair operator on partial assignments allows leaps to distant areas of the search space, overcoming poor search decisions made during partial assignment construction. The variable domain information maintained in the constructive stage can potentially be exploited for guiding the reparative stage, as is explained in Sect. 5.

The generic CR algorithm is described in Fig. 3(a). The **extend** function is inherited from constructive search and implements the construction operator, whereas the **repair** function is a generalized version of the operator encountered in reparative search which can also be applied on partial assignments. Different implementations of these abstract functions give rise to different specializations of the generic CR-search framework. Constructive search itself can be obtained from CR by using backtracking as the repair operator. Reparative search can also be obtained from CR by applying the repair operator only on complete assignments. This means that CR is strictly more general that constructive or reparative search alone.

```
cr-search (α) {
    L ← ∅
    while (not solution(α)) {
        if (consistent(α))
            α ← extend(α, L)
        else
            α ← repair(α, L)
    }
    return α
}
```

(a)

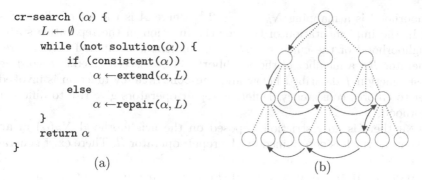

(b)

Fig. 3. Construction-Repair search. (a) The generic search algorithm and (b) an illustration of the manner in which the search tree is traversed.

```
CNR-extend(α, L) {                CNR-repair(α, L) {
    v ← h_v(α)                        α ← arg min_{α'∈N(α)} f(α')
    ℓ ← h_ℓ(α, v)                     return consistency(α)
    return consistency(α ⊙_{v_i} ℓ)  }
}
```

(a)   (b)

Fig. 4. Implementation of the (a) constructive and (b) reparative stages. Applying the operator $\odot_{v_i}$ on an assignment α instantiates the i-th variable of α.

5　Search by Construction and Neighborhood Repair

In this section, we provide implementations for both the construction and repair operators of the CR framework, thus obtaining a concrete search algorithm called CNR-search (construction-neighborhood repair).

5.1　Constructive Stage

The implementation of the extend function in the constructive stage is contained in Fig. 4(a). The variable ordering heuristic function h_v selects an uninstantiated variable and the value ordering heuristic function h_ℓ selects a value out of the domain of a variable. The selected variable is instantiated with the selected value and the consistency function is invoked in order to propagate the effects of the instantiation to the domains of the other variables. Note that in our implementation, the consistency function implements a modified version of *arc consistency* which does not terminate when an inconsistency is detected. Instead, propagation continues without taking into account any variables with an empty domain. The remaining domain information is to be exploited during the reparative stage.

5.2　Reparative Stage

The *neighborhood* $N_R(\alpha)$ of an assignment α is the set of assignments which are accessible from α in a single application of the repair operator R. Formally, a neighborhood is a mapping $N_R : \mathcal{A} \to 2^{\mathcal{A}}$, where $\mathcal{A}$ is the set of all assignments. In the implementation of the repair function in the reparative stage, the neighborhood of the current *partial* assignment is computed (given a repair operator R), a member of the neighborhood is selected greedily according to a cost function f described below and the consistency function is invoked in order to enforce consistency. Different repair operators give rise to different neighborhoods.

In CNR there is no restriction imposed on the neighborhood $N_R(\alpha)$ of an assignment α, which is determined by the repair operator R. There exist general neighborhoods which are applicable to arbitrary CSPs and are often encountered in the literature. In this research, the ALTER repair operator has been employed, yielding a neighborhood $N_a(\alpha)$ which contains any assignment obtainable from α by modifying the value of a single instantiated variable. The domains of all variables uninstantiated in α are reset to their original domains.

The cost function $f : \mathcal{A} \to \mathbb{R}$ evaluates the partial assignments in a neighborhood in order to guide the reparative process towards consistent partial assignments. Therefore, f must evaluate the *extent* of constraint violation in an assignment and must be minimized for consistent assignments. Along the same lines, a well-known function described in [7] returns the number of violated constraints but is not directly applicable on partial assignments. We propose that, given an assignment $\alpha = \langle a_1, a_2, \ldots, a_n \rangle$ where a_i is the domain of variable v_i, the cost function evaluating α be:

$$f(\alpha) = \rho \cdot |\{v_i \in V \mid a_i' = \emptyset\}| - \prod_{v_i \in V} \max\{|a_i'|, 1\}$$

where $\alpha' = \texttt{consistency}(\alpha)$, and ρ a large penalty constant. The first term pertains to the number of variables with an empty domain. The greater the number of such variables in an assignment, the more this assignment is penalized. The second term is a tie-breaker and pertains to the product of domain sizes. This product reflects the number of complete assignments which are extensions of α and the greater this number is, the less *constrained* is the assignment. Recall from Sect. 5.1 that this function is applicable because we use a modified version of arc-consistency.

In practice, the neighborhood can be prohibitively large to compute. Its size can be reduced if a window of w variables is selected and the repair operator is only applied to them, disallowing any modifications to variables outside the window. In addition to reducing the size of the neighborhood, using a window also allows for consistency to be enforced in a more efficient manner. The selection of the window size w is critical: computational performance is improved as w decreases but the repair operator becomes less effective since a smaller neighborhood is available. Except for the size of the window, there is also the issue of which variables to include in it. The simplest method is to order the variables lexicographically, include w consecutive variables in the window and slide the window so that it contains a different set of variables in every execution of the reparative stage. This produces an effect similar to that of tabu search: a recently modified variable leaves the window and will not be modified again for a number of iterations. As a result, it is highly unlikely that the same assignment is reached more than once or that an infinite loop is entered.

6   Experimental Results on a Scheduling Problem

In this section, we present experimental results from the application of CNR to *open-shop*, a scheduling problem. In open-shop, a set of n jobs, each consisting of m tasks, must be processed on a set of m machines. Task i of job j requires processing time t_{ij} and must be executed by machine i. Each machine can execute one task at a time and no two tasks of the same job can be executed simultaneously. Our goal is to find a non-preemptive schedule that minimizes the *makespan*, that is the finish time of the latest task. For $m > 2$ non-preemptive open-shop is NP-hard [8] and problems of very small size still remain unsolved. This is a problem particularly appropriate for methods utilizing repair operators.

6.1   Application of the Search Method

In the experiments performed with CNR, open-shop is handled as a general CSP and no problem-specific techniques are employed:

Constructive Stage. In this stage, the variable ordering heuristic selects the variable with the smallest domain, whereas the value ordering heuristic selects the smallest value in the domain (which is only reasonable when minimizing the makespan). Both ordering heuristics are elementary.

Repair Stage. In this stage, the ALTER neighborhood with first improvement selection is used. Experiments with alternative neighborhoods have been performed, although not extensively, since it immediately became apparent that the ALTER neighborhood is particularly well-suited for the problem at hand. Due to the large number of values in each domain, only a small number of randomly selected values is examined for each variable and, in addition, a sliding variable window of size $w = 1$ is employed. Experiments with larger windows showed that the increase in window size hampers computational performance without improving solution quality.

To minimize the makespan, CNR is coupled with *branch-and-bound*. After each run of CNR, a constraint is added which enforces new solutions to be of better quality, rendering the current assignment infeasible. Search continues by repairing this assignment, which is of good quality and likely to be repaired easily.

Since CNR is not complete, a stopping criterion must be used: in our experiments, the search was interrupted after 120 minutes of computation and only if the time elapsed after the last improvement exceeded 30 minutes. In some cases where the best known solution is available, search was interrupted when this solution was obtained.

6.2   Experiments

We applied CNR on three sets of benchmark problems from the literature:

- 40 instances by Taillard, contained in [9], with sizes ranging from 4×4 to 10×10 and known optimal solutions.
- 52 instances by Brucker, contained in [10], with sizes ranging from 3×3 to 8×8. The optimal solution is not always known but all instances have a classical lower bound of 1000.
- 80 instances by Guéret & Prins, presented in [11] along with an improved lower bound for open-shop. These instances are especially designed so that the proposed bound differs significantly from the classical one.

For these benchmark instances, the quality of the final solutions obtained with CNR is compared against that of a diverse range of algorithms for open-shop:

- the genetic algorithm GA of Prins [12],
- the decision-repair algorithm TDR of Jussien and Lhomme [6],
- (only for the Taillard instances) two specialized tabu search methods TS-A and TS-L, of Alcaide et al. [13] and Liaw [14] and
- (only for the Guéret & Prins instances) the improved branch-and-bound algorithm BB of Guéret & Prins [15].

Experimental results for these algorithms have been published collectively in [6] (available at http://njussien.e-constraints.net/palm-os.html). Note that in open-shop scheduling, the quality of the final solution obtained is of primary interest, regardless of the time required to obtain it. Open-shop is a hard problem where quality is considered more important than efficiency. Besides, the execution time of some algorithms strongly depends on the particular instance, while in some cases it is not reported at all. The two hour limit on the execution time of CNR is strict, compared to that of most other algorithms.

Results for the Taillard benchmarks are displayed in Table 1. Except for the 10×10 instances, the performance of CNR is excellent. Results for the Brucker benchmarks are displayed in Table 1. Once again CNR exhibits prime performance for all sets of instances up to size 7×7, whereas for the 8×8 instances, GA is only slightly better.

Results for the Guéret & Prins instances are presented in Table 2 and are outstanding, since CNR prevails over all other methods in every problem size. In fact, CNR yields the best solution quality for all instances in the set, except for a single 9×9 instance. Moreover, the solution quality obtained for all instances of size 10×10, is strictly better than that of any other algorithm. Together with TDR, CNR solves the greatest number of instances to optimality. It is clear that CNR is particularly well-suited for this series of problems.

The qualitative performance of CNR is also underlined by the fact that it managed to improve the best known solution for many instances, in both series with existing open problems. Table 3 shows the number of open problems for each series as well as the number of improved ones.

Table 1. Results for the Taillard and Brucker instances. Each column corresponds to a particular method and contains the average and maximum percent deviation from the optimum, as well as the number of instances solved to optimality (in parentheses). In the cases where the optimum is not known, the classical lower bound is used. An asterisk marks the method(s) exhibiting the best performance across a row.

size	TS-A	TS-L	GA	TDR	CNR
4×4	–	$0/0(10)^*$	$0.31/1.84(8)$	$0/0(10)^*$	$0/0(10)^*$
5×5	–	$0.09/0.93(9)$	$1.26/3.72(1)$	$0/0(10)^*$	$0/0(10)^*$
7×7	$0.75/1.71(2)$	$0.56/1.77(6)$	$0.41/0.95(4)$	$0.44/1.92(6)$	$0.25/0.95(6)^*$
10×10	$0.73/1.67(1)$	$0.29/1.41(6)$	$0/0(10)^*$	$2.02/3.19(0)$	$0.69/2.04(2)$
3×3	–	–	$0/0(8)^*$	$0/0(8)^*$	$0/0(8)^*$
4×4	–	–	$0/0(9)^*$	$0/0(9)^*$	$0/0(9)^*$
5×5	–	–	$0.36/2.07(6)$	$0/0(9)^*$	$0/0(9)^*$
6×6	–	–	$0.92/2.27(3)$	$0.71/3.5(6)$	$0.08/0.76(8)^*$
7×7	–	–	$3.82/8.2(4)$	$4.4/11.5(3)$	$3.22/8.2(5)^*$
8×8	–	–	$3.58/7.5(5)^*$	$4.95/11.8(1)$	$3.64/8.2(4)$

Table 2. Results for the Guéret & Prins instances. Each column corresponds to a particular method and contains the number of instances in which the best known results were obtained (or even improved, in the case of CNR), as well as the number of instances solved to optimality.

size	BB	GA	TDR	CNR
3×3	$10/10^*$	$10/10^*$	$10/10^*$	$10/10^*$
4×4	$10/10^*$	$10/10^*$	$10/10^*$	$10/10^*$
5×5	$10/10^*$	$8/8$	$10/10^*$	$10/10^*$
6×6	$9/7$	$2/1$	$10/8^*$	$10/8^*$
7×7	$3/1$	$6/3$	$10/4^*$	$10/4^*$
8×8	$2/1$	$2/1$	$10/4^*$	$10/4^*$
9×9	$1/1$	$0/0$	$8/2$	$9/2^*$
10×10	$0/0$	$0/0$	$0/0$	$10/0^*$

Table 3. For a number of *open* instances (unknown optimal solution), CNR managed to improve the best known solution.

Series	Open Inst.	Improved Inst.
Taillard	0	–
Brucker	8	3
Guéret & Prins	32	12

7   Conclusions

In this work, we describe the general CR framework which allows for the combination of constructive and reparative features into a hybrid abstract search method. The most characteristic feature of the CR framework is that a repair operator is applied on *partial* (rather than complete) inconsistent assignments, obtained by construction. Such an approach retains many of the advantages of both constructive and reparative methods. By specifying some of the abstract parameters of the CR framework, we obtain a search method called CNR-search. The main difference between CNR-search and the relevant approaches in [5, 6] is the nature of the repair operator, which does not perform backtracking. The extensive experimental results presented Sect. 6 clearly exhibit that CNR-search can be effective in a hard combinatorial problem such as open-shop, prevailing even over closely related methods such as TDR.

References

1. Nareyek, A., Smith, S.F., Ohler, C.M.: Integrating local-search advice into refinement search (or not). In: Proceedings of the CP 2003 Third International Workshop on Cooperative Solvers in Constraint Programming. (2003) 29–43
2. Zhang, J., Zhang, H.: Combining local search and backtracking techniques for constraint satisfaction. In: AAAI-96. (1996) 369–374
3. Schaerf, A.: Combining local search and look-ahead for scheduling and constraint satisfaction problems. In: IJCAI-97. (1997) 1254–1259
4. N. Roos, Y.P. Ran, H.v.d.H.: Combining local search and constraint propagation to find a minimal change solution for a dynamic csp. In: AIMSA. (2000)
5. Prestwich, S.: Combining the scalability of local search with the pruning techniques of systematic search. Annals of Operations Research **115** (2002) 51–72
6. Jussien, N., Lhomme, O.: Local search with constraint propagation and conflict-based heuristics. Artificial Intelligence **139** (2002) 21–45
7. Minton, S., Johnston, M., Philips, A., Laird, P.: Minimizing conflicts: a heuristic repair method for constraint satisfaction and scheduling problems. Artificial Intelligence **58** (1992) 161–205
8. Gonzalez, T., Sahni, S.: Open shop scheduling to minimize finish time. Journal of the ACM **23** (1976) 665–679
9. Taillard, E.: Benchmarks for basic scheduling problems. European Journal of Operational Research **64** (1993) 278–285
10. Brucker, P., Hurink, J., Jurich, B., Wostmann, B.: A branch-and-bound algorithm for the open-shop problem. Discrete Applied Mathematics **76** (1997) 43–59
11. Guéret, C., Prins, C.: A new lower bound for the open-shop problem. Annals of Operations Research **92** (1999) 165–183
12. Prins, C.: Competitive genetic algorithms for the open shop scheduling problem. Mathematical Methods of Operations Research **52** (2000) 389–411
13. Alcaide, D., Sicilia, J., Vigo, D.: A tabu search algorithm for the open shop problem. Trobajos de Investigación Operativa **5** (1997) 283–297
14. Liaw, C.F.: A tabu search algorithm for the open shop scheduling problem. Computers and Operations Research **26** (1999) 109–126
15. Guéret, C., Jussien, N., Prins, C.: Using intelligent backtracking to improve branch-and-bound methods: An application to open-shop problems. European Journal of Operational Research **127** (2000) 344–354

Arc Consistency in Binary Encodings of Non-binary CSPs: Theoretical and Experimental Evaluation

Nikos Samaras[1] and Kostas Stergiou[2]

[1] Department of Applied Informatics
University of Macedonia
[2] Department of Information and Communication Systems Engineering
University of the Aegean

Abstract. A Non-binary Constraint Satisfaction Problem (CSP) can be solved by converting the problem into an equivalent binary one and applying well-established binary CSP techniques. An alternative way is to use extended versions of binary techniques directly on the non-binary problem. There are two well-known computational methods in the literature for translating a non-binary CSP to an equivalent binary CSP; (i) the hidden variable encoding and (ii) the dual encoding. In this paper we make a theoretical and empirical study of arc consistency for the binary encodings. An arc consistency algorithm for the hidden variable encoding with optimal $O(ekd^k)$ worst-case time complexity is presented. This algorithm is compared theoretically and empirically to an optimal generalized arc consistency algorithm that operates on the non-binary representation. We also describe an arc consistency algorithm for the dual encoding with $O(e^2 d^k)$ worst-case complexity. This gives an $O(d^k)$ reduction compared to a generic arc consistency algorithm. Both theoretical and computational results show that the encodings are competitive with the non-binary representation for certain classes of non-binary CSPs.

Keywords: Constraint Programming, Constraint Satisfaction, Search

1 Introduction

Many problems from the real world can be represented as CSPs. For example, timetabling, scheduling, resource allocation, planning, circuit design etc. Most of these problems can be naturally modelled using $n-ary$ or non-binary constraints. Research efforts in the past had focused only on binary constraints $(2 - ary)$. The simplicity of dealing with binary constraints compared to $n - ary$ ones is the commonly given explanation. Another reason is the fact that any non-binary CSP can be converted into an equivalent binary one. A review techniques for CSP can be found in [11].

The most often used binary translations are the Dual Encoding (DE) [7] and the Hidden Variable Encoding (HVE) [13]. Recently, the efficiency of the above encodings has been studied theoretically and empirically [1], [2], [10] and [14].

G.A. Vouros and T. Panayiotopoulos (Eds.): SETN 2004, LNAI 3025, pp. 352–361, 2004.

It has been proved that arc consistency (AC) on the HVE achieves exactly the same consistency level as Generalized Arc Consistency (GAC) on the non-binary CSP [14]. Also, AC on the DE achieves a stronger level of consistency than GAC on the non-binary problem.

In this paper an extended study on binary encodings is presented. We describe an algorithm that enforces AC on the HVE of an arbitrary $n - ary$ CSP. We prove that this algorithm has $O(ekd^k)$ time complexity, where e denotes the number of non-binary constraints and d the maximum domain size of the variables. This result gives an $O(d)$ reduction compared to the asymptotic complexity of a generic AC algorithm. We also describe a specialized algorithm that achieves AC on the DE with $O(e^2d^k)$ worst-case time complexity. This is a a significant reduction compared to the $O(e^2d^{2k})$ complexity of a generic optimal AC algorithm. Finally, a computational study of the MAC algorithm is presented. Computational results show that the HVE can be competitive and often superior than the non-binary representation in cases of tight CSPs.

Apart from the theoretical interest, this study is also of practical importance. The similarity of AC on the HVE and GAC on $n - ary$ problems means that a generic GAC algorithm can be encoded as a binary AC algorithm on the HVE without losing anything in terms of consistency level achieved or time complexity. In fact, this is the approach favored in some constraint programming toolkits, including the most commercially successful; ILOG Solver.

The paper is organized as follows. Following this introduction a brief description of mathematical notations is given in Section 2. In Section 3 we study AC for the HVE. In Section 4 we repeat the study for the DE. In Section 5 we present experimental results that demonstrate the practical value of the HVE. Finally, in Section 6 we conclude and discuss future work.

2 Preliminaries

A CSP is stated as a triple (X, D, C), where X is a set of n variables, $D = \{D(x_1), \ldots, D(x_n)\}$ is the domain of each variable $x_i \in X$ and C is a set of c $k - ary$ constraints. Each $k - ary$ constraint c is defined over a set of variables $(x_1, \ldots, x_k)$ by the subset of the *Cartesian* product $D(x_1)\mathrm{x} \ldots \mathrm{x}D(x_k)$ which are consistent tuples. In this way, each constraint c implies the allowed combination of values for the variables $(x_1, \ldots, x_k)$. The verification procedure whether a given tuple is allowed by c or not is called a consistency check. An assignment of a value a to variable $x_i, i = 1, 2, \ldots, n$ is denoted by (x_i, a).

CSPs are usually represented as graphs, where nodes correspond to variables and edges to constraints. A solution of a CSP $G = (X, D, C)$ is an instantiation of the variables $x \in X$, such that all the constraints $c \in C$ are satisfied. A value $a \in D(x_i)$ is consistent with a binary constraint c_{ij} iff $\exists\ b \in D(x_j)$ such that $(a, b) \in c_{ij}$. In this case the value b is called a support for (x_i, a) on the constraint c_{ij}. A value $a \in D(x_i)$ is *valid* iff it has support in all $D(x_j)$ such that constraint $c_{ij} \in C$. A variable x is consistent with a constraint c if $D(x) \neq 0$ and all its values are consistent with c.

A CSP G is arc consistent iff all the values in all the domains are valid. A constraint c_{ij} is arc consistent if $\forall\ a \in D(x_i)$, $\exists\ b \in D(x_j)$ such that b is a support for (x_i, a). In this case b is a support for a on c and a is a support for b on the symmetric constraint (x_2, x_1). A method to achieve AC in G is by removing every value which is not valid. The above definitions have been extended to non-binary CSPs. A non-binary constraint is GAC iff for any variable in the constraint and and any value of that variable, there exist compatible values for all the other variables in the constraint.

The HVE changes the set P of variables x of the original $n - ary$ CSP. The variables of the new binary CSP P are all the original variables plus a new set of variables called hidden variables. Each hidden variable v_c corresponds to a constraint c of the original CSP. The domain of each hidden variable consists of the allowed tuples in the original constraint. For every hidden variable v_c, there is a binary constraint between the v_c and each of the original variables x_i involved in constraint c. Each constraint specifies that the tuple assigned to v_c is consistent with the value assigned to x_i.

In the DE [7] the variables are swapped with constraints and vice versa. Each constraint c of the original n-ary CSP is represented by a dual variable v_c. The domain of each dual variable consists of the set of allowed tuples in the original constraint. Binary constraints between two dual variables v_{c_1} and v_{c_2} exist iff the original constraints c_1 and c_2 share one or more variables. These binary constraints disallow pairs of tuples in which shared variables have different values.

3   Hidden Variable Encoding

Applying GAC on a set of non-binary constraints achieves the same level of consistency as AC on HVE of the same constraints. This means that they both delete the same values from the domains of variables. Several AC algorithms for binary CSPs have been proposed in the literature [4], [9] and [12]. Recently, the non-optimal AC-3 algorithm has been modified to yield an algorithm with optimal complexity [6] and [15]. The AC-3 algorithm can be extended to non-binary CSPs resulting in an optimal GAC algorithm. In this section we will show that AC on the HVE can be achieved with the same worst-case time complexity as GAC. The optimal worst-case time complexity of achieving GAC is $O(ekd^k)$.

The HVE is a binary CSP. One way to apply AC is using the optimal algorithm of [6] and [15]. However, this results in redundant processing. The number of binary constraints in the HVE of a $k - ary$ CSP is ek. For one constraint, AC can be enforced with $O(dd^k)$ worst-case time complexity. To apply AC to whole problem, the time complexity is $O(ekd^{k+1})$. In the following, we describe a binary AC algorithm which operates on the HVE and achieves the same worst-case time complexity as the optimal GAC algorithm. This AC algorithm is based on variable propagation. Figure 1 gives a sketch of the algorithm. $currentSupport_{x,a,v}$ points to the last tuple in $D(v)$ supporting value a of variable x, where x is an original variable constrained with hidden variable v.

```
1 function Propagation
2       While Q ≠ ∅
3             pick hidden variable v from Q
4             for each uninstantiated x constrained with v
5                   if Revise(x,v) = TRUE then
6                         if D(x) = ∅ then return INCONSISTENCY
7                         Q ⟵ vᵢ
8       Return CONSISTENCY

9 function Revise(x,v)
10      DELETION ⟵ FALSE
11            for each a ∈ D(x)
12                  if currentSupportₓ,ₐ,ᵥ is not valid then
13                        if ∃ tuple > currentSupportₓ,ₐ,ᵥ then
14                        currentSupportₓ,ₐ,ᵥ ⟵ tuple
15                        else D(x) ⟵ D(x) \ a
16                        for all v constrained with x remove from D(v)
17                        all tuples that include (x,a)
18                        DELETION ⟵ TRUE
19      Return DELETION
```

Fig. 1. An optimal AC algorithm for the hidden variable encoding.

The algorithm of Figure 1 works as follows. If a value a of original variable $x_i \in X$ has no support then it is deleted from the domain of x_i. In this case each hidden variable v that is constrained with x is added to the queue of the hidden variables Q (line 7 of pseudocode). Then, hidden variables are removed from the Q sequentially and revised (lines 3 to 6). During the execution of the revision of a hidden variable v, the following cases can hold. If there is no supporting tuple for value a of original variable x, then a is removed from $D(x)$ (line 16). In that case, all tuples that include the value a are removed from the domains of the hidden variables that are constrained with original variable x (lines 17 and 18). This can result in new hidden variables being added to the Q and so on. The AC algorithm terminates either (i) if all the values from a domain are deleted, (problem is not AC), or (ii) if the queue Q becomes empty (problem is AC).

3.1 Worst-Case Time Complexity

In this section we discuss the worst-case time complexity of the AC algorithm for HVE.

Theorem 1. *The worst-case time complexity of the AC algorithm on the HVE is $O(ekd^k)$.*

Proof. Each hidden variable v can be revised at most kd times. Particularly, one for every deletion of a value from the domain of one of the k original variables constrained with v. This means that the function *Revise* can be called at most kd times for each hidden variable v. For each value a we perform $O(d)$ checks to verify if $currentSupport_{x,a,v}$ is valid (line 12). In case that $currentSupport_{x,a,v}$ is not valid we try to find a new supporting tuple in $D(v)$ for value a of a variable x. In order to check if a tuple supports value a we need to check if the tuple is valid. If a tuple is not valid then one of its values has been removed from the domain of the corresponding variable. Also, the tuple has been removed from the domain of the hidden variable (see lines 17, 18). In order to check the validity of a tuple, we only need to look at the $O(d^{k-1})$ subtuples that contain the assignment (x, a). Using the variable $currentSupport_{x,a,v}$ at each call of function $Revise$ and for each pair (x, a) we only check tuples that have not been checked before. This means that we can check of the $O(d^{k-1})$ tuples at most once for each value a of an original variable. For kd values we have $O(kd(d + d^{k-1})) = O(kdd^{k-1}) = O(kd^k)$ checks for one hidden variable in the worst-case. In generic case, for e hidden variables, the worst-case time complexity is $O(ekd^k)$. $Q.E.D$

The AC algorithm can be viewed as a GAC algorithm that operates on the non-binary representation. Two changes we need to make; (i) to exchange hidden variables with $n - ary$ constraints in lines 3, 4 and 7 of the above pseudocode and (ii) remove lines 17 and 18. Also, the $currentSupport_{x,a,v}$ will point to the last tuple in constraint c that supports value a of variable x.

4   Dual Encoding

We know ([14]) that AC on the DE is strictly stronger than GAC on the n-ary representation and AC on the HVE. We now describe an algorithm that enforces AC on the DE of a n-ary CSP with $O(e^2d^k)$ worst-case time complexity. If we apply a generic optimal AC algorithm (e.g. AC-2001) then we can enforce AC on the DE with $O(e^2d^{2k})$ worst-case complexity. The $O(e^2d^k)$ complexity of the algorithm we will describe is a considerable improvement. The improvement is based on the the observation that the constraints in the DE are piecewise functional. A constraint c on variables x_i and x_j is called *piecewise* if the domains of x_i and x_j can be partitioned into groups such that the elements of each group behave similarly with respect to c [9]. A *piecewise functional* constraint c on variables x_i and x_j is a constraint where the domains of x_i and x_j can be decomposed into groups such that each group of $D(x_i)$ (resp. $D(x_j)$) is supported by at most one group of $D(x_j)$ (resp. $D(x_i)$) [9].

We can partition the tuples in the domains of dual variables into groups where all tuples in a group are supported by the same tuple in some other variable. If two dual variables v_i and v_j share f original variables of domain size d then we can partition the tuples of each variable in $O(d^f)$ groups where all tuples in a group include the same sub-tuple of the form $< a_1, \ldots, a_f >$. The tuples in such a group s will only be supported by all tuples in a group s' of the other variable, where tuples in s' include the sub-tuple $< a_1, \ldots, a_f >$. In other words, group s in variable v_i will only be supported by a corresponding group in variable v_j (and vice versa). This means that the constraints in the DE are piecewise functional.

Example 1. Assume we have two dual variables v_1 and v_2. v_1 encodes constraint (x_1, x_2, x_3), and v_2 encodes constraint (x_1, x_4, x_5), where the original variables $x_1, \ldots, x_5$ have the domain $\{a, b, c\}$. We can partition the tuples in each dual variable into 3 groups. The first group will include tuples of the form $< a, -, - >$, the second will include tuples of the form $< b, -, - >$, and the third will include tuples of the form $< c, -, - >$. A dash $(-)$ means that the corresponding variable can take any value. Each group is supported only by the corresponding group in the other variable. Note that the tuples of a variable v_i are partitioned in different groups according to each constraint that involves v_i. If there is a additional dual variable v_3 encoding constraint (x_6, x_7, x_3) then the partition of tuples in v_1 according to the constraint between v_1 and v_3 is into groups of the form $< -, -, a >, < -, -, b >, < -, -, c >$.

To achieve the $O(e^2 d^k)$ complexity bound we need an AC algorithm that processes variable-tuple pairs or constraint-tuple pairs, instead of variables (or constraints) as in the algorithm of Figure 1. This is because each time we revise a variable we need to know which tuple deletion caused the revision so that we can avoid redundant checks. For each deletion of a tuple τ from a variable v_i we add to a queue the variable-tuple pair (v_i, τ). Such pairs are removed from the queue sequentially and all variables connected to v_j are revised. Assume the variable-tuple pair (v_i, τ) is removed from the queue. In the revision of a variable v_j connected to v_i we may only check for support the group of v_j that is supported by the group of v_i where τ belongs. All other groups are definitely supported. To check if a group s is supported by a group s' we only need to check if s' is empty or not. If there is at least one tuple in its domain then group s is definitely supported.

In Figure 2 we sketch a specialized AC algorithm for the DE. δ is a set of tuples and it is used to deliver the set of deleted tuples after a revision. The domain $D(v_i)$ of variable v_i denotes the current domain, i.e. the tuples that are valid at any time. $GroupOf(v_i, v_j, \tau)$ is a function that returns the group of variable v_i where tuple τ belongs according to the partition of v_i for constraint C_{ij}. This function can be implemented using a two-dimensional array which for each constraint and each value holds the group where the value belongs. In this way the $GroupOf$ function takes constant time. If a tuple τ is deleted from variable v_i during propagation then the variable-tuple pair (v_i, τ) is added to the queue.

Theorem 2. *The worst-case time complexity of the AC algorithm on the DE is* $O(e^2 d^k)$.

Proof. To measure the complexity of the algorithm we make the same assumptions as in [9], where algorithm AC-5 is described. Namely, the test $s = \emptyset$ of line 1 can be done in constant time. This can be achieved using a counter for each group that decreases when elements are removed from the group. Line 2 $(\delta \leftarrow s' \cap D(v_j))$ of function *Revise* takes $O(d^{k-f})$ operations in the worst case, since the maximum size of the groups in the worst case is $O(d^{k-f})$. Function $Revise(v_i, v_j, \tau, \delta)$ can be called at most $O(d^k)$ times for each constraint, one

function *Propagation*
    While Q is not empty
        pick variable-tuple pair (v_i, τ) from Q
        for each variable v_j constrained with v_i
          $\delta \leftarrow \emptyset$
          if $Revise(v_i, v_j, \tau, \delta) = TRUE$ **then**
             if $D(v_j)$ is empty **then return** INCONSISTENCY
             $D(v_j) = D(v_j) - \delta$
             for each $\tau \in \delta$ put (v_j, τ) in Q
    Return CONSISTENCY

function $Revise(v_i, v_j, \tau, \delta)$
    DELETION $\leftarrow$ FALSE
    $s \leftarrow GroupOf(v_i, v_j, \tau)$
    $s' \leftarrow GroupOf(v_j, v_i, \tau)$
1   **if** $s = \emptyset$
2       $\delta \leftarrow s' \cap D(v_j)$
       DELETION $\leftarrow$ TRUE
    Return DELETION

Fig. 2. An AC algorithm for the DE with low complexity.

for every deletion of a value from the domain of a variable. All operation in *Revise* are executed in constant time except line 2. Line 2 will be executed at most $O(d^f)$ times, once for each group (since each group can become empty only once). Therefore, the $O(d^k)$ calls to *Revise* cost $O(d^f d^{k-f})=O(d^k)$ operations. There are $O(e^2)$ constraints in the dual encoding in the worst case, so the complexity of the algorithm is $O(e^2 d^k)$.   *Q.E.D*

5 Experimental Study

In this section an experimental computational study of search algorithms that run on the HVE compared to their non-binary counterparts is presented. Two major categories of test problems were used in our study; (i) randomly generated problems and (ii) benchmark crossword puzzle generation problems. The constraints in crossword puzzles are by nature tight. We also focus our attention on tight instances of the first category. The reason being that the HVE cannot be practical in problems with loose constraints, where the domains of the hidden variables are prohibitively large.

    Random instances were generated using the extended *model B* as it is described in [5]. We summarize this model generation as follows. A random CSP is defined by the following five input parameters: n - number of variables, d - domain size, k - arity of the constraints, p - density percentage of the generated graph, q - looseness percentage of the constraints. We ensure that the generated graphs are connected. In this study (on randomly generated problems) we compared algorithms MGAC and MHAC, which stands for MAC in the encoding that only instantiates original variables. Both algorithms use the dom/deg heuristic for variable ordering and lexicographic value ordering. We do not include results on algorithms that can instantiate hidden variables as well as original, because experiments showed that such algorithms have very similar behavior to the corresponding algorithms that instantiate only original variables.

Table 1 reports the statistics on the randomly generated test problems used in our study. Classes 1, 2 and 3 are sparse, class 4 is extremely sparse and class 5 is much denser with much looser constraints than the others. Sparse matrices are widely used in scientific computations, especially in large-scale applications. All problems are from the hard phase transition region. For each class we ran 100 instances. The CPU times are in seconds. For nodes and checks, we give mean numbers for the executed instances. The symbol M stands for x10^6.

Table 1. Comparison of algorithms MGAC and MHAC on sparse random CSPs.

	MGAC	MHAC
class 1: $n = 30$, $d = 6$, $k = 3$, $p = 1.847$, $q = 50$		
nodes	3430	3430
sec	2.08	1.90
checks	20M	14M
class 2: $n = 75$, $d = 5$, $k = 3$, $p = 0.177$, $q = 41$		
nodes	7501	7501
sec	4.09	3.41
checks	24M	15M
class 3: $n = 50$, $d = 20$, $k = 3$, $p = 0.3$, $q = 5$		
nodes	1488	1488
sec	64.15	28.10
checks	173M	110M
class 4: $n = 50$, $d = 10$, $k = 5$, $p = 0.001$, $q = 0.5$		
nodes	16496	16496
sec	74.72	22.53
checks	847M	628M
class 5: $n = 20$, $d = 10$, $k = 3$, $p = 5$, $q = 40$		
nodes	4834	4834
sec	5.75	8.15
checks	151M	119M

From the results of Table 1 we can see that MHAC performs fewer checks than MGAC in all classes. This is due to the ability of MHAC to detect a domain wipeout early at dead ends. MHAC performs better than MGAC on the sparser CSPs in terms of CPU time. This is reversed in the denser class 5. As the number of constraints in the problems is increased the phase transition moves to a location where the constraints are loose (i.e. they allow many tuples). As a result, the overhead of updating the domains of the hidden variables overweighs the gains of early domain wipeout detections.

Table 2. CPU times of algorithms MGAC, MHAC and hMAC on benchmark crossword puzzles.

puzzle	n	m	MGAC	MHAC	hMAC
15.05	78	181	3	3.1	2.2
15.07	74	193	670	335	376m
15.08	84	186	2.32	2.27	2.89
15.09	82	187	2.24	2.3	2.45
19.01	128	301	7.6	7.3	6.9
19.02	118	296	198	204	—
19.06	128	287	5.9	4.7	5.8
19.07	134	291	3.4	3.4	4.4
19.08	130	295	—	—	5.45
19.09	130	295	3.64	5	4.2
puzzleC	78	189	77.5	107	—
6×6	12	36	84	55	64
7×7*	14	49	120m	75m	96m
8×8*	16	64	45m	29m	42m

Crossword puzzle generation problems have been used for the evaluation of algorithms and heuristics for CSPs [3] and binary encodings of non-binary problems [1] and [14]. In crossword puzzle generation we try to construct puzzles for a given number of words and a given grid which has to be filled in with words. Particularly, in the non-binary representation there is a variable for each letter to be filled in and a $n - ary$ constraint for each set of k variables that form a word in the puzzle. The domain size of each variable can be the lower case letters from the English alphabet. In this case the domain size is 26. The allowed tuples of such a constraint are all the words with k letters in the dictionary used. There are 26^k possible combinations of letters. This means that the constraints are very tight.

Tables 2 shows the performance of the algorithms MGAC and MHAC on various crossword puzzles. We solved hard puzzles from [8]. Apart from algorithms that instantiate only original variable we tested a version of MAC which may also instantiate hidden variables. This algorithm is denoted by hMAC. All algorithms use the dom/deg heuristic for variable ordering. For each benchmark we give the number of words, n and the number of blanks m. All CPU times are in seconds. Benchmark problems marked by (*) are insoluble. An em-dash (−) is placed wherever the method did not manage to find a solution within 5 hours of CPU time.

From Table 2 we can observe that MHAC usually performed better than MGAC in terms of CPU time. MHAC and MGAC visit exactly the same number of nodes. In many cases hMAC managed to find a different solution than MGAC and MHAC. This result means that we can benefit from a method that instantiates hidden variables. In puzzle 19.08 hMAC managed to find a solution fast, while the other MAC based algorithms thrashed. Further investigation in the possibilities offered by such algorithms is required.

6   Conclusion

In this paper a theoretical and empirical investigation of arc consistency algorithms for binary encodings of non-binary CSPs is presented. We proved that the worst-case time complexity of AC on the HVE is $O(ekd^k)$, which is the same as the complexity of an optimal GAC on the non-binary representation. We also presented an AC algorithm on the DE with $O(e^2d^k)$ complexity. Computational results showed that binary encodings are competitive with the non-binary representation for tight classes of non-binary constraints. In order to obtain more specific conclusions about the practical performance of algorithms on the encodings, a more extensive computational study is needed. Also, we intend to investigate the implications and possibilities offered by the choice to instantiate hidden variables in the HVE.

References

1. F. Bacchus and P. Van Beek. On the Conversion between Non-Binary and Binary Constraint Satisfaction Problems. In *Proceedings of AAAI'98*, pages 310–318.
2. F. Bacchus, X. Chen, P. van Beek and T. Walsh. Binary vs. Non-Binary CSPs. Artificial Intelligence, 2002.
3. A. Beacham, X. Chen, J. Sillito and P. Van Beek. Constraint Programming Lessons Learned from Crossword Puzzles. In *Proceedings of the 14th Canadian Conference in AI'2001, Canada*.
4. C. Bessière, E. C. Freuder and J. C. Régin. Using Inference to reduce Arc Consistency Computation. In *Proceedings of IJCAI'95*, pages 592–599.
5. C. Bessière, P. Meseguer, E. C. Freuder and J. Larrosa. On Forward Checking for Non-binary Constraint Satisfaction. In *Proceedings of CP'99*, pages 88–102.
6. C. Bessière and J. C. Régin. Refining the basic constraint propagation algorithm. In *Proceedings of IJCAI'2001*.
7. R. Dechter and J. Pearl. Tree Clustering for Constraint Networks. *Artificial Intelligence*, 38:353–366, 1989.
8. M. Ginsberg, M. Frank, M. Halpin and M. Torrance. Search Lessons learned from Crossword Puzzles . In *Proceedings of AAAI'90*, pages 210–215.
9. P. Van Hentenryck, Y. Deville and C. Teng. A Generic Arc Consistency Algorithm and its specializations. *Artificial Intelligence*, 57:291–321, 1992.
10. N. Mamoulis and K. Stergiou. Solving non-binary CSPs using the Hidden Variable Encoding. In *Proceedings of CP'2001*.
11. I. Miguel and Q. Shen. Solution Techniques for Constraint Satisfaction Problems: Foundations. *Artificial Intelligence Review*, 15:243–267, 2001.
12. R. Mhor and G. Masini. Arc and Path Consistency revisited. *Artificial Intelligence*, 28:225–233, 1986.
13. F. Rossi, C. Petrie, and V. Dhar. On the equivalence of constraint satisfaction problems. In *Proceedings of ECAI'90*, pages 550–556.
14. K. Stergiou and T. Walsh. Encodings of Non-Binary Constraint Satisfaction Problems. In *Proceedings of AAAI'99*, pages 163–168.
15. Y. Zhang and R. Yap. Making AC-3 an optimal algorithm. In *Proceedings of IJCAI'2001*.

Inherent Choice in the Search Space of Constraint Satisfaction Problem Instances

George Boukeas, Panagiotis Stamatopoulos,
Constantinos Halatsis, and Vassilis Zissimopoulos

Department of Informatics and Telecommunications, University of Athens
Panepistimiopolis, Athens 15784, Greece
{boukeas,takis,halatsis,vassilis}@di.uoa.gr

Abstract. Constructive methods obtain solutions to constraint satisfaction problem instances by iteratively extending consistent partial assignments. In this research, we study the *solution paths* in the search
space of constructive methods and examine their distribution among the
assignments of the search space. By properly employing the *entropy* of
this distribution, we derive measures of the average amount of *choice*
available within the search space for constructing a solution. The derived quantities directly reflect both the number and the distribution
of solutions, an "open question" in the phase transition literature. We
show that *constrainedness*, an acknowledged predictor of computational
cost, is an aggregate measure of choice deficit. This establishes a connection between an algorithm-independent property of the search space,
such as the inherent choice available for constructing a solution, and the
algorithm-dependent amount of resources required to actually construct
a solution.

Keywords: search, constraint satisfaction, mathematical foundations

1 Introduction

A constraint satisfaction problem consists of a set of variables and a set of constraints. A variable which has been given a value is said to be *instantiated* and
a set of i instantiated variables is an *assignment* α_i of size i. Assignments α_i
which satisfy all problem constraints are called *consistent* and assignments α_n
in which all n problem variables are instantiated are called *complete*. Given an
instance of a constraint satisfaction problem, the goal is to obtain a consistent
complete assignment (a solution) or to prove that none exists. In order to accomplish this goal, *constructive* methods iteratively extend consistent partial
assignments, whereas methods based on *repair* iteratively transform inconsistent complete assignments. The search spaces explored by methods belonging to
these categories overlap but do not coincide. The focus here is on constructive
methods but the fact remains that any particular search space offers a set of
alternative ways for obtaining a solution, a set of *solution paths*.

This research is prompted by the observation that both the number and distribution of solution paths play a significant role. A search space with scarce

G.A. Vouros and T. Panayiotopoulos (Eds.): SETN 2004, LNAI 3025, pp. 362–370, 2004.

solution paths offers very little choice for constructing a solution: a correct decision must be made at almost every choice point due to the lack of alternatives. On the other extreme, a search space with an abundance of solution paths offers ample choice for constructing a solution: decisions made at choice points are almost inconsequential due to the multitude of alternatives. The aim of this research is to quantify and investigate the amount of choice inherently available within the search space of a problem instance for constructing a solution.

In the context of constructive methods, Sect. 2 describes the composition and size of the search space, along with the notion of paths for constructing assignments. Our view of the search space is similar to the *deep structure* of [1] and allows for an abstraction away from problem-specific and algorithm-dependent features. The structure of the search space, that is the distribution of solution paths therein, is discussed in Sect. 3. By properly employing the *entropy* of this distribution, we derive measures of the average amount of choice inherently available at each level of the search space for constructing a solution, as explained in Sects. 3 and 4. Aggregate quantities over the entire search space are discussed in Sect. 5. Recall that entropy is a measure of information and uncertainty but it is also a measure of choice [2]. Relevant information-theoretic approaches have been employed in order to characterize system structure in [3]. The introduced measures directly reflect not only the number but also the distribution of solutions to a problem instance. In fact, Sect. 6 explains how the average amount of choice available on each level of the search space is identical only among instances with isomorphic solution sets. In Sect. 7, the nature of constrainedness [4–6] as an aggregate measure of choice deficit is elucidated, which serves to explain the successful application of constrainedness as a generic predictor of computational cost and yields a number of contributions. Throughout this paper, all proofs have necessarily been omitted due to space restrictions.

2   The Search Space of Constructive Methods

The search space of a problem instance consists of the complete set of states that may be explored in the attempt to obtain a solution to the problem instance. In the case of constructive methods, obtaining a solution is apparently synonymous to *constructing* a solution and the set of states constituting the search space is the set of assignments α_i, with size i ranging from 0 (empty assignment) to n (complete assignments). This is because the process of constructing a solution is initiated at assignment α_0, where no variables are instantiated, encounters a particular assignment α_i after the performance of i successive variable instantiations and eventually leads to a complete assignment α_n belonging to the solution set $\mathcal{S}$. The notion of search space *paths* is pertinent to this constructive process: a path is an ordered set of instantiations. There are $n!$ paths towards any complete assignment α_n, corresponding to the $n!$ distinct ways of ordering the instantiations of problem variables. Each path is essentially a different way of constructing a complete assignment and therefore all paths are disjoint, although they may overlap. Figure 1 illustrates the search space for a small problem in-

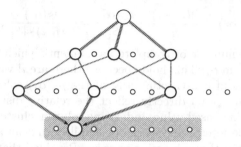

Fig. 1. The search space of a constructive method for instances with $n = 3$ binary variables. Circles at level i denote assignments of size i and lines between them denote variable instantiations. The $n!$ alternative paths available for constructing a particular complete assignment are also depicted. The complete assignments in the shaded rectangle form the search space of a repair method.

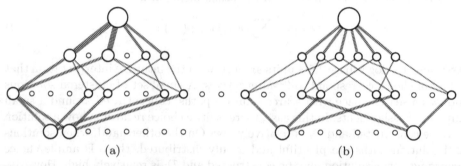

Fig. 2. The search space and solution paths for instances with $n = 3$ binary variables and $|\mathcal{S}| = 2$ solutions, with the distance between the solutions being (a) minimal: one instantiation and (b) maximal: n instantiations. Circle area and line thickness reflect the distribution of solution paths among assignments and instantiations.

stance, as well as the alternative paths available for constructing a particular complete assignment. Note how the assignments in the search space are partitioned into disjoint levels according to size: there are $C(n, i) \cdot 2^i$ assignments of size i, corresponding to the $C(n, i) = n!/i!(n - i)!$ different ways of selecting i variables out of n and the 2^i different instantiations of these i binary variables.

3   Choice in the Search Space

A search space inherently offers *choice* to any constructive algorithm in the sense that it contains a set of alternative paths available for constructing a solution. In the search space of a problem instance with n variables, there are $n!$ paths towards any complete assignment and a total of $n!|\mathcal{S}|$ solution paths. Figure 2 contains the search spaces of two problem instances with $n = 3$ binary variables and $|\mathcal{S}| = 2$ solutions, as well as all solution paths contained therein. Evidently, the solution paths need not be evenly distributed throughout the search space. The fraction $\wp(\alpha_i)$ of solution paths intersecting assignment α_i is:

$$\wp(\alpha_i) = \frac{i!(n-i)!}{n!} \cdot \frac{\rho_S(\alpha_i)}{|S|} = \frac{\rho_S(\alpha_i)}{C(n,i) \cdot |S|} , \tag{1}$$

where $\rho_S(\alpha_i)$ is the number of complete assignments which are solutions of S and are reachable from α_i. This holds because there are $i!$ ways of constructing α_i and $(n-i)!$ ways of constructing any of the $\rho_S(\alpha_i)$ solutions from α_i. By definition, $\rho_S(\alpha_i)$ and $\wp(\alpha_i)$ directly reflect the relative distances between the solutions in S, with increased values indicating solution clustering under α_i. The $\wp(\alpha_i)$ fraction can be interpreted as the probability that an arbitrarily selected solution is constructed through assignment α_i. Provided that a solution exists, $\sum_{\alpha_i} \wp(\alpha_i) = 1$ holds for every level i. Essentially, the $\wp(\alpha_i)$ fractions describe the distribution of solution paths among the assignments of level i. The entropy of this distribution, called *solution path diversity* $\mathcal{D}_i$, is a concise quantitative measure of the average amount of choice inherently available in the search space for constructing a solution through the assignments of level i:

$$\mathcal{D}_i = -\sum_{\alpha_i} \wp(\alpha_i) \log \wp(\alpha_i) . \tag{2}$$

Assuming the log is base 2, its units are *bits*, with the intuitive interpretation that x bits of choice correspond to 2^x alternatives. A small set of clustered solutions induces a search space with scarce solution paths, concentrated around a small number of assignments. In this case, there is little choice regarding how a solution may be constructed and $\mathcal{D}_i$ is relatively low. On the other hand, when solutions and solution paths are plentiful and evenly distributed, there is ample choice regarding how a solution may be constructed and $\mathcal{D}_i$ is relatively high. However, bear in mind that solution path diversity $\mathcal{D}_i$ is a *relevant* quantity: its value becomes meaningful only when compared to the *general path diversity* $\mathcal{G}_i$, a measure of the average amount of choice available for constructing any complete assignment (not necessarily a solution), through the assignments of level i:

$$\mathcal{G}_i = \log \left[C(n,i) \cdot 2^i \right] = i + \log C(n,i) . \tag{3}$$

The general path diversity reflects the size of the search space (the total number of paths) and determines the maximal attainable value for the solution path diversity. The maximum is observed in the case where all complete assignments are solutions and all paths are thus solution paths. In every other case, there exists a *choice deficit* $\mathcal{H}_i$ in the average amount of choice available for constructing a solution through the assignments of level i:

$$\mathcal{H}_i = \mathcal{G}_i - \mathcal{D}_i . \tag{4}$$

The definition of the choice deficit $\mathcal{H}_i$ can be interpreted as "the difference between the greatest amount of choice that can possibly be available at level i and the amount of choice actually available at level i". The deficit rises as the solution path diversity $\mathcal{D}_i$ drops. It is maximal when there are no solutions and minimal when there are no infeasible assignments. It also rises along with the size of the search space, which manifests itself through the general path diversity

$\mathcal{G}_i$. The choice deficit $\mathcal{H}_i$ is a monotonic increasing function with respect to the search level i, due to the fact that solution paths tend to spread and become scarce at deeper levels of the search space.

4   Conditional Measures of Choice

A conditional version of solution path diversity $\mathcal{D}_i$ can be derived using the distribution of solution paths among the *instantiations* leading to level i. The conditional entropy of this distribution is called *conditional solution path diversity* $\Delta\mathcal{D}_i$ and is a more refined measure (in *bits per level* units) of the average amount of choice inherently available for constructing a solution through the assignments of level i, having reached level $i-1$. It is a monotonic decreasing function with respect to i. The direct definition of $\Delta\mathcal{D}_i$ is straightforward but it is more convenient to express it in terms of $\mathcal{D}_i$, since it can be proved that:

$$\Delta\mathcal{D}_i = \mathcal{D}_i - \mathcal{D}_{i-1} + \log i . \tag{5}$$

The $\log i$ term appears because the search space implicitly contains all possible variable orderings, offering alternative paths for constructing an assignment.

The *conditional general path diversity* $\Delta\mathcal{G}_i$ at level i, is a measure of the average amount of choice available for constructing a complete assignment through the assignments of level i, having reached level $i-1$, and is a monotonic decreasing function with respect to i:

$$\Delta\mathcal{G}_i = \mathcal{G}_i - \mathcal{G}_{i-1} + \log i = 1 + \log(n - i + 1) . \tag{6}$$

This finally leads to the definition of the *conditional choice deficit* $\Delta\mathcal{H}_i$, a monotonic increasing function with respect to i:

$$\Delta\mathcal{H}_i = \Delta\mathcal{G}_i - \Delta\mathcal{D}_i = \mathcal{H}_i - \mathcal{H}_{i-1} . \tag{7}$$

It is interesting to read (5), (6) and (7) as: "choice (or deficit) at level i minus choice (or deficit) removed having reached level $i-1$," which offers an intuitive explanation as to why these conditional measures are refined enough to measure choice (or deficit) at a single level.

5   The Sum Property

Conditional measures of choice pertain exclusively to a single level of the search space. It is therefore acceptable to sum such conditional measures over all levels, obtaining aggregate quantities. Summing (5) over all levels yields the *total solution path diversity* $\mathbf{D}^n$, which is the total amount of choice available for constructing a solution. Not surprisingly, $\mathbf{D}^n$ depends upon $n!|\mathcal{S}|$, the number of solution paths:

$$\mathbf{D}^n(\mathcal{S}) = \sum_{i=1}^{n} \Delta\mathcal{D}_i = \log(n!|\mathcal{S}|) . \tag{8}$$

Table 1. Conditional and aggregate measures of choice and deficit for the two instances of Fig. 2. The total amounts of choice $\mathbf{D}^n$ and deficit $\mathbf{H}^n$, which are identical for both instances, are expended in a different manner among the individual search space levels, due to the difference between the two instances in the distribution of solutions.

i	$\Delta \mathcal{G}_i$	$\Delta \mathcal{D}_i$		$\Delta \mathcal{H}_i$	
		2(a)	2(b)	2(a)	2(b)
1	2.58	1.92	2.58	0.67	0.00
2	2.00	1.33	1.00	0.67	1.00
3	1.00	0.33	0.00	0.67	1.00
sum	5.58	3.58	3.58	2.00	2.00

Note that $\mathbf{D}^n$ exhibits the *sum property*: it remains invariant among problem instances with the same number of variables n and the same number of solutions $|\mathcal{S}|$, even though it is an aggregate quantity comprising individual, per-level amounts of choice $\Delta \mathcal{D}_i$ which need not be identical among all such instances. In the same manner, summing (7) over all levels yields the *total choice deficit* $\mathbf{H}^n$, for which the sum property also holds:

$$\mathbf{H}^n(\mathcal{S}) = \sum_{i=1}^{n} \Delta \mathcal{H}_i = \sum_{i=1}^{n} \Delta \mathcal{G}_i - \sum_{i=1}^{n} \Delta \mathcal{D}_i = n - \log |\mathcal{S}| . \tag{9}$$

To provide a concrete example, conditional and aggregate measures of choice and deficit for the instances in Fig. 2 have been computed and included in Table 1. Interpreting the numbers in Table 1 using Fig. 2 is instructive. Notice how there is no choice deficit $\Delta \mathcal{H}_1$ for instance 2(b) since there are no instantiations at that level not included in a solution path. Note also how, for the same instance, there is no choice $\Delta \mathcal{D}_3$ since, having reached an assignment at the second level, there is only one instantiation in each case leading to a solution. Finally, notice how one bit of choice for $\Delta \mathcal{D}_2$ corresponds to exactly two alternative instantiations extending each assignment at the first level. This is half of the instantiations generally available for extending each assignment at this level and this is why the choice deficit $\Delta \mathcal{H}_2$ is equal to $\Delta \mathcal{D}_2$ and half of $\Delta \mathcal{G}_2$.

6   The Distribution of Solutions

The search spaces in Fig. 2 both correspond to instances with $n = 3$ variables and $|\mathcal{S}| = 2$ solutions. The number of solution paths is identical for the two instances and so is the aggregate amount of choice $\mathbf{D}^n$ available for constructing a solution. It is only the relative distance between the solutions in $\mathcal{S}$ which differentiates the two instances and yet the distribution of solution paths in the search space is notably dissimilar. The values of $\mathcal{D}_i$ for these instances are also dissimilar since $\mathcal{D}_i$ is, by definition, sensitive to the relative distances between the solutions and the distribution of solution paths (this carries on to $\Delta \mathcal{D}_i$, $\mathcal{H}_i$ and $\Delta \mathcal{H}_i$ as well). It turns out that the aggregate amount of choice $\mathbf{D}^n$ and the way this

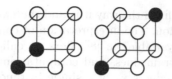

Fig. 3. The distribution of solutions for the two example instances of Fig. 2, with the distance between the solutions being (a) minimal: one instantiation and (b) maximal: n instantiations.

is distributed among the search space levels through the $\Delta\mathcal{D}_i$'s coincides only among *isomorphic* instances. In order to obtain a definition of isomorphism, map the 2^n complete assignments of a n-variable problem instance to the 2^n vertices of a n-hypercube. To map the solution set $\mathcal{S}$, let the vertices which correspond to solutions be colored black and the rest of the vertices be colored white. Such a colored hypercube reflects the *distribution of solutions*, the relative distances between them. For example, Fig. 3 contains the distribution of solutions for the two example instances of Fig. 2, with the distance between the solutions being (a) minimal: one instantiation and (b) maximal: n instantiations. Two problem instances are *isomorphic* iff the corresponding distributions of solutions (colored hypercubes) are isomorphic. It is straightforward to show that if two instances S and T are isomorphic, then for every level i of the search space it holds that $\Delta\mathcal{D}_i^S = \Delta\mathcal{D}_i^T$. In addition, the inverse has also been invariably observed (no formal proof is currently available): given two instances S and T, if for every level i of the search space it holds that $\Delta\mathcal{D}_i^S = \Delta\mathcal{D}_i^T$, then S and T are isomorphic. It is not uncommon for entropy to be an invariant of isomorphic structures [7]. The point is that solution path diversity, the measure of the average amount of choice available in a level of the search space for constructing a solution, is *necessary and sufficient for discriminating between non-isomorphic instances*. In contrast to cruder aggregate measures which only reflect the number of solutions, it is a refined indicator of their distribution. This is a significant development in itself and will also prove useful in the following section.

7   Constrainedness

The *constrainedness* κ of an ensemble of problem instances is defined as:

$$\kappa \equiv 1 - \frac{\log\langle|\mathcal{S}|\rangle}{n}, \tag{10}$$

where $\langle|\mathcal{S}|\rangle$ is the average number of solutions over all instances of the ensemble and n is the number of variables in each instance [4]. Ensemble constrainedness has been successfully employed in a variety of problem classes as a predictor of computational cost. Its wide applicability is due to the fact that the parameters it involves, that is number of variables n and average number of solutions $\langle|\mathcal{S}|\rangle$, are problem-independent. However, there exists no formal justification as to why constrainedness is defined the way it is and therefore no formal explanation for its successful application. The interpretation of constrainedness as "average information content per variable" in [8] offers no enlightenment regarding the connection between constrainedness and computational cost. Nevertheless, using (9) and the constrainedness κ_p of a single instance p, an interpretation in terms of the total choice deficit $\mathbf{H}^n$ is provided.

$$\kappa_p = 1 - \frac{\log|S_p|}{n} = \frac{n - \log|S_p|}{n} = \frac{\mathbf{H}^n(S_p)}{n} . \tag{11}$$

Evidently, instance constrainedness κ_p is the average choice deficit per search space level or, in other words, the deficit of choice available in the search space for constructing a solution, averaged over all levels of the search space. When it comes to ensemble constrainedness κ, choice deficit is also averaged over all instances in the ensemble. This result reveals that constrainedness is a reliable and widely applicable predictor of computational cost because it reflects an intrinsic property of search spaces: deficit in the amount of choice available for constructing a solution. This verifies the claim in [4] about constrainedness being "a fundamental property of problem ensembles". Note that the amount of choice offered in the search space of an instance is independent of the manner in which a particular algorithm may make use of such choice. Choice deficit characterizes the search space of an instance and is insufficient, by itself, for determining the exact value of computational cost. However, there is logic to *comparing* the choice deficit among instances: the lower the amount of choice available for constructing a solution path, the higher the amount of resources an algorithm is expected to expend in order to obtain such a path and vice versa.

Unfortunately, both $\mathbf{H}^n$ and κ suffer from the same deficiency: they are not refined enough to *distinguish between instances with non-isomorphic solution sets*. They are aggregate quantities which depend only on the number of solutions while failing to retain any information about their distribution. According to [9], it is an important "open question" to derive a "better specification of the number and location of solutions". Having introduced the individual quantities $\Delta\mathcal{D}_i$'s and $\Delta\mathcal{H}_i$'s, a direct reflection of the distribution of solutions is now available. Moreover, it can be argued along the lines of [3], that a single aggregate quantity such as the sum of $\mathcal{H}_i$'s can capture additional information about the distribution of solutions. In such a case, the instances offering the least amount of choice (among all instances with the same number of solutions $|S|$) and are expected to require increased computational effort are the ones in which the solutions are *clustered*, which is in accordance with [10].

8   Conclusions

The solution set S of a n-variable constraint satisfaction problem instance induces a search space common to all constructive methods. This search space contains $n!|S|$ solution paths, distinct alternative instantiation orderings which lead to solutions in S. The structure of the solution set S directly determines the structure of the search space, that is the distribution of solution paths among the assignments of each search space level. The entropy of this distribution yields a measure of the average amount of choice available at each search space level for constructing a solution. Aggregate measures of choice for the entire search space, as well as measures of choice deficit are also defined. Such application of entropy as a means to study the structure of problem instance search spaces is completely novel and so is the notion of choice which is inherently available within the search space for constructing solutions. All the derived quantities directly reflect not only the number but also the distribution of solutions and are, in fact, refined enough to distinguish between instances with non-isomorphic solution sets. This is a contribution to research in *phase transitions*, where structural parameters of problem instances are investigated in order to predict the expected computational cost of solving them [11] and the "better specification of the number and location of solutions" is considered to be an "open question" [9]. Another contribution of this work is the interpretation of constrainedness, an acknowledged predictor of computational cost [4–6], as an aggregate measure of choice deficit. This establishes a connection between an algorithm-independent property of the search space, such as the inherent choice available for constructing a solution, and the algorithm-dependent amount of resources required to actually construct a solution. It also underlines how the simplicity of a measure such as constrainedness incurs certain limitations and explains how these can be alleviated using the introduced measures of inherent choice.

References

1. Williams, C., Hogg, T.: Exploiting the deep structure of constraint problems. Artificial Intellingence **70** (1994) 73–117
2. Shannon, C.E.: A mathematical theory of communication. The Bell Systems Technical Journal **27** (1948) Reprinted with corrections.
3. Crutchfield, J., Feldman, D.: Regularities unseen, randomness observed: Levels of entropy convergence. Chaos **13** (2003) 25–54
4. Gent, I.P., MacIntyre, E., Prosser, P., Walsh, T.: The constrainedness of search. In: AAAI/IAAI. Volume 1. (1996) 246–252
5. Gent, I.P., MacIntyre, E., Prosser, P., Walsh, T.: The constrainedness of arc consistency. In: Principles and Practice of Constraint Programming. (1997) 327–340
6. Walsh, T.: The constrainedness knife-edge. In: AAAI/IAAI. (1998) 406–411
7. Ornstein, D.: Bernoulli shifts with the same entropy are isomorphic. Adv. in Math. **4** (1970) 337–352
8. Slaney, J.: Is there a constrainedness knife-edge? In: Proceedings of the 14th European Conference on Artificial Intelligence. (2000) 614–618
9. Hogg, T.: Refining the phase transitions in combinatorial search. Artificial Intelligence **81** (1996) 127–154
10. Parkes, A.J.: Clustering at the phase transition. In: AAAI/IAAI. (1997) 340–345
11. Hogg, T., Huberman, B., Williams, C.: Phase transitions and the search problem. Artificial Intelligence **81** (1996) 1–15

Part-of-Speech Tagging in Molecular Biology Scientific Abstracts Using Morphological and Contextual Statistical Information

Gavrilis Dimitris and Dermatas Evangelos

Department of Electrical & Computer Engineering, University of Patras
26500 Patras, Hellas
gavrilis@george.wcl2.ee.upatras.gr

Abstract. In this paper a probabilistic tagger for molecular biology related abstracts is presented and evaluated. The system consists of three modules: a rule based molecular-biology names detector, an unknown words handler, and a Hidden Markov model based tagger which are used to annotate the corpus with an extended set of grammatical and molecular biology tags. The complete system has been evaluated using 500 randomly selected abstracts from the MEDLINE database. The F-score for the molecular-biology names detector was 0.95, and the annotation rate was greater than 93% in all experiments using the Viterbi algorithm. The best annotation rate of 97.34% is achieved using a Pubmed dictionary.

Keywords: Part-of-Speech Tagging, Natural Language Processing, HMM.

1 Introduction

In recent years a huge amount of molecular-biology knowledge has been collected and freely distributed to the research community through Internet services (e.g. MEDLINE) in electronic form. The number of scientific papers is growing extremely fast, thus efficient information extraction and data mining processes is used to reduce the information retrieval time, minimizing also the presence of irrelevant data. In the near future, data processing methods will produce automatically molecular-biology interaction networks by processing the enormous size of knowledge collected in the scientific papers. The complexity of this problem requires the development of complex and multi-level corpus processing systems. The general structure of such systems is the following: an accurate and efficient recognizer of the important entities, proteins, genes, interaction verbs, cell type and chemical names and their synonyms in free text [1-9] detects the most important tokens, a Part-of-Speech tagger annotates the corpus in the level of sentences, a semantic analyzer identifies the relations and interactions between molecular biology tokens and a network contractor unifies the distributed scientific knowledge describing the molecular-biology interactions for each gene.

As a first step towards automatic information extraction on various interactions between biological entities in Molecular Biology scientific abstracts (e.g. MEDLINE),

G.A. Vouros and T. Panayiotopoulos (Eds.): SETN 2004, LNAI 3025, pp. 371–380, 2004.
© Springer-Verlag Berlin Heidelberg 2004

this paper presents a natural language processing system for biological entities identification, e.g. gene, protein, chemical, cell and organism names, and a part-of-speech tagger based on the hidden Markov model (HMM). The probabilistic tagger annotates scientific abstracts according to an extended set of grammatical and biology-chemical-species related tags. Few probabilistic assumptions have been used to annotate the unknown words. The reliability of the assumptions has been verified in extended experiments.

A few biological name entity recognition tools exist which were developed as an integral part of different information extraction applications. Some of the tools use statistical or machine learning approaches in identifying names from biological texts. Collier et al [7] presents the results of extracting technical terminology from MEDLINE abstracts and texts in the molecular-biology domain using a linear interpolating hidden Markov model (HMM). The training set used in their experiments consisted of 100 Medline abstracts. The results are given as F-scores, combining recall and precision rates. A Support Vector Machine application to a biomedical named entity recognition problem is presented in [1]. The training and evaluation was performed on the 670 abstracts of the GENIA corpus giving F-score rates of 50.2.

The recognition of newly proposed technical terms identified initially as proper names is studied in [6]. The proposed rule-based method is applied to unknown words, coinages, long compound words, and variations in expression. The experiments carried out by processing 30 abstracts on the SH3 domain and 50 abstracts on the signal transduction domain retrieved from MEDLINE. Hanisch et al [3] shown that dictionary-based recognition of names leads to poor sensitivity when simply searching methods are used, whereas naïve search of protein synonyms incurs a loss in specificity. To face this problem they build a large, automatically created, "curated" dictionary of protein and gene names from the HUGO nomenclature, SWICCPROT and TREMBL databases, with the corresponding token-based search algorithm. The combined dictionary consists of approximately 38,200 entries with 151,700 synonyms.

In the symbolic approach of Narayaswamy etal [4] a set of manually developed rules exploit surface clues and simple linguistic and domain knowledge in identifying the relevant terms in the biomedical papers. In the recognition process context and surrounding words were used for categorization of named entities in six classes (protein/gene, protein/gene parts, chemical, chemical parts, source, general biology) and find the results obtained are encouraging. Preliminary experiments on a collection of 55 manually annotated MEDLINE-abstracts gave precision, recall and f-score of 90.39%, 95.64%, and 92.94% respectively.

Improving the processing speed by avoiding part-of-speech taggers and syntactic parsers Kazukiro and Javed [8] proposed hand-crafted rules based on heuristics and a dictionary to extract protein names from biological texts. The dictionary, consists of 114,876 protein names and their synonyms, is created by combining the information included in the SWISSPROT, the TrEMBL and the WordNet dictionaries. The evaluation gives best precision, recall and f-score in 70, 92 and 79.5 per cent respectively.

The structure of this paper is as follows: In the next section a detailed presentation of the rule based molecular-biology names detector, the unknown words handler and the probabilistic tagger for molecular biology related abstracts is given. A presentation

of the corpus and biology names databases used to build-up and to evaluate the proposed automatic system is described in section 3. In the last part of this work the experimental results are presented and discussed.

2 System Description

The complete system consists of a rule based molecular-biology names detector, an
unknown-word tag handler, and the stochastic tagger. The detector recognizes names
such as genes, proteins, mRNA, Cell types and biology functions using a look-up table
of gene/protein names and a dictionary of common words of the English language. A
set of token-based context sensitive rules is used to resolve ambiguities appearing in
abstract corpora. Assuming that the remaining unknown tokens are names from biology, chemical, species domain the appropriate set of expected tags is assigned to the
unresolved tokens. In the last processing module an HMM-based tagger extracts the
most probable sequence of tags, which describes the grammatical structure of each
sentence enriched by molecular biology related tags.

2.1 Molecular-Biology Names Detector

The molecular-biology names detector (MBND) is based on rules and a reference
database containing 217 Kwords gene/protein names obtained from the NCBI's LocusLink names database. The detector recognizes names as genes, proteins, mRNA,
Cell types and biology functions. A dictionary of 1930 words, extracted form the
Wall-street Journal corpus and from other sources, is used to recognize the common
words of the English language. The MBND general architecture is shown in fig. 1.

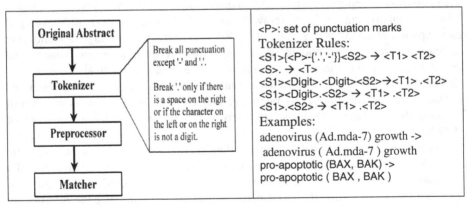

Fig. 1. Flowchart of the proposed molecular-biology names detector (left), the tokenization
rules and two examples (right).

TOKENIZER: Initially, the original abstract is processed by the tokenizer (figure 1),
which splits the text into tokens. In all punctuation marks, except characters '-' and '.',

the word entries are split into tokens. If the punctuation mark '.' is the last character in a word entry or the neighbour character is not a digit, the word entry is split into tokens. The last rule is applied due to the special morphological characteristics of gene/protein and other biology specific entities.

Preprocessor Rules:	Examples:
[Rule 1] <T>-, <T>-, ... AND <T>-<T2> → <T>-<T2> AND <T>-<T2> <T>- , <T>- , ... OR <T>-<T2> → <T>-<T2> AND <T>-<T2> AND ... [Rule 2] <T>-<T2> AND <T2> : activat* , regulat* , inhibit* , activat* , induc* , transcri* , phospho* , bind* , suppress* , indepen* , specifi* → <T> - <T2> [Rule 3] if <T2><T> != Gene or Protein → <T2> - <T> if<T2>-<T> != Gene OR Protein AND <T2> : dn , dp → <T2> - <T> [Rule 4] if <><T2><T3> AND <T2> : -/- , +/+ , -/+ , +/- → <N> <T2> <T3> [Rule 5] IF <T> : Gene OR Protein AND <T><D1>/<D2> → <T><D1> AND <T><D2> [Rule 6] <T><T2> AND <T2> NOT Greek Letter AND <<T><T2>> NOT Gene OR Protein → <T> <T2>	Ha- and Ki-ras -> Ha-ras and Ki-ras Ras-activated -> Ras – activated dnRas -> dn – Ras p21-/- -> p21 -/- MEK1/2 -> MEK1 and MEK2 HNF-1alpha -> HNF-1 alpha

Fig. 2. Preprocessor rules (left) and typical examples (right).

PREPROCESSOR: After tokenization, a set of rules is applied in a specific order in the abstract using the preprocessor module. The main goal of this module is to handle the tokens (<T>) containing the punctuation mark '-'. Taking into account that character '-' plays an important role in biological text, the preprocessor perform a crucial transformation task. The complete set of pre-processor rules can be viewed in Figure 2.

BIOLOGICAL ENTITY RECOGNIZER: In the current state of processing, each abstract is a sequence of tokens. The biological entity recognizer uses two dictionaries: the 217125 gene/proteins names extracted from the LocusLink names database and a set of approximately 1930 common words of the English language.

For each token a simply search is performed in both dictionaries. If the token exists in both dictionaries an ambiguity is recognized: the token is annotated as a common English word and a gene/protein name. If the token exists in the gene/protein dictionary and it is not a common English word, is annotated as a protein if it's first letter is capital, otherwise is annotated as gene.

The proposed annotation method identifies gene and protein entities in text, but it won't always differentiate correctly between them. This is due to the fact that genes share their names with proteins, so an ambiguity problem exists. The Biologists recognize the class of the name by the first letter's case (uppercase for proteins and low-ercase for genes), but unfortunately the authors do not always follow this rule.

The biological entity recognizer detects the presence of prefixes and suffixes. If a prefix or suffix is detected, the token is split and the recognizer annotates again the new token. The list of prefixes/suffixes is given in fig. 3. The gene-protein interaction tokens are recognized using a look-up table.

The biological entity recognizer module also detects the cell-types names. A sig-nificantly simpler process is developed due to the fact that cell-type names have a significantly complex and irregular morphology that gene and protein names. There-fore, each token is annotated as cell-type by a string-matching search to the cell-types dictionary (5826 entries).

POSTPROCESSOR: This module improves the entity detection process by identify-ing acronyms in the abstract and replacing them throughout the same abstract.

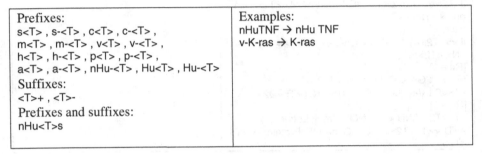

Fig. 3. Recognized prefixes and suffixes (left) and typical examples (right).

2.2 Handling the Unknown Word Tags

Taking into account the experimentally verified hypothesis, that the molecular-biology tokens, which are not included in the Wall Street Journal (WSJ), are almost exclu-sively biology-species-chemical names, the possible tags for the unknown tokens were part of gene, protein, mRNA names. This assumption introduces a small annotation error, but reduces significantly the annotation perplexity.

2.3 Stochastic Tagging

The stochastic tagger is based on the HMM and estimates the most probable sequence of tags using the Viterbi algorithm. In the training process a great number of NLP databases have been used to estimate the HMM parameters:

- The Celex Lexicon consists of 116 Kwords manually splitting from their prefixes.
- The PUBMED_STATS consists of 35 Kwords from molecular biology texts anno-tated by a restricted set of Biological tags, the frequency of occurrence of each tag and the word-end estimated by the Porter stemmer.
- The WSJ corpus annotated by a set of grammatical categories, and the correspond-ing dictionary of approximately 72 Kwords.

- The WSJ_STATS, which consists of approximately 19Kwords from the WSJ corpus annotated by a set of grammatical categories tags, the frequency of occurrence of each tag and the word-end estimated by the Porter Stemmer.

The stochastic tagger can be used to simultaneously recognize the biological entities for the unknown words and to annotate the corpus.

3 System Build-up

In our implementation we downloaded 110373 PUBMED abstracts and stored it in a mysql database. The information extraction software is based in the JAVA programming language. The software uses the tokenizer, preprocessor, the recognizer, the postprocessor and the POS tagger that are applied over pure and annotated abstracts. In the user interface the biologist have the ability to enable/disable on-line certain features on each module like certain rules on the preprocessor module. Different rules and modules can be easily embodied in the JAVA code. All these different features can be applied dynamically from the user interface giving the ability to evaluate its aspect of the system easily and fast. The abstracts' screen can also be separated in two individual parts where the original abstract and the annotated text is displayed. Thus, the expert can be easily compare the original abstract with the one are experimenting with.

During start-up, the program loads the gene/protein database on a tree in memory because the matcher and the rule matcher modules use it extensively. The databases loaded consist of 217125 gene/protein names, 5826 cell type names and 1909 common English words.

In order to increase the program's flexibility, during the tokenization process we convert the abstract into XML. The XML parsers we use later to parse the abstract are SAX and a custom XML parser is developed. We chose SAX because it is fast although it has limited capabilities. SAX is used to retrieve the processed text that will be displayed and annotate the entities found. The need for a more sophisticated XML parser drove us to write a custom one. Our custom XML parser loads the document in a tree (like DOM) but we have implemented certain features (mostly about token matching).

The biological entity recognition system is written in Java (Fig. 4) and uses the modules described above applied in the same order. Apart from the molecular biology abstracts, we also used the already tagged WSJ corpus (containing 3M tokens), which contains 48 grammatical categories.

The stochastic tagger was written in Java and uses 6 biological tags (Gene, Protein, mRNA, Biological Function, Cell Type, Species) plus 48 grammatical categories and it is used for biological-names recognition in the unknown words and for annotating the scientific abstracts (Fig. 5). The tagger was trained using 2000 molecular biology abstracts containing 3.9M entries. The Segmental K-means algorithm was used to estimate the model parameters. The Viterbi algorithm detects the most probable tag sequence.

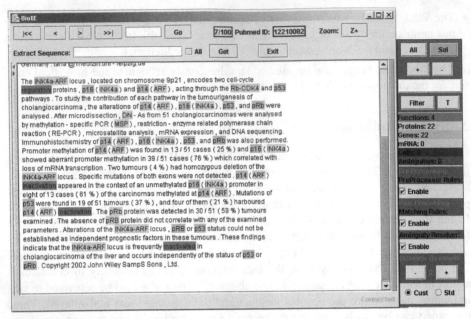

Fig. 4. User interface of the proposed molecular-biology name detection system.

On [DT] basis [NN] of [IN] discovering [VBG] the [DT] mutation [NN] in [IN] 12th [JJ] codon [NN] of [IN] K-ras [Gene] in [IN] endometrial [Gene] carcinoma [NN] cell [NN] line [NN] , [,] HEC-1A [Protein] , [,] we [PP] explored [VBD] the [DT] carcinogenesis [NN] and [CC] molecular [JJ] mechanism [NN] of [IN] mutant-type [NP] [[(] 12Asp [NP]] [)] K-ras4B [Gene] gene [NN] . [.]

Fig. 5. Typical example of the statistical POS tagger.

4 Experimental Results

We evaluated the Molecular biology names detector on 200 randomly selected abstracts from a database retrieved from the PUBMED database using the keyword K-ras. In Table 1 the precision, recall and f-score rates are shown, when different modules of the proposed information retrieval system are activated.

The f-score combines recall and precision rates into a single measurement defined by the following equation:

$$F - score = 2\frac{precision\_X\_recall}{precision + recall} \ .$$

Before applying the preprocessor rules, high precision is obtained while significantly lower recall rate is measured. After applying the preprocessor rules the precision rate is slightly decreased and the recall rate is increased by more than 10%. If the matching rules are applied, precision decreases by about 0.6% and recall levels increase again by more that 10%. The proposed rules have slightly decreased our precision levels but have significantly increased the recall levels (from 0.760 to 0.975). The improvement is clearly shown in the F-score rates.

Table 1. Precision, Recall and F-score for the Molecular biology names detector.

Modules involved	Precision	Recall	F-score
Tokenizer&Recognizer	0.976	0.760	0.8546
Tokenizer&preprocessor&Recognizer	0.974	0.864	0.9157
Complete names detector	0.968	0.975	0.9515

Additionally, the proposed recognizer was tested against a simple tokenizer (that breaks all punctuation) using 50 randomly selected abstracts. We noticed that although the standard tokenizer managed in most cases to identify the same or more number of genes and proteins, in cases where the gene or protein name has a complex morphology, the gene or protein identified was a subset of the correct one (e.g.: K-Ras -> Ras), or it identified wrongly more that one genes and proteins (e.g.: Ink4a-Arf -> Ink4a – Arf). Our results showed that our tokenizer increase the correct f-score for at least 20%.

In the HMM training process the transition probabilities and the observation probabilities are estimated from training data. The absence of annotated corpora with the desired grammatical and biological tags introduces significant difficulties in the training process. A number of novel training techniques can be implemented using resources available in the Internet and other dedicated electronic libraries.

The HMM-based biological entities recognizer for unknown words (T1) uses 6 biological tags: Gene, Protein, Species, Cell Type, mRNA, Biological Function and two POS tags: Common Word and Number, the BLG tagset. The entity recognition system and the biological abstract tagger has been evaluated using two different tagsets, training and testing corpora.

- **T1:** This tagger has been trained using the 2000 molecular biology abstracts, which were annotated using the BLG tagset. In case that an unknown token is met (the word is not included in the WSJ and Pubmed dictionaries), the Gene, Protein and mRNA tags are assigned.
- **T2:** This tagger has been trained using the WSJ corpus annotated by a set of 48 grammatical categories. In this corpus the 2000 molecular biology abstracts, annotated using the 6 biological categories, where added to the training corpus. In this implementation a unique grammatical category is assigned to each word included in the WSJ corpus, the most frequently met in the corpus.

In T1 and T2, both transition and observation probabilities were estimated using the Segmental K-means algorithm. After the algorithm converged, the zero probabilities were normalized: the zero transition and observation probabilities have been replaced by the minimum non-zero transition probability found. The probabilities of the new models (T1N, T2N) were normalized to satisfy the mutual exclusive restrictions for the hidden and observation events.

The four HMM tagger models were used in conducting the following experiments:

In the first experiment, the tagger is used for entity recognition. The Viterbi algorithm annotates 500 molecular biology abstracts (containing 135K tokens) using the T1 and T1N taggers using the BLG tagset. In the evaluation process two approaches were implemented: 1) Every tag can annotate every token, 2) The tags used to annotate the tokens found in the training data (2000 abstracts) were used to annotate the testing corpus (Table 2).

In the second experiment, the tagger is used for corpus annotation using (48 grammatical categories plus the 6 biological categories). The Viterbi algorithm annotates 100 (26K total tokens, 1512 evaluation tokens), 200 (54K total tokens, 3246 evaluation tokens) and 500 (135K total tokens, 8770 evaluation tokens) using the T1N and T2N taggers. In the evaluation process the tags used to annotate the tokens found in the WSJ and the 2000 abstracts were used to annotate the testing corpus (Table 3).

In both experiments, the tagging error is measured by estimating the false annotated biological tokens.

5 Discussion of the Experimental Results

The proposed system gives excellent biological-names detection rate when the rule based modules and the dictionaries are used (Table 1).

In the case of a biological abstract contains unknown words, the normalization process for the zero transition and observation probabilities decreases significantly (6.33% to 2.66%) the biological entity recognition error for the unknown words as shown in Table 2.

Table 2. Annotation error of the first experiment.

Training process	Annotation Error (%)
First experiment - T1 Tagger	6.36
First experiment - T1N Tagger	5.28
Second experiment - T1 Tagger	6.33
Second experiment - T1N Tagger	2.66

When a subset of the training corpus is used by the Segmental K-means algorithm for the estimation of the HMM model parameters, lower tagging error rate is measured compared to the error rate obtained by statistical estimation of the model probabilities (using the frequency of occurrence in the 2000 biological abstracts). The error rate decreases from 45.37% to 44.7%. When the training corpus increases (from 100 to 500 abstracts), the improvement rate increases also in both T1 and T2 taggers (Table 3).

The complete system is available at http://www.wcl2.ee.upatras.gr

Table 3. Experimental results of the second experiment.

| Number of Abstracts | Training process | | | Annotation Error (%) | |
	Tagger	Segmental K-means (Convergence rate)		Initial Estimation	Segmental K-Means
100	T1N	Slow		45.37	44.77
200	T1N	Slow		42.02	41.21
500	T1N	Slow		43.78	41.64
100	T2N	Fast		42.79	41.73
200	T2N	Fast		41.62	38.63
500	T2N	Fast		39.24	37.77

References

1. Junichi Kazama, Takaki Makino, Yoshihiro Ohta, and Junichi Tsujii, «Tuning Support Vector Machines for Biomedical Named Entity Recognition», Proceedings of the Workshop on Natural Porcessing in the Biomedical Domain, Philadelphia, USA, 1-8, 2002.
2. Cohen, B., Dolbey, A., Acquaah-Mensah, G., Hunter, L.: Contrast And Variability In Gene Names. Proceedings of the Workshop on Natural Porcessing in the Biomedical Domain, Philadelphia, USA (2002) 14-20.
3. Hanisch, D., Fluck, J., Mevissen, T., Zimmer, R.: Playing Biology's Name Game: Identifying Protein Names in Scientific Text. Proceedings of the Pacific Symposium on Biocomputing, (2003) 403-414.
4. Narayanaswamy, M., Ravikumar, K., Vijay-Shanker, K.: A Biological Named Entity Recognizer. Proceedings of the Pacific Symposium on Biocomputing, Hawaii (2003).
5. Fukuda, K., Tsunoda, T., Tamura, A., Takagi, T.: Toward Information Extraction: Identifying protein names from biological papers. Proceedings of the Pacific Symposium on Biocomputing, PSB'98 3 (1998) 705-716.
6. Tanabe, L., Wilbur, W.: Tagging Gene and Protein Names in Full Text Articles. Proceedings of the Workshop on Natural Porcessing in the Biomedical Domain, Philadelphia, USA (2002) 9-13.
7. Collier, N., Nobata, C., Tsujii, J.: Extracting the Names of Genes and Gene Products with a Hidden Markov Model. COLING, (2000) 201-207.
8. Seki, K., Mostafa, J.: An Approach to Protein Name Extraction using Heuristics and a Dictionary. Laboratory of Applied Information Research Tech Report 2003-2. Indiana University, Bloomington, IN, USA, 2003.
9. Seki, K., Mostafa, J.: A Probabilistic Model for Identifying Protein Names and their Name Boundaries. *http://lair.indiana.edu/research/capris/papers.html*.

A Name-Matching Algorithm
for Supporting Ontology Enrichment

Alexandros G. Valarakos[1,2], Georgios Paliouras[1],
Vangelis Karkaletsis[1], and George Vouros[2]

[1] Software and Knowledge Engineering, Laboratory
Institute of Informatics and Telecommunications,
National Centre for Scientific Research "Demokritos",
153 10 Ag. Paraskevi, Athens, Greece
{alexv,paliourg,vangelis}@iit.demokritos.gr
[2] Department of Information and Telecommunication Systems Engineering,
School of Sciences, University of the Aegean,
83200, Karlovassi, Samos, Greece
georgev@aegean.gr

Abstract. Ontologies are widely used for capturing and organizing knowledge of a particular domain of interest. This knowledge is usually evolvable and therefore an ontology maintenance process is required. In the context of ontology maintenance we tackle the problem that arises when an instance/individual is written differently (grammatically, orthographically, lexicographically), while representing the same entity/ concept. This type of knowledge is captured into a semantic relationship and constitutes valuable information for many intelligent methods and systems. We enrich a domain ontology with instances that participate in this type of relationship, using a novel name matching method based on machine learning. We also show how the proposed method can support the discovery of new entities/concepts to be added to the ontology. Finally, we present experimental results for the enrichment of an ontology used in the multi-lingual information integration project CROSSMARC.

1 Introduction

Ontologies are becoming an essential component of knowledge-intensive methods and systems because of their potential to capture and represent domain knowledge in a machine understandable and processable format. According to the most cited definition [4] in the literature, an ontology is an explicit specification of a domain conceptualization. It denotes and organizes entities/concepts that exist in a domain of interest, using a formal declarative language. Ontologies provide a common basis of understanding through their structure and vocabulary, facilitating information/knowledge dissemination and reuse.

A domain ontology usually consists of concepts/entities/types of the domain which are captured and organized by various types of relationships that hold between them. Relationships which organize concepts hierarchically are called

G.A. Vouros and T. Panayiotopoulos (Eds.): SETN 2004, LNAI 3025, pp. 381–389, 2004.

vertical relationships (e.g. the 'is-a'relationship) in contrast to horizontal relationships (e.g. the 'synonymy' relationship) which link entities across the hierarchy. The instantiation of the concepts in a particular domain is performed by instances/objects/individuals that are members of concepts.

A domain ontology captures knowledge in a static way, as it is a snapshot of knowledge from a particular point of view that governs a certain domain of interest in a specific time-period. However, this knowledge changes according to the needs of the method/system that uses the ontology as well as the evolutionary tendency of the already captured knowledge. Ontology maintenance is defined as the task of adapting the captured knowledge to some specifications, performing the appropriate interventions in its structure and content. It is a difficult and expensive task as it requires the collaboration of both knowledge engineers and domain experts. Ontology learning can facilitate the maintenance process by using machine learning techniques to obtain knowledge from data.

One problem that is often encountered in many knowledge-intensive applications is related to the different appearance (orthographically, lexicographically) of an instance. For example, the processor name 'Pentium 2' can be written differently as 'Pentium II'or 'p2' or 'P II' or 'Intel Pentium 2' etc. The poor performance of many intelligent systems and methods, in particular information extraction, retrieval and integration systems, is due to their inability to handle such cases. A domain ontology can handle this by relating the appropriate instances through predefined relationships denoting this regularity. In the multi-lingual information integration project CROSSMARC[1], an ontology was used that defines a horizontal relationship named 'synonymy' to cope with this. The task of maintaining this aspect of the ontology is generally addressed by work on ontology enrichment, which aims at the extension and updating of the ontology avoiding duplicate instances.

In this article we present a method for enriching a domain ontology with instances participating in the relationship 'synonymy' of the CROSSMARC ontology. This work follows naturally from the work in [8] which deals with the enrichment of a multi-lingual ontology with new instances participating in the vertical 'instance-of' relationship. We drive a machine learning-based algorithm to identify new instances by training it on positive examples of instances. The algorithm that we present in this paper uses information compression principles, in order to classify the new instances into existing concepts, e.g. the new instance 'P2' belongs in concept 'Intel Pentium II', and to discover new concepts by grouping lexicographically similar instances. This task is known as name matching and in the context of natural language processing, it aims to detect orthographic co-references between named entities [1] in a text. Also, this task is encountered in the data base community, where its goal is to identify data records that describe the same object keeping the number of duplicates to a minimum [3] or performing normalization to the data.

---

[1] IST (IST 2000-25366) EU-founded project:
http://www.iit.demokritos.gr/skel/crossmarc

Section 2 describes the overall structure of the CROSSMARC ontology, whereas section 3 presents our method for ontology enrichment. Section 4, introduces the machine learning algorithm that performs name matching and in section 5 we expose the results of the conducted experiment. Finally, we conclude in section 6 in which we present also our plans for future work.

2   CROSSMARC Ontology

The main aim in the design of the CROSSMARC ontology was sufficient flexibility in order to secure: (a) customizability to different domains and languages and (b) quick maintainability by modifying only a limited set of features. For these reasons, the architecture of the ontology consists of four layers:

- The *meta-conceptual layer*, which defines the generic ontological commitments of the CROSSMARC ontology architecture. It includes three meta-elements: Feature, Attribute and Value. These are used in the conceptual layer to assign computational semantics to elements of the ontology.
- The *conceptual layer*, which comprises the concepts that populate the specific domain of interest. The internal representations of these concepts as well as their relations comply with the commitments defined in the meta-conceptual layer.
- The *instances layer*, which represents domain-specific individuals. Therefore, this layer instantiates each concept.
- The *lexical layer* provides the multi-lingual surface realization (lexicalization) of ontologies' concepts and instances in the natural languages that are being supported by the project, currently English, Greek, French and Italian.

The ontology that we used in our case study describes laptop products and has been manually constructed using the Protege-based [6] management system developed in the context of the CROSSMARC project. The ontology consists of 'part-of' relationships, which link the main concept, namely laptop, with its parts (e.g. processor, screen, battery, price etc.) Additionally, there is a 'has attribute' relationship for each concept which links them with other concepts (e.g. processor is linked with processor name), an 'instance-of' relationship that denotes the instances (members) of the concepts, e.g. 'Pentium 3' and 'amd k6' instantiates the concept 'processor name'. Furthermore, a 'synonymy[2]' relationship (non-taxonomic, horizontal relationship) links the appropriate different surface appearances - lexicalizations - of an entity that is classified to be an instance of a concept. All the above relationships are defined in the ontology's XML schema. The ontology consists of 119 instances for English and 116 for Greek. Also, instances are available for the Italian and French language. For the purposes of our case study, we use only the English instantiation of the ontology.

---

[2] The meaning of this word is overridden; it refers to the surface appearance of an instance rather to its meaning.

3   Name-Matching for Ontology Enrichment

3.1   Ontology Enrichment

The ontology enrichment task is initiated when the knowledge captured in an ontology is out-of-date or incomplete for the task at hand. In our case study, we are interested in enriching the ontology with new instances, focusing on particular instances of the ontology that participate in the 'synonym' relationship. This is a strong relationship underlying the data of a domain and is part of many real-life domain ontologies. The laptop domain that we study here is a highly evolving one, as new laptop products appear in the market almost daily. Thus, the quick and accurate maintenance of the ontology is vital to the performance of the various modules [5] that use it, e.g. information extraction. For example, if the ontology is not aware of the new Intel's processor names and their different typographic appearances, the information extraction task will not be able present this information in a normalized form to the user.

The aim of our method is to discover different surface appearances of an instance by employing a learning algorithm on candidate instances that are produced by a well-defined methodology for ontology enrichment [9]. The overall methodology to ontology enrichment iterates through four stages:

1. Use the domain ontology to semantically annotate a domain-specific corpus.
2. Use the annotated corpus to train a Hidden Markov Model to locate new instances.
3. Extract new candidate instances from the corpus, using the trained Hidden Markov Model.
4. Use domain experts to validate the new instances and manually add them to the domain ontology.

The aim of the research proposed in this paper is to perform the fourth stage in a more robust, tolerant and therefore effective way, clustering different surface appearances of an instance via the synonym relationship. This will further reduce the involvement of domain experts in the whole process and ease the frequent update of the ontology with buzzwords appearing in publications.

3.2   Name Matching

The name matching task fits well with the problem of discovering instances that differ typographically (different surface appearance) but represent the same concept/entity. The task of matching entities has been researched by various communities, including statistics, databases, and artificial intelligence proposing different techniques. Cohen et. al [2] give a short survey on these techniques.

The novel algorithm that we use for name matching is based on the assumption that different lexicalizations of an entity use more-or-less a common set of 'core' characters. Therefore lexicalizations that are 'close' to this set are potential alternative appearances of the same entity, while those that are 'far' from this set are potentially related to another concept.

Specifically, the proposed algorithm classifies the candidate instances generated in the third stage of the ontology enrichment methodology, by employing a compression-based score function. The instances that already exist in the ontology, grouped by the concept they belong to, constitute the initial clusters. Each surface appearance of an instance is included only once in the cluster. Each of the initial clusters is coded by a codebook, which is defined by a Huffman tree created by the cluster's members. A new instance, with an unknown surface appearance, is assigned to a cluster if its addition to the codebook does not increase the size of the coded cluster by more than a pre-specified threshold. Otherwise, a new cluster is created which defines a new concept containing initially a single instance. It should be stressed that in this method we do not incorporate domain knowledge but we handle only strings as they appear in the text. Therefore, the proposed algorithm cannot compute clusters of lexicalizations of the same entity whose 'core characters' differ radically. Hence, synonymy relationships that are not based on surface appearance cannot be identified and homonymy ambiguities cannot be resolved.

4   Compression-Based Name Matching

In this section we present the **COCLU** (**CO**mpression-based **CLU**stering) algorithm that we propose for the discovery of typographic similarities between strings (sequences of elements-letters) over an alphabet (ASCII or UTF character set), which are candidate instances for a domain ontology, the CROSSMARC ontology. It is a partition-based clustering algorithm which divides the data into several subsets and searches the space of possible subsets using a greedy heuristic. Each cluster is represented by a model, rather than by the collection of data assigned to it. This property classifies the algorithm to the conceptual or model-based learning algorithms. The cluster model is realized by a corresponding Huffman tree which is incrementally constructed, as the algorithm dynamically generates and updates the clusters by processing one string (instance's surface appearance) at a time.

The algorithm employs a new score function that measures the compactness and homogeneity of a cluster. This score function is termed herein *Cluster Code Difference (CCDiff)* and is defined as the difference of the summed length of the coded string tokens that are members of the cluster, and the length of the same cluster updated with the candidate string. This score function groups together strings that contain the same set of frequent characters according to the model of a cluster. A string/instance belongs in a particular cluster when its *CCDiff* is below a specific threshold and the smallest between the *CCDiff*'s of the given string with all existing clusters. A new cluster is created if the candidate string cannot be assigned to any of the existing clusters. As a result, it is possible to use the algorithm even when no initial clusters are available.

Similar to many incremental algorithms, the order in which the strings are encountered influences the performance of the proposed algorithm. For this reason, when many candidate strings are available, as is usually the case in the ontology enrichment process, we iteratively select the candidate instance that is more reliably assigned to a particular cluster. The instance that is selected in each iteration is the one that maximizes the difference between its two smallest *CCDiff's* from the existing clusters.

The algorithm implements a hill-climbing search in the subset space for locating the best partition. It iteratively computes the *CCDiff* for all the existing clusters and for all candidate strings/instances and selects the instance that can be more reliably assigned to a cluster. If the corresponding *CCDiff* is greater than a user-defined threshold then a new cluster is created. The pseudo-code of the COCLU algorithm is presented below:

```
0. Given CLUSTERS and candidate INSTANCES
1. while INSTANCES do
     a. for each instance in INSTANCES
          i.   compute  CCDiff for every cluster in CLUSTERS
     b.  end for each
     c.  select instance from INSTANCES that maximizes
          the difference between its two smallest CCDiff's
     d.  if min(CCDiff) of instance > threshold
          i.   create new cluster
          ii.  assign instance to new cluster
          iii. remove instance from INSTANCES
          iv.  calculate code model for the new cluster
          v.   add new cluster to CLUSTERS
     e.  else
          i.   assign instance to cluster of min(CCDiff)
          ii.  remove instance from INSTANCES
          iii. recalculate code model for the cluster
2. end while
```

If the CLUSTERS set is empty at the beginning, the algorithm chooses the longest string, in order to construct the first cluster. This part of the algorithm can be improved by defining a reasonable heuristic for choosing a "good" string to start with.

5   Experimental Results

We have evaluated the performance of the algorithm using the enrichment methodology presented in section 3 on the laptop domain ontology of CROSS-MARC. The evaluation included two scenarios. In the first scenario, we evaluated the ability of the algorithm to discover new clusters (cluster generation), by hiding one or more of the existing clusters in each run. In the second scenario we evaluated the ability of the algorithm to assign a string/instance to the appropriate cluster, while decreasing proportionally the number of instances available initially in the cluster. In the first scenario we set the CCDiff threshold to 20 whereas in the second one high enough to avoid creating new clusters.

Table 1. Statistical data about the clusters that were used

Cluster's Name	Cluster's Type	Number of Instances
Amd	Processor Name	19
Intel	Processor Name	8
Hewlett-Packard	Manufacturer Name	3
Fujitsu-Siemens	Manufacturer Name	5
Windows 98	Operating System	10
Windows 2000	Operating System	3

Table 1 presents some statistics about the clusters we used in our experiments. In this you can find the cluster's name and type, as well as the number of instances in it. The identifier attribute is used as reference to the cluster in the following sections.

5.1 Concept Generation Scenario

In this experiment we hide incrementally one cluster at a time and measure the ability of the algorithm to discover the hidden clusters. A cluster is characterized by the majority of its instances. For example, a cluster which contains 6 instances of 'Windows 2000' and 3 of 'Windows 98' is characterized to be mostly a 'Windows 2000' cluster, rather than a 'Windows 98' cluster. We use three measures to evaluate the cluster generation process: 'correct' measures the clusters that were correctly generated according to the initial partition, 'wrong' measures the erroneously generated clusters and 'missed' measures the clusters that the algorithm did not manage to generate.

Initially, we conducted 6 different experiments, in which we hid a different cluster each time. The COCLU algorithm generated 2 wrong clusters while it succeeded not to miss any cluster. The two clusters that were wrongly generated correspond to instances of 5 and 6. In other words, the members of each of these two clusters were incorrectly further subdivided into two smaller clusters. The same phenomenon was observed in all of the experiments that we did, where we hid from 2 up to all 6 clusters. At each step, we enumerated all possible combinations of the 6 clusters and did the experiments. No missed clusters were observed in any experiment, while the 'wrong' clusters that were generated corresponded consistently to the subdivision of clusters 5 and 6. In standard information retrieval terms, the recall of the algorithm was 100%, as it managed to generate all the required clusters, while its precision was 75% in all of the experiments. The fact that the two figures remain unaffected by the number of hidden clusters indicates the robustness of the algorithm, which remains to be proven by more extended experimentation.

5.2 Instance Matching Scenario

In this experiment we measured the ability of the algorithm to assign an instance to the correct cluster (accuracy) reducing proportionally the instances in the

Table 2. Results of the instance matching experiments

Instance Reduction (%)	Correct	Accuracy (%)
90	3	100
80	11	100
70	15	100
60	19	100
50	23	95,6
40	29	96,5
30	34	94,1

initial clusters. By doing this, we tested the performance of our algorithm to handle cases where little background knowledge is used. Table 2 presents the results measuring the accuracy of the algorithm.

As expected, the accuracy of the algorithm decreases as the size of the initial clusters is decreasing. However, it is very encouraging that, despite the small number of clusters, their size can be further reduced to almost half without any loss in accuracy. Additionally, the accuracy of the algorithm is preserved at a high level (above 90%) even when the size of the original clusters is reduced to less than a third of the initial.

6   Conclusions

We have presented a novel algorithm (COCLU) for the discovery of typographic similarities between strings facilitating in this way the enrichment of a domain ontology. We have integrated COCLU into a well-defined methodology for ontology enrichment in order to support a non-taxonomic relationship, namely 'synonym' (in the context of the CROSSMARC ontology), between instances. The algorithm performed very well obtaining remarkably good results both in terms of generating new clusters, as well as in assigning new strings to the correct clusters. Thus, the initial results are very encouraging, although further experimentation with larger and noisy datasets is needed, in order to prove the value of the method. Furthermore, the method will need to be compared experimentally with other similar methods that may be used to tackle the same problem.

In addition to the need for further experimentation, we are planning to improve and extend the algorithm in several ways. One issue that we are studying is a good heuristic for choosing a "good" string to start with when no cluster is given apriori. Furthermore, we are investigating the possibility of extending the algorithm beyond typographic clustering and into other interesting synonymy relationships. In order to do this, we will need to take into account contextual information that will allow us to identify higher-order semantic relationships among the clusters.

References

1. Bontcheva, K., Dimitrov, M., Maynard, D., Tablan, V., Cunningham, H., Shallow Methods for Named Entity Co-reference Resolution, In Proceedings of TALN 2002, Nancy, 24-27 June 2002
2. Cohen, W., Ravikumar, P., Fienberg, S., A Comparison of String Distance Metrics for Name-Matching Tasks, In Proceedings of IIWeb Workshop, 2003
3. Galhardas, H., Florescu, D., Shasha, D., Simon, E., An extensible framework for data cleaning, In Proceedings of ICDE, 2000
4. Gruber, T. R., A translation approach to portable ontologies, Knowledge Acquisition, 5(2):199-220, 1993
5. Hachey, B., Grover, C., Karkaletsis, V., Valarakos, A., Pazienza, M. T., Vindigni, M., Cartier, E., Coch, J., Use of Ontologies for Cross-lingual Information Management in the Web, In Proceedings of the Ontologies and Information Extraction International Workshop held as part of the EUROLAN 2003, Romania, July 28 - August 8, 2003
6. Noy, N. F., Fergerson, R. W., MusenM. A., The knowledge model of Protege-2000: Combining interoperability and flexibility, In Proceedings of EKAW 2000, Juan-les-Pins, France, 2000
7. Pazienza, M. T., Stellato, A., Vindigni, M., Valarakos, A., Karkaletsis, V., Ontology Integration in a Multilingual e-Retail System, In Proceedings of the HCI International Conference, Volume 4, pp. 785-789, Heraklion, Crete, Greece, June 22-27 2003
8. Valarakos, A., Sigletos, G., Karkaletsis, V., Paliouras, G., Vouros, G., A Methodology for Enriching a Multi-Lingual Domain Ontology using Machine Learning, In Proceedings of the 6th ICGL workshop on Text Processing for Modern Greek: from Symbolic to Statistical Approaches, held as part of the 6th International Conference in Greek Linguistics, Rethymno, Crete, 20 September, 2003
9. Valarakos, A., Sigletos, G., Karkaletsis, V., Paliouras, G., A Methodology for Semantically Annotating a Corpus Using a Domain Ontology and Machine Learning, In Proceedings of the International Conference in Racent Advances in NLP (RANLP), Borovest, Bulgaria, 2003

Text Normalization for the Pronunciation
of Non-standard Words in an Inflected Language

Gerasimos Xydas, Georgios Karberis, and Georgios Kouroupertroglou

National and Kapodistrian University of Athens
Department of Informatics and Telecommunications
Speech Group
{gxydas,grad0350,koupe}@di.uoa.gr

Abstract. In this paper we present a novel approach, called "Text to Pronunciation (TtP)", for the proper normalization of Non-Standard Words (NSWs) in unrestricted texts. The methodology deals with inflection issues for the consistency of the NSWs with the syntactic structure of the utterances they belong to. Moreover, for the achievement of an augmented auditory representation of NSWs in Text-to-Speech (TtS) systems, we introduce the coupling of the standard normalizer with: i) a language generator that compiles pronunciation formats and ii) VoiceXML attributes for the guidance of the underlying TtS to imitate the human speaking style in the case of numbers. For the evaluation of the above model in the Greek language we have used a 158K word corpus with 4499 numerical expressions. We achieved an internal error rate of 7,67% however, only 1,02% were perceivable errors due to the nature of the language.

1 Introduction

Unrestricted texts include Standard Words (Common Words and Proper Names) and Non-Standard Words (NSWs). Standard Words have a specific pronunciation that can be phonetically described either in a lexicon, using a disambiguation processing to some extent, or by letter-to-sound rules. By definition, NSWs comprise numerical patterns and alphabetical strings that do not have a regular entry in a lexicon and their pronunciation needs to be generated by a more complicated natural language process. In inflected languages word sequences that result from NSWs need to be proper inflected and converted into the right gender in order to match the syntactic structure of the sentences and the target noun they refer to. Even so, there are still some Text-to-Speech (TtS) oriented issues concerning the style, the rate and the format of the pronunciation of NSWs that have not been addressed yet. For example, humans tend to read out long numbers slowly and with pauses between groups of digits.

Most of the previous works deal with NSWs' pronunciation in Text-to-Speech systems, however, NSWs constitutes a problem in the fields of information retrieval and speech recognition [6]. Most of the proposed approaches are language specific as the problem depends on language properties. Even so, there are some issues, like the inflection of the NSWs, which have been partially solved. For example, in the German language there are two systems that deal with normalization: Bell Labs TtS [1] and FELIX [2]. FELIX analyzes the text syntactically using the Zingle [3] algorithm and the utterance pronunciation is determined by the Part-of-Speech information. In

G.A. Vouros and T. Panayiotopoulos (Eds.): SETN 2004, LNAI 3025, pp. 390–399, 2004.

the Bell Labs approach, there is an attempt here to deal with ambiguities but the lack of syntactical analysis limits the capabilities of the system. In the Japanese language [4] every possible role of a word in a sentence is scored and, after analysis, the role with the highest dependency score is selected. Thus, the appropriate pronunciation is applied for the normalization of the NSWs. A model that uses a pre-processor performing syntax analysis of sentences was presented in [5] for English. Though it is presented to be a language independent solution, there is no care for inflections.

The Johns Hopkins University Summer Workshop (WS99) research project [6] made a systematic effort to build a general solution of the NSW's normalization problem in the English language. Later on, this was applied to the Asian languages in [7]. The application of this model to the Greek language has the major drawback of the inflection.

In the "Text to Pronunciation" (TtP) work we deal with three important elements in the normalization of texts. The first is the dynamic definition of the pronounceable format of NSWs through a Language Generator model, leading to increased semantics in the synthesized speech. The second deals with the inflection of word lattices that are generated during the expansion of NSWs, so that normalized expressions are consistent with the syntax structure of the utterances they belong to and to ensure the sequence of tenses and genders in nominal phrases. Other important issues that have not been addressed before and we accommodate in this work are the capability of inserting SSML [10] (or VoiceXML or any other speech markup language, SAPI etc) tags mainly for defining short breaks between groups of digits in cases of long numbers. The rest of the paper focuses on the numerical's problem, which is (a) more general, (b) more important and (c) shares similar, if not more complex, methods to the alphabetical cases. Thus, the same methodology can be and has been applied to alphabetical expressions as well.

2 The TtP Model

Figure 1 presents the block diagram of the TtP model. The individual components and the data used by them can by either domain specific (e.g. in economical texts there are several numerical patterns that have a different pronunciation in the sports domain) or generic. The first yields better performance and supports disambiguation.

2.1 Tokenizer, Splitter and Classifier

These have been described in [6]. Their functionality differs in Greek but the model works similar. The main purpose of the Tokenizer is to successfully identify End of Sentences (EoS) and to create tokens from the given sentence. We use the EoS of the Greek TtS system DEMOSTHeNES [8]. In cases of dot punctuation, two lists are parsed for EoS disambiguation: acronyms ("\\([A–Ω]\\.\\)*[A–Ω]\\.?") and a list of abbreviations. We consider them as EoS if the next token starts with a capital letter and it is not an Out-of-Vocabulary (OOV) word (i.e. likely to be a proper name). For example "ο κ. Νικολάου" and "το Ι.Κ.Α. Αθήνας" are not EoS. This is not optimum; however, the evaluation showed that it does not affect the model for the specific task (2 errors in 4499 cases).

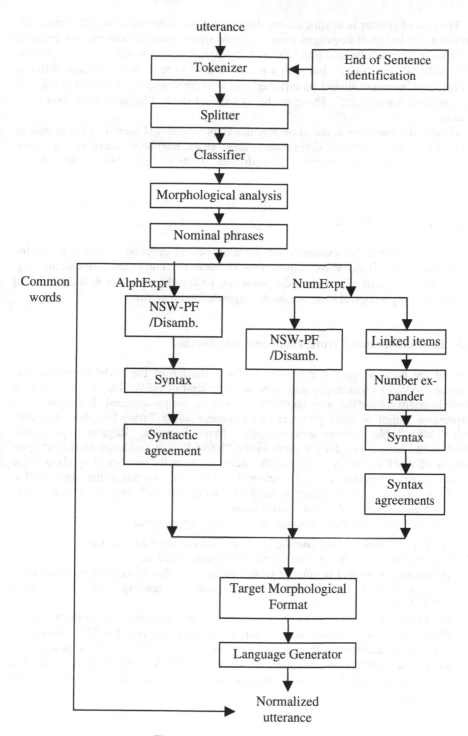

Fig. 1. The architecture of the NfP.

The role of splitter is to split tokens that are not pure numerical or alphabetical expressions. In inflected languages there are some more issues to address. For example "25χρονος" can not be split into "25" and "χρονος " and "3-4 ώρες" can be split into "3", dash, "4" and "ώρες", but with a mark, because even if they constitute different tokens, both numbers should be inflected and converted into the gender that matches the common noun "ώρες". These are being handled in the Language Generator component.

Finally, the classifier is based on Regular Expressions and identifies (a) in case of numerics: cardinal, ordinal, dates, hours, time, years, telephone, currencies, percentages, postal codes, street number, IP addresses, digits and (b) abbreviations: to expand, as words and as letters.

2.2   Expansion of NSWs

Firstly, we perform the expansion on the alphabetical expressions and then on the numerical ones. Thus, abbreviations that characterize numerical expressions (e.g. "5 δις") are normalized prior to these numerics, so that the numerics would be able to inherit the morphological structure on the expanded abbreviation.

2.3   The Non-standard Word Pronounceable Format

One of the main aspects of this work is the definition of the NSW Pronounceable Format (NSW-PF) that might accommodate any kind of NSW. This format allows a flexible control over the way numbers and strings are pronounced. It assigns to an expression a digit or alpha grouping and a corresponding Target Morphological Format (TMF). Table 1 shows some examples. Symbols on the "Regular Expressions" field should have a matching symbol in the "NSW-PF". A sequence of similar symbols in NSW-PF defines a number of that many digits as the number of symbols in the sequence (e.g. ## defines a 2-digit number) and this corresponds to the same number of digits in the Regular Expression. Thus, wildcards and ranges of digits (e.g. "[0-9]*") are not allowed in this specification.

The NSW Pronounceable Format allows five things to happen:

1. To deal with ambiguities, like the last two numerics on the table below.
2. To mix plain text with annotated text in the format section.
3. To segment a number to smaller groups of digits so that it could be pronounced in a relaxed and understandable way (imagine reading out the number "456675342345" as a single entity).
4. To define the morphology of the sub-groups in specific cases and domains, where the user ensures the right pronunciation of a NSW in terms of the TMF. According to the above definitions, the telephone number "210-7275320" will be pronounced as "two ten seventy two seventy five three twenty". The NSW-PF grammar has some restrictions itself, but these are not evaluated here and are out of the scope of this paper.

5. To incorporate SSML (or VoiceXML or any other speech markup, SAPI etc) tags in the NSW-PF so that, for example, the TtS is forced to pause in specific points, like humans do when reading long numbers. The above telephone example will be read out in a 20% decreased rate (which is a natural behavior; humans speaks slow in order for the number to be easier to be memorized by the interlocutor) and with medium and long pauses between the group of digits: "two ten// seventy two/ seventy five/ three/ twenty".

Table 1. Examples of the Non-Standard Pronounceable Format. In the *telephone* example SSML tags have been incorporated to be parsed latter by the TtS system.

Reg. Expr.	Class	NSW-PF
##/#/####	Date	<tmf gender="neutral" case="nominative" number="singular">##</tmf> <tmf gender="neutral" case="genitive" number="singular">#</tmf> <tmf gender="feminine" case="nominative" number="singular">####</tmf>
###- #######	Tel.	<ssml:prosody rate="-20%"> <tmf gender="neutral" case="nominative" number="singular">#</tmf> <tmf gender="neutral" case="nominative" number="singular">##</tmf> <ssml:break time="long"/> <tmf gender="neutral" case="nominative" number="singular">##</tmf> <ssml:break/> <tmf gender="neutral" case="nominative" number="singular">##</tmf> <ssml:break/> <tmf gender="neutral" case="nominative" number="singular">#</tmf> <ssml:break/> <tmf gender="neutral" case="nominative" number="singular">##</tmf> </ssml:prosody>
##ωρος	AlfNum Stem	<tmf gender="masculine" case="nominative" number="singular" type="alphanum_stem">##</tmf>ωρος
στις #/#	Date	στις <tmf gender="neutral" case="nominative" number="singular">#</tmf> <tmf gender="neutral" case="genitive" number="singular" type="ordinal">#</tmf>
το#/#	Ord.	το <tmf gender="neutral" case="nominative" number="singular">#</tmf> <tmf gender="neutral" case="nominative" number="singular" type="ordinal">#</tmf>

where # = 0..9.

2.4 The Target Morphological Format

The Target Morphological Format (TMF) has been introduced to allow the definition of the pronunciation format of NSWs. The TMF entries have an XML form (the <tmf> entity in Table 1) and might include as attributes any field from the morphological lexicon. In the Language Generator component the enclosed words will be converted in order to conform to these directives.

2.5 The Number Expander

In cases of numerical expressions that are not defined in the NSW-PF, we use a dynamic Number Expander that differs from the Language Generator as the linguistic nature of numbers can be characterized as "non-normal". Numerics have three states: cardinal, ordinal and alphanumeric (e.g. "14ωρο"). Consider the string "των 1636 ανθρώπων". After all the above steps and dealing with the exceptions we will generate "των {χίλια} {εξακόσια τριάντα έξι} ανθρώπων". The cardinal, ordinal or alphanumeric information is passed to the Syntactic Agreement component for further processing.

2.6 Syntactical Analysis

Syntactical analysis is being performed using templates for the Greek language. Each template defines a sequence of POS occurrences and can determine the subject and the object or the link verb complement. Table 2 shows some templates that determines the object. Many of the templates that stand for the object are common for the predicate as well. Though the covering achieved by this approach is small for the richness of the Greek language, however, this seems adequate for the specific problem we deal with: the normalization errors caused by faulty syntax were 4,47% while the noticeable errors were only 0,89%. This is because the syntax information we mainly look for is the identification of nominal phrases that can be predicted by such an approach.

Table 2. Syntactic templates (sequences of POS) for the Object.

Object
At+No+Pn+Cj+Pn
At+No+Cj+Pn
Pn+Cj+Ar+No+Pn
Pn+Cj+Ar+No
...

Syntactical analysis is also important in inflected languages for another reason: assume the text "3-4 ώρες". The splitter will split these in "3", dash, "4" and "ώρες". Both numbers should be inflected and match the gender of "ώρες". There are other cases as well of conjunctive numbers with a common noun. This are dealt by the following directive {NSW+ [lnk+NSW] *+No}, where lnk is a defined set of links between consecutive NSW: "-", ",", "&", "και", "εώς", "ως", "μέχρι", "στα", "στις", "προς", "με", "ή".

2.7 Syntactic Agreement

We collected a number of main rules found in the grammar of Modern Greek [9]. These proved to achieve the desired consistency between numerics and nouns. Cases of syntactic agreement constitute 1635 out of 4499 numerics in the corpus (36,34%) and raised errors otherwise. These agreements are:

2.7.1 Agreement within Nominal Phrases

The gender, case and number of the noun must agree with the gender, case and number of its specifiers (in our case numbers). Thus, we can determine the gender, number and case of numbers if we know the morphological information of the noun they specify or the determiner of the noun (in case the head-noun itself is missing). For instance, the above example will produce a TMF of:
"των <tmf gender='masculine' number='plural' case ='genitive'> χίλια </tmf> <tmf gender = 'masculine' number ='plural' case='genitive'> εξακόσια τριάντα έξι </tmf> ανθρώπων".

2.7.2 Agreement between Subject and Verb

The verb of a sentence inherits the number and the person of the subject. Moreover, the tokens that constitute the subject are transformed to the nominative case. This rule we deal with cases of ambiguities in the morphology of words that constitute the subject. For example: "Τα 1500 έφτασαν εχθές.". In order to form the number "1500" we look in the nominal phrase "τα 1500". However, "τα" can be either in the nominative or the accusative case. Since this nominal phrase is the subject of the sentence, the case of the tokens in it is chosen to be the nominative.

2.7.3 Object in the Accusative Case

The object of a sentence is always in the accusative case. Thus, all the tokens that constitute the object are considered to be in the accusative case: "Το μουσείο δέχεται καθημερινά 1500 επισκέπτες".

2.7.4 Predicate in the Nominative Case

On the other hand, the predicate of a sentence is always in the nominative case. Furthermore, it inherits the case and the gender of the subject, as complement describe or identifies the subject: "Οι επιτυχόντεσ είναι 1501".

2.8 The Language Generator

The Language Generator component is able to parse sequences of TMFs and generate the word lattices with the corresponding morphological features. For Greek, this is achieved by using of a morphological lexicon that includes (per word):

- Word
- Morpheme information
- Inflection code
- Stem
- Lemma

The Inflection code field corresponds to a template of affixes. Thus, given a word we retrieve its stem and following the template instructions we form the target word. All the inflectional affixes in any applicable gender can be dynamically generated for any word in this lexicon. Table 3 shows some entries of this lexicon, while Table 4 illustrates the corresponding templates.

Table 3. Entries in the morphological lexicon.

Word	Morph	Infl. Code	Stem	Lemma
εξάρτημα	NoNeSgNm	O49	εξάρτημ	Εξάρτημα
σελίδα	NoFeSgNm	O26	σελίδ	Σελίδα

Table 4. Desinence's templates. S1 to S4 and P1 to P4 stand for the singular and plural cases.

Infl. Code	S1	S2	S3	S4	P1	P2	P3	P4
O49	α	ατος(+1)	α	α	ατα(+1)	ατών	ατα(+1)	ατα(+1)
O26	α	Aς	α	α	ες	ων	ες	Eς

The lexicon defines 53 affix templates, covering all Greek nouns and 17 templates for the adjectives and the participles. The total amount of word covering is currently 1.077.458 words. Articles have been encoded separately. Numbers are formed depending whether they are cardinal, ordinal or alphanumerical. Default type is cardinal. Default gender is neutral. Default case is nominative. These "default" assumptions have very impressive effects on the overall evaluation as most of the numerical NSW fail into them.

3   Evaluation

During the evaluation, we distinguish between "system errors" and "perceivable errors". Due to the fact that in cases of weakness to predict or generate the correct normalized form of a NSW the system assumes that the token should be rendered in the corresponding neutral, singular and nominative form, there are errors that are not noticeable, because this assumption stands for the majority of the cases: e.g. only numbers ending in "1", "3" or "4" have different forms in male, female and neutral genders. Thus, system errors refer to "wrong or uninformed prediction but possibly right pronunciation" while perceivable errors refer to "wrong pronunciation". The size of the corpus used for evaluation (158557 words - 4499 NSWs) verifies this.

Evaluation involves only the standard normalization procedures and not the pronunciation oriented ones. Firstly, we built and hand annotated a corpus in the Speech Group of the University of Athens. The corpus was selected from 4 major on-line newspapers and the subjects covered were:

Table 5. Statistics of the NSW in the collected corpus.

Category	Total Words	Nums	%
Sports	35994	1225	3,40
Social issues	27825	531	1,91
Politics	29190	482	1,65
Economy	55772	2013	3,61
Science	4826	118	2,45
Weather	3432	130	3,79
TOTAL	158557	4499	2,84

Table 6. Statistics of the NSWs. The classification of the NSWs is presented here. The last case (Discourse, mainly surface anaphora) could not be currently handled by the system.

Category	Nums	AlphNum		Regular Expr.		Nominal phrases		Discourse	
Sports	1225	357	29,14%	247	20,16%	343	28,0%	278	22,69%
Social issues	531	42	7,91%	203	38,23%	277	52,17%	9	1,70%
Politics	482	71	14,73%	257	53,32%	136	28,22%	18	3,73%
Economy	2013	57	2,83%	1158	57,53%	761	37,80%	37	1,84%
Science	118	5	4,24%	42	35,59%	69	58,47%	2	1,69%
Weather	130	60	46,15%	20	15,38%	49	37,69%	1	0,77%
TOTAL	**4499**	**592**	**13,16%**	**1927**	**42,83%**	**1635**	**36,34%**	**345**	**7,67%**

The current implementation of the TtP is able to handle in generic or domain specific environments most of the NSWs. Table 6 illustrates the kind of numerical NSWs and how they were classified. The last column shows the actual errors of the model and need discourse analysis to be handled. However, only a 1,02% was actual perceivable errors.

Comparing against a legacy model of DEMOSTHeNES based on the UoA Transcriber (FSA engine), the improvements were dramatics: the UoA Transcriber is able to handle all of the alphanumerics cases, most of the Regular Expressions but there is not any provision for nominal phrases and of course discourse analysis. Thus, the optimum error rate for the UoA Transcriber is 44,0%.

The introduction of the NSW-PF provides improved effects: "2107275320" is not pronounced like "δύο δισσεατομμύρια εκατόν επτά εκατομμύρια διακόσιες εβδομήντα πέντε χιλιάδες τριακόσια είκοσι"   but   slowly   "δύο δέκα {pause} εβδομήντα δύο {pause} εβδομήντα πέντε {pause} τρία {pause} είκοσι".

4 Conclusions

We presented a novel model for the normalization of NSWs that achieves improved semantics of the synthesized speech by dealing with inflection issues and enhanced auditory representation in cases of NSWs by (a) defining the NSW Pronounceable Format and (b) incorporating VoiceXML attributes to the normalized tokens. The evaluation of the model for the Greek language showed the drastically improvement of 36,33% in correct normalization over a legacy model of the DEMOSTHeNES Speech Composer, while the auditory enhancements have not been evaluated.

Acknowledgements

We would like to thank Pepi Stavropoulou for her significant contribution during the evaluation.

References

1. B. Mobius, R. Sproat, J. van Santen, J. Olive: The Bell Labs German Text-To-Speech system: An overview. In Proceedings of EUROSPEECH '97, Volume IV, p. 2443-2446, (1997).
2. G. Fries and A. Wirth: FELIX – A TTS System with Improved pre-processing and source signal generation. In Proceedings of EUROSPEECH '97, Vol. II, p. 589-592, (1997).
3. H. Zingle: Traitement de la prosodie allemande dans un systeme de synthese de la parole. These pour le 'Doctorat d'Etat, Universite de Strasbourg II, (1982).
4. Y. Ooyama, M. Miyazaki, S. Ikehara: Natural Language Processing in a Japanese Text-To-Speech System. In Proceedings of the Annual Computer Science Conference, p. 40-47, ACM, (1987).
5. D. Coughlin: Leveraging Syntactic Information for Text Normalization. Lecture Notes in Artificial Intelligence (LNAI), Vol. 1692, p.95-100, (1999).
6. Richard Sproat, Alan Black, Stanley Chen, Shankar Kumar, Mari Ostendorf, and Christopher Richards: Normalization of non-standard words. Computer Speech and Language, 15(3), p. 287-333, (2001).
7. Olinsky, G. and Black, A.: Non-Standard Word and Homograph Resolution for Asian Language Text Analysis. In Proceedings of ICSLP2000, Beijing, China, (2000).
8. Xydas G. and Kouroupetroglou G.: The DEMOSTHeNES Speech Composer. In Proceedings of the 4th ISCA Tutorial and Research Workshop on Speech Synthesis, Perthshire, Scotland, August 29th - September 1st, pp 167-172, (2001).
9. Babiniotis, G. and Christou, K.: The Grammar of Modern Greek, II. The verb. Ellinika Grammata, (1998).
10. Burnett, D., Walker, M. and Hunt, A.: Speech Synthesis Markup Language Version 1.0. W3C Working Draft, http://www.w3.org/TR/speech-synthesis.

Multi-topic Information Filtering
with a Single User Profile

Nikolaos Nanas[1], Victoria Uren[1], Anne de Roeck[2], and John Domingue[1]

[1] Knowledge Media Institute, The Open University, Milton Keynes, MK7 6AA, UK
{N.Nanas,V.S.Uren,J.B.Domingue}@open.ac.uk
[2] Computing Department, The Open University, Milton Keynes, MK7 6AA, UK
A.DeRoeck@open.ac.uk

Abstract. In Information Filtering (IF) a user may be interested in several topics in parallel. But IF systems have been built on representational models derived from Information Retrieval and Text Categorization, which assume independence between terms. The linearity of these models results in user profiles that can only represent one topic of interest. We present a methodology that takes into account term dependencies to construct a single profile representation for multiple topics, in the form of a hierarchical term network. We also introduce a series of non-linear functions for evaluating documents against the profile. Initial experiments produced positive results.

1 Introduction

In recent years, advances in digital media, network and computing technologies have caused an exponential growth of the digital information space that is accessible to individuals. We are facing the cumbersome task of selecting out of this glut of accessible information, information items that satisfy our interests, i.e. "relevant information". This is the problem that is usually referred to as "Information Overload" [9].

Research in Information Filtering (IF) tackles information overload through a tailored representation of a user's interests called, a "user profile". User interests however, are by nature dynamic. During an IF system's lifecycle, a user may develop or loose interest in various topics. For example, a general interest in *Knowledge Management* can trigger an interest in *Intelligent Information Agents*, which may evolve to include related topics like *Information Retrieval* and *Information Filtering*. The latter may develop further, causing a decay in the initial interest in *Knowledge Management* and the emergence of other topics of interest like *Term Weighting*, *Complex Adaptive Systems* and so on. A user's interests co-evolve, affected by changes in the user's environment and knowledge. Therefore, it would be legitimate for a single user profile to be able to: a) represent a user's multiple topics and subtopics of interests and their interrelations and b) to adapt to their changes over time.

In this paper we focus on the first of the above issues, i.e. multi-topic IF with a single profile. More specifically, we present part of our work on the de-

G.A. Vouros and T. Panayiotopoulos (Eds.): SETN 2004, LNAI 3025, pp. 400–409, 2004.

velopment of a document filtering system that we call Nootropia[1]. In contrast to traditional approaches to IF that adopt linear, single-topic representations for user profiling (section 2), in Nootropia, we employ a hierarchical term network to represent multiple topics of interest with a single profile (section 3). A spreading activation model is then used to establish a series of non-linear document evaluation functions (section 4). Experiments performed using this novel IF approach to represent two topics of interest with a single profile, have produced positive results (section 5). Adaptation to changes in the user's interests is briefly discussed in the concluding section.

2   The Dominance of Single-Topic Representations

Traditionally, IF systems inherit profile representations, that ignore term dependencies, from research in Information Retrieval (IR) and Text Categorisation (TC). These include the dominant vector space model [18], probabilistic IR models [16], and linear classifiers like naive Bayes, decision trees, nearest-neighbour classification and others [20]. Even in the case of connectionist approaches to IR, like neural networks [23] and semantic networks [4, 6], links between terms are ignored. Such linear representations can only estimate the relevance of a document to a single topic of interest. Typically, a separate profile is built for each topic of interest based on documents that the user has pre-classified according to these topics [1, 15, 7]. Alternatively, online clustering algorithms can be employed to incrementally identify document classes. Nevertheless, the number of classes is either predefined [11, 8] or is determined by a fixed relevance threshold [3]. Finally, evolutionary approaches maintain a population of linear profiles that collectively represent the user interests [12, 21].

The above tendency to break a user's multiple interests into distinct topics that can then be represented by linear, single-topic profiles, can only yield partial solutions to the problem at hand. The topics of interest are assumed to be independent. Neither their relative importance nor their topic-subtopic relations are represented. Practically, it implies a large number of parameters, like number of terms in each profile, relative profile weights etc., that have to be fine tuned for each individual user.

As we will see, to represent multiple topics of interest with a single profile, term dependencies must be taken into account. These include both lexical correlations and topical correlations between terms [5]. Recently, lexical correlations have been represented with connectionist profiles, which associate terms that appear in the same phrase [22, 10]. Nevertheless, both approaches employ a separate profile for each topic of interest. Topical correlations between terms and more specifically topic-subtopic relations between them, may be expressed using a *concept hierarchy*. One method for the automatic construction of a concept hierarchy is through the use of subsumption associations between terms ("Subsumption Hierarchies") [19]. Another approach generates "Lexical Hierarchies"

---

[1] Greek word for: "an individual's or a group's particular way of thinking, someone's characteristics of intellect and perception"

based on frequently occurring words within phrases or lexical compounds [2, 14]. So while subsumption hierarchies do not take into account the lexical correlations between terms, lexical hierarchies are only based on such correlations. In IR, concept hierarchies have been used for the organisation and interactive access to information, but their computational use for IF has so far not been explored. To our knowledge, no existing IF system exploits both kinds of term dependencies to represent a user's multiple topics of interest with a single profile.

3   Building a Hierarchical Profile

In previous work, we presented a methodology that generates a hierarchical term network from a set of user specified documents, through a series of three processes [13]. Initially, stop word removal and stemming is applied to reduce the number of unique terms in the documents. The remaining terms are then weighted using a term weighting method called Relative Document Frequency (RelDF) [13]. Given a number R of documents that a user has specified as relevant and a general collection of documents, RelDF assigns to a term t in the documents, a weight $w_t \in (-1, 1)$, according to equation 1: where N is the number of documents in the collection and r and n are respectively the number of user specified documents and the number of documents in the collection that contain the term. While the first part of the equation $(\frac{r}{R})$ favours those terms that exhaustively describe the user specified documents and therefore the underlying topic of interest, the second part $(-\frac{n}{N})$ biases the weighting towards terms that are specific within the general collection. The assigned weights can be used to extract the most competent terms on the basis of an appropriate threshold.

$$w_t = \frac{r}{R} - \frac{n}{N} \qquad (1)$$

Extracted terms are added to the profile. If term independence between the extracted terms is assumed, then they can be used for evaluating documents, using for example the inner product. For binary indexing of documents, the inner product of a document D can be defined using equation 2, where NT is the number of terms in the document. In section 5 we will use this traditional approach to IF as a baseline for our experimentation.

$$S0_D = \frac{\sum_{t \in D} w_t \cdot 1}{log(NT)} \qquad (2)$$

Having selected the profile terms, a sliding window comprising 10 contiguous words is used to identify dependencies between them. Two extracted terms are linked if they appear at least once within the sliding window. A weight $w_{ij} \in (0, 1]$ is then assigned to the link between two extracted terms t_i and t_j using equation 3. fr_{ij} is the number of times t_i and t_j appear within the sliding window, fr_i and fr_j are respectively the number of occurrences of t_i and t_j in the user specified documents and d is the average distance between the two linked terms. The above process connects the extracted profile terms with symmetric,

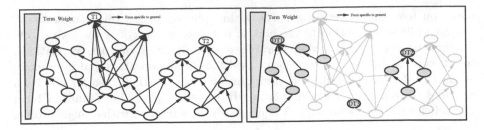

Fig. 1. Hierarchical Term Network: (a) deactivated, (b) activated

associative links. The first fraction of equation 3 measures the likelihood that the two extracted terms will appear within the sliding window. The second fraction on the other hand is a measure of how close the two terms usually appear. As a result, a link's weight is a combined measure of the statistical dependencies caused by both lexical and topical correlations.

$$w_{ij} = \frac{fr_{ij}^2}{fr_i \cdot fr_j} \cdot \frac{1}{d} \tag{3}$$

In the past, we had adopted the document frequency of terms in the specified documents as a measure of their generality [13]. Here, the third process involves ordering terms according to decreasing weight. So the ordering takes into account both the generality of terms and their specificity in the complete collection. This yields a network of terms (nodes) and links between them, which formulates a separate hierarchy for each general topic discussed in the user specified documents. Figure 1(a) depicts an example network constructed from a set of documents about two overlapping topics. The two topics are reflected by two hierarchical sub-networks that share a small number of common terms. Each of the formulated hierarchies can be identified by a term that is only connected to lower terms with smaller weights (fig. 1(a): terms T1 and T2). These "dominant" terms can be used to identify the profile's "breadth", i.e. the number of general topics represented. A hierarchy's "depth", on the other hand, is proportional to the number of terms with smaller weights that are explicitly or implicitly connected to dominant terms. A topic of interest discussed in the majority of the user specified documents will be reflected by a hierarchy with larger depth. A hierarchy's depth is therefore a measure of a topic's importance within the profile.

The above hierarchical network complies with most of the design principles set by Sanderson and Croft for the generation of a concept hierarchy using subsumption [19]. General informative terms are linked to related, less general or informative terms. If in addition a link between two terms has a large weight, then one can confidently assume that a topic-subtopic relation exists between the two. In contrast, however, to subsumption hierarchies that only exploit the stochastic dependencies between terms, link weighting is based on both the lexical and topical correlation between terms. In the next section we will discuss how the above characteristics of the constructed hierarchical network allow its computational use for non-linear document evaluation. Other applications of the hierarchical network, which are not discussed in this paper, include, automatic summarisation, expert finding and collaborative filtering.

4 Document Evaluation

The above methodology generates, from a set of user specified documents, a concept hierarchy of weighted terms that takes into account both lexical and topical correlations. In this section, we address how to use this profile representation for document filtering. We introduce a series of document evaluation functions, based on a spreading activation model that draws ideas from the application of neural networks [23] and semantic networks [4,6] to IR. But as already mentioned, these connectionist approaches ignore links between terms, which leads them to adopt a linear evaluation function through energy dissemination from a query towards the documents. Spreading activation on associative term networks has been employed by the INFOrmer [22] filtering system. Due to the inherent lack of direction in this kind of networks, an initial energy is assigned to the terms that appear in a specific document and is then iteratively disseminated through the network until an equilibrium is reached. In our case, document evaluation is based on a directed, spreading activation model that combines the characteristics of the above approaches. Although the network contains only terms, the direction imposed by the hierarchy is taken into account.

Given a document D, an initial energy of 1 (binary document indexing), is deposited with those profile terms that appear in D. In figure 1(b), activated terms are depicted by shadowed nodes. Subsequently, energy is disseminated sequentially, starting with the activated term with the smallest weight and moving up the weight order. If, and only if, an activated term t_i is directly linked to another activated term t_j higher in the hierarchy, is an amount of energy E_{ij} disseminated by t_i to t_j through the corresponding link. E_{ij} is defined by equation 4, where E_i^c is t_i's current energy, w_{ij} is the weight of the link between t_i and t_j, and A^h is the set of activated terms higher in the hierarchy that t_i is linked to. The purpose of the normalization parameter $\sum_{k \in A^h} w_{ik}$ is to ensure that a term does not disseminate more than its current energy. The current energy of term t_i is $E_i^c = 1 + \sum_{m \in A^l} E_{mi}$, where A^l is the set of activated terms lower in the hierarchy that t_i is linked to. After the end of the dissemination process the final energy of a term t_i is $E_i^f = E_i^c - \sum_{k \in A^h} E_{ik}$.

$$
E_{ij} = \begin{cases} E_i^c \cdot w_{ij} & \text{if } \sum_{k \in A^h} w_{ik} \leq 1 \\ E_i^c \cdot \left(\dfrac{w_{ij}}{\sum_{k \in A^h} w_{ik}} \right) & \text{if } \sum_{k \in A^h} w_{ik} > 1 \end{cases} \tag{4}
$$

We have experimented with three different ways for assessing a document's relevance score S_D, based on the final energy of activated terms. The simplest variation is defined by equation 5, where A is the set of activated profile terms,

NT the number of terms in the document, and w_i is the weight of an activated term t_i.

$$S1_D = \frac{\sum_{i \in A} w_i \cdot E_i^f}{log(NT)} \tag{5}$$

The above process establishes a non-linear document evaluation function that takes into account the term dependencies which the concept hierarchy represents. Its effect can be demonstrated with the following example. Consider the simple case of a document that has activated two profile terms t_1 and t_2, with $w_2 > w_1 > 0$. If the terms are not connected, then no dissemination takes place and so the final energy of the terms is equal to their initial energy. The document's relevance would then be $S_D^u = 1 \cdot w_1 + 1 \cdot w_2$. On the other hand, if the terms were connected, then their final energy would be $E_1^f = 1 - (1 \cdot w_{12})$ and $E_2^f = 1 + (1 \cdot w_{12})$ respectively. Since $E_2^f > 1 > E_1^f$ and $w_2 > w_1$ it is obvious that $S_D^c = E_1^f \cdot w_1 + E_2^f \cdot w_2$ is greater than S_D^u. So if two terms are linked by a topic-subtopic relation they contribute more to the document's relevance than two isolated terms with the same weights. The difference in the contribution is proportional to the weight of the link between the terms which, as already mentioned, measures the statistical dependence caused by both topical and lexical correlations.

The overall effect is visible in figure 1(b). Activated profile terms define subhierarchies for each topic of interest discussed in the document. The dominant terms $DT1$, $DT2$ and $DT3$ can be defined as those activated terms that didn't disseminate any energy. The number of dominant terms measures the document's breadth b, i.e. the number of topics discussed in the document. For each dominant term the depth of the corresponding subhierarchy is equal to the number of activated terms from which energy was received. The document's depth d can thereafter be approximated as the number of activated terms that disseminated energy. Obviously, $b + d = a$, where a is the total number of activated terms. The total amount of energy that a subhierarchy contributes to a document's relevance, is analogous to its depth, and the weight of the terms involved. The document's relevance increases if it activates profile terms that formulate connected subhierarchies with large depths, and not isolated profile terms. In this latter case, the document's breadth increases without a corresponding increase in depth. $DT3$ represents an example of such an isolated term.

We also experimented with two normalized versions of the initial function, that explicitly take into account the above measures. The first is defined by equation 6. Here, the document breadth is used to normalize the document's score. The idea is to penalize documents that activate many unconnected terms. In the second case, the document's score is multiplied by the factor $log(1 + (b + d)/b)$ which favors documents with large depths and small breadths (eq. 7). Logarithmic smoothing is applied to avoid very large document scores.

$$S2_D = S_D \cdot \frac{1}{b} \tag{6}$$

$$S3_D = S_D \cdot log(1 + \frac{b+d}{b}) \tag{7}$$

Table 1. Two-Topic Combinations: codes, subjects and statistical characteristics

Combination	Topics	Subject	Code	Training	Test
I	R1	STRATEGY/PLANS	C11	597	23651
	R2	LEGAL/JUDICIAL	C12	351	11563
II	R10	CREDIT RATINGS	C174	212	5625
	R32	CONSUMER PRICES	E131	140	5492
III	R6	INSOLVENCY/LIQUIDITY	C16	42	1871
	R20	MARKET SHARE	C313	38	1074
IV	R41	INDUSTRIAL PRODUCTION	E311	35	1658
	R79	WELFARE, SOCIAL SERVICES	GWELF	42	1818

5   Experimental Evaluation

The shortage of multi-topic profile representations is unfortunately coupled with a lack of appropriate evaluation methodologies. We have attempted to establish such a methodology using a variation of the TREC-2001 routing subtask[2]. TREC-2001 adopts the Reuters Corpus Volume 1 (RCV1), an archive of 806,791 English language news stories that has recently been made freely available for research purposes[3]. The stories have been manually categorised according to topic, region, and industry sector [17]. The TREC-2001 filtering track is based on 84 out of the 103 RCV1 topic categories. Furthermore, it divides RCV1 into 23,864 training stories and a test set comprising the rest of the stories

To evaluate the proposed approach on a multi-topic filtering problem we experimented with profiles trained on combinations of RCV1 topics. Here we present results for four two-topic combinations. Table 1 presents for each combination the involved topics, their subject, RCV1 code and number of documents in the training and test set. A single profile was built for each one of these combinations. The training set comprised only the first 30 training documents corresponding to each topic in a combination (a total of 60 documents)[4]. This amount was considered a reasonable approximation of the number of documents that a user might actually provide. RelDF weighting was used to extract the most competent terms, based on the following thresholds: 0, 0.1, 0.15, 0.2, 0.25 and 0.3. We experimented with both unconnected profiles that use the inner product (S0) and connected profiles using the introduced functions (S1, S2 and S3). This allowed a direct comparison between a traditional linear approach to user profiling and our non-linear approach. Profiles were tested against the test set and evaluated on the basis of an ordered list of the best 3000 scoring documents, using the *Average Uninterpolated Precision* (AUP) measure. The AUP is defined as the sum of the precision value–i.e. percentage of filtered documents that are relevant–at each point in the list where a relevant document appears, divided by the total number of relevant documents. A separate AUP score was calculated for each topic in a combination and was then averaged into a single

---

[2] For more details see: http://trec.nist.gov/data/t10_filtering/T10filter_guide.htm

[3] http://about.reuters.com/researchandstandards/corpus/index.asp

[4] The user does not have to categorize the specified documents

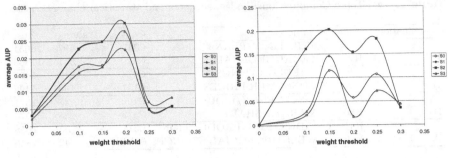

Fig. 2. Results for topics R1/R2(I)   **Fig. 3.** Results for topics R10/R32(II)

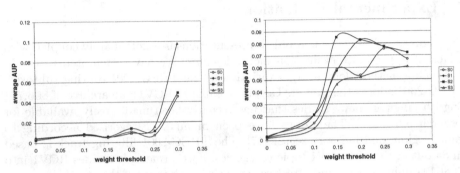

Fig. 4. Results for topics R6/R20(III)   **Fig. 5.** Results for topics R41/R79(IV)

score. Figures 2 to 5 present for each weight threshold and topic combination this average AUP score. Note, that due to the above differences in the evaluation methodology, a direct comparison to other IF systems, evaluated according to the standard TREC-2001 routing subtask, is not possible.

For combination I (fig. 2), S1 and S2 exhibit almost identical performance[5] and outperform S0 for most weight thresholds. S3 is also better than S0 for large threshold values and slightly worse for small values. The difference in the performance between S1, S2 and S0 is even larger for combination II (fig. 3). For the same combination S3 is now better than S0 for small thresholds and worse for large ones. In figure 4, the results for combination III indicate similar performance for all four functions and small weight thresholds, but for larger thresholds S1, S2 and clearly S3 are better than S0. Finally, for combination IV, S1 and S2 are in general better or at least as good as S0, but S3 is worse.

Overall, the above experiments on multi-topic information filtering with a single profile, indicate that the use of a hierarchical term network for profile representation is advantageous over a profile containing the same unconnected terms. The non-linear document evaluation functions we introduced, and especially S1 and S2, outperform the linear, inner product (S0). As already mentioned, since the same terms are used in both cases, any difference in performance is caused

---

[5] Note that in most graphs there is no visible difference between S1 and S2

by taking into account term dependencies. Documents containing profile terms that are linked score higher than documents containing non-correlated profile terms.

6   Summary and Further Work

We have presented a methodology that generates out of a set of user specified documents a hierarchical term network that represents the topics and subtopics that these documents discuss. A spreading activation model on this weighted network then establishes a series of non-linear document evaluation functions. Term dependence representation allows this kind of profile to filter documents according to multiple topics of interest. Experiments performed on combinations of two topics, revealed that this non-linear profile outperforms a traditional linear profile that ignores term dependencies. Further experiments with combinations of three topics have since confirmed the positive results.

Nootropia's profile represents a significant step towards tackling the dynamic nature of user interests. In addition to its ability to represent multiple topics of interests, adaptation to their changes can be achieved through a process of self-organisation, where based on user feedback, term and link weights are constantly calibrated, incompetent terms and their links removed, and new terms and links generated. New hierarchies develop to represent emerging topics of interest and hierarchies representing lapsed topics progressively disintegrate and are eventually forgotten. Experiments using virtual users have produced positive results.

References

1. G. Amati, D. D' Aloisi, V. Giannini, and F. Ubaldini. A framework for filtering news and managing distributed data. *Journal of Universal Computer Science*, 3(8):1007–1021, 1997.
2. P. Anick and S. Tipirneri. The paraphrase search assistant: Terminological feedback for iterative information seeking. In M. Hearst, F. Gey, and R. Tong, editors, *22nd Annual International ACM SIGIR Conference on Research and Development in Information Retrieval*, pages 153–159, 1999.
3. D. Billsus and M. Pazzani. A personal news agent that talks, learns and explains. In *3rd International Conference on Autonomous Agents*, Seattle, WA, 1999.
4. F. Crestani. Application of spreading activation techniques in information retrieval. *Artificial Intelligence Review*, 11(6):453–482, 1997.
5. L. B. Doyle. Semantic road maps for literature searchers. *Journal of the ACM*, 8:553–578, 1962.
6. W. P. Jones and G. W. Furnas. Pictures of relevance: A geometric analysis of similarity measures. *Journal of the American Society of Information Science*, 38(6):420–442, May 1986.
7. B. Krulwich and C. Burkey. The InfoFinder agent: Learning user interests through heuristic phrase extraction. *IEEE Expert*, pages 22–27, 1997.
8. K. Lang. NewsWeeder: Learning to filter netnews. In *12th International Conference on Machine Learning (ICML95)*, 1995.

9. P. Maes. Agents that reduce work and information overload. *Communications of the ACM*, 37(7):30–40, 1994.
10. M. McElligott and H. Sorensen. An evolutionary connectionist approach to personal information filtering. In *4th Irish Neural Networks Conference '94*, University College Dublin, Ireland, 1994.
11. J. Mostafa, S. Mukhopadhyay, M. Palakal, and W. Lam. A multilevel approach to intelligent information filtering: model, system, and evaluation. *ACM Transactions on Information Systems (TOIS)*, 15(4):368–399, 1997.
12. A. Moukas and P. Maes. Amalthaea: An evolving multi-agent information filtering and discovery system for the www. *Autonomous Agents and Multi-Agent Systems.*, 1(1):59–88, 1998.
13. N. Nanas, V. Uren, A. D. Roeck, and J. Domingue. Building and applying a concept hierarchy representation of a user profile. In *26th Annual International ACM SIGIR International Conference on Research and Development in Information Retrieval*, pages 198–204. ACM press, 2003.
14. C. G. Nevill-Manning, I. H. Witten, and G. W. Paynter. Lexically-generated subject hierarchies for browsing large collections. *International Journal on Digital Libraries*, 2(2-3):111–123, 1999.
15. M. Pazzani, J. Muramatsu, and D. Billsus. Syskill & webert: identifying interesting web sites. In *13th National Conference on Artificial Intelligence*, Portland, Oregon, 1996.
16. S. E. Robertson and K. Sparck Jones. Relevance weighting of search terms. *Journal of the American Society for Information Science*, 27:129–146, 1976.
17. T. Rose, M. Stevenson, and M. Whitehead. The Reuters Corpus Volume 1 - from yesterday's news to tomorrow's language resources. In *3rd International Conference on Language Resources and Evaluation*, 2002.
18. G. Salton and M. J. McGill. *Introduction to Modern Information Retrieval.* McGraw-Hill Inc., 1983.
19. M. Sanderson and B. W. Croft. Deriving concept hierarchies from text. In *22nd Annual Internation ACM SIGIR Conference on Research and Development in Information Retrieval*, pages 206–213, Berkeley, California, United States, 1999. ACM Press.
20. F. Sebastiani. Machine learning in automated text categorization. *ACM Computing Surveys*, 34(1), 2002.
21. B. D. Sheth. *A Learning Approach to Personalized Information Filtering.* Master of Science, Massachusetts Institute of Technology, 1994.
22. H. Sorensen, A. O' Riordan, and C. O' Riordan. Profiling with the informer text filtering agent. *Journal of Universal Computer Science*, 3(8):988–1006, 1997.
23. R. Wilkinson and P. Hingston. Using the cosine measure in a neural network for document retrieval. In *14th Annual Internation ACM SIGIR conference on Research and Development in Information Retrieval*, pages 202–210. ACM Press, 1991.

Exploiting Cross-Document Relations
for Multi-document Evolving Summarization

Stergos D. Afantenos[1], Irene Doura[2],
Eleni Kapellou[2], and Vangelis Karkaletsis[1]

[1] Software and Knowledge Engineering Laboratory
Institute of Informatics and Telecommunications,
National Center for Scientific Research (NCSR) "Demokritos"
{stergos,vangelis}@iit.demokritos.gr
[2] Institute of Language and Speech Processing
intoura@isll.uoa.gr, kotkap@teiath.gr

Abstract. This paper presents a methodology for summarization from multiple documents which are about a specific topic. It is based on the specification and identification of the cross-document relations that occur among textual elements within those documents. Our methodology involves the specification of the topic-specific entities, the messages conveyed for the specific entities by certain textual elements and the specification of the relations that can hold among these messages. The above resources are necessary for setting up a specific topic for our query-based summarization approach which uses these resources to identify the query-specific messages within the documents and the query-specific relations that connect these messages across documents.

1 Introduction

In the process of reading a text, we come to realize that several textual elements have a sort of connection with other textual elements. That is not a coincidence. Mann and Thompson (1988), in fact, have proposed a theory, the *Rhetorical Structure Theory (RST)*, according to which sentences or phrases are connected with some *relations*, from a set of predefined relations. This theory has been exploited, by Marcu (2000) for example, for single-document summarization.

We do believe that something similar happens across documents, at least when they are on the same topic. In other words, several *"elements"* in one document are *"connected"* with several other *"elements"* in another document. The point, of course, is to define those "elements" and "connections".

The aim of this paper is an attempt to remove the quotes from the words "elements" and "connections", *i.e.* try to make a little bit more explicit what such elements and connections can be, as well as suggest possible ways of how they can be used for multi-document summarization.

The motivation behind this work is presented in the following section, in which the related work will be presented as well. The general methodology of our work, as it has been formed until now, is given in section 3. This methodology is made more explicit through a case study in section 4.

G.A. Vouros and T. Panayiotopoulos (Eds.): SETN 2004, LNAI 3025, pp. 410–419, 2004.

2   Related Work – Motivation

As mentioned in the introduction, in this paper we consider the question of whether something similar to the RST can hold for more than one documents, and if that is so, how can that theory be exploited for the automatic creation of summaries. Of course, we are not the only ones who have given this matter some consideration. Radev (2000), inspired by Mann and Thompson's (1988) RST, tried to create a similar theory which would connect multiple documents. He called his theory *Cross-document Structure Theory (CST)*.

In his endeavor Radev (2000) proposed a set of relations which bear a certain similarity to the RST relations, such as *Elaboration, Contradiction, Equivalence, Agreement*, etc[1]. These relations are not applied to phrases or sentences of one document anymore, but, depending on the relation, they can be applied across documents to words, phrases, sentences, paragraphs or even entire documents. Radev claims that Cross-document Structure Theory can be the basis for multi-document summarization.

Since this theory was merely a proposition by Radev, Zhang *et al.* (2002) tried to put that theory to test by conducting an experiment, according to which subjects (judges) were asked to read a set of news articles and write down the CST relations they observed. The set of documents contained 11 news articles that were on the same topic but which originated from different sources. Five pairs of documents were given to 9 subjects, along with instructions on how to annotate the documents with the proposed relations. The instructions contained the set of 24 relations, along with examples on their use. It was clearly mentioned that the set of those relations was simply a "proposed" set and that they should feel free to use their own relations, should they wish to.

The results of this experiment can be summarize them as follows[2]:

- The inter-judge agreement was very low.
- Only a small subset of the proposed relations was used by the judges.
- No new relations were proposed.
- Only sentences were connected with each other; relations between words or phrases or paragraphs and documents were ignored.

We believe that the reasons for these results lie not in the fact that certain "elements" of one document are not "connected" with other "elements" in another document, but in the following.

First of all, the relations that Radev (2000) proposes seem to be similar to the ones that Mann and Thompson (1988) have proposed for the *Rhetorical Structure Theory*, only that they are extended to include multiple documents. While this seems reasonable at first sight, if we delve a little bit more in the details we will see that it is somewhat problematic. RST is based on the assumption of a *coherent text*, whose meaning needs further clarification when extended to include

---

[1]For more information on the RST relations see Mann and Thompson (1988) or http://www.sil.org/~mannb/rst.

[2]For more details, the reader is encouraged to consult Zhang *et al.* (2002).

multiple documents written by different authors, under different conditions and in a different context.

A second potential cause for the above results we consider to be the fact that CST concentrates on textual spans, and not — instead — on what these textual spans *represent*. In the context of multiple documents, the connection of textual spans seems more logical if what we connect is what is being *represented* by the textual spans and not the textual spans *themselves*.

The problem, of course, is that in order to find what the textual spans represent, one has to focus on a specific topic. And at this point comes our proposition, that to study the cross-document relations one has to begin with a specific topic, before generalizing, if that is possible.

In the next section we propose a general methodology for the manual specification of the cross-document relations. We also present the architecture of a query-based summarization system that exploits such relations. This system is currently under development. In section 4 we will give a particular example of this methodology in the topic of the description of football matches.

3   Methodology for Identifying Cross-Document Relations

The conclusion that can be drawn from the previous section is that the study of general cross-document relations, at least in the sense that Radev (2000) proposes it, is still premature. Instead we propose to concentrate on the identification of the *nature of what* can be connected between the documents first, as well as how that can be connected in each particular topic, and then try to generalize. Before continuing with the presentation of our methodology, we would like to put it in the context of our approach to multi-document summarization. Our approach is a query-based summarization one, which employs: a) an Information Extraction (IE) system for extracting the messages that are needed for the summarization task; this system is used off-line for the processing of the documents before the submission of the query. b) a Natural Language Generation (NLG) system for presenting the summary, exploiting those messages that are relevant to the query within a document and the relations that connect these messages across documents; the NLG system is used on-line after the submission of the query.

We have to stress here that despite the fact that this paper concentrates on the presentation of the methodology and not on the query-based summarization system, which is currently under development. The basic stages of our methodology are presented below.

Collection of corpus. The first stage of our methodology involves the collection of the corpus to be summarized. The corpus should be on a certain topic in which several events — that we want to summarize — are evolving and are being described by more than one source. Although this process can be automated using text classification techniques, we currently do not plan to do so and the collection of the corpus is done manually.

Creation of a topic-specific ontology. The next step involves the specification of the types of entities in the corpus that our summaries will concentrate on, as well as the specification of the events, and the entities' attributes or their roles in those events. For example, in the topic of football matches' descriptions (see the following section), important entity types are team, player, etc; important events are foul, penalty, etc; important entities' roles are the winner team, the player that shot the penalty, etc. In other words we have to set up the topic's *ontology*. The specification of the entity types and the ontology structure is done manually. Yet, there are several ontology editors that enable the building of the ontology using a specific knowledge representation format. In our case, we use the *Protégé*-based ontology editor developed in the CROSSMARC project (Pazienza et al. 2003).

Specification of the topic-specific message types. Our summarization system employs an NLG component which generates text from a set of messages that convey the meaning of the text to be generated (Reiter and Dale 2000). Therefore, the next step in our methodology is to specify the message types in the specific topic where our summarization system will be applied. Those message types should contain entity types and event-specific roles from the ontology that was built beforehand. The specification of the message types and their precise definition results through a study of the corpus.

We consider this step of the methodology as an IE task, which can be performed off-line before the query submission. Once the message types have been specified, the IE sub-system will locate the textual elements which instantiate particular messages and fill in the arguments for each message. For this purpose we use the Greek IE system developed in the context of the CROSSMARC project (Karkaletsis and Spyropoulos 2003), which is currently being adapted to the topics.

Specification of the topic-specific relations. Once we have finalized the set of topic-specific message types that occur within the documents of our corpus, we should try to specify what sort of relation types can connect those messages across the documents, again in relation to our summarization task. The set of relations can be a general one, similar to that of Radev's (2000) CST or Mann and Thompson's (1988) RST, or it can be topic-specific.

In order to define the relations we rely on the message types and the values that they can have in their arguments. Thus, we devise a set of rules to identify the relations connecting the messages. Once the instances of the relations have been identified, the relevant to the query messages and relations can be passed to the NLG system.

The above constitute our general methodology for specifying cross-document relations and exploiting them by a query-based summarization system. Those relations are not a rigid set that will be exactly the same, independently of the summarization task. Instead, they are quite flexible and can be customized for whatever application of summarization one has to deal with. In our case we were interested in the creation of *evolving summaries, i.e.* summaries of events within a topic which evolve through time, so our relations are customized for this.

In the next section we will make the above more explicit by presenting our initial steps towards the application of the above methodology to a specific topic: that of the description of football matches.

4   Case Study: Descriptions of Football Matches

Our choice for the topic of descriptions of football matches was influenced by the fact that we were interested in the study of *evolving summaries*. In that topic the main events that evolve can easily be isolated from the rest of the events in order to be studied separately, which made it suitable for an initial study.

The target language of this topic was Greek. The first step in the methodology is the collection of the corpus. The corpus we collected originated from three different sources: a newspaper, a sports magazine and the official internet site of a team[3], and it contained descriptions of football matches for the Greek football Championship of the first division for the years 2002–2003. The total number of documents that we studied was 90; they contained about 67,500 tokens totally.

For every team, we organized the descriptions of the matches in a way which reflects a *grid* and is depicted in Fig. 1. Note that if in a particular championship N teams compete, then the total number of rounds will be $(N - 1) \times 2$. This grid organization reflects the fact that for a certain team we have two axes in which we can view the descriptions of its matches. The first, *horizontal axis*, contains the descriptions of the *same match* but from *different sources*. The second, *vertical axis*, contains the descriptions from the *same source* but for all the *series* of matches during the championship. It should also be noted that if the grids of the teams are interposed on top of each other, the result will be a *cube* organization for the whole championship.

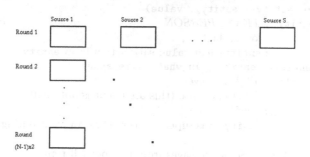

Fig. 1. Organization of the corpus in a grid

The next step involves the building of an ontology. Some of the main entities that we have decided to include in the ontology are shown in Fig. 2. Although this ontology is still in its first version and further refinement is still needed, it is in a state that it can be used for our experiments, as we describe below.

---

[3]One could argue that each of our source constitutes a different *genre* of text, since each source has a different target readership and a different purpose.

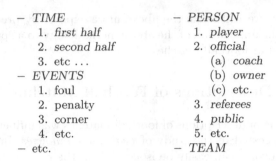

     − TIME   − PERSON
       1. *first half*   1. *player*
       2. *second half*   2. *official*
       3. etc ...   (a) *coach*
     − EVENTS   (b) *owner*
       1. foul   (c) etc.
       2. penalty   3. *referees*
       3. corner   4. *public*
       4. etc.   5. etc.
     − etc.   − TEAM

Fig. 2. A high level excerpt of the ontology

This ontology is related to the specification of the message types, which constitutes the next step in our methodology. In Fig. 3 several message types are presented in detail. The complete list of the message types is the following:

performance, satisfaction, blocks, superior, belongs, final_score, opportunity_lost, change, cancelation_of_goal, surprise, injured, alias, penalty, card, behavior, foul, selection_of_scheme, win, comeback, absent, successive_victories, refereeship, hope_for, scorer, expectations, conditions

  − **performance** (entity, in_what, time_span, value)
    entity   : *TEAM, PERSON*
    in_what   : offense, defense, general etc.
    value   : bad, good, moderate, excellent
    time_span : *TIME*
    Comment : entity had value performance in_what during time_span
  − **satisfaction** (entity₁, entity₂, value)
    entity₁, entity₂ : *TEAM, PERSON*
    value   : low ... high
    Comment   : entity₁ had value satisfaction from entity₂
  − **superior** (entity₁, entity₂, in_what, time_span)
    entity₁, entity₂ : *TEAM, player*
    in_what   : defense, offense (this argument is optional)
    time_span   : *TIME*
    Comment   : entity₁ was superior to entity₂ in_what during time_span

Fig. 3. Some messages from the football topic

It cannot be claimed that this set of messages is final, since changes in the ontology might result in further refinement of the messages.

    The final step of our methodology involves the identification of the relation types that exist between the messages. As it has been noted before, the relations can be similar to Radev's (2000) CST or to Mann and Thompson's (1988) RST, but they can also be different, depicting the needs for summarization that one has. In our case, the *grid* organization of our corpus, along with the fact that

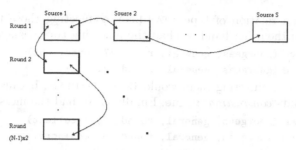

Fig. 4. Relations in two axes

we were interested in the study of *evolving summarization*, has led us to create relations across two axes, the *horizontal* and the *vertical* (See Fig. 4).

Relations on the horizontal axis are concerned with the *same* match as it was described by *different sources*, while relations on the vertical axis are concerned with the *different* matches of a certain team as described by the *same source*. We call the relations on the horizontal axis *synchronic* and the relations on the vertical axis *diachronic*. Those last relations, one could argue, concern the *progress* of a certain team, or of a certain player, which reflects our endeavor for *evolving summarization*. Examples of synchronic and diachronic relations are given in Table 1.

Table 1. Examples of synchronic and diachronic relations

Synchronic Relations	Diachronic Relations	
– IDENTITY	– STABILITY	– VARIATION
– EQUIVALENCE	– ANTITHESIS	– IDENTITY
– ELABORATION	– POSITIVE GRADUATION	– ANALOGY
– CONTRADICTION	– NEGATIVE GRADUATION	
– PRECISENESS		

Each relation connects messages of the *same* type. In contrast to Radev's (2000) CST relations, our synchronic–diachronic relations are not dependent on the semantics of the sentences in order to be established, because they do not connect sentences. Instead, we have strict rules which connect certain messages according to the *values of their arguments*, which are predefined since they are taken from the ontology.

Things will become clearer with an example. Let us assume that we have the following two messages taken from the descriptions of two consecutive matches of the same team and from the same source:

performance (georgeas, general, round_17, excellent)
performance (georgeas, general, round_18, excellent)

What those messages state is that a certain player had, according to the author(s) of the articles, excellent performance in both the 17th and 18th round. According to our rules, given that the **value** and **entity** argument of this message are the same, we have a relation of type STABILITY connecting those two particular messages. If, on the other hand, we had the following two messages

performance (georgeas, general, round_17, excellent)

performance (georgeas, general, round_18, bad)

then the relation connecting them would be ANTITHESIS, because we have the same entity but *"contrasting"* value. Finally, if we had the messages

performance (georgeas, general, round_17, excellent)

performance (georgeas, general, round_18, mediocre)

then the resulting relation would be NEGATIVE GRADUATION since we have the same entity but *"close"* values. We have to note here that what is meant by *"contrasting"* and *"close"* values is something which is defined in the ontology, although here it is quite intuitively understood. Similarly, we have exact rules for each message, according to which the synchronic and diachronic relations are established. The rules take into account the values of the messages' arguments, as these are defined in the ontology.

But how does all that relate to summarization? As it has previously been stated, our system is query-based and relies on NLG for the production of the summary. The following example will explain how the above can be used for the creation of the summary. Let us assume that a user asks the question: *"What was the performance of Georgeas like during the first three rounds?"* In order to answer that question we analyze the query and we can see that we have to pinpoint the **performance** messages that are related to Georgeas for the first three rounds of the championship. For the sake of argument, let us assume that we only have three sources describing the matches of his team, and that we have already specified the messages and relations connecting them. In addition, the IE system has already identified the messages within the documents of our corpus. For each source, the query-specific messages are the following (what precedes each message is an identifier for it):

Source 1:
s1.1 **performance** (georgeas, general, round_1, excellent)
s1.2 **performance** (georgeas, general, round_2, excellent)
s1.3 **performance** (georgeas, general, round_3, mediocre)

Source 2:
s2.1 **performance** (georgeas, general, round_1, excellent)
s2.2 **performance** (georgeas, general, round_2, good)
s2.3 **performance** (georgeas, general, round_3, bad)

Source 3:
s3.1 **performance** (georgeas, general, round_1, excellent)
s3.3 **performance** (georgeas, general, round_2, excellent)
s3.3 **performance** (georgeas, general, round_3, bad)

Concerning the synchronic relations, for the first round all sources have exactly the same message, which means that there is a relation IDENTITY connecting those messages:

IDENTITY(s1.1, s2.1)   IDENTITY(s1.1, s3.1)
IDENTITY(s2.1, s3.1)

For the second and third round, not all sources agree, so the relations that exist
are the following:

IDENTITY(s1.2, s3.2)   CONTRADICTION(s1.2, s2.2)
CONTRADICTION(s2.2, s3.2)   CONTRADICTION(s1.3, s2.3)
IDENTITY(s2.3, s3.3)   CONTRADICTION(s1.3, s3.3)

Concerning the diachronic relations, the relations that hold are the following:

NEGATIVE GRADUATION(s1.2, s1.3)   STABILITY(s3.1, s3.2)
NEGATIVE GRADUATION(s2.1, s2.2)   STABILITY(s1.1, s1.2)
NEGATIVE GRADUATION(s2.2, s2.3)
NEGATIVE GRADUATION(s3.2, s3.3)

The above information can be used by the NLG system for the *content selection*
phase. The NLG system, of course, will have to make more choices depending
on several factors, such as the compression rate that the user wishes, etc. A
candidate final summary can be the following:

*Georgeas's performance for the first two rounds of the championship was almost
excellent. In the third round his performance deteriorated and was quite bad.*

A more concise summary could be:

With the exception of the third round, Georgeas's performance was very good.

From these examples the reader can glimpse the advantages that an abstractive
summary has over an extractive one. The above summaries could not possibly
have been created with an extractive approach since the generated sentences
simply could not exist in the source documents. Furthermore, the manipulation
of the relevant information for the creation of two different summaries, as hap-
pened above, cannot happen with an extractive approach. This means that, at
least qualitatively, we achieve better results compared with an extractive system.

5   Conclusion

The aim of the paper is to propose a new approach for the specification and
identification of cross-document relations which will enhance multi-document
summarization.

Currently the methodology is being applied to a specific topic, that of the
descriptions of football matches, and has produced some promising results. We
have to note though that not all of the stages of the methodology are fully
automated yet; so far we have designed the architecture of the summarization
system that we build, and collected its components. Our query-based summarization system involves an IE and an NLG system. These are currently being
customized to the needs of our task. The ontology is currently being built using
the CROSSMARC ontology management system.

In the future we plan to examine the application of the methodology in
other topics, in order for its strengths and weaknesses to be identified. For this

reason we plan to create the infrastructure needed for the adaptation of this methodology to other topics, *i.e.* to provide the infrastructure to support the creation of new entity types, message types and relation types.

References

Karkaletsis, V., and C. D. Spyropoulos. 2003, November. "Cross-lingual Information Management from Web Pages." *Proceedings of the 9th Panhellenic Conference in Informatics (PCI-2003)*. Thessaloniki, Greece.

Mann, W. C., and S. A. Thompson. 1988. "Rhetorical Structure Theory: Towards a Functional Theory of Text Organization." *Text* 8 (3): 243–281.

Marcu, D. 2000. *The Theory and Practice of Discourse Parsing and Summarization*. The MIT Press.

Pazienza, M. T., A. Stellato, M. Vindigni, A. Valarakos, and V. Karkaletsis. 2003, June. "Ontology Integration in a Multilingual e-Retail System." *Proceedings of the Human Computer Interaction International (HCII'2003), Special Session on Ontologies and Multilinguality in User Interfaces*. Heraklion, Crete, Greece.

Radev, D. 2000, October. "A Common Theory of Information Fusion from Multiple Text Sources, Step One: Cross-Document Structure." *Proceedings of the 1st ACL SIGDIAL Workshop on Discourse and Dialogue*. Hong Kong.

Reiter, E., and R. Dale. 2000. *Building Natural Language Generation Systems*. Studies in Natural Language Processing. Cambridge University Press.

Zhang, Z., S. Blair-Goldensohn, and D. Radev. 2002. "Towards CST-Enhanced Summarization." *Proceedings of AAAI-2002*.

Diagnosing Transformer Faults with Petri Nets

John A. Katsigiannis[1], Pavlos S. Georgilakis[1],
Athanasios T. Souflaris[2], and Kimon P. Valavanis[1]

[1] Technical University of Crete, University Campus, Kounoupidiana, Chania, Greece
{katsigiannis,pgeorg,kimonv}@dpem.tuc.gr
[2] Schneider Electric AE, Elvim Plant, P.O. Box 59, 32011, Inofyta, Viotia, Greece
thanassis_souflaris@mail.schneider.fr

Abstract. Transformer fault diagnosis and repair is a complex task that includes many possible types of faults and demands special trained personnel. In this paper, Petri Nets are used for the simulation of transformer fault diagnosis process and the definition of the actions followed to repair the transformer. An integrated safety detector relay is used for transformer fault detection. Simulation results for the most common types of transformer faults (overloading, oil leakage, short-circuit and insulation failure) are presented. The proposed methodology aims at identifying the transformer fault and estimating the duration for transformer repair.

1 Introduction

The process of Electric utilities restructuring, privatization, and deregulation has created a competitive, global marketplace for energy [1]. Early preparation to market competition and best use of technology will drive success in this new and challenging environment. Twenty-first century utilities will try to further improve system reliability and quality, while simultaneously being cost effective.

Power system reliability depends on components reliability. As the ultimate element in the electricity supply chain, the distribution transformer is one of the most widespread apparatus in electric power systems. During their operation, transformers are subjected to many external electrical stresses from both the upstream and downstream network. The consequences of transformer fault can be significant (damage, oil pollution, etc). Transformers must, therefore, be protected against attacks of external origin, and be isolated from the network in case of internal failure.

It is the electrical network designer's responsibility to define the measures to be implemented for each transformer as a function of such criteria like continuity and quality of service, cost of investment and operation and safety of property and people as well as the acceptable level of risk. The solution chosen is always a compromise between the various criteria and it is important that the strengths and weaknesses of the chosen compromise are clearly identified [2]. The high reliability level of transformers is a decisive factor in the protection choices that are made by electrical utilities, faced with the unit cost of the protection devices that can be associated with them.

G.A. Vouros and T. Panayiotopoulos (Eds.): SETN 2004, LNAI 3025, pp. 420–431, 2004.

In spite of the high reliability of transformers, in practice, various types of faults (e.g. insulation failure, overloading, oil leakage, short-circuit, etc) can occur to the transformers of an electrical utility. Failure of these transformers is very costly to both the electrical companies and their customers.

When a transformer fault occurs, it is important to identify the fault type and to minimize the time needed for transformer repair, especially in cases where the continuity of supply is crucial. Consequently, it should not come as a surprise that transformer fault diagnosis forms a subject of a permanent research effort.

Various transformer fault diagnosis techniques have been proposed in the literature, for different types of faults [3]. For thermal related faults, the most important diagnostic method is the gas-in-oil analysis [4-5], while other methods such as the degree of polymerization, the furanic compounds analysis and the thermography are also applicable [6]. For dielectric related faults, it is necessary to localize and to characterize the partial discharge source, in order to give a correct diagnosis after receiving an alarm signal via sensors or via gas-in-oil sampling [7]. For mechanical related faults, the frequency response analysis and the leakage inductance methods are the more frequently used transformer fault diagnosis techniques [8]. Finally, for transformer general degradation, the dielectric response, the oil analysis and the furanic compounds analysis methods are applicable [9].

In spite of the wide range of the transformer fault diagnosis methods, the diagnostic criteria developed till today are not fully applicable to all faulty cases, and consequently, the experience of experts still play an important role in the diagnosis of the transformer faults. Dismantling the suspected transformers, performing internal examinations, and holding a group discussion are usually the procedure to conclude the diagnosis.

Expert systems and artificial intelligence techniques have already been proposed to understand the obvious and non-obvious relationships between transformer failures and the causes of failures (i.e. internal or external causes) [10-13]. Preliminary results, obtained from the application of these techniques, are encouraging, however some limitations exist. Knowledge acquisition, knowledge representation and maintenance of a great number of rules in the expert systems require plenty of efforts [14].

In this paper, Petri Nets are proposed for modeling of transformer fault diagnosis process. Petri Nets are both a mathematical and graphical tool capable of capturing deterministic or stochastic system behavior and modeling phenomena such as sequentialism, parallelism, asynchronous behavior, conflicts, resource sharing and mutual exclusion [15]. The proposed method offers significant advantages such as systematical determination of the sequence of fault diagnosis and repair actions, visual representation of the above actions, as well as estimation of the time needed for transformer repair.

The paper is organized as follows: Section 2 describes the Petri Nets methodology. The application of Petri Nets to transformer fault diagnosis and the obtained results are described in Section 3. Finally, Section 4 concludes the paper.

2 Overview of Petri Nets

Petri Nets (PNs) were introduced in Carl A. Petri's 1962 Ph.D. dissertation [16]. Since that time, they have proved to be a valuable graphical and mathematical modeling tool applicable to many systems. As a graphical tool, PNs can be used as a visual communication aid similar to flow charts, block diagrams, and networks. As a mathematical tool, it is possible to set up state equations, algebraic equations, and other mathematical models governing the behavior of systems. For a formal introduction to PNs the reader is referred to [15, 17].

A PN is a particular kind of directed graph, together with an initial marking, M_0. The underlying graph of a PN is a directed, weighted, bipartite graph consisting of two kinds of nodes, called places and transitions, where arcs are either from a place to a transition or from a transition to a place. In graphical representation, places are drawn as circles, and transitions as either bars or boxes. If a marking (state) assigns to each place p a nonnegative integer k, it is called that p is marked with k tokens. Pictorially, k black dots (tokens) are placed in p.

Places are used to describe possible local system rates, named conditions or situations. Transitions are used to describe events that may modify the system state. Arcs specify the relation between local states and events in two ways: they indicate the local state in which the event can occur, and the local state transformations induced by the event.

The presence of a token in a place is interpreted as holding the truth of the condition associated with the place. The only execution rule in a PN is the rule for transition enabling and firing. A transition t is considered as enabled if each input place p of t is marked with at least $w(p,t)$ tokens, where $w(p,t)$ is the weight of the arc from p to t. An enabled transition may or may not fire. A firing of an enabled transition t removes $w(p,t)$ tokens from all its input places p, and adds $w(p,t)$ tokens to each of its output places, where $w(t,p)$ is the weight of the arc from t to p. The movement of tokens through the PN graph represents the flow of information or control in the system [18-20].

Fig. 1 presents an example of a PN. The input place for transition t_0 is place p_0, and the set of output places for t_0 is $[p_1, p_2]$.

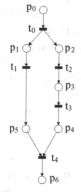

Fig. 1. Petri Net.

For problems that include the completion of an activity, it is necessary and useful to introduce time delays associated with transitions (activity executions) in their net models. Such a PN model is known as a deterministic timed net if the delays are deterministically given, or as a stochastic net, if the delays are probabilistically specified. In both cases, boxes of thick bars graphically represent transitions [17, 19].

The Stochastic Petri Net (SPN) model provides a more realistic representation of matter [21]. In SPNs transitions are associated with random variables that express the delay from enabling to the firing of the transition. The type of distribution in random variables can be uniform, exponential, etc.

Reachability is a useful concept of PNs. Each initial marking M_0 has a reachability set associated with it; this set consists of all the markings which can be reached from M_0 through the firing of one or more transitions.

Each marking, which can be reached from the initial marking, is referred to as a state. The reachability information is represented through a reachability graph, in which each node corresponds to a state, and the edges are associated with transitions. A directed edge is incident out of node M_i and into node M_{i+1} if and only if there exists a transition t_j whose firing changes the initial marking M_i to the marking M_{i+1}; the edge bears the label t_j. Reachability graphs enable as to find all the nodes which can be reached from M_i by the traversal of directed paths [22].

A PN is safe if the number of tokens in each place does not exceed 1 for any marking reachable from an initial marking M_0. A PN is live if, no matter what marking has been reached from M_0, it is possible to ultimately fire any transition of the net by progressing through some further firing sequence. A PN is reversible if, for each possible marking M, M_0 is reachable from M [17].

3 Fault Diagnosis Using Petri Nets

This paper simulates the actions that are followed by the transformer maintenance personnel in order to diagnose the fault and repair the transformer. It is important to notice that the maintenance staff is not able to know the exact problem from the beginning of the diagnosis process; there is crucial information that is obtained during the whole transformer fault diagnosis process.

To better model the transformer fault diagnosis process, stochastic PNs are used in this paper. These nets provide a structural tool, like flow charts, with the additional advantages of simulating dynamic and concurrent actions, and they provide the simulation results using stochastic times for a number of transitions.

Fig. 2 presents the proposed PN model for transformer fault diagnosis, Fig. 3 shows the "not on-site repair" subnet (i.e. in case that the transformer repair is implemented in the factory), and Table 1 describes all places and transitions that constitute the PN models of Fig. 2 and 3. Places in shadow boxes represent the crucial information that is obtained during the transformer fault diagnosis process; these places represent two opposite events, so tokens can be placed only in one of the places.

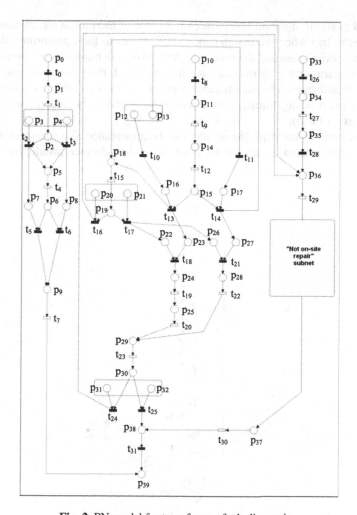

Fig. 2. PN model for transformer fault diagnosis.

The proposed PN models the following transformer faults: short-circuit, overloading, oil leakage and insulation failure. The protection equipment that is used for detection of all the faults mentioned above is an integrated safety detector. This device contains four switches: a pressure switch, which trips the transformer operation in case of a strong short-circuit; a thermostat switch which alarms when oil temperature exceeds a predetermined temperature level; another thermostat switch that stops the transformer operation when oil temperature reaches the trip level; and an alarm switch that operates when oil is reduced to a specified level. The last switch also detects an insulation failure, as the generated bubbles reduce the oil level. The activation of the above switches notifies the personnel, and makes it capable of understanding the general type of the problem. The possible initial warnings are a) alarm of the thermostat switch (thermostat switch cannot trip without earlier alarm), b) trip of the pressure switch, and c) alarm of the oil level detector. In case of thermostat switch alarm, it can be a change to trip when the maintenance staff arrives to the transformer, depending on problem's seriousness and the time required arriving in transformer's area.

When the alarm or trip thermostat switch is activated, there is an overloading problem in the transformer. The maintenance staff has to check if the loads are over the transformer overloading limits, reduce the loads accordingly and restart the transformer (in case of trip).

If the pressure switch trips, the problem is the appearance of a strong short-circuit. The repair of the damage can not be done in the transformer installation area; the transformer must be disconnected and transferred in a dedicated repairing area (e.g. in a transformer factory).

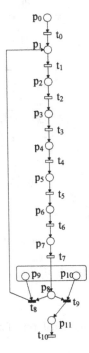

Fig. 3. PN model for the "not on-site repair" subnet.

The handling of the maintenance staff is more complex, in case of alarm of the oil level detector. The possible problems can be oil leakage or insulation failure. Initially, the maintenance staff has to check the exact kind of damage. There are two possible contingencies: either the level of the oil indicator is low (p_{12}), or there are air bubbles behind the observation glass (p_{13}). In the first case, the problem is oil leakage, otherwise there is insulation failure. The operation of transformer has to stop and it is checked if it is possible to repair the transformer on-site. This depends on a) the type of problem: the repair can be done if the oil leakage is not wide (i.e. the size of hole in the tank is very small) or if the insulation failure is on a part outside the tank, and b) the existence of suitable tools. The capability of on-site repair enables repairing possibilities for the two possible problems (p_{22} and p_{26}) and the specific type (p_{23} or p_{27}) enables the transition t_{18} or t_{21} (on-site repair of the damage is possible). Then the staff works on the problem (in the case of oil leakage, the lost oil has also to be replaced). Finally, there is a check if everything works right. If there is still a problem, then the transformer must be sent to a dedicated repairing area (i.e. on-site repair is not possible). The "not on-site repair" subnet of Fig. 3 is then models the transformer fault diagnosis and repair process.

When the transformer arrives in the dedicated repairing area (not on-site repair), before opening the tank, oil has to be removed. Fault diagnosis follows, and next transformer repair is done. The time needed for transformer diagnosis and repair depends on many factors, such as seriousness of the problem, availability of spare parts, working load of factory personnel, etc. After repair, the transformer is reassembled and is filled with oil, and the repaired transformer passes through quality control tests. If the transformer passes successfully all the quality control tests, then it is sent back in its area and is reinstalled (see Fig. 2), otherwise the repairing procedure is repeated.

Considering the sequence of transition firings and all marking reachable from the initial marking, the reachability graph of the Petri subnet of Fig. 3 is drawn in Fig. 4 for the case of non-existence of any fault after the repair. The dotted arc represents the modification carried out on the individual subnet, in order to validate its proper

Table 1. Description of PN places and transitions.

Main Petri net	
p_0:	Thermostat switch alarms
t_0:	Alarm is activated
p_1:	Personnel is notified
t_1:	Personnel is moving to transformer area
p_2:	Existence of alarm or trip?
p_3:	Thermostat switch still alarms
t_2:	Alarm is still activated
p_4:	Thermostat switch tripped
t_3:	Trip is activated
p_5:	Need to check the loads
t_4:	Loads are checked
p_6:	Does transformer need to restart?
p_7:	It doesn't need to restart
t_5:	No restart is needed
p_8:	It needs to restart
t_6:	Transformer is restarting
p_9:	Loads have to be reduced properly
t_7:	Loads are reduced properly
p_{10}:	Oil level detector alarms
t_8:	Alarm is activated
p_{11}:	Personnel is notified
t_9:	Personnel is moving to transformer area

Table 1. Description of PN places and transitions (cont'd).

p_{12}:	Low level of oil indicator
t_{10}:	Oil volume has reduced
p_{13}:	Air bubbles in oil indicator's glass
t_{11}:	Air bubbles are observed
p_{14}:	Transformer needs to stop
t_{12}:	Transformer is stopped
p_{15}:	Existence of oil leakage or insulation failure?
p_{16}:	Oil leakage
t_{13}:	Existence of oil leakage
p_{17}:	Insulation failure
t_{14}:	Existence of insulation failure
p_{18}:	Check for the exact type of fault
t_{15}:	Transformer is checked
p_{19}:	Is it possible repair fault on the spot?
p_{20}:	It is not possible to repair
t_{16}:	Fault cannot be repaired on the spot
p_{21}:	It is possible to repair
t_{17}:	Fault can be repaired on the spot
p_{22}:	Possibility for repairing oil leakage
p_{23}:	Problem of oil leakage
t_{18}:	Repair of oil leakage is possible
p_{24}:	Personnel prepares to repair transformer
t_{19}:	Transformer is repaired
p_{25}:	Lost oil needs to be replaced
t_{20}:	Lost oil is replaced
p_{26}:	Possibility for repairing insulation failure
p_{27}:	Problem of insulation failure
t_{21}:	Repair of insulation failure is possible
p_{28}:	Need to replace problematic external parts
t_{22}:	Parts are replaced
p_{29}:	Check if everything works properly
t_{23}:	Transformer is checked
p_{30}:	Is transformer working properly?
p_{31}:	It is not working properly
t_{24}:	Fault still exists
p_{32}:	It is working properly
t_{25}:	Fault is repaired
p_{33}:	Pressure switch trips
t_{26}:	Trip is activated
p_{34}:	Personnel is notified
t_{27}:	Personnel is moving to transformer area
p_{35}:	Identification of transformer's fault
t_{28}:	Existence of a powerful short-circuit
p_{36}:	Transformer needs to disconnect
t_{29}:	Transformer is disconnected

Table 1. Description of PN places and transitions (cont'd).

p_{37}:	Transformer arrives in area of installation
t_{30}:	Transformer is reinstalled
p_{38}:	Transformer is ready to work
t_{31}:	Transformer is restarted
p_{39}:	Transformer reworks properly

"Not on-site repair" subnet

p_0:	Transformer is sending to repairing area
t_0:	Transformer arrives to repairing area
p_1:	Oil has to be removed
t_1:	Oil is removed
p_2:	Inside search is needed
t_2:	Tank is opened
p_3:	Check for the exact type of fault
t_3:	Check is done
p_4:	Identification of fault
t_4:	Fault is repaired
p_5:	Transformer has to be reassembled
t_5:	Transformer is reassembled
p_6:	Oil has to be added
t_6:	Oil is added
p_7:	Check for the proper operation
t_7:	Check is done
p_8:	Is transformer working properly?
p_9:	It is not working properly
t_8:	Fault still exists
p_{10}:	It is working properly
t_9:	Fault is repaired
p_{11}:	Transformer is ready to be sent back in its area
t_{10}:	Transformer is transferred

Table 2. Simulation results.

Fault	Duration
Oil leakage	7 hours
Oil leakage (not on-site repair)	7 days
Overloading	4 hours
Insulation failure (bushings)	5 hours
Insulation failure (not on-site repair)	7 days
Short-circuit	7 days

ties. By examining this reachability graph, it is validated that the constructed model is safe, live and reversible. The verification of these important PN properties assures that our subnet is feasible and deadlock-free [18].

In the proposed PN modeling, immediate, deterministic and stochastic transitions are used, which take integer values that represent hours. For stochastic transitions, uniform distribution is assumed (i.e. the duration for transition t_4 of main net can take an integer value from interval [1 5]). In Table 2, simulation results for fault diagnosis and repair are presented.

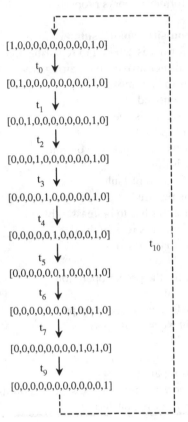

Fig. 4. Reachability graph for the "not on-site repair" subnet.

4 Conclusions

Transformer fault diagnosis and repair is a complex task that includes many possible types of faults and demands special trained personnel. This paper is concentrated on the investigation of the applicability of Stochastic Petri Nets in the modeling of transformer fault diagnosis and repair process. Simulation results for the most common types of transformer faults (overloading, oil leakage, short-circuit and insulation failure) are presented. The proposed methodology aims at identifying the transformer fault and estimating the duration for transformer repair.

As future research objectives, the modeling of other uncommon transformer faults and the more detailed analysis of the not on-site repair process would help in better understanding the diagnosis and repair and in acquiring better simulation results (by improving the accuracy of the stochastic transitions).

References

1. Georgilakis, P.S., Doulamis, N.D., Doulamis, A.D., Hatziargyriou, N.D., Kollias, S.D.: A novel iron loss reduction technique for distribution transformers based on a combined genetic algorithm-neural network approach. IEEE Trans. Systems, Man, and Cybernetics, Part C: Applications and Reviews **31** (2001) 16-34.
2. Fulchiron, D.: Protection of MV/LV Substation Transformers. Schneider Electric (1998), Cahier Technique no 192.
3. Bengtsson, C: Status and trends in transformer monitoring. IEEE Trans. Power Delivery **11** (1996) 1379-1384.
4. Pugh P.S., Wagner H.H.: Detection of incipient faults in transformer by gas analysis. AIEE Trans. **80** (1961) 189-195.
5. Kelly, J.J.: Transformer fault diagnosis by dissolved gas analysis. IEEE Trans. Industry Applications **16** (1980) 777-782.
6. Oommen T.V. et al: Analysis of furanic compounds from cellulose aging by GC-MS, and attempts to correlate with degree of polymerization. CIGRE Berlin Symposium, Paper 110-2, April 1993.
7. Eriksson, T., Leijon, M., Bengtsson, C.: PD on-line monitoring of power transformers. IEEE Stockholm Power Tech, 1995.
8. Hanique, E., Reijnders, H., Vaessen, P.: Frequency response analysis as a diagnostic tool. Elektrotechniek **68** (1990) 549.
9. Ildstad, E., Gäfvert, U., Thärning, P.: Relation between return voltage and other methods for measurement of dielectric response. IEEE Int. Symposium on Electrical Insulation, June 1994.
10. Wang, Z., Liu, Y., Griffin, P.J.: A combined ANN and expert system tool for transformer fault diagnosis. IEEE Trans. Power Delivery **13** (1998) 1224-1229.
11. Zhang, Y., Ding, X., Liu, Y., Griffin, P.J.: An artificial neural network approach to transformer fault diagnosis. IEEE Trans. Power Delivery **11** (1996) 1836-1841.
12. Lin, C.E., Ling, J.-M., Huang, C.-L.: An expert system for transformer fault diagnosis using dissolved gas analysis. IEEE Trans. Power Delivery **8** (1993) 231-238.
13. Tomsovic, K., Tapper, M., Ingvarsson, T.: A fuzzy information approach to integrating different transformer diagnostic methods. IEEE Trans. Power Delivery **8** (1993) 1638-1646.
14. Farag, A.S., Mohandes, M., Al-Shaikh, A.: Diagnosing failed distribution transformers using neural networks. IEEE Trans. Power Delivery **16** (2001) 631-636.
15. Peterson, J.L.: Petri Net theory and the modeling of systems. Prentice-Hall Inc., N.J. (1981).
16. Petri, C.A.: Kommunikation mit Automaten. Institut für Instrumentelle Mathematik, Bonn (1962). Also, English translation: Communication with Automata. Griffiss Air Force Base, New York (1966).
17. Murata, T.: Petri Nets: properties, analysis and applications. Proceedings of the IEEE **77** (1989) 541-580.

18. Fountas, N.A., Hatziargyriou, N.D., Valavanis, K.P.: Hierarchical time-extended Petri Nets as a generic tool for power system restoration. IEEE Trans. Power Systems **12** (1997) 837-843.
19. Marsan, M.A., Balbo, G., Conte, G., Donatelli, S., Franceschinis, G.: Modelling with generalized stochastic Petri Nets. Wiley, Chichester (1995).
20. Zhou, M.C., Zurawski, R.: Introduction to Petri Nets in flexible and agile automation. In: Zhou, M.C. (ed.): Petri Nets in flexible and agile automation. Kluwer Academic Publishers, Boston (1995) 1-42.
21. Moloy, M.K.: Performance analysis using stochastic Petri Nets. IEEE Trans. Computers **31** (1987) 913-917.
22. Jenkins, L., Khincha, H.P.: Deterministic and stochastic Petri Net models of protection schemes. IEEE Trans. Power Delivery **7** (1992) 84-90.

Short-Term Load Forecasting
Using Radial Basis Function Networks

Zbigniew Gontar[1], George Sideratos[2], and Nikos Hatziargyriou[2]

[1] Dept. of Computer Science, University of Lodz, Poland
[2] School of Electrical & Computer Engineering, National Technical University of Athens
Greece

Abstract. This paper presents results from the application of Radial Basis Function Networks (RBFNs) to Short-Term Load Forecasting. Short-term Load Forecasting is nowadays a crucial function, especially in the operation of liberalized electricity markets, as it affects the economy and security of the system. Actual load series from Crete are used for the evaluation of the developed structures providing results of satisfactory accuracy, retaining the advantages of RBFNs.

1 Introduction

Short-term load forecasting is one of the most significant functions of contemporary energy management systems. The hourly load forecasting of the next 24 up to 48 hours ahead or more is needed to support basic operational planning functions, such as spinning reserve management and energy exchanges, as well as network analysis functions related to system security, such as contingency analysis. Especially in the liberalized energy market operation, load forecasting plays a significant role in market operation and in the resulting prices. Reliable load forecasting forms the basis for the economic and secure operation of the system.

A number of algorithms employing artificial intelligence techniques have been published in the literature [1-6]. In this paper the application of Radial Basis Function Networks to the short-term load forecasting is proposed. RBFNs were chosen for the following reasons:

- RBFNs are universal approximators, i.e. they provide techniques for approximating non-linear functional mappings between multidimensional spaces.
- RBFNs are faster than other ANN models in the sense of neural learning. A typical ANN learning algorithm follows a scheme with: random initial estimates, case by case updating formulas, and slow convergence (or non-convergence). Contrary to that learning scheme, RBFN usually applies classical optimising techniques. They are not only faster, but also more understandable and easier to operate for end-users.

In the framework of the Greek-Polish joint Research & Technology Programme two RBFN structures were developed by the research teams of the University of Lodz (UL) and the National Technical University of Athens (NTUA) and applied to actual Greek and Polish load time-series [7]. In this paper results from the application to the load time series of the island of Crete are presented. The power system of Crete was chosen as a study case. Crete is the largest Greek island with the highest growth in

G.A. Vouros and T. Panayiotopoulos (Eds.): SETN 2004, LNAI 3025, pp. 432–438, 2004.

peak load and energy nation-wide. There is a large variance between the maximum and minimum load values throughout the year and even in a typical day. In summer's days the peak exceeds 450 MW, while the low load is about 100 MW. These large variations make STLF more difficult. The system base load is covered by steam turbines and the combined cycle plant, while for the peak, gas turbines at multiple cost are used. Accurate STLF for efficient operational planning of the system is therefore of vital importance.

2 Architectures of RBFN Models

2.1 RBFN Developed at NTUA

For one hour-ahead load forecasting the system comprises a combination of Radial Basis (RBF) neural networks. In the input of the system, there are five RBFNs, which accept the same input vector. Four of them have the same structure and each one is trained with load time-series corresponding to each season of the year, in order to give a better prediction in the period for which they have been trained. The fifth network is trained with the load values that correspond to weekends and special days. The five same networks consist of two layers and 48 neurons and the network's spread is 256. The input of the system, that is the input vector for all networks, consists of nine values: eight previous load values of the current point and the hour (1-24) that we want to make the prediction for. The eight load values are the two latest hours' values of the current point and the three respective hours' values of the past two days. For example, if the load at 7:00a.m. on Friday is predicted, the input includes load values at 6:00a.m., 5:00a.m. of the current day and at 7:00a.m., 6:00a.m. and 5:00a.m. of the previous two days.

$$P1(t+1)=\{L(t),L(t-1),L(t-24),L(t-25),L(t-26),L(t-48),L(t-49),$$

$$L(t-50),H(t)\} \tag{1}$$

- L , previous load value
- P1, first system's prediction
- H, time of day

The above networks provide five outputs and the system keeps the one with the minimum distance from the average value of these outputs. The variance of the predicted value with the previous hour's value and the respective hour's value of the last day is calculated next together with the cumulative probability density function of the data. The predicted value, the five first elements of the input of the system, the minimum and maximum values of the current day's temperature, the cumulative density function and the variances are provided as input to an RBFN that makes the final prediction.

$$P2=f\{P1,L(t), L(t-1), L(t-24), L(t-25), L(t-26),CPDF,V1,V2,TMP\}$$
$$\tag{2}$$

- CPDF, cumulative density function,
- V1,V2, variances between predicted value and previous load value.

The output network of the system has 96 neurons and the spread is 314.

2.2 RBFN Developed at UL

Forecasting models based on ANN methods, are organised as follows:

- Separate models were used for the prediction of the load at typical days. These models consist of 24 equations (one equation for each hour). The equations were modelled using separate neural networks, all with one hidden layer and the same structure.
- For the special days the forecasting models were slightly modified. All equations have been modelled by separate neural networks with one hidden layer and the same structure each (however different, than in the previous case). In models for special days, some heuristic adjustments associated with interpretation of input variables and selection of training data were used:
  - Holidays were treated as Sundays, i.e. training and validation sets have included both, Sundays and holidays, i.e. the last Sunday before holiday and the second working day before holiday.
  - The days after holiday were treated as Mondays, i.e. training and validation sets have included both, Mondays, and the days after holiday, as above.
  - The days two-day after holiday were treated as Tuesdays, i.e. training and validation sets have included both, Tuesdays, and the days two-day after holiday.

The model of one hour ahead STLF consists of 24 equations (one for each hour):

- $ED_k(t) = f(ED(t-1)_k, ED(t)_{k-1}, ED(t)_{k-7}, ED(t)^{a1}_{k-1}, ED(t)^{a1}_{k-7})$ (3)
- $ED_k(t)$ - energy demand at hour t in k-th day,
- $ED(t)^{a1}_{k-1}$ - average energy demand at the period, to which the given hour t belongs (morning peak, night valley) in k-1-th day
- $ED(t)^{a2}_{k-7}$ - average energy demand at the period, to which the given hour t belongs (morning peak, night valley) in k-7-th day.

All equations have been modelled by different RBFN with the same structure each. The used training data contained all days of the week (including Saturdays and Sundays).

The model of 24 hours ahead STLF consists of 24 equations (one forr each hour):

$$ED_k(t) = f(ED(t)_{k-1}, ED(t)_{k-7}, ED(t)^{a1}_{k-1}, ED(t)^{a1}_{k-7})$$ (4)

- $ED_k(t)$ - energy demand at hour t in k-th day,
- $ED(t)^{a1}_{k-1}$ - average energy demand at the period, to which the given hour t belongs (morning peak, night valley) in k-1-th day
- $ED(t)^{a2}_{k-7}$ - average energy demand at the period, to which the given hour t belongs (morning peak, night valley) in k-7-th day.

All equations have been modelled by different RBFN of the same structure each. The used training data contained all days of the week (including Saturdays and Sundays).

The model of 48 hours ahead STLF consists of 24 equations (one per each hour):

$$ED_k(t) = f(ED(t)_{k-2}, ED(t)_{k-7}, ED(t)_{k-2}^{a1}, ED(t)_{k-7}^{a1}) \tag{5}$$

- $ED_k(t)$ - energy demand at hour t in k-th day,
- $ED(t)_{k-1}^{a1}$ - average energy demand at the period, to which the given hour t belongs (morning peak, night valley, ... – described in the section of data presentation) in k-1-th day
- $ED(t)_{k-7}^{a2}$ - average energy demand at the period, to which the given hour t belongs (morning peak, night valley) in k-7-th day.

All equations have been modelled by different RBFN with the same structure each. The used training data contained all days of the week (incl. Saturdays and Sundays).

3   Evaluation of Forecasting Methods

3.1   Evaluation of the RBFN Developed at NTUA

In order to predict the load of the power system of Crete for one hour ahead, the five networks of the system's input were trained with the time-series of 1999 and part of 2000 and for testing the residual time-series of 2000. The time-series were divided to the five learning sets, corresponding to the four sessions of year and to all special days of year. The four learning sets contain about 1000 samples each and the rest 1430 samples. From the following tables it can be seen that the system can predict better in the hours of the night and it is unstable in the morning hours (5:00a.m.-10:00am) and in the evening hours (after 19:00)

Table 1. One-hour ahead forecasting results.

Hour	MAPE	MAXAPE	Hour	MAPE	MAXAPE
1	1.92%	8.00%	13	1.70%	10.45%
2	1.48%	8.50%	14	2.06%	13.95%
3	1.96%	9.12%	15	1.98%	12.21%
4	1.33%	8.52%	16	1.95%	12.08%
5	1.50%	9.39%	17	1.70%	13.08%
6	1.76%	11.96%	18	1.86%	12.49%
7	2.33%	13.49%	19	1.75%	12.19%
8	4.56%	15.14%	20	1.62%	11.45%
9	2.74%	15.25%	21	1.73%	11.10%
10	2.21%	13.74%	22	2.18%	14.10%
11	2.41%	12.71%	23	1.95%	13.77%
12	1.97%	11.26%	24	1.62%	10.11%

Table 2. 24-hours ahead forecasting results.

Hour	MAPE	MAXAPE	Hour	MAPE	MAXAPE
1	4.17%	28.01%	13	6.34%	34.92%
2	4.11%	24.40%	14	6.92%	40.68%
3	4.65%	26.34%	15	7.34%	46.23%
4	4.77%	24.69%	16	7.62%	44.25%
5	4.51%	23.03%	17	7.11%	38.36%
6	4.46%	22.84%	18	6.87%	36.02%
7	4.55%	23.24%	19	6.06%	27.55%
8	4.72%	22.44%	20	5.65%	29.17%
9	6.67%	28.26%	21	6.04%	32.12%
10	6.69%	34.63%	22	6.47%	32.35%
11	6.07%	27.02%	23	5.26%	24.74%
12	5.92%	32.95%	24	5.51%	37.15%

Table 3. 48-hours ahead forecasting results.

Hour	MAPE	MAXAPE	Hour	MAPE	MAXAPE
1	4.46%	27.73%	13	7.45%	23.78%
2	4.26%	23.07%	14	6.86%	30.51%
3	4.41%	26.89%	15	7.11%	28.57%
4	4.55%	25.64%	16	7.26%	30.24%
5	4.61%	25.46%	17	6.89%	31.89%
6	4.73%	28.76%	18	6.75%	33.24%
7	4.91%	27.33%	19	6.29%	32.54%
8	4.96%	22.21%	20	6.04%	33.04%
9	6.51%	40.11%	21	7.75%	29.70%
10	7.01%	33.72%	22	6.82%	38.74%
11	6.48%	32.49%	23	6.47%	54.02%
12	7.28%	26.46%	24	6.13%	48.69%

Table 4. Forecasting errors for 48-hour ahead hourly energy demand.

Hour	MAPE	MAXAPE	Hour	MAPE	MAXAPE
1	3,47%	28,87%	13	4,39%	26,90%
2	3,45%	27,36%	14	4,49%	30,19%
3	3,23%	31,17%	15	4,94%	29,32%
4	3,28%	31,63%	16	5,13%	39,64%
5	3,32%	33,49%	17	5,27%	57,64%
6	3,38%	33,02%	18	6,47%	48,58%
7	3,29%	31,17%	19	4,92%	51,79%
8	3,95%	32,53%	20	4,57%	42,97%
9	4,21%	30,95%	21	3,88%	32,04%
10	4,34%	32,53%	22	3,94%	24,15%
11	4,26%	22,97%	23	3,76%	21,76%
12	4,29%	25,59%	24	3,84%	58,41%
Average over all 24 hours				4,17%	34,02%

3.2 Evaluation of the RBFN Developed at UL

STLF models have been modelled by separate RBF with one hidden layer and structure {19-10-1} each, trained by incremental learning procedure. The obtained results are summarized in Table 4. The average error of the prediction over all hours is 9.34 MW (4.17%). The best results were obtained for night hours with low dynamics of load process (Fig.1). The worst hour is 6 p.m. with 6.47% average percentage error. This is due to unexpected fluctuations in load process in that hour. For comparison, prediction with MLP network with the same structure {19-10-1} has been made. In this case, the average error of the prediction over all hours was 10.12 MW (4.42%). The results reported in Table 4 indicate big maximum errors for some hours (for example: 58.41% for 12 p.m., 57.64% for 5 p.m. or 51.79% for 7 p.m.). Such errors are caused mainly by unexpected fluctuations observed in the load process (e.g. Fig.2). These unexpected fluctuations have important influence on the generalization performance of the proposed models.

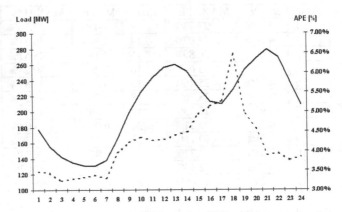

Fig. 1. Daily load variation (solid) and Average Percentage Errors (dotted curve).

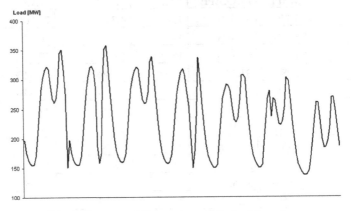

Fig. 2. Unexpected fluctuations of Crete data series.

4 Conclusions

This paper presents RBFNs models for short-term load forecasting developed at the University of Lodz and the National Technical University of Athens, respectively. Results from the application and evaluation of the two models on load series from Crete are presented. The obtained Mean Absolute Errors (MAE) for the next hour, 24-hours and 48-hours ahead are summarized in Table 5. It can be seen that both models provide results of satisfactory accuracy, retaining the advantages of RBFNs.

Table 5. Summary of Evaluation results.

	MAE for Crete Load Series	
	RBFN by NTUA	RBFN by UL
Next hour	2,01%	2,56%
24-hours	5,77%	4,94%
48-hours	6,08%	5,23%

Acknowledgement

The authors wish to thank the General Secretariat for Research and Technology of Greece for partially funding this work within the Greek-Polish Joint Research and Technology Programme, 2001-2002.

References

1. X. Wang, T.Y.C. Wei, J. Reifman, and L.H. Tsoukalas, "Signal trend identification with fuzzy methods", Proc. 1999 IEEE Int. Conf. Tools with Artificial Intelligence, Chicago, IL, 9-11 Nov. 1999, pp. 332-335, 1999.
2. A.G. Dutton, G. Kariniotakis, J.A. Halliday, and E. Nogaret, "Load and wind power forecasting methods for the optimal management isolated power systems with high wind penetration," Wind Eng., vol. 23, no. 2, pp. 69-88, 1999.
3. Hippert, H.S., Perdeira, C.E., Souza, R.C., "Neural Networks for Short-Term Load Forecasting: A Review and Evaluation", IEEE Trans. on Power Systems, Vol.16, No 1, February 2001, pp. 44-55.
4. Witold Bartkiewicz, Zbigniew Gontar, Bożena Matusiak, Jerzy S. Zieliński: "Short-Term Load Forecasting in Market environment", Med Power 02, Athens.
5. Zbigniew Gontar: Short Term Load Forecasting with Radial Basis Function Network, 2001 IEEE Porto Power Tech, Porto, Portugal, 2001.
6. Zbigniew Gontar: Notes of Application Rbf Network to Short Term Electrical Load Forecasting Problems, 10th International Conference on System Modelling Control – SMC, Zakopane, 2001.
7. "Short-Term Load Forecasting in the Growing Energy Market", Final Technical Report, Poland-Greece Joint Research&Technology Programme, October 2003.

Reinforcement Learning (RL) to Optimal Reconfiguration of Radial Distribution System (RDS)

John G. Vlachogiannis[1] and Nikos Hatziargyriou[2]

[1] Industry & Energy (IEI) Lab
Dept. of Informatics & Computer Technology
Technological Educational Institute (TEI) of Lamia, Greece
[2] Power Systems Lab
School of Electrical & Computer Engineering
National Technical University of Athens (NTUA), Greece

Abstract. This paper presents a Reinforcement Learning (RL) method for optimal reconfiguration of radial distribution system (RDS). Optimal reconfiguration involves selection of the best set of branches to be opened, one from each loop, such that the resulting RDS has the desired performance. Among the several performance criteria considered for optimal network reconfiguration, an important one is real power losses minimization, while satisfying voltage limits. The RL method formulates the reconfiguration of RDS as a multistage decision problem. More specifically, the model-free learning algorithm (Q-learning) learns by experience how to adjust a closed-loop control rule mapping operating states to control actions by means of reward values. Rewards are chosen to express how well control actions cause minimization of power losses. The Q-learning algorithm is applied to the reconfiguration of 33-bus RDS busbar system. The results are compared with those given by other evolutionary programming methods.

1 Introduction

The reconfiguration of radial distribution systems (RDS) aims at its optimal operation satisfying physical and operating constraints. One of the criteria for optimal operation is the minimization of the real power losses satisfying simultaneously operating limits of voltages. A number of algorithms based on evolutionary computation techniques [1-5] have been developed to solve this problem. These methods however are inefficient in providing optimal configurations for a whole planning period. In this paper the RDS problem is solved by means of Reinforcement Learning (RL) [6-9]. RL originates from optimal control theory and dynamic programming and aims at approximating by experience solutions to problems of unknown dynamics [8]. From a theoretical point of view, many breakthroughs have been realized concerning the convergence of the RL approach and their application to nonlinear systems [6, 8], leading to very efficient algorithms. Also the rapid increase in computer capacities makes RL methods feasible and attractive in the power system community [6, 8].

In order to apply RL, the reconfiguration problem is formulated as a multistage decision problem. Optimal control settings are learnt by experience adjusting a closed-

G.A. Vouros and T. Panayiotopoulos (Eds.): SETN 2004, LNAI 3025, pp. 439–446, 2004.
© Springer-Verlag Berlin Heidelberg 2004

loop control rule, which is mapping operating states to control actions (set of branches switched off one by one at each loop of RDS). The control settings are based on rewards, expressing how well actions work over the whole planning period. As a reward function minimization of real power losses is chosen. Moreover all voltage limits must be satisfied. In the paper the model-free learning algorithm (Q-learning) [6] is applied to reactive power control, however the algorithm is general and can be applied to a wide variety of constrained optimization problems in planning or operational planning.

The paper is organized in 5 sections. Section 2 describes the Reinforcement Learning approach. In Section 3, Q-learning algorithm is implemented to optimal reconfiguration of RDS. In Section 4, the results obtained by the application of the Q-learning algorithm to the 33-bus RDS are presented. The results are compared with those obtained by the evolutionary programming algorithm [1], showing the superiority of RL. Moreover the superiority of Q-learning algorithm in providing optimal reconfiguration over the whole planning period is depicted. In Section 5, general conclusions are drawn.

2   Reinforcement Learning (RL)

Reinforcement Learning (RL) techniques are simple iterative algorithms that learn to act in an optimal way through experience gained by exploring an unknown system [6-9]. RL assumes that the "world" can be described by a set of states S and an "agent" can choose one action from a set of actions A. The operating range is divided into discrete learning-steps. At each learning-step the agent observes the current state s of the "world" ($s \in S$), and chooses an action $a \in A$ that tends to maximize an expected long-term value function [6-8]. After taking action (a), the agent is given an immediate reward $r \in \Re$, expressing the effectiveness of the action and observing the resulting state of the "world" $s' \in S$. The particular RL algorithm used in this work is the Q-learning algorithm [6]. The Q-learning optimal value function is defined by means of the Bellman equation, as:

$$Q^*(s,a) = E\left(r(s,a) + \gamma \max_{a'} Q^*(s',a')\right) \tag{1}$$

This represents the expected sum of rewards, when starting from an initial state (s) taking action (a), and performing optimal actions (a′) in next searches, until the optimal value of Q-function, (Q*(s,a)) is reached. The discount parameter γ (0≤γ≤1) is used to exponentially decrease the weight of rewards received in next searches [6-8].

Once we have the optimal value $Q^*(s,a)$, it is easy to determine the optimal action a* using a greedy policy [6-9]. A simple way is to look at all possible actions (a) from a given state (s) and select the one with the largest value:

$$a^* = \arg\max_a Q^*(s,a) \tag{2}$$

The Q-function (Q-memory) is typically stored in a table, indexed by state and action. Starting with arbitrary values, we can iteratively approximate the optimal Q-function based on our optimality criteria. The table entry for state (s) and action (a) is then updated according to [6]:

$$Q(s,a) = (1-\alpha) \cdot Q(s,a) + \alpha \left(r + \gamma \max_{a'} Q(s',a') \right)$$ (3)

It is important to note that the new value for $Q(s,a)$ memory is based both on the current value of $Q(s,a)$, and the values (immediate rewards) of control actions obtained by next searches. So, the parameter α ($0 \leq \alpha \leq 1$) plays a critical role representing the amount of the updated Q-memory (3) and affects the number of iterations. The parameter $(1-\alpha)$ represents the total amount of Q-values still remaining as a memory in the Q-function [6].

Table 1. Q-Learning algorithm applied to optimal reconfiguration of RDS.

1) Initialize memory $Q(s,a)$ and immediate rewards $r(s,a)=0.0$, $\forall\, s \in S$, $\forall\, a \in A$
2) Repeat for a given number of operating points over the whole planning period (load variations)
2.1) Repeat
2.1.1) Observe the state (s) of load flow solution
2.1.2) Choose an action vector (a)
2.1.3) Execute load flow
2.1.4) Observe state (s´) resulting from load flow and calculate the reward (6)
2.1.5) Update Q-function using (3)
2.1.6) Set s←s´
until optimal Q-function is achieved (no change in reward or in action vector)

3 Q-Learning Applied to Optimal Reconfiguration of RDS

For the purpose of our analysis a two-class classification is assumed. The "world" of RL solution states ($s \in S$) is binary, comprising acceptable operating points characterized by satisfaction of all constraints and unacceptable, when any constraint is violated. The control vectors that combine discrete values of control adjustments are the actions ($a \in A$), and the Q-learning algorithm is the "agent". The algorithm proceeds as follows: An operating point comprising a load and generation pattern including a set of control actions is randomly created. The agent observes the state (s) of the system, as obtained by the load flow solution, and chooses one control action (a) from the control vector. A new load flow is executed. The agent observes the resulting state of the solution (s´) and provides an immediate reward (r): $SxA \rightarrow \Re$ expressing the reduction of power losses. A new control (switching) action is selected next, leading to a new load flow solution and a new reward. Selection of new control actions is repeated until no more changes in the reward value or in control action can be achieved. The goal of the agent is to learn the optimal Q-function ($Q^*(s,a)$) using the mappings of states to actions ($S \rightarrow A$) such that the long-term reward is maximized. The procedure is repeated for a large number of operating states covering the whole planning period. The agent finds the optimal control settings (a^*) [6] using the optimal policy described by (3). Table I shows the Q-learning algorithm applied in the optimal reconfiguration of RDS.

3.1 State Vectors

In order to confine the constrained variable within its operating limits, the states of the system are discretized as follows:

When one of the variables (e.g voltage magnitude) lies outside its operating limits, the state is considered as -1 level-state, otherwise it is considered at the zero level-state. Consequently, if we have n-constrained variables, the total number of states is:

$$\overline{\overline{S}} = 2^n \tag{4}$$

In our application the lowest voltage in each loop is constrained within operating limits.

3.2 Action Vectors

If each control variable u_i is discretized in d_{u_i} levels (e.g branches to be opened one at each loop of RDS), the total number of action-vectors affecting the load flow is:

$$\overline{\overline{A}} = \prod_{i=1}^{m} d_{u_i} \tag{5}$$

m expresses the total number of control variables (e.g total number of branches to be switched out).

3.3 Rewards

Optimal reconfiguration involves selection of the best set of branches to be opened, one from each loop, such that the resulting RDS has the desired performance. Amongst the several performance criteria considered for optimal network reconfiguration, the one selected is the minimization of real power losses, while satisfying operating limits of voltages. Application of the Q-learning algorithm to optimal reconfiguration of RDS is linked to the choice of an immediate reward (r), such that the iterative value of Q-function (3) is maximized, while the minimization of total real power losses (TPRL) is satisfied over the whole planning period. So the immediate reward (r) is computed as:

$$r = - \text{Total Losses} \tag{6}$$

4 Performance Results

The Q-learning algorithm is applied to the optimal reconfiguration of the 33-bus RDS. The line diagram is shown in the Appendix and also in [1] together with the transmission line and load data. The control variables comprise the sets of branches to be opened, one from each loop. There are five loops, therefore each control action of Q-learning vector comprises five branches. Table 2 shows the branches comprising each loop. According to this Table, the total number of control action vectors is calculated

10x7x7x16x11= 86240. Since the lowest voltage magnitudes (v_j) in each loop are constrained within operating limits [0.96pu, 1.05pu], the total number of solution states is calculated 2^5= 32. The Q-learning algorithm (Table 1) can be implemented in a large number of load combinations (operating points) selected over the whole planning period.

Table 2. Branches to be opened at each loop of 33-bus RDS.

Loops	Branches
1	2-3-4-5-6-7-18-19-20-33
2	9-10-11-12-13-14-34
3	8-9-10-11-21-33-35
4	6-7-8-15-16-17-25-26-27-28-29-30-31-32-34-36
5	3-4-5-22-23-24-25-26-27-28-37

We first apply the Q-learning algorithm for a particular load profile. In this case we set the Q-learning parameters $\alpha = 0.99$ and $\gamma = 0.01$. Figure 1 shows the obtained immediate reward r (6) at each Q-learning step, corresponding to the upper values of load. Each Q-learning step corresponds to an iteration of the Q-learning algorithm (Table 1). The agent made approximately 46000 Q-learning steps to find the optimum control actions. The whole computing time was 100 sec in a 1.4-GHz Pentium-IV PC. This figure also depicts the convergence of Q-learning algorithm in a maximum reward value (-0.354), mapping the optimum control action to the best solution state.

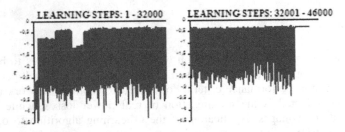

Fig. 1. Immediate rewards of Q-learning algorithm.

Table 3 shows the optimum control action (best set of branches switched out) 7-10-13-31-25 and the total real power losses calculated at 110,05 kW. Moreover, Table 3 shows the voltage magnitude achieved by the evolutionary programming algorithm reported in [1]. The latter proposes as best control action the set of branches to be opened: (6-14-9-32-37). Table 3 also gives the load voltage magnitudes of 33-bus RDS at the base case of branches switched out: (33-34-35-36-37).

The optimal solution of Q-learning compared to the evolutionary programming optimal solution is better, since all voltage constraints are satisfied and the total of real power losses are smaller (110.05 kW compared to 118.37 kW [1]).

The Q-learning algorithm also provides on-line control under non-autonomous environment [8]. Such case study is considered when the system load varies over a period. The load variation is cyclic with period of 50 Q-learning steps (ls) and it is modeled according to the equation:

$$z(\text{ls}) = z_{max} \cdot \sin\left(\frac{2 \cdot \pi \cdot \text{ls}}{50}\right) \qquad (7)$$

z stands for the real or reactive parts of load. In this case we set the Q-learning parameters $\alpha = 0.1$ and $\gamma = 0.98$.

Table 3. Load bus voltages under the optimal control action given by Q-learning and programming evolutionary algorithm

Method	Q-learning	Evolutionary Programming [1]	Base Case
Optimum Control Action	7-13-10-31-25	6-14-9-32-37	33-34-35-36-37
Total real power losses	110.05 kW	118.37 kW	181.53 kW
Load Bus		Voltages	
1	1.020	1.020	1.020
2	1.017	1.017	1.017
3	1.007	1.007	1.003
4	1.005	1.003	0.996
5	1.003	1.000	0.990
6	0.998	0.991	0.974
7	0.998	0.982	0.972
8	0.986	0.984	0.961
9	0.981	0.981	0.956*
10	0.982	0.982	0.952*
11	0.986	0.983	0.952*
12	0.987	0.984	0.951*
13	0.985	0.980	0.946*
14	0.976	0.979	0.945*
15	0.977	0.979	0.944*
16	0.974	0.977	0.944*
17	0.969	0.973	0.943*
18	0.968	0.972	0.944*
19	1.015	1.015	1.016
20	0.997	0.995	1.012
21	0.992	0.990	1.010
22	0.988	0.986	1.009
23	1.001	1.004	0.999
24	0.989	0.997	0.990
25	0.980	0.993	0.985
26	0.982	0.989	0.972
27	0.982	0.987	0.970
28	0.980	0.978	0.960
29	0.978	0.971	0.953*
30	0.976	0.968	0.949*
31	0.974	0.965	0.944*
32	0.966	0.965	0.943*
33	0.967	0.971	0.942*

Voltage magnitude violates lower limit

The progressive learning of the control agent over the whole planning period is illustrated in Figure 2. The convergence of Q-learning algorithm took about 78000 steps. Each Q-learning step corresponds to an iteration of the Q-learning algorithm (Table 1). The whole computing times were 190 sec in a 1.4-GHz Pentium-IV PC. This figure also depicts the convergence of Q-learning algorithm in a maximum range of rewards [-0.467, -0.155] over the whole planning period, mapping the optimum control action to the best solution state. The greedy-optimum control action includes the branches to be switched out (6-10-8-32-37), satisfying all voltage constraints over the whole planning period.

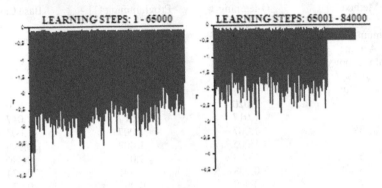

Fig. 2. Immediate rewards of Q-learning algorithm over the whole planning period.

5 Conclusions

In this paper the RL method was applied to the optimal reconfiguration of RDS. An iterative Q-learning algorithm is implemented in order to provide the optimal control action (set of branches to be opened one from each loop of RDS), satisfying all operating limits of the constrained variables (voltages) simultaneously with the minimum total of real power losses. Optimal control settings are learnt by experience adjusting a closed-loop control rule, which is mapping operating states to control actions by means of reward values. As a reward function the total of real power losses was chosen. The Q-learning algorithm was applied to the 33-bus RDS. The results have shown that Q-learning algorithm is able to provide better control settings than other evolutionary programming algorithms. Moreover, the RL approach provided on-line optimal reconfiguration of the 33-bus RDS over the whole planning period.

References

1. Venkatesh, B., Ranjan, R.: Optimal Radial Distribution System Reconfiguration using Fuzzy Adaption of Evolutionary Programming. Int. J. Electrical Power & Energy Systems 25 (2003) 775-780.
2. Baran, M.E., Wu, F.F.: Network reconfiguration in distribution systems for loss reduction and load balancing. IEEE Trans. on Power Delivery 4 (1989) 1401-1407.

3. Shirmohamaddi, D., Hong, H.W.: Reconfiguration of electric distribution networks for resistive line losses reduction. IEEE Trans. on Power Delivery, 4 (1989) 1484-1491.
4. Peponis, G.P., Papadopoulos, M.P., Hatziargyriou, N.D.: Distribution networks reconfiguration to minimize resistive line losses. IEEE Trans. on Power Delivery, 10 (1995) 1338-1342.
5. Kashem, M.A., Ganapathy, V., Jasmon, G.B., Buhari, M.I.: A novel method for loss minimization in distribution networks. Proc of Inter. Conf. on Electric Utility Deregulation and Restruct. and Power Tech., London (2000) 251-255.
6. Watkins, C.J.C.H., Dayan, P.: Q-learning. Machine Learning 8 (1992) 279-292.
7. Kaelbling, L.P., Littman, M.L., Moore, A.W.: Reinforcement Learning: A Survey. Journal of Artificial Intelligence Research 4 (1996) 237-285.
8. Sutton, R.S., Barto, A.G.: Reinforcement Learning: An Introduction, Adaptive Computations and Machine Learning. MIT Press Cambridge MA (1998).
9. Bertsekas, D.P., Tsitsiklis, J.N.: Neuro-Dynamic Programming. Athena Scientific Belmont MA (1996).

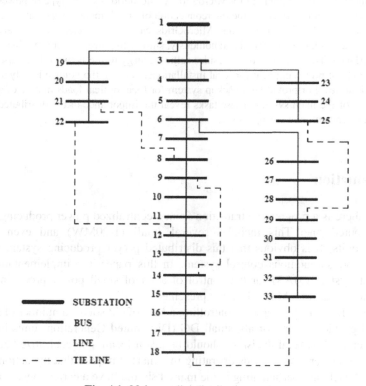

Fig. A1. 33-bus radial distribution system.

A Multi-agent System for Microgrids

Aris Dimeas and Nikos Hatziargyriou

National Technical University of Athens, Department of Electrical and Computer Engineer
Iroon Polytechniou 9, 157 73 Zografou, Athens, Greece
{adimeas,nh}@power.ece.ntua.gr

Abstract. This paper presents the capabilities offered by MultiAgent System technology in the operation of a Microgrid. A Microgrid is a new type of power system, which is formed by the interconnection of small, modular generation to low voltage distribution systems. MicroGrids can be connected to the main power network or be operated autonomously, similar to power systems of physical islands. The local DG units besides selling energy to the network have also other tasks: producing heat for local installations, keeping the voltage locally at a certain level or providing a backup system for local critical loads in case of a failure of the main system. These tasks reveal the importance of the distributed control and autonomous operation.

1 Introduction

Nowadays there is a progressive transition from a centralized power producing system to a distributed one. This includes several small (1-20MW) and even smaller (<0.5MW) units. It is obvious that this distributed power producing system needs a distributed and autonomous control system. In this paper, the implementation of a MultiAgent System (MAS) for the control of a set of small power producing units, which could be part of a MicroGrid, are presented.

The use of MAS technology in controlling a MicroGrid solves a number of specific operational problems. First of all, small DG (Distributed Generation) units have different owners, and several decisions should be taken locally, so centralized control is difficult. Furthermore, Microgrids operating in a market require that the actions of the controller of each unit participating in the market should have a certain degree of intelligence. Finally, the local DG units next to selling power to the network have also other tasks: producing heat for local installations, keeping the voltage locally at a certain level or providing a backup system for local critical loads in case of main system failure. These tasks suggest the importance of distributed control and autonomous operation.

This paper is organized as follows: the main market operations of the MAS are discussed in Section II. The software that was developed for the MAS system is described in Section III. In Section IV the implementation and operation of the MAS in the laboratory Microgrid installed at NTUA is presented. The last section concludes.

G.A. Vouros and T. Panayiotopoulos (Eds.): SETN 2004, LNAI 3025, pp. 447–455, 2004.

2 Market Operation of the MicroGrid

This section describes a possible market operation of a Microgrid. The market model that is used in this application is simple since our focus is on the operation of the agents. The basic rule of the market is that if the MicroGrid is connected to the Grid then there is no limit to the power that can be sold or bought from it (as long there are no technical constraints). It should be noted that the product traded is the energy (kWh) and not the power (kW). This is happening because it is very difficult to keep the production, especially of a small unit, constant for a long period due to technical reasons. However considering that energy is the interval of the power it is easier to produce an exact amount of energy in a certain period of time (in our case 15 minutes). It is assumed that the Grid Operator announces two prices: the price for selling kWh and the price for buying kWh. The production units that belong to the MicroGrid adjust their set points, after negotiation with the other units, based on the Grids prices, their operational cost and the local demands.

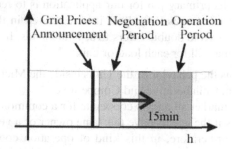

Fig. 1. The actions sequence for the Market Operation in the time domain.

The overall procedure, which is based on the FIPA English Auction Protocol [2], is the following:

1. The Grid Operator announces the prices for selling (SP) or buying (BP) energy to the MicroGrid. Normally it is SP>BP.
2. The local loads announce their demands for the next 15 minutes and an initial price DP for the kWh. DP>BP and DP<SP.
3. The production units accept or decline the offer after comparing it with the acceptable internal price (AP).
4. The local loads keep making bids according to the English Auction Protocol for a specific time (3 minutes). This means that the load increases its offer as long DP<SP or no production unit has accepted the offer.
5. After the end of the negotiation time all the units know their set points. If there is no production unit of the Microgrid to satisfy the load demand the power is bought from the Grid. Furthermore if the AP power is lower than the BP the production unit starts selling energy to the network.

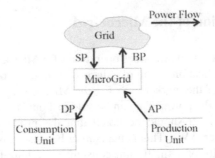

Fig. 2. Power flows and bids in the Microgrid.

For the previous model of operation the following remarks should be made.

- There is no need to send a Schedule to the Grid Operator since the only limits for taking or sending energy to the network is the technical constraints of the installation.
- In the Microgrid MAS there is an extra Agent who is called MGCC (MicroGrid Central Controller). Its primary job for our application is to record the bids and the power flow. A transaction is valid only if it is registered in the MGCC agent and this is vital in order to avoid double offers to separate loads. In Market Operation its job is to create the final bill for each load or unit.

The next critical point is the behavior of the Units inside the MicroGrid. There are two basic ways of operation: Collaborative and Competitive.

In the collaborative market all agents cooperate for a common operation. It is obvious that this case exists if the agents have the same owner or a very strong operational or legal connection. Furthermore, in this kind of operation coordination among the production units could take place in order to achieve a better operation and maximize the gain of selling energy to the Main Grid.

In the competitive market each microsource has its own interests. This does not necessarily mean that the other agents are opponents. If the microsource is a battery system and its primary goal is to feed a number of computers with uninterruptible power, then the behavior of this particular unit in the market would be very passive. On the other hand, if the microsource is a CHP and its primary objective is the heating of the local installation, then it might become a very aggressive player. The operational cost for this unit is reduced since it incorporates savings from heating. Furthermore, we should consider that some rules of the traditional Power Market are very hard to apply. For example, the bid in the traditional market is not allowed to be lower than the actual cost something that is very hard to apply in a Microgrid: in a CHP occasionally the cost might be lower than the fuel cost in comparison to a simple gas turbine.

In the application presented in this paper the market is assumed competitive and the players focus mainly in the market.

3 Software Implementation of the MAS

3.1 The MAS Technology in MicroGrids

The MAS theory appears to be a very useful tool for the operation and control of a MicroGrid. Before continuing with the presentation of our implementation, it is useful to provide a short description of the main theoretical principles of the agent theory, as linked to our application [3,4].

The main element of a MAS is the agent, which is a physical entity that acts in the environment or a virtual one without physical existence. In our case the physical entity is a microsource, e.g. a Microturbine and a virtual one a piece of software that makes bids to the energy market.

An agent is capable of acting in the environment, which means that the agent changes its environment with its actions. A diesel generator by altering its production changes the setpoints of other units, changes the voltage level in the adjacent buses and in a more global point of view changes the security level of the system [affects the stability of the system in case of a short circuit for example].

Agents communicate with each other and this is part of their capability for acting in the environment. Consider a system that includes a wind generator and a battery system: the battery system receives some power from the wind turbine to charge and to provide it back to the system in time with no wind. In order to achieve this operation, the two agents have to exchange several messages and, of course, this is a type of action because the environment is altered in a different way than if the two agents were acting without any kind of coordination.

Agents have a certain level of autonomy, which means that they can take decisions without a central controller or commander and to achieve that, they are driven by a set of tendencies. For a battery system a tendency could be: "charge the batteries when the price for the kWh is low and the state of charge is low too". The system decides when to start charging based on its own rules and goals and not by an external command. In addition, the autonomy of every agent is related to the resources that it possesses and uses. These resources could be the available fuel for a diesel generator, the bandwidth in the communication channel or the processor time.

Another significant characteristic of agents is that they have partial or none at all representation of the environment. For example in a power system the agent of a generator knows only the voltage level at its own bus and maybe it can estimate what is happening in some certain buses, but it does not know what is happening in the whole system. This is the core of the MAS theory, since the goal is to control a very complicated system with minimum data exchange and minimum computational demands.

Finally, another significant characteristic of an agent is that it has a certain behavior and tends to satisfy certain objectives using its resources, skills and services. One skill could be the ability to produce or store power and a service could be selling power in a market. The way that the agent uses the resources, skills and services presents its behavior. As a consequence it is obvious that the behavior of every agents is formed by its goals. An agent that controls a battery system and its goal is to supply uninterruptible power to a load will have different behavior than a similar battery system whose primary goal is to increase its profit by participating in the energy market.

3.2 Description of the MAS

In this section the specific MAS implementation is presented. For the implementation the JADE Agent Management Platform was used. JADE (Java Agent Development Framework) is a software development framework for developing MAS and applications conforming to FIPA (Foundation for Intelligent Physical Agents) standards for intelligent agents.

Four kinds of agents are developed:

- Production Unit: This agent controls the Battery Inverter of the Microgrid. The main tasks of this agent are to control the overall status of the Batteries and to adjust the power flow depending on the Market Condition (prices).
- Consumption Unit: This agent represents the controllable loads in the system. This agent knows the current demand and makes estimations of energy demand for the next 15 minutes. Every 15 minutes it makes bids to the available Production Units in order to cover the estimated needs.
- Power System: This agent represents the Main Grid to which the Microgrid is connected. According to the Market Model presented in Section II the Power System Agent announces to all participants the Selling and the Buying price. It does not participate in the market operation since it is obliged to buy or sell any amount of energy it is asked for (as long as there is no security problem for the network)
- MGCC: This agent has only coordinating tasks and more specifically it announces the beginning and the end of a negotiation for a specific period and records final power exchanges between the agents in every period.

3.3 Services

According to the Agent Directory Service Specifications every agent announces to the DF agent the services that it can offer to the MAS. The available services are:

- Power_Production: This agent is a power producer.
- Power_Consumption: This agent is a load.
- Power_Selling: This agent can operate in the Energy Market and can sell power.
- Power_Buying: This agent can operate in the Energy Market and can make bids for buying power.
- MGCC. This agent is the MGCC.

It should be mentioned that Power Production is a different service than the Power Selling since the Power System agent produce power but it does not participate in the Market. The same applies for the loads.

3.4 Ontology

According to the FIPA specification agents that wish to make a conversation need to share the same ontology. The ontology used in the application has four main parts.

3.4.1 Concepts
- **Agent** that operates in the MAS. This ontology includes information like Name, Description, Available Services etc.
- **Bid** that the agents exchange during the Market negotiation and includes information about the amount of energy that is requested or offered, the price for this amount and the period of time for which this bid is valid.
- **EnergyPackage** which is the amount of energy that is going to be exchanged between **Seller** and **Buyer** after a transaction in the energy market.
- **GridPrices** which are the prices for selling or buying electric energy from the main power network (grid).

3.4.2 Predicates
- **Buyer** is an **Agent** that **Buys** energy from another **Agent**
- **Seller** is an **Agent** that **Sells** energy to another **Agent**

3.4.3 Agent Actions
- **Buy EnergyPackage** from an **Agent**
- **Sell EnergyPackage** to an **Agent**
- **Record Bid** and **EnergyPackage** which is an order to MGCC indicating that a deal came to an agreement.
- **Accept** a **Bid**
- **Deny** a **Bid**
- **Request** an **EnergyPackage.**
- **Make** a **Bid**
- **BidStart** is an announcement that the agents can start making bids
- **BidEnd** is an announcement that the agents should stop making bids

3.4.4 Behavior and Actions
In this section the behavior and the actions of the agents are described. The behavior of every agent has two main parts:

- Initialization in which every agent announces its services to the DF agent.
- Normal Operation which includes all the tasks and actions that every agent performs. In the following paragraph the behavior of each agent is presented separately. All the agents use cyclic behavior.

MGCC: The first task of this agent is to record every message of type "**Record**" and the second is to announce the period of the negotiation. According to the market model adopted, and in order to avoid double assignments, no energy exchange inside the Microgrid happens unless it is recorded in the MGCC.

Power System: This agent announces the Grid sell/buy price to all agents that participate (according to their service declarations) in the Market. The announcement is made just after the end of the negotiation period or whenever we have a change in the prices. In order to simplify the start up of the other agents, it is not allowed for a market agent to bid in the market if it has not received at least one announcement for the grid prices. This means that the new agent launched will bid in the next period.

Consumption Unit: This agent has currently two tasks. The first task is to estimate its energy needs for the next period and the second is to bid in the market.

- Energy estimation: In our application the "persistence" method is used, i.e. estimation is based on the current power demand assuming that this demand will be the same in the next 15-20 minutes.
- Market operation: The agent sends an offer to all available sellers for price higher than the price BP that the Grid would buy. If the agent does not receive any "accept" message then increases the bid a bit more. This cycle continues, as long the bid is lower than the sell price SP of the grid. After this it is obvious that it is in the interest of the agent to buy energy directly from the Grid.

Production Unit: This agent just receives offers from the consumption units. The agent decides based on its operational cost and the available capacity, if this is acceptable or not.

4 The NTUA Microgrid

The MAS system that was developed for controlling the operation of Microgrid was tested in the Laboratory Microgrid of the NTUA.

4.1 Equipment Description

The composition of the microgrid system is shown in Fig 3. It is a modular system, comprising a PV generator as the primary source of power. Both microsources are interfaced to the 1-phase AC bus via DC/AC PWM inverters. A battery bank is also included, interfaced to the AC system via a bi-directional PWM voltage source converter. The Microgrid is connected to the local LV grid, as shown in Fig 3 [1].

When the system is connected to the grid, the local load receives power both from the grid and the local micro-sources. In case of grid power interruptions, the Microgrid can transfer smoothly to island operation and subsequently reconnect to the public grid.

The active power control is primarily performed by their power frequency control characteristics, known as droop curves.

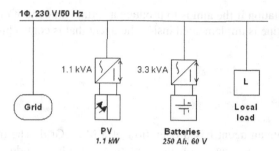

Fig. 3. The laboratory Microgrid system.

4.2 Communication between Agents and Local Sources/Loads

One of the main difficulties for the development of our system is to establish the communication between the agents and the inverters. The main method for communication is through OPC [OLE for Process Control and OLE stands for Object Linking and Embedding] servers/clients. This method was selected since the manufacturer of the inverter has available an OPC server suitable for his device.

4.3 Software Operation

In the Fig. 4 a display of the GUI of the agents is presented. From this screen the operational cost can be adjusted. Similar forms have been developed for the Loads and the Main Grid.

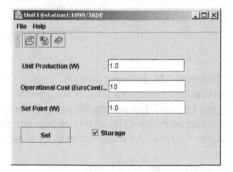

Fig. 4. Screenshot of the GUI for the Production Unit.

In the implementation developed, the main target is to produce or store a certain amount of energy in a specific time period and this is done with a procedure that calculates the droop frequency set point. This calculation is very fast, however due to communication limitations the resulting set point can be sent to the inverter only every 4-5 seconds. This long period of time does not allow us to have a steady power production since the grid frequency changes very fast. On the other hand, the 4-5 seconds delay is not a limitation if the aim is to produce a certain amount of energy in 10 or 15 minutes. This routine is implemented inside the agent that is controlling the production units.

5 Conclusions

This paper presents an agent based operation of a MicroGrid. The main focus so far has been on the communication of an agent that controls a production unit with its market environment. Preliminary results have shown the feasibility of this approach. Work is in progress in order to build controllable loads linked to the Consumption Unit agents. The most efficient and cheap method to achieve this is by using a PLC (Programmable Logical Controller). The Consumption Unit agent will have measurements in order to estimate the consumption and to make more realistic bids. Furthermore, this agent will have the ability to control the load and to limit it according to the market status or the MicroGrid security. In addition, more sophisticated market operations are tested in order to reveal potential technical problems, like the one presented before (keeping the power at a certain level).

Acknowledgements

The authors wish to thank the European Commission, DG Research for funding the project "MICROGRIDS: Large Scale Integration of Microgeneration to Low Voltage Grids", Contract No: ENK-CT-2002-00610.

References

1. S. Papathanassiou, D. Georgakis, N. Hatziargyriou, A. Engler, Ch. Hardt, Operation of a prototype Micro-grid system based on micro-sources equipped with fast-acting power electronics interfaces. Available On line http://microgrids.power.ece.ntua.gr.
2. FIPA English Auction Interaction Protocol. Available on line: http://www.fipa.org.
3. Jacques Ferber. Multi-Agent Systems. An introduction to Distributed Intelligence. Addison-Wesley.
4. Jeffrey M. Bradshaw. Software Agents. MIT Press.

Automated Medical Image Registration
Using the Simulated Annealing Algorithm

Ilias Maglogiannis[1] and Elias Zafiropoulos[2]

[1] University of the Aegean, Dept. of Information and Communication Systems Engineering
83 200 Karlovassi, Samos, Greece
imaglo@aegean.gr
[2] National Technical University of Athens, School of Electrical and Computer Engineering
ezafir@power.ece.ntua.gr

Abstract. This paper presents a robust, automated registration algorithm, which may be applied to several types of medical images, including CTs, MRIs, X-rays, Ultrasounds and dermatological images. The proposed algorithm is intended for imaging modalities depicting primarily morphology of objects i.e. tumors, bones, cysts and lesions that are characterized by translation, scaling and rotation. An efficient deterministic algorithm is used in order to decouple these effects by transforming images into the log-polar Fourier domain. Then, the correlation coefficient function criterion is employed and the corresponding values of scaling and rotation are detected. Due to the non-linearity of the correlation coefficient function criterion and the heavy computational effort required for its full enumeration, this optimization problem is solved using an efficient simulated annealing algorithm. After the images alignment in scaling and rotation, the simulated annealing algorithm is employed again, in order to detect the remaining values of the horizontal and vertical shifting. The proposed algorithm was tested using different initialization schemes and resulted in fast convergence to the optimal solutions independently of the initial points.

1 Introduction

Within the current clinical setting, medical imaging is a significant component of a medical practice. Medical images are widely used by physicians not only for diagnostic purposes, but prominently in the areas of therapy planning, or carrying out and evaluating surgical and therapeutical procedures. The imaging modalities employed in such images are mostly anatomical depicting primarily morphology of objects i.e. tumors, bones, lesions. Medical images are frequently used in follow up studies for monitoring the progress of such modalities.

Image registration is the procedure of finding correspondence between two different images acquired at different time or by different devices in order to correct transpositions of image modalities [1]. Several methods of image registration have been presented in literature, which can be broadly classified in local and global methods [2], [3], [4]. Local registration methods extract image distinctive features, using a subset of the original image information, and the correspondence between the images is performed only on these extracted features. These methods are usually based on

G.A. Vouros and T. Panayiotopoulos (Eds.): SETN 2004, LNAI 3025, pp. 456–465, 2004.

rules for both identification of features and determination of the correspondence. Therefore local registration methods are difficult to generalize and deal with various problem types. In contrast, global methods use all of the original image pixel values within both images in order to determine the optimal set of transformation parameters for an image pair. Global methods do not include any decision process for identifying image features and can be generalized easily. However, these methods cannot be practically applied in the cases where the unregistered images are also scaled or rotated apart from being translated (horizontally and vertically shifted), due to the high computational effort.

In the present paper, an effective global image registration procedure is described. The input of the image registration procedure consists of the two images and the output is the values of four parameters: Scaling ratio, Rotation angle, horizontal shifting and vertical shifting [5]. The measurement of similarity between the two images is based on the correlation coefficient function of the two images, which is a reliable similarity criterion but it has the disadvantage of being sensitive to rotation and scaling. Fourier Transform is used in order to diminish the effect of vertical and horizontal shifting on the image pair. The computational effort of the full enumeration for the correlation coefficient function as well as its non-linearity is the main reason for adopting a random search optimization. The use of random search algorithms is a generally acceptable technique for the optimization of non-linear problems. Their major advantage is easy implementation and speed. On the other hand, their efficiency is based on probability factors and their behavior is not predictable. An optimization procedure based on the simulated annealing algorithm is developed and applied for the maximization of the correlation coefficient function. The optimal values of scaling and rotation are introduced for the initial image alignment and the optimization procedure is applied again to find the optimal values of horizontal and vertical shifting. Thus the registration procedure is divided in two stages: the first stage deals only with scaling ratio and rotation angle, while the second stage computes horizontal and vertical shifting. The complete image registration procedure is depicted in Figure 1.

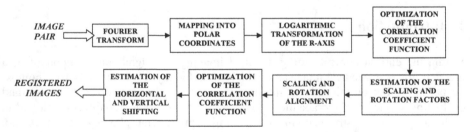

Fig. 1. The proposed image registration procedure.

The above registration algorithm may be applied in several medical imaging types including X-rays, MRIs (Magnetic Resonance Imaging), US (Ultrasounds) and digital skin images containing cutaneous lesions [6]. The rest paper is organized as follows: Section 2 discusses the log-polar transform and the methodology. Section 3 presents the general aspects of the simulated annealing algorithm. Section 4 provides results from the image registration procedure applied in several types of medical images and, finally, section 5 concludes the paper.

2 Image Registration Method Based on Log-Polar Transform

A typical technique in order to estimate the correspondence of two images is the calculation of the cross correlation function or the correlation coefficient function. The two images may differ due to possible translation (horizontal and vertical shifting), scaling (the one image is magnified towards the other) and rotation (the one image is rotated towards the other). The correlation coefficient function is a normalized similarity criterion, reliable and immune to white noise, but it has the disadvantage of being sensitive to rotation and scaling. A very effective deterministic algorithm, which transforms the Fourier functions of the images into the log-polar domain described in [7], is used to overcome this problem. The algorithm diminishes the effect of translation on the images and converts the scaling and rotation into independent shifts in orthogonal directions.

Let us consider two images of the same object represented as functions f(x,y) and f'(x,y) that are related through a four-parameter geometric transformation, described by the following equation:

$$f'(x, y) = f(\alpha\,(x\cos b + y\sin b) - \Delta x, \alpha\,(-x\sin b + y\cos b) - \Delta y) \tag{1}$$

where Δx and Δy are the parallel shifting, α is the scaling factor and b is the rotation angle. The Fourier spectrums of the two images are related by the following equation:

$$|F'(u,v)| = \frac{1}{a^2}\left|F\left(\frac{(u\cos b + v\sin b)}{a}, \frac{(-u\sin b + v\cos b)}{a}\right)\right| \tag{2}$$

In equation (2), the Fourier spectrums of the two images are independent of the horizontal or vertical shifting of the images and are influenced only by the scaling and rotation factors α and b. Then, the polar transformation of the Fourier spectrums is described by the following equations:

$$|F'(r,\theta)| = \frac{1}{a^2}\left|F\left(\frac{r}{a}, \theta + b\right)\right| \qquad \text{where} \qquad r = \sqrt{u^2 + v^2}, \qquad \theta = \tan^{-1}\frac{v}{u} \tag{3}$$

In equation (3), the effect of scaling and rotation are completely decoupled, since the r-axis is affected only by the scaling factor α and the polar angle θ is affected only by the rotation angle b. The final step of the images transformation is the logarithmic transformation of the r-axis. Then, equation (3) can be expressed as:

$$|F'(\rho,\theta)| = \frac{1}{a^2}\left|F(\rho - \ln(a), \theta + b)\right| \qquad \text{where } \rho = \ln(r) \tag{4}$$

The remaining step is the selection of a similarity criterion for the two images in the Log- Polar domain of their Fourier spectrum. The maximization of this criterion proclaims the values of scaling ratio α and rotation angle b. A commonly used criterion is the cross-correlation coefficient function, which, in the present case, is defined as:

$$CC(R,T) = \frac{\sum_{\rho=\rho_{\min}}^{\rho_{\max}}\sum_{\theta=0}^{2\pi}[F'(\rho,\theta) - \overline{F'(\rho,\theta)}][F(\rho + R, \theta + T) - \overline{F(\rho + R, \theta + T)}]}{\left\{\left(\sum_{\rho=\rho_{\min}}^{\rho_{\max}}\sum_{\theta=0}^{2\pi}[F'(\rho,\theta) - \overline{F'(\rho,\theta)}]^2\right)\left(\sum_{\rho=\rho_{\min}}^{\rho_{\max}}\sum_{\theta=0}^{2\pi}[F(\rho + R, \theta + T) - \overline{F(\rho + R, \theta + T)}]^2\right)\right\}^{1/2}} \tag{5}$$

where the parameters are the log-difference of the scale factors R and the difference of the rotation angle T. The values ρ_{min} and ρ_{max} are the lower and upper values of the transformed images in the log-r axis respectively. The detection of the optimal values R and T that maximize the correlation coefficient function of equation (5) can lead to the estimation of scaling and rotation factors α and b respectively, using equation (4). After applying the computed scaling and rotation factors, the two images $f_{new}(x,y)$ and f'(x,y) differ only by the horizontal and vertical shifting Δx and Δy, as it is shown by the following equation:

$$f'(x,y) = f_{new}(x - \Delta x, y - \Delta y) \tag{6}$$

Therefore, the problem is now reduced to finding the horizontal and vertical shifting, which is a much simpler problem than the initial, as it involves only two independent parameters. The calculation of the similarity criterion between two windows is required. These windows are:

$$\begin{bmatrix} (m,m)........................(m,k-m+1) \\ (k-m+1,m)...(k-m+1,k-m+1) \end{bmatrix}$$ of the first image and

$$\begin{bmatrix} (m+i,m+j)........................(m+i,k-m+1+j) \\ (k-m+1+i,m+j)...(k-m+1+i,k-m+1+j) \end{bmatrix}$$ of the second image

where p is the assumed limit of shifting. The similarity criterion used in this case is the following:

$$CC(\Delta X, \Delta Y) = \frac{\sum_x \sum_y [f'(x,y) - \overline{f'(x,y)}][f(x-\Delta x, y-\Delta y) - \overline{f(x-\Delta x, y-\Delta y)}]}{\left\{ \left(\sum_x \sum_y [f'(x,y) - \overline{f'(x,y)}]^2 \right) \sum_x \sum_y [f(x-\Delta x, y-\Delta y) - \overline{f(x-\Delta x, y-\Delta y)}]^2 \right\}^{1/2}} \tag{7}$$

The detection of the optimal values Δx and Δy that maximize the correlation coefficient function of equation (7) can lead to the estimation of horizontal and vertical shifting. The full enumeration of the potential problem solutions requires the calculation of the similarity criterion $4 \times p^2$ times in a window of $(k-2 \cdot m) \times (k-2 \cdot m)$ pixels. This could also be a complex and resources consuming problem in case we select a big value for p. Therefore we used the simulated annealing algorithm.

3   The Simulated Annealing Algorithm

Optimization methods can be broadly classified into two classes: the gradient-based methods and the direct search methods. Gradient-based methods use the first-order or higher derivatives of an objective function to determine a suitable search direction. Direct search methods require only the computation of the objective(s) function(s) values to select suitable search directions. Since evaluating derivatives of the objective(s) function(s) is usually laborious, and in some cases impossible, this gives an advantage to the direct search class of algorithms [8]. However, conventional search techniques, such as hill climbing, are often incapable of optimizing non-linear multi-modal functions, such as the correlation coefficient function employed in our case.

Directed random search techniques however, such as Genetic Algorithms, Simulated Annealing and Tabu search can find the optimal solution in complex search spaces.

The simulated annealing algorithm is based on the analogy between a combinatorial problem and physical systems integrating a large number of particles [9, 10]. The algorithm consists of a sequence of iterations. Each iteration includes a random change of the current solution to create a new solution in its "neighborhood", which is defined by the choice of the generation mechanism. The objective function for the newly produced solution is computed to decide whether it can be accepted as current. In the case of maximization problems, if the value of the objective function for the newly produced solution is greater than the value for the current, the newly produced solution is directly taken as current and the optimal solution is updated. Otherwise, the newly produced solution may be accepted as current according to Metropolis's criterion based on Boltzman's probability [10]. In accordance to Metropolis's criterion, if the objective function value of the current solution minus the respective value of the newly produced one is equal or larger than zero, a random number δ in [0,1] is generated from a uniform distribution and if $\delta \leq e^{(-\Delta E/kT)}$ then the newly produced solution is accepted as current. If not, the current solution remains unchanged. The parameter k is a constant and T is the temperature parameter that is updated after n_{max} iterations according to a certain schedule ("cooling schedule"). ΔE is the difference of the new solution's objective function value and the respective value for the current. The parameters to be optimized are usually represented in a string form using various binary coding schemes.

The above presented simulated annealing algorithm has been employed for the estimation of the scaling factor and the rotation angle of the image pair in the first stage and the horizontal and vertical shifting in the second stage. During implementation four principal choices were adopted:

1. *The representation of solutions:* The solutions are represented in a bit string of 8 bits length, while each bit may be in 4 levels and take the values 0, 1, 2, 3.
2. *The definition of the objective function:* The correlation coefficient function is selected as the objective function. In the case of detecting the scaling and rotation factors, the images are previously transformed in the log-polar Fourier domain in order to eliminate the effect of horizontal and vertical shifting.
3. *The definition of the generation mechanism:* New solutions are produced by randomly selecting a bit in the bit string of the current solution and then randomly flipping its value one level up or down.
4. *The design of a cooling schedule:* This issue requires the determination of the initial (T_{init}) and the lowest temperature (T_{fin}), the parameter n_{max} of the maximum number of iterations for each temperature level, the maximum number of accepted "worst-than-current" solutions (CW_{max}) and the temperature update rule. The temperature update rule employed here is the following

$$T_{i+1} = cT_i, i = 0,1,... \tag{8}$$

where c is a temperature factor which is a constant smaller than 1 but close to 1. The parameters used in the developed simulated annealing algorithm are: k=0.005, n_{max}=60, CW_{max}=40, c=0.9, T_{init}=500, T_{fin}=50.

A flow chart showing the steps of the algorithm is presented in Figure 2.

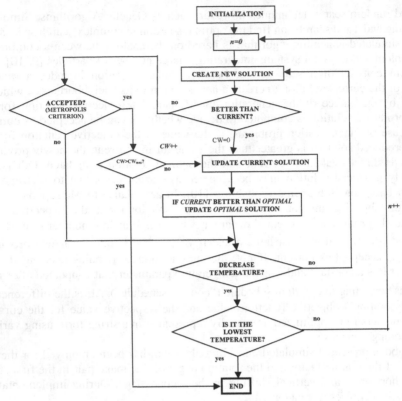

Fig. 2. Simulated Annealing Implemented Algorithm Flowchart.

4 Case Studies Application and Results

The proposed image registration algorithm has been applied in four indicative types of medical images depicted in Figure 3. In order to reach in comparable results all images had a resolution of 256×256 pixels in a grayscale mode.

The algorithm has been introduced in several scenarios of image translation, rotation and scaling. The upper and lower values of expected scaling ratio are 0.1 up to 1 and the corresponding values of rotation angle are kept to −30 till 30 degrees. Three scenarios of image scaling and rotation for each image are investigated and several runs of the algorithm have been tried for each scenario. The results of these runs are summarized in Table 1. The mean values of the optimal solutions are close to the actual values. The maximum error observed is 0.01 for the scaling factor and 1.46 degrees for the rotation factor. In the above runs, the simulated annealing algorithm did not require more than 1320 iterations of the similarity criterion calculation to find the optimal solution, while the full enumeration requires $4^8=65536$ calculations. Therefore, the simulated annealing algorithm resulted in an acceptable solution demanding only 2% of the time needed for the complete enumeration. In Figure 4(a) the solutions examined as current solutions during the progression of the algorithm's search are presented in the case of the MRI image. It can be seen that the total number of solutions examined is significantly low, but very well distributed in the whole solution space.

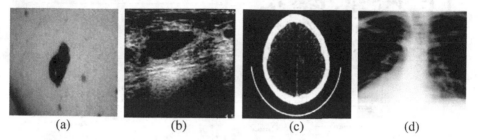

(a)   (b)   (c)   (d)

Fig. 3. The medical images used as a case studies: (a) Dermatological image, (b) Ultrasound image, (c) Magnetic Resonance Image (d) X-ray image.

Table 1. Results of the simulated annealing algorithm for the estimation of scaling and rotation factors.

Image Type	Actual Values		Results (mean values)		Error		Stand. Deviation	
	Scaling	Rotation (°)	Scaling	Rotation (°)	Scaling	Rotation (°)	Scaling	Rotation (°)
Skin	0.8	20	0.7882	20.6352	0.0118	0.6352	0.0223	1.0708
	0.9	10	0.8976	9.7777	0.0024	0.2223	0.0193	1.8793
	0.7	15	0.7049	14.4708	0.0049	0.5292	0.0163	1.1647
X-ray	0.8	20	0.7918	19.9766	0.0082	0.0234	0.0056	1.1719
	0.9	10	0.8856	10.2822	0.0144	0.2822	0.0047	0.9468
	0.7	15	0.7014	15.5530	0.0014	0.5530	0.0019	0.4587
US	0.8	20	0.7974	19.6472	0.0026	0.3528	0.0081	1.2562
	0.9	10	0.8913	10.8940	0.0087	0.8940	0.0030	0.8710
	0.7	15	0.6965	14.7530	0.0035	0.2470	0.0071	1.2714
MRI	0.8	20	0.8002	21.4590	0.0002	1.4590	0.0040	1.2045
	0.9	10	0.8955	10.0471	0.0045	0.0471	0.0054	1.4827
	0.7	15	0.7014	15.6412	0.0014	0.6412	0.0019	0.9149

Figure 4(b) displays the correlation coefficient values for the solutions considered as optimal. The depicted scenario refers in 80% scaling and 20 degrees clockwise rotation for the dermatological image in Figure 3(a). It can be noticed in Figures 4(c) and 4(d) that in some cases a latter optimal solution's value for the scaling factor or the rotation angle separately may be further away from the value of a former value. However, the corresponding value of the correlation coefficient function, as it can be seen in Figure 4(b), is always improving.

The second stage of the registration procedure refers to the detection of the horizontal and vertical shifting. The maximum horizontal and vertical shifting expected is p=60 pixels in all directions. Several runs of the simulated annealing algorithm have been tried for three scenarios in order to test the robustness of the algorithm. The results are summarized in Table 2. The maximum error observed is 1.4 pixels for the horizontal and 2.2 pixels for the vertical shifting. In the above runs, the simulated annealing algorithm did not need more than 1100 iterations to find the optimal solution. According to the analysis in section 2, the full enumeration requires $4p^2=14400$ calculations of the objective function. Therefore, the simulated annealing algorithm resulted in a good solution demanding only 7.6% of the computational time needed

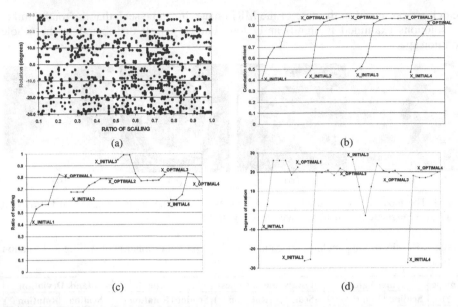

Fig. 4. (a) Solutions examined for the estimation of scaling and rotation factors in the case of the Magnetic Resonance image of Figure 3(c), (b) Convergence of the simulated annealing algorithm for various initial points in the case of the dermatological image (representation of the correlation coefficient function), (c) Convergence of the simulated annealing algorithm for various initial points in the case of the dermatological image (representation of the scaling ratio), (d) Convergence of the simulated annealing algorithm for various initial points in the case of the dermatological image (representation of the rotation angle).

for the complete enumeration. In Figure 5(a), the examined current solutions in the case of the Ultrasound image are presented. The total number of solutions examined is very well distributed in the solution space.

As it was done previously, the simulated annealing was applied to the different scenarios of the horizontal and vertical shifting using different initial solutions. In Figure 5(b), the correlation coefficient values for the solutions considered as optimal during the algorithm's search are presented, for four runs with different initial solutions. The scenario presented analytically is −20 pixels horizontal shifting and 10 pixels vertical shifting for the case of the MRI in Figure 3(c). In Figure 5(b) the objective function (correlation coefficient) is presented while Figures 5(c) and 5(d) provide the corresponding values of horizontal and vertical shifting.

5 Conclusion

In the present paper, an efficient algorithm that overcomes the increased complexity problem of global image registration methods is proposed. The algorithm is based on Log-Polar transform to decouple the effect of translation, scaling and rotation on the image pair and on a fast simulated annealing algorithm to maximize the non-linear

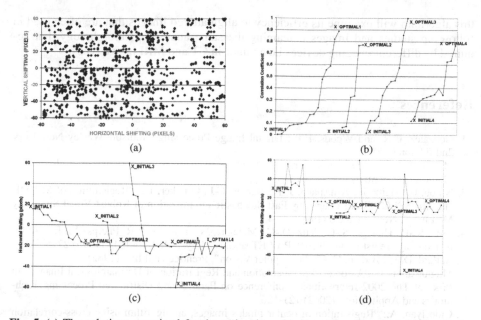

Fig. 5. (a) The solutions examined for the estimation of horizontal and vertical shifting in the case of the Ultrasound image of Figure 3(b), (b) Convergence of the simulated annealing algorithm for various initial points in the case of the MR image (representation of the correlation coefficient), (c) Convergence of the simulated annealing algorithm for various initial points in the case of the MR image (representation of the horizontal shifting), (d) Convergence of the simulated annealing algorithm for various initial points in the case of the MR image (representation of the vertical shifting).

Table 2. Results of the simulated annealing algorithm for the estimation of translation.

Image Type	Actual Shifting in pixels		Results (mean values)		Error		Stand. Deviation	
	Horizontal	Vertical	Horizontal	Vertical	Horizontal	Vertical	Horizontal	Vertical
Skin	10	20	9.4	20.4	0.6	0.4	1.673	1.140
	-20	10	-19.8	10.8	0.2	0.8	0.447	1.304
	-15	-5	-14.6	-4.4	0.4	0.6	1.517	1.140
X-ray	10	20	9.6	20.8	0.4	0.8	2.881	0.837
	-20	10	-20.4	9.8	0.4	0.2	1.140	1.095
	-15	-5	-14.6	-4.8	0.4	0.2	0.548	0.447
US	10	20	8.6	18	1.4	2	2.302	1.225
	-20	10	-20.8	10	0.8	0	1.789	1.000
	-15	-5	-14.8	-4.2	0.2	0.8	1.095	0.447
MRI	10	20	10	22.2	0	2.2	1.225	1.643
	-20	10	-19.8	9.8	0.2	0.2	1.304	2.387
	-15	-5	-16.2	-4	1.2	1	1.095	1.000

correlation coefficient similarity criterion. The registration procedure and the corresponding optimization is divided in two consecutive stages; the first stage the scaling and rotation factors are computed while in the second stage the horizontal and vertical shifting are detected. The image registration algorithm has been applied to a variety of medical images for several scenarios of image modalities. In all cases the image registration algorithm performed very well exhibiting low level of error. Future work on this algorithm will examine its efficiency to align altered images that are often used in follow up studies and images containing the same anatomical morphology, but acquired by different imaging devices i.e a tumor in CT and MRI image types.

References

1. Gonzalez, C.R. and Woods, E.R.: Digital Image Processing. Addison–Wesley New York 2nd Edition (2000).
2. Maintz, J. B. A., Max Viergever, A.: "A survey of medical image registration" Journal of Medical Image Analysis Vol. 2 1 (1998) pp 1–36.
3. Nikou, C., Heitz, F., Armspach, J.-P., Namer, I.-J., Grucker, D.: "Registration of MR/MR and MR/SPECT Brain Images by Fast Stochastic Optimization of Robust Voxel Similarity Measures", Neuroimage 8 (1998) 30–43.
4. Liny, K.-P., Huangz, S.-C., Yuz, D.-C., Melegaz, W., Barrioz, J. R, Phelpsz M. E.: "Automated image registration for FDOPA PET studies", Phys. Med. Biol. 41 (1996) 2775–2788
5. Ballard, D. H., Brown, C. M.: "Computer Vision", Prentice Hall Inv. (1982).
6. Maglogiannis I.: "Automated Segmentation and Registration of Dermatological Images" In Proc. of The 2002 International Conference on Parallel and Distributed Processing Techniques and Applications (2002) 121-126.
7. Cideciyan, A.: "Registration of ocular fundus images, an algorithm using cross-correlation of triple invariant image descriptors." IEEE Eng. Med. Biol. 14 1 (1995).
8. Rao S. S.: "Engineering Optimization", John Wiley and Sons, New York, (1996).
9. Pham D. T., Karaboga D.:"Intelligent Optimisation Techniques: Genetic Algorithms, Tabu Search, Simulated Annealing and Neural Networks", Springer, Great Britain (2000).
10. Aarts E., Korst J.: Simulated Annealing and Boltzman Machines, John Wiley & Sons, New York, (1990).
11. Papadogiannis K. A., Hatziargyriou N. D., and Saraiva J. T.: "Short Term Active/Reactive Operation Planning in Market Environment using Simulated Annealing", 12th Intelligent Systems Application to Power Systems Conference 2003 Limnos Greece (2003).

Adaptive Rule-Based Facial Expression Recognition

Spiros Ioannou, Amaryllis Raouzaiou, Kostas Karpouzis, Minas Pertselakis,
Nicolas Tsapatsoulis, and Stefanos Kollias

Department of Electrical and Computer Engineering
National Technical University of Athens
Heroon Polytechniou 9, 157 73 Zographou, Greece
Phone: +30-210-7723039, Fax: +30-210-7722492
{sivann,araouz,kkarpou,ntsap}@image.ntua.gr, mper@cslab.ntua.gr,
stefanos@cs.ntua.gr

Abstract. This paper addresses the problem of emotion recognition in faces
through an intelligent neuro-fuzzy system, which is capable of analysing facial
features extracted following the MPEG-4 standard and classifying facial images
according to the underlying emotional states, following rules derived from expression profiles. Results are presented which illustrate the capability of the developed system to analyse and recognise facial expressions in man-machine interaction applications.

1 Introduction

Current information processing and visualization systems are capable of offering
advanced and intuitive means of receiving input and communicating output to their
users. As a result, Man-Machine Interaction (MMI) systems that utilize multimodal
information about their users' current emotional state are presently at the forefront of
interest of the computer vision and artificial intelligence communities. Such interfaces
give the opportunity to less technology-aware individuals, as well as handicapped
people, to use computers more efficiently and thus overcome related fears and pre-
conceptions. Besides this, most emotion-related facial gestures are considered to be
universal, in the sense that they are recognized along different cultures. Therefore, the
introduction of an "emotional dictionary" that includes descriptions and perceived
meanings of facial expressions, so as to help infer the likely emotional state of a specific user, can enhance the affective nature of MMI applications.

Automatic emotion recognition in faces is a hard problem, requiring a number of
pre-processing steps which attempt to detect or track the face, to locate characteristic
facial regions such as eyes, mouth and nose on it, to extract and follow the movement
of facial features, e.g., characteristic points in these regions, or model facial gestures
using anatomic information about the face.

Most of the above techniques are based on a well-known system for describing "all
visually distinguishable facial movements", called the Facial Action Coding System
(FACS) [4], [6]. FACS is an anatomically oriented coding system, based on the definition of "action units" that cause facial movements. The FACS model has inspired
the derivation of facial animation and definition parameters in the framework of the
ISO MPEG-4 standard [7]. In particular, the Facial Definition Parameter (FDP) set

G.A. Vouros and T. Panayiotopoulos (Eds.): SETN 2004, LNAI 3025, pp. 466–475, 2004.

and the Facial Animation Parameter (FAP) set were designed in the MPEG-4 framework to allow the definition of a facial shape and texture, as well as the animation of faces reproducing expressions, emotions and speech pronunciation. By monitoring facial gestures corresponding to FDP feature points (FP) and/or FAP movements over time, it is possible to derive cues about user's expressions/emotions [1], [3].

In this work we present a methodology for analysing expressions. This is performed through a neuro-fuzzy system which first translates FP movements into FAPs and reasons on the latter to recognize the underlying emotion in facial video sequences.

2   Representation of Emotion

The obvious goal for emotion analysis applications is to assign category labels that identify emotional states. However, labels as such are very poor descriptions, especially since humans use a daunting number of labels to describe emotion. Therefore we need to incorporate a more transparent, as well as continuous representation, that matches closely our conception of what emotions are or, at least, how they are expressed and perceived.

Activation-emotion space [3] is a representation that is both simple and capable of capturing a wide range of significant issues in emotion. It rests on a simplified treatment of two key themes:

- *Valence:* The clearest common element of emotional states is that the person is materially influenced by feelings that are "valenced", i.e. they are centrally concerned with positive or negative evaluations of people or things or events; the link between emotion and valencing is widely agreed.
- *Activation level:* Research has recognized that emotional states involve dispositions to act in certain ways. A basic way of reflecting that theme turns out to be surprisingly useful. States are simply rated in terms of the associated activation level, i.e. the strength of the person's disposition to take some action rather than none.

The axes of the activation-evaluation space reflect those themes. The vertical axis shows activation level, the horizontal axis evaluation. A basic attraction of that arrangement is that it provides a way of describing emotional states which is more tractable than using words, but which can be translated into and out of verbal descriptions. Translation is possible because emotion-related words can be understood, at least to a first approximation, as referring to positions in activation-emotion space. Various techniques lead to that conclusion, including factor analysis, direct scaling, and others [16].

A surprising amount of emotional discourse can be captured in terms of activation-emotion space. Perceived full-blown emotions are not evenly distributed in activation-emotion space; instead they tend to form a roughly circular pattern. In this framework, identifying the center as a natural origin has several implications. Emotional strength can be measured as the distance from the origin to a given point in activation-evaluation space. The concept of a full-blown emotion can then be translated roughly as a state where emotional strength has passed a certain limit. An interesting implication is that strong emotions are more sharply distinct from each other than weaker emotions with the same emotional orientation. A related extension is to think of primary or basic emotions as cardinal points on the periphery of an emotion circle (see Figure 1).

Activation-evaluation space is a surprisingly powerful device, and it has been increasingly used in computationally oriented research. However, it has to be emphasized that representations of that kind depend on collapsing the structured, high-dimensional space of possible emotional states into a homogeneous space of two dimensions. There is inevitably loss of information; and worse still, different ways of making the collapse lead to substantially different results. Extreme care is, thus, needed to ensure that collapsed representations are used consistently.

Fig. 1. The Activation-emotion space.

3 Modelling Facial Expressions Using FAPs

Two basic issues should be addressed when modelling archetypal expression:

(i) estimation of FAPs that are involved in their formation,
(ii) definition of the FAP intensities.

Table 1 illustrates the description of "anger" and "fear", using MPEG-4 FAPs. Descriptions for all archetypal expressions can be found in [1].

Table 1. FAP vocabulary for description of "anger" and "fear".

Anger	lower_t_midlip (F_4), raise_b_midlip (F_5), push_b_lip (F_{16}), depress_chin (F_{18}), close_t_l_eyelid (F_{19}), close_t_r_eyelid (F_{20}), close_b_l_eyelid (F_{21}), close_b_r_eyelid (F_{22}), raise_l_i_eyebrow (F_{31}), raise_r_i_eyebrow (F_{32}), raise_l_m_eyebrow (F_{33}), raise_r_m_eyebrow (F_{34}), raise_l_o_eyebrow (F_{35}), raise_r_o_eyebrow (F_{36}), squeeze_l_eyebrow (F_{37}), squeeze_r_eyebrow (F_{38})
Fear	open_jaw (F_3), lower_t_midlip (F_4), raise_b_midlip (F_5), lower_t_lip_lm (F_8), lower_t_lip_rm (F_9), raise_b_lip_lm (F_{10}), raise_b_lip_rm (F_{11}), close_t_l_eyelid (F_{19}), close_t_r_eyelid (F_{20}), close_b_l_eyelid (F_{21}), close_b_r_eyelid (F_{22}), raise_l_i_eyebrow (F_{31}), raise_r_i_eyebrow (F_{32}), raise_l_m_eyebrow (F_{33}), raise_r_m_eyebrow (F_{34}), raise_l_o_eyebrow (F_{35}), raise_r_o_eyebrow (F_{36}), squeeze_l_eyebrow (F_{37}), squeeze_r_eyebrow (F_{38})

Although FAPs are practical and very useful for animation purposes, they are inadequate for analysing facial expressions from video scenes or still images. In order to measure FAPs in real images and video sequences, it is necessary to define a way of describing them through the movement of points that lie in the facial area and that can be automatically detected. Such a description could gain advantage from the extended research on automatic facial point detection [10].

Quantitative modelling of FAPs can be implemented using the features labelled as f_i $(i=1...15)$ in the third column of Table 2 [11]. The feature set employs FDP feature points that lie in the facial area. It consists of distances (noted as $s(x,y)$, where x and y correspond to FDP feature points ranked in terms of their belonging to specific facial areas [13]), some of which are constant during expressions and are used as reference points. It should be noted that not all FAPs can be modelled by distances between facial protuberant points (e.g. *raise_b_lip_lm_o*, *lower_t_lip_lm_o*). In such cases, the corresponding FAPs are retained in the vocabulary and their ranges of variation are experimentally defined based on facial animations. Moreover, some features serve for the estimation of the range of variation of more than one FAP (e.g. features f_{12}-f_{15}).

Table 2. Quantitative FAP modelling: (1) $s(x,y)$ is the Euclidean distance between FPs x and y, (2) $D_{i\text{-NEUTRAL}}$ refers to distance D_i with the face in neutral position.

FAP name	Main Feature for description	Utilized Main Feature
squeeze_l_eyebrow (F_{37})	$D_1=s(4.6,3.8)$	$f_1 = D_{1\text{-NEUTRAL}} - D_1$
squeeze_r_eyebrow (F_{38})	$D_2=s(4.5,3.11)$	$f_2 = D_{2\text{-NEUTRAL}} - D_2$
lower_t_midlip (F_4)	$D_3=s(9.3,8.1)$	$f_3 = D_3 - D_{3\text{-NEUTRAL}}$
raise_b_midlip (F_5)	$D_4=s(9.3,8.2)$	$f_4 = D_{4\text{-NEUTRAL}} - D_4$
raise_l_i_eyebrow (F_{31})	$D_5=s(4.2,3.8)$	$f_5 = D_5 - D_{5\text{-NEUTRAL}}$
raise_r_I_eyebrow (F_{32})	$D_6=s(4.1,3.11)$	$f_6 = D_6 - D_{6\text{-NEUTRAL}}$
raise_l_o_eyebrow (F_{35})	$D_7=s(4.6,3.12)$	$f_7 = D_7 - D_{7\text{-NEUTRAL}}$
raise_r_o_eyebrow (F_{36})	$D_8=s(4.5,3.7)$	$f_8 = D_8 - D_{8\text{-NEUTRAL}}$
raise_l_m_eyebrow (F_{33})	$D_9=s(4.4,3.12)$	$f_9 = D_9 - D_{9\text{-NEUTRAL}}$
raise_r_m_eyebrow (F_{34})	$D_{10}=s(4.3,3.7)$	$f_{10} = D_{10} - D_{10\text{-NEUTRAL}}$
open_jaw (F_3)	$D_{11}=s(8.1,8.2)$	$f_{11} = D_{11} - D_{11\text{-NEUTRAL}}$
close_t_l_eyelid (F_{19}) –close_b_l_eyelid (F_{21})	$D_{12}=s(3.2,3.4)$	$f_{12} = D_{12} - D_{12\text{-NEUTRAL}}$
close_t_r_eyelid (F_{20}) –close_b_r_eyelid (F_{22})	$D_{13}=s(3.1,3.3)$	$f_{13} = D_{13} - D_{13\text{-NEUTRAL}}$
stretch_l_cornerlip (F_6) (stretch_l_cornerlip_o)(F_{53}) – stretch_r_cornerlip (F_7) (stretch_r_cornerlip_o) (F_{54})	$D_{14}=s(8.4,8.3)$	$f_{14} = D_{14} - D_{14\text{-NEUTRAL}}$
squeeze_l_eyebrow (F_{37}) AND squeeze_r_eyebrow (F_{38})	$D_{15}=s(4.6,4.5)$	$f_{15} = D_{15\text{-NEUTRAL}} - D_{15}$

3.1 Profiles Creation

An archetypal *expression profile* is a set of FAPs accompanied by the corresponding range of variation, which, if animated, produces a visual representation of the corresponding emotion. Typically, a profile of an archetypal expression consists of a subset of the corresponding FAPs' vocabulary coupled with the appropriate ranges of variation. Table 3 and Figure 2 illustrate different profiles of "fear". Detailed description of profiles creation can be found in [13].

Table 3. Profiles of the expression "fear".

Profiles	FAPs and Range of Variation
Fear ($P_F^{(0)}$)	$F_3 \in$ [102,480], $F_5 \in$ [83,353], $F_{19} \in$ [118,370], $F_{20} \in$ [121,377], $F_{21} \in$ [118,370], $F_{22} \in$ [121,377], $F_{31} \in$ [35,173], $F_{32} \in$ [39,183], $F_{33} \in$ [14,130], $F_{34} \in$ [15,135]
$P_F^{(1)}$	$F_3 \in$ [400,560], $F_5 \in$ [307,399], $F_{19} \in$ [-530,-470], $F_{20} \in$ [-523,-463], $F_{21} \in$ [-530,-470], $F_{22} \in$ [-523,-463], $F_{31} \in$ [460,540], $F_{32} \in$ [460,540], $F_{33} \in$ [460,540], $F_{34} \in$ [460,540], $F_{35} \in$ [460,540], $F_{36} \in$ [460,540]
$P_F^{(2)}$	$F_3 \in$ [400,560], $F_5 \in$ [-240,-160], $F_{19} \in$ [-630,-570], $F_{20} \in$ [-630,-570], $F_{21} \in$ [-630,-570], $F_{22} \in$ [-630,-570], $F_{31} \in$ [460,540], $F_{32} \in$ [460,540], $F_{37} \in$ [60,140], $F_{38} \in$ [60,140]
$P_F^{(3)}$	$F_3 \in$ [400,560], $F_5 \in$ [-240,-160], $F_{19} \in$ [-630,-570], $F_{20} \in$ [-630,-570], $F_{21} \in$ [-630,-570], $F_{22} \in$ [-630,-570], $F_{31} \in$ [460,540], $F_{32} \in$ [460,540], $F_{33} \in$ [360,440], $F_{34} \in$ [360,440], $F_{35} \in$ [260,340], $F_{36} \in$ [260,340], $F_{37} \in$ 0, $F_{38} \in$ 0
$P_F^{(4)}$	$F_3 \in$ [400,560], $F_5 \in$ [-240,-160], $F_8 \in$ [-120,-80], $F_9 \in$ [-120,-80], $F_{10} \in$ [-120,-80], $F_{11} \in$ [-120,-80], $F_{19} \in$ [-630,-570], $F_{20} \in$ [-630,-570], $F_{21} \in$ [-630,-570], $F_{22} \in$ [-630,-570], $F_{31} \in$ [460,540], $F_{32} \in$ [460,540], $F_{33} \in$ [360,440], $F_{34} \in$ [360,440], $F_{35} \in$ [260,340], $F_{36} \in$ [260,340], $F_{37} \in$ 0, $F_{38} \in$ 0

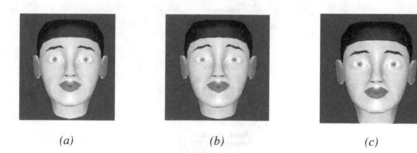

(a)   *(b)*   *(c)*

Fig. 2. MPEG-4 face model: animated profiles of "fear".

The rules used in the facial expression recognition system have derived from the created profiles.

4 The Facial Expression Recognition System

In general, six general categories are used, each one characterized by an archetypal emotion. Within each category, intermediate expressions are described by different emotional and optical intensities, as well as minor variations in expression details.

A hybrid intelligent emotion recognition system is presented next, consisting of a connectionist (subsymbolic) association part and a symbolic processing part as shown in Figure 3. In this modular architecture the *Connectionist Association Module* (CAM) provides the system with the ability to ground the symbolic predicates (associating them with the input features), while the *Adaptive Resource Allocating Neuro Fuzzy Inference System* (ARANFIS) [14] implements the semantic reasoning process.

The system takes as input a feature vector $\underline{f}$ that corresponds to the features f_i shown in the third column of Table 2. The particular values of $\underline{f}$ are associated to the symbolic predicates – i.e., FAP values shown in the first column of the same table– through the CAM subsystem. The CAM's outputs form the input vector $\underline{G}$ to the fuzzy inference subsystem, with the elements of $\underline{G}$ expressing the observed value of a corresponding FAP. The CAM consists of a neural network that dynamically forms the above association, providing the emotion analysis system with the capability to adapt to peculiarities of the specific user. In the training phase, the CAM learns to analyse the feature space and provide estimates of the FAP intensities (e.g. low, high, medium). This step requires: (a) Using an appropriate set of training inputs f, (b) Collecting a representative set T_I of pairs (f, s) to be used for network training, and (c) Estimating a parameter set $\mathbf{W_I}$, which maps the input space $\boldsymbol{F}$ to the symbolic predicate space S.

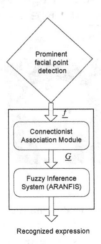

Fig. 3. The emotion analysis system.

ARANFIS evaluates the symbolic predicates provided by the CAM subsystem and performs the conceptual reasoning process that finally results to the degree at which the output situations – expressions- are recognised. ARANFIS [14] is a variation of the SuPFuNIS system [5] that enables structured learning. ARANFIS embeds fuzzy rules of the form "If s_1 is LOW and s_2 is HIGH then y is [expression - e.g. anger], where LOW, and HIGH are fuzzy sets defined, respectively, on input universes of discourse (UODs) and the output is a fuzzified expression.

Input nodes represent the domain variables-predicates and output nodes represent the target variables or classes. Each hidden node represents a rule, and input-hidden node connections represent fuzzy rules antecedents. Each hidden-output node connection represents a fuzzy-rule consequent. Fuzzy sets corresponding to linguistic labels of fuzzy *if-then* rules (such as LOW and HIGH) are defined on input and output UODs and are represented by symmetric Gaussian membership functions specified by a center and spread. Fuzzy weights w_{ij} from input nodes i to rule nodes j are thus modeled by the center w_{ij}^c and spread w_{ij}^s of a Gaussian fuzzy set and denoted by $w_{ij}=(w_{ij}^c , w_{ij}^s)$. In a similar fashion, consequent fuzzy weights from rule nodes j to output nodes k are denoted by $v_{jk} = (v_{ij}^c , v_{ij}^s)$. The spread of the i-th fuzzified input element is denoted as s_i^s while s_i^c is obtained as the crisp value of the i-th input element. Knowledge in the form of *if-then* rules can be either derived through clustering of input data or be embedded directly as a-priori knowledge.

It should be noted that in the previously described emotion analysis system, no hypothesis has been made about the type of recognizable emotions, that can be either archetypal or non-archetypal ones.

5 Application Study

Let us examine the situation where a PC camera captures its user's image. In the preprocessing stage, skin color segmentation is performed and the face is extracted. A snake is then used to smooth the face mask computed at the segmentation subsystem output. Then, the facial points are extracted, and point distances are calculated. Assuming that the above procedure is first performed for the user's neutral image, storing the corresponding facial points, the differences between them and the FPs of the current facial image of the user are estimated.

An emotion analysis system is created in [12]. In the system interface shown in Figure 4, one can observe an example of the calculated FP distances, the rules activated by the neurofuzzy system and the recognised emotion ('surprise').

To train the CAM system, we used the PHYSTA database in [2] as training set and the EKMAN database [4] as evaluation test. The coordinates of the points have been marked by hand for 300 images in the training set and 110 images in the test set. The CAM consisted of 17 neural networks, each of which associated less than 10 FP input distances (from the list of 23 distances defined as in Table 1 and mentioned in Table 4) to the states (high, medium, low, very low) of a corresponding FAP, and was trained using a variant of backpropagation learning algorithm [15]. Moreover, 41 rules were appropriately defined, half of them taken from the associated literature and half of them derived through training [13], and inserted in the ARANFIS subsystem.

Table 5 illustrates the confusion matrix of the mean degree of beliefs (*not the classification rates),* for each of the archetypal emotions *anger, joy, disgust, surprise* and the *neutral* condition, computed over the EKMAN dataset, which verifies the good system performance, while Table 6 shows the more often activated rule for each of the above expressions.

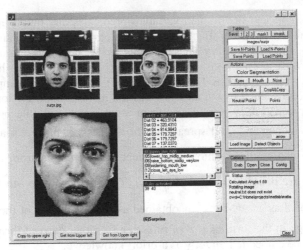

Fig. 4. System Interface.

Table 4. Training the CAM module.

FAP name	Primary distance	Other distances	States (VL-VeryLow, L-Low, M-Medium, H-High)
Squeeze_l_eyebrow (F_{37})	d_2	d_6, d_8, d_{10}, d_{17}, d_{19}, d_{15}	L, M, H
Squeeze_r_eyebrow (F_{38})	d_1	d_5, d_7, d_9, d_{16}, d_{18}, d_{15}	L, M, H
Lower_t_midlip (F_4)	d_3	d_{11}, d_{20}, d_{21}	L, M
Raise_b_midlip (F_5)	d_4	d_{11}, d_{20}, d_{21}	VL, L, H
Raise_l_I_eyebrow (F_{31})	d_6	d_2, d_8, d_{10}, d_{17}, d_{19}, d_{15}	L, M, H
Raise_r_I_eyebrow (F_{32})	d_5	d_1, d_7, d_9, d_{16}, d_{18}, d_{15}	L, M, H
Raise_l_o_eyebrow (F_{35})	d_8	d_2, d_6, d_{10}, d_{17}, d_{19}, d_{15}	L, M, H
Raise_r_o_eyebrow (F_{36})	d_7	d_1, d_5, d_9, d_{16}, d_{18}, d_{15}	L, M, H
Raise_l_m_eyebrow (F_{33})	d_{10}	d_2, d_6, d_8, d_{17}, d_{19}, d_{15}	L, M, H
Raise_r_m_eyebrow (F_{34})	d_9	d_1, d_5, d_7, d_{16}, d_{18}, d_{15}	L, M, H
Open_jaw (F_3)	d_{11}	d_4	L, M, H
close_left_eye (F_{19}, F_{21})	d_{13}	-	L, H
close_right_eye (F_{20}, F_{22})	d_{12}	-	L, H
Wrinkles_between_eyebrows (F_{37}, F_{38})	d_{15}	d_1, d_2, d_5, d_6, d_7, d_8, d_9, d_{16}, d_{17}, d_{18}, d_{19}	L, M, H
Raise_l_cornerlip_o (F_{53})	d_{23}	d_3, d_4, d_{11}, d_{20}, d_{21}, d_{22}	L, M, H
Raise_r_cornerlip_o (F_{54})	d_{22}	d_3, d_4, d_{11}, d_{20}, d_{21}, d_{23}	L, M, H
widening_mouth (F_6, F_7)	d_{11}	d_3, d_4, d_{14}	L, M, H

Table 5. Results in images of different expressions.

	Anger	Joy	Disgust	Surprise	Neutral
Anger	0.611	0.01	0.068	0	0
Joy	0.006	0.757	0.009	0	0.024
Disgust	0.061	0.007	0.635	0	0
Surprise	0	0.004	0	0.605	0.001
Neutral	0	0.123	0	0	0.83

Table 6. Activated rules.

Expressions	Rule more often activated (% of examined photos)
Anger	[*open_jaw_low, lower_top_midlip_medium, raise_bottom_midlip_high, raise_left_inner_eyebrow_low, raise_right_inner_eyebrow_low, raise_left_medium_eyebrow_low, raise_right_medium_eyebrow_low, squeeze_left_eyebrow_high, squeeze_right_eyebrow_high, wrinkles_between_eyebrows_high, raise_left_outer_cornerlip_medium, raise_right_outer_cornerlip_medium*] (47%)
Joy	[*open_jaw_high, lower_top_midlip_low, raise_bottom_midlip_verylow, widening_mouth_high, close_left_eye_high, close_right_eye_high*] (39%)
Disgust	[*open_jaw_low, lower_top_midlip_low, raise_bottom_midlip_high, widening_mouth_low, close_left_eye_high, close_right_eye_high, raise_left_inner_eyebrow_medium, raise_right_inner_eyebrow_medium, raise_left_medium_eyebrow_medium, raise_right_medium_eyebrow_medium, wrinkles_between_eyebrows_medium*] (33%)
Surprise	[*open_jaw_high, raise_bottom_midlip_verylow, widening_mouth_low, close_left_eye_low, close_right_eye_low, raise_left_inner_eyebrow_high, raise_right_inner_eyebrow_high, raise_left_medium_eyebrow_high, raise_right_medium_eyebrow_high, raise_left_outer_eyebrow_high, raise_right_outer_eyebrow_high, squeeze_left_eyebrow_low, squeeze_right_eyebrow_low, wrinkles_between_eyebrows_low*] (71%)
Neutral	[*open_jaw_low, lower_top_midlip_medium, raise_left_inner_eyebrow_medium, raise_right_inner_eyebrow_medium, raise_left_medium_eyebrow_medium, raise_right_medium_eyebrow_medium, raise_left_outer_eyebrow_medium, raise_right_outer_eyebrow_medium, squeeze_left_eyebrow_medium, squeeze_right_eyebrow_medium, wrinkles_between_eyebrows_medium, raise_left_outer_cornerlip_medium, raise_right_outer_cornerlip_medium*] (70%)

6 Conclusions

Facial expression recognition has been investigated in this paper, based on neuro-fuzzy analysis of facial features extracted from a user's image following the MPEG-4 standard. A hybrid intelligent system has been described that performs extraction of fuzzy predicates and inference, providing an estimate of the user's emotional state. Work is currently been done, extending and validating the above developments in the framework of the IST ERMIS project [12].

References

1. N. Tsapatsoulis, A. Raouzaiou, S. Kollias, R. Cowie and E. Douglas-Cowie, "Emotion Recognition and Synthesis based on MPEG-4 FAPs," in *MPEG-4 Facial Animation*, Igor Pandzic, R. Forchheimer (eds), John Wiley & Sons, UK, 2002.
2. EC TMR Project "PHYSTA: Principled Hybrid Systems: Theory and Applications," *http://www.image.ece.ntua.gr/physta*.
3. R. Cowie, E. Douglas-Cowie, N. Tsapatsoulis, G. Votsis, S. Kollias, W. Fellenz and J. Taylor, "Emotion Recognition in Human-Computer Interaction", *IEEE Signal Processing Magazine*, 18 (1), p. 32-80, January 2001.

4. P. Ekman and W. Friesen, *The Facial Action Coding System*, Consulting Psychologists Press, San Francisco, CA, 1978 (*http://www.paulekman.com*).
5. S. Paul and S. Kumar, "Subsethood-Product Fuzzy Neural Inference System (SuPFuNIS)," *IEEE Trans. on Neural Networks*, vol. 13, no 3, pp. 578-599, May 2002.
6. ISO/IEC JTC1/SC29/WG11 N3205, "Multi-users technology (Requirements and Applications)", December 1999, Maui.
7. A.M. Tekalp, J. Ostermann, "Face and 2-D mesh animation in MPEG-4", *Signal Processing: Image Communication,* Vol. 15, No. 4-5 (Tutorial Issue on the MPEG-4 Standard), pp. 387-421, January 2000.
8. EC TMR Project PHYSTA Report, "Development of Feature Representation from Facial Signals and Speech," January 1999.
9. P. Ekman, "Facial expression and Emotion," *Am. Psychologist*, vol. 48 pp.384-392, 1993.
10. P. Chellapa, C. Wilson and S. Sirohey, "Human and Machine Recognition of Faces: A Survey," *Proceedings of IEEE*, vol.83, no. 5, pp. 705-740, 1995.
11. K.Karpouzis, N. Tsapatsoulis and S. Kollias, "Moving to Continuous Facial Expression Space using the MPEG-4 Facial Definition Parameter (FDP) Set," *in Proc. of the Electronic Imaging 2000 Conference of SPIE,* San Jose, CA, USA, January 2000.
12. IST Project: Emotionally Rich Man-Machine Interaction Systems (ERMIS), 2001-2003.
13. A. Raouzaiou, N. Tsapatsoulis, K. Karpouzis and S. Kollias, "Parameterized facial expression synthesis based on MPEG-4", EURASIP Journal on Applied Signal Processing,Vol. 2002, No. 10, pp. 1021-1038, Hindawi Publishing Corporation, October 2002.
14. M Pertselakis, N. Tsapatsoulis, S. Kollias and A. Stafylopatis, "An Adaptive Resource Allocating Neural Fuzzy Inference System," *in Proc. of "IEEE Intelligent Systems Application to Power Systems" (ISAP'03)*, Lemnos, Greece, 2003.
15. S. Haykin, "Neural Networks: a Comprehensive Foundation", Macmillan College Publishing Company, Inc., New York, 1994.
16. C. M. Whissel, "The dictionary of affect in language", in R. Plutchnik & H. Kellerman (Eds), *Emotion: Theory, research and experience: vol 4, The measurement of emotions*, Academic Press, New York 1989.

Locating Text in Historical Collection Manuscripts

Basilios Gatos[1], Ioannis Pratikakis[1,2], and Stavros J. Perantonis[1]

[1] Computational Intelligence Laboratory
Institute of Informatics and Telecommunications
National Research Center "Demokritos"
153 10 Athens, Greece
{bgat,ipratika,sper}@iit.demokritos.gr
[2] Department of Information and Communication Systems Engineering
University of the Aegean
83 200 Karlovassi, Samos, Greece
yipratik@aegean.gr

Abstract. It is common that documents belonging to historical collections are poorly preserved and are prone to degradation processes. The aim of this work is to leverage state-of-the-art techniques in digital image binarization and text identification for digitized documents allowing further content exploitation in an efficient way. A novel methodology is proposed that leads to preservation of meaningful textual information in low quality historical documents. The method has been developed in the framework of the Hellenic GSRT-funded R&D project, D-SCRIBE, which aims at developing an integrated system for digitization and processing of old Hellenic manuscripts. After testing of the proposed method on numerous low quality historical manuscripts, it has turned out that our methodology performs better compared to current state-of-the-art adaptive thresholding techniques.

1 Introduction

Historical document collections are a valuable resource for human history. It is common that documents belonging to historical collections are poorly preserved and are prone to degradation processes. This work aims to leverage state-of-the-art techniques in digital image binarization and text identification for digitized documents allowing further content exploitation in an efficient way. The method has been developed in the framework of the Hellenic GSRT-funded R&D project, D-SCRIBE, which aims to develop an integrated system for digitization and processing of old Hellenic manuscripts.

Binarization (threshold selection) is the starting step of the most document image analysis systems and refers to the conversion of the gray-scale image into a binary image. Binarization is a key step in document image processing modules since a good binarization set the base for successful segmentation and recognition of characters. In

G.A. Vouros and T. Panayiotopoulos (Eds.): SETN 2004, LNAI 3025, pp. 476–485, 2004.

old document processing, binarization usually distinguishes text areas from background areas, so it is used as a text locating technique. In the literature, the binarization is usually reported to be performed either globally or locally. The global methods (global thresholding) use one calculated threshold value to classify image pixels into object or background classes [1-5], whereas the local schemes (adaptive thresholding) can use many different adapted values selected according to the local area information [6,7]. Most of the proposed algorithms for optimum image binarization rely on statistical methods, without taking into account the special nature of document images [8-10]. However, recently some document directed binarization techniques have been developed [11-14]. Global thresholding methods are not sufficient for document image binarization since document images usually have poor quality, shadows, nonuniform illumination, low contrast, large signal-dependent noise, smear and strains. The most famous and efficient global thresholding technique is this of Otsu [2].

In this paper, a novel adaptive thresholding scheme is introduced in order to binarize low quality historical documents and locate meaningful textual information. The proposed scheme consists of four basic steps. The first step is dedicated to a denoising procedure using a low-pass Wiener filter. We use an adaptive Wiener method based on statistics estimated from a local neighborhood of each pixel. In the second step, we use Niblack's approach for a first rough estimation of foreground regions. Usually, the foreground pixels are a subset of Niblack's result since Niblack's method usually introduces extra noise. In the third step, we compute the background surface of the image by interpolating neighboring background intensities into the foreground areas that result from Niblack's method. A similar approach has been proposed for binarizing camera images [15]. In the last step, we proceed to final thresholding by combining the calculated background surface with the original image. Text areas are located if the distance of the original image with the calculated background is over a threshold. This threshold adapts to the gray-scale value of the background surface in order to preserve textual information even in very dark background areas. The proposed method has been tested with a variety of low quality historical manuscripts and has been reported to work better than the most famous adaptive thresholding techniques.

2 Previous Work

Among the most known approaches for adaptive thresholding is Niblack's method [8] and Sauvola's method [11].

Niblack's algorithm [8] calculates a pixel-wise threshold by shifting a rectangular window across the image. The threshold T for the center pixel of the window is computed using the mean m and the variance s of the gray values in the window:

$$T = m + k\,s \qquad (1)$$

where k is a constant set to -0.2. The value of k is used to determine how much of the total print object boundary is taken as a part of the given object. This method can distinguish the object from the background effectively in the areas close to the objects.

The results are not very sensitive to the window size as long as the window covers at least 1-2 characters. However, noise that is present in the background remains dominant in the final binary image. Consequently, if the objects are sparse in an image, a lot of background noise will be left. Sauvola's method [11] solves this problem by adding a hypothesis on the gray values of text and background pixels (text pixels have gray values near 0 and background pixels have gray values near 255), which results in the following formula for the threshold:

$$T = m + (1 - k (1 - s/R)) \qquad (2)$$

where R is the dynamics of the standard deviation fixed to 128 and k is fixed to 0.5. This method gives better results for document images.

3 Methodology

The proposed methodology for low quality historical document binarization and text preservation is illustrated in Fig. 1 and it is fully described in this section.

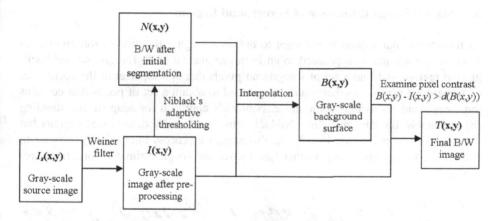

Fig. 1. Block diagram of the proposed methodology for low quality historical document text preservation.

3.1 Stage1: Pre-processing

Since historical document collections are usually of very low quality, a pre-processing stage of the grayscale source image is essential in order to eliminate noise areas, to smooth the background texture and to highlight the contrast between background and text areas. The use of a low-pass Wiener filter [16] has proved efficient for the above goals. Wiener filter is commonly used in filtering theory for image restoration. Our pre-processing module implements an adaptive Wiener method based on statistics estimated from a local neighborhood around each pixel. The grayscale source image I_s is transformed to grayscale image I according to the following formula:

$$I(x,y) = \mu + (\sigma^2 - v^2)(I_s (x,y) - \mu) / \sigma^2 \qquad (3)$$

where μ is the local mean and σ^2 the variance at a NxM neighborhood around each pixel. We used a 5x5 Wiener filter for documents with thick characters or an alternative 3x3 for documents with thin characters. Fig. 2 shows the results of applying a 3x3 Wiener filter to a document image.

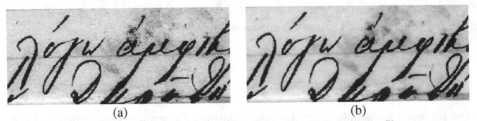

(a)   (b)

Fig. 2. Image pre-processing. (a) Original image; (b) 3x3 Wiener filter.

3.2 Stage2: Rough Estimation of Foreground Regions

At this step of our approach, we want to obtain a rough estimation of foreground regions. Our intention is to proceed to an initial segmentation to foreground and background regions and find a set of foreground pixels that is a superset of the correct set of foreground pixels. In other words, we intend to obtain a set of pixels that contains the foreground pixels plus some noise. Niblack's approach for adaptive thresholding [8] is suitable for this case since Niblack's method usually detects text regions but introduces extra noise (see Fig. 3). At this step, we process image $I(x,y)$ in order to extract the binary image $N(x,y)$ that has 1's for the rough estimated foreground regions.

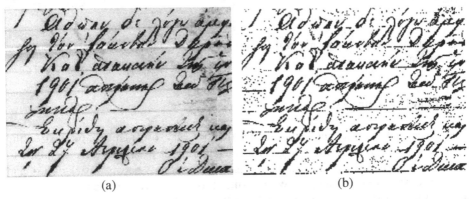

(a)   (b)

Fig. 3. Adaptive thresholding using Niblack's approach (a) Original image; (b) Estimation of foreground regions.

3.3 Stage3: Background Surface Estimation

At this stage, we compute an approximate background surface $B(x,y)$ of the image. The pixels of the pre-processed source image $I(x,y)$ belong to the background surface $B(x,y)$ only if the corresponding pixels of the resulting rough estimated foreground image $N(x,y)$ have zero values. The remaining values of surface $B(x,y)$ are interpolated from neighboring pixels. The formula for $B(x,y)$ calculation is as follows:

$$B(x,y) = \begin{cases} I(x,y) & \text{if } N(x,y) = 0 \\ \dfrac{\displaystyle\sum_{ix=x-dx}^{x+dx}\sum_{iy=y-dy}^{y+dy}(I(ix,iy)(1-N(ix,iy)))}{\displaystyle\sum_{ix=x-dx}^{x+dx}\sum_{iy=y-dy}^{y+dy}(1-N(ix,iy))} & \text{if } N(x,y) = 1 \end{cases} \tag{4}$$

The interpolation window of size $dx \times dy$ is defined to cover at least two image characters. An example of the background surface estimation is demonstrated in Fig. 4.

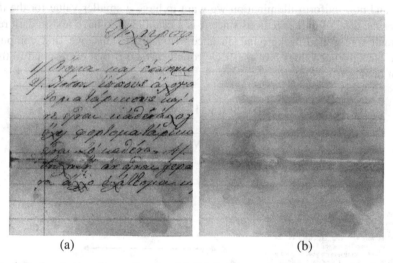

(a)   (b)

Fig. 4. Background surface estimation (a) Original image I; (b) Background surface B.

3.4 Stage4: Final Thresholding

In the last step, we proceed to final thresholding by combining the calculated background surface B with the original image I. Text areas are located if the distance of the original image with the calculated background is over a threshold d. We suggest the threshold d must change according to the gray-scale value of the background surface B in order to preserve textual information even in very dark background areas. For this reason, we propose a threshold d that has smaller values for darker regions. The final binary image T is given by the following formula:

$$T(x,y) = \begin{cases} 1, & \text{if } B(x,y) - I(x,y) > d(B(x,y)) \\ 0, & \text{otherwise} \end{cases} \tag{5}$$

A typical histogram of a document image (see Fig. 5) has two peaks, one for text regions and one for background regions. The average distance δ between the foreground and background can be calculated by the following formula:

$$\delta = \frac{\sum_x \sum_y (B(x,y) - I(x,y))}{\sum_x \sum_y N(x,y)} \tag{6}$$

For the usual case of document images with uniform illumination, the minimum threshold d between text pixels and background pixels can be defined with success as $q \cdot \delta$ where q is a variable near 0.8 that helps preserving the total character body in order to have successful OCR results [15]. In the case of very old documents with low quality and non-uniform illumination we want to have a smaller value for the threshold d for the case of darker regions since it is a usual case to have text in dark regions with small foreground-background distance. To achieve this, we first compute the average background values b of the background surface B that correspond to the text areas of image N:

$$b = \frac{\sum_x \sum_y (B(x,y)(1 - N(x,y))}{\sum_x \sum_y (1 - N(x,y))} \tag{7}$$

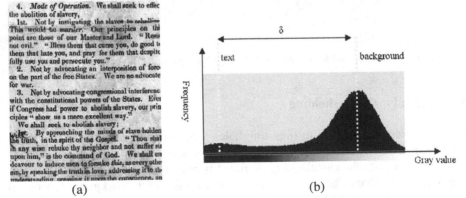

(a)   (b)

Fig. 5. Document image histogram (a) Original image; (b) Gray level histogram.

We wish the threshold to be approximately equal to the value $q \cdot \delta$ when the background is large (roughly greater than the average background value b) and approximately equal to $p_2 \cdot q \cdot \delta$ when the background is small (roughly less than $p_1 \cdot b$) with $p_1, p_2 \in [0,1]$. To simulate this desired behaviour, we use the following logistic sigmoid function that exhibits the desired saturation behaviour for large and small values of the background as shown in Fig. 6:

$$d(B(x, y)) = q\,\delta \left(\frac{(1 - p_2)}{1 + \exp(\dfrac{-4\,B(x, y)}{b\,(1 - p_1)} + \dfrac{2(1 + p_1)}{(1 - p_1)})} + p_2 \right) \tag{8}$$

After experimental work, for the case of old manuscripts, we suggest the following parameter values: $q = 0.6$, $p_1 = 0.5$, $p_2 = 0.8$.

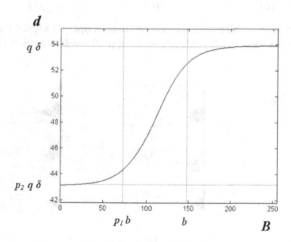

Fig. 6. Function $d(B(x,y))$.

4   Experimental Results

In this section, we compare the performance of our algorithm with those of Otsu [2], of Niblack [8] and of Sauvola *et al.* [11]. We also give the results of the application of a global thresholding value. The testing set includes images from handwritten or typed historical manuscripts. All images are of poor quality and have shadows, non-uniform illumination, smear and strain. Fig. 7 demonstrates an example of a typed manuscript, while Fig. 8 demonstrates an example of handwritten characters. As shown in all cases, our algorithm out-performs all the rest of the algorithms in preservation of meaningful textual information.

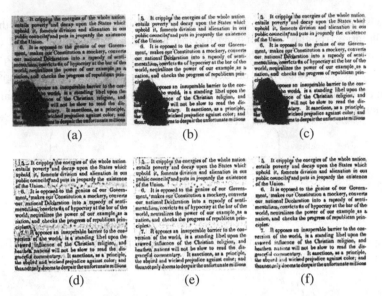

Fig. 7. Experimental results - binarization of a typed manuscript (a) Original image; (b) Global thresholding; (c) Otsu's method; (d) Niblack's method; (e) Sauvola's method; (f) The proposed method.

Fig. 8. Experimental results - binarization of a handwritten manuscript (a) Original image; (b) Global thresholding; (c) Otsu's method; (d) Niblack's method; (e) Sauvola's method; (f) The proposed method.

To quantify the efficiency of the proposed binarization method, we compared the results obtained by the well-known OCR engine FineReader 6 [17], using the binarization results of Niblack [8], Sauvola *et al.* [11] and the proposed method, as the inputs of this engine. To measure the quality of the OCR results we calculated the Levenshtein distance [18] between the correct text (ground truth) and the resulting text. As shown at Table 1, the application of the proposed binarization technique has shown the best performance regarding the final OCR results.

Table 1. Representative OCR results after applying several binarization schemes.

	Levenshtein Distance from the Ground truth			
	Document 1	Document 2	Document 3	Document 4
Niblack's method	228	619	513	447
Sauvola's method	60	394	276	694
The proposed method	**56**	**207**	**177**	**153**

5 Conclusions

In this paper, we present a novel methodology that leads to preservation of meaningful textual information in low quality historical documents. The proposed scheme consists of four (4) distinct steps: a pre-processing procedure using a low-pass Wiener filter, a rough estimation of foreground regions using Niblack's approach, a background surface calculation by interpolating neighboring background intensities and finally a thresholding by combining the calculated background surface with the original image. Text areas are located if the distance of the original image with the calculated background is over a threshold. This threshold adapts to the gray-scale value of the background surface in order to preserve textual information even in very dark background areas. The proposed methodology works with great success even in cases of historical manuscripts with poor quality, shadows, nonuniform illumination, low contrast, large signal-dependent noise, smear and strain. Experimental results show that our algorithm out-performs the most known thresholding approaches.

Acknowledgment

The authors would like to thank Dr. Ergina Kavallieratou for providing us samples from her private historical document collection.

References

1. Rosenfeld, A., Kak, A. C.: Digital Picture Processing, 2nd edition, Academic Press, New York (1982).
2. Otsu, N.: A threshold selection method from gray-level histograms. IEEE Trans. Systems Man Cybernet. 9 (1) (1979) 62-66.

3. Kittler, J., Illingworth, J.: On threshold selection using clustering criteria. IEEE Trans. Systems Man Cybernet. 15 (1985) 652-55.
4. Brink, A. D.: Thresholding of digital images using two-dimensional entropies. Pattern Recognition 25 (8) (1992) 803-808.
5. Yan, H.: Unified formulation of a class of image thresholding techniques. Pattern Recognition 29(12) (1996) 2025-2032.
6. Sahoo, P. K., Soltani, S., Wong, A. K. C.: A survey of Thresholding Techniques. Computer Vision, Graphics and Image Processing, 41(2) (1988) 233-260.
7. Kim, I. K., Park, R. H.: Local adaptive thresholding based on a water flow model. Second Japan-Korea Joint Workshop on Computer Vision, Japan (1996) 21-27.
8. Niblack, W.: An Introduction to Digital Image Processing. Englewood Cliffs, N. J., Prentice Hall (1986) 115-116.
9. Yang, J., Chen, Y., Hsu, W.: Adaptive thresholding algorithm and its hardware implementation. Pattern Recognition Lett. 15(2) (1994) 141-150.
10. Parker, J. R., Jennings, C., Salkauskas, A. G.: Thresholding using an illumination model. ICDAR'93 (1993) 270-273.
11. Sauvola, J., Seppanen, T., Haapakoski, S., Pietikainen, M.: Adaptive Document Binarization. International Conference on Document Analysis and Recognition (1997) 147-152.
12. Chang, M., Kang, S.,Rho, W., Kim, H., Kim, D.: Improved binarization algorithm for document image by histogram and edge detection. ICDAR'95 (1993) 636-643.
13. Trier, O. D., Jain, A. K.: Goal-Directed Evaluation of Binarization Methods. IEEE Trans. on Patt. Anal. and Mach. Intell., 17(12) (1995) 1191-1201.
14. Eikvil, L., Taxt, T., Moen, K.: A fast adaptive method for binarization of document images. Int. Conf. Document Analysis and Recognition, France (1991) 435-443.
15. Seeger, M., Dance, C.: Binarising Camera Images for OCR. Sixth International Conference on Document Analysis and Recognition (ICDAR'01), Seattle, Washington (2001) 54-58.
16. Jain, A.: Fundamentals of Digital Image Processing. Prantice Hall, Englewood Cliffs, NJ (1989).
17. www.finereader.com
18. Levenshtein, V. I.: Binary codes capable of correcting deletions, insertions and reversals. Sov. Phys. Dokl., 6 (1966) 707-710.

Semi-automatic Extraction of Semantics from Football Video Sequences

Vassilis Tzouvaras, Giorgos Stamou, and Stefanos Kollias

Image, Video and Multimedia Laboratory
Institute for Computer and Communication Systems
Department of electrical and Computer Engineering
National Technical University of Athens, Greece
tzouvaras@image.ntua.gr
{gstam,stefanos}@softlab.ntua.gr

Abstract. In this paper we use a knowledge based inference model in combination with knowledge stored in a domain specific ontologies to organize and combine semantically-related entities, within multimedia documents in order to extract semantics from video sequences. The simulation results demonstrate that is possible to extract high-level information from video if low-level features are extracted with high precision. Within the scope of this work we are not particularly interested in the method by which the low level features are extracted from the video.

1 Introduction

Researchers in content-based retrieval are concentrating on extracting semantics from multimedia documents so that retrievals using concept-based queries can be tailored to individual users. Following the semantic web paradigm, techniques for video annotation are now deployed. Manual annotation however, is time consuming and therefore expensive task. Fully automatic annotation of video, on the other hand, despite many efforts, is not feasible. Currently, all the efforts are focused on creating semi-automatic tools for annotation of multimedia content. New application in the context of the semantic web have renewed interest in the creation of knowledge based systems, and in particular on the exchange of information for different applications. As a result, new tools for creating and maintaining ontologies (formal explicit specifications of domain) have been developed, and there are many efforts to create domain specific ontologies.

In parallel with advancements in the development of the Semantic Web, is a rapid increase in the size and range of multimedia resources being added to the web. Archives museums and libraries are making enormous contributions to the amount of multimedia on the Internet through the digitization and online publication of their photographic, audio, film and video collection.

Although significant progress has been made in recent years on automatic segmentation, scene detection, and the recognition and detection of low level features from multimedia content, comparatively little progress has been made on machine genera-

G.A. Vouros and T. Panayiotopoulos (Eds.): SETN 2004, LNAI 3025, pp. 486–495, 2004.

tion of semantic descriptions of audiovisual information. The representation of the semantics of MPEG-7 terms within machine processable ontologies facilitates efficient knowledge based multimedia systems, which are capable of automatically extracting and aggregating semantic information about the audiovisual data.

Within this paper we attempt to exploit all these developments- the rapid growth in multimedia content, the standardization of the content description and the semantic web infrastructure – to develop a system which will automatically retrieve related multimedia entities and generate knowledge through neurofuzzy inferencing and domain specific ontologies.

The work presented in this paper differs from previous works in two major aspects: (1) we produce dynamic inferencing in the sense that the system is using predefined mapping rules extracted from an ontology knowledge database, which can be adapted to specific context and user through a learning procedure provided by a new mathematical model. (2) using the combination of domain specific multimedia ontologies we can generate real time-semantic inferencing in multimedia documents, which can be used for searching and efficient retrieval in multimedia content.

2 Related Background

In order to achieve the above tasks we have combined a number of related technologies and research areas, such as the semantic web initiative, artificial intelligent techniques, knowledge based systems and knowledge management techniques.

2.1 Neurofuzzy Inferencing

Fuzzy systems are numerical model-free estimators. While neural networks encode sampled information in a parallel-distributed framework, fuzzy systems encode structured, empirical (heuristic) or linguistic knowledge in a similar numerical framework. Although they can describe the operation of the system in natural language with the aid of human-like if-then rules, they do not provide the highly desired characteristics of learning and adaptation. The use of neural networks in order to realize the key concepts of a fuzzy logic system enriches the system with the ability of learning and improves the subsymbolic to symbolic mapping. One of the key-aspects of the present work is the description of semantic events and composite objects, in terms of rules employing fuzzy hypotheses (the degree of belief of the presence of specific objects and their interrelations). For the above representation, a neurofuzzy network is used in order to preserve the symbolic nature of the information, also providing learning capabilities. The proposed inference model can be seen in Figure 1.

The input of the system is the evaluated predicates (semantic entities) and the output a new recognized entity. The inferencing procedure is completed through IF-THEN rules, which are stored in a semantic knowledge container. The semantic knowledge is an ontology infrastructure.

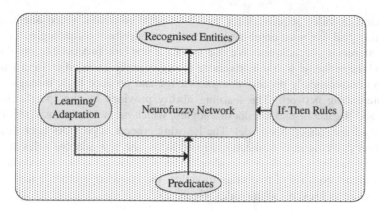

Fig. 1. The neurofuzzy model.

2.2 Semantic Web Activity and Multimedia Ontologies

Currently computers are changing from single isolated devices into entry points to worldwide network of information exchange and business transactions called the World Wide Web (WWW). For this reason, support data, information, and knowledge exchange has become a key issue in current computer technology. The success of the WWW has made it increasingly difficult to find, access, present and maintain the information required by a wide variety of users. In response to this problem, many new researchers initiatives and commercial enterprises have been set up to enrich available information with machine processable semantics. The semantic web will provide intelligent access to heterogeneous, distributed information enabling software products (agents) to mediate between user needs and information sources available.

One of the cornerstones of the Semantic Web is the Resource Description Framework (RDF). RDF provides a common underlying framework for supporting semantically rich descriptions, or metadata, which enables interoperable XML data exchange. The Web Ontology group are currently developing a Web Ontology Language (OWL), based on RDF Schema for defining Structured, Web-based ontologies which will provide richer integration and interoperability of data among descriptive communities.

An ontology is a formal, explicit specification of a domain. Typically, an ontology consists of concepts, concept properties and relationship between concepts. In a typical ontology concepts are represented by terms. In a multimedia ontology concepts might be represented by multimedia entities (images, video, audio, segments, etc.). In this paper we use textual and non-textual representation of multimedia knowledge for multimedia applications. Multimedia ontologies have many application areas such as content visualization, content indexing, knowledge sharing, learning and reasoning.

3 The Model

The aim of our model is to produce semantic inferencing, using knowledge stored in an ontology network. The output will be semantic events and composite object, which are detected in video sequences for real-time semi-automatic video annotation. To achieve this goal, we must combine knowledge management technologies and mathematical inferencing techniques. We use OWL, a machine processable ontology language and the semantic web initiative/idea to organise the knowledge. In this way, our model can automatically process this knowledge and produce logic through a neurofuzzy inferencing network. The learning ability provided by the specific inference network and the use of multimedia ontologies, which are not previously reported, are the major advantages of this model. The learning procedure provides context adaptivity and alternative definition matching. In addition, the new adapted rules are replacing the old rules in the ontology providing knowledge evolution and maintenance. The proposed model consists of two main modules, the knowledge module and the inferencing module and several submodules (figure 2).

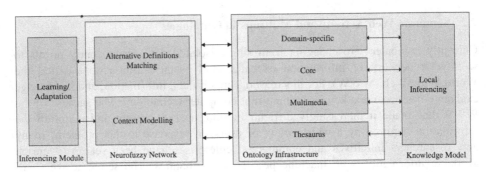

Fig. 2. The model.

3.1 Modes of Operation

The operation of the proposed model is divided into four modes. The initialisation of the neurofuzzy network is the first mode. Rules describing situations are stored in the knowledge database. These rules are transformed into numerical data and are used to initialise the neurons weights. The learning procedure is the second operation mode. The initialisation rules are adapted to the context and environmental conditions of the current application through a learning algorithm. Input-output data sets are put in the knowledge database to facilitate the adaptation of the existed knowledge. The new adapted rules are replacing the old rules in the knowledge. This procedure is human assisted since the new data might be incorrect. In this way we achieve semi-automatic knowledge evolution and maintenance. In case the knowledge is externally modified, then all the modes of operations must run from the beginning. Every time we insert new learning data into the knowledge then we must the start system operation from the learning mode.

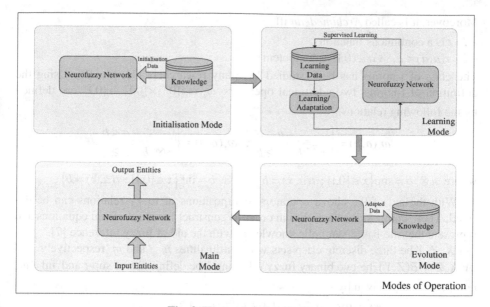

Fig. 3. The modes of operation.

4 Two-Layered Fuzzy Compositional Neural Networks

Let $y = [y_1, y_2, ..., y_m]$ denote a fuzzy set defined on the set of output predicates, the truth of which will be examined. Actually, each y_i represents the degree in which the i-th output fuzzy predicate is satisfied. The input of the proposed system is a fuzzy set $x = [x_1, x_2, ..., x_n]$ defined on the set of the input predicates, with each x_i representing the degree in which the i-th input predicate is detected. The proposed system represents the association $f : X \rightarrow Y$ which is the knowledge of the system, in a neurofuzzy structure. After the evaluation of the input predicates, some output predicates represented in the knowledge of the system can be recognized with the aid of fuzzy systems' reasoning [3]. One of the widely used ways of constructing fuzzy inference systems is the method of approximate reasoning which can be implemented on the basis of compositional rule of inference [3]. The need for results with theoretical soundness lead to the representation of fuzzy inference systems on the basis of generalized sup-t-norm compositions [4],[2]. A t-norm (triangular norm) is a function $t : [0,1] \times [0,1] \rightarrow [0,1]$ satisfying for any $a, b, d \in [0,1]$ the next four conditions:

1. $t(a,1) = a$ and $t(a,0) = 0$
2. $b \leq d$ implies $t(a,b) \leq t(a,d)$
3. $t(a,b) = t(b,a)$
4. $t(a,t(b,d)) = t(t(a,b),d)$

Moreover, it is called *Archimedean* iff

1. t is a continuous function

2. $t(a,a) < a,\ \forall a \in (0,1)$ (idempotent)

The class of t-norms has been studied by many researchers [1], [5], [2]. Using the definition of t-norms, two additional operators $\hat{\omega}_t, \check{\omega}_t : [0,1] \times [0,1] \to [0,1]$ are defined by the following relations:

$$\hat{\omega}_t(a,b) = \begin{cases} 1 & a < b \\ a \hat{\otimes}^t b & a \geq b \end{cases}, \quad \check{\omega}_t(a,b) = \begin{cases} 0 & a < b \\ a \check{\otimes}^t b & a \geq b \end{cases}$$

where $a \hat{\otimes}^t b = \sup\{x \in [0,1] : t(a,x) = b\}$, $a \check{\otimes}^t b = \inf\{x \in [0,1] : t(a,x) = b\}$.

With the aid of the above operators, compositions of fuzzy relations can be defined. These compositions are used in order to construct fuzzy relational equations and represent the rule-based symbolic knowledge with the aid of fuzzy inference [7].

Let X, Z, Y be three discrete crisp sets with cardinalities n, l and m respectively, and $A(X,Z)$, $B(Z,Y)$ be two binary fuzzy relations. The definitions of sup-t and inf$-\hat{\omega}_t$ compositions are given by

$$(A \circ^t B)(i,j) = \sup_{k \in N_l} t\{A(i,k), B(k,j)\}, i \in N_n, j \in N_m$$

$$(A \circ^{\hat{\omega}_t} B)(i,j) = \inf_{k \in N_l} \hat{\omega}_t\{A(i,k), B(k,j)\}, i \in N_n, j \in N_m.$$

Let us now proceed to a more detailed description of the proposed neurofuzzy architecture (Figure 1). It consists of two layers of *compositional* neurons which are extensions of the conventional neurons [7]. While the operation of the conventional neuron is described by the equation:

$$y = \alpha \left(\sum_{i=1}^{n} w_i x_i + \vartheta \right),$$

where α is non-linearity, ϑ is threshold and w_i are the weights, the operation of the sup-t compositional neuron is described by the equation:

$$y = a' \left\{ \sup_{j \in N_n} t(x_i, w_i) \right\},$$

where t is a fuzzy intersection operator (a t-norm) and α is the following activation function $a'(z) = \begin{cases} 0 & x \in (-\infty,0) \\ x & x \in [0,1] \\ 1 & x \in (0,+\infty) \end{cases}$.

A second type of compositional neuron is constructed using the $\hat{\omega}_t$ operation. The neuron equation is given by:

$$y = a' \left\{ \inf_{j \in N_n} \hat{\omega}_t(x_i, w_i) \right\}$$

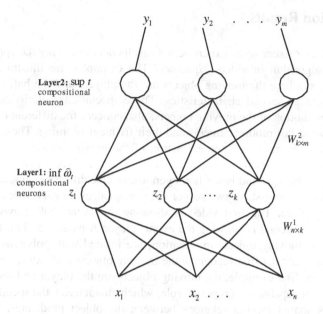

Fig. 4. The Neurofuzzy network.

The proposed architecture is a two-layer neural network of compositional neurons. The first layer consists of the $\inf - \widehat{\omega}_t$ neurons and the second layer consists of the sup-t neurons. The system takes as input, the input predicates and gives to the output the recognized output predicates. The first layer computes the antecedents of the fuzzy rules, while the second implements the fuzzy reasoning using the modus ponens schema.

The rules describing the events are generally of the form "if *input predicate (1)* and ... and *input predicate (n)* then *output predicate (i)*". Each rule consists of an antecedent (the *if* part of the rule) and a consequence (the *then* part of the rule). The set of the rules of the system is given in symbolic form by the expert and is used in order to initialize the neurofuzzy network (giving its initial structure and weights). During the learning process the number of neurons in the hidden layer and the weights of the two layers may change with the aid of a learning with the objective of the error minimization. The learning algorithm that supports the above network is applied in each layer independently. During the learning process, the weight matrices are adapted in order to approximate the solution of the fuzzy relational equation describing the association of the input with the output. Using a traditional minimization algorithm (for example the steepest descent), we cannot take advantage of the specific character of the problem. The algorithm that we use is based on a more sophisticated *credit assignment* that "blames" the neurons of the network using the knowledge about the topographic structure of the solution of the fuzzy relation equation [7]. After the learning process, the network keeps its transparent structure and the new knowledge represented in it can be extracted in the form of fuzzy IF-THEN rules.

5 Simulation Results

In this section we present some experimental results demonstrating the applicability of the proposed algorithm in video sequences. The examples are illustrated in soccer video sequences, where the moving objects are the players and the ball. That kind of sequences has some special characteristics. These special characteristics, apart from the size and the motion of the moving objects, also concern the different camera views of the game, some fast motion cameras and their frequent zooming. These characteristics are used as constraints for the extraction of the moving objects. An appropriate parameter tuning is performed to detect and localize the objects even if their size is very small or the background is not homogenous, or else different cameras capture an event. The example consists of two soccer video sequences. In each video sequence an event is taking place. The first video is showing the event 'ball draws away from player', while the second is showing the event 'player A passes the ball to player B'. In each case the moving objects in attention, are located with polygons. In order to detect an event, we must first recognize the moving objects and extract them as fuzzy predicates. In the first example, the moving objects are the player and the ball. These predicates are not capable to compose a rule, which characterize the specific event. An event requires spatiotemporal relations between the object predicates. In the event 'ball drawing away from player', the relation is the distance between the two objects, and it is calculated from the position of their metacenter. Furthermore, the timing of the detected predicates is a vital factor for the detection of an event. For example, the predicates 'player', 'ball' and the 'distance between them' cannot be used to detect the event 'ball drawing away from the player'. The distance of the ball from the player must be increasing. The subsymbolic module gives degrees of confidence for each fuzzy predicate every one-second. These degrees are stored into a buffer and fed into the neurofuzzy network. In Fig. 5 the distances in pixels are: (a) 12, (b) 23, (c) 40, (d) 60, (e) 90, (f) 140. These numbers are normalized and transformed in degrees of confidence for the predicate 'distance between the ball and the player.

In Fig. 6, a more complicated event is shown. The ball is drawing away from player A, moving in a certain direction and when a new player appears (player B), it is concluded that the ball is approaching him. The incorporated fuzzy predicates in this example are: 'player A', 'player B', 'ball', 'distance of the ball from player A', 'distance of the ball from player B' and 'playerA and playerB same team'. The localization of the concerned objects is shown in boxes and for the description of this event some more information, apart from the objects relative positions, is needed. Firstly, the objects included in the event are recognized and the distances are calculated in pixels, showing that the ball is going from player A to player B: (a) player A − ball = 21, (b) player A − ball = 61, ball − player B = 88, (c) player A − ball = 64, ball − player B = 85, (d) player A − ball = 72, ball − player B = 77, (e) player A − ball = 81, ball − player B = 67, (f) player A − ball = 87, ball − player B = 61. In Fig 6(a) the ball is set given the description 'close to player A', in Figs. 6(b-d) the ball is described as 'drawing away from player A', in Figs. 6(e-f) the ball is described as 'moving towards player B' and in Fig. 6(f) the ball is 'close to player B'. Also, if we extract some extra features for the moving objects, like the mean intensity of the regions inside the bounding polygons, we can conclude that players A and B belong to the same team and thus the event 'player A passes to player B' is detected.

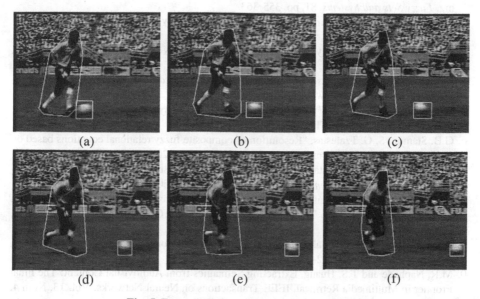

Fig. 5. Event 'ball draws away from player A'.

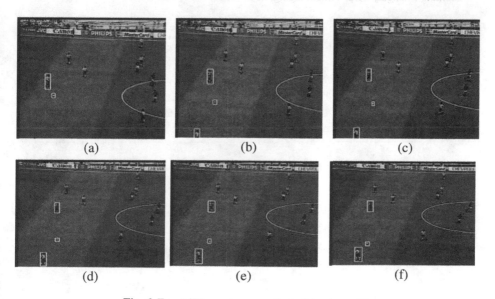

Fig. 6. Event 'Player A passes the ball to player B'.

References

1. Hirota, K. and W. Pedrycz (1996), Solving fuzzy relational equations through logical filtering, *Fuzzy Sets and Systems* 81, pp. 355-363.
2. Jenei, S., (1998) "On Archimedean triangular norms." Fuzzy Sets and Systems, 99, pp. 179-186.
3. G. Klir and Bo Yuan, Fuzzy Sets and Fuzzy Logic: Theory and Applications, New Jersey, Prentice Hall, 1995.
4. Kosko, B., *Neural networks and fuzzy systems: a dynamical approach to machine intelligence*, Prentice Hall, Englewood Cliffs (1992).
5. C.-T. Lin, C.S. Lee, *Neural fuzzy Systems: A neuro-fuzzy synergism to intelligent systems*, Prentice-Hall, Englewood Cliffs, NJ, 1995.
6. G.B. Stamou, S. G. Tzafestas, "Resolution of composite fuzzy relational equations based on Archimedean triangular norms", Fuzzy Sets and Systems, 120, pp. 395-407, 2001.
7. G.B. Stamou, S. G. Tzafestas, "Neural fuzzy relational systems with a new learning algorithm", *Mathematics and computers in simulation,* pp. 301-304, 2000.
8. G. B. Stamou and S. G. Tzafestas, Fuzzy Relation Equations and Fuzzy Inference Systems: an Inside Approach, IEEE Trans. on Systems, Man and Cybernetics, Vol. 99, Num. 6, (1999), 694-702.
9. R.L. Graham. An efficient algorithm for determining the convex hull of a finite planar set. Inform. Process. Lett., 1:132-133, 1972.
10. M.R. Naphade and T.S. Huang, Extracting Semantics from Audiovisual Content: The Final Frontier in Multimedia Retrieval, IEEE Transactions on Neural Networks, Vol. 13, Num 4, July 2002.
11. A. Makarov, J.M. Vesin and F. Reymond, "Intrusion Detection Robust to Slow and Abrupt Lighting Changes," Real-Time Imaging, SPIE-2661, 1996, 44-54.

Agents and Affect:
Why Embodied Agents Need Affective Systems

Ruth S. Aylett

CVE, University of Salford
Salford, M5 4WT, UK
r.s.aylett@salford.ac.uk

Abstract. This paper discusses why intelligent embodied agents – concentrating on the case of graphically-embodied agents – require affective systems. It discusses the risks involved in attempting to produce naturalistic expressive behaviour, and examines the specific case of facial expression generation. It considers the approach taken by the EU Framework 5 project VICTEC to facial expressions and then discusses some of the issues in affective architectures needed to drive facial expressiveness in an autonomous Intelligent Virtual Agent (IVA).

1 Introduction

Unlike software agents in general, intelligent virtual agents (IVAs) – or synthetic characters, or virtual humans - have an important characteristic in common with robots. This is embodiment, albeit in virtual form. Embodiment has a number of consequences. It means that an IVA typically interacts with its virtual world through sensors, of greater or less elaboration, and requires a perceptual component in its architecture to handle this. It raises sometimes complex control issues as limbs, trunks and heads have to move in a competent and believable fashion. However the consequence that we will concentrate on in this paper is the use of embodiment as a communication mechanism for the internal state of the agent, complementing its explicit communication mechanisms such as natural language.

Why might one want to communicate an IVA's internal state to a human user? One important reason is to support the continuing human process of inferring the intentions of an IVA – it motives and goals. This can help to produce a feeling of coherent action which is required for the user to feel that in some sense they 'understand' what an IVA is doing. We argue that a vital component of this process for the user is recognising the emotional state of the IVA and relating it to their own affective state. If in turn the IVA is able to recognise the affective state of the user and perform an equivalent integrative process, then one could speak of an 'affective loop' [12] between user and IVA.

Affective computing is a new but growing area within computer science, often dated to the seminal work of Picard in 1997 [20]. It encompasses a large number of research topics: some human-centred - sensing human affect and affective responses, modelling the user state; and some technological - from affective wearable computers to synthesising emotional systems on machines. Affect impinges directly upon work with IVAs at the latter end of this list: in the expression of affective state, and in the synthesis of the states that are to be expressed.

G.A. Vouros and T. Panayiotopoulos (Eds.): SETN 2004, LNAI 3025, pp. 496–504, 2004.

Where software agents in general can often be thought of as communicating mostly with each other, embodied agents are more and more expected to function in the human social context. Emotional expressiveness in such a context is not an optional add-on but a fundamental requirement for competence and acceptability [21]. Consider for example the acceptability of a virtual newsreader who announces the collapse of the World Trade Centre in the same equable manner as the winner of a multi-million pound lottery.

Moreover once an agent is embodied, the issue of trust is no longer merely a rational calculation, but is based on the perceived personality of the agent, in turn intimately connected to its emotional expressiveness. Thus an IVA that offers the 'human touch' can only do so if its expressive behaviour is consistent and appropriate. For example, selling property, as does REA [4], cannot be carried out in the same way as selling newspapers. The difference is not merely about the length of the dialogue between user and IVA but about the affective engagement of the user in the process, in turn partly dependent on the feeling that the IVA 'cares' about the seriousness of the transaction. Other potential IVA applications have even greater requirements for expressive accuracy – consider for example the level of social immersion required of a user in an interactive narrative. Here, any feeling that the IVAs are 'wooden' or 'robotic', and not emotionally engaged with other IVAs and with their own choices, may completely undermine the user's own engagement in the story-telling process.

2 Expressive Behaviour

The main channels or modes available to an IVA for affective display are the obvious visual ones of facial expression, posture, and gesture, plus in a few cases, voice. In this section we will discuss facial expression as a way of illustrating the main issues as this is the mode that has been researched most up to now. Less work has been carried out on posture (Badler's EMOTE system [5] is a seminal work here) and there is no agreed method for describing or classifying gesture as yet. Work in expressive voice is at a still earlier stage.

First it is worth highlighting an important generic issue for all modes – how far naturalism is an appropriate or realistic aim. In the graphics world, a driving force has been the attempt to achieve photo-realism, firstly in graphical worlds, and more recently in graphical characters. The 2001 animated film "Final Fantasy- The Spirits Within" is one example of such a search for photo-realism. On the other hand, many researchers in IVAs are actually striving for believability [2], where an IVA is perceived by the user as a compelling and engaging character.

The history of animation demonstrates that believability does not require naturalism – Mickey Mouse, probably the most successful animated character ever, looks nothing like a real mouse. A comparison between the films "Toy Story" and "Final Fantasy" demonstrates that in some cases a non-naturalistic character can be more believable than a naturalistic one – certainly Buzz Lightyear in the former has made a far greater impact than any of the characters in the latter.

An implicit assumption behind the striving for photo-realism is the reverse argument that a more naturalistic character must also be a more believable one. However seminal work by Mori [17] in relation to robots, discussed in [6] in the context of the 'life-like agents hypothesis', demonstrates that this is not always true. Mori predicted that the more life-like a robot became, that is, the more naturalistically human, the more *familiar* it would also become. However, he argues that just short of 100% naturalism, there is actually a sharp drop in familiarity – or we might now say believability; a drop so deep that it forms what he calls 'the uncanny valley'. An explanation of this effect suggests that a nearly-naturalistic character is capable of invoking standard human-to-human responses up to the point where these heightened expectations are jolted by some minor inconsistency. This jolt is experienced as a highly negative reaction to the IVA.

Mori actually broke down his overall curve into two separate ones for movement and appearance, and suggested that in fact the appearance curve was the dominant one of the pair. Since real-time interactive behaviour is a good deal more challenging than either static photo-realism or pre-rendered animation, the uncanny value is a persistent risk in the drive to naturalistic IVAs.

2.1 Facial Expression

The risks of near-naturalism are perhaps not so widely perceived among those researching facial expressiveness for IVAs. Certainly much of this work draws directly upon human psychology and the categorisation of human facial expressions.

The Facial Action Coding System (FACS) is a method of describing facial movement based on an anatomical analysis of facial action. This was systemised by Ekman and Friesen, [9], but in fact goes all the way back to a French anatomist of the 19thC – Duchenne de Boulogne; the author of "Mecanisme de la physionomie humaine". Duchenne had a patient with facial paralysis and was able to produce particular expressions on this man's face by administering an electrical shock to different facial muscles. He then photographed the results to produce a catalogue of human expressions.

Fig. 1. GRETA [Pelachaud et al 01].

Affective facial expressions are defined in FACS not directly by muscle values but by 46 Action Units (AUs), relating to whole groups of muscles. Duchenne identified a particular type of smile ascribed to an unqualified feeling of happiness – still called the *Duchenne smile* to differentiate it from all the other types of smiles that humans display [13]. A Duchenne smile (Figure 1) is produced by two AUs or muscle groups. One group around the mouth, called the zygomatic pulls up the lip corners; the other, around the eyes, called the orbicularis, produces a lifting of the cheeks, narrowing of the eye opening and that gathering of the skin around the eye called 'crows feet wrinkles'. Later research has shown that while a human subject can consciously control the mouth AU, the orbicularis only responds to a genuine emotion of happiness.

FACS has been used for some time to visually code for affective expressions in human subjects from video. It can be used to define the six 'primitive emotions' identified by Ekman [10] – anger, fear, disgust, joy, sadness and surprise – as recognised across all human cultures. It has also heavily influenced the design of the MPEG4 facial animation system with its Facial Definition Parameters (FDPs) and Facial Animation Parameters (FAPs). This in turn has provided a mechanism for researchers to produce facial animation in IVAs.

A good example of the use of MPEG4 as a basis for an expressive facial display in an IVA can be seen in GRETA (Figure 2) [19]. This uses expressive folds and wrinkles in the model to achieve an equivalent effects to FACS using MPEG4 FAPs and XML language annotation to invoke the desired effect for a particular piece of speech output.

It can be considered perhaps the best such 'talking head' in the current state of the art, yet even the small – scale illustration of Figure 2 shows that it some way from photo-realism. It tackles a problem of naturalistic facial expression not so far mentioned – the dynamism of affective facial expression. While primitive emotions may be recognisable across cultures from photographs, no real-world face holds such am emotion for more than a fleeting second before moving on to the next. GRETA combines affective expressions with many other factors such as glance and head movement, yet the overall effect is still some way from that of a real human face. Producing a naturalistic dynamic in real;-time interaction is an extremely challenging problem.

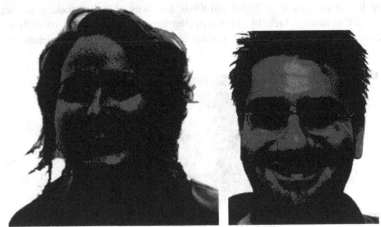

Fig. 2. Examples of the Duchenne smile.

2.2 Avoiding Naturalism

The IVAs being developed in the EU FP5 project VICTEC – Virtual ICT with Empathic Characters [23] – represent a very different position on facial expressiveness. In this project, IVAs act out short improvisational episodes on the theme of bullying, with a child user interacting with the victimised character between episodes to act as an 'invisible friend' and offer advice, influencing its behaviour in the next episode. Here, the expressiveness of the characters is required in order to engage the user in dramatic interaction of the episodes and to develop a feeling of empathy and thus of commitment towards the victim.

The approach just discussed in which FAPs are used to animate the structure of an IVA's face is clearly expensive in terms of rendering since it requires enough polygons in the facial model to support the number of parameters in use. Where an IVA is essentially a 'talking head' as in the case of GRETA, this level of detail is feasible, but once several characters must interact in a virtual world that is itself contributing substantially to the polygon count, this becomes very much less feasible. In addition, the user's viewpoint is very much further from the faces of the characters, making it harder to recognise the expressions being displayed.

The VICTEC characters are deliberately cartoon-like in design, as can be seen from the top-left component of Figure 3. In tune with this design, facial expressions have been designed as textures rather than polygonal animations, with a small set of primitives, some of which are shown in Figure 3. This is not only economical, but the expressions are dramatically obvious to users, and preliminary evaluation [24] has shown that believability is high even though naturalism is clearly not present.

Fig. 3. VICTEC facial expressions and cartoon-like character design.

3   Do the Right Thing?

Superficially, expressive behaviour may seem to belong entirely to the domain of animation: after all, to move the features of a face, make a gesture, adopt a particular posture is, for graphical characters, a graphical problem. While this is true for pre-rendered animated characters in film, once a character has to interact in real-time the problem is no longer merely one of graphically displaying an affective state, but of generating the affective state in the first place. So the XML annotation used by GRETA above to invoke facial expressions has to be generated 'on the fly' if it is to interact with a user. In other words, expressive behaviour is an instance of the generic problem of behaviour for an autonomous agent: how to select the appropriate behaviour, or in the now classic phrase 'do the right thing' [15].

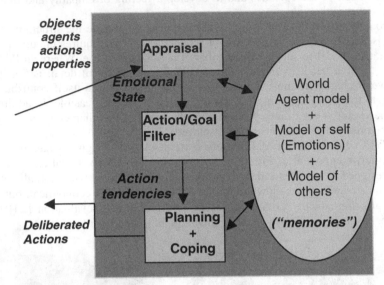

Fig. 4. The VICTEC 'Agent Mind'.

Affect, however, has a special status as a behaviour – it is not only an output from a behaviour selection system, but is itself an input into that selection mechanism. As argued by Damasio [7], affect should not be seen as the antithesis of rational decision-making but as a vital part of ensuring that decisions are timely and relevant to the situation of an agent. From this viewpoint, the expressive behaviour discussed above acts as a window for the user into the decision-making process of the IVA, giving it a leading role in supporting the decoding of motive and intention referred to above.

Where affective expressiveness is being generated by an internal architecture in which behaviour is being autonomously selected, two overall approaches can be discerned. One might be termed the 'low-level' account of affect and frequently implements models of IVA physiology, for example the endocrine system [3,22]. Such architectures are very successful in handling changes in affective state since they are normally based on continuously-valued variables and reject affective labels such as the six primitive emotions already referred to in favour of emergent states resulting from the interaction of much lower-level processes.

However, difficulties emerge in applying such models successfully once IVAs must act at the higher cognitive level of responding to each other's goals and intentions. Thus in the VICTEC domain, a bullying action may cause physical pain if one character punches another, but more significant is the social humiliation of the exercise of power by the bully over the victim. Here, higher-level models taken from psychology have some advantages, since they are based on the concept of appraisal in which a person, event or situation is evaluated in relation to an IVA's own goals. Appraisal can be thought of as acting as a high-level filter on perceptual input to an agent (high-level because it uses far-from basic categories such as events, situations and persons) via an emotional state which constrains the possible behaviours to be selected for immediate execution. Figure 4 gives an example of the functional architecture that might result, as used in the VICTEC project.

The taxonomy of Ortony, Clore and Collins [18] – often abbreviated to OCC - has been used in a number of IVA systems since it supplies straightforward rules for the appraisal process. OCC divides the possible reactions of an agent into those in Table 1.

Table 1. OCC Appraisal categories.

Reaction Type	Definition
Attraction reactions	Which entities the agent likes or hates
Event reactions	How important are particular events to the agent?
Prospect-based reactions	How important are the agent's goals?
Attribution reactions	What are the agent' norms or standards of behaviour?

The OCC model was not in fact originally intended for the generation of affective state, but as a means of recognising it in other agents, and it has a number of weaknesses as an affective mechanism. One is that it has nothing concrete to say on how affective state produces behaviour selection. Here other work, for example that of Lazarus [14], is more useful since it introduces the concept of *coping behaviour* – behaviour that tries to equalise an imbalance between the external situation of an agent and its internal affective state. This approach has been used very successfully in the Mission Rehearsal Exercise system of USC [11] as well as in Carmen' Bright IDEAS [16].

An alternative is to define a behaviour repertoire indexed by the OCC taxonomic emotions, and how this might work for the type of emotions require3d for IVAs in the bullying scenarios of the VICTEC project is shown in Table 2.

Table 2. Associating actions with OCC emotions in the bullying case.

OCC emotion	Appropriate actions/behaviours
Joy	Smile, dance, laugh, wave
Happy-for	Felicitate, encourage
Sorry-for	Apologise, encourage, protect
Anger	Ignore, hit, avoid, aggress, humiliate
Distress	Cry, sit on the floor, beg

4   Conclusions

In this paper we have argued that affective systems are not optional extras for IVAs but a requirement from at least two angles. The first is in the generation of the type of expressive behaviour that allows a user to understand an IVA in terms of its motivations and goals. The second is precisely in generating these motivations and goals as an input into the behaviour selection process of the IVA. In both cases, relevant work from psychology can be drawn upon, though in both cases this work undergoes modification for the purpose of IVA development.

One should note however that psychological theory is necessarily naturalistic, that is, it seeks to model and explain the natural behaviour of humans. In some sense then, the use of such theories - as against work in animation or indeed in drama, - is an implicit choice by IVA researchers in the direction of naturalism. Yet Mori's work shows that naturalism and believability are far from the same thing. It may in fact be that the aesthetic choices of the artist are at least as important as the scientific framework of the psychologist in IVAs, and that in expressive affective behaviour, narrative and drama require something that is 'larger than life' rather than the everyday norms of behaviour.

Acknowledgement

The presentation of this work has been funded by the University of Piraeus Research Centre.

References

1. Badler, N. I; Reich, B. D. and Webber, B. L. (1997) Towards Personalities for Animated Agents with Reactive and Planning Behaviors, in Creating Personalities for Synthetic Actors, eds. Trappl, R. and Petta, P. Springer-Verlag pp43—57 1997.
2. Bates, J. (1994), The Role of Emotion in Believable Agents Communications of the ACM v37, n7 pp122—125 1994.
3. Canamero, D. (1998) Modeling Motivations and Emotions as a Basis for Intelligent Behaviour, Proceedings of the First International Conference on Autonomous Agents eds. Johnson, W. L. and Hayes-Roth, B. ACM Press pp148—155, 1998.
4. Cassell, J., Bickmore, T., Billinghurst, M., Campbell, L., Chang, K., Vilhjálmsson, H. and Yan, H. (1999). "Embodiment in Conversational Interfaces: Rea." Proceedings of the CHI'99 Conference, pp. 520-527. Pittsburgh, PA.
5. Chi, D; M. Costa, L. Zhao, and N. Badler (2000) The EMOTE model for Effort and Shape, ACM SIGGRAPH '00, New Orleans, LA, July, 2000, pp. 173-182 2000.
6. Dautenhahn, K. (2002) The Design Space of Life-Like Robots. Proc. 5th German Workshop on Artificial Life, Lübeck 18th - 20th March, 2002, IOS Press, Eds D. Polani, J. Kim, T. Martinetz, pp. 135-142.
7. Damasio, A. (1994)Descartes Error. Avon Books. 1994.
8. Duchenne (de Boulogne), G.-B. (1876). Mecanisme de la Physionomie Humaine. Atlas. Deuxieme edition. J.-B. Bailliere et Fils.
9. Ekman,P. and Friesen, W.V (1978) Manual for the Facial Action Coding System, Consulting Psychology Press, Palo Alto, Calif., 1978.
10. Ekman, P. (1982) Emotions on the Human Face. Cambrdige University Press.
11. Gratch, J; Rickel, J; & Marsalla, S. (2001) Tears and Fears, 5Th International Conference on Autonomous Agents, pp113-118 2001.
12. INVOLVE group http://www.dsv.su.se/research/k2lab/involve_group.htm.
13. LaFrance, M. (2002) What's in a Robot's Smile? The Many Meanings of Positive Facial Display In: eds D..Canamero, R.S.Aylett, proceedings, Aimating Expressive Characters for Social Interraction, AISB Symposia, April 2003 Imperial College London.
14. Lazarus, R.S& Folkman, S. (1984). Stress, appraisal and coping. New York: Springer.
15. Maes, P. (1990) How to do the right thing. Connection Science. 1990.

16. Marsella, S; Johnson, L.W. & LaBore, C. (2000) Interactive Pedagogical Drama Proceedings, Autonomous Agents 2000.
17. Mori, M. (1982), The Buddha in the Robot, Charles E. Tuttle Co.
18. Ortony, A; Clore, G. L. and Collins, A. (1988) The Cognitive Structure of Emotions, Cambridge University Press 1988.
19. Pelachaud,C; E. Magno-Caldognetto, C. Zmarich, P. Cosi, [01] Modelling an Italian Talking Head, Audio-Visual Speech Processing, Scheelsminde, Danemark, 7-9 septembre 2001.
20. Picard, R. (1997), Affective Computing, MIT Press 1997.
21. Sloman, A. and Croucher, M. (1981), Why Robots Will Have Emotions IJCAI81, PP197--202, Vancouver, B.C 1981.
22. Velasquez, J.D. (1997) Modeling Emotions and Other Motivations in Synthetic Agents. Proceedings, 14th National Conference on AI, AAAI Press, pp10-16.
23. VICTEC www.victec.org.
24. Woods, S; Hall, L; Sobral, D, Dautenhahn, K. & Wolke, D. (2003) Animated characters in bullying intervention. In: T.Rist, R.S.Aylett, D.Ballin (eds) Proceedings, IVA2003 Springer LNAI 2003.

Synthetic Characters with Emotional States

Nikos Avradinis, Themis Panayiotopoulos, and Spyros Vosinakis

Knowledge Engineering Lab, University of Piraeus, Department of Informatics
80, Karaoli & Dimitriou Street, 185 34, Piraeus, Greece
{avrad,themisp,spyrosv}@unipi.gr

Abstract. A new trend that has emerged in the field of applied artificial intelligence in the past few years is the incorporation of emotion emulation mechanisms in situated agent systems. Several researchers in the field of psychology and neural science agree that emotion is an essential aspect of human intelligence, diverging from the traditional treatment of emotion as something that inhibits rational thinking. This argument has also influenced the area of artificial intelligence and especially the young, yet vibrant field of Intelligent Virtual Agents, where it has become accepted that emotion is a key issue to achieve believable agent behaviour. The increased interest for emotions has resulted in several computational emotional models having been presented, with diverse approaches, generically classified into cognitive and non-cognitive, inspired by areas such as neural science. Hybrid approaches have also appeared, combining both cognitive and non-cognitive elements in an attempt to accurately describe the inner workings of emotional mechanisms. Such a hybrid model is the one we adopt in this paper, aiming to apply it to SimHuman, an intelligent virtual agent platform, in order to introduce emotion awareness and affective behaviour to the agent architecture.

Introduction

Emotion has been traditionally treated as a factor that inhibits rational thinking. Considered as a disorganized human response, emotion was labelled inappropriate for decision-making, and although it might be suitable for art or entertainment, it had better be kept out of scientific work.

This long-standing view on emotions has lately been strongly questioned. Researchers, mainly from the area of psychology and neural science, agree that emotion is an essential aspect of human intelligence. Particularly influential towards establishing this notion were two popular works by Le Doux and Damasio in the mid-1990's [1,2].

Long before Damasio's and Le Doux's works, various researchers had argued about the importance of emotions [3, 4, 5]. However, conclusions drawn from research in neurology and psychology started having a stronger influence in the early nineties, when several works on intelligent agents adopting ideas from the field of psychology were presented [6, 7, 8, 9]. The AI research community started showing an increased interest for the incorporation of emotion-handling mechanisms into embodied intelligent agent systems, which had as a result the evolution of emotional agents into a new, highly active research field. The importance of emotions became

G.A. Vouros and T. Panayiotopoulos (Eds.): SETN 2004, LNAI 3025, pp. 505–514, 2004.

even more apparent with the appearance of virtual agent systems, as they provided a basic feature classic agent systems lacked-embodiment. By assuming the existence of a virtual body, agent systems moved from merely textual forms of communication to highly expressive non-verbal communication means, such as body posture or eye gaze [10]. These new ways of communication were particularly suitable to express emotions, which provided a strong motivation to continue and expand research work in this field.

Defining Emotions

While there is a lot of talk going on about emotions, a universal and authoritative definition is difficult to be given. Many attempts to define emotion have been made, with more than ninety of them having been reviewed in [11]. In the same paper, Kleinginna and Kleinginna propose what is considered one of the most comprehensive definitions of emotions:

"Emotion is a complex set of interactions among subjective and objective factors, mediated by neural/hormonal systems, which can:

(a) give rise to affective experiences such as feelings of arousal, pleasure/displeasure;
(b) generate cognitive processes such as emotionally relevant perceptual effects, appraisals, labeling processes;
(c) activate widespread physiological adjustments to the arousing conditions; and
(d) lead to behavior that is often, but not always, expressive, goal directed, and adaptive".

The above approach defines emotions as relevant with cognitive as well as subcognitive processes, placing subcognitive systems at an entry level, driving the higher level subsystems. Although including goal-oriented behaviour, the definition differentiates from other approaches such as Oatley's one [12], where goal management is considered an essential attribute of emotions.

A lot of the confusion about emotions is attributed to the fact that, being a common word in every day language, the term is used to describe various closely related, yet not identical concepts, such as moods, drives or emotional states. As a general rule, emotions are responses to environmental input that produce an intense short-term affective state-an emotional state [8]. So, if one experiences fear because of a threatening event, he is afraid. A mood, on the other hand, is a longer-term affective state, that cannot be clearly attributed to a specific cause-for example, depression, in its common rather than its clinical definition can be considered a mood. Drives are mainly physical and although not emotions themselves, they can activate or influence affective processes-for example, hunger can make somebody irritated.

Do Agent Systems Really Need Emotions?

One could understandably pose the question "Why should I bother to put emotions in an agent system? After all, I want my computer to be able to assist my work in an efficient way-I don't need an agent greeting me with a smile every time I switch it on or start nagging whenever I make a mistake".

This can be easily answered when one considers applications involving some sort of social interaction among agent and environment, agent and human user or agents among themselves. When social issues emerge, purely rational agents prove insufficient, as the focus is not on providing the best solution to a well-defined problem, but rather producing an output that is suitable and in context. Applications like interactive storytelling [13], education, training in social and everyday skills [14] are examples where awareness on emotions is essential.

The need for mechanisms that can model and handle emotions is even more apparent in applications that include naturalistic animated visual representations of the agent, where the issue of believability comes to surface. Even the simplest forms of such applications, like two-dimensional talking heads, require attention so that the agent's representation does not seem robotic and lifeless. Animation sequences should be coherent with the action the agent is performing or the message it is trying to communicate. A virtual newscaster, for example, would seem absolutely fake if it was presenting breaking news about a tragic accident with a bright, smiling face. Being able to assume a suitable facial expression requires emotion-understanding skills from the part of the agent system, so that it can recognize the emotional impact of the news it is attempting to present.

The importance of emotions is even more apparent in Virtual Reality applications where full-scale agent embodiment raises believability standards even higher. Providing multi-modal means of communication, 3D models of agents situated in virtual environments are expected by the user not only to look realistic, but, more important, demonstrate believable reactions and behaviour, consistent with the states they are in, their own internal attributes as well as the stimuli they receive.

Physical Aspects of Emotion in Synthetic Agents

Having established the value of incorporating emotions into software agent applications, one has to consider what characteristics an agent should have in order to be considered "emotionally aware". A first look into the issue reveals two aspects of it: Emotion Recognition and Emotion Expression.

Emotion recognition implies the ability to guess the emotional state of the agent itself, as well as other agents situated in the environment either human or synthetic. Recognition can be performed by observing a wide range of signals as well as reasoning about situations that generate emotions. A list of such signals is presented below, based on a list of *sentic modulations* presented by Picard in [8], The list refers to humans and is classified into two categories according to how easily these signs can be perceived by an external observer.

Physical Signs of Emotions

Easy to perceive	Difficult to perceive
Facial expression	Respiration rate
Voice intonation	Heart/pulse rate
Gestures	Temperature
Movement	Perspiration
Posture	Muscle
Eye gaze	Blood Pressure
	Body Odour

In order to recognise emotional states, an agent should be able to perceive the above signs in addition to verbal emotional expressions and reason about them in context with the environment. However, just being able to recognise emotions is not enough for an emotional agent. It should also be able to express emotions in a way perceptible by other agents, which means that at a physical level it should be able to produce signs such as the above.

Expressing Emotions in Virtual Agents

Not all of the above features are easy or even feasible to be modelled and communicated with existing technology. However, most current virtual agent systems support all or some of the following:

- Facial expressions
- Movement
- Gestures
- Head orientation & Eye gaze
- Posture
- Vocal intonation
- Linguistic expression
- Odour emission

It is easily understood that emotion expression is finally a compound product, emerging as a resultant of the synthesis of more than one of the above expressive means. Expressing an emotion can either be a deliberate and conscious act, like a willingly generated smile, or a spontaneous one, as a result of a certain emotional state, like a shaking hand because of nervousness.

Emotion Generation in Synthetic Agents

Assuming a synthetic agent system incorporates all necessary means of emotion recognition and expression, there is still something missing so that it can be characterized as a full scale emotional agent. This is a mechanism to handle and generate emotions in a believable way, consistent with the input received from the environment. This mechanism should interact with the decision-making and motor components of the agent, so that emotional effects on the agent's actions can be taken into account and properly manipulated. In [8] the basic characteristics of an emotional computer-based system is presented, summarized in the five generic principles shown below:

1. The system should demonstrate behaviour that appears to an external observer as a result of emotional processes.
2. The system should have spontaneous, low level emotional responses to certain stimuli.
3. The system should be able to cognitively process and generate emotions by reasoning about situations, especially when these concern its goals, standards, preferences and expectations in some way.

4. The system should be able to have an emotional experience and be aware of its cognitive, physiological and subjective feeling aspects.
5. The system's emotions should interact with other processes that imitate human functions, including cognitive ones such as memory, perception, decision making, learning, but also physical ones, such as sentic modulations.

Most of the emotional agent implementations presented up to date incorporate some sort of mechanism that partially supports the above principles. In an attempt to produce more realistic emotional responses, the AI community has turned towards the field of psychology and neuroscience, adopting theories and models devised by researchers in these areas. Custom emotional models are not uncommon, but the majority of them are in some way or another based on or influenced by established emotion theories.

Models of Emotion

Theories about emotion generation are not a new development in science. Philosophical approaches concerning emotion first appeared in ancient times, with more comprehensive theories based on scientific observation rather than philosophy becoming available in the 19th century, such as Darwin's research on animal and human emotional expressions. However, the majority of the modern emotional theories are dated to the 1960's and forth.

The numerous different approaches presented so far can be roughly classified into two broad categories-cognitive and non-cognitive theories. The distinction between cognitive and sub-cognitive is directly analogous to the brain and body separation, and is part of a long-standing debate on whether emotions are cognitive, therefore a mental process or physical, therefore a bodily process.

The former approach is a high-level one, treating emotions as a result of symbolic, cognitive processing that involves reasoning. Examples of this category are Frijda's [15] and Lazarus'[16] emotional theories, while the most representative example and the most widely applied one in computer systems is the OCC model by Ortony, Clore and Collins [17].

Sub-cognitive approaches, mainly inspired by the field of neural science, treat emotion as a result of physiological processes that involve issues such as electrical signal transmission and changes in body chemistry. Examples of this category are Damasio [1] and Le Doux's [2] theories.

Designing an Emotional Agent System

A hybrid approach, combining ideas from both cognitive and non-cognitive theories of emotion activation was presented in an influential work by Carroll Izard in 1993 [18]. Attempting to bridge the gap between two strong standing, independent approaches, Izard proposes that emotions cannot be simply treated as something belonging to the realm of either the cognitive or the sub-cognitive, and that the final state and response of an emotional agent is the resultant of a multi-stage process involving cognitive and non-cognitive functions. Izard argues there are numerous sources of emotion activation, falling into four broad classes: Neural, sensorimotor, motivational and cognitive.

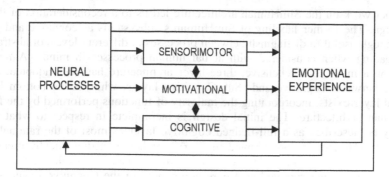

Fig. 1. Carroll Izard's four systems of emotion activation *(Izard, 1993)*.

The neural subsystem includes processes such as neural signal transmission, temperature effects, hormone-affected functions or sleep, diet, environmental conditions. The sensorimotor system includes processes such as facial expressions, body posture or activity that can either elicit emotion or affect ongoing emotional experiences. The motivational subsystem includes drives that can lead to emotion generation, such as thirst or hunger, or processes where emotions like sadness can activate others like anger. The cognitive subsystem includes higher-level processes, like appraisal of situations, belief revision or causal attributions.

Although Izard's model does not include implementation details, it illustrates the importance of multiple levels of emotion activation processes, as well as establishing a body-mind connection, by attributing emotion elicitation either to cognitive or non-cognitive processes.

Combining Izard's Theory with SimHuman

Adopting Izard's ideas, we are currently working on an emotional agent model we intend to apply over the existing SimHuman architecture. SimHuman, described in [19], is an implemented virtual agent architecture as well as a tool for the creation of virtual agent environments, supporting real-time animation features and incorporating. The SimHuman platform allows users to define and animate three-dimensional scenes with an arbitrary number of objects, virtual agents and user-controlled avatars and has embedded characteristics such as Inverse Kinematics, Physically Based Modeling, Collision Detection and Response, and Vision. SimHuman agents have perception and task control capabilities that can be programmed using SLaVE, a custom high level scripting language [20].

SimHuman's architecture allows the implementation of intelligent virtual agents that are easily adjusted and reprogrammed and can be further connected to more complex AI modules. The agents' functionality is divided into two independent layers with several modules that communicate with each other using certain protocols. The basic layer is the physical *layer*, which contains the modules that can directly control the agent's body and communicates with the environment through sensing and acting. Above the physical layer there is a cognitive one responsible for higher level functions, such as establishing beliefs through perceptive processes and controlling the agent's behavior using decision or task monitoring and control functions.

Further work on the SimHuman architecture led us to a reconsideration of the initial design. The former labeling of SimHuman's subsystems as cognitive and physical, although useful to distinguish between processes at different levels of abstraction, is misleading when considered with actual human processes in mind. A new approach on a more comprehensive, three-layer architecture has been adopted, distinguishing between Cognitive and Sub-Cognitive layers, while at the bottom level a Physical layer exists, incorporating the majority of functions performed by the former SimHuman architecture. The initial design is incomplete in respect to what would formally be described as a full-fledged cognitive layer as most of the rational processes in SimHuman are pre-scripted in SLaVE rather than dynamically created. A dynamic action selection and decision making mechanism like a full-scale intelligent planner has to be incorporated as a core component of the Cognitive Layer, so that high-level, deliberative decision-making functions of the agent can be simulated.

Further work was also considered necessary in respect to the reactive control capabilities of the agent, so that lower-level, spontaneous behaviour can be generated according to appropriate stimuli from the environment. The redesign of the initial agent architecture presented in the current work aims towards addressing problems such as the above and providing a unified framework that will incorporate all basic agent functions.

The lack of any emotion-awareness or emotion-handling capabilities, is addressed by the incorporation of an emotional subsystem, inspired by Izard's ideas. In a way similar to works like Cathexis [21], the model designed for the emotional system is a simplification of Izard's four-system model and consists of two generic components, a cognitive and a non-cognitive one. Emotional components in the newly adopted architecture cannot be distinguished as discrete modules, in accordance with the concept of emotion as a necessary ingredient for intelligence. Emotional processes intertwined with deliberative and reactive decision-making processes as parts of the cognitive and the non-cognitive layers, respectively. This approach raises the need for a unified mechanism that can handle emotions along with rational decision making functions. Parallel work is being conducted towards this direction on a continuous planning system taking emotion into account as a necessary element that can affect goal generation and action selection [22].

The new architecture takes into account various constituents of an emotional experience and how that can affect decision making, incorporating basic emotions [23], personality models, basic physical, emotional and mental attributes, as well as low and high level drives. The incorporation of these concepts is of major importance, as they are factors that can influence the generation or selection of goals and actions by the agent, but also affect emotion elicitation.

There is substantial interaction between different components of the architecture. As shown in Fig.2,3, process flow in the system does not follow a straightforward in/out execution cycle; several loops might occur in the process, instead. Actions generated in either the Cognitive or the Non-Cognitive Layers can either be extrovert, sending tasks for execution to the Physical Layer, or introvert, actions to be performed by other components. These can either be instructions for further reasoning, or plain information update and communication instructions.

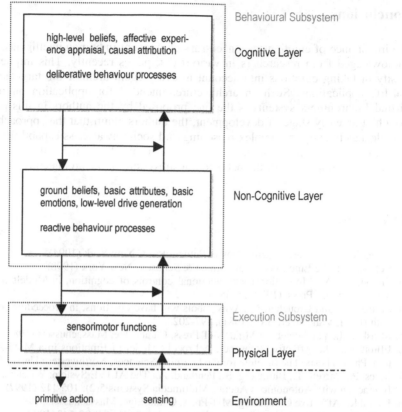

Fig. 2. Information flow among system layers.

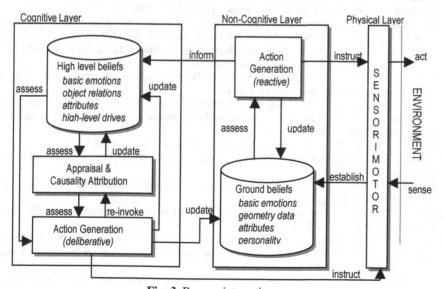

Fig. 3. Process interaction.

Conclusions

The importance of emotions as a necessary component in human intelligence has been acknowledged from researchers in various disciplines recently. This implies the necessity of taking emotions into account in every agent architecture targeted towards real-life applications. Such an architecture, intended for application on Intelligent Virtual Environment systems is the one proposed by the authors in this paper. Although at an early stage of development, the authors claim that the approach adopted can adequately support complex reasoning and social awareness capabilities, through the incorporation of an emotion-handling mechanism intertwined with the deliberative and reactive components of the behavioural subsystem of the architecture.

References

1. Damasio, A.: Descartes' Error, Gosset/Putnam Press, New York (1994).
2. LeDoux, J.: The Emotional Brain, Simon & Schuster, New York (1998).
3. Simon, H. A.: Motivational and emotional controls of cognition, in Models of Thought, Yale University Press, (1979) 29-38.
4. Sloman, A. and Croucher, M.: Why robots will have emotions, in Proceedings of the Seventh IJCAI, Vancouver, B.C. (1981), 197-202.
5. Minsky, M.: The Society of Mind, MIT Press, Cambridge, Massachussets (1985).
6. Elliott, C.: The Affective Reasoner: A Process Model of Emotions in a Multi-Agent System. Ph.D. Thesis, The Institute for the Learning Sciences, Northwestern University, 1992.
7. Maes, P., Darrell, T., Blumberg, B., Pentland, A.: The ALIVE System: Wireless, Full-Body Interaction with Autonomous Agents. Multimedia Systems 5(2): 105-112 (1997).
8. Picard R.: Affective Computing, MIT Press, Cambridge, Massachussets, 1997.
9. Reilly W. S., Bates, J.: Building Emotional Agents, CMU-CS-92-143, 1992.
10. Luck, M., Aylett, R.: Applying Artificial Intelligence to Virtual Reality: Intelligent Virtual Environments. Applied Artificial Intelligence 14(1): 3-32 (2000).
11. Kleinginna, P. & Kleinginna, A.: A categorized list of emotion definitions with suggestions for a consensual definition. Motivation and Emotion, 5, 345-379.
12. Oatley, K.: Emotions, in the MIT Encyclopedia of Cognitive Sciences, R.A. Wilson, F. Kiel (Eds), MIT Press, Cambridge, Massachussets, 1999.
13. Cavazza, M., Charles, F., Mead, S.J.: Character-Based Interactive Storytelling, IEEE Intelligent Systems, July/August 2002, pp 17-24.
14. Marsella S., Gratch, J.: Modeling the Interplay of Emotions and Plans in Multi-Agent Simulations, in Proceedings of the 23rd Annual Conference of the Cognitive Science Society, Edinburgh, Scotland, 2001.
15. Frijda, N.: The Emotions, Cambridge University Press, 1986.
16. Lazarus, R.E.: Cognition and motivation in emotion, American Psychologist, 46(4):352-367, 1991.
17. Ortony, A., Clore, G., Collins, A.: The Cognitive Structure of Emotions, Cambridge University Press, Cambridge, 1988.
18. Izard, C.E.: Four Systems for Emotion Activation: Cognitive and Noncognitive Processes, Psychological Review, 100 (1), pp 68-90.
19. Vosinakis, S., Panayiotopoulos, T.: SimHuman : A Platform for real time Virtual Agents with Planning Capabilities, IVA 2001, 3rd International Workshop on Intelligent Virtual Agents, Madrid, Spain, September 10-11, 2001.
20. Vosinakis, S., Panayiotopoulos, T.: Programmable Agent Perception in Intelligent Virtual Environments. IVA 2003: 202-206.

21. Velasquez, J. D.: Modeling emotions and other motivations in synthetic agents. In AAAI 97, pages 10-15. ACM 1997.
22. Avradinis, N., Aylett R.: Agents with No Aims: Motivation-Driven Continuous Planning. In: IVA 2003: 269-273.
23. Ekman, P.: Basic emotions. In T. Dalgleish and T. Power (Eds.) The Handbook of Cognition and Emotion. Pp. 45-60. John Wiley & Sons Ltd, Sussex, U.K, (1999).

Control and Autonomy
for Intelligent Virtual Agent Behaviour

Daniel Thalmann

EPFL, VRlab
CH 1015 Lausanne, Switzerland
Daniel.Thalmann@epfl.ch
http://vrlab.epfl.ch

Abstract. This paper discusses some issues for animating Virtual Characters. It emphasizes the duality between control and autonomy. Specific problems and examples are addressed like generic motion engine, environment-based motion control, autonomous behaviors, and cooperation between the user and an autonomous agent.

1 Introduction

The main goal of computer animation is to synthesize the desired motion effect which is a mixing of natural phenomena, perception and imagination. The animator designs the object's dynamic behavior with his mental representation of causality. He/she imagines how it moves, gets out of shape or reacts when it is pushed, pressed, pulled, or twisted. So, the animation system has to provide the user with motion control tools able to translate his/her wishes from his/her own language. Traditionally, the virtual characters are controlled by three main approaches:

1. Scripting. Scripting allows very detailed level of control, but is very inflexible.
2. Reactive agents: they are not scripted, but react to the changing environment according to the sets of rules.
3. BDI logic: similar to reactive agents, most popular implementation is probably the game "The Sims".

2 Motion Control Methods

In any case, there is a need for a Motion Control Method behind. It specifies how a Virtual Human is animated and may be characterized according to the type of information it privileged in animating the character. For example, in a keyframe system for an articulated body, the privileged information to be manipulated is the angle. In a forward dynamics-based system, the privileged information is a set of forces and torques; of course, in solving the dynamic equations, joint angles are also obtained in this system, but we consider these as derived information. In fact, any Motion Control Method will eventually have to deal with geometric information (typically joint angles), but only geometric Motion Control Methods explicitly privilege this information at the level of animation control. Typically, motion is defined in terms of coordi-

G.A. Vouros and T. Panayiotopoulos (Eds.): SETN 2004, LNAI 3025, pp. 515–524, 2004.
© Springer-Verlag Berlin Heidelberg 2004

nates, angles and other shape characteristics. A physical Motion Control Method uses physical characteristics and laws as a basis for calculating motion. Privileged information for these Motion Control Methods include physical characteristics such as mass, moments of inertia, and stiffness. The physical laws involved are mainly those of mechanics, and more particularly dynamics.

But, how to do it? A database of motion capture sequences is not the solution, key frame is not the solution, inverse kinematics is not the solution. But, they are part of the solution. Once an acceptable motion segment has been created, either from keyframing, motion capture or physical simulations, reuse of it is important. By separating motion or skeleton generation into a time-consuming preprocess and a fast process based on efficient data representation, it fits well to real-time synthesis for applications such as game and virtual reality while taking advantage of a rich set of examples. Much of the recent research in computer animation has been directed towards editing and reuse of existing motion data. Stylistic variations are learned from a training set of very long unsegmented motion-capture sequences [1]. An interactive multi-resolution motion editing is proposed for fast and fine-scale control of the motion [2].

3 Generic Motion Engines

One promising way is the development of a methodology to generate generic real-time motion. This is the approach developed by Glardon et al. [3] for the simulation of human locomotion. Any motion engine needs input data on which it will create new motion by interpolation and extrapolation. The first step consists of getting through motion capture a database of walking and running motions at various speed and height jumps (without initial speed).

In this approach, the Principal Component Analysis (PCA) method is used to represent the motion capture data in a new, smaller space. As the first PC's (Principal Components) contain the most variance of the data, an original methodology is used to extract essential parameters of a motion. This method decomposes the PCA in a hierarchical structure of sub-PCA spaces. At each level of the hierarchy, an important parameter (personification, type of motion, speed) of a motion is extracted and a related function is elaborated, allowing not only motion interpolation but also extrapolation. Moreover, effort achieved concerning the possibility not only to qualify a parameter but also to quantify it improves this method in comparison to other similar works. Generic animation, applicable to any kind of human size, is another important aspect of such a research. The method cannot only normalize a generated motion, it may animate human with a large range of different size. In order to have a complete locomotion engine, transitions between different motions should be handled. The PCA structure offers the capability to perform transition from a specific movement to another one in a very smooth and efficient way. Indeed, as coefficient vectors represent a motion, interpolation between these vectors is sufficient to generate intermediate motion, without computing into the joint angle space. Glardon et al. applied these new concepts on a home-made motion database composed of walking and running motion on a treadmill, at different specific speeds. They developed engine proposes real-time variation of high-level parameters (style, speed, type of motion, human size), generating a smooth animation (Fig.1).

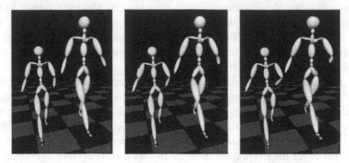

Fig. 1. Postures at identical moment in the walk cycle, with two different skeleton sizes.

4 Environment-Based Motion Control

The Virtual Human is moving in an environment and he is conscious of this environment. This implies that the motion of the actor is dependent on parts of the environment. The actor will avoid obstacles or collide with them, grasp objects etc. This dependence on the environment can be understood from a geometric, a physical or a behavioral point of view. We will illustrate the concept with two case studies: reaching objects and animation of musicians from the music data.

4.1 Reaching Objects

One typical challenge of environment-based motion control is the automatic synthesis of collision-free reaching motions for both arms, with automatic column control and leg flexion. Generated motions are collision-free, in equilibrium, and respect articulation range limits. In order to deal with the high (22) dimension of our configuration space, we bias the random distribution of configurations to favor postures most useful for reaching and grasping. In addition, extensions are presented in order to interactively generate object manipulation sequences: a probabilistic inverse kinematics solver for proposing goal postures matching pre-designed grasps; dynamic update of roadmaps when obstacles change position; online planning of object location transfer; and an automatic stepping control to enlarge the character's reachable space. This is, to our knowledge, the first time probabilistic planning techniques are used to automatically generate collision-free reaching motions involving the entire body of a human-like character at interactive frame rates [4]. Figure 2 shows an example.

4.2 Sound-Based Animation

Real-time systems must react fast enough to events, to keep a good immersion. This is particularly true when animation should "stick" to sound events, which is deeply affected by any delay in the processing. In the case of virtual orchestra, we need to synchronize the musician's animation with the corresponding sound. Due to real-time restrictions it's impossible to predict the transition of states, and thus we cannot prepare the right key-frame at a certain time. A careful management of the sound and animation databases is crucial to reduce latency [5].

Fig. 2. Reaching an object in an environment.

Such An experience has been proposed by for drums [6]. A prototype was also created for piano by Esmerado et al. [7]. The piano skill Execution model generally obeys the following procedural pattern:

- Transform Note Input into structured note data
- Generation of a music interpretation
- Hand/Finger attribution to the note
- Schedule time for note execution
- Feed time and note to the instrument model
- Feed finger and time to the Virtual Human animation unit
- Generate animation for Virtual Pianist
- Generate animation for Virtual Piano
- Check end of execution for each time-scheduled note set for both Virtual Pianist and Virtual Piano

Inverse kinematics techniques are used to generate the final gestures associated to the placement of the fingers on the desired (virtual) keys, these being in their pressed-down position. The inverse kinematics algorithm conversion is normally insured by the specification of a number of controlling points (end-effectors) situated at the fingertips and wrists of the virtual human pianist. The resulting gestures are combined with in-between gestures and interpolated so that a smooth gesture sequence and transitions results.

Schertenleib et al. [8] extended the work by adding more flexibility and independence on the musician attributes while relying on current hardware. The system relies on pre-ordering data using statistical information based on Markov chains. Some similar works have already been done in persistent worlds [9] with the difference that they need to quickly transfer small amounts of information through network from a complex database. In our case the data is locally stored but we must provide close to instantaneous access to the current state depending on external events. Instead of trying to follow the animation with the sound processing, we used the sound information to reflect and blend the right animation. A selected note within a music score will trigger the events allowing the manipulation of the different skeleton's bones of a specified musician [H-Anim]. Thus, as the system is managed through sound events (see figure 3), we can avoid delays in the sound processing; even though we will degrade a bit the animation's smoothness. However, this is less important, as human senses are more affected by sound distortion than by visual artifacts.

Fig. 3. Music-based pianist animation.

Fig. 4. Autonomous flutist and the system installation: large projection screen, 5.1 Dolby digital speakers.

5   Autonomous Behavior

The computer graphics approach makes use of different artificial intelligence techniques (reinforcement learning, genetic algorithms, and neural networks) to generate behavioral animation. However, to the best of our knowledge, no work has been targeted to generate spontaneous (without specific goal) gestures as reaction to internal and external stimuli. Most of the research is focused on goal-directed behavior: behavioral animation.

By behavioral animation we refer to the techniques applied to the synthesis of autonomous animation of virtual characters. Autonomy is one of the most priced goals in the field of character animation. We generally consider autonomy as the quality or state of being self-governing. Perception of the elements in the environment is essential, as it gives the agent the awareness of what is changing around it. It is indeed the most important element that one should simulate before going further. Most common perceptions include (but are not limited to) simulated visual and auditive feedback. Adaptation and intelligence then define how the agent is capable of reasoning about what it perceives, especially when unpredictable events happen. On the other hand, when predictable elements are showing up again, it is necessary to have a memory capability, so that similar behaviour can be selected again. Lastly, emotion instantaneously adds realism by defining affective relationships between agents. Figure 5. shows autonomous Virtual Humans.

Fig. 5. Autonomous Virtual characters.

The subtle and spontaneous gestures are part of low-level behaviors, and they are essential to communicate any message and convey emotions. These ideas are just beginning to be explored by the scientific community, some studies focus on non-human characters, like dogs or other virtual animals [10], while others put special attention on human-like facial gestures.

Continuous animation (low level behavior) as the result of proprioception (this includes motivations, internal "mental" or emotional states, etc.), and reactions to external stimuli.

The low-level behavioral animation is an open research avenue. Creating virtual characters able to select the action to perform in an automatic way is not new. State of the art autonomous characters and Virtual Humans are able to perform a variety of tasks, and have some level of autonomy in their decision making, but still they don't look like real people. One of the problems is that the virtual humans don't display the subtle gestures and mannerisms that characterize a real human being: facial expressions, body language, etc.

Several studies and implementations have been done with the objective of giving a virtual character the ability to perceive its virtual environment and react to it by means of executing adequate tasks [11, 12], creating the illusion that the synthetic character is alive: it moves by itself and achieves relatively complex tasks. The AVA explores an unknown environment constructed on mental models as well as a "cognitive map" based on this exploration. Navigation is carried out in two ways: globally (pre-learned model of the virtual environment, few changes and the search for performance with a path planning algorithm) and locally (direct acquisition of the virtual environment.) A 3D geometrical model in the form of a grid is implemented with the help of an octree combined with the approach proposed by Noser [13] and Kuffner [14]. Nevertheless, this approach requires a filtering of irrelevant information from the variable positions of the virtual sensors, Elfes [15]. A Virtual Human is situated in a Virtual Environment (VE) equipped with sensors for vision, audition and touch, informing it of the external VE and its internal state. A Virtual Human possesses effectors, which allow it to exert an influence on the VE and a control architecture, which coordinates its perceptions and actions. The behaviour of a Virtual Human can be qualified as being adaptive as long as the control architecture allows it to maintain its variables in their validity zone. Learning methodologies can modify the organization of the control architecture. We will then integrate them in the further pursuit of our research. Our *Artificial Life Environment* framework equips a Virtual Human with the main virtual sensors, based on an original approach inspired by neuroscience in the form of a small *nervous system* with a simplified control architecture to optimise the management of its virtual sensors as well as the virtual perception part. The processes of filtering, selection and simplification are carried out after obtaining the sensorial information; this approach allows us to obtain some persistence in the form of a "cognitive map" and also serves as a pre-learning framework to activate learning methods of low and high level concerning the behaviour of an Virtual Human.

The objective pursued is to allow the Virtual Human to explore virtual environments until then unknown and to construct *mental structures and models, cognitive maps or plans from this exploration.* Once its representation has been constructed, this knowledge can be passed on to other Virtual Humans. The Autononmous Virtual Human perceives objects and other Virtual Humans with the help of its virtual environment, which provides the information concerning the nature and position of the latter. The behavioural model to decide which actions the Virtual human should take such as walking, handling an object, etc then uses this information.

6   User – Autonomous Agent Collaboration in VR

Let us start with a scenario that we implemented for the need of a medical European project dedicated to the training of paramedical personnel to emergency rescue [16]. The aim of this scenario is to train the Basic Life Support medical procedure. The trainee is immersed in a virtual office and discovers a man lying on the ground. He has to give BLS to the victim by giving orders to a young Virtual Assistant (Fig.6). The VA possesses all the skills required (mouth-to-mouth, chest compression) but highly hesitates on the procedure order; this is the job of the trainee. The latter will interact with the VA to apply his theoretical knowledge of the BLS procedure. This scenario consists of a dozen steps. At each step, the trainee has to make a (fast) decision. It does not present many possibilities because the BLS guidelines give no alternative. The scenario we implemented does not explore all the incorrect possibilities, which would all lead to a negative learning ('learn by errors'), but gives an example where the Social Channel can be used to orient the user in an Interactive Narration Space ('learn by success').

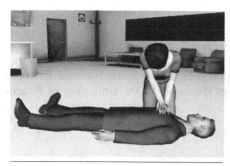 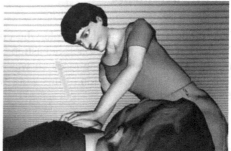

Fig.6. Use of a Virtual Assistant.

In many situations, autonomous agents should work as a team with the user to solve the problem at hand. In general, there was a plenty of work done on both multi-agent systems (mostly AI) and collaborative VR (mostly multi-user systems), but nobody tried to use collaborative agents for VR applications and have them collaborate with the human operator to solve a problem. This approach has a large potential for training applications (emergency response, medical training, air traffic control, even military) or for simulations (crowd control for example).

The three approaches mentioned in Section 1 (scripting, reactive agents, BDI) are difficult to use for collaborating agents, because there is no notion of the "global goal" or "global state" shared among the agents. There were attempts to generalize these techniques for collaboration, but it works only in carefully crafted environments (e.g. the collaborating agents have to know about each other in advance) and it is difficult to drive a purely reactive system to the desired goal.

Finally, it is usually not important who does the job, but that the job is done. For example, in emergency response simulation, we are usually not interested that a specific medical person arrives to rescue an injured person, but that some (closest, not busy, etc.) medical staff arrives and rescues the injured. In a similar case, the user does not care which virtual human shows him the place he is looking for, but that someone does it.

Traditional systems solve this by using broadcasting architectures which impose a lot of overhead and sometimes do not produce good results – e.g. every medic will rush to rescue the injured person upon receiving the event, not just one or two needed, or they have to coordinate among themselves who is going to do what imposing even more overhead. Delegated computing achieves this by using a facilitator – something like an oracle, which coordinates things "automagically" and keeps the information about the global state of the system. The coordination process is invisible to the agents and they do not have to care about it, this greatly simplifies the implementation. The collaboration will then be possible via either direct interaction with the virtual environment (e.g. by direct interaction with the virtual human or object on the screen) or by asking the facilitator for help with some problem. The facilitator then distributes the work among the agents. Each agent is capable of solving some small portion of the problem, but usually cannot solve the problem completely and has to collaborate with others and the user.

Acknowledgments

The author is grateful to the people who contributed to this research, especially Toni Conde, Jan Ciger, Tolga Abaci, Sebastien Schertenleib, Frederic Vexo, Bruno Herbelin, and Michal Ponder. The research was sponsored by the Swiss National Research Foundation. The presentation of this work was sponsored by the University of Piraeus Research Centre.

References

1 M. Brand and A. Hertzmann, "Style machines", Proc. SIGGRAPH 2000, 2000, pp. 183 – 192.
2 J. Lee and S. Y. Shin, "A hierarchical approach to interactive motion editing for human-like figures", Proc. SIGGRAPH 1999, 1999, pp. 39 –48.
3 P. Glardon, R.Boulic, D.Thalmann, PCA-based Walking Engine using Motion Capture Data (to be published).
4 M. Kallmann, A. Aubel, T. Abaci, and D. Thalmann, Planning Collision-Free Reaching Motions for Interactive Object Manipulation and Grasping, Proc. Eurographics 2003.
5 Y. Arafa, B. Kamyab, E. Mamdani, S. Kshirsagar, N. Magnenat-Thalmann, A.Guye-Vuilleme, D. Thalmann, Two Approaches to Scripting Character Animation, Proc. Workshop "Embodied Conversational Agents", Italy, 2002.
6 M. Kragtwijk, A. Nijholt & J. Zwiers. "Implementation of a 3D Virtual Drummer", Proceedings CAS2001, Eurographics Workshop on Animation and Simulation 2001, Manchester, UK, Springer-Verlag, 2001, pp.15-26.
7 J. Esmerado; F. Vexo, D. Thalmann, "Interaction in Virtual Worlds: Application to Music Performers", CGI, UK 2002.
8 S. Schertenleib, M. Gutierrez, F. Vexo, D.Thalmann, Conducting a Virtual Orchestra: Multimedia Interaction in a Music Performance Simulator (to be published).
9 K. Wilson; Game Object Structure, GDC 2003.
10 D. Isla, B. Blumberg. Object Persistence for Synthetic Creatures. In the Proceedings of the International Joint Conference on Autonomous Agents and Multiagent Systems (AAMAS), Bologna, Italy. July 2002.
11 B. Blumberg and T. Galyean. Multi-level Direction of Autonomous Creatures for Real-Time Virtual Environments. In Proceedings of SIGGRAPH 95.
12 X. Tu and D. Terzopoulos. "Artificial Fishes: Physics, Locomotion, Perception, Behavior", ACM Computer Graphics, Proceedings of SIGGRAPH'94, July 1994.

13 H. Noser, O. Renault, D. Thalmann, N. Magnenat Thalmann, "Navigation for Digital Actors based on Synthetic Vision, Memory and Learning", Computers and Graphics, Pergamon Press, Vol.19, No 1, 1995, pp. 7-19.

14 J.-J. Kuffner, J.-C. Latombe, "Fast Synthetic Vision, Memory, and Learning Models for Virtual Humans", Proc. Of Computer Animation, IEEE, pp. 118-127, May 1999.

15 A. Elfes, "Occupancy Grid: A Stochastic Spatial Representation for Active Robot Perception", 6th Conf. on Uncertainly in AI, 1990.

16 B. Herbelin, M. Ponder , D. Thalmann, Building Exposure: Synergy of Interaction and Narration through Social Channels (annexe), Second International Workshop on Virtual Rehabilitation (IWVR2003).

Reflex Movements for a Virtual Human:
A Biology Inspired Approach

Mario Gutierrez, Frederic Vexo, and Daniel Thalmann

Virtual Reality Laboratory (VRlab)
Swiss Federal Institute of Technology Lausanne (EPFL)
CH-1015 Lausanne Switzerland
{mario.gutierrez,frederic.vexo,daniel.thalmann}@epfl.ch

Abstract. This paper presents the results of a method to produce autonomous animation of virtual humans. In particular, the proposed methodology is focused on the autonomous synthesis of non-voluntary gestures such as reflexes and subtle movements which provide a noticeable impression of realism and naturalness. The final goal of this technique is to produce virtual humans with a more spontaneous, non preprogrammed behaviour. For the moment, the technique is applied to the synthesis of reflex movements of the arm, in reaction to thermic stimuli. Nevertheless, a general architecture is outlined.

1 Introduction

The animation of virtual humans and computer animation in general have always searched to produce realistic imagery and true naturalness in the motions.

One particularly difficult problem is to provide automatic animation of a virtual human displaying a behaviour that truly resembles a real human [1, 2]. Our goal is to animate virtual humans (body gestures) in an autonomous way, giving the illusion that the artificial human being is a living creature displaying spontaneous behaviour according to its internal information and external stimuli coming from its virtual environment.

The proposed method is a real-time, distributed control system inspired in the human nervous system, which will be able to produce natural movements in response to external and internal stimuli. The advantage of the real-time control techniques over the "Computer Graphics movie" approach is their promise of combined autonomy and realism as well as their focus on reusability. The autonomous control system we are presenting could be instantiated and used to animate several different characters in a variety of situations.

This paper is organized according to the following structure: in the next section we present an overview of the existing techniques used in the synthesis of human postures and gestures. The third part is the detailed description of the proposed approach and methodology; the fourth section presents the results that have been obtained. We conclude with a discussion on the results and the future developments of the methodology.

G.A. Vouros and T. Panayiotopoulos (Eds.): SETN 2004, LNAI 3025, pp. 525–534, 2004.

2   State of the Art

In this section we present an overview of the different scientific developments focused on the study and generation of human postures and gestures. We distinguish two main trends: the biology (biomechanics studies) and the non-biology based (more computer-graphics-oriented) approach.

2.1   The Biology Based Approach

Many biomechanical models have been developed to provide partial simulations of specific human movements: walking/running models, or simulations of dynamic postural control under unknown conditions [3, 4].

The biology based approach has been used in the research of biomechanical engineering, robotics and neurophysiology, to clarify the mechanisms of human walking [5], and modelling the muscular actuation systems of animals [6, 7] and human beings [8, 9]. The biologically inspired control architectures are one of the most recent trends in the field of robotics [10]. Models of the human nervous system, in conjunction with fuzzy logic, neural networks and evolutionary algorithms have been used to better understand and control the way humans and animals move and execute typical actions such as walking, running, reaching or grasping [11, 12, 4]. Some other studies focus on the analysis of the human motion to extract parametric models for posture recognition [13].

None of these developments has been specifically applied to create a general autonomous control system to drive the animation and behaviour of a virtual human in the framework of a virtual reality application. However, they can provide the basis for a general motion control model.

2.2   The Computer Graphics Approach

In contrast with the above mentioned studies, the following citations are more related to the development of virtual reality and computer graphics applications in general. The most "traditional" techniques used to synthesize human gestures include the use of kinematics, dynamics or a combination of them [14]. Inverse Kinematics has been used for animation of complex articulated figures such as the human body, balance control, motion and postures correction are some of their applications [15–17]. These techniques are focused on the correction of predefined postures or common actions such as walking to make them more natural; however, they require specific goals to be predefined and don't consider spontaneous movements. They can be used as tools for animators but don't provide a system for autonomous motion.

Another approach is the use of statistical analysis of observation data acquired by different means: motion capture systems, video or photographs. These methods use in different ways a database of pre-recorded movements to mix them, readapt them and reuse them in a variety of environments where the same kind of actions are required. Again, the main type of movements that are studied are walking sequences and standard combinations of movements: walk-sit, sit-walk, etc. [1, 18, 19]. These approaches are not very suitable to be used as part of a system for the automatic generation of gestures.

Synthesizing autonomous gestures is related to the area of behavioural animation. By behavioural animation we refer to the techniques applied to the synthesis of autonomous animation of virtual characters. Autonomy is one of the most priced goals in the field of character animation. Several studies and implementations have been done with the objective of giving a virtual character the ability to perceive its virtual environment and react to it by means of executing adequate tasks [20, 21], creating the illusion that the synthetic character is alive: it moves by itself and achieves relatively complex tasks.

The subtle and spontaneous gestures are part of low-level behaviors, and they are essential to communicate any message and convey emotions. These ideas are just beginning to be explored by the scientific community, some studies focus on non-human characters, like dogs or other virtual animals [22].

One particularly difficult issue is the problem of what to do with the characters when there is no pre-defined task assigned to them. Research has been done to produce the so-called "idle animation": generating behavior to make the character move when there's no specific action to do. Some work has focused on adding a pseudo-random "perturbation" to an idle posture [23], avoiding "frozen" characters. However, real people perform very different gestures when waiting for something or while attending or listening to someone. The gestures performed during "idle states" depend on a variety of factors: emotional state, cultural background, the current situation (waiting for something, listening, or thinking), unexpected events (a change in the environment), etc. and can be classified as low-level behavior.

Despite the advances in behavioural animation, autonomous virtual humans are not yet able to display the whole range of subtle gestures and mannerisms that characterize a real human being: facial expressions, body language, autonomous reactions, etc. Our work intends to advance the state of the art on the last category: providing virtual humans with the ability to react to unexpected events through reflex movements.

After analyzing some of the existing techniques applied to the control and synthesis of human gestures, we observe a promising way in the biologically inspired systems, especially when the goal of autonomy and naturalness in the motions is the first priority.

In the state of the art we observe that the metaphor of the nervous system has been used to simulate and control the motion of a specific limb with applications to medicine and/or robotics. We have followed this approach to build a general architecture for the synthesis of autonomous gestures. In the next section we describe our proposal in detail.

3   The Virtual Human Neuromotor System

The main innovation of this work is the design of a distributed control architecture based on autonomous entities that intercommunicate with each other in a self-similar hierarchy (fractal architecture). We propose a control system inspired in the human nervous system which will be used to generate autonomous behaviour on virtual humans. Biologically based control systems have been applied mainly to simulations oriented to robotics or for biomechanics applications.

The human nervous system (HNS) is divided into the central and peripheral nervous systems (CNS and PNS, respectively). The PNS consists of sensory neurons running from stimulus receptors that inform the CNS of the stimuli; and motor neurons running from the CNS to the muscles and glands - called effectors - that take action. The CNS consists of the spinal cord and the brain [24]. The CNS is a control centre which receives internal and external stimuli and sends orders to the effectors by means of the motor neurons. We are using this principle as the basic building block for a simplified model of the nervous system (NS) that will act as an animation controller for a virtual human.

The proposed model of the Virtual Human NS is a distributed system capable to produce autonomous gestures (reflex movements) in reaction to a defined set of stimuli: external forces, temperature, and muscle effort. This NS model constitutes what we call the distributed animation control system (DACS). In conjunction with the DACS we have implemented a simplified model of the human locomotion system in order to provide the DACS with a set of effectors to move the different body parts. The Virtual Human Locomotion System (VHLS) models the human musculo-skeletal system as a skeleton structure, compliant with the H-Anim specification [25], whose joints can be moved by pairs of antagonist muscles, one pair for each degree of freedom. The implementation of the muscles gives importance to the effect they produce on the virtual humans joints, that's why they are called effectors.

The main idea behind the DACS is the definition of a minimum control entity constituted by three main sub entities or components: sensors, analyzers and effectors, defined as follows:

The Sensors are the virtual devices capable of gathering information from the exterior world of the virtual human, such as temperature, contact with other objects, external forces, etc.; and also from the interior of the virtual human: stress, muscle effort, etc. They store the acquired information in the form of a stimulus vector, containing information on the intensity, direction and orientation of the received stimulus.

The Analyzers are entities which concentrate information coming from one or many sensors or analyzers. An analyzer's main function is to calculate the cumulative effect of the sensors attached to it. The reaction vector calculated by the analyzer is used by the effectors to generate the adequate reaction as a function of the intensity, direction and orientation of the stimulus received.

The Effectors: these entities are black boxes capable to affect one or more degrees of freedom of the virtual human joints to which they're attached. Currently, they're implemented as inverse kinematics controllers that calculate the position of the joints as a function of the reaction vector calculated by the analyzer attached to them.

The components of the minimum control entity – sensors, analyzers and effectors – which will constitute the basic building block of the DACS are shown on figure 1.

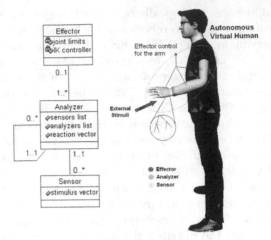

Fig. 1. The basic control entity and the hierarchical structure of the DACS.

This scheme will be replicated at different hierarchic levels providing main control centres (analyzers which will be linked to lower level analyzers) capable of taking high level decisions.

The control entity is capable to receive (sense) a set of stimuli or information, process them and generate a reaction, which can be an order to an effector (a muscle or set of muscles) or a message to another control entity in the same or in a different hierarchic level.

Each control entity (c.e.) is usually responsible of controlling one limb of the virtual human (arms, legs). The basic c.e. will be reproduced in different hierarchic levels in order to coordinate the whole body. The figure 1 illustrates this idea: a hierarchy of control entities following a fractal like structure (self-similar hierarchy). Each component works in an independent way, this characteristic allows for distributing the system.

The communication between control entities will takes place depending on the intensity of the received stimuli, this will emulate the neurotransmitters effect (the chemical substances which act as communication channels between neurons) and allow or avoid communication at different levels. The simulation of the neurotransmitters effect will allow for modifying the intensity of the response to a given stimulus. For example, if the virtual human touches a hot object such as the grill of a stove, it will react with different speed or intensity depending on the actual temperature, it's different to touch a grill at 20°C than trying to do it when the object is at 150°C. Spontaneous behaviour can be generated depending on the overall conditions of the virtual human. Spontaneous movements such as balancing the arms or changing the body weight from one leg to another in a stand up posture, vary depending on the muscular and/or mental stress. People display different gestures when they stop after running or walking depending on the amount of energy they have spent, among many other factors. These gestures can be also considered as reactions to a certain kind of stimuli as well.

Until now we have explained the general principles of the DACS which will constitute the nervous and motor system and provide autonomous animation to a virtual human, depending on the internal and external stimuli and information coming from its environment.

In the next section we describe a test application that shows the feasibility of the proposed model.

3.1   Test Application: Reaction to Thermic Stimuli

To show the feasibility of using the Distributed Animation Control System as the neuromotor system for a virtual human, we have implemented a demonstration application which generates reflex movements for the arm as reaction to thermic stimuli. The virtual human will stand in front of a stove with its left hand over one of the burners. The temperature of the burner will be modified in the different tests.

The objective is to see different levels of reaction depending on the perceived temperature. The reaction levels have been classified intro 3 main regions depending on the stimulus intensity: green zone -no reaction is required-, yellow zone -controlled reaction, the speed of the motion starts to increase depending on the stimulus intensity-, red zone -the reaction is more "violent" since the stimulus intensity reaches the highest values, in this level the joint limits are usually reached and a "bounding" motion is produced as a reaction.

If the temperature of the burner is above 40°C, the reflex movements start to appear, ranging from a slight movement of the wrist to separate the hand from the burner level, up to a violent fast movement involving all the arm joints in order to retire the hand as soon as possible if the temperature raises to values around the 100°C.

We used an H-Anim compliant virtual human model and implemented an animation control for one arm (see figure 2), with temperature sensors (to receive external stimuli) in the palm of the hand.

The general algorithm used to calculate the reflex movement is the following: Analyzers and sensors are arranged in a tree structure. The sensors are sampled at each animation frame. The analyzer-sensor tree is traversed in post-order (first children, then the local parent). Allowing each analyzer to gather the information of the sensors attached to it. The process is recursively repeated letting the analyzers concentrate the information coming from the lower levels. Each segment of the articulated character has a main analyzer. Segment analyzers are associated to the main limb analyzer, the one for the arm in this case.

The limb analyzers are usually the local root of the sensor-analyzer tree and contain the overall reaction vector specifying the velocity of the reflex movement. The reaction vector contains the orientation and direction to be followed by the limb in order to react as required – rejecting the thermic stimuli.

The orientation and direction of the stimulus vector depend on the position of the sensor relative to the stimulus source – orientation is inverted representing the need for rejecting the stimulus source. The stimulus vectors are calculated as follows: the vector magnitude – stimulus intensity – is a function of the Euclidean

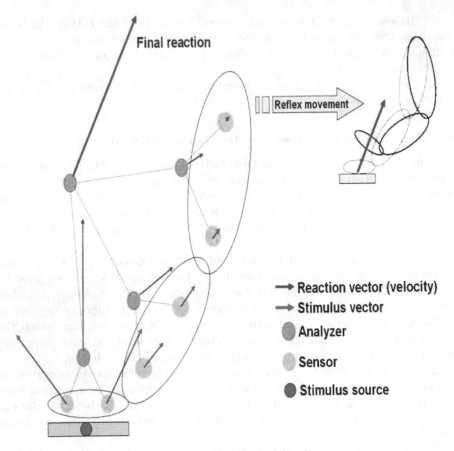

Fig. 2. The animation control for the arm.

distance between the sensor and the stimulus source – represented by a point in the 3D space. The intensity decreases with the distance – in our tests this is done in a linear way. The analyzers compute the reaction vector by calculating a vector addition of the stimulus vectors from their associated sensors.

The actual movement of the arm is calculated using inverse kinematics (IK) [26, 27]. The end effector required by the IK algorithm is the segment receiving the highest stimulus intensity – magnitude of the reaction vector –, as calculated by the segment analyzers. The trajectory to be followed by the limb – end effector – is defined by the reaction vector computed by the main limb analyzer. The motion speed is directly proportional to the intensity of the reaction vector. As explained in the previous section, the reaction speed can range from no reaction at all – when intensity falls into the tolerance interval – up to a very fast reaction causing the limb to reach the joint limits very fast, even before the sensors detect there is no need to reject the stimulus source anymore. In the later case, the effector nodes – not shown in figure 2, but associated to each joint, force the limb to recover a comfortable posture – under the joint limits.

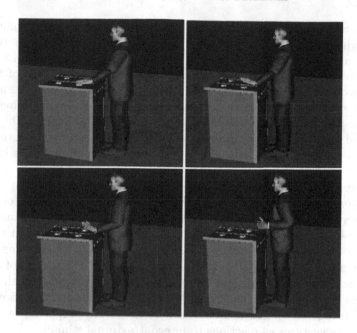

Fig. 3. Snapshots of the test application.

3.2   Technical Details of the Implementation

The demonstration application has been implemented as a java applet. The 3D animation is done using a 3D rendering engine for java [28]. The components of the basic control entity are java classes which extend the thread class in order to be instantiated and run as independent threads. The analyzer objects monitor continuously their attached components (effectors, sensors or other analyzers) and establish the required communications. The virtual human model is an H – Anim VRML file, the stove is a conventional VRML'97 file. The demonstration was run on a PC workstation with a bi-Xeon at 1.2Mhz processor and 1Gb of RAM using MS-Windows 2000. The animation runs at 30 frames per second and the gives the impression of a natural reaction speed. The figure 3 shows different levels of reaction depending on the preset temperature. For each test the simulation is reset to the initial posture of the virtual human with its left hand over the stove burner.

4   Conclusions

The work presented in this paper is still in an early stage and many more stimuli-response pairs must be modelled. One of the most important questions to solve is the modelling of internal stimuli such as emotions, stress and other cognitive processes. Our research is not advanced enough to give a precise answer at this moment. Nevertheless, the arm implementation with sensors and effectors driven by the fractal hierarchy of basic control entities has shown the feasibility of this system architecture to be implemented at larger scale (full body control). The test application provides a way for the virtual human to react in an automatic way to a certain kind of stimuli in the virtual environment. One of the main drawbacks of our current model is the fact that the reflex movements are deterministic; to a given stimulus there is always the same reaction. A higher level control must be put in place to take into account the stress induced by previous stimuli and the variations it produces on subsequent gestures. In future developments, a central control unit will be implemented to emulate the brain as a main control centre and reach a higher level of autonomy: based not only on reflex gestures, but able to generate more complex behaviour driven by high level directives or intentions. Implementing virtual senses such as vision or audition will let us synthesize more advanced reactions, e.g. the virtual human could be able to raise its arms to protect itself from an object being thrown toward it. This kind of reflex movement would require a set of rules for selecting the kind of gesture in function of the stimulus being received – e.g. detection of an object being thrown towards us triggers a predefined defensive gesture of the arms to protect the body part being menaced. We believe this kind of behaviour can be generated using the virtual neuromotor system we are proposing by means of modelling the gestures as reactions to internal/external stimuli.

References

1. Badler, N., Chi, D., Chopra-Khullar, S.: Virtual human animation based on movement observation and cognitive behavior models. In: Computer Animation 1999. (1999) 128–137
2. Perlin, K.: Building virtual actors who can really act. In: 2nd International Conference on Virtual Storytelling. (2003)
3. Gorce, P.: Dynamic postural control method for biped in unknown environment. In: IEEE Transactions on Systems, Man and Cybernetics. (1999) 616–626
4. Kubica, E., Wang, D., Winter, D.: Feedforward and deterministic fuzzy control of balance and posture during human gait. In: IEEE International Conference on Robotics and Automation. (2001) 2293–2298
5. Ok, S., Miyashita, K., Hase, K.: Evolving bipedal locomotion with genetic programming - a preliminary report. In: Congress on Evolutionary Computation. (2001) 1025–1032
6. He, J., Levine, W., Loeb, G.: The modeling of the neuro-musculo-skeletal control system of a cat hindlimb. In: IEEE International Symposium on Intelligent Control. (1988) 406–411
7. Garcia-Cordova, F., Guerrero-Gonzalez, A., Pedreno-Molina, J., Moran, J.: Emulation of the animal muscular actuation system in an experimental platform. In: IEEE International Conference on Systems, Man, and Cybernetics. (2001) 64–69
8. Brown, I., Loeb, G.: Design of a mathematical model of force in whole skeletal muscle. In: IEEE 17th Annual Conference on Engineering in Medicine and Biology Society. (1995) 1243–1244
9. Guihard, M., Gorce, P.: Dynamic control of an artificial muscle arm. In: IEEE Transactions on Systems, Man and Cybernetics. (1999) 813–818

10. Northrup, S., Sarkar, N., Kawamura, K.: Biologically-inspired control architecture for a humanoid robot. In: IEEE/RSJ International Conference on Intelligent Robots and Systems. (2001) 1100–1105
11. Karniel, A., Inbar, G.: A model for learning human reaching-movements. In: 18th Annual International Conference of the IEEE on Engineering in Medicine and Biology Society. (1996) 619–620
12. Andry, P., Gaussier, P., Moga, S., Banquet, J., Nadel, J.: Learning and communication in imitation: An autonomous robot perspective. In: IEEE Transaction on Systems, Man and Cybernetics, Part A: Systems and Humans. (2001) 431–444
13. Hu, C., Yu, Q., Li, Y., Ma, S.: Extraction of parametric human model for posture recognition using genetic algorithm. In: Fourth IEEE International Conference on Automatic Face and Gesture Recognition. (2000) 518–523
14. Kacic-Alesic, Z., Nordenstam, M., Bullock, D.: A practical dynamics system. In: Proceedings of the 2003 ACM SIGGRAPH/Eurographics Symposium on Computer Animation, Eurographics Association (2003) 7–16
15. Boulic, R., Mas, R.: Hierarchical kinematics behaviors for complex articulated figures. In: Interactive Computer Animation, Prentice Hall. (1996) 40–70
16. Rodriguez, I., Peinado, M., Boulic, R., Meziat, D.: Reaching volumes generated by means of octal trees and cartesian constraints. In: CGI 2003. (2003)
17. Komura, T., Kuroda, A., Kudoh, S., Lan, T., Shinagawa, Y.: An inverse kinematics method for 3d figures with motion data. In: Computer Graphics International, 2003. (2003) 242–247
18. Tanco, L., Hilton, A.: Realistic synthesis of novel human movements from a database of motion capture examples. In: Workshop on Human Motion. (2000) 137–142
19. Ashida, K., Lee, S.J., Allbeck, J., Sun, H., Badler, N., Metaxas, D.: Pedestrians: Creating agent behaviors through statistical analysis of observation data. In: Computer Animation 2001. (2001)
20. Blumberg, B., Galyean, T.: Multi-level direction of autonomous creatures for real-time virtual environments. In: SIGGRAPH 1995. (1995)
21. Tu, X., Terzopoulos, D.: Artificial fishes: physics, locomotion, perception, behavior. In: Proceedings of the 21st annual conference on Computer graphics and interactive techniques, ACM Press (1994) 43–50
22. Isla, D., Blumberg, B.: Object persistence for synthetic creatures. In: International Joint Conference on Autonomous Agents and Multiagent Systems (AAMAS). (2002)
23. Perlin, K.: Real time responsive animation with personality. In: IEEE Transactions on Visualization and Computer Graphics. (1995) 5–15
24. Kimball, J.: (Organization of the Nervous System, Kimball's Biology Pages. 2003) http://users.rcn.com/jkimball.ma.ultranet/BiologyPages.
25. H-Anim: (The humanoid animation working group. http://www.h-anim.org)
26. Deepak, T., Goswami, A., Badler, N.: Real-time inverse kinematics techniques for anthropomorphic limbs. In: Graphical Models and Image Processing. (2000)
27. IKAN: (Inverse kinematics using analytical methods. http://hms.upenn.edu/software/ik/software.html)
28. Shout3D: (Shout3D, Eyematic Interfaces Inc. (2001)) http://www.shout3d.com.

Integrating miniMin-HSP Agents in a Dynamic Simulation Framework

Miguel Lozano[1], Francisco Grimaldo[2], and Fernando Barber[1]

[1] Computer Science Department, University of Valencia,
Dr.Moliner 50, (Burjassot) Valencia, Spain
{Miguel.Lozano}@uv.es
[2] Institute of Robotics, University of Valencia,
Pol. de la Coma s/n (Paterna) Valencia, Spain

Abstract. In this paper, we describe the framework created for implementing AI-based animations for artificial actors in the context of IVE (Intelligent Virtual Environments). The minMin-HSP (Heuristic Search Planner) planner presented in [12] has been updated to deal with 3D dynamic simulation environments, using the sensory/actuator system fully implemented in UnrealTM and presented in [10]. Here, we show how we have integrated these systems to handle the necessary balance between the reactive and deliberative skills for 3D Intelligent Virtual Agents (3DIVAs). We have carried out experiments in a multi-agent 3D blocks world, where 3DIVAs will have to interleave sensing, planning and execution to be able to adapt to the enviromental changes without forgetting their goals. Finally, we discuss how the HSP agents created are adequated to animate the intelligent behaviour of 3D simulation actors.

1 Introduction and Previous Work

Artificial humans and other kinds of 3D intelligent virtual agents (IVA) normally display their intelligence through their navigation skills, full-body control, and decision-taking formalisms adopted. The complexity involved in these agents, normally suggests designing and executing them independently of the 3D graphics engine, so the agent could be focussed on their behavioural problems (see figure 1).

There are numerous applications that would require these kinds of agents, especially in fields such us, entertainment, education or simulation [2]. We are working towards the creation of a robust simulation framework for IVE simulations, where different 3D embodied agents are able to sense their environment, to take decisions according to their visible states, and finally to navigate in a dynamic scenario performing the actions which will animate their behaviours in real time.

There has been a great amount of research along the main behavioural requirements of 3DIVA systems, from their physical appearance and motor system to the cognitive one, as described in the spectrum introduced by Ayleth in [1].

G.A. Vouros and T. Panayiotopoulos (Eds.): SETN 2004, LNAI 3025, pp. 535–544, 2004.

Early work in AI planning archiectures for 3DIVAs was undertaken by Badler et al. They proposed an architecture based mainly on two components: a) Parallel state-machines (PaT-Nets), which are good at sequencing actions to support Jack's high level behaviours, and b) the low level (reactive) loop (sense-control-act, SCA) used to handle low level information mainly used for locomotion. [2]. SodaJack [5] and Hide-and-Seek [3] systems are created through a combination of two planners: a hierarchical planner (ItPlans [4]), which controls the main agent behaviours, and a specific purpose search planner, devoted to help Jack in locating objects or other agents. In SodaJack, the character interleaves planning and execution in a single-agent simulation, where reactivity and interaction wasn't considered. On the other hand, Hide-and-Seek simulations introduce a multi-agent framework in a dynamic environment, although the planning schema remains the same. In this case, agent reactivity is achieved by comparision between the perceived world state and the partial hierarchical plan, that is regularly revised [3].

Behavioural animation based on Situation Calculus is another cognitive approach which has been adapted to virtual creatures [9]. However, the state space model designed is more close to a declarative language than an agent centered behavioural system.

Interacting Storytelling systems integrate AI techniques such as planning with narrative representations to generate stories [14]. In [13], we discuss the use of HTN's [6] and HSP planning formalisms in Interactive Storytelling from the perspective of story generation and authoring. The main difference between these systems and the one presented here lies in the introduction of the perception system presented in [10] which let the agents deal with partially observable 3D dynamic environments.

Beliefs-Desires-Intentions (BDI) has adopted a significant number of implemetations in order to build cognitive agent architectures. A reduced number of them has also been applied to the current context, as VITAL [7] and SimHuman [8] platforms have shown. SimHuman shows a real-time platform for 3D agents with planning capabilities, which represents from a 3DIVE perspective, a similar approach to the multi-agent system presented in this paper. However, we will concentrate on the planning formalism introduced and also how agents deal with reactivity in the behavioural system designed.

Accordingly to this, the aim of this paper is to present a new agent system which interleaves sense, plan, and execution tasks to deal with normal 3DIVE's multi-agent simulations, where normally intelligent characters modify and interact autonomously with the 3D environment, guided by their AI based formalisms.

The next section shows an overview of the 3D multi-agent architecture implemented, where the world modelling and sensory system fully integrated in UnrealTM are briefly explained. Section 3 is focussed on the behavioural control of the simulation agents created. We analyse the planning algorithm for dynamic environments and the behavioural system designed to handle reactivity and goal direction for 3DIVAs. Finally, section 4 shows the results obtained from this

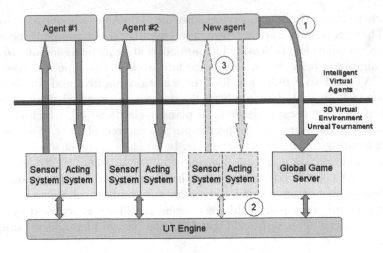

Fig. 1. System architecture overview

framework in a *shared* blocks world, where several agents have been introduced to create an intelligent simulation environment.

2 System Architecture Overview

The multi-agent system designed is based on a distributed model that figure 1 shows. As mentioned before, this modular structure is adequate for 3D real time graphic simulations, as it provides for a scalable and reusable framework for both, 3D agents and environments.

As figure 1 shows, the architecture implemented is mainly divided into two components: the world manager, responsible for managing the information flow between the agent and the 3D environment (sense/act) [10], and the behavioural system of the agent, devoted to handling reactivity and planning for the 3DIVAs created (possibly running on a separate process or machine).

2.1 Behavioural Agent System

This system is the responsible for controlling the main components of the task-oriented agent architecture that figure 2 shows. The main components are briefly described now:

- **The Agent Control Module** contains two important agent components: a) the Agent Memory (perceived world and internal state) and b) the Task Control Model.
  The Agent Memory is a dynamic object container, which asynchronously receives and updates new information from the perception module. We maintain two representation levels: low level information (location, size, ...) and symbolic object centered data (properties and their perceived values).

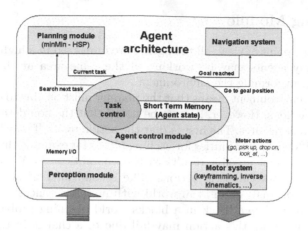

Fig. 2. Internal agent architecture

The Task Controller governs the agent activity anytime and it decides what to do depending on the agent and world states. Figure 3 shows the Finite State Machine (FSM) designed for general simulation task monitorization. We are using a classical task definition, so tasks consist of several primitive actions to be executed by the agent sequentially. IDLE will be the initial and the final state, where the agent has nothing to do. Anytime the agent generates a plan it goes to the WORKING state, and start sequencing the current task in its corresponding actions. WORKING is designed to transite to NAVIGATE or EXECUTE depending on the current action to carry out. NAVIGATE is simply used to undertake the *go_to* action, and EXECUTE will send an action request to the motor agent system and will wait until the results are known. To detect when the current task (and plan) should be aborted, the preconditions of the current task are regularly revised in these states (WORKING, NAVIGATE, EXECUTE). SLEEP is a state where the agent has no plan to carry out, normally this situation is motivated by world changes that finally hide the agent's goal states. To animate this situation the agent will look at the desired object and it will wait until a new possible plan to carry out is achieved. In order to do this, the agent will periodically translate from this state to the SEARCH one.

– **The Reactive Navigation System** of the agents created is based on the 3-layered Feed Forward Nerural Network presented in [11]. This local navigation system is allowed to access the agent memory, where visible and remembered objects are located. The main objective of this system is to guarantee NAVIGATION free of obstacles in a multi-agent environment.

– **Planning module** starts from the miniMin-HSP planner shown in [12], and it will be described in further detail in the next section.

3   Planning Module

From planning's point of view, all the agents are immersed in a highly dynamical scenario - many agents may be working in the same area at the same time, continuously transforming the environment.

A dynamic environment means that the planner must be able to deal with non deterministic actions. However, it must be noted that the non determinism may be of two different natures. The first is that the action by itself may have different results with different probabilities for each result, as for example throwing a dice, which has six different possible results with probabilities 1/6. We will call these actions pure non deterministic actions. The second kind of nondeterministic action is an action that, in an ideal world with no interferences is deterministic (for example, to *pickup* a block in a blocks world planning problem), but in a real multi agent world, this action may fail due to a change in the world that doesn't allow the action to be finished (other agent got the block), or the action may succeed but the resulting state is a state that comes from a composition of different actions, that are casually executed at a similar time by different agents. We will call these actions casual non deterministic actions.

The way to deal with pure non deterministic actions is to model the problem as a Markov Decision Problem (MDP) or a Partially Observable Markov Decision Problem (POMDP) [16] where the possible states resulting from the actions have a probability, and an optimal solution is a policy that has a minimum expected cost. Algorithms that deal with these problems are the Minimax Real Time Heuristic Search [17] and the RTDP [16].

However, in a virtual environment, the most common kinds of actions are the casual non deterministic actions. These kinds of actions have one expected resulting state with high probability and many unexpected resulting states with low probability. During the planning process, we consider these actions as deterministic ones, so each agent starts planning from the current state perceived from its sensors under classical planning assumptions. In this way, planning is used to generate the necessary agent intentions.However, it is necessary to choose a robust algorithm in order to recover from *perturbations*, normally when the expected results are not achieved.

Another challenge that the planner must face is that it must work in real time. The planner is used for a visual simulation, so it shouldn't take more than a few seconds to choose the action to execute.

The technique commonly used to solve these problems is to interleave planning and plan execution. In this way, it is not necessary to obtain a complete plan from the initial state to the goal state before beginning the execution of the first action. The agent only needs to advance the plan sufficiently to choose the first action, then it can execute the action and continue the planning from the resulting execution state, until it is able to choose the next action, repeating the cycle until the goal state is reached.

The algorithm we use to control the interleaving of planning and action execution is a greedy search, as described in [16]. We have also included memory facilities to avoid past states. The different steps of the algorithm are represented

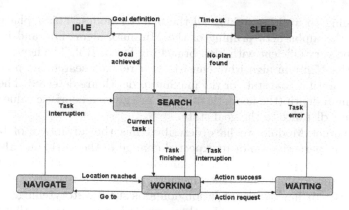

Fig. 3. Task Controler

1. Evaluate each task a applicable in current state s as

$$Q(a, s) = c(a, s) + h(s_a)$$

where s_a is state predicted after doing a in s.

2. Apply action a that minimizes $Q(a, s)$, breaking ties randomly
3. Observe the resulting state s'.
4. Exit if resulting state s' is a goal state, else set s to s' and go to 1.

Fig. 4. Greedy Search Algorithm

in figure 4, where $c(a, s)$ is the cost of applying the task a in the state s, and $h(s_a)$ is an estimation of the cost from state s_a to the goal state.

It can be clearly seen that this algorithm implements a sense - plan - act cycle. Step 1 corresponds to the planning phase, step 2 to the action execution and step 3 to the sensorization phase. The sensorization is fundamental for dealing with the non determinism of the actions, as the agent can't know the resulting state of an action. If the action observed in step 3 (s') is not the same as the predicted state (s_a) the algorithm continues the search from s'. To deal with the possible failure of the actions, we have made step 2 of the algorithm interruptible. For example, in the multi-agent blocks world scenario, agent1 may plan the task of *Picking up block*1. This task is translated into two primitive actions: *go_to block*1 and *pick_up block*1. But it may happen that while agent1 is going to *block*1, another agent takes it. In this case the task is no longer possible and the current action is interrupted, so the algorithm continues with step 3 for identifying the new state and planning once again.

For the planning phase of the algorithm, which corresponds with step 1 of the previous algorithm, we use the Minimin algorithm [15], which is similar to the Minimax algorithm but more oriented to single agent real time search. This algorithm searches forward from the current state to a fixed depth and applies the heuristic evaluation function to the nodes at the search frontier. We use an alpha pruning to avoid searching all the frontier nodes. This alpha pruning is similar to the alpha-beta pruning of the Minimax algorithm, and it has been shown to be very efficient with high branching factor [15]. The heuristics we are using for the Minimin algorithm consists of a relaxed search (no preconditions considered) until a goal state or the maximum depth are detected. The nodes at this maximum depth (the heuristic frontier) are given a heuristic value according to the atoms distance to the goal state.

The Planner Module we have described has the advantage of being very robust at any perturbation or unexpected change in the world and also efficient enough for the purpose of the module, although the quality of the solution (with respect to the optimal one) relies heavily on the heuristic used. However as occurs in other behavioural simulation domains such as storytelling, the optimal plan is not really a requirement. Furthermore, it is easy to realise that to extract plans in a multiagent environment it is insuficcient to guarantee that the goal state will be reached by the agent, as it is always possible to create another agent (*agent2*) that undoes the actions done by the *agent1*, independently of the algorithm used.

Other similar algorithms to the one presented here are the RTA* or LRTA* [15]. Although they need some adjustment to be able to function in a highly dynamical environment.

4   Results

The flexibilty of the simulation system created lets us design a high number of experiments in different 3D simulation environments. Furthermore, as occurs in storytelling, the full potential of story generation derives from the interaction of character behaviours while they compete for action resources (pre-conditions). As occurs in storytelling, in this case, the story can only carry forward if the character has re-planning capabilities.

Figure 5 shows the trace of one of the simulations performed in a BlocksWorld inspired 3D environment, composed of 4 tables, 4 cubes and two agents. The initial state perceived by both agents is the same, however their goals are independent. Agent1 has to invert the cubes0-3 which are placed on table0, and Agent2 will do it with cubes2-1, placed on table2 (tables1,3 are free). Although it is clear that an optimal plan, in terms of the total number of actions performed by all actors is possible to achieve, we are more interested now in checking the robustness of the planning system created, as it will have to face complex situations where the goal state can move away or even disappear. For example, initially the Agent2 decides to move the cube3 to the cube2, however Agent1 gets the cube2 before. This situation is detected by Agent2 who aborts its current plan and searchs again from the new state perceived, deciding this time to drop the picked cube(2) on the cube1, as it is now free.

As there is no muti-agent task coordination[1] between the agents, a conflict situation is generated again when both agents drop their cubes and they disturb

---

[1] we can consider the current agent task as its short-term intentions, while complete plans can be viewed as long-term ones

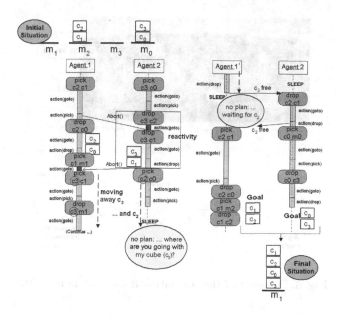

Fig. 5. Simulation trace example

themselves. Agent1 faces this situation, moving away cube3, while Agent2 picks up cube2. At this moment Agent2 searchs again, however, a plan can not be provided, as Agent1 is moving cube3, son Agent2 has no way to know its final location. Once Agent1 drops cube3 on one of the free tables, Agent2 decides to drop the cube previously picked on cube1 (so it will produce a new initial state from Agent1's point of view) and finally, it achieves its goals as it moves cube0 to its final position on cube3. Agent1 can finish now without more problems, so that finally all cubes are compiled in a single stack, which is a possible solution to the 2-Agent problem designed.

5   Conclusions

We have described an agent architecture that interleaves perception, planning and action, to be able to adapt itself to the changes produced by users or agents. We have shown how to combine planning and reactivity (based on the precondition checking performed by the agents while they are working) in order to manage complex environmental simulations in 3D. This can be also very useful for behavioural character animation, for example when a character detects that another one is moving the cube that it will need in the future, we can animate this situation through a suprise agent dialogue (eg: ... where are you going with this cube?). Reactivity tunning can be also easily introduced, as the agents can always try to follow their current task, and anly re-plan after their actions. Furthermore, it is easy to see how new informative heuristic functions can be introduced in the planning system to finally influence the agent behaviour(in a

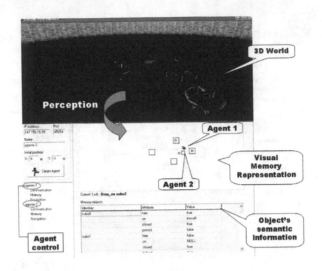

Fig. 6. Snapshot of the simulation framework in real time

similar way as narrative concepts can guide actor's decision taking in storytelling domains). Heuristics can derive mainly from two information soruces: a) from perception: where typically object distances or other kind of situation recognition can be easily introduced, b) from the agent internal state: as showed in [13], agents could also manage some *fluents* (eg. *mood*, etc.) which finally assist its decision taking. From storytelling system's point of view, the behavioural approach presented lets the agents to autonomously deal with reactivity and long-term dependencies in similar 3D simulation scenarios (in storytelling domains, normally is the *author* who apriori introduces the narrative content using AND/OR graphs composed by independent sub-problems, so agent behaviours based on long-term dependencies can not be considered).

Summarizing, the storytelling inspired agents created are able to adapt themselves to the enviromental changes they are producing anytime, which is an important point when simulating intelligent and *believables* character's behaviours.

References

1. Aylett R. Luck M. *Applying Artificial Intelligence to Virtual Reality: Intelligent Virtual Environments*. Applied Artificial Intelligence, 2000.
2. N. Badler, M. Palmer, R. Bindiganavale. *Animation control for real-time virtual humans*. Communications of the ACM, 42(8). August 1999.
3. Badler, N., Webber, B., Becket, W., Geib, C., Moore, M. Pelachaud, C., Reich, B., and Stone, M., *Planning for Animation* in D. Thalmann and N. Magnanat-Thalmann (eds.), Computer Animation, New York: Prentice Hall Inc., 1995.
4. Geib, C. *The intentional planning system: Itplans*. Proceedings of the 2nd Artificial Intelligence Planning Systems Conference. 1994.

5. C. Geib and L. Levison and M. Moore, *Sodajack: An architecture for agents that search and manipulate objects.* Technical Report MS-CIS-94-16/LINC LAB 265, Department of Computer and Information Science, University of Pennsylvania, 1994.

6. Cavazza, M., Charles, F. and Mead, S.J., 2001. *AI-based Animation for Interactive Storytelling.* Proceedings of Computer Animation, IEEE Computer Society Press, Seoul, Korea, pp. 113-120.

7. George Anastassakis and Tim Ritchings and Themis Panayiotopoulos. *Multi-agent Systems as Intelligent Virtual Environments* Lecture Notes in Computer Science, Vol. 2174, Springer-Verlag, pp.381-395, 2001.

8. S. Vosinakis, T. Panayiotopoulos, *SimHuman : A Platform for real time Virtual Agents with Planning Capabilities*, IVA 2001, 3rd International Workshop on Intelligent Virtual Agents, Madrid, Spain, September 10-11, 2001.

9. John Funge, Xiaoyuan Tu, and Demetri Terzopoulos (1999). *Cognitive Modeling: Knowledge, Reasoning and Planning for Intelligent Characters in Computer Graphics.* Volume 33 Annual Conference Series (Proceedings of SIGGRAPH 99) pages 29-38.

10. M. Lozano et al. *An Efficient Synthetic Vision System for 3D Multi-character Systems.* 4th International Workshop of Intelligent Agents (IVA03),Springer-LNAI Munchen 2003.

11. M. Lozano, F.Grimaldo, J. Molina. *Towards reactive navigation and attention skills for 3D intelligent characters.* International Work-conference on Artificial and Natural Neural Networks (IWANN). June 3-6, 2003 Mahn, Menorca (Balearic Islands, Spain).

12. M. Lozano, Mead, S.J., Cavazza, M. and Charles, F. *Search Based Planning: A Model for Character Behaviour.* Proceedings of the 3rd on Intelligent Games and Simulation, GameOn-2002, London, UK, November 2002.

13. Charles, F., Lozano, M., Mead, S.J., Bisquerra, A.F., and Cavazza, M. *Planning Formalisms and Authoring in Interactive Storytelling.* 1st International Conference on Technologies for Interactive Digital Storytelling and Entertainment, Darmstadt, Germany, 2003.

14. Michael Young *An Overview of the Mimesis Architecture: Integrating Intelligent Narrative Control into an Existing Gaming Environment* In The Working Notes of the AAAI Spring Symposium on Artificial Intelligence and Interactive Entertainment, Stanford, CA, March 2001.

15. R. E. Korf. *Real-Time Heuristic Search* Artificial Intelligence 42, pp 189-211, 1990.

16. B. Bonet, H. Geffner. *Planning and Control in Artificial Intelligence: A Unifying Perspective* Applied Intelligence 14 (3), pp 237-252, 2001.

17. S. Koenig. *Minimax Real-Time Heuristic Search* Artificial Intelligence 129, pp 165-197, 2001.

Author Index